Introduction to

Environmental Health

Joe E. Beck

Kendall Hunt
publishing company

Kendall Hunt
publishing company

www.kendallhunt.com
Send all inquiries to:
4050 Westmark Drive
Dubuque, IA 52004-1840

Copyright © 2013 by Joe E. Beck

ISBN 978-1-4652-1850-6

Printed in the United States of America
10 9 8 7 6 5 4 3 2 1

Contents

Contents

Acknowledgments

My most sincere thanks to Mrs. Jamie Hisle, administrative assistant, and Mr. Cody Buell, MPH student, for reviewing chapters and making suggestions for format changes. They were willing, with the utmost grace, to review these chapters in spite of their very busy work schedules.

I would also like to think the employees of the EPA, the CDC, the FDA, and the USPHS for their generosity in allowing us to use the material from their well-developed webpages. And last, I would like to give a profound thanks to the contributing authors for their willingness to develop and turn their chapters around on a very short time schedule.

Joe Beck

Foreword

When I was preparing for a career as a sanitarian as an undergraduate at the University of Georgia, I was extremely fortunate to attend a new course on ecosystem ecology taught by Eugene P. Odum (1913–2002). Dr. Odum was notably the "Father of Ecology" and wrote the first textbook on the subject in 1953: *Fundamentals of Ecology*. The book introduced us to ecosystems and their interaction with the world around them. and particularly their interaction with our modern, engineered community. At the time, ecology was considered no more than a pastiche of natural history. However, over the 60 years since the book's introduction, we have realized and understand the splendid impact it had on everything we do in public and environmental health. It fundamentally changed the way we view our world. We transformed our science from a pedantic approach to a topic alive with change and interaction.

In the preface to his text, Dr. Odum included a nursery rhyme attributed to Jonathan Swift, aptly titled "The Siphonaptera":

Big fleas have little fleas,
Upon their backs to bite 'em,
And little fleas have lesser fleas,
and so, ad infinitum.

This little couplet, which embodies the world of ecology, influenced my approach to environmental health more than any single course, event, lecture, or reading. To this end, it defines our modern view of environmental health and its place in today's society.

This book, *Introduction to Environmental Health*, embraces this unique approach. The well-known and respected authors of the individual book chapters skillfully used this concept and made every effort to provide you, the reader, with a global view of their subject matter and how it interacts with individual health and well-being regardless of the setting.

This book introduces you to new and emerging as well as classical environmental health issues faced by the world community, including risk and sustainability. It teaches various practical and oftentimes futuristic approaches and concepts to manage and control environmental problems brought about by the advancement of civilizations. But beyond its being a new and invaluable educational adjunct to the applied science of environmental health, this book also serves as a motivational tool for those contemplating a career in the public health allied profession. I welcome you to read and enjoy this book, and I particularly welcome you into the exciting world of environmental health science.

Robert W. Powitz, PhD, MPH, RS, DLAAS
Sanitarian

About the Contributors

Joe E. Beck, R. S., D.E.A.A.S.

Prof. Beck, Eastern Kentucky University, RS DAAS, holds an undergraduate degree in biology with concentrations in chemistry and geology and a graduate degree from the University of Illinois in Public Administration and Political Science. He earned 120 hours of Preventive Medicine training from the United States Army Medical School at Fort Sam Houston and their advanced certificate. He holds the current position, of Professor Environmental Health Science and has held past positions as a Senior Research Staff Scientist and project manager at the Pacific Northwest laboratory, Battelle, and other past positions as academic Department Head of Environmental Sciences and Health and field practice positions with the Illinois Department of Public Health and the McCracken County Health Department in Kentucky. He also has served as a full graduate faculty member in the Department of Political Science and Public Administration at Western Carolina University and as a Graduate Faculty of Washington State University School of Business. He has served numerous terms on the National Council on Accreditation of Environmental Health Sciences Curricula and several as its past Chair. Professor Beck has been a member of the Academy of Sanitarians since 1982 and has also served as its Chair. He has also served as Past environmental advisor to the Governor of North Carolina, chair of the North Carolina Solid and Hazardous Council and served on the North Carolina Department of Crime Controls Emergency Response Personnel Standards Committee. He was recognized as recipient of Western Carolina University's distinguished teaching award it is him the recipient of Eastern Kentucky's universities Apple award for teaching.

Dr. Eric C. Brevik

Eric C. Brevik is a professor of geology and soils at Dickinson State University, North Dakota, United States. Dr. Brevik earned his BS and MA degrees in geology from the University of North Dakota and his PhD in soil science (soil morphology and genesis) from Iowa State University. He has taught courses in soil science and geology at Valdosta State University (Georgia, United States) and Dickinson State University since 2001. His research interests include carbon sequestration by soil, soil health and productivity, soils and society, and the integration of geological and soils information. He is active professionally, having published over 160 peer-reviewed articles, abstracts, and other publications. He is also active both in the United States and internationally in researching the historical and sociological aspects of soil science. He served as the vice chair and then the chair for the Soil Science Society of America's (SSSA's) Council on the History, Philosophy, and Sociology of Soil Science from 2004 to 2006 and currently serves as the SSSA historian. He has organized and chaired several sessions at meetings of professional groups including SSSA and the European Geosciences Union, including a session on soils and human health at the 2006 SSSA meeting in Indianapolis, Indiana, United States. Dr. Brevik received the Soil Science Educator award from SSSA in 2012 and the Distinguished Professor of the Year award from Dickinson State University in 2010.

Dr. D. Gary Brown, RS, CIH, DAAS

Dr. D. Gary Brown is currently a Professor at Eastern Kentucky University (EKU) in the Department of Environmental Health Science (EHS). He is a certified industrial hygienist (CIH), registered sanitarian (RS) and a diplomate of the American Academy of sanitarians. Dr. Brown is Past President of the Association of Environmental Health Academic Programs. Dr. Brown received the distinguished educational leader award in 2003 and 2005 from the EKU Student Government Association; only four distinguished educational leader awards given out by the SGA University wide per semester. Dr. Brown received the EKU University Housing 2010 College of Health Sciences Golden Apple Award; annually, six awards are given University wide. Dr. Brown was named a 2012 EKU Star recognizing the top 10% of faculty from graduating seniors polled. He has presented at numerous national and international conferences.

He is actively involved with undergraduate student research. Dr. Brown was a founding member of the National Environmental Health Diversity Recruitment Task Force (NEHDRTF), a task force centered on making diversity a positive reality within the Environmental Health workforce and of EKU's Undergraduate research/scholarship day committee. In addition, he is on the staff of the OSHA Training Institute located at EKU. He teaches annually at the University of West Indies Occupational and Environmental Safety and Health (OESH) program at Mona.

Dr. Brown has over 20 years' experience in the field of environmental/occupational health and safety spanning both academic and practical fields in the United States and throughout the Caribbean. Dr. Brown still provides consulting for from government and private entities. Prior to arriving in Eastern Kentucky, he had over 10 years professional experience in the environmental, industrial hygiene and safety arenas.

Dr. Brown is extremely interested in the promotion of the field of environmental health and increasing the number of EHS majors nationally.

Dr. Lynn C. Burgess

Lynn C. Burgess is a professor of biology at Dickinson State University, North Dakota. Dr. Burgess earned his BS degree in zoology from Utah State University, his MS degree in biology from Eastern Washington University, and his PhD in toxicology from Utah State University. Before working in academia, he was an air-force officer and pilot, and business owner, and managed both milk processing and feed-production plants. He has taught courses in biology and environmental health at Dickinson State University since 1999. He is the director of the university's Environmental Health Program, which is nationally accredited. He was a member of the National Environmental Health Science and Protection Accreditation Council for six years and he is the past-president of the board of directors of the Association for Environmental Health Academic Programs. His research interests include the cancer preventative properties of natural compounds, the toxicological effect of heavy metals on gap junctional communications, and the angiogenesis involved in the exuberant granulation tissue in equines. His research is funded by the NIH specifically for undergraduate students. Dr. Burgess is involved in the Society of Toxicology and their subcommittee on undergraduate education, and in the National Environmental Health Association.

Sheila Davidson Pressley, DrPH, REHS/RS, DAAS, CPH

Dr. Pressley is an Associate Professor in the Department of Environmental Health Science at Eastern Kentucky University (EKU) in Richmond, Kentucky. She teaches undergraduate and graduate courses in environmental health science. Her courses include *Diseases and Hazards of Leisure, Solid and Hazardous Waste Management, African/African American Health Issues, Toxicology,* and *Food/Waterborne Disease Control.* Her specific research interests are in children's environmental health issues such toxic substance exposures from lead and illegal drug lab environments, and other environmental exposures.

Dr. Pressley received her BS degree in Environmental Health Science from Western Carolina University, her MS degree from the Department of Civil Engineering at Tufts University, and her DrPH degree in Preventive Medicine and Environmental Health from the University of Kentucky's College of Public Health. She also holds a number of professional certifications such as the Registered Environmental Health Specialist/Registered Sanitarian (REHS/RS), Diplomate of the American Academy of Sanitarians (DAAS), and the Certified in Public Health (CPH) credential from the National Board of Public Health Examiners.

Dr. Douglas G. Draper, Certified Health Physicist

Mr. Draper currently works as a Senior Health Physicist for consulting company Dade Moeller and Associates, assigned to support the US Environmental Protection Agency Environmental Response Team. He graduated from Eastern Kentucky University with a BS in Chemistry. He later received his MS in Chemistry from Xavier University in Cincinnati, Ohio. Following a period where he taught high school chemistry and physics, he accepted a job as a radiochemist with the Kentucky Radiation Control Branch. During this period he performed environmental monitoring, emergency response planning, and radioactive materials inspections. He later accepted a Health Physicist position with a major Department of Energy facility where he became the Health Physics Operations manager. During his career, he has served as an officer in the US Army Reserve with a specialty in nuclear weapons employment and in Chemical, Biological and Nuclear defensive operations. He has supported numerous overseas missions as a consultant to the International Atomic Energy Agency, a branch of the United Nations. He also teaches classes in Radiological Health for the Environmental Health Sciences Program at Eastern Kentucky University. Mr. Draper was certified by the Health Physics Society in 1984.

Larry Gordon, M.S., M.P.H., D.H.L., D.E.A.A.S.

Larry Gordon, M.S., M.P.H., D.H.L., D.E.A.A.S., has devoted more than 60 years to environmental health and protection including roles as a county sanitarian, district sanitarian, state sanitarian, chief sanitarian in a municipal health department, founding Director of the Albuquerque-Bernalillo County Environmental Health Department, PHS consultant, PHS Commissioned Officer (Captain), frequent lecturer for CDC training courses, Director of the first Governor's Conference on Environmental Health Planning, founding Director of the NM Environmental Improvement Ageny (Environment Department), founding Director of the NM Scientific Laboratory System, President of the American Public Health Association, NM Cabinet Secretary for Health and Environment, Chair of the National Committee on the Future of Environmental Health, UNM Visiting Professor of Public Administration, Senior Fellow of the UNM Institute for Public Policy, and UNM Adjunct Professor of Political Science.

He was one of the 12 Founders and is one of five Diplomates Laureate and one of five Diplomates Emeritus of the American Academy of Sanitarians. He is a recipient of numerous state and national professional awards, as well as an Honorary Doctorate in 2007.

He was a founder of the Council on Education for Public Health, as well as a long time member of the National Environmental Health Science and Protection Accreditation Council.

He developed, testified and gained enactment of numerous state and local environmental health measures, testified before the Presidential Committee on Executive Reorganization regarding the creation and scope of EPA, and testified before Congressional Committees regarding several major environmental health issues.

He has over 240 publications and policy papers, many of which may be accessed at: http://hsc .unm.edu/library/development/endowment/Gordon/index.shtml , and http://www.sanitarians .org/gordon.html

Vonia L. Grabeel, REHS/RS, MPH

Vonia L. Grabeel, REHS/RS, MPH, graduated from Eastern Kentucky University (EKU) with Bachelors of Science degrees in Biology and Environmental Health Sciences, as well as a Masters of Public Health. She joined the staff at EKU in 2005 and is currently serving as an Associate Professor in the Environmental Health Sciences Department.

Vonia began her professional career in 1993 with the Broward County Health Department in Ft. Lauderdale, Florida as an Environmental Health Specialist. After returning to her native state, Kentucky, Vonia had the opportunity to work for the Lexington-Fayette County Health Department as a Health Environmentalist. She worked there from 1998 to 2005 and rose in the ranks from a field inspector to the Environmental Health Director. In 2005, she joined the Department for Public Health as a section supervisor in the Division of Public Health Protection and Safety's Environmental Management Branch. This position has afforded her many opportunities from affecting policies statewide, regulations and training fledgling environmental health professionals.

She has been active in the state and national organizations that support and promote Environmental Health since beginning her career. She truly has a passion for our vocation and a love of mentoring new people in the Environmental Health profession.

Nancy Haberstich, RN

Nancy Haberstich is a registered nurse, a self-employed infection preventionist, health educator, and consultant. She was employed for 17 years as the infection control coordinator in a 300-bed municipal hospital in Lincoln, Nebraska.

Nancy has lectured and consulted with hospitals in six countries on five continents. She served as a volunteer in Liberia, West Africa for one year to reopen a school of nursing and paramedical training programs that had been destroyed by civil war. The project was funded by a grant from the government of Denmark. At the invitation of the Canadian Ministry of Health, Nancy spent one month providing infection control consultation for one of the four hospitals involved in the SARS crisis in Toronto, Canada in 2003. In 2004 Nancy developed the curriculum and served for 4 years as the coordinator of *The IPC Classroom* in Japan—a 78-hour comprehensive infection prevention and control training course for Japanese nurses and doctors. *The IPC Classroom* graduated 162 nurses and 2 doctors.

Nancy was the technical advisor and scriptwriter for 13 training videotapes on infection control topics that are utilized by many hospitals throughout the United States. Nancy has been a long-time member of APIC—Association for Professionals in Infection Control and Epidemiology—serving the international organization on the Board of Directors, the Certification Board of Infection Control and as a chapter president. Nancy was awarded the Carole DeMille Award from APIC in 1992 for her "knowledge of the present and her vision for the future".

Nancy Haberstich, founder and CEO of Nanobugs, inc., lives in Lincoln, Nebraska.

Tom Hatfield R.S. DAAS

DEGREES: BS, Biological Sciences, Stanford University 1976; MPH, Environmental. Health, UCLA 1978; Dr.PH, Environmental Health, UCLA 1985.

CURRENTLY: Professor, Dept of Environment and Occupational Health, California State University, Northridge, CA.

PREVIOUSLY: NSF, Orange County, Southern California Association of Governments, University of Oklahoma.

PROFESSIONAL AFFILIATIONS: REHA, CA.

Carolyn Hester Harvey, PhD, CIH, RS, DAAS

Carolyn Hester Harvey First Vice President—Carolyn Hester Harvey, PhD, CIH, RS, DAAS, CHMM Professor, Director of MPH Program Department of Environmental Health, Eastern Kentucky University. Dr. Carolyn Harvey is currently a full professor of Environmental Health at Eastern Kentucky University and Interim Director of the Master of Public Health program, where she has been a Professor since 2001. Before coming to EKU, she also taught at East Tennessee State University, also in the Environmental Health Department. Her teaching and research interests include: Occupational Health & Safety, Hazardous Materials Management, Air Pollution, Solid Waste, Industrial Hygiene Sampling & Analysis, HAZWOPER, and Industrial Ventilation, as well as farm safety, ergonomics and worker exposure assessment. Before joining the world of academia, she worked for the Galveston County Health Department in Texas, Union Carbide Corporation as an

Environmental Engineer and Industrial Hygienist, and several other environmental health corporations. Harvey began her education at ETSU, and went on to get a Masters in Environmental Management from the University of Houston, and then her Ph.D. from the University of Texas, School of Public Health. She has previously been a Council Member and Board Member for the National Environmental Health Science & Protection Accreditation Council. Harvey has also served on the Board of the Association of Environmental Health Academic Programs, and is a member of the National Environmental Health Association, the Academy of Hazardous Materials Managers and the American Board of Industrial Hygiene. She currently resides in Richmond, Kentucky.

Jason W. Marion, PhD

Jason W. Marion, PhD, has been actively involved in environmental health and epidemiology research. His work has been published in *Water Research* and *Environmental Science & Technology*, focusing on recreational water quality and waterborne disease risk. He has co-authored papers appearing in *Applied and Environmental Microbiology* and the *Journal of Water and Health*, while also having served as a peer-reviewer for the *International Journal of Environmental Research and Public Health*. Dr. Marion has had held a variety of positions including an Infectious Diseases Fellowship for the Public Health Preparedness for Infectious Diseases program at The Ohio State University. Outside of academia, from 1999 to 2012, he held multiple positions with the Ohio Department of Natural Resources (ODNR) and the Ohio Department of Agriculture. During his tenure with ODNR, he was the lead worker on waste management issues in his region in Southwest Ohio. While working in Ohio, Dr. Marion received a M.S. from Morehead State University in Morehead, Kentucky, and M.S. and Ph.D. degrees from The Ohio State University in Columbus. He currently serves as an assistant professor of environmental health science at Eastern Kentucky University in Richmond, where he teaches courses in toxicology and epidemiology.

Dr. David McSwane RS, CFP

Dr. David McSwane is Professor of Public Health and Chair of the Department of Epidemiology and Environmental Health Science in the Richard M. Fairbanks School of Public Health. He teaches courses in environmental health, food safety, and environmental health policy at the undergraduate and graduate levels. His research targets environmental hazards that cause illness and injury with a specific focus on food safety and defense. Dr. McSwane has published numerous articles in peer-reviewed journals in the fields of environmental health and food protection. He is the lead author of the SafeMark—Food Safety Fundamentals and the SafeMark Guide to Food Safety textbooks, which are published by the Food Marketing Institute and used by retail food managers to prepare for Food Protection Manager Certification examinations.

Dr. McSwane holds a bachelor's degree in Biology from Wabash College and Master of Public Health and Doctor of Health and Safety degrees from Indiana University. He is a Registered Environmental Health Specialist and a Certified Professional in Food Safety. Prior to joining the faculty at Indiana University, Dr. McSwane was Administrator of the Monroe County Health Department in Bloomington, Indiana, and he also worked as a Public Health Sanitarian with the Indiana State Department of Health.

Dr. McSwane is Past-President of the Indiana Environmental Health Association and the Indiana Public Health Association. He currently serves as the Executive Director of the Conference for Food Protection. He has received a variety of awards such as the Walter S. Mangold Award presented by the National Environmental Health Association, the Tim Sullivan Food Safety Award presented by the Indiana Environmental Health Association, the St. George Medal presented by the American Cancer Society, and the Indiana Public Health Foundation's Tony and Mary Hulman Health Achievement Award in recognition of his contributions to public health and environmental health.

Priscilla Oliver, PhD

Priscilla Oliver, PhD. is currently the Treasurer of the National Environmental Health Science and Protection Accreditation Council (EHAC). Dr. Oliver has been dedicated to teaching and speaking on environmental health and protection issues in her community. She serves as a peer reviewer of the Journal of Environmental Health, Technical Advisor of the Hazardous Materials and Toxic Substances Section of the National Environmental Health Association (NEHA) and a charter member of the National Council on Diversity in Environmental Health (N-CODE Health).

Dr. Oliver has taught Grant Writing, Fundraising and Development, Health Policy, and Managing Staff and Volunteers at Kennesaw State University in Graduate Public Administration in Marietta and at Troy University in Atlanta. She taught Academic Medicine and Environmental Health at the Morehouse School of Medicine in Atlanta. She has several years of work experience with government and is also a guest lecturer at several colleges. She is a graduate of the University of Alabama and Georgia State University.

Robert W. Powitz, RS & CSFP, ABSA, RBSP, CHSP, CHMM, CHCM, WQA, CWS-V

DEGREES: AAS, Agriculture, S.U.N.Y. 1962; BSA, Agriculture, University of Georgia 1964; MPH, Environmental Health, University of Minnesota 1974; PhD, Environmental Health, University of Minnesota 1978

CURRENTLY: Forensic Sanitarian, R.W. Powitz & Assoc, P.C., PO Box 502, Old Saybrook, CT 06475-0502; (work) 860-388-0893; (fax) 860-388-9566; (e-mail) sanitarian@juno.com or powitz@nsf.org Health Director, towns of Franklin, Lebanon, Salem, Sprague & Westbrook, CT.

PREVIOUSLY: Biosafety Officer, USDA, Plum Island Animal Disease Center, NY; Director, Environmental Health & Safety; Associate Professor-College of Engineering, Wayne State University, MI; Hospital Epidemiologist, Mercy Hospital, MI; Health Officer, Borough of Ringwood, NJ; Senior Sanitarian, State of New Jersey.

PROFESSIONAL AFFILIATIONS: American Academy of Sanitarians, Chairman 2001-04; Underwriter Laboratory Consumer Advisory Council; NSF International, Council of Public Health Consultants; NEHA; Davis Calvin Wagner Award 1996 AAS; Walter F Snyder Award 2001 NEHA/NSF; President's Award ACHMM 1990; Harry Bliss Journal Tech Editor's Award, NEHA, 1998; RS, CT, MI, Ohio, NY, PA; NEHA, RS & CSFP; ABSA, RBSP; CHSP, CHMM, CHCM, WQA, CWS-V.

Lauren Reno

Lauren Reno is a graduate from EKU, in both the Bachelor's (2006) and Master's (2011) programs of Environmental Health Science/Public Health. She has worked at Hitachi Automotive Systems Americas, Inc. in Berea, KY for 5 years, and was a Safety Intern at Smurfit Stone Container Corp. in Fernandina Beach, FL (now RockTenn). She obtained her Master's degree in Public Health while working full time at Hitachi as the Environmental/ISO Coordinator. Lauren has extensive experience in solid/hazardous waste management, air quality, water quality, groundwater remediation, environmental reporting, DOT regulations, OSHA regulations, and ISO 14001 standards. She is also HAZWOPER trained. Lauren currently is a member of the EHS Bachelor's degree curriculum advisory committee for EKU as well, which is made up of faculty and alumni. Lauren was born and raised on a farm in Flemingsburg, KY and graduated from Fleming County High School in 2002. She attended EKU and was a member of the EKU dance team for one year. Lauren was also a member of the Kappa Delta Tau service sorority, which solely focuses on community service projects. She now lives in Berea, KY with her husband and daughter.

History of Environmental Health

Joe E. Beck, RS, DEAAS

In spite of failures which I lament, of errors which I now see and acknowledge, or of the present aspect of affairs, do I despair the future? The truth is this: the march of Providence is so slow, our desires so impatient, the work of progress is so immense, and our means of aiding it so feeble, the life of humanity is so long, that of the individual so brief, that we often see only the ebb of the advancing wave and are thus discouraged. It is history that teaches us to hope.

— General Robert E. Lee
(near end of life)

Key Performance Outcome Indicators:

1. Understand the scope/definition of environmental and public health
2. Be able to visualize the impact of the environment on human life span through the ages
3. Be capable of discussing the significance of the impacts and evolution of environmental health over history
4. Understand the drivers and constraints facing environmental health professionals
5. Be able to identify key milestones in environmental health.

Historic Life Expectancy

During the Roman Empire, Romans had a approximate life expectancy of 22 to 25 years. In 1900, the world life expectancy was approximately 30 years and in 1985 it was about 62 years, just two years short of today's life expectancy.

Table 1.1 Human Life Expectancy at Birth

ERA	AVERAGE LIFESPAN AT BIRTH (YEARS)
Upper Paleolithic	33
Neolithic	20
Bronze Age	18
Bronze Age, Sweden	40–60
Classical Greece	28
Classical Rome	28
Pre-Columbian North America	25–30
Medieval Islamic caliphate	35+ The average life spans of the elite class were 59–84.3 years in the Middle East and 69–75 in Islamic Spain and medieval Britain (20–30)
Early twentieth century	30–45
Current world average	66.58 2009 established

Aging

Life expectancy changes as one gets older. By the time a child reaches their first year, their chances of living longer increase. By the time of late adulthood, ones chances of survival to a very old age are quite good. For example, although the life expectancy from birth for all people in the United States is 77.7 years, those who live to age 65 will have an average of almost 18 additional years left to live, making their life expectancy almost 83 years.

What Is Environmental Health?

The protection of populations and individuals from chemical, biological, radiological, and physical threats to their health and well-being.

—**J. Beck, 1976**

This definition was developed out of desperation when I began teaching environmental health at the university. It was necessary to define the scope of my responsibility and our mission. The older definitions assigned to our profession were in flux due to the creation of three new federal agencies that were formerly parts of the public health domain. These three agencies forced changes throughout state and local government. Public health lost many of its first-line employees to these new agencies.

What Is Public Health?

The definition of public health, as stated by Charles-Edward A. Winslow, in 1920:

The science and art of preventing disease, prolonging life, and promoting physical health and efficiency through organized community efforts for the sanitation of the environment, the control of community infections, the education of the individual in principles of personal hygiene, the organization of medical and nursing service for the early diagnosis and preventive treatment of disease, and the development of the social machinery which will ensure to every individual in the community a standard of living adequate for the maintenance of health.

His work provided the basis for the World Health Organization's definition of health: "A state of complete physical, mental, and social well-being and not merely the absence of disease or infirmity" **(UN, WHO, 1948).**

Environmental Health and History

Most infectious diseases that plague developing countries are associated with poverty, crowded and unsanitary living conditions, lack of clean water, failure to properly dispose of human waste and garbage, lack of protection against disease-bearing insects (window screens, mosquito nets, repellents and insecticides). An estimated 300–500 million people contract malaria each year. Every day 3,000 children die of malaria—mostly in sub-Saharan Africa. Malaria *kills* more than 13 million people a year (most of these deaths could be prevented with little more than a $10 mosquito net). Today in America 725,000 people die annually from heart disease, and about 540,000 die from cancer. While these diseases kill *less than 1%* of the population, tuberculosis will infect 1 billion new people and kill 35 million. AIDS is rapidly becoming the greatest threat to health, economic development, and national stability in many African and Asian countries. Dengue fever, which occurs primarily in tropical and subtropical countries, will total 50 million cases, with more than 25,000 dengue-related fatalities each year.

It was the exigencies of urban living, not considerations of health and disease, that necessitated sanitary engineering. Supernatural explanations of disease did not evoke or require an environmental origin for disease. However, in the fifth and fourth centuries B.C., in Greece, an empirical explanation of disease was proposed by the physician Hippocrates and his followers, who described diseases in objective terms, and rejected supernatural causes. In his book *On Airs, Waters, and Places,* the relations of disease to physical, social, and behavioral settings are presented for the first time. This book served as a guide for decisions regarding the location of urban sites in the Greco-Roman world, and may be considered the first rational guide to the establishment of a science-based public health.

However, the earliest recorded mention of any form of health control is contained in the Bible under *Leviticus.* When Moses led the children of Israel out of Egypt, the eating of the flesh of swine was forbidden because the animal was considered "unclean." The modern logic for this decision is: Pigs are scavengers and as result many parasites are known for carrying the tapeworm egg *Cystercircus cellulosae,* which infests man as *Taenia solium.* In *Leviticus* 14:1, the commentary in the *Expositor's Bible (a 12-volume reference that is a comprehensive and scholarly tool used for debating and explaining the Scriptures)* states: "Priests were public health officers in addition to their religious role." Religious leaders in ancient Israel taught people *not to eat* unclean animals (*Leviticus* 11; *Deuteronomy* 14). These included scavengers, shellfish, and shrimp. Many of these animals carry disease-causing organisms.

The ancient source of wisdom for this taboo is that the animals are scavengers that eat others that die of disease or are filter feeders that thrive in contaminated waters often containing human waste. The blood vessels in pigs are small and numerous, and it is therefore difficult to bleed the animal after slaughter. Blood was considered unclean; the meat either went sour rapidly or could cause food poisoning. Biblical guidance and directives also include *avoiding contact* with animals that are found dead without injury (*Leviticus* 11:32–40). The Israelites were prohibited from using porous earthen vessels because these could not be cleaned. The biblical regulations are consistent with many of today's practices and are based upon sound microbiological principles. It was the priests' job to teach and explain these laws. Priests were to designate as unclean those who had contagious diseases characterized by skin rashes, such as leprosy, measles, smallpox, and scarlet fever. This required some people to be isolated from others to prevent the spread of disease (see *Leviticus* 13). These later became the basis for quarantine procedures. Bible guidelines include limiting contact with property of sick people (*Leviticus* 13:47–59). Contaminated items were to be washed or burned (which destroys microorganisms). Health instructions also applied to dwellings. The Bible acknowledges that body fluids can be a vehicle for transmitting disease (*Leviticus* 15). Those coming into contact with fluids from a sick person had to wash their hands and clothes in water, bathe, and remain isolated from other people until evening as a precaution against spreading disease (*Leviticus* 15:11). These were the first universal fluid precautions, which were not recognized until the early 1980s due to AIDs.

The priest functioned as a *public health educator*, a sanitarian, and a building inspector, to promote health and prevent disease. The priest instructed that mold or fungal growth had to be scraped off and cleaned, or a house would be quarantined or demolished. Again, it was not until the 1980s that this issue started receiving appropriate attention, when we found that certain molds give off neurotoxins and could cause infections of the lungs and brain. The removal of the building approach is still used today when the mold cannot be contained. Openings to the outside of a building which would allow entrance to vermin, ticks and other disease-bearing bugs were to be sealed (*Leviticus* 14:33–48). Another major advance in promoting environmental health came with the Romans; we believe that the Babylonians and the Romans devised the first water carriage sewage disposal, hot and cold running water, central heating, and regular bathing. Evidence of these advances can be seen in the remains found in the Euphrates Valley and in Roman settlements.

With the fall of the Roman Empire, the world sank into the Dark Ages for several hundred years. The Stuart kings of England were a new beginning in health regulations. The air in London at that time was often lethal and obscured the sun because of the use of high-sulfur coal. This coal was the primary heating and cooking fuel. The king appointed his own inspector to ensure that burning trash and rubbish did not pollute the air in London, though the king's inspector does not appear to have had much success. The government started applying taxes to regulatory programs and soon forgot that the prime reason for the regulation was health; instead it became about the money. The stated purpose of the tax was to improve the standard of living. An example was the appointment of inspectors of the customs and excise tax to ensure the strength of the beer. This was one of the more successful taxes. The testing was not quite scientific; the inspector—wearing leather breeches—poured the beer on a seat and sat on it. If the beer was up to strength, he would stick to the seat; otherwise he could stand without difficulty. When the newly formed United States attempted to pass and enforce a similar beer tax, it nearly led to the breakup of the new country. The term *baker's dozen* also came from this period. Bakers sold bread by weight and were convicted for short measure or cheating the buyer, hence the term. They would add an extra roll to the dozen, making the measure to 13. Another more serious example of regulation from this time involves shipped fertilizer. Before 1943 acronyms were called *initialisms* when pronounced as a word, meaning the use of a word made from the initial letters or syllables of other words. The fertilizer bags were a major fire hazard aboard ship, so loading ships were inspected to make sure the bags were properly stored high, away from water so they would not get wet. Wet manure would start decomposing, which would cause the manure or guano (bird waste is very high in nitrogen) to generate heat, toxic/explosive gas, and fire. It is believed that failure to properly store these bags resulted in a major fine. Bags of fertilizer were said to be stamped SHIT, or *ship high in transit*.

Basic hygiene was nonexistent in the Dark Ages. Chamber pots containing the night soil were emptied out of windows to join all the other refuse in the streets and sidewalks. This gave rise to custom of the gentleman walking on the outside when on the street to protect the woman from splash. The more fortunate people lived in areas that had a central channel cut into road for drainage along which passed the waste and filth to discharge at the nearest convenient stream or containment basin. The occasional shallow drinking water well was dug for the residents, but sadly the source of water in the well was contaminated or the nearest convenient water was from a drainage ditch.

Epidemics such as the Black Death, caused by *Yersinia pestis*, carried by the flea, were a common occurrence of medieval times. The Black Death is estimated to have killed 30% to 60% of Europe's population, reducing the world's population from an estimated 450 million to between 350 and 375 million in 1400. This has been seen as creating a series of religious, social, and economic upheavals that had profound effects on the course of European history. It took over 150 years for Europe's population and society to recover. The plague returned at various times, particularly the sixteenth century, resulting in a larger number of deaths, until it disappeared from Europe in the nineteenth century. During that time, very few people reached any great age, and infant mortality was as high as could be expected. Frequently, over 50% of children would be dead before passing adolescence.

The housing boom brought on by industrialization resulted in hundreds of houses being built to meet the needs of the workers—somewhere to eat and steep, and for the lucky ones, some form of sanitation. However, the design of the houses was such that they were reservoirs of disease, being built back-to-back with common courtyards and invariably, earth closets or outhouses. Most of these were just a hole in the ground with a seat over it. The drinking water source was a communal pump which took its water from a similar hole in the ground. Some idea of the situation that prevailed can be gained from the Aldgate Pump Epidemic, where several hundred people died as a result of drinking polluted water containing the cholera organism from the communal pump well. Often waterborne disease outbreaks today have similar counterparts. As recently as 1936, Croydon (located in South London) was almost the subject of a similar epidemic, when it was discovered that one worker, a carrier of typhoid, had urinated at the bottom of a well he was helping to construct. This well would have supplied a large proportion of the population's water requirements and would likely have made thousands ill.

The Father of Public Health, Edwin Chadwick, wrote an article in *Westminster Review* entitled *"The Means of Assurance against the Casualties of Sickness, Decrepitude and Morality."* He urged the collection of accurate records and statistics about sickness and death. In 1831, a cholera epidemic resulted in the establishment of a **Consultative Board of Health**. The following year, Chadwick was appointed to the **Royal Commission on the Poor**, and together with the epidemic was responsible for the Report of the Commission and the terms of the Poor Law Amendment Act 1834. This act created a central department that was to end the poorly working system of the parish poor relief effort by amalgamating (combining) the parishes into larger unions, the forerunners of the present-day local government authorities.

1837: A bad harvest, rising prices, and unemployment coincided with an outbreak of typhus in London. (Typhus is closely allied to poor, overcrowded living conditions, as happened in Naples in 1944, and is carried by body lice.) This prompted more action from Chadwick, who persuaded the government to institute an inquiry into the cause of the outbreak. The panel was formed of Drs. Neil Amott, Kay, and Southwood Smith, and their report was submitted to the home secretary in 1838. *Note: The widespread use of the pesticide DDT saved many lives in Europe during World War II by preventing massive out breaks of typhus. While this pesticide is now banned from use because of environmental impacts, without a doubt it saved many lives.*

1839: Formation of the **Health of Towns Association**, which led to the appointment of a Select Committee. Its recommendation in 1840 was that there should be a general Building Act, Sewage Act, and the creation of **a board of health in every town**. Some states in the United States copied this idea.

1838: As a result of the findings and report of the panel of doctors, a further *Report on the Sanitary Condition of the Laboring Population of Great Britain* was issued in 1842, which was to have a far-reaching effect in the cause of public health. It is worth noting at this stage that these enlightened men were concentrating on the conditions of the working classes, the members of the population least able to fend for themselves, and the most prone to epidemics and poor living conditions. However, Chadwick was about to hit out again with even more far-reaching results, forming a team with Dr. Southwood Smith, who was later superseded by Dr. John Simon.

1840, 19th Century Deck Prism. First evidence of use of sensors used to alert crews of a fire below deck. On coal ships, prisms were also used to reflect light originating in the cargo hold; light from a fire would be collected by the prism and be reflected onto the deck. The nautical terms "deck light" and "dead light" or "deadlight" created, The surviving deck prisms with evidence of age or provenance date to the 1840s. In normal usage, the prism would protrude below the ceiling to allow it to pick up any light; the top or table of the prism is flat and flush with the deck to prevent creating a tripping hazard. If plain flat glass were were to be used it would just form a single bright spot below—not very useful general illumination—hence the prismatic shape.

Before 1943s acronyms were called initialisms when pronounced as a word, meaning the use a word made from the initial letters or syllables of other words. Bags of fertilizer would be shipped to various islands, but they we a major fire hazard The bags were a major fire hazard aboard ship so loading ships were inspected to make sure the bags were properly stored high away from water which would cause the manure or guano (bird waste high in nitrogen,) to generate tremendous heat, toxic/explosive gas and fire. Failure to properly store these bags resulted in a major fine, Bags of fertilizer were said to be stamped S.H.I.T, or ship high in transit.

1843: A Commission on the Health of Towns was set up and its first report was issued in 1844, with a second report nine months later. However, many towns and cities were beginning to appreciate the findings of Chadwick, Snow, and Simon, and embarked on their own to do something positive, by obtaining private legislation empowering the appointment of a medical officer of health and inspector of nuisances. The forerunner in this effort was Liverpool, whose act required the council to appoint one or more persons to supervise and enforce the due execution of all the duties to be performed by the inspectors appointed under this act, and report to the Council and Health Committee all breaches of the bylaws, rules, and regulations of the Council and Health Committee. Nationally very little progress was made until, in 1847, a financial crash, a famine, and a threatened epidemic of cholera joined forces to start some positive action.

1846: A temporary measure known as the **Nuisances Removal and Diseases Prevention Act** for the removal of nuisances and prevention of epidemic diseases was proposed and made permanent in 1848 under the title of the **Public Health Act of 1848** which, at last, began the move in the right direction. Most county health boards in the United States passed similar acts. It allowed for the creation of the local boards of health, and the setting up of a General Board of Health. Unfortunately, between 1848 and 1849 an epidemic of cholera coincided with the setting up of this board, which bore the brunt of blame for the epidemic and failure to control it, despite the fact that at that time medical knowledge was at a very low level, with the cause of many diseases being virtually unknown.

1854, London Cholera outbreak. John Snow was a British physician known as the father of epidemiology because of his work in tracing the source of a cholera outbreak in the Soho district of London, England. The 1854 a severe outbreak of cholera, occurred near Broad Street in Soho. John Snow's discoved that cholera is spread by contaminated water. Many areas in London as well as building basements had cesspools of night soil (human waste} underneath their floorboards. Many of the cesspools were overflowing and running down the middle of the street, the London government in an attempt to clean up the city decided to dump the waste into the River Thames. This action further contaminated the water supply, leading to the cholera outbreak. Dr Snow called it "the most terrible outbreak of cholera which ever to occurred in the United Kingdom. Over three days, 127 people on or near Broad Street died. In the next week, three quarters of the residents had fled the area. By 10 September, 500 people had died and the mortality rate was 12.8 percent in some parts of the city. At the end of the outbreak, 616 people died. As a result of this outbreak the educated Sanitary Inspector, the precursor to the modern English Environmental Health Officer was coming of age.

1875: They were assigned responsibility for the regulation of the Sale of Food and Drugs Act.

1876: They were assigned responsibility for the Pollution of Rivers Act and the Factories and Workshops Acts, 1878.

1877: The Royal Sanitary Institute established a simple examination to qualify inspectors. It was now becoming obvious that an unqualified person was no longer able successfully to hold these scientific and engineering responsibilities. Despite this move, it was not until 1997 that a certificate of competency was obligatory for all new appointments of inspectors of nuisances in London and for the remainder of the country.

1884: Sir Edwin Chadwick became the founding president of the Association of Public Sanitary inspectors, which today is the Chartered Institute of Environmental Health.

1895: The certificate of the Royal Sanitary Institute was awarded upon successful examination. In an effort to standardize enforcement, a set procedure of training and more comprehensive examination was set up for the sanitary inspector. The Royal Sanitary Institute and Sanitary Inspectors' Examination joint board allowed the holder to practice the profession of sanitary inspector. Invariably this was followed by a qualification of diploma for inspector of meat and other foods, or meat ticket, and for some a similar qualification of smoke inspector. This body has now been superseded by the Public Health Inspectors Examination Board, and has now incorporated a degree course in environmental health.

1956: UK public health inspector. In keeping with the upgraded qualifications by the United Kingdom, the title of sanitary inspector was changed, to show the expanded role of the profession to EHO. This is a designation of considerable prestige and influence in the United Kingdom, very similar to an inspector with New Scotland Yard, some of the world's most respected law enforcement officials.

Environmental Health in the United States

The environmental health profession in the United States had its modern-day roots in the sanitary and public health movement of the United Kingdom. In many ways the British efforts influenced the early growth of the profession in the United States. U.S. environmental health addresses all human health-related aspects of both the natural environment and the built environment. Our EH professionals are required to be licensed by exam in most states, and several levels of certificates are available. These include the diplomate status of the American Academy of Sanitarians, the certified occupational health and safety professional, and the food safety professional. The typical areas assigned to the U.S. environmental health specialist include those listed below and some that are of questionable environmental health concern.

- Air quality, including both ambient outdoor air and indoor air quality, which also comprises concerns about environmental tobacco smoke
- Body art safety, including tattooing, body piercing, and permanent cosmetics
- Climate change and its effects on health
- Disaster preparedness and response.
- Food safety, including in agriculture, transportation, food processing, wholesale, and retail distribution and sale
- Hazardous materials management, including hazardous waste management, contaminated site remediation, the prevention of leaks from underground storage tanks, the prevention of hazardous material releases to the environment, and responses to emergency situations resulting from such releases
- Housing, including substandard housing abatement and the inspection of jails and prisons
- Childhood lead poisoning prevention
- Land use planning, including smart growth
- Liquid waste disposal, including city wastewater treatment plants and on site waste water disposal systems, such as septic tank systems and chemical toilets
- Medical waste management and disposal
- Noise pollution control
- Occupational health and industrial hygiene
- Areas of homeland security
- Radiological health, including exposure to ionizing radiation from X-rays or radioactive isotopes

- Recreational water illness prevention, including from swimming pools, spas, and ocean and freshwater bathing places
- Safe drinking water.
- Solid waste management, including landfills, recycling facilities, composting, and solid waste transfer stations
- Toxic chemical exposure whether in consumer products, housing, workplaces, air, water, or soil
- Vector control, including the control of mosquitoes, rodents, flies, cockroaches, and other animals that may transmit pathogens.

Our early heath departments were nearly all created to deal with preventable environmental illness such as cholera, yellow fever and typhoid.

1793: Baltimore, first city board of health. The board of health was formed to fight a potential outbreak of cholera. Taking innovative strides to save lives, health officials posted signs on lampposts, held meetings, and led an early-day public information campaign to reduce deaths due to cholera, a highly preventable but often lethal communicable disease. The Baltimore City Health Department holds claim to being the oldest, continuously operating health department in the United States. The governor appointed the city's first health officers in response to a yellow fever outbreak in the Fells Point neighborhood along the northwestern branch of the Patapsco River.

1793–1799: Boston also holds claim to being the nation's first city health department. John Ross and John Worthington had been acting as quarantine physicians since 1792, and it is apparent that they served under the Committee of Health that was set up in September 1793. This is prior to the state legislation on the authorization of the health department.

1798: USPHS established. The Public Health Service Act structured the United States Public Health Service (PHS) as the primary division of the Department of Health Education and Welfare (HEW), which later became the United States Department of Health and Human Services. The origins of the Public Health Service can be traced to the passage of an act in 1798 that provided for the care and relief of sick and injured merchant seamen. The earliest marine hospitals created to care for the seamen were located along the east coast, with Boston being the site of the first such facility; later they were also established along inland waterways, the Great Lakes, and the Gulf of Mexico and Pacific coasts.

1799: Paul Revere was named Boston's first health officer.

1854: Massachusetts; first milk laws established.

1855: Louisiana; first State board of health established in the United States. The establishment of the Louisiana State Board of Health was authorized by Act 336 of March 15, 1855, primarily to manage epidemics, which endangered the state as well as New Orleans. New Orleans had failed to maintain a board of health for any length of time due to powerful local political resistance. The state finally acted because of the yellow fever epidemic of 1853.

This resulted in the creation of the Sanitary Commission of New Orleans, which then recommended the establishment of a city board of health. In order to negotiate the opposition from the commercial interests which had destroyed previous city boards of health, the state government resolved the problem by creating a state board of health.

1859: Boston; first milk inspector hired.

1863: Washington, D.C.; first nuisance law passed.

1866: New York; Metropolitan Health Act established.

1830: William Alcott wrote hundreds of articles on cleanliness, health, and virtue, the law of cleanliness.

1840: Sylvester Graham wrote on cholera and hygiene.

1844: John H. Criscom, *The Sanitary Condition of the Laboring Population of New York.*

1850: Lemuel Shattuck, *Report of the Massachusetts Sanitary Commission.*

1851: Dr. J.C. Simonds, *The Sanitary Condition of New Orleans* (tuberculosis).

1859: Florence Nightingale the apostle of cleanliness. Studied death rate from communicable diseases (principally cholera and typhus) among wounded British soldiers during the Crimean War and proved that improvements in sanitation at hospitals led to a decrease in the death rate. Human health is first linked to environmental conditions. The United States Sanitary Commission was an official agency of the United States government, created by legislation signed by President Abraham Lincoln on June 18, 1861, to coordinate the volunteer efforts of women who wanted to contribute to the war effort of the Union states during the American Civil War. Founded by Henry Whitney Bellows and William H. Van Buren, the Sanitary Commission was one of the great triumphs of private humanitarian enterprise during the Civil War. It was created to make up for grievous shortcomings of the Union Army's small and inefficient Medical Bureau. The commission, along with its impressive women's auxiliary, soon became the largest and most advanced national agency devoted to the care of casualties of war, supplying ambulances and medicines, staffing hospitals with doctors and nurses, inspecting camps, and much, much more. Provided most medical and sanitary supplies until the battle of Chancellorsville in 1863. The lessons of cleanliness were brought home from the war: Rural and urban public health initiatives were started.

1863: General Joseph K. Barnes was, by a special order of the War Department, empowered to take charge of the bureau of the Medical Department of the Army. For the remainder of his term of office he exhibited the greatest interest in the health and hygienic conditions of the army, in the comfort and welfare of the sick and wounded. Standardized field sanitation. On August 22, 1864, he was advanced to the position of surgeon general.

1870: The federal government converted the loose network of locally controlled hospitals into a centrally controlled Marine Hospital Service, with its headquarters in Washington, D.C. The position of supervising surgeon (later surgeon general) was created to administer the service, and John Maynard Woodworth was appointed as the first incumbent in 1871. He moved quickly to reform the system and adopted a military model for his medical staff, instituting examinations for applicants and putting his physicians in uniforms. Woodworth created a cadre of mobile, career service physicians who could be assigned as needed to the various marine hospitals. The commissioned officer corps (now known as the Commissioned Corps of the U.S. Public Health Service) was established by legislation in 1889. At first open only to physicians, over the course of the twentieth century, the corps expanded to include dentists, physician assistants, sanitary engineers, pharmacists, nurses, sanitarians, scientists, and other health professionals *Note*: U.S. Public Health Commissioned Corps emergency response teams are managed by the Office of the Surgeon General. They are trained and equipped to respond to public health crises and national emergencies, such as natural disasters, disease outbreaks, or terrorist attacks. The teams are multidisciplinary and are capable of responding to domestic and international humanitarian missions. Officers have responded to many such emergencies in the past, including: 1999, hospital center at Fort Dix, NJ, for Kosovo refugees; 2001, terrorist attacks; 2001 anthrax attacks; 2004/2005 tsunami and earthquake in Indonesia.

1863: Joseph K. Barnes, medical inspector of the Army. On August 22, 1864, he was advanced to the position of surgeon general, with the grade of brigadier general and on March 13, 1865, he received the brevet of major general for faithful and meritorious service during the war. He was at President Lincoln's bedside as he died of the gunshot to the head.

1872: American Public Health Association founded.

1875: Alabama; first rural public health department.

1879: National Board of Health created. In 1874 the National Association of State Health Commissioners was formed, and the need for a central federal health agency became more and more apparent. At that time the threat of yellow fever led to a sudden and widespread development of legislation—on both state and local levels—for the establishment of permanent boards of health. This fear led to a meeting attended by many of the existing state and city health departments in 1875 to discuss plans for a federal health organization. This convention met with little success due to interagency politics. The three existing national government departments that already possessed medical officers, the Army, the Navy, and the Marine Hospital Service, got into a dispute as to which should be charged with the new responsibilities. Political differences resulted in the closing of the National Board of Health in 1893.

1881: New York; first effective food control laws in the United States.

1882: Newark; first dairy inspections.

1883: Robert Koch; 1877 Koch's postulates. Koch pioneered the use of microbiologic techniques still used today. Developed agar growth media, petri dishes; bacterial purification and staining techniques.

1888: Louis Pasteur, Father of the Germ Theory and modern microbiology Pasteurization process for beer and milk. Discovered aeromicrobial utilization of oxygen, filterable viruses (1877). Defined fermentation, and developed rabies and anthrax vaccines and the basis for aseptic surgery.

1900: Major Walter Reed; yellow fever. Reed's research on yellow fever was the seminal work on vector-borne disease transmission. Yellow fever was a dreaded disease that had killed 90,000 people in the United States alone. Thousands of American soldiers in Cuba had died also. Reed observed that people who cared for the patients with yellow fever did not usually get the disease. His conclusion: People did not catch it from each other. In October 1900, Major Reed was able to announce to the annual meeting of the American Public Health Association that "the mosquito serves as the intermediate host for the parasite of yellow fever." Reed's success with stopping the spread of yellow fever made it possible for the United States to build the Panama Canal, a project previously attempted by France.

1910: Charles-Edward Amory Winslow; founded the Yale Department of Public Health, 1915. He had a major impact on housing and urban renewal policy.

1927: Victor Marcus Ehlers and E. W. Steel, *Municipal and Rural Sanitation* (sanitary science and water engineering). First nationally used book on sanitation and engineering, Used extensively for years to train early sanitarians. One of first texts to deal with rural environments. Writing of book started in 1897; first edition in 1927, fifth editions in total. Last published in 1965.

1930: The term *sanitarian* replaced the title of *inspector*.

1930: The journal *Sanitarian* was published. The first editor was Walter S. Mangold. (1932–1947). He later became senior sanitarian for the U.S. Public Health Service (Reserve); was widely quoted and a highly respected and influential public health pioneer.

1900–1910: Several states enact mandatory licensing for sanitary inspectors.

1930: The Dust Bowl lasted about a decade, displacing and impacting the health of over a million people from dust exposure and lack of water.

1935: The Soil Conservation Service was created and placed in the Department of Agriculture under the direction of Hugh H. Bennett,

1937: The California Association of Sanitarians, with members from nine states, changed its name and formed the National Association of Sanitarians (NAS) incorporated in California. The association had a printed magazine and four sections (chapters): Northern California, Southern California, San Diego, and Pennsylvania. The first president of the new national organization was Herbert A. Jewlett,

1939: John Steinbeck wrote his 1939 novel *The Grapes of Wrath*. The book dealt with the misery of the Dust Bowl, the depression, and the profound relocation and movement of people on the Plains.

1946: Communicable Disease Center created in Atlanta, Georgia.

1946–1961: CDC Field Training Program instructors Frank Bryan, PhD, MPH, (Capt., USPHS ret.), Richard Clapp, DSc, MPH (Capt., USPHS ret.), and Frank Bryan, PhD, MPH, (Capt., USPHS ret.), and Jerrold Michael, DrPH, ScD, PE, assistant surgeon general (Rear Admiral, USPHS ret.). Provided standardized environmental health practice in the United States, and laid the foundation for the professionalization of environmental health with the establishment of a network of undergraduate degrees in environmental health. During that time, nearly 38,000 local, state, and international public health workers took more than 1,600 courses.

1956: The Sanitarian Joint Council formed; sanitarians from Public Health Association, International Association of Food and Environmental Sanitarians, National Association of Sanitarians. Mission was to define role and qualifications for sanitarians.

1955: Indian Health Service (IHS) was established to take over health care of American Indians and Alaska Natives from the Bureau of Indian Affairs. The provision of health services to members of federally recognized tribes grew out of the special government-to-government relationship between the federal government and Indian tribes. This relationship, established in 1787, is based on Article I, Section 8 of the Constitution, and has been given form and substance by numerous treaties, laws, Supreme Court decisions, and executive orders.

1956: Frank Bryan, food safety leader, established the technique of hazard analyses (HCCP) in homes and at street-vending stands in developing countries. Then started setting up HACCP systems in food service establishments and chains.

1957: Ben Freedman, MD, MPH. Wrote *The Sanitarian's Handbook*, the first truly comprehensive book on how to be a sanitarian in the United States.

1958: Joe Salvato, P.E. *Environmental Engineering and Sanitation*, six editions and still in print, though the content of book shifted toward engineering after the 5th edition. First five editions contain critical knowledge for sanitarians and environmental health specialists. *Supplement to Environmental Engineering and Sanitation* published 1994, by Joe Beck and Joseph Salvato.

1966: Establishment of American Academy of Sanitarians, an organization that elevates standards, improves practice, advances professional proficiency, and promotes the highest levels of ethical conduct among professional sanitarians in every field of environmental health.

1967: The National Accreditation Council for Environmental Health Curricula was established to implement a program accrediting undergraduate and graduate programs environmental health. The name of the council was changed to the National Environmental Health Science and Protection Accreditation Council in 1991 to better reflect the entire discipline considered by the council. Promotes undergraduate curricula of a quality and content compatible with admission prerequisites of graduate programs in environmental health science and protection. Evaluates academic programs in environmental health science, and protection using criteria established by the Council.

1970: The NAS was composed of 41 affiliates, including a California state affiliate known as CAS, and over 5,000 members. In 1970, the NAS was renamed the National Environmental Health Association (NEH) and the CAS affiliate was renamed the California Environmental Health Association (CEHA)

1999: The Association of Environmental Health Academic Programs (AEHAP) was formed to address decreasing enrollment in environmental health undergraduate academic programs, and a severe workforce shortage of environmental health professionals.

2005: Joe Beck's *The Healthy Housing Reference Manual* published. A joint work of CDC, EPA, and HUD. Government Printing Office. This manual replaces the 1976 publication, *Basic Housing Inspection*.

2010: NEHA now has 4,500+ members who practice their profession in the public and private sectors as well as in academia and the uniformed services, with a majority being employed by state and local county health departments. In addition, NEHA's *Journal of Environmental Health* has subscribers in over 40 countries around the world. It is still the only organization that encompasses the entire environmental health profession.

Food/product Safety Milestones

1862: President Lincoln appoints a chemist, Charles M. Wetherill, to serve in the new Department of Agriculture (USDA). This was the beginning of the Bureau of Chemistry, the predecessor of the Food and Drug Administration.

1880: Peter Collier, chief chemist, U.S. Department of Agriculture, recommends passage of a national food and drug law, following his own food adulteration investigations. The bill was defeated, but during the next 25 years more than 100 food and drug bills were introduced in Congress.

1888: Dr. Harvey W. Wiley becomes chief chemist, expanding the Bureau of Chemistry's food adulteration studies. Campaigning for a federal law, Dr. Wiley is called the crusading chemist and father of the Pure Food and Drugs Act.

1902: Congress appropriates $5,000 to the Bureau of Chemistry to study chemical preservatives and colors and their effects on digestion and health. Dr. Wiley's studies draw widespread attention to the problem of food adulteration. Public support for passage of a federal food and drug law grows.

1902: Association of Official Agricultural Chemists (now AOAC International) establishes a Committee on Food Standards headed by Dr. Wiley. States begin incorporating these standards into their food statutes.

1906: On June 30, 1906, Teddy Roosevelt signed the Pure Food and Drug Act, establishing the nation's very first regulatory agency, This agency promulgated the early federal food laws. The Food and Drug Administration is the oldest comprehensive consumer protection agency in the U.S. federal government. Theodore Roosevelt was well versed about dangerous food; during the Spanish-American War he witnessed his Rough Riders made ill by canned meat. Roosevelt examined the slimy, stringy rations and instantly understood why his men were ill. The act prohibits interstate commerce in misbranded and adulterated foods, drinks, and drugs. The Meat Inspection Act is passed the same day.

The origins of the FDA can be traced back to the appointment of Lewis Caleb Beck in the Patent Office in 1848 to carry out chemical analyses of agricultural products, a function that the newly created Department of Agriculture inherited in 1862. Although it was not known by its present name until 1930, the FDA's modern regulatory functions began with the passage of the 1906 Pure Food and Drugs Act, a law a quarter-century in the making.

1905: *The Jungle*, a novel written by author and journalist Upton Sinclair. Sinclair wrote this novel to highlight the plight of the working class and to remove from obscurity the corruption of the American meat-packing industry during the early twentieth century. He made shocking disclosures of unsanitary conditions in meat-packing plants, the use of poisonous preservatives and dyes in foods, and cure-all claims for worthless and dangerous patent medicines. Sinclair intended for his novel to highlight the plight of the working class and reveal the corruption of the American meat-packing industry.

1911: In Milwaukee, Wisconsin; October, 35 men from Australia, Canada, and the United States, interested in improving the quality of milk, organized the International Association of Dairy and Milk Inspectors. By 1936, the association had become the International Association of Milk Sanitarians. In 1947, its name changed to the International Association of Milk and Food Sanitarians, Inc. Again in 1966, the association changed to the International Association of Milk, Food and Environmental Sanitarians. In October 1999, members voted to accept the current name, International Association for Food Protection.

1912: Congress enacts the Sherley Amendment to overcome the ruling in *United States v. Johnson*. It prohibits labeling medicines with false therapeutic claims intended to defraud the purchaser, a standard difficult to prove. This law was passed because of a common medicine called Mrs. Winslow's Soothing Syrup for teething and colicky babies; it was unlabeled yet laced with morphine, which resulted in the deaths of many teething infants.

1913: Gould Amendment requires that food package contents be "plainly and conspicuously marked on the outside of the package in terms of weight, measure, or numerical count."

1924: In *United States v. 95 Barrels Alleged Apple Cider Vinegar*, the Supreme Court rules that the Food and Drugs Act condemns every statement, design, or device on a product's label that may mislead or deceive, even if technically true.

1937: The elixir sulfanilamide disaster of 1937 was one of the most consequential mass poisonings of the twentieth century. This tragedy occurred shortly after the introduction of sulfanilamide, the first antimicrobial drug, when diethylene glycol (antifreeze) was used as the solvent in the formulation of a liquid preparation of sulfanilamide known as elixir sulfanilamide. One hundred five patients died from its therapeutic use. Under the existing drug regulations, premarket toxicity testing was not required. In reaction to this calamity, Congress passed the 1938 Federal Food, Drug and Cosmetic Act, which required scientific proof of safety before the release of a new drug.

1938: The Federal Food, Drug, and Cosmetic (FDC) Act of 1938 is passed by Congress. The new provisions:

- Extend control to cosmetics and therapeutic devices.
- Require new drugs to be shown safe before marketing, starting a new system of drug regulation.
- Eliminate the Sherley Amendment requirement to prove intent to defraud in drug-misbranding cases.
- Provide that safe tolerances be set for unavoidable poisonous substances.
- Authorize standards of identity, quality, and fill-of-container for foods.
- Authorize factory inspections.
- Add the remedy of court injunctions to the previous penalties of seizures and prosecutions.

1943: In *United States v. Dotterweich*, the Supreme Court rules that the responsible officials of a corporation, as well as the corporation itself, may be prosecuted for violations. It need not be proven that the officials intended, or even knew of, the violations.

1950: Oleomargarine Act requires prominent labeling of colored oleomargarine, to distinguish it from butter. Margarine was not always the preferred tables spread in the United States. In 1930, per capita consumption of margarine was only 2.6 pounds (vs. 17.6 pounds of butter). Times have changed, though. Today, per capita consumption of margarine is 8.3 pounds (including vegetable oil spreads), whereas butter consumption is down to about 4.2 pounds. Margarine was invented in 1870 by Hippolyte Mège-Mouriez from Provence, France.

1886: New York and New Jersey prohibited the manufacture and sale of yellow-colored margarine.

1902: Thirty two states and 80% of the U.S. population lived under margarine color bans. While the Supreme Court upheld such bans, it did strike down forced coloration (pink) which had begun in an effort by the dairy industry to discourage people from using margarine. During this period coloring in the home began, with purveyors providing capsules of food coloring to be kneaded into the margarine. This practice continued through World War II.

Claims that the butter yellow artificial coloring causes cancer in test animals were one of the drivers of the Delany Clause. The Delaney Committee starts congressional investigation of the safety of chemicals in foods and cosmetics, laying the foundation for the 1954 Miller Pesticide Amendment, the 1958 Food Additives Amendment, and the 1960 Color Additive Amendment.

1953: The FDA, now the Federal Security Agency, becomes the Department of Health, Education, and Welfare (HEW). Factory Inspection Amendment clarifies previous law and requires

FDA to give manufacturers written reports of conditions observed during inspections and analyses of factory samples.

1954: Miller Pesticide Amendment spells out procedures for setting safety limits for pesticide residues on raw agricultural commodities.

1958: Food Additives Amendment enacted, requiring manufacturers of new food additives to establish safety. The Delaney proviso prohibits the approval of any food additive shown to induce cancer in humans or animals. FDA publishes in the *Federal Register* the first list of substances generally recognized as safe (GRAS). The list contains nearly 200 substances.

1959: U.S. cranberry crop recalled three weeks before Thanksgiving for FDA tests to check for aminotriazole, a weed-killer found to cause cancer in laboratory animals. Cleared berries were allowed a label stating that they had been tested and had passed FDA inspection, the only such endorsement ever allowed by FDA on a food product.

1960: Color Additive Amendment enacted, requiring manufacturers to establish the safety of color additives in foods, drugs, and cosmetics. The Delaney proviso prohibits the approval of any color additive shown to induce cancer in humans or animals.

1960: Reorganization of federal health programs places FDA in the Public Health Service. under Section 512 of the Food, Drug, and Cosmetic Act, making approval of animal drugs and medicated feeds more efficient.

1969: FDA begins administering sanitation programs for milk, shellfish, food service, and interstate travel facilities, and for preventing poisoning and accidents. These responsibilities were transferred from other units of the Public Health Service. The White House Conference on Food, Nutrition, and Health recommends systematic review of GRAS substances in light of the FDA's ban of the artificial sweetener cyclamate. President Nixon orders FDA to review its GRAS list.

1972: The Consumer Product Safety Commission (CPSC) was signed into law by President Nixon; commission was created when Congress passed the Consumer Product Safety Act to protect the public "against unreasonable risks of injuries associated with consumer products." The CPSC began its oversight in 1973. As an independent agency, the CPSC does not report to any federal department or agency.

1977: Saccharin Study and Labeling Act passed by Congress to stop the FDA from banning the chemical sweetener but requiring a label warning that it has been found to cause cancer in laboratory animals.

1982: Tamper-resistant packing regulations issued by FDA to prevent poisonings such as deaths from cyanide placed in Tylenol capsules. The Federal Anti-Tampering Act passed in 1983 makes it a crime to tamper with packaged consumer products.

FDA publishes first Red Book (successor to 1949 Black Book), officially known as *Toxicological Principles for the Safety Assessment of Direct Food Additives and Color Additives Used in Food.*

1988: Food and Drug Administration Act of 1988 officially establishes the FDA as an agency of the Department of Health and Human Services, with the commissioner of food and appointed by the president with the advice and consent of the Senate, and broadly spells out the responsibilities of the secretary and the commissioner for research, enforcement, education, and information.

1996: Saccharin Notice Repeal Act repeals the saccharin notice requirements.

The Food Quality Protection Act amends the Food, Drug, and Cosmetic Act, eliminating application of the Delaney proviso to pesticides.

2000: The U.S. Supreme Court, upholding an earlier decision in *Food and Drug Administration v. Brown & Williamson Tobacco Corp. et al.*, ruled 5–4 that FDA does not have authority to regulate tobacco as a drug. Within weeks of this ruling, FDA revokes its final rule, issued in 1996, that restricted the sale and distribution of cigarettes and smokeless tobacco products to children and adolescents, and that determined that cigarettes and smokeless tobacco products are combination products consisting of a drug (nicotine) and device components intended to deliver nicotine to the body.

2004: Legislation passed to help consumers choose heart-healthy foods. The Department of Health and Human Services announces that FDA will require food labels to include transfat content, the first substantive change to the nutrition facts panel on foods since the label was changed in 1913.

2004: The National Academy of Sciences releases *Scientific Criteria to Ensure Safe Food*, a report commissioned by FDA and the Department of Agriculture, which buttresses the value of the Hazard Analysis and Critical Control Point (HACCP) approach to food safety already in place at FDA and invokes the need for continued efforts to make food safety a vital part of the overall public health mission.

2004: The Animal Drug User Fee Act permits FDA to collect subsidies for the review of certain animal drug applications from sponsors, analogous to laws passed for the evaluation of other products FDA regulates, ensuring the safety and effectiveness of drugs for animals and the safety of animals used as foodstuffs.

2004: Passage of the Food Allergy Labeling and Consumer Protection Act requires the labeling of any food that contains a protein derived from any one of the following foods that, as a group, account for the vast majority of food allergies: peanuts, soybeans, cow's milk, eggs, fish, crustacean shellfish, tree nuts, and wheat.

Occupational Health and Safety Timelines

1970: The Occupational Safety and Health Act of heralded a new era in the history of public efforts to protect workers from harm on the job. The act established for the first time a nationwide federal program to protect almost the entire workforce from job-related death, injury, and illness. Secretary of Labor James Hodgson, who had helped shape the law, termed it "the most significant legislative achievement" for workers in a decade.

1867: Massachusetts institutes the first factory inspections for safety hazards.

1869: 179 workers burned to death in the Avondale Mine in Luzerne County, PA, because the mine owners had refused to build an escape exit.

1870: The Pennsylvania legislature passed the first mine safety act in the country (legislation that was rejected prior to the Avondale Mine disaster).

1877: Massachusetts enacts legislation requiring guarding of hazardous parts of machinery.

1893: The first federal law requiring safety equipment on railroad engines (law due to numerous explosions).

1907: Upton Sinclair's *The Jungle* aroused public sympathy for workers in the packing house industry, where the joints in the fingers of worker might be eaten by the acid or cuts mutilated their hands.

1907: 26 states passed legislation making it easier for workers to sue employers if injured or killed on the job.

1911: Fire at Triangle Shirtwaist factory where 146 women and children workers are killed, in part because the fire escape doors were locked to prevent unauthorized breaks by workers.

1911: National Safety Council (pro-business workplace safety organization) is established.

1915: Oil workers in Bayonne, NJ, go on strike over heat stress that reached as high as 250 degrees.

1918: U.S. and Canadian insurance companies refused to sell life insurance policies to asbestos workers due to the high mortality rate.

1920: All but eight of the states had passed workmen compensation laws. True purpose was to prevent workers from suing their employers. Two of the biggest supporters were U.S. Steel and the National Association of Manufacturers.

1933: The National Safety Council (business organization) says "safety can never be legislated and enforced to individuals. Safety must be sold and taught into individuals."

1935: Up to 2,000 workers died in the United States from exposure to high levels of silica.

1935: 108 black steelworkers (furnace cleaners) in northern Indiana sued subsidiaries of U.S. Steel for failing to provide healthful working conditions (leading to silicosis and other lung diseases). They settle out of court in 1938 for an undisclosed amount.

1936: Walsh-Healy (public contracts) Act is passed, the first national standards for workplace safety (only for corporations getting federal contracts). An employer found guilty of violating the act could be "blacklisted" from federal contracts for three years.

1950: Mechanization of the cotton industry increases incidence of respiratory symptoms similar to byssinosis.

1952: Coal Mine Safety Act passed.

1955: It was established unequivocally that exposure to asbestos causes lung cancer.

1956: The World Health Organization discovered an alarming number of cases of mesothelioma (a rare cancer caused by asbestos exposure) due to asbestos exposure that was less than the amount that causes asbestosis.

1960: Specific safety standards promulgated comprehensive safety and health regulations for shipyard and longshore industries.

1968: 78 coal miners killed in mine explosion in Farmington, West Virginia.

1968: Surgeon general reports that 65% of workers studied were exposed to toxic materials or harmful physical agents, with only 25% adequately protected.

1969: Construction Safety Act passed.

1970: Occupational Safety and Health Act (OSHA) enacted with the active support of the Oil Chemical and Atomic Workers, Ralph Nader, the Steelworkers, the UAW, and the AFL-CIO (signed into law by President Nixon after his weaker bills were defeated).

1974: OSHA adopted health standards for 14 carcinogens.

1974: Karen Silkwood dies in a mysterious car accident. Silkwood helped organize the union at Kerr McGee and was active in health and safety organizing when she died.

1976: Eula Bingham is appointed head of OSHA. New Directions grant program helps fund training for thousands of workers about workplace hazards and their legal rights.

1086: After years of lawsuits and passage of local legislation, federal right-to-know standard is established.

1986: After years of lawsuits and passage of local legislation, federal asbestos in schools regulations are established.

Environmental Protection Timelines

1947: Los Angeles Air Pollution Control District created the first air pollution agency in the United States.

1948: Federal Water Pollution Control Act

1955: National Air Pollution Control Act

1965: National Emissions Standards Act

1965: Motor Vehicle Air Pollution Control Act

1965: Solid Waste Disposal Act

1967: Air Quality Act (amendment to CAA)

1969: Federal Coal Mine Health and Safety Act

1970: Created by President Nixon. A time when rivers caught fire and cities were hidden under dense clouds of smoke. We've made remarkable progress since then in protecting human health and safeguarding the natural environment. The U.S. Environmental Protection Agency was established in 1970 to consolidate in one agency a variety of federal research, monitoring, standard-setting, and enforcement activities to ensure environmental protection. EPA's mission is to protect human health and to safeguard the natural environment—air, water, and land.

1970: Williams-Steiger Occupational Safety and Health Act created OSHA and NIOSH.

1970: Lead-Based Paint Poisoning Prevention Act

1972: Federal Insecticide, Fungicide, and Rodenticide Act (FIFRA) (amended by Food Quality Protection Act of 1996)

1973: Endangered Species Act

1974: Safe Drinking Water Act

1975: Hazardous Materials Transportation Act

1976: Resource Conservation and Recovery Act (RCRA)

1976: Toxic Substances Control Act (TSCA)

1977: Clean Water Act

1977: Surface Mining Control and Reclamation Act

1978: National Energy Conservation Policy Act

1980: The Superfund law is passed to clean up old, abandoned waste sites. EPA and communities begin emergency response planning in the event of environmental accidents. States begin to run their own hazardous waste programs. Risk science begins to help EPA set priorities. Thirty years after Valley of the Drums in Bullitt County became the nation's poster child for industrial negligence and helped push Congress to enact a toxic dump cleanup program, the EPA has raised new concerns about conditions at the Kentucky site.

1980: Comprehensive Environmental Response, Compensation, and Liability Act (CERCLA) created the Superfund program.

1980: Fish and Wildlife Conservation Act

1982: Nuclear Waste Policy Act

1986: Emergency Planning and Community Right-to-Know Act (EPCRKA)

1986: Superfund Amendments and Reauthorization Act (SARA)

1989: Montreal Protocol on ozone-depleting chemicals enters into force.

1990s: The Clean Air Act Amendments set the stage for further protections, such as dust and soot. Pollution prevention reduces pollution before it begins. EPA partners with companies to explore and test innovative, voluntary approaches to environmental protection.

1990: Clean Air Act Amendments of 1990 Set new automobile emissions standards, low-sulfur gas, required Best Available Control Technology (BACT) for toxins, reduction in CFCs.

1991: Intermodal Surface Transportation Efficiency Act (ISTEA)

1992: Residential Lead-Based Paint Hazard Reduction Act

1993: North American Free Trade Agreement Implementation Act

1994: Executive Order 12898 on Environmental Justice

1996: Mercury-containing and Rechargeable Battery Management Act (PL 104–19)

2000: Mercury emissions; visibility rules further improve air quality. EPA responds to 9/11. Clean diesel engines cut emissions from trucks.

2002: Small Business Liability Relief and Brownfields Revitalization Act (amended CERCLA)

2003: Clear Skies Act (proposed) The Clear Skies Initiative was President George H.W. Bush's proposed strategy for air regulation. It is proposed legislation that mandates a 70% cut in air pollution from power plants.

The Role of the Environmental Health Officer

Who fits the role of an EHO? Typically an overworked, underpaid soul who loves the job. This may sound big-headed and simplified, but nevertheless is more than somewhat true. By virtue of the nature of the employment, an EHO (also known by over 100 titles such as sanitarian, a title once used by M.D.s while apparently working a set number of hours per week). The EHO must be part engineer, scientist, investigator, and educator. The EHO is never off duty. Depending on the authority and the nature of work, they are on call 24 hours per day, 365 days per year, and it is not unknown, albeit under exceptional circumstances, for EHOs to be called back from holiday. Equally, an experienced EHO cannot "turn off" at the end of a working day, but finds that eyes and ears remain working, even when engaged in a leisure pursuit. After all, a meal in a restaurant still has to be prepared and served, and the eyes still watch what is going on. Infectious diseases know no time barrier, and an outbreak of food poisoning or Noro virus has to be investigated forthwith.

Similarly the underpaid genius, EHOs are required to deal with so many trades and professions, ranging from medical practitioner to plumbers, architects, and civil engineers to refuse collectors, that they have to have a wide-ranging variety of subjects at their fingertips to ensure understanding between both parties.

It is now generally accepted that the EHO is a highly qualified individual with worldwide respect. EHOs, under whatever name, operate throughout the world and are recognized as professionals. The profession is wide open to both men and women. The number of women students increases annually, and it is estimated that some 2,500 new graduating students in the United States and 250 students per year in the United Kingdom are required to maintain the yearly expansion of EHO classifications. We currently come nowhere close to filling the openings.

REFERENCES

Hippocrates, 460 B.C.–357 B.C., head portrait, Library of Congress, Prints & Photographs Online Catalog, 1 photomechanical print, BIOG FILE [item] LC-USZ62-51385 (b&w film copy neg.)

John Moffat, *The Prognostics and Prorrhetics of Hippocrates*; translated from the original Greek: with large annotations, critical and explanatory: to which is prefixed a short account of the life of Hippocrates, Printed by T. Bensley, for C. Elliot, T. Kay, and Co., 1788.

Central Intelligence Agency (CIA), *The World Factbook*, Life Spans 2009, accessed 11/12/09, https://www.cia.gov/library/publications/the-world-factbook/index.html.

Life expectancy. Life expectancy over human history: Encyclopedia II: Life expectancy—Life expectancy over human history, accessed 08/26/09, adapted from the Wikipedia article "Life expectancy over human history," under the GNU Free Documentation License; also see http://en.wikipedia.org/wiki.

Mary C. Gillett, U.S Army Medical Department. Office of Medical History, Library of Congress Cataloging in Publication, Data History—19th century. 2. Medicine, Military—United States- History—19th century. I. Title. II. Series. UH223.G543 1987 355.3'45'0973 87-600095, First Printing-CMH Pub 30–8

Association of Environmental Health Academic Programs (AEHAP), accessed 10/23/09, http://www.aehap.org/.

National Environmental Health Association (NEHA) web site, accessed 03/08/10, http://www.neha.org/index.shtml.

National Environmental Health Science & Protection Council (EHAC), web accessed 12/23/09, http://www.ehacoffice.org/.

United States Environmental Protection Agency (EPA), updated 12/10/09, accessed. 03/08/10, http://www.epa.gov/history/.

United Nations, World Health Organization (WHO), updated 2010, accessed 03/06/10, http://www.who.int/about/history/en/index.html.

Consumer Product Safety Commission (CPSC), The Consumer Product Safety Improvement Act (CPSIA) and Legislation and Amended Statutes, accessed 01/23/10, http://www.cpsc.gov/ABOUT/cpsia/legislation.html.

Federal Food and Drug Administration (FDA), updated 03/03/08, accessed 02/05/10, http://www.fda.gov/.

CDC (1999). "Ten great public health achievements—United States, 1900–1999". MMWR Morb Mortal Wkly Rep 48 (12): 241–3. PMID 10220250. Reprinted in: *JAMA* 281 (16): 1481. 1999. doi:10.1001/jama.281.16.1481. PMID 10227303, web accessed 12/03/08, http://cdc.gov/mmwr/preview/mmwrhtml/00056796.htm.

Encyclopedia of Public Health, Winslow, Charles-Edward Amory, accessed 11/24/09, http://www.enotes.com/public-health-encyclopedia/winslow-charles-edward-amory.

UK History of Environmental Health, States of Jersey, British Crown Dependency, web accessed 02/01/10; the official website for public services and information online is: http://www.gov.je/Health/HealthProtection/About/Pages/History .aspx.

Occupational Safety and Health Administration (OSHA), The Labor Department in the Carter Administration: A Summary Report—January 14, 1981, accessed 11/25/09, http://www.dol.gov/oasam/programs/history/carter-osha.htm.

Careers in Environment Health

2

Joe E. Beck, RS, DEAAS

Comparative Summary of Environmental Health Sciences

Joe E. Beck, RS, DEAAS

A Day in the Life of an Environmental Public Health Practitioner

Vonia L. Grabeel, RS, MPH

A Day in the Life of an Industrial Environmental Health Practitioner

Lauren K. Reno, MPH

Three-Dimensional Career Planning: "What do I want to be when I grow up?"

Joe E. Beck, RS, DEASS

"The creatures that inhabit this earth—be they human beings or animals—are here to contribute, each in its own particular way, to the beauty and prosperity of the world."

—Dalai Lama

Key Performance Outcome Indicators:

1. Understand the definition of environmental health;
2. Understand the difference between environmental health and environmental science
3. Be able to define a professional in environmental health and professionals working in environmental health
4. Understand the various job titles that environmental health people work under
5. Be aware of the differences of educational process for environmental health and environmental science

What Is Environmental Health?

Environmental Health is about protecting human health from the environment. Environmental science is about protecting the environment from primarily human threats and actions. There are a lot of areas in which common goals can be found, but in the end humans are always going to be the chief threat to environmental protection. Environmental scientists will tell you that without population control, humans will always be the chief threat. The progress in expanding human life expectancy impacts environmental science in many negative ways due to the increase in natural resources used for that purpose. Many short-term goals of environmental health and environmental science may seem compatible, but when viewed under scientific scrutiny will often be found in conflict. One partial answer to this conundrum can be found in the sustainability movement. As much damage to the environment has been done by well-intentioned people as by those exploiting our resources. We may discover that we need to rip up many parking lots and other concrete and asphalt surfaces in order to plant things which will remove mass quantities of CO_2 from the atmosphere to restore a balance in the carbon cycle and begin the control of greenhouse gases, but only if we act in time! The issues of atmospheric and oceanic degradation and the wasting of the resources of the planet are areas where environmental science and environmental health collectively share interest. Our foolishness in not being careful stewards to the environment was apparent to many far before recent times. The quotations given below seem quite appropriate, particularly because they were written by a prominent life science scholar, Lewis Thomas, in his famous book, The Lives of a Cell: Notes of a Biology Watcher.

The greatest of all the accomplishments of 20th century science has been the discovery of human ignorance.

The oldest, easiest to swallow idea was that the earth was man's personal property, a combination of garden, zoo, bank vault, and energy source, placed at our disposal to be consumed, ornamented, or pulled apart as we wished.

This chapter discusses the different career options and academic path for becoming a qualified environmental health professional or an environmental protection scientist. It does not mean that one could not get a degree in environmental health and work in environmental science or get a degree in environmental science and work in environmental health. It only serves to show the difference between the two academic criteria and why environmental health is often identified as an engineering discipline.

Environmental Health

Due to a national shortage of trained environmental health professionals, earning a degree in environmental health from a program accredited by the National Environmental Health Science and Protection Accreditation Council (environmental health AC) offers many career opportunities. This career selection is a great career choice. You can find a list of programs at: http://www.ehacoffice.org/accred-prog/under-prog.php

What Is an Environmental Health specialist?

Environmental health is a branch of public health protection that is concerned with all aspects of the natural and built environment that may affect human health. Other terms that refer to the discipline of environmental health include environmental public health, industrial hygiene, and environmental health and protection. Environmental health is a field of science that studies how the environment influences human health and disease. "Environment" in this context means identifying and addressing how the environment impacts human health. Environmental health is a very diverse field where professionals perform a variety of tasks, such as inspecting public and work facilities investigating disease outbreaks, emerging communicable diseases, workplace hazards, and environmental pollution, providing education, conducting environmental cleanups follow-ups, and more.

There are two primary types of professionals working in environmental health today. One has an education in environmental health, and the other an education that is supportive of environmental health. Environmental health and protection professionals may have education in many areas critical to the practice of environmental health, such as engineering or air quality. Professionals with environmental health and protection degrees are typically licensed and are essential to the success of a comprehensive program.

Environmental health professionals are well known for their efforts to ensure the safety of what we eat, breathe, touch, and drink. Environmental health professionals monitor air quality, water and noise pollution, toxic substances and pesticides, conduct restaurant inspections, carry out vector control, and promote healthy land use and housing. Environmental health professionals also perform research on a variety of topics, including environmental toxins, communicable diseases, and the human health impacts of environmental catastrophes such as tornados, nuclear accidents, product hazards, hurricanes, and health threats under homeland security. The increase in environmental health threats includes the reoccurrence of bedbugs after 50 years, contaminated food disease outbreaks such as Escherichia coli 159 H, failing private waste water systems, West Nile virus, SARS (severe acute respiratory syndrome), bio/agro-terrorism (intentional poisoning of food), and the human health impacts of terrorist attacks and environmental catastrophes. The newspapers each day have articles that result in a demand for more trained professionals in the field of environmental health.

Environmental health and protection professionals have been adequately educated in environmental health and protection and hold a degree in environmental health. They are specifically educated in the technical (programmatic) components, as well as in epidemiology, biostatistics, toxicology, management, public policy, risk communication, risk management, environmental law, and environmental finance. Environmental health professionals are routinely called upon to apply forensic skills in the investigation of the sources of disease outbreaks.

Other professionals working in environmental health and protection include chemists, geologists, biologists, meteorologists, physicists, physicians, nurses, economists, engineers, attorneys, planners, epidemiologists, social scientists, political scientists, toxicologists, public administrators, veterinarians, and planners.

Environmental health is concerned with all aspects of the natural and built environment that may affect human health. Other phrases that concern or refer to the discipline of environmental health include environmental public health and environmental health and protection.

Here are two good definitions for you to consider. Environmental health is defined as:

The protection of populations and individuals from chemical, biological, radiological, and physical threats to their health and well-being. (J. Beck, 1976)

Environmental health services are defined as:

Those services which implement environmental health policies through monitoring and control activities. They also carry out that role by promoting the improvement of environmental parameters and by encouraging the use of environmentally friendly and healthy technologies and behaviors. They also have a leading role in developing and suggesting new policy areas in health.(World Health Organization)

Environmental health practitioners may be known as sanitarians, public health inspectors, environmental health specialists, environmental health officers, or environmental health practitioners. In many European countries physicians and veterinarians are involved in environmental health. Many states in the United States require that individuals have professional licenses in order to practice environmental health.

Environmental health epidemiology studies the relationship between environmental exposures (including exposure to chemicals, radiation, and microbiological agents) and human health. Observational studies, which simply observe exposures that people have already experienced, are common in environmental epidemiology because humans cannot ethically be exposed to agents that are known or suspected to cause disease. While the inability to use experimental study designs is a limitation of environmental epidemiology, this discipline directly observes effects on human health rather than estimating effects from animal studies. (Referenced from Wikipedia)

Toxicology studies how environmental exposures lead to specific health outcomes, generally in animals, as a means to understand possible health outcomes in humans. Toxicology has the advantage of being able to conduct randomized controlled trials and other experimental studies because they can use animal subjects. However, there are many differences in animal and human biology, and there can be a lot of uncertainty when interpreting the results of animal studies for their implications for human health. (Referenced from Wikipedia)

The B.S. in Environmental Health and Job Opportunities

Currently there are fewer than 40 accredited environmental health programs in the United States providing bachelor's degrees. Due to the academic difficulty of the academic programs, there is not an adequate number of graduates available for the current positions. These academic programs offer a significant amount of instruction in engineering, biology, chemistry, physics, and math. As a result, many positions are filled with underqualified individuals. The U.S. Department of Health and Human Services estimates that there is a need of 25,000 new environmental health professionals each year. The accredited programs graduate fewer than 800 graduates each year. A 1987 study by the Bureau of Health Professions, Health Resources and Services Administration, determined that 121,000 additional environmental health specialists were needed (environmental scientists, geologists, chemists, biologists, toxicologists). The profession has lost ground in the years since trying to recruit an additional workforce. (To read more, refer to the website of the Association of Environmental Health Academic Programs: http://aehap.org/#)

Unlike many BS degree programs, the baccalaureate degree in environmental health fully qualifies individuals for professional-level positions upon graduation. The degree exceeds most employment requirements due to its intensity in science and the shortage of qualified applicants. Many of us in academia would recommend, after a little job experience, seeking a master's degree in a specialty area.

Individuals electing to pursue a degree in environmental health sciences can look forward to employment opportunities in four primary areas:

1. Industry
2. Government
3. Consulting organizations
4. Third-party certification organizations

The curricula of these accredited programs are configured to ensure that the graduates of the programs have multiple career-growth options upon graduation. Students have been extremely successful both in graduate study and professional positions.

All of the students in accredited programs participate in experiential learning during before they graduate. Most of the accredited programs provide opportunities for interested students to have an external professional mentor. The mentors are selected from highly successful professionals whose primary role is to provide friendly insights on developing career plans and long-term career goals, and to encourage the development of effective networking skills. Past mentors have included national research scientists, senior technical editors of international publications, heads of corporations, high-ranking governmental officials, including high-ranking military personnel, and even two assistant surgeon generals of the U.S. Public Health Service.

In today's world, few professions can promise that the job you start with can or will be the job in which you end your career. However, we can document that the majority of our graduates have the opportunity to spend their careers in the same positions but with salary and responsibility growth. Our surveys also reveal that the profession provides numerous growth, pay, and career-expansion opportunities to students willing to market themselves and take advantage of those opportunities.

The following are a few of the many positions that environmental health professionals currently hold:

Environmental Health Officer
Emergency Management Specialist
Emergency Response Specialist
Environmental Health Educator
Environmental Health and Safety Officer
Disease Control Office
Environmental Health Science Officer
Environmental Health Scientist
Environmental Health and Protection Consultant
Environmental Health Sanitarian
Environmental Health Specialist
Risk-Assessment Specialist
Environmental Toxicologist
Epidemiologist
Ergonomist
Industrial Hygienist
Institutional Environmental Health Injury Control Officer
Food Safety Officer
HACCP Consultant
Hazardous Waste Specialist
Health Physicist
Housing Code Enforcement Official
Onsite Waste Control Officer
Pollution Control Officer
Air Pollution Control Officer
Occupational Health and Safety Trainer
Public Water Supply Control Officer
Solid Waste Specialist
Swimming Pool and Spa Consultant
Risk-Communication Specialist
Vector Control Specialist
Consumer Product Safety Officer
Public Health Pest Control Consultant
Air Pollution Control Officer
Industrial Hygienist
Institutional Environmental Health Manager
Injury Control Officer
Food Safety Officer

Third-Party Product Certifier
Preventive Medicine Specialist
Supply Control Officer
Public Health Pest Control Consultant

The Registered Environmental Health Specialist/Registered Sanitarian Exam (NEHA S/RS)

The NEHA S/RS is the premier environmental health credential in the United States, only superseded by membership in the Academy of Sanitarians. It is available to a wide range of environmental health professionals. Individuals holding the environmental health S/RS credential demonstrate competency in environmental health issues, direct and train personnel to respond to routine or emergency environmental situations, and frequently provide education to their communities on environmental health concerns. The advantage of NEHA's environmental health S/RS registration program is that it demonstrates your competency and capabilities in the environmental health field. NEHA provides continual update of the environmental health S/RS examination and develops a study guide based on an ongoing assessment of the environmental health field; it also tracks individuals continuing education (to read more, go to the web page of NEHA http://www.neha.org/credential/#rehsrs_cred).

What Is a Registered Sanitarian?

A sanitarian is an individual licensed by the state "who, through education, training or experience in the natural sciences and their application and through technical knowledge of prevention and control of preventable diseases, is capable of applying environmental control measures so as to protect human health, safety and welfare." Becoming a registered sanitarian confirms that the individual possesses knowledge on a variety of environmental and public health issues and can properly take corrective action to protect human health. Registered sanitarians work in the public and private sectors. Many are employed by state and local government in regulatory programs such as food safety, drinking water regulation, wastewater systems, radiation protection, housing, and occupational safety. Below is an outline of the 15 different content areas the examination covers and the percentages allotted to each area.

Task/ Knowledge Statement % of Exam (# of Questions)

I. GENERAL ENVIRONMENTAL HEALTH 14% (35 questions)
   A. Conduct Environmental Health Investigations, Inspections, and Audits
   B. Conduct Epidemiological Investigations
   C. Collect Samples and Specimens for Lab Analysis
   D. Perform Routine Field Tests and Measurements
   E. Plan Land Use
   F. Review Construction Plans
   G. Environmental Microbiology
   H. Contamination Control

II. FOOD PROTECTION 14% (35 questions)
   A. Inspection and Investigation of Food Establishments
   B. Food Safety, Protection, Quality, and Storage
   C. Temporary Events with Food Service
   D. Transportation of Food

III. WASTEWATER 8% (20 questions)
   A. Conduct Investigations of Wastewater Management Systems

IV. SOLID AND HAZARDOUS WASTE 4% (10 questions)
   A. Knowledge of Waste Management Systems
   B. Conduct Waste Management Investigations
   C. Public Education

V. POTABLE WATER 8% (20 questions)
   A. Conduct Sanitary Surveys of Potential or Existing Water
   B Evaluate Systems and Watersheds

VI. INSTITUTIONS AND LICENSED ESTABLISHMENTS 12% (30 questions)
   A. Understand the Health Hazards and Sanitation Problems of Institutions
   B. Conduct Epidemiological Investigations of Institutions
   C. Conduct Investigations of Facilities, Institutions and Licensed Establishments

VII. VECTORS, PESTS, AND POISONOUS PLANTS 6% (15 questions)
   A. Develop Controls for Vectors, Pests, and Poisonous Plants

Please see the NEHA website about this essential credential often required to practice as a sanitarian: http://www.neha.org/credential/

B.S in Environmental Health Science

An accredited program in environmental health leading to a bachelor of science degree is only offered by a small number of nationally accredited programs. Some of those programs have been previously listed in this chapter . The typical program includes general education and supporting courses in biology, chemistry, and mathematics, plus a variety of environmental health courses dealing with air quality, water quality, wastewater disposal and treatment, hazardous and solid waste management, risk assessment and epidemiology, industrial hygiene, control of disease vectors, food hygiene, radiological health, environmental health program planning and law, terrorism, institutional health, housing, and toxicology. During upper-division study, the student must complete six credit hours of supervised field experience (internship) with appropriate agencies.

A Typical Environmental Health Curriculum and Courses:

280 Introduction to Environmental Health Science (3) A. Elements of environmental health, including water and waste treatment, air pollution, food sanitation, vector control, solid waste disposal, and general sanitation problems.

285 Environmental Health Professional Standards (1) A. Provides the student with the personal and professional tools to succeed as an environmental health professional. Information related to required professional certifications, ethical demands, and professional standards and practices will be provided.

300 Water Supplies and Waste Disposal (4) I, II. Prerequisite: Environmental Health 280. Corequisite: BIO 320 or CLT209 and CLT211. Drinking water safety in both individual private systems and larger public systems. Maintenance of raw water quality. Water purification, delivery systems, and surveillance. Techniques for collection, treatment, and disposal of sewage.

330 Environmental Control of Disease Vectors. (3) II. Prerequisite: BIO121. The identification and control of arthropods, arachnids, rodents, and other vectors of disease. Safe use of pesticides will also be discussed.

335 Hazardous and Solid Waste Management (3) II. Prerequisites: CHE 111, 116, and environmental health S 280; or departmental approval. Nature of toxic and hazardous wastes and methods for their disposal to protect health and the environment and to prevent contamination of groundwater. The environmental health and safety aspects of solid waste collection, treatment and disposal, and regulations governing waste management are also covered.

340 Industrial Hygiene (3) I, II. Prerequisite: BIO 121, CHE 111, 115 and environmental health S 280; or departmental approval. The impact of the workplace on safety and health, and methods for avoiding work-related illnesses. Emphasis will be on the evaluation and the control of the work environment to protect worker health.

360 Air Pollution and Health (4) A. Prerequisite: CHE 112,116, PHY 131, Environmental Health 280; or departmental approval. Health effects of air pollution, including a discussion of the primary sources of airborne pollutants, their transport and transformation, the control of air pollution, state and national standards.

370 Risk Assessment and Environmental Epidemiology (3) I, II. Prerequisites: Environmental Health 280 and STA215; or departmental approval. The use of data to define the health effects of exposed individuals or populations to hazardous materials and situations.

380 Food Hygiene (3) I, II. Prerequisites: BIO 320 or CLT209 and CLT211, and Environmental Health 280; or departmental approval. A study of the health effects of food and milk-borne disease, including a discussion of milk and foods as vehicles of infection, essentials of milk and food quality, standards for dairy, milk, and food service equipment.

410 Radiological Health (3) I. Prerequisites: environmental health S 280, MAT 107, AND PHY 131. Corequisite: PHY 131. A discussion of the health effects from ionizing radiation, including radiation sources, detection, measurement, control, and safety devices.

425 Environmental Health Program Planning (3) A. Prerequisite: Environmental Health 280, 300, and 335. Administration, planning, implementation, and evaluation of environmental health programs. Discussion of resources and promotional techniques, and the role of the environmental health specialist dealing with community, state, and regional agencies.

440 Environmental and Industrial Toxicology (3) II. Prerequisites: CHE 112, 116 and Environmental Health 280; or departmental approval. Health effects and nature of toxic substances with discussions of dose-response relationships, latency, target organs, and potential exposures in the environment.

460 Housing and Institutional Environments (3) A. Prerequisites: Environmental Health 280, or departmental approval. discusses the requirements for healthful housing means of attaining and maintaining these requirements. Reviews environmental health concerns relating to daycare centers, schools, hospitals, nursing homes, and prisons. Describes surveillance, evaluative, and corrective methods.

463 Field Experience in Environmental Health (6) A. Prerequisites: Environmental Health 300, 335, 380, and departmental approval. Supervised and directed field experience in local, state, regional environmental health agencies, or with appropriate industries. Eight to twelve weeks full-time required depending on workplace.

485 Environmental Health Professional Practice Seminar (1) A. Prerequisite: 90 hours. Provides the graduating student a certification and licensure review for the required state and national exams. The student will also be taught how to develop professional-success strategies and long-range career plans.

Environmental Science Careers

What can you do with an environmental science degree? Websites are easily found that include information on employment areas, employers, and employment strategies.

Environmental Career Opportunities at http://www.ecojobs.com/ is primarily a subscription site, although there is limited job listing information available to nonsubscribers. Subscribers will receive over 500 current environmental jobs every two weeks at our password-protected website by subscribing to Environmental Career Opportunities, the only comprehensive source of environmental job vacancies. Environmental job vacancies are from all sectors of the job market, including nonprofits, corporations, professional firms, institutions, and federal, state, and local governments.

Opportunities for College Students and College Graduates at EPA Student Opportunities at EPA—Numerous opportunities are available within the Environmental Protection Agency for students to gain vital career experience while contributing to the mission of protecting human health and safeguarding the environment. Internships, fellowships and other opportunities are available in Washington, D.C., laboratories, and at regional EPA locations nationwide. Go to: http://www .epa.gov/careers/stuopp.html.

Opportunities for graduates are available at EPA with an emphasis on the graduate's career and leadership development. http://www.epa.gov/careers/gradopp.html

- EPA Intern Program (EIP) Federal Career Intern Program (FCIP) Presidential Management Fellows Program (PMFP) Office of Research and Development Post-Doctoral Program
- Environmental careers can be found at Environmental Science Jobs
- Outdoor Educators and How They Affect Our Forestry
- ELOSH Wild Population Monitoring
- A Habitat Garden Educator for Neighborhoods
- Health and Safety Manager—A Great Job for a Highly Motivated Individual
- Soil Scientist
- Trail Coordinator
- Water Analysts Hold Positions of Responsibility to Protect Our Water Supply
- Pollution Control Design
- Recycle Coordinator
- Park Ranger Jobs are Scarce
- Maine Biologists
- Land Managers
- Land Surveyors
- Field Science Educators
- Environmental Technicians Research the Problem of Pollution
- Environmental Research Assistants
- Environmental Restoration Planners
- Environmental Enforcement Officers Work to Protect Our Forests
- Environmental, Health & Safety Analysts:
- Entomologists
- Botanists
- Bird-Bander Jobs
- Air Quality Control,
- Storm Chasers—Meteorologists
- Environmental Systems Analyst
- Fish Hatchery Technician
- Ecologist
- Green Educators
- Environmental Lobbyist
- Environmental Educator
- Climatologist
- Air Quality Specialist

- Fisheries Technician
- Ecologist
- Forester
- Science Teacher

The above career information comes from a website that advertises thousands of entry-level jobs each day. It is highly recommended that you visit this site: http://www.indeed.com/q-Entry-Level-Environmental-l-Illinois-jobs.html

Conclusion

While both fields of study appear the same on the surface, there are definite differences. Environmental health positions are located in almost every industry and company in the world. This is due to the incredible number of federal, state, and local regulations covering impact of the work environment for both the population and the worker. Of the evolution of academic programs in environmental health, the bachelor's degree holder is typically far better educated technically, while the advanced degree holder is typically far better educated in project management and advanced planning. There is not seen to be a solution in sight for the limited workforce available in environmental health due to the lack of institutions offering accredited environmental health BS degrees. There has been a trend recently for BS holders in environmental health to also be hired for environmental science positions. This could be related to the applied engineering courses often taken by environmental health students.

Comparative Summary of Environmental Health Sciences

Joe E. Beck, RS, DEASS

Overview

Environmental Health Specialist

Environmental health specialists are concerned with the environmental quality of a community and the health and safety of the workers in that community. They are responsible for enforcing local, state, and federal regulations that pertain to the sanitation of food and water, handling of hazardous and infectious wastes, and cleanliness and safety of housing and institutional environments. They may also be in charge of collecting and analyzing samples to determine if a hazard to public health exists. Environmental health specialists need to be comfortable with computers and other high-tech devices because they may be called upon to prepare and calibrate the equipment used to collect and analyze the samples. Another major function of these specialists is to consult with and advise physicians and other medical personnel about potential community environmental health hazards. Environmental health specialists may specialize in any area of environmental health, particularly milk and dairy production, food protection, sewage disposal, pesticide management, air and water pollution, hazardous waste disposal, occupational health, and wildlife health/management. These professionals need to possess good social skills, as well as oral and written communication skills, because they may have to conduct, analyze, and dispense epidemiologic data regarding disease outbreaks within a community. Individuals must also have good analytical and problem-solving skills, work well with other people, and have a commitment to creating a safe environment.

Work Environment

Environmental health specialists may work in state, county, or local health departments, hospitals, private businesses, major theme and amusement parks, and environmental enforcement agencies. They are often employed as educators, consultants, and/or interpreters.

High School Preparation

Students interested in becoming environmental health specialists would be recommended to take high school courses in algebra, geometry, trigonometry, calculus, biology, chemistry, physics, English, literature, computer skills, and health occupations/medical professions education.

College Requirements

Individuals interested in environmental health must have a high school diploma or the equivalent. Most environmental health specialists earn a bachelor's degree in environmental health, but some have a degree in a related field such as biological/chemical sciences or environmental engineering. Career opportunities can be greatly advanced by having an environmental health degree.

29

The earning of a master's or doctoral degree will assist in this specialty. Optional certification may be obtained through the National Environmental Health Association and is often required by the states.

Schools offering Environmental Health Degrees

Students interested in environmental health should contact the National Environmental Health Science & Protection Accreditation Council (EHAC) to find quality programs in environmental health or accredited schools of public health. ASPH represents the CEPH-accredited schools of public health.

You can find a list of environmental health programs at: http://www.ehacoffice.org/accred-prog/under-prog.php

Environmental Health Careers Path

Since math comes in to play in a lot of environmental health scientists' daily tasks, it's important to have a strong foundation in math and statistics. If you picture yourself as part of the lawmaking process, it would behoove you to take some courses dealing with the law as well.

Often beginning their careers as field analysts or as research assistants, environmental health scientists may see the opportunity to advance their career as they gain relevant work experience.

If you're interested in furthering your education to the graduate level, consider a school with a concentration in environmental health or science. Here you will gain the critical knowledge necessary to advance your career quickly.

Environmental Health Careers: Compatible Personality Traits

Analytical, detail-oriented, good communication skills, passion for the environment, and a patient personality.

Environmental Health Careers: Salary Expectations

In May 2009, environmental scientists held roughly 83,530 positions throughout the United States. The average annual income was $67,360, and the middle 50% earned between $46,000 and $81,500. The lowest 10% earned less than $37,120, and the highest 10% earned more than $107,190. Pay will depend on willingness to travel and dedication to position.

Environmental Health Careers: Job Outlook

According to the Bureau of Health Manpower, employment for environmental scientists is expected to grow 28% over the 2008–2018 decade, which is much faster than average for all occupations. This growth is due to new demands on the safety of the environment and the rising population. Additionally, new demands for laws and regulations affecting the environment are expected to spur new positions within the field. Job prospects for those in environmental science are expected to be best in federal, state, and local governments, as they employ roughly 44% of all environmental scientists and specialists.

Career Outlook:

Employment opportunities for environmental health specialists are expected to grow between 10% and 25% through the year 2015. Because the majority of environmental health specialists are employed by local, state, and federal agencies, job security is usually relatively high. With an increasing amount of environmental protection legislation being passed, demand for these health professionals should increase steadily well into the twenty-first century. Demand should also increase due to individuals retiring or leaving the profession for other reasons.

Professional Organizations

National Environmental Health Association
720 South Colorado Blvd. South Tower, Suite 970
Denver, CO, 80246-1925, Phone: (303) 756-9090
Fax: (303) 691-9490
www.neha.org

National Institute of Environmental Health Sciences
111 Alexander Drive
PO Box 12233
Research Triangle Park, NC 27709
Phone: (919) 541-3345
www.niehs.nih.gov

American Board of Industrial Hygiene
6015 West St. Joseph, Suite 102
Lansing, MI 48917-3980
Phone: (517) 321-2638
Fax: (517) 321-4624
www.abih.org

Employment Forecast Summaries

Environmental Health

Environmental scientists and specialists analyze samples of air, water, and other substances to identify, assess, and control threats to people and the environment.

Environmental Health Scientists and Specialistsii

2010 Median Pay	$81,500 10 + years of experience
Entry-Level Education	Bachelor's degree in environmental health
Work Experience in a Related Occupation	None
On-the-Job Training	State Licensure or NEHA Registration Certified Industrial Hygienist Certification
Number of Jobs, 2010	83,400 government equal number in industry
Job Outlook, 2010–2020	28%
Employment Change, 2010–2020	25,000 +

Environmental Science and Specialists

Environmental Science and specialists enforce and develop standards impacting health and safety standards for both the public and

Environmental Scientists and Specialists

2010 Median Pay	$61,700 per year $29.66 per hour
Entry-Level Education	Bachelor's Degree
Work Experience in a Related Occupation	None
On-the-Job Training	None
Number of Jobs, 2010	89,400
Job Outlook, 2010–2020	19% (about as fast as average)
Employment Change, 2010–2020	16,700

http://www.indeed.com/q-Entry-Level-Environmental-l-Illinois-jobs.html

A Day in the Life of an Environmental Public Health Practitioner

Vonia L. Grabeel, RS, MPH

Key Concepts:

1. Be able to discuss the different career paths in Environmental Health.
2. Be able to discuss what may occur during a typical day of Environmental Public Health Practitioner
3. Discuss the Core Competencies that an Environmental Public Health Practitioner should possess.

Have you ever thought about what an environmental public health practitioner does for you or the community in which you live? What duties they perform? What impact they have on your daily lives? What exactly is environmental public health? If you haven't, then don't feel alone, because most people have not. During the course of this chapter, I hope to answer these and other questions concerning the environmental public health practitioner.

Our profession is routinely called the "silent profession" because we are not very good at promoting ourselves. We tend to work behind the scenes, do our jobs, and move on to the next task at hand. I am asked on a fairly routine basis what environmental health is and what exactly environmental public health practitioners actually do on a daily basis. There are numerous definitions of environmental health, all of which are very good descriptions of what environmental health is, but in its most basic form, environmental health is the application of science for the protection of humans from the environment in which they live, work, and play.

The more complicated question to answer is, What exactly does a health environmentalist do? The reason this is so difficult to answer is because the field of environmental health is extremely varied. There are many different avenues that a student may explore upon graduation. One may chose to go into industrial hygiene, private industry, consulting, public health, or one of the many other career options within this vocation. The reason one has so many choices is because of the diverse subject matter that is encompassed in the field. Areas of interest include (Morgan):

- Air Pollution Control
- Milk Sanitation
- Solid and Hazardous Waste Management
- Occupational Safety and Health
- Noise Control

- Food Safety
- Onsite Waste Disposal
- Insect and Rodent Control
- Water Pollution Control
- Environmental Design Engineering and Accident Prevention

- Housing Hygiene
- Recreational Sanitation
- Product Safety
- Interstate and International Travel Sanitation

- Radiological Health Control
- Institutional Health
- Consumer Protection
- Land Use Management and Environmental Planning

Once a person chooses a career, there are many different options they may explore, such as public health. One can work for the federal, state, or local government. One may practice as a generalist or specialize in one of the many different areas within the purview of public health. One may also become an epidemiologist, work in the preparedness arena, and prepare state and local employees for all hazards and disasters.

Environmental health programs are virtually the same in most state and local programs. The programs may be spread over different agencies depending on the state in which the environmental public health practitioner works. The typical programs that fall under the purview of the department for public health are:

- Food Protection Program
- Milk Protection Program
- Motel/Hotel Sanitation Program
- School Sanitation Program
- Boarding Homes
- Tanning Salons
- Recreational Vehicle Communities
- Lead Abatement Programs
- Rabies Control Programs
- Nuisance Control Program
- Core training course for new employees

- Onsite Septic Systems
- Radiation Control Programs
- Swimming Pool/Bathing Facilities
- Bed and Breakfast
- Tattoo Studios
- Manufactured Mobile Home Communities
- Radon Awareness Program
- Lead Awareness Program
- Indoor Air Programs
- Preparedness Programs
- Refresher trainings for seasoned employees

Most of these programs have multiple divisions within them, such as the food protection and swimming pool programs. For example, within these programs there are inspectional and plan-review programs for:

- retail food facilities,
- food manufacturing facilities,
- food service facilities,
- combination food service and retail food facilities,
- temporary food booths,
- concession stands,
- special events,
- farmers markets,
- swimming pools,
- beaches, and
- swimming pool/bathing facilities construction programs.

Most states require their environmental public health practitioners to be graduates of an accredited college or university with a certain amount of hours in environmental health, biological, or natural sciences. They must also pass a certification exam to be able to practice within the state.

Some states have their own credentialing programs or they may use the National Environmental Health Association (NEHA) exam in order to credential their employees.

How does an environmental public health practitioner affect your life or the community in which you live? Have you ever eaten a meal, drank a glass of water, or swam in a swimming pool? The following was adapted from a presentation that can be found on the Clark County Health Department's website in Washington State, http://www.clark.wa.gov/public-health/FoodWaterCat.html

- Let's start when you get out of the bed in the morning. Drink that first glass of water or take a shower. If you use a private well or cistern to provide water to your home, then the local environmental public health practitioner at your request will collect a water sample from your home to test it for bacteriological quality (E. coli and total coliforms). If municipal water is the primary source of potable water to the home, then periodic water samples are collected to ensure that the water meets both the bacteriological and disinfectant quality.

- After the morning shower you share a nice breakfast with the family. The food you prepare for your morning breakfast comes from a grocery store. Environmental public health practitioners have been to the grocery stores and processing plants to conduct inspections and provide food managers and food handlers with a course to ensure a safe and sanitary food supply.

- After breakfast is eaten, the kids head out for the bus stop. Schools are yet another facility that environmental public health practitioners have inspected—both the physical plant and the cafeteria—in order to ensure compliance with the state laws and regulations.

- You attend a luncheon with friends or with work colleagues. We inspect and permit the restaurant you eat at to ensure safe food-handling standards and sanitation; and we provide food manager and food handlers' course.

- Your spouse calls to tell you the neighbor's dog bit the mail carrier. By law an animal bite has to be reported to the health department within 12 hours of the bite. Dogs, cats, or ferrets must be quarantined for 10 days to ensure they were not transmitting rabies at the time of the bite. The environmental public health practitioner's responsibility is to see the animal is quarantined and released at the end of the quarantine period. If the animal is healthy at the end of the quarantine period, then it could not have transmitted rabies when it bit the mail carrier. The animal may then be released to the owner.

- The kids have swim practice today at the local recreational center. The health department environmental public health practitioners routinely inspect public swimming pools and spas to ensure compliance with state and local laws and regulations for safety and sanitation and work with the operators to make any needed corrections. Pool operator training is offered to new and seasonal operators covering the laws and regulations, proper chemicals levels, safety issues, pool filtration systems, recirculation systems, and related matters.

- On your way home from work you pass a billboard that reminds citizens to test their homes for radon. Radon is a colorless, odorless, naturally occurring radioactive gas that comes from the breakdown of uranium from rocks and soil, according to the EPA is the second lung cancer, and could be present in your home. Testing is easy, inexpensive, and can help you live a healthier life. Environmental public health practitioners present at various public meetings to raise awareness of the health hazards of radon and many states/counties offer free radon test kits to all residents.

- After dinner you settle down to read the evening news paper, the leading story is about a Shigella outbreak in five area daycare centers. Environmental public health practitioners collaborate with the epidemiologists, daycare owners, parents, and doctors to determine the cause of the outbreak. The environmental public health practitioners along with the epidemiologists investigate the disease outbreak, disseminate health education information, advise the daycare centers on proper sanitation, and emphasize handwashing to prevent further contamination. You also notice that the county fair starts on Saturday. The local environmental public health practitioners inspect each of the food booths to ensure the food is safe for you and your family to eat. The handwashing stations they require at the petting zoo and at the bathrooms are there so you and your family can properly wash your hands to prevent exposure to harmful bacteria.

- Planning for the family vacation has begun. With the destination chosen, what is left is to decide on whether to stay at a hotel or a recreational vehicle park. The health department inspects recreational vehicle parks for sanitation purposes. They are checked for lot spacing, dump stations, and water hook-ups, and, if present, sanitation in the shower houses. Inspections of hotels are also conducted to ensure the public clean and healthy lodging places.

- The kids are planning on going to camp during the summer. The health department environmental public health practitioner reviews the building constructions plans, the inspections of all swimming areas, the cafeteria, the cabins/tents, and any sanitation concerns.

- On the late news you see stories about H1N1 flu, and another meth lab bust. The environmental public health practitioner performs public education on meth labs and participates when necessary during flu clinics and outbreaks.

Environmental public health practitioners touch virtually every part of our everyday lives, and as a general rule they go unnoticed unless something goes wrong. This is the fault of the profession; we don't market the profession well enough. Awareness of the important role that environmental public health practitioners play in the lives of our citizens and communities will only increase the knowledge base and an understanding of the public health significance of the requirements of laws and regulations.

Education is a vital part of this profession. Providing workforce development training for all new and seasoned environmental public health practitioners is essential to prepare them to face the challenges of the ever changing face of environmental health. They also conduct research or perform investigations for the purpose of identifying, diminishing, and/or eliminating sources of pollutants and hazards that affect either the environment or the health of the population. They may collect, synthesize, study, report, and take action based on data derived from measurements or observations of air, food, soil, water, and other sources.

A typical day in the life of a field environmental public health practitioner at a local health department:

- Arrive at work ready and eager to face the challenges of the day promptly at 8:00 a.m.

- By 8:00 there are already two onsite sewage installers and a local plumber waiting to pull permits for an onsite sewage system and to have plumbing plans for a new commercial building reviewed.

- The phone rings with another onsite sewage installer needing you to meet him to lay out a system.

- The administrative assistant comes in with three animal bite reports, which have to be quarantined by the end of the work day.

- By 9:25 a.m. you are done with the two onsite sewage installers plus an additional two onsite sewage installers that followed and have reviewed three sets of plans for new commercial buildings. The three sets of plans are sent to the state plumbing office for review.

- 10:00 am: reschedule 10:00 a.m. appointment, leave for the field to quarantine the three dogs.

- If the three dog quarantines (all dogs, cats, and ferrets are required to be quarantined for a mandatory 10 days) go without any problems, you work in a couple of pool inspections.

- 12:05 p.m.: Go through the drive-through and enjoy lunch to the next appointment.

- 12:45 p.m.: Meet with the rescheduled 10:00 a.m. appointment to conduct a site evaluation for a new home requiring an onsite sewage system.

- 1:30 p.m.: The director called and wants you to drop everything to investigate a rat infestation at the nursing home.

- 2:45 p.m.: Finish up with the nursing home director, advise him to get a pest control company, and schedule a follow-up appointment in 10 days.
- 3:05 p.m.: Meet with the installer that called at 10:00 a.m. and assist him in laying out his onsite sewage system.
- 4:00 p.m.: Make way back to the office to turn in paperwork, telephone calls, and prepare for the next day's adventure.
- 4:30 p.m.: Go home!

Core Competencies

According to the National Environmental Health Science & Protection Accreditation Council (EHAC), there are 32 accredited undergraduate and eight graduate environmental health science programs across the country. Even with the growing number of accredited programs, it is difficult to produce enough classically trained environmentalists to fill all of the available positions in the workforce. After assessing the general makeup of the workforce of local health departments, the National Center for Environmental Health (NCEH), Centers for Disease Control and Prevention (CDC), and the American Public Health Association (APHA) sponsored the Environmental Health Competency Project. This document outlines the core competencies that every environmentalist should have to be an effective and competent employee of local health departments. It is the opinion of the author that these are the core competencies that all environmentalists should possess. There are 14 competencies in three different areas: assessment, management, and communications. The committee identified the following core competencies in this living document:

- **Assessment**
  - Information Gathering
    - Environmentalists are sleuths of a sort. Understanding where to obtain information and the ability to discern pertinent information is imperative.

  There are times when an EPHP will have to track down an owner of a property to issue a Notice of Violation to the owner of an animal; someone that has been exposed to rabies. One such time occurred when a person was exposed to a bat that tested positive for rabies. This person, however, decided to leave the state before finding out the results of the test. It took us several hours on the telephone to track this person down and to arrange for them to start the post exposure propolaxis. In the end we found his mother who once she knew the situation found her child. This person took the series of shots and never contracted rabies. Morale of this story you cannot hide from a worried mother.

  - Data Analysis and Interpretation
    - When determining trends in disease outbreaks, being able to make connections in different data sets, looking at the whole to recognize relationships in the data, and being able to use the information gleaned to report the results and make the appropriate decisions.
  - Evaluation
    - Conducting programs the same way for years may be routine, but it may not be the most efficient use of resources. All programs, interventions, policies, and procedures need to be evaluated for effectiveness.
- **Management**
  - Problem-Solving
    - Developing the ability to look at the whole to see the pieces is essential to all Environmentalists. The goal should be to reach the appropriate solution to the problem at hand. Developing that insight is an essential skill to hone.

The ability to see the big picture is an invaluable tool in the environmental public health practitioner's toolbox. Standing back and looking at the whole, then at the pieces. You get a call that there is something terribly wrong with the environment because all of the leaves are falling off the trees. You have to step back and consider some things, like it may be October and it's time for the leaves to fall off the trees. Step back and gather the facts before reacting.

- Economic and Political Issues
  - Every decision made by environmentalists affects someone's pocketbook. When money is involved, then politics comes on its heels. One has to be cognizant of the political climate. One's decisions must be based in fact, law, and common sense.
- Organizational Knowledge and Behavior
  - The ability to work within the organizational structure to become a valuable team member will aid in developing an effective creative team. Knowing one's place in the organization and the role one plays is very important.

Knowing one's place within the organization is extremely important. As a young environmental public health practitioner I worked on a state attorney taskforce which included eight other agencies. We were to meet at a prearranged spot covertly before going to the facility, I and the news team arrived first. The reporter asked who was the lead for the health department, and I looked at him and said, "I don't know." The truth of the matter was, I didn't know. But then the state attorney called me to the front of the group, saying, "Vonia, come on up here, you are the lead for health department." When I saw the look on the reporter's face, I wished I had known the answer to his question.

- Project Management
  - Being able to juggle not only your regular duties but the added duties of managing a special project or an added program is essential when your are the project manager. The project manager has to ensure the project/program carries out its intended function and meets all of its objectives and goals; adhere to the budget; write and submit any required reporting; and still complete their daily duties within the health department.
- Computer and Information Technology
  - We live in an age that if you cannot use a computer, then you will be left behind. A good portion of the data we collect in the field can now be made available virtually in real time. With the advances in smart phones, a field person can document a situation and send directly to the supervisor for advice or evaluation.
- Reporting, Documentation, and Record-Keeping
  - Keeping proper records is vital in documenting actions or in determining trends. The files are legal records and are evidence in any type of legal action that may be taken against the owner. It is also very important to be able to use the information in the files to inform different audiences.
- Collaboration
  - Forming partnerships with other agencies and community organizations makes it easier to solve issues that cross jurisdictional boundaries. During emergencies, if the responders are acquainted, it makes handling the task at hand less difficult.

- **Communications**
  - Educate.
    - Every time we encounter someone during the course of our job it is an opportunity to educate the public. Effectively explaining the public health rationale for recommendations issued by the environmental public health practitioner to owners/managers of the facilities

that are regulated by the health departments is essential. Understanding the rationale behind regulations may not please those being regulated, but they will understand the public health importance behind them.

- ○ Communicate
  - ■ Due to the wide variety of the people that environmental public health practitioners come in contact on a daily basis, they need to possess the ability to communicate with all educational levels and in any setting. Whether it is public speaking, print, or electronic media the ability to effectively communicate health risks and exchange information is a critical tool.

Picture a downpour, a dairy barn, 50 Amish gentlemen, high-ranking state legislators, the deputy commissioner of health, his assistant, the director of public protection and safety, reporters, and myself. It almost sounds like a bad joke but, in fact iwas the setting for a meeting we were asked to speak at concerning controversial regulations regrading schools. The look on my superiors' faces was priceless when we were told the meeting was going to be held in the hay loft of a dairy milk barn! It was great! Having dealt with the Amish community for years, I was prepared for such a meeting place. My superiors, dressed in their suits, and I had to walk through a muddy feed lot to get to the barn, and they had sat up hay bales for everyone to sit on during the meeting; very cozy really. The rain was so loud on the roof that we had to scream just to be heard, but all in all it was an effective meeting. The moral of the story is, you never know the situation you are walking into, so be able to go with the flow no matter the setting and effectively get the message across to all of the parties in attendance.

- ○ Conflict Resolution
  - ■ From the time the sun comes up, there is conflict of some sort in our lives. Honing one's skills in facilitating resolutions to conflicts within the agency, the community, and with regulated parties will be of benefit to an environmental public health practitioner.
- ○ Marketing
  - ■ The ability to articulate the concepts of environmental and public health in a way in which its importance is understood by the clients of the health department and the community at large. These concepts need to be presented in a variety of medias (print, web, social media, etc.). Most people do not know what environmental public health practitioners do or even what environmental health encompasses. This profession needs to come out of the shadows to market itself so that the public will know who they may rely on to aid them with their issues or connect them to other necessary resources.

Environmental public health practitioners touch virtually every part of our daily life, and before now you may have only had a cursory knowledge of these professionals and the work they do behind the scenes. There are numerous career paths an environmental health student can explore, public or private industry, government the possibilities are vast. The environmental public health practitioner has to be versed in a wide variety of subjects: biology, chemistry, microbiology, and construction among many others. Not only do they inspect the environment we live, work, and play in, but they are also first responders to such emergencies as floods, hurricanes, tornadoes, and Anthrax (white powder) incidents. These professionals have to possess many qualities, a few of which are flexibility, common sense, willingness to collaborate, focus on the big picture to reach fair and equitable solutions to various issues. It is a noble profession that can trace its origin back to early recorded history; its members have been given many different titles throughout the years, but the goal has always been and always will be to prevent illness and protect the public from the hazards where we live, work, and play.

A Day in the Life of an Industrial Environmental Health Practitioner

Lauren Reno

Figure 2.1. A Love Canal protestor.

Key Performance Outcome Indicators;

1. Be able to discuss the different career paths in industrial environmental health
2. Be able to discuss what may occur during a typical day in the life of an industrial environmental health professional
3. Discuss the traits and characteristics that an environmental health specialist should possess

A story on the front page of the *New York Times on* August 1, 1978, describes the notorious Love Canal, located in Niagara Falls, New York. As an environmental health student and professional, you will learn about this tragedy, which took place in the 1920s. It was "one of the most appalling environmental tragedies in U.S. history" (Beck). For industrial environmental health professionals, Love Canal is a particularly interesting story. Why? Because that's what we do—we protect the environment from industrial pollution. This is really only one facet of the profession, but it's the basis for need of an environmental professional in an industrial facility. These days, the protection of the environment is a hot topic, so corporations try to ensure they stay out of trouble with the EPA. This is where we enter the scene.

Industrial health professionals are usually the heroes behind the scenes. They keep companies in compliance with a variety of regulations, and consequently help save a significant amount of money in the process. So what exactly is the difference between public and industrial environmental health careers? Well, public health officials are typically the enforcers of regulations set forth by the state and/or federal government. They protect the public from environmental influences such as lead, radiation, insect vectors, and disease or illness caused by food, pools, sewage, and the like. Industrial professionals protect the environment from the by products of manufacturing, assembling, and packaging of commodities we all depend on.

As you read "A Day in the Life of an Environmental Public Health Practitioner" by Vonia Grabeel, you will see how varied the field of environmental health can be. There are so many choices as to which area of industrial environmental health you can choose to go into. They include, but aren't limited to:

- Industrial Hygiene
- Environmental Compliance
- Occupational Safety/ Health

- Environmental Engineering
- Project Management and Consulting
- Remediation and Cleanup

As an environmentalist in the private sector of industry, you will likely wear several hats. As companies are forced to go lean (meaning cutting costs as much as possible in order to maximize profit), the environmental, health, and safety positions are typically combined into one. This isn't always the case, but is typical of smaller companies with lower profit margins. Responsibilities that can be expected are:

- Ensuring required permits are filed and maintained
- Completing required reports for local, state, or federal regulations
- Management of hazardous and solid wastes
- Responding to customer requests on environmental issues
- Maintain the facility's safety data sheets and hazard communication program
- Incident investigation
- Responding to spills within the facility
- Overseeing wastewater-treatment operations
- Monitoring environmental data associated with permits
- Serving as a liaison between regulators and the company
- Upholding confidentiality of employees and the company
- Managing the environmental management system (such as ISO 14000)
- Serving as an emergency contact or coordinator
- Training employees on legally required subjects
- Interpreting regulations set forth by the
  - Environmental Protection Agency (EPA)
  - Occupational Safety and Health Association (OSHA)
  - Department of Transportation (DOT)
- Management of hazardous materials in the facility
- Industrial hygiene (including air monitoring, chemical exposure, and ventilation)
- Managing worker's compensation claims
- Facility safety audits to ensure conditions are safe for employees
- Leading inspections by regulatory officials

This list is not all-inclusive but gives you an idea of what to expect in industry. Most companies and corporations require the environmental health professional to be a graduate of an accredited college or university with a certain amount of hours in environmental health and biological or natural sciences. Certifications are always a plus, such as the Certified Safety Professional (CSP) or Certified Hazardous Materials Manager (CHMM). It's common for certification boards to require a number of years of experience in the field, as well as a bachelor's degree.

Let's go through some scenarios that might be encountered by an industrial environmental, safety, and health professional on any given day:

- A new waste is discovered and needs to be disposed of properly. A sample must be sent to a lab to determine whether it is be a hazardous waste or not. You must obtain the sample and ensure it gets to the lab promptly. Once the results are received, you must then create a profile based on the contents (metals, volatile organic compounds, etc.), ignitability, corrosivity, reactivity, and toxicity. Using what you've learned from training, you profile this waste and determine the best, most economical way to dispose of it.

- Someone announces over the intercom that there's been a spill in the facility. You drop what you're doing and respond to the area immediately. Since you manage the company's hazard communication program, you are very familiar with the chemicals that are used. After running to the spill area, you learn that the spill is hydrochloric acid. After you clear the area of employees, you and the facility's emergency responders put on proper personal protective equipment and work to clean up the spill, then ensure that it's disposed of properly.

- A wastewater-treatment operator informs you that an excess of chromium was released to the sanitary sewer, which flows to the city's wastewater-treatment plant. This is a problem because the facility has a permit from the city utility and cannot exceed the limits set forth by the permit. You must notify the utility immediately of the release and determine the root cause for it. Within seven days you must send a report to the utility explaining what you found and what countermeasure you have implemented to fix the problem so that it doesn't happen again.

- An employee trips and falls in the facility and hits his head, causing a deep gash. His supervisor brings him to your office, and he is bleeding badly. You must quickly clean and dress the wound so that you can get him to the emergency room to get stitches. But your job isn't done yet—you need to make sure the supervisor fills out an injury report so that you can file the claim with worker's compensation.

- The local emergency planning committee (LEPC) is meeting soon and you are invited to attend as an industrial ambassador. This committee prepares for local emergencies involving hazardous materials, whether from industry, train derailments, highway spills, or other disasters. As a representative of industry, your presence shows support to the community. For more information on LEPCs, go to http://www.epa.gov/oem/content/epcra/epcra_plan.htm.

- You receive a phone call from the security guard that an OSHA inspector has arrived at the facility for a surprise inspection. Since you keep your records updated, you aren't worried. You go greet the inspector in the lobby and ask her to take a few minutes to review the company's safety video before entering the factory. Once she's finished with the video, you double-check to make sure she has the proper shoes, safety glasses, and earplugs. She then asks for a plant tour to see the processes and safety procedures in action. Once finished, she asks for records, such as the injury log (called the OSHA 300 log). The inspection is completed and no violations were observed, so the inspector leaves the facility. You write up an internal memo on the inspection and results and send it to management.

- An employee complains to you that he feels like he's being overexposed to the smoke from the welder machine he works on. The machine has an exhaust fan leading to the roof, but you investigate the situation to ensure it's working properly. The exhaust doesn't seem to be pulling the smoke from the welder, so you ask maintenance to look at it. As it turns out, the fan motor was bad, so the smoke wasn't being exhausted. To be safe, you ask an industrial hygienist to come in and perform air monitoring at the weld lines to ensure the exposure levels are within limit.

- You realize that a reporting deadline is fast approaching and you haven't started on compiling the data yet. You have several other items that are also priority. In a professional field such as environmental health, you must learn to prioritize your schedule and be efficient in time management.

Now that you've learned a little about what we do, let's take a look at what a typical day may be like for an industrial environmental health professional:

8:00 a.m.	Arrive at work promptly and begin the day by reading emails
8:30 a.m.	Attend the daily management meeting to discuss any injuries from the day/night before, as well as any current environmental issues
9:00 a.m.	Return to your desk to work on necessary paperwork and finish responding to emails
10:00 a.m.	The local fire chief and crew arrive at the facility to do their annual inspection. You lead them on the tour and take notes on any findings they point out. After the tour is over, you have a closing meeting to discuss a plan of action for fixing the issues that were found.
12:00 p.m.	Lunch!
1:00 p.m.	You send an email with a memo describing the fire inspection findings to your boss and the maintenance manager, and a few other key managers, so that work can begin on fixing the problems
1:30 p.m.	A required annual report for the division of air quality is coming due soon. You begin preparing and compiling information for the report now to ensure it won't be late. Submitting a report past deadline can cost the company a fine.
3:30 p.m.	Once a week you do a documented walk through of the facility to look for any issues that need correction. Of course, every time you walk out on the production floor, you're constantly looking for problems.
4:30 p.m.	When finished with the walk-through, you put together a file with any pictures you took and list the issues you found. This will be discussed in the morning meeting, as well as emailed to all managers.
5:30 p.m.	After staying a little late to finish up your report, you can now go home and enjoy your evening.

One other aspect in the industrial field that you may be responsible for managing is the ISO 14001 Environmental Management System. The International Organization for Standardization (ISO) is based in Geneva, Switzerland, and is a developer and publisher of standards that ensure that products and services are safe, reliable, and of good quality (www.iso.org). The ISO 14001 standard is basically a framework that a company can follow to set up an effective environmental management system. It can be used by any company no matter what industry it may be, and is used around the world.

The benefits of being certified to ISO 14001 include:

- Reduced cost of waste management and waste minimization
- Reduced utility usage and costs associated
- Can be a business requirement, especially in the automotive industry
- Improved corporate image among regulators, customers, and the public

There's also another standard that is becoming more popular among organizations. It's not associated with ISO, but is very similar. It was created by the Occupational Health and Safety Advisory

Services (OHSAS) and is called OHSAS 18001. This standard is a tool to help companies create a safety management system, and is usually combined into the EMS (www.ohsas.org).

Traits and Characteristics of an Effective Environmental Health Practitioner

In February 2000, environmental health experts from 13 national environmental/health organizations came together in Washington to begin the work of defining core competencies for local-level environmental health practitioners. APHA's Public Health Innovations Project, with funding from the National Center for Environmental Health (NCEH) at the Centers for Disease Control and Prevention (CDC), convened the meeting.

The expert panel members and several federal agency representatives met for two days to identify the core competencies local environmental health practitioners needed to be effective in their work. You read about these competencies in "A Day in the Life of an Environmental Public Health Practitioner" by Vonia Grabeel. Below are the traits and characteristics that the group of experts developed for environmental health practitioners (www.cdc.gov).

- Positive attitude
  - You must always try to keep a positive attitude, even when you're stressed. Negativity is like a virus that spreads to others and is not productive or becoming of anyone.
- Versatility and flexibility
  - Remember that everything won't always happen the way you want it to, but you have to work together in order to accomplish a common goal.
- Practical perspective and common sense
  - Don't overthink situations. Use your common sense!
- Strong principles and ethics
  - Very important in this field. You must uphold the highest ethics and resist the temptation to do something the easy way. This field will require you to challenge yourself every day.
- Practitioner integrity
  - As a professional in this field, you must represent others as well. Uphold your integrity and maintain the morals that been instilled throughout your education.
- Tenacity
  - Don't give up. Sometimes it may take a while for others to see your vision, but stay tenacious.
- Willingness to learn
  - A bachelor's degree is only the beginning of your education. Never stop learning, for the field of environmental health is always changing.
- Focus on fair solutions
  - This goes along with being flexible. Sometimes a compromise is the best that you'll get, so you must learn to focus on the positive and go with it.
- Collaborative spirit
  - Teamwork is vital in this field. We are constantly learning from other colleagues. Companies want team players and not people who are only out for themselves.
- Willingness to embrace change
  - I am guilty of not handling change very well. It's difficult and you must learn to overcome it because it will only hold you back.
- Involvement with community

- The environment is a key topic and the community wants reassurance that companies are doing everything possible to prevent negative effects on the environment.
- Calmness during conflict
  - You'll run into many situations where you are the leader in an emergency situation. This takes practice and experience to learn, but you must remain calm. Everyone else's energy will feed off of you.
- Understanding of other points of view
  - This is important in everyday life, and sometimes it helps to have a second set of eyes looking at a situation with you.
- Ability to observe
  - Sometimes you must be the observer, not the teacher. Learning to watch employees and take notes without interrupting is crucial for accident investigations.
- Focus on team accomplishments
  - "There is no I in team"
- Appropriate appearance and body language
  - As a professional you must dress appropriately and learn to use your body to express the right body language. Standing with your arms folded across your chest gives people the impression that you don't want to be bothered. Eye contact is positive body language.
- Ability to lead
  - You will learn to be a leader. As a professional you will lead meetings, conduct trainings, and have to lead projects. Public speaking ability also ties into this. Trust me, it comes with practice!
- Big-picture perspective
  - You must focus on the big picture and try not to be close-minded. Think about how one decision will affect the overall outcome later on.
- Respect for diversity
  - More and more international companies are opening up facilities in the United States. Japan, China, and Germany hold a major presence in the U.S. industrial marketplace. Working for an international company can be somewhat different than working for an American company. There are cultural differences that you will learn to uphold.
- Knowledge of when to ask for help
  - Just because you have a degree in environmental health doesn't mean you will always have the answers. Don't be afraid to use your resources and network with others in the field when possible.

Develop Your Own Career Plan

After reading this, many of you may feel that environmental health is the profession that you want to spend your life working. Let me caution you at this point that the field requires individuals who want to provide benefit to others, continually solve new and unique problems, spend most of their time working outside, and meeting and working with people who often do not want to do things correctly. It is a job for an educator, a law enforcement officer, and a negotiator combined. Those who desire to help others will typically find this profession to be a delight to work in.

Below I have provided an article with instructions on how to do three-dimensional career planning that takes into consideration the other two sectors of your life, the personal and the spiritual. After reading the article, please go to the forms located at the end of the chapter and follow the instructions meticulously to create your own lifelong career plan.

Three-Dimensional Career Planning: "What do I want to be when I grow up?"

Joe E. Beck, RS, DEASS

A life-shattering event occurred last week in the Beck household, one that put me in a grumpy mood all weekend. I thought that I had managed to keep the fact that I had turned age 50 this past Christmas a closely guarded secret but discovered that the world knew it when I received the dreaded letter from AARP! I am told that this organization is called the American Association of Retired Persons; however, I am not really sure about its name. I do know that it must have illegal access to some government computer file to discover the deeply guarded secret of my age. This reality forced me to realize that I am on the entry point of what, according to demographics, is the last third of my life span and that I still have things to do that I have not completed in my personal strategic plan.

Before going further into this article, let it be known that I am quite pleased to reach the age of 50; the obvious alternative is not one that I am in a rush to visit. I am just having too much fun at the present time! The secret to having fun is having a balanced life and having some idea of where you think you would like to go with it. I would like to share with you one of the tools to achieve this balance and of developing your own personal strategic plan.

Let me start the process this way, if you were going to take a trip to Richmond, Kentucky, to visit me, what is the process that you would follow? Life is also like a trip, only that you are traveling at the speed of time, starting at a given point and ending at another. Getting back to the trip, you would first locate Richmond, Kentucky, on the map and you would then move your finger back toward your current location, noting the major roads that would provide the most direct route. You would then likely take a marker and trace the route with the best roads that go there, beside other attractions that you would like to visit. To maximize the trip you might even be wise enough to involve your spouse to ensure that her/his expectations of the trip will be enhanced. If this is the way that you do travel planning, then you are a "natural" at strategic planning. Let me explain:

You have discovered where you want to go and what you expect to gain as a result of the trip. To accomplish this you walk into the future and locate Richmond, Kentucky. In strategic planning this is referred to as "Development of the Vision." A route is them identified between Richmond and where you live, the obstacles identified that you might encounter, and substrategies developed to navigate them. After you are comfortable with the reality that your future trip is understood, you start to maximize the experience to ensure that the time, energy, and money expended are maximized. In strategic planning this is called "Identification of Strategic Goals."

One important aspect that age and time teach is to ensure that other stakeholders are also excited and satisfied with the trip. This is done by ensuring that the trip meets their values (why travel), their interest (what is in it for me), and their expectations (If I am going to travel it must also be worthwhile to me). In strategic planning this is called a "Stakeholder Involvement."

The next step in the travel process is to examine your current state. Will the car get us there? is the weather likely to be acceptable for travel? how long will it take to get there? how long will we stay? do we have the money to travel with security? These are only some of the potential questions. In strategic planning this is called a "Situational Analysis."

After going through this thought process (it is wise to do this with the other critical stakeholders), identify the unresolved issues or gaps between where you want to go and where you are now. Become aware of the gaps in your plan. In this case they might be: (1) making sure Joe will be at home; (2) getting time off from work to take the trip; (3) your spouse getting time off from work; and (4) checking on the realistic attainment of the strategic goals. In strategic planning this is called a "Gap Analysis." The thought process of dealing with the three above issues is known as "Strategy Development."

Though you may not have committed any of this to paper, a functional strategic plan has been developed. Now you know the process is easy, flexible, and an ongoing process, I would like to provide some insights of how to use this with your own life planning. The first step is to realize that there are at least three dimensions to your personality: (1) a spiritual or emotional side; (2) a personal side; and (3) your professional side. I intentionally listed the professional side last and do this for several reasons. When doing career-planning workshops, I do not find a lot of happy campers. I find a lot of successful people attend, but discussions with them reveal a great deal of regret and pain about their priorities. Evidence of the truth of this could be reflected in our national divorce rate , which is now exceeding 50%. The following is a step-by-step process that I developed at the National Research Lab to assist displaced executives during the downsizing binge of the 1990s. If, after reading this article, you are interested in using the work sheets that I have developed, please do not hesitate to ask and I will send them to you for free.

Step No. 1 (Very important!)
Walk forward in time to near the end of your life and look back over it from the mindset of an appraiser and answer the following questions:

Step No. 2
What are the top five values that, if you had another chance at life, would be accomplished in each of the three spheres (spiritual, personal, and professional)? Are any of them in conflict with each other? If so, understand why and the rest will take care of itself as a result of the designed thought process.

Step No. 3
From the perspective of this appraisal, write one sentence for each of the three spheres that captures the most important accomplishments that you want to leave as a legacy.

Step No. 4
Now combine these three sentences into a paragraph that places the sentences into context with the richness and flavor of life that are to be achieved in this second chance. Take time to make this paragraph elegant (it should even make you blush a bit). Remember that this paragraph is a future vision of what will be your legacy, The paragraph should not be modest and should express your desire for achievement in all three spheres. Note: Remember, the future is a blank sheet, nothing exists there except what is placed in it. The filling-the-blanks sheet will represent the only place you know to travel to in the future. For those of you who are religious, all of the primary world religions acknowledge that if you describe your quest you can have it. I was once working with a pastor, helping him design his personal strategic plan, and I asked him whether prayer changes the mind of our maker or helps us discover what the creator of the universe wants. That question provided both of us with a personal discovery! I believe that it is a tool given to us to discover within the frame of religious values what we are to do with our lives. In short, do not underestimate the power of a vision. The likelihood that we can create the reality of a nightmare through negatives is also valid, so be careful negative thinkers. Accept my assurance that whatever vision you will develop will actualize itself ,and be careful with this powerful tool. We always travel, when given the option, from one known place to another. If you dream of castles in the sky, make sure you also dream of the bathrooms, septic tanks, and heating/cooling systems they require to make it livable.

Step No. 5
Identify what strategic goals are essential to make the vision real! Limit the number of goals to seven or fewer to ensure you can keep them in your memory without great stress. Each day you will make decisions that impact your progress toward these goals. This will happen without intent as long as you remember your goals. This phase of the planning process is the building of a clear road from the future to your current state or time. It provides the pathway to the future. It will also drive daily decisions made through both conscious and unconscious thought.

Step No. 6
The most difficult sections of the process have now been completed and you are beginning the downslope run. Now identify personal, professional, and spiritual weaknesses and strengths, primary constraining fears, what factors push to succeed, the individuals that contribute to your success, the primary obstacles that you must overcome or navigate to achieve the vision.

Step No 7
Take the listing in Step 6 and pick the top five critical issues to be overcome.

Step No. 8
Develop strategies to resolve or navigate the top five critical issues identified above. The elements of a good strategy are: listing of the issue; a statement of strategy to overcome the issue; a listing of short-term actions that wear down the issue and a listing of similar long-term actions; and the identification of time-lines or milestones when each long-term and short-term activity should take place.
The career-planning process that I have sketched in this article is one chapter of a book that should be published in the near future. The book will be entitled *Walking Backwards: A Guide to Rediscovering Your Lost Creativity*.

References

1. Beck, Eckardt C. "The Love Canal Tragedy," *United States Environmental Protection Agency Journal*, January 1979. Web. Retrieved October 20, 2012. From http://www.epa.gov/history/topics/lovecanal/01.html

2. Centers for Disease Control and Prevention. National Center for Environmental Health, Centers for Disease Control and Prevention, American Public Health Association. "Environmental Health Competency Project Recommendations for Core Competencies for Local Environmental Health Practitioners," May 2001. Web. Retrieved October 20, 2012. From http://www.cdc.gov/nceh/ehs/Corecomp/Core_Competencies_environmental health _Practice.pdf

3. International Organization for Standardization. Web. Retrieved October 20, 2012. From http://www.iso.org/iso/home.html

4. Occupational Health and Safety Advisory Services. Copyright 2011. Web. Retrieved October 20, 2012. From http://www.ohsas.org/

5. U.S. Environmental Protection Agency. Love Canal, Press Releases and Articles. Web. Retrieved October 20, 2012. From http://www.epa.gov/history/topics/lovecanal/

References Part 1

1. Wikipedia—May 2001. http://www.wikipedia.org/wiki/Wikipedia:Announcements_May_2001., wikipedia.org

2. National Environmental Health Association **http://www.neha.org/credential/**

3. National Environmental Health Science & Protection Accreditation Council (environmental health AC) http://www.ehacoffice.org/about/8620 Roosevelt Way NE, Suite A Seattle, WA 98115

4. Environmental Jobs and Careers, Environmental Health Jobs.co http://www.ehscareers.com/

5. 2012 American Dental Education Association, http://explorehealthcareers.org/en/Field/11/Public_ Health ExploreHealthCareers is sponsored in part, by the Institute for Oral Health.

6. Bureau of Labor Statistics, U.S. Department of Labor, *Occupational Outlook Handbook*, B2012-13 Edition, Environmental Scientists and Specialists, on the Internet at http://www.bls.gov/ooh/ life-physical-and-social-science/environmental-scientists-and-sp

7. *Dictionary of Literary Biography*: Vol. 275: *Twentieth-Century American Nature Writers: Prose*, 2003. Succinct review of Thomas's life and of the books listed above. Retrieved 2008-11-08

8. Eastern Kentucky University's Environmental Health Science BS program is accredited by the National Environmental Health and Protection
Accreditation Council. http://eh.eku.edu/accreditation

References: Part 2

1. Morgan, Monroe T. (2003). *Environmental Health Third Edition*. Belmont, CA: Wadsworth/Thomson Learning.

2. Clark County Health Department Washington State. "Environmental Public Health and You." Web. Retrieved October 15, 2012. From http://www.clark.wa.gov/public-health/FoodWaterCat.html

3. Centers for Disease Control and Prevention. National Center for Environmental Health, Centers for Disease Control and Prevention, American Public Health Association. "Environmental Health Competency Project Recommendations for Core Competencies for Local Environmental Health Practitioners" May 2001. Web. Retrieved October 15, 2012. From http://www.cdc.gov/nceh/ehs/Corecomp/Core_ Competencies_environmental health _Practice.pdf

4. National Environmental Health Sciences & Protection Accreditation Council (environmental health AC). environmental health AC Undergraduate Programs. October 3, 2012. Web. Retrieved October 15, 2012. From http://www.ehacoffice.org/accred-prog/under-prog.php

5. National Environmental Health Sciences & Protection Accreditation Council (environmental health AC). environmental health AC Undergraduate Programs. October 3, 2012. Web. Retrieved October 15, 2012. From http://www.ehacoffice.org/accred-prog/grad-prog.php

Microbiology

3

Joe E. Beck, RS, DEASS

"But however secure and well-regulated civilized life may become, bacteria, protozoa, viruses, infected fleas, lice, ticks, mosquitoes, and bedbugs will always lurk in the shadows ready to pounce when neglect, poverty, famine, or war lets down the defenses."

—Hans Zinsser

Key Performance Outcome Indicators:

1. Understand the scope of microbiology;
2. Be able to define the difference between bacteria, viruses, fungi and protozoa:
3. Know what a prion is;
4. Know the various shapes of different types of bacteria;
5. Be able to draw and label the parts of a cell;
6. Know how they move, reproduce, and the typical time required;
7. Be capable of discussing the growth curve of bacteria and its various stages;
8. Be able to list the major environmental diseases;
9. Understand the factors affecting the growth of microorganisms;
10. Know and be able to discuss the factors influencing the rate of destruction of bacteria.

INTRODUCTION

Misunderstood bacteria

We usually associate bacteria with dirt, disease, and death. They generally get a bad rap and suffer from negative public relations. You probably associate bacteria with the three Ds: dirt, disease, and death. And indeed, for centuries bacterial infections were the major cause of infant and child mortality worldwide. Child mortality began to decline after people were educated about better hygiene. The decline continued with the introduction of antibiotics for better treatment and vaccination for prevention of common deadly diseases.

Bacteria are certainly present in dirt, disease, decay, and death. Spoilage of leftover food, decomposition of garden compost, decay of dead organisms, stale water in a forgotten vase, are all the result of bacterial activity. As are body odor, caries, strep throat, or bubonic plague. No wonder that bacteria receive a bad press. Commercials want us to believe that the only good bacterium is a dead bacterium. Antimicrobial agents are added to toothpaste, soaps, detergents, and plastics. There is no Society for the Protection of Bacteria. However, some bacteria may hover on the edge of extinction, and it is no coincidence that these are pathogenic (disease-causing) bacteria such as *Salmonella typhi* (the cause of typhoid fever) or Yersinia pestis (the cause of plague). Fortunately for the little critters, populations survive in remote areas where they are not efficiently hunted with vaccines and antimicrobials, and people are still at risk for the diseases they cause in these places.

Many environmental health concerns stem from the adverse effect microorganisms can have on the health of people. To understand and control these environmental diseases and conditions, a basic knowledge of microbiology is necessary. The term microbiology is derived from the Greek words *micro* (very small); *bios* (life); and *ology* (the study of). Microbiology usually is concerned with organisms so small they cannot be seen distinctly with the unaided eye; thus a microscope must be used.

Although a tree can kill a person when it falls, we usually don't regard trees as harmful. The same is true for most bacteria—although they may cause problems under specific conditions, they usually live their lives without interfering with ours. An example is Pseudomonas aeruginosa, which commonly lives in soil without doing harm. However, if a person with a suppressed immune system (such as can be caused by cystic fibrosis), inhales it it can colonize their lungs and cause lethal infections.[1]

For many bacteria, the human body is not the right place to live in at all:

They couldn't cope with the lack of oxygen (inside our cells the oxygen concentration is lower than that of air) or with the presence of oxygen (for bacteria that live in oxygen-deprived environments, oxygen is toxic).

The human body is not the natural environment for many bacteria.

They couldn't withstand our defense mechanisms such as the salt present on our skin and in our tears, the lack of iron (a smart device keeps iron, an element vital to all living organisms, inaccessible to most microorganisms in our body), or with the toxic radicals that cells release when under attack of bacteria.

It could be too warm for them, or too cold, as certain bacteria have specific temperature requirements to grow.

Or they could be deprived of food, as the members of the bacterial kingdom have specialized to live on almost anything, but each species has specific nutrient needs.

We have little to fear from most bacteria that we encounter because our bodies can resist most bacterial attacks.

Father of Food Science and Germ Theory

Louis Pasteur was born in 1822 in Dole, France. Louis Pasteur's name is forever cemented in the history of medicine. He, along with Alexander Fleming, Edward Jenner, Robert Koch and Joseph Lister, is of great importance when studying medical history. Pasteur's discovery—that of germs—may seem reasonably tame by the standards of 2010, but his discovery was to transform medicine and see his name forever immortalized on a day-to-day basis in pasteurized milk, named in his honor.

Pasteur showed that airborne microbes were the cause of disease. He built on the work of Edward Jenner and helped to develop more vaccines. Pasteur's career showed how conservative the medical establishment was at the time.

As a young man, he became Dean of the Faculty of Science at the University of Lille. At this time, Lille was the centre of alcohol manufacture in France. IN 1856, Pasteur received a visit from a man called Bigo who worked at a factory that made alcohol from sugar beets. Bigo's problem was that many of his vats of fermented beer were turning sour and, as a result, the beer had gone off and had to be thrown away. From a business point of view, this was a disaster. Bigo asked Pasteur to find out why this was happening.

After using a microscope to analyze samples from the vats, Pasteur found thousands of tiny microorganisms. He became convinced that they were responsible for the beer going sour. Pasteur believed that they caused the putrefaction of the beer—not that they were the result of the putrefaction.

Pasteur continued his work on this theme by studying other liquids such as milk, wine and vinegar. In 1857, he was appointed Director of Scientific Studies at the Ecôle Normale in Paris. Between 1857 and 1859, Pasteur became convinced that the liquids he had studied were being contaminated with microbes that floated in the air. The medical establishment ridiculed him.

Types of Microbiological Organisms

It is no big surprise that we are relatively resistant to bacteria. After all, mammals have evolved in the presence of bacteria, and have developed specialized strategies to keep them under control. In contrast to what your mother taught you, soap is not essential to survive. Our body can resist the bombardment of bacteria it receives every day quite efficiently. Just as well that we can't see them (for the idea is unpleasant) but with every breath of air, every bite we take, little bugs are unknowingly entering our body. And this shouldn't worry you in the least. As long as you keep the troublemakers—the real pathogens—out.

The following are the major groups of microorganisms that are important in environmental health, shown to right in order of listing:

- Bacteria
- Viruses
- Fungi
- Protozoan

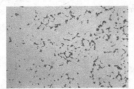  

Centers for Disease Control

Bacteria and fungi traditionally have been included in the plant kingdom because their characteristics most resemble single-celled plants rather than animals. Contrary to these, protozoa are definitely in the animal kingdom. However, viruses possess characteristics similar to both. Viruses can be subdivided into two groups: plant and animal. This means that they attack and reproduce only in those groups. A currently minor category of agent related to human illness is the *prion*. According to Dr. Stanley Prusiner, prion are "small proteinaceous infectious particles which are resistant to inactivation by most procedures that modify nucleic acids." Little is known of these particles but they are believed to have a relationship to several diseases transmitted by food sources. This chapter will address the primary properties and characteristics of each of the four major groups. Because bacteria are the causative agents for most environmental diseases the majority of the chapter will be focused on them.

Bacteria

The most commonly encountered of bacteria can the following shapes:

1. *Cocci (coccus is singular)* are roughly spherical (round like a ball) when mature can exist as individual cells.
2. *Bacilli (bacillus is singular)* are straight (rod shaped).
3. Spirals, or helics
4. *Vibrios* are rod shaped and curved to distinctive commas.
5. *Fusiforms* are spindle shaped.

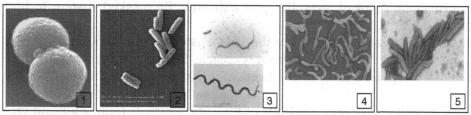

Centers for Disease Control

Diplococci arise when remaining together to form pairs, appearing as paired balls. *Streptococci* appear as long chains of spheres, while *Micrococci* appear square groups of four cells in clusters. Those referred to *Staphylococcus* appear as irregular grape-like clumps.

Bacteria are also classified by their ability to accept or reject staining. Staining helps increase visibility under the microscope and to preserve them for future use. The most widely used staining procedure today is the gram stain, which divides bacteria into two separate groups: gram positive (accepts and retains the gram stain) or gram negative (does not retain the gram stain).

Bacteria reproduce asexually: They are neither male nor female. The most common method of asexual reproduction is binary fission. This is a division process where a single cell divides into two genetically identical daughter cells. The structure of a bacterial cell will vary, but all will typically have the following components:

- A cell wall which supports the cell and imparts shape to it
- A plasma membrane which helps control cell physiology
- A cytoplasmic matrix which contains water and functional organs
- A capsule which surrounds the cell as a slime layer and acts as a protective coating
- A nucleiod which contains the genetic material
- Flagella which provide the power of movement
- Granules that serve as reserve food for the cell

Bacteria are usually measured in micrometers (μm) or nanometers. A micrometer is equal to 1/1,000,000 of a meter while a nanometer is equal to 1/1,000,000,000 of meter. They usually range in length from 0.25 μm to 30 μm, with the *bacillus* averaging about 8 μm in length. A red blood cell is about 7 μm in length.

Most bacteria do not have the ability to move themselves and those that do can only move short distances, primarily when in a liquid medium. Bacteria which are able to move on their own, utilize one of several different methods of locomotion.

- *Flagella*
- *Axial filaments*
- *Gliding motility*

Since most bacteria do not have means of locomotion, they must move principally as passengers, rather than on their own. They get from place to place by becoming hitch hikers on other objects such as fingers, utensils, soiled linen, soiled dishes, dust particles, and insects.

If growth conditions are favorable, bacteria can double in number each generation. This is known as generation time or doubling time. Because the population is doubling every generation this increase is expressed as 2^n. Thus, 2 cells become 4, 4 become 8. The resulting population increase is exponential or logarithmic. Under optimal conditions a generation span may only be 20 minutes. Therefore, one cell may become 250,000 in 6 hours and 280 trillion in 24 hours! Cells normally reproduce faster in a culture than in the human body. The "Growth Curve" in a microbiological culture is seen in Figure 1.1 as four distinct phases.

- The lag phase occurs when the organism is introduced into a medium with little immediate activity.
- The exponential phase occurs when the organisms are growing and dividing at the maximal rate possible under the given conditions.
- In the stationary phase population growth ceases. This is primarily due to nutrient limitation—in other words a change or reduction in the food supply.
- The death phase occurs due to nutrient deprivation and a buildup of toxic waste. In order to grow and reproduce, bacteria must have suitable conditions, which include variations of the following.

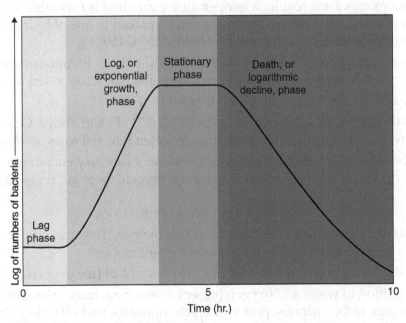

Figure 1.1 The microbial growth curve

Table 3.1 Environmentally Related Bacterial Diseases

Typhoid fever	*Salmonella typhi* (food, milk or waterborne plus direct and indirect contact)
Paratyphoid fever	*Salmonella paratyphi* (food, milk or waterborne plus direct and indirect contact)
Cholera	*Vibrio cholera* (primarily food, milk or waterborne plus direct contact)
Shigellosis	*Shigella* species (27 types) (fecal-oral, indirect contact, food, water, flies)
Campylobacteriosis	*Campylobacter jejuni* (food, milk and waterborne, direct contact with infected pets)
Tuberculosis	*Mycobacterium tuberculosis* (airborne droplets, milk, indirect contact)
Leptospirosis	*Leptospira interogans et al.* (*direct contact with infected animals, waterborne*)
Epidemic typhus	*Rickettsia prowazeki* (vectorborne—*Pediculus humanus*, body louse)
Endemic typhus	*Rickettsia typhi* (vectorborne—*Xenophylla cheopis*, Oriental rat flea)
Scrub typhus	*Rickettsia tsutsumagushi* (vectorborne—bite of larval *Leptotrombidium akumushi*)
Anthrax	*Brucella anthracis* (airborne, foodborne, dermal transmission)
Relapsing fever	*Borrelia recurrentis* (vectorborne—bite of *Peduculus humanus* body louse) *and* bite or coxal fluid of argasid tick (Orntihodoros *turicata* et al.)
Rocky Mountain spotted fever	*Rickettsia rickettsii* (vectorborne—bite/tissue/fecal material of *Dermacentor sp.*and *Amblyomma americanum*
Tetanus	*Clostridium tetani* (dermal transmission from injury)
Plague	Yersinia pestis (vectorborne—bite of Oriental rat flea, *Xenopsylla cheopis*) (airborne—droplets and fomites of pneumonic plague cases dermal—handling of tissues of infecting animals)

Factors Affecting the Growth of Microorganisms

1. *Temperature:* Microorganisms require a temperature range that is favorable to their growth. Regarding temperature, most microorganisms can be placed in one of four classes.
   - *Psychrophiles* (cold loving), which grow best below 150 C (59° F);
   - *Facultative psychrophiles*, which are optimal at 20–30°C (68–86° F), but can grow at 0° C (32° F). These bacteria and fungi are major factors in the spoilage of refrigerated foods.
   - *Mesophilesic*, which grow best at 20° C–45° C (68–113° F);
   - *Thermophiles* (heat loving), which can grow at 55° C (131° F) and above. Organisms that grow moderately well at refrigeration temperatures are often referred to as *psychrotrophs*.

2. *Atmosphere:* The presence or absence of oxygen or other gases may encourage or discourage the growth of a particular type of organism. Regarding oxygen, there are three basic divisions of organisms.
   - *Aerobes* that require the presence of free oxygen in order to grow.
   - *Anaerobes* that can grow only in the absence of free oxygen. The amount of carbon dioxide (CO_2) present may also play a role in the growth of anaerobes.
   - *Facultatives*, since they grow with or without the presence of free oxygen.

3. *Nutrients:* In addition to water and oxygen (except anaerobes), most microbes need external sources of nitrogen, carbohydrates, proteins, lipids, minerals, and vitamins. These nutrients may come from food sources such as host tissue, blood, and plant matter. Bacteria which require many organic growth factors are termed *fastidious*.

4. *Moisture:* It is not the total amount of moisture present which determines the limit of microbial growth, but the amount of moisture that is readily available for metabolic activity. *Relative humidity* also plays a role in moisture, as the optimal relative humidity for bacteria is 92% of higher. Organisms vary in the amount of moisture required; this is referred to as *water activity* (a_w). The approximate lower a_w limit for a bacterium is 0.75.

5. *Osmotic pressure:* High concentrations of salt and sugar usually do not favor bacterial growth. Species, which require high concentrations of salt, are referred to as *halophilic*. Those that require high concentrations of sugar are called *saccharophilic*. The utilization of high concentrations of salt or sugar has been used historically as a means of food preservation.

6. *pH:* This is a measure of hydrogen ion activity. The internal pH of most microorganisms is close to neutrality. Most bacterial species pathogenic to man grow best in environments which are between 7.0 and 7.4 pH. Acids or strong bases usually do not favor bacterial growth. For instance, foods with high vinegar (acid) content do not spoil as easily as other foods.

7. *Pressure:* Most organisms thrive and spend their lives at a pressure of 1 atmosphere (atm). Pressure changes such as in certain laboratory conditions may suppress growth or kill the organisms.

8. *Time:* The amount of time required for bacterial growth is a function of the other factors mentioned. To a limit, the more favorable the conditions the less time will be required for bacterial growth to accelerate to large numbers. The time needed for cell division and thus for a population to double is referred to as *generation time*.

If any of the listed items are unfavorable, bacterial growth may be hampered or controlled altogether.

Factors Influencing the Rate of Destruction of Bacteria

1. *Concentration of an antimicrobial agent:* The more concentrated an agent is, generally the more rapid its action. Over the short range, a small increase in concentration leads to an exponential rise in effectiveness. However, increasing the concentration of disinfectant beyond a certain point may accomplish nothing. An example is 70% ethanol alcohol, which is more effective than 95% ethanol alcohol.

2. *Time:* The longer a population is exposed to a chemical or physical antimicrobial agent, the more organisms are killed. Sufficient time for contact and for resultant chemical and physical reactions to occur must be allowed. Time required will depend on concentration, temperature, nature of the organism, and physiological factors. Exposure duration sufficient to reduce the probability of survival to 10^{-6} or less should be used.

3. *pH (hydrogen ion concentration):* Lethal or toxic action of harmful agents, both physical and chemical, is effected by the concentration of H^+ or of OH^-. For example, both acidity and alkalinity increase the lethal effect of heat. However, the activity of microbial agents that occur as different species within a pH range can be influenced dramatically by pH changes of the medium. It is noted that chlorine and iodine compounds will, as the pH increases, generally decrease in effectiveness. On the other hand, quaternary ammonium compounds are effective at higher pH's and have good stability against heat.

4. *Temperature:* Temperature and time are used jointly in the reduction of bacterial count. They are inversely related. As a rule, the lower the temperature, the longer the time required to kill the organism. Usually 140° F–150° F or above is necessary to kill nonspore bacteria even over long time periods. Higher temperature and pressure are recommended for spores. The time required to exterminate 90% of the vegetative cell at a certain temperature is known as the *decimal reduction time,* or *D value*. This is a key factor utilized in the canning industry. When using chemical microbiocides, frequently a lower concentration of disinfectant can be used at higher temperatures. In this respect, the warmer a disinfectant the more effective it is. However, certain chemicals such as chlorine and iodine can be adversely affected by

water temperature. Chlorine can be driven off as the temperature increases, and its solubility decreases and corrosiveness increases. In addition, iodine in solution is lost very rapidly when the temperature of the solution is in excess of 50° C (122° F). This is due to the tendency of iodine to sublime.

5. *Nature of the organism:* An organism's resistance to chemicals, drugs, and physical agents depends on many factors. The spore form of a bacteria μm is much more resistant than the vegetative form; younger organisms are usually more susceptible than older ones. Endospores are actually a survival mechanism for the entire cell. When growth conditions become hostile to the cell, such as at the end of the log phase of growth, some bacteria have the ability to build a protective coat around their nucleic material. In this form, the nuclear core is able to survive changes in temperature, moisture, pH, and nutrient levels. When growth conditions become favorable, the spore will change back to the vegetative or normal form of the bacteria. Endospores are extremely resistant to heat, ultraviolet light, x-rays, chemicals, and desiccation (drying). Special care must be exercised to assure that when something is "sterilized," it is free of all living organisms in both vegetative and spore forms. In addition, some species are generally more resistant than others. The causative agent for tuberculosis, *Mycobacterium tuberculosis*, is one of the most resistant to antimicrobial agents, particularly disinfectants that are aqueous. This occurs because the cell wall contains wax-like lipids that make the cell surface hydrophobic.

6. *Presence of extraneous materials:* Organic matter can cause coagulation of agents. The presence of considerable quantities of extraneous proteins or colloids, such as blood serum, mucus, and feces in any materials being disinfected will protect the organisms to a great extent. The extraneous material combines with the chemical disinfectant before it reaches the organism. Some disinfectants are more sensitive than others to organic material. For instance, quaternary ammonium compounds are less impaired by organic material than chlorine and iodine. Physical antimicrobial processes are also diminished since the extraneous material insulates the microbe from the effects of heat, steam, and other processes.

7. *Population size:* The larger the population of microorganisms the more time it requires to reduce the population to a given number: An equal fraction of the population is killed during each time interval of exposure to the agent. This principle is applicable to both physical and chemical antimicrobials.

Practical Methods of Microbial Reduction and Elimination

Microbes are reduced in number or eliminated entirely by one of two methods, physical or chemical. Reduction in numbers can be attained by the use of certain chemicals. When a chemical antimicrobial is used only on inanimate objects it is referred to as a *disinfectant*. Disinfectants do not kill all of the organisms since viable spores and a small number of vegetative forms may remain. When a chemical antimicrobial is used on living tissue it is called an *antiseptic*. Again, these normally kill microbes and suppress pathogen development. They are normally less toxic than disinfectants as their usage is on living tissue. If a disinfectant is utilized merely to reduce the population of microbes to a certain acceptable public health level this is termed *sanitization*. A cleaning process (soap and water) which reduces the number of organisms should first accompany this process by removal. If an object is rendered entirely free of all living forms of microbes, both spores and vegetative cells, the process is called *sterilization*. This term stems from the Latin word, sterlis, meaning unable to produce offspring. Sterilization can be accomplished by both physical and chemical means. The following are the primary methods of sterilization.

Physical Methods

Burning:
This is essentially dry heat sterilization. Burning destroys bacteria as long as the item burned is completely incinerated. For highly infectious wastes from health care facilities, proper high temperature, gas-fired incineration is required.

Hot Air:

This is also a form of dry-heat sterilization. It requires a dry oven heated to 165° C (330° F) for a minimum of two hours and can only be used on dry heat–resistant items (glassware, instruments). It requires a longer period and a higher temperature than moist heat since heat in water is conveyed to a body, more easily which is cool then heat from air. Solutions containing water, alcohol, or other volatile substances boil away and are ruined.

Moist Heat:

This process occurs due to the coagulation of microbial proteins. Boiling (212° F/100° C at sea level) in water will kill vegetative bacteria, but spores and some viruses will remain alive after hours of boiling. Certain spores are known to survive in excess of 20 hours of boiling temperatures. For ordinary household purposes of disinfection—*not sterilization*—boiling for 5 minutes will disinfect most surfaces.

Pasteurization:

This is a process applied to many food items in today's market, including eggs, juice and milk. The process is best known with milk and it classically requires that milk be subjected to temperatures of 145° F for 30 minutes. Currently, the high-temperature short-time (*HTST*) process is used, which requires 161° F (70° C) for 15 seconds. This process does not sterilize the milk; it only eliminates disease-producing organisms. There will remain heat-resistant organisms, also known as *thermoduric* organisms. Sterilization can be accomplished using the ultra-high temperature (*UHT*) method. This requires temperatures of 140° F (284° F) for less than a second.

Live Steam:

This is applied in a covered container that will hold steam but not pressure; the boiling water and steam never reach a temperature above 212° F or 100° C. Therefore it is not a reliable sporicidal process.

Steam under Pressure:

The autoclave and the home pressure cooker use this method to produce higher steam and water temperatures. The steam coagulates (cooks) and kills the bacterial cytoplasm. The higher the steam pressures the higher the temperature. The temperature is the most important item in sterilization, but steam under pressure aids the process. Temperatures of 121° C–125° C (250° F–251° F) for 15 to 45 minutes, depending on the package size, wrapping, etc., work for most fluids and freely exposed surfaces. Steam pressure should be 15–20 pounds per square inch (psi). This system with the above parameters is effective on all endospores and organisms and is considered the most reliable system for reaching sterility.

Radiation:

Ionizing and nonionizing radiation can be used to sterilize items. They are not routinely used in institutional settings but are common in large commercial processes. Commercial food processes utilize ionizing radiation such as gamma rays or high-energy electron beams. These have the capability to penetrate through the product. Nonionizing radiation, such as ultraviolet (UV) light, has very slight powers of penetration. The wavelength of 260–400 nanometers is known as UVC or the germicidal spectrum. UVC lamps have returned in recent years as a method of controlling airborne *Mycobacterium tuberculosis*. However, bacteria hidden by a dust particle may escape this type of radiation.

Chemical Methods

Ethylene Oxide:

The chemical *ethylene oxide (ETO)* can be used to sterilize a wide variety of items that are sensitive to high heat or other chemical-sterilizing agents. This agent (toxic and explosive) is used in a closed container mixed with a nonflammable agent such as nitrogen or carbon dioxide. It is valued in part due to its penetrating power, plus low requirement for heat and moisture. Ethylene oxide concentrations should be approximately 900 milligrams per liter at temperatures over 37° C

(98.6° F) for 3–12 hours. Gas sterilization can also be accomplished by using propylene oxide and betapropiolactone.

Glutaraldehyde:
This product is related to, but more effective than formaldehyde, yet it is less irritating. If used as a 2% solution, with 10 minutes exposure it can be bactericidal, tuberculocidal, and virucidal and if exposed for three to ten hours it is sporicidal. This is known as cold sterilization.

Fungi

Fungi are a group of plants with a diverse morphology varying from yeasts to molds. Members of this group deviate from mildew mold to fleshy fungi such as mushrooms and coral fungi. Fungi are heterotrophic, indicating they are decomposers of the hard parts of plants by using enzymes. This decomposition is accomplished either as a *saprobe* of dead tissue or as a *parasite* of living tissue. Fungi are not known to be totally anaerobic, thus they are either aerobic or facultatively anaerobic.

While there are in excess of 100,000 species of fungi, a mere 100 species are known to produce disease in man or other animals. Entry into humans is accomplished by inhalation of the spore form, through a break or opening in the skin, or less prominently on a mucosal surface. *Mycosis* is the term for a fungal infection. Infections that occur deep within the body are referred to, as *systemic mycoses* while *subcutaneous mycoses* are infections of the skin. The former tends to be more serious, the latter attributed to saprophytic fungi that are reservoired in the soil and plants. With the exception of some *dematophytes*, such as athlete's foot and ringworm of the scalp, pathogenic fungi are not deemed to be communicable. Thus, the environmental health practitioner must consider these diseases to be a threat primarily from the soil, most frequently obtained by way of inhalation.

Viruses

Viruses are considered *obligatory intracellular parasites*, meaning they need a living host cell for multiplication to occur. It is known that viruses infect humans, other animals, plants, bacteria, fungi, and protists, which include some molds, protozoans, and some algae.

Viruses enter the body primarily through the respiratory, gastrointestinal, and integumentary systems. Once in the body they find a complementary plasma receptor site protein, which is specific for the virus. This allows the virus to bind to the cell, which is necessary in order to infect it. This process relates to the differences in the nature of diseases such as measles and polio. For example, measles virus receptors are found in a number of tissues; the human spinal cord, nasopharynx, and gut are the only places poliovirus receptors are found, explaining the effect of the poliovirus and its means of transmission. Once attached to the cell they enter by being carried into the cell (endocytosis) with other surface molecules or by fusion, in which the viral envelope fuses with the plasma membrane.

Table 3.2 Environmentally Related Mycotic Diseases

DISEASE	ORGANISM	TRANSMISSION
Cryptococcosis	*Cryptococcus neoformans*	Inhalation: pigeon droppings/soil
North American	*Blastomyces dermatitis* Blastomycosis	Inhalation: soil
Histoplasmosis	*Histoplasma capsulatum*	Inhalation: bat and soil enriched with bird droppings
Coccidioidomycosis	*Coccidioides immitis*	Inhalation: soil
South American	*Paracoccidioides brasiliensis* Blastomycosis	Inhalation: soil

Once inside the host cell they undergo a complicated process of replication resulting in cell damage and cytocidal infection. This cell damage can have several effects including a toxic effect on the organism, chromosomal effects, and transformation into a malignant cell.

Protozoa

Protozoa are unicellular organisms found in soil, water, and the intestinal systems of animals. They constitute a significant portion of plankton, which plays an integral part in aquatic food chains. The classification of protozoans is based upon their motility mode. The protozoans that cause disease are found in four phyla: the *sporozoa*, which cannot move independently; the *mastigophora*, which move by flagella; the *sarcodina*, which are amoebas and move by pseudopods; and the *ciliate*, which move by cilia.

Protozoans typically live in habits that are water rich and are primarily aerobic, but numerous protozoa that inhabit the intestines are competent anaerobes. One characteristic possessed by some protozoa of environmental interest is their ability to form a cyst or protective capsule. This can occur when the protozoa must survive outside of a host or when basic life requirements such as temperature, food, oxygen, or water are not available. This trait can make the organism difficult to destroy when considering public health problems.

Emerging and Reemerging Pathogens

According to the Institute of Medicine,[2] "Emerging infectious diseases are diseases of infectious origin whose incidence in humans has increased within the past two decades and threatens to increase in the near future." The emergence of new pathogens or the reemergence of old pathogens may be influenced by several factors. These include societal changes, human behavior, health care changes, public health infrastructure changes, and microbial adaptation. The environmental practitioner should be aware that environmental changes such as deforestation/reforestation, famine, ecosystem changes, flood/drought and global warming are also influencing these developments. Table 1.3 lists of emerging/reemergening infectious organisms/diseases of environmental origin that the environmental health practitioner should be cognizant of when investigating an outbreak or reviewing data.

Table 3.3 Environmentally Related Viral Diseases

Alphvirus	Eastern, Western and Venezuela equine encephalitis (mosquito borne)
Flavivirus	Yellow fever, Dengue fever, St. Louis encephalitis (mosquito borne), Powassan encephalitis (tickborne), Russian spring-summer encephalitis (tickborne) and Japanese encephalitis (mosquitobourne)
Lyssavirus	Rabies (various mammalian vectors, airbore, and corneal transplants)
Adenoviruses	Gastroenteritis (fecal-oral)
Bunyaviruses	California encephalitis (mosquitobourne), Sandûy fever (*Phlebotomus papatasil*), Rift Valley fever (contact and mosquito), Crimean-Congo hemorrhagic fever (tickborne), Lacross encephalitis (mosquitobourne), Hantavirus (airborne/rodent excreta)
Rotaviruses	Infantile gastroenteritis (fecal-oral)
Enteroviruses	Hepatitis A (fecal-oral)
Calcirirus	Norwalk agent (fecal-oral)
Orbivirus	Colorado tick fever (tickborne)

Table 3.4 Environmentaly Related Protozoan Diseases

DISEASE	ORGANISM	TRANSMISSION
Amoebic dysentery	*Entamoeba histolytica*	Fecal/oral
Primary amoebic meningoencephalitis	*Naegleria fowleri*	Mucosal passage: swimming
Amoebic meningoencephalitis	Acanthamoeba *castellani*	Unknown
Giardiasis	*Giardia lamblia*	Fecal-oral Water Person-person
Malaria	*Plasmodium falciparium P. vivax P. ovale P. malariae*	*Anopheles mosquito*
Leishmaniasis a. Cutaneous *Phlebotomus Lutzomyia* b. Visceral	*Leishmania braziliensis L. tropica L. mexicana L. donovani*	Sandfly
Trypanosomiasis American (Chagas Disease)	*Trypanosoma cruzi*	Reduivid (cone-nosed) bug feces
African (Sleeping sickness)	*T. brucei rhodesinse T. b. gambiense*	Tsetse (Glossina fly)
Toxoplasmosis	*Toxoplasma gondi*	Ingestion/mucosal/ Congenital/blood Transfusion/tissue Transplant/cats
Cyclosporosis	*Cyclospora cayetanensis*	Water/food
Cryptosporidiosis	*Cryptosporidium parvum*	Water/food

Table 3.5 Emerging Infectious Diseases

ORGANISM	TYPE	PRIMARY TRANSMISSION
E.coli 0157:H7	Bacteria	Foodborne
Cyclospora cayetanensis	protozoa	water/food
Cryptosporidium parvum	protozoa	water/food
Borrelia burgdorfei	bacteria	*loxides dammini tick I. pacifica*
Bartonella quintana	bacteria	*Pediculus humanus lice*
Vibrio cholera 0139	bacteria	water/foodborne
Listeria monocytogenes	bacteria	foodborne
Norwalk	virus	foodborne
Yersina enterocolitica	bacteria	foodborne
Salmonella enteritidis	bacteria	foodborne
Campylobacter jejuni	bacteria	foodborne
Coccidioides immitis	fungi	inhalation/soil
Histoplasma capsulatum	fungi	inhalation avian/bat feces
Brucella abortis	bacteria	milk/direct contact
Salmonella typhimurium	bacteria	foodborne
Mad cow disease/Bovine spongiform encephalopathy	prion	foodborne/beef

Methicillin-resistant *Staphylococcus* aureus (MRSA)

Methicillin-resistant *Staphylococcus aureus* (MRSA) is a type of staph bacteria that does not react to certain antibiotics and will normally cause skin infections, but MRSA can also cause other infections, including pneumonia. MRSA can be fatal. In 1974, MRSA infections accounted for 2% of the total number of staph infections; in 1995 it was 22%; in 2004 it was 63%. CDC estimated that 94,360 invasive MRSA infections occurred in the United States in 2005; 18,650 of these were associated with death. MRSA is resistant to antibiotics including methicillin, oxacillin, penicillin, and amoxicillin.

Since these strong drugs are not effective with MRSA, these infections are sometimes called multidrug-resistant organisms (MDROs). Staph infections, including MRSA, occur most often among people in hospitals and health care facilities (such as nursing homes and dialysis centers) who have weakened immune systems. The infection can be spread by skin-to-skin contact, sharing or touching a personal item with someone with infected skin, or touching a surface or item that has been in contact with someone with MRSA.

Community-associated MRSA

MRSA infections that occur in otherwise healthy people who have not been recently hospitalized (within the past year) or had a medical procedure (such as dialysis, surgery, catheters) are known as community-associated MRSA infections (CA-MRSA). These infections are usually skin infections such as abscesses, boils, and other pus-filled lesions, but these infections may also lead to more serious illness, such as pneumonia.

Most staph infections, including MRSA, will grow as a bump or infected area on the skin. You should look for skin that is:

- Red
- Swollen
- Painful
- Warm to the touch
- Full of pus or other drainage
- Accompanied by a fever

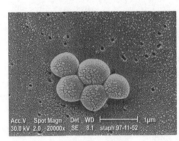
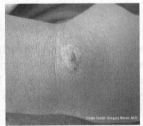

| Staph bacteria | Early MRSA infection | Early progression |

Gregory Moran, MD, Public Health Image Library (PHIL) CDC

Prions

A prion (pronounced pr_-_än) is an infectious agent that is composed primarily of protein. To date, all such agents that have been discovered propagate by transmitting a misfolded protein state; as with viruses the protein itself does not self-replicate. Rather it induces existing polypeptides in the host organism to take on the rogue form. The misfolded form of the prion protein has been implicated in a number of diseases in a variety of mammals, including bovine spongiform encephalopathy. Prion diseases or transmissible spongiform encephalopathies (TSEs) are a family of rare progressive neurodegenerative disorders that affect both humans and animals. They are distinguished by long incubation periods, characteristic spongiform changes associated with neuronal loss, and a failure to induce inflammatory response. One of the issues that make this particle so dangerous is that heat by cooking seems to have no impact on the protein.

The causative agent of TSEs is believed to be a prion. A prion is an abnormal, transmissible agent that is able to induce abnormal folding of normal cellular prion proteins in the brain, leading to brain damage and the characteristics signs and symptoms of the disease. Prion diseases are usually rapidly progressive and always fatal.

A List of Prion Diseases

Listed below are the prion diseases identified to date. Click the linked diseases to go to their respective topic sites. The CDC does not currently offer information here on every prion disease listed.

Human Prion Diseases

- Creutzfeldt-Jakob disease (CJD)
- Variant Creutzfeldt-Jakob disease (vCJD)
- Gerstmann-Straussler-Scheinker syndrome
- Fatal familial insomnia
- Kuru

Animal Prion Diseases

- Bovine spongiform encephalopathy (BSE)
- Chronic wasting disease (CWD)
- Scrapie
- Transmissible mink encephalopathy
- Feline spongiform encephalopathy
- Ungulate spongiform encephalopathy

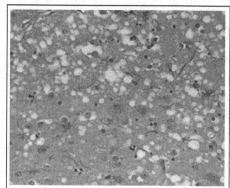

Microscopic "holes" are characteristic in prion-affected tissue sections, causing the tissue to develop a "spongy" architecture.
U.S. Centers for Disease Control

References

Note: this book has been done in consultation with the Environmental Health Officers of the United States Public Health Service, Indian Health Service, and various Civil Service employees of other federal agencies. The 1994 edition of the *Handbook of Environmental Health Field Technician Handbook* was used as a guide and resource in identifying the needs of the field practitioner. Our thanks to that generous sharing of information.

1. Boyd, R. F. and Marr, J. J. 1980. *Medical Microbiology*. Boston: Little, Brown.
2. Prescott, L.M., Harley, J.P., and Klein, D.A., *Microbiology, 2nd edition*, Wm C. Brown Publishers, Dubuque, Iowa, 1993.
3. Starr, C. and Taggert, R., *Biology: The Unity and Diversity of Life, 5th edition*, Wadsworth Publishing Company, Belmont, California, 1989.
4. Marriott, N.G., *Principles of Food Sanitation, 3rd edition*, Chapman & Hall, New York, 1994.
5. Tortora, G.J., Funke, B.R., and Case, C.L., *Microbiology: An Introduction, 4th Edition*, The Benjamin/Cummings Publishing Company, Redwood City, California, 1992.
6. Institute of Medicine, Emerging *Infections: Microbial Threats to Health in the United States*, National Academy Press, Washington, D.C., 1992.
7. Rhodes, R., *Deadly Feasts: Tracking the Secrets of a Terrifying New Plague*, Simon & Schuster, New York, 1997.

The Earth: Its Soil, Water, and Atmosphere

4

Lynn C. Burgess, PhD

Eric C. Brevik, PhD

The human brain now holds the key to our future. We have to recall the image of the planet from outer space: a single entity in which air, water, and continents are interconnected. That is our home.

David Suzuki

Key Performance Outcome Indicators:

1. Understand the scope/definition of the human environment
2. Be able to understand how air, water, and soil contribute to the human environment
3. Be capable of discussing the significance of the impacts of humans on the earth
4. Understand how pollution and other changes to the air, water, and soil impact human health
5. Understand how the profession of environmental health can control, mitigate, or prevent damage to the human environment

Introduction

The earth is the only place that humans live. We cannot at present move to anyplace else. All of us are intertwined with the earth in a symbiotic relationship where everything we do as living organisms has an effect on the earth and every other living organism on the earth. The earth's air, water, and soil, along with the sun, provide us with everything we need to survive, and with the exception of the sun, we interact with these components directly. This means that the earth is our environment, and that the quality of its air, water, and soil is what lets us survive and thrive.

The purpose of this chapter is to introduce you to the study of the human environment, or the field called **environmental health**. Environmental health is the science that studies how to protect the human environment and how to provide a healthy place for humans to live. This chapter will cover the most basic components of the human environment, the earth's air, water, and soil, how these components can be damaged, and how we use each of them to live. We will see how air, water, and soil support life. We will learn how these components can be changed and damaged by human activity, and how the profession of environmental health works to protect human life by protecting our air, water, and soil.

The World Population

The human population is over 7 billion, and the United Nations projects 9 billion by 2050 (Figure 4.1). This growth is only sustainable due to our modern technology and the use of fossil fuels. Both of these are limited, and without them the earth's population would be a fraction

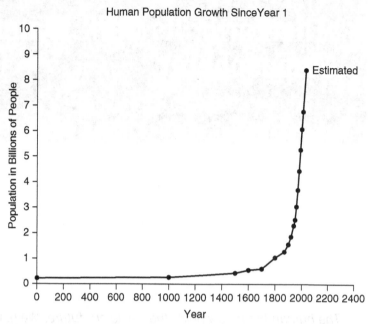

Figure 4.1 World population in modern times, population growth from 7 to 9 billion people is estimated by 2050. Figure by Lynn Burgess with data from U.S Census Bureau.

of what it is today. This growth rate is fueled by a worldwide birth rate of 19.2 births/1,000 population as of 2011. The population declines by a worldwide death rate of 8.12 deaths/1,000 population; therefore, there is a net gain of 11.08 people/1,000 population each year. Even if the world were to control the number of births, as China has done, and lower the birth rate to replacement level, the population would continue to grow for 50 to 70 years. The **replacement rate** is the number of births per female needed to replace her and one male plus the number of persons who die during the childbearing years, which end at 44–49 years old. It also includes those who are inhibited to procreate or have other dysfunctions that prevent childbearing and some adjustments, since the number of male births is slightly higher than female births. The replacement rate is 2.1 births per women in industrialized countries and ranges from 2.5 to 3.3 in developing countries due to a higher death rate.

China has had a one-child limit for urban couples and a two-child limit for rural couples for over 40 years. China's present birth rate is 1.09/1,000 population. Its **population momentum** (population growth at the national level that would occur even if levels of childbearing immediately declined to replacement level) will continue to increase its population until 2030 before it stabilizes or declines. This increase will be about 9%. But it will have taken China almost 60 years to stabilize its population, and this can only be done with a strict dictatorial government.

We have a finite supply of air, water, and soil, and as the world population grows exponentially, we continue to displace other living organisms, use up the available fresh water and tillable soil, and pollute everything. Even our living space is becoming limited. Even if the human population suddenly ceased to increase, there would still be an increasing demand for the earth's resources. People in the developing countries are demanding more and more of the lifestyle enjoyed by citizens of the industrial world. People everywhere want to improve their standard of living and have more luxury items and larger homes. The size of the average home in the United States more than doubled between 1950 and 2010 (Figure 4.2). At the same time, the number of people who live together has decreased from an average of 3.37 in 1950 to 2.63 in 2010.

Let's consider a single consumer item like cellphones, since they are relatively new but are seen everywhere. Cellphone companies are offering cellphone service to 193 of the 196 countries in the world. Only three areas in the world have no cellphone service; these are the Falkland Islands,

Norfolk Island, and the Western Sahara. These areas can still be covered with Internet phone service and satellite phones. China has over twice as many cellphones as the United States. So how does a cellphone affect the earth's resources? Each phone requires plastic and some scarce metals called **rare earth metals** (set of 17 chemical elements in the periodic table, specifically the 15 lanthanides plus scandium and yttrium). Energy to manufacture the phone and more energy each day to run the phone and the systems to operate it are also required. Mining of the rare earth metals is limited to a few areas and has a long history of environmental damage and illegal operations. There is limited recycling of these phones (and other electronic devices), and the disposal of electronic devices and their batteries is a significant source of pollution.

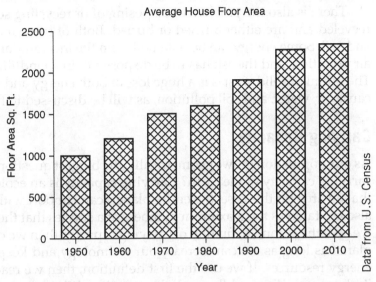

Figure 4.2 Increasing size of the average home in the United States by floor area over the last 60 years. Figure by Lynn Burgess

Therefore the trend is for each person on the planet to require more of our resources each year. From the soil to grow the food we need to the metals being mined, each of us will make a bigger impact on the earth than our ancestors did. Our demand for energy grows even faster than the population, and we use very little **renewable** or **green energy**. Most of our energy is derived from fossil fuels or hydroelectric dams which impact the air, water, and soil. A hydroelectric dam may be "cleaner" than a coal-fired electric plant but it is not without an environmental impact. Much of the water behind the dam is lost to evaporation and is warmed as it sits in the reservoir, the wildlife of the area is changed, the reservoir slowly fills in with silt, and soil erosion downstream is increased.

Every person on earth requires a certain amount of clear air, freshwater, and food. They need healthy soil and freshwater to grow their food. Each person contributes wastes that pollute and change the air, water, and soil. Even the most "green" person on the planet still pollutes and contributes wastes. Everyone breathes out CO_2 and creates urine and fecal wastes. The CO_2 adds to global climatic change and the bodily wastes must be recycled in the **ecosystem** (a system formed by the interaction of a community of organisms with their environment). This is not a problem when there are few humans spread over a large area, but as the population increases there are very few areas left where the population density is low enough that waste is not a problem. The urban areas where most people live are growing rapidly and have created a major challenge for environmental professionals, engineers, and government officials to find ways of treating and disposing of the human wastes. When the other wastes that are produced by our technology, such as plastics, burned fossil fuels, and old electronic components, are added, then the problem of disposal and recycling becomes huge, and at present we are not keeping up with the task.

Many urban areas in the United States have to reuse the water from their wastewater treatment plants as part of their domestic water supply. Many are only using the wastewater for irrigation for places like golf courses, but a few are using it as drinking water, and more will be using it for this purpose in the future as the growth of urban areas outstrips their freshwater supply. In reality, wastewater reuse is not new. Many communities with municipal wastewater treatment facilities discharge their water into a river or lake and then another community downstream takes its water from the same river or lake. Just think about the entire Mississippi River system and all of the cities upstream. Where does their wastewater go to after treatment? The exceptions are those cities that discharge into the ocean, but we then swim and eat fish caught from the ocean.

There is also the problem of disposing of or recycling solid wastes. Most of these wastes are not recycled and are either burned or buried. Both of these methods create pollution of the air, water, and soil. Some energy can be obtained from the incineration of solid wastes, but it is also a source of air pollution, and the ash has to be disposed of in a landfill, creating additional pollution problems. The burial of solid wastes is a huge loss of both energy and material resources. This process can also cause air, water, and soil pollution, as will be discussed in further chapters.

Carrying Capacity

As our population grows geometrically, the biggest question we face is, Have we reached the human carrying capacity of the earth? **Carrying capacity** is an ecological term that refers to the population that an area (in this case, the entire planet) can support without environmental deterioration. It can also be stated as the maximum numbers of a species that the environment can sustain indefinitely. If we take the second definition of carrying capacity, then we can continue to put more humans on this planet as long as we can increase our technology and keep finding either fossil fuel or alternative energy resources. If we use the first definition, then we reached the earth's human carrying capacity long ago. We need then ask the question, When does the displacement of many other species and serious pollution and degradation of the air, water, and soil become irreversible environmental deterioration? Other animal populations are controlled by predation, infective diseases, food and water availability and other resource limitations associated with space, like nesting sites or cover. Humans have lost their predators and have learned to control many of the infective diseases to such a point that chronic diseases of aging, heart disease and cancer are our biggest killers. These diseases generally occur after the childbearing age and have less effect on population growth than infectious diseases had in the past. The biggest threats to our growing population, or what is contributing to our carrying capacity, are food, freshwater, and space. Pollution-caused climatic changes are also limiting our population growth. We are building cities and houses on our farmland and therefore reducing the amount of area we have to grow food. Freshwater is in very limited supply in most areas of the world. In the sub-Saharan areas of Africa, a person may have to walk 8 or 10 miles a day to get water, and many times the water is polluted or has parasites.

As space is reduced in cities and farms are lost, there is a direct reduction in the quality of life and the standard of living. In the United States, we are now experiencing a reduction in the per capita number of homeowners and an increase in apartments and other multi-unit housing. Most of the people in multi-unit housing rent rather than own their homes. So what faces humans as we reach our maximum carrying capacity on the earth? The predictions vary between (1) increased frequency and extent of war (i.e., humans acting as their own predators), (2) new and old diseases that will cause worldwide pandemics, (3) increased areas of famine due to drought, higher temperatures, desertification, and loss of available fertilizers (phosphate supplies are very close to this today), and (4) overwhelming pollution and degradation of our air, water, and soil. With the possible exception of war, all of the predictions pertaining to a dramatic reduction in quality of life can be moderated by the environmental health profession.

What Is Soil?

The Soil Science Society of America defines **soil** as "a naturally occurring surface layer formed by complex biogeochemical and physical weathering processes that contains living matter and is capable of supporting plant life." Note that there are several important parts to this definition. Soil is something we find in nature created by natural processes, it is not something that humans make. Soil is found on the surface of our planet, not at great depths. While there is no single depth that all soils go down to, in most of the United States the "bottom" of the soil is found about 1.2–1.8 m (4–6 ft) below the surface (Figure 4.3). However, the depth can be greater than 1.8 m or less than 1.2 m depending on local conditions. Soils are formed by complex biogeochemical and physical weathering processes, meaning that soils have been significantly altered from the original materials, or parent materials, they formed in through biological, chemical, and physical processes. Chemical processes include the **dissolution** (the process of breaking a compound material into its individual elements or parts), **precipitation** (the process by which a solid substance separates, or is separated from, a liquid it is in), and **alteration** (changing the chemical composition of a material through the introduction of other chemical species) of materials found in the soil. Physical processes involve breaking large materials into smaller materials without changing their chemical composition, and the movement of materials within the soil profile. Biological processes involve anything driven by living organisms, which can include chemical and physical processes driven by organisms (Figure 4.4). Finally, to be considered soil, a material must be associated with living organisms (Figure 4.5).

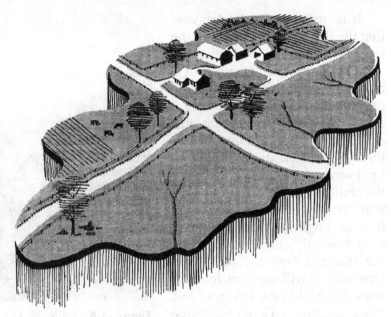

Figure 4.3 The concept of soils as a thin covering on the surface of our planet. The figure shows a cutaway view of the Earth. The thin black line running around the upper edge of the cutaway view is the soil, while the vertical lines beneath it show geological materials, or parent material, the soil formed in. Figure courtesy of U.S. Department of Agriculture.

Photo by Eric Brevik

Figure 4.4 Organisms such as these trees can break down, or weather, geologic materials such as the rocks in the picture both physically and chemically. As the tree roots grow in cracks in the rock, they push on the cracks, which can help to widen them and break up the rock. Organic acids released from the tree roots and from the needles as they decompose also chemically break down the rock. Eventually, some of the broken-down rock will transform into soil as it is weathered, and organic materials are added through the needles that fall off the trees and as roots die and decompose. This process can already be seen happening in some of the cracks (shown by the A symbols) along the rock. Photo by Eric Brevik

It is important to understand that the definition of soil is not the same for everyone. Soil scientists use the definition given above, but engineers define soils as all unconsolidated materials found above bedrock. Notice that this definition is considerably different then the soil scientists' definition. Engineers are not concerned with the ability of soil to support life or with the processes that form soil. Instead, engineers are concerned with how difficult it is to move the material (soil vs. rock) and how well it will support foundations for buildings, bridges, and other structures. Geologists have another definition again, so in working with people from different professions it is important to clarify just what is meant when the term "soil" is used. Without that clarification it is possible to have two people using the same term but discussing completely different ideas.

Figure 4.5. Soils in the bottom of this valley support lush forest growth. The rock walls on the upper part of the valley do not have a soil cover and support very little life. Photo by Eric Brevik

Soils are widespread on the surface of our planet, but they are not found everywhere (Figure 4.6). When working with materials on the earth's surface, it is important to be able to tell the difference between soils and geologic materials, such as **sediments** (pieces of broken and weathered

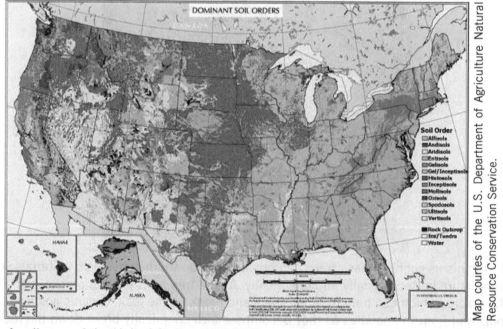

Figure 4.6. A soil map of the United States. While soils are extensive across the map, note that there are areas of rock at the surface, especially in the mountainous areas of the western conterminous United States, Alaska, and the Big Island of Hawaii (shown in black). There are also areas of ice in Alaska (shown in white). Worldwide, about 86% of land is covered with soil and about 14% is composed of nonsoil surfaces, such as rock and ice. Map courtesy of U.S. Department of Agriculture Natural Resource Conservation Service.

rock that have been carried by water, wind, or ice and then deposited [left behind]) or **regolith** (a layer of loose or broken up rock above solid bedrock). Soils have horizons, or layers, in them that form roughly parallel to the earth's surface (Figure 4.7, Table 4.1). These layers are created by the physical and biogeochemical weathering processes that formed the soil from parent materials (Table 4.2). Geologic sediments may have layers in them (Figure 4.8), but these layers are created by processes such as moving water, wind, or ice that left the sediments behind (Table 4.2). The properties of soils are very different than the properties of sediments and regolith, and these differences are important in some environmental health applications, such as the placement of septic systems.

Important Properties and Functions of Soil

Soils possess physical, chemical, and biological properties that are important to their various functions. While this chapter does not have space to cover these properties in detail, some of the most important routinely measured properties are listed in Table 4.3. An introduction to soil science textbook can be consulted for a more complete discussion of these properties.

Photo by Eric Brevik

Figure 4.7. A soil profile, or vertical exposure of the soil, in Iowa. This picture shows the layering typical of soils, indicated with the lines and A, B, and C horizon notation. The black tape is graduated in 0.2 m depth increments.

Table 4.1 Soil horizons shown in their common order from the surface down. It is important to note that not all of these horizons are usually found in a single typical soil, but various combinations of these horizons are found in all soils. The R horizon is not an official horizon but is commonly used, the other horizons are all official horizon names.

HORIZON	CHARACTERISTICS
O	A layer dominated by organic materials, frequently greater than 35% organic material although it can be as low as 25% given certain other conditions. Can be very thin, such as a layer of leaves on the forest floor, or several meters thick, such as the accumulation of organic material in a bog.
A	A mineral-based horizon that also contains significant amounts of organic material, this is usually less than 5% organics although it can contain as much as 35% organic material given certain conditions
E	A light colored mineral horizon, characterized by intense leaching and the loss of clay (eluviation) to lower horizons. Common beneath forest vegetation.
B	A zone marked by a significant accumulation due to soil forming processes. These accumulations can be silicate clays (Bt horizon), pigmenting minerals marked by a color change relative to the horizons above and below (Bw horizon), or a number of other materials. The lower case letter behind the upper case B tells a soil scientist what has accumulated to create the B horizon.
C	Slightly altered parent material, represents the geologic sediment that was present prior to soil formation.
R	A layer of consolidated rock within the soil profile.

Table 4.2 Classification of soil parent materials.

PARENT MATERIAL	MODE OF CREATION
Aeolian	Sediments that were transported (moved) and deposited (left behind) by wind. A commonly known example would be sand in sand dunes.
Alluvium	Sediments that were transported and deposited by flowing water (rivers or streams).
Colluvium	Sediments that were transported and deposited by gravity, usually found at the base of high spots such as mountains or hills.
Lacustrine	Sediments that were deposited in lakes.
Marine	Sediments that were deposited in oceans.
Organic	Created when organic materials, primarily plant debris, accumulate to thicknesses that can be several meters, thick deposits are common in wet areas (i.e., swamps).
Outwash	Sediments that were deposited by water (rivers or streams) flowing off of melting glaciers. The glacial source typically gives these sediments different properties than alluvium derived from non-glacial sources, thus the separate classification.
Residuum	Forms when solid rocks weather (break down) in place, leaving behind loose material.
Till	Sediments that were transported and deposited by glacial ice.

One of the most important properties of the soil from an environmental health perspective is the organic matter content. This is because organic matter has such wide-ranging influences on other soil physical, chemical, and biological properties. In fact, most of the properties (about 80%) listed in Table 4.3 are directly or indirectly influenced by organic matter. Organic matter comes from life in the soil, such as plants (both above- and below-ground portions), earthworms, and a myriad of other organisms. Most scientists believe there is a greater diversity of life in the soil below our feet than on the earth's surface. In fact, a single tablespoon of good soil can contain billions of individual organisms. Another important property is the clay content, which is a part of the soil texture, or the distribution of sand, silt, and clay particles in the

Photo by Eric Brevik

Figure 4.8 Geologic sediments deposited by flowing water. The arrows point to an area with curved beds, or layers. These layers were created by geologic processes rather than soil processes. Learning how to tell the difference between soils and geologic sediments such as these is one of the more difficult field skills for young scientists to master, but is very important for many environmental health applications.

Table 4.3 Examples of some commonly measured chemical, physical, and biological properties of the soil.

CHEMICAL PROPERTIES	PHYSICAL PROPERTIES	BIOLOGICAL PROPERTIES
pH	Texture	Microbial biomass
Organic matter	Bulk density	Earthworm populations
Total carbon	Penetration resistance	Nematode populations
Total nitrogen	Aggregate stability	Arthropod populations
Cation exchange capacity	Water holding capacity	Mycorrihizal fungi
Major and minor nutrients	Infiltration rate	Respiration rate
Electrical conductivity	Depth to hardpan	Soil enzyme activities
Heavy metals and other plant toxins	Depth to water table	Pollutant detoxification
	Porosity	Decomposition rate
	Erosive potential	
	Aeration	

soil (Figure 4.9, Table 4.4). Organic matter and clay combine to give soils many of their most important chemical properties. This is because organic matter and clays are **colloids** (very small particles). Chemical reactions occur on surfaces, and colloids have very large surface areas relative to their volume (Table 4.5). One of the important chemical properties for environmental health applications

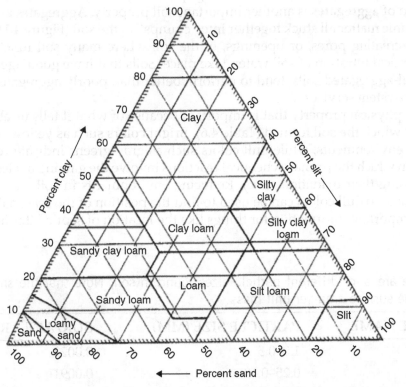

Figure 4.9 The percentage of sand, silt, and clay-sized particles in the mineral component of a soil is used to determine the soil's texture. A textural triangle, such as the one in the figure, shows the various possible soil textures. Texture is an important soil property because it determines many of the physical and chemical properties of a soil. Textural analysis is probably the single most conducted test in soil science. U.S. Department of Agriculture.

Table 4.4 Soil texture refers to the proportions of sand, silt, and clay found in the soil. There are different breaks between textural classes used by different professional groups so it is important to know which system is being used when discussing soil texture. Examples of the different size ranges used by some common systems for classifying mineral particle sizes are given here. In all cases gravel is the coarsest material, followed by sand and silt with clay being the finest particle size.

	SIZE RANGE (MM) BY SYSTEM				
Particle Size Name	United States Department of Agriculture	International Society of Soil Science	American Assoc. of State Highway and Transportation Officials	Udden-Wentworth Scale	Unified System
Gravel	>2.0	>2.0	>2.0	>2.0	>5.0
Sand (total)	0.05–2.0	0.02–2.0	0.074–2.0	0.0625–2.0	0.074–5.0
Silt (total)	0.002–0.05	0.002–0.02	0.005–0.074	0.0039–0.0625	(silt and clay are combined)
Clay (total)	<0.002	<0.002	<0.005	<0.0039	<0.074

is **cation exchange capacity** (the degree to which a soil can adsorb and exchange cations; cations are positively charged ions). The surfaces of most clays and organic matter have a net negative charge, giving them the ability to attract, hold, and exchange positively charged ions, or cations (Figure 4.10).

The formation of **aggregates** is another important soil property. Aggregates are masses of sand, silt, clay, and organic matter all stuck together into "clumps" in the soil (Figure 4.11). Soil aggregates are important in creating pores, or openings, in the soil where many soil functions, such as the physical and chemical filtration of soil water, take place. Soils that have good aggregate formation, referred to as well-aggregated soils, tend to perform better than poorly aggregated soils in providing important ecosystem services.

Soil color is a physical property that is important because of what it tells us about the chemical conditions under which the soil formed (Table 4.6). Bright colors such as yellows and reds indicate well-oxygenated environments, while dull colors such as gray-greens indicate **reducing environments** (a setting in which the primary chemical reactions involve the gaining of electrons by electron receptors, decreasing their oxidation state). Reducing environments in soil are usually associated with wet conditions, so dull colors can be used to find the position of the seasonal high water table in a soil. This is important information for things like the location of septic filter fields.

Table 4.5 Surface areas for different particle sizes found in soil. Note that the smaller the particle size, the larger the surface area per unit mass.

PARTICLE SIZE NAME	PARTICLE SIZE (MM)	SURFACE AREA (M²/G)
Coarse sand	1.0–0.5	0.0023
Fine sand	0.25–0.10	0.0091
Silt	0.05–0.002	0.0454
Clay	<0.002	10 to 820

Source: Brevik, E.C. 2012. An Introduction to Soil Science Basics. In: E.C. Brevik and L.C. Burgess (Eds). Soils and Human Health. Taylor Francis Press, Boca Raton, FL. 2013.

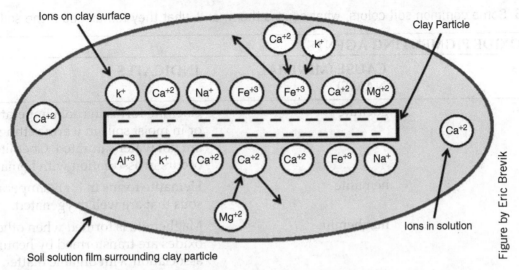

Figure 4.10 The concept of cation exchange on clay surfaces. Clays have a net negative charge, which attracts cations to them. Cations can be exchanged (note the Mg^{+2} exchanging for the Ca^{+2} and the Ca^{+2} and K^+ exchanging for the Fe^{+3}) between the soil solution (water plus dissolved ions) and the clay surface on a charge-for-charge basis. Figure by Eric Brevik

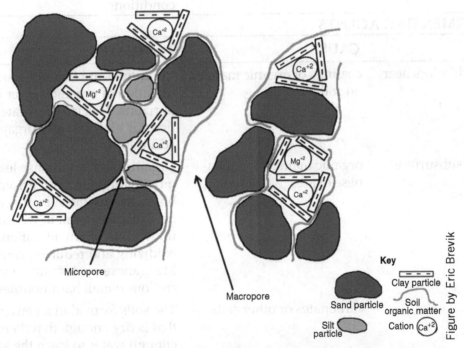

Figure 4.11 Soil aggregates are composed of individual sand, silt, and clay particles that are held together by soil organic matter "glues" and electrostatic attraction between negatively charged clay particles and cations. The large pore, or opening, between the two aggregates shown here is a macropore. Macropores serve as pathways for air, water, and many organisms to move through the soil as well as places for the penetration of plant roots. The small pores within the aggregates are micropores that store water, some of which can be accessed by plants during dry periods. Figure by Eric Brevik

Table 4.6 Some common soil colors, what causes them, and what they tell us about the soil.

IRON OXIDE PIGMENTING AGENTS

COLOR	CAUSE (MINERAL NAME)	INDICATES
yellow	goethite	Goethite forms in cool temperatures, or in moist soils in warm settings that are not water saturated. Goethite often occurs in association with hematite.
red	hematite	Hematite forms in high temperature soils that are well oxygenated.
brown	maghemite	Maghemite is formed when other iron oxides are transformed by heating in association with organic matter, i.e., in forest fires.
orange	lepidocrocite	Lepidocrocite forms in a local zone of oxidation in soils that are otherwise reduced, i.e., around the roots of wetland plants.
gray-green	hydromagnetite	Hydromagnetite forms in soils that are frequently saturated, creating reducing conditions.

OTHER PIGMENTING AGENTS

COLOR	CAUSE	INDICATES
black or dark colors near the surface	coatings of organic matter on soil particles	Conditions are favorable for the accumulation of organic matter in surface horizons. This may indicate wet conditions or high levels of organic matter additions.
black in the subsurface	organic matter or manganese oxides	Organic matter—intense leaching is moving organic matter from surface horizons into the subsurface. Manganese oxides—form in wet soils that undergo frequent alterations between oxidizing and reducing conditions. Manganese oxides often occur as concretions (small hard nodules).
white	carbonates or other salts	The soils formed in an environment that is dry enough that there was not enough water to leach the salts from the soil.

Source: Brevik, E.C. 2012. An Introduction to Soil Science Basics. In: E.C. Brevik and L.C. Burgess (Eds). Soils and Human Health. Taylor Francis Press, Boca Raton, FL. 2013.

Organisms in Soil

Organisms that live in the soil also provide important contributions from an environmental health perspective. Microorganisms found in soil can neutralize the toxic effects of some chemicals, such as spilled petroleum products, and consume organic material and related contaminants released from septic systems. Because of this, humans frequently use soils as a natural disposal location for waste products, with the expectation that the soil will clean up the wastes. **Metal hyperaccumulating plants** have the ability to remove heavy metals from soils; some of these plants can accumulate metals in such high concentrations that the plant itself can be harvested and used as an ore. Properties such as these make soil organisms very important from an environmental health perspective.

Soils and Human Health

Many things are likely to come to mind when people think about their health, such as an active exercise program, wise food choices, good medical care, and proper sanitation. Few people recognize the connection between soils and human health, even though soils are actually very important to human health. Soils influence health through the nutrients taken up by plants and the animals that eat those plants, nutrients that are needed by humans for adequate nutrition for growth and development. Soils have the ability to purify water and to neutralize or sequester a wide range of contaminates. Many of our modern medicines come from soil or soil organisms. In fact, the only Nobel Prize won by a soil scientist to date was awarded to Dr. Selman Waksman in 1952 for his work in isolating antibiotic compounds from soil actinomycetes. Soils can also act to harm human health in three major ways: (1) toxic levels of substances or disease-causing organisms may enter the human food chain from the soil, (2) humans can encounter pathogenic organisms through direct contact with the soil or inhaling dust from the soil, and (3) degraded soils produce nutrient-deficient foods leading to malnutrition. Therefore, soils are an integral link in the holistic view of human health.

Soils and Water

Soil is an important part of the **hydrologic cycle** (the natural sequence through which water passes into the atmosphere as water vapor, precipitates to the earth in liquid or solid form, and ultimately returns to the oceans). As water comes in contact with soil, it has the opportunity to pick up materials from the soil that can be detrimental to human health when present in high-enough concentrations, including heavy metals, organic pollutants, and soil pathogens. These materials and organisms then have the potential to end up in potable surface or groundwater sources and cause adverse effects on human health. Contaminated water can also be introduced to the soil system by accident via sewage spills, breaching or leaching of manure pits or lagoons, or the washing of surface-applied manure into streams by rainwater. However, the physical, chemical, and biological properties of soil also allow soil to function as a natural filter, purifying water that moves through it. We make use of these capabilities in many applications, including septic systems, the use of artificial wetland systems for sewage processing, and land application of manures (Figure 4.12). Using the soil system to clean such contaminated water sources works well if the application system is properly designed and sited, and the soil is not overwhelmed with an overload of contaminates, but the potential for ecosystem contamination is a constant concern.

Heavy Metals

Exposure to **heavy metals** (metal elements that have densities greater than $4500 kg/m^3$) through soil contact is a major human health concern (Table 4.7). Arsenic is actually a **metalloid** (a chemical element with properties that are in-between or a mixture of those of metals and nonmetals), but is commonly grouped with the heavy metals for the purpose of human health discussions. Heavy metals can originate naturally from the weathering of rocks, but have also been introduced to soils through human activity. Heavy metals may occur as a byproduct of mining ores and are therefore

Photo by Tim McCabe, U.S. Department of Agriculture, Natural Resources Conservation Service.

Figure 4.12 A manure slurry being applied to an agricultural field in Arkansas. Land application of manures is done to add nutrients to the soil, but it is also an economical means of disposing of the waste products that takes advantage of the natural filtration capacity of soil. This can be an environmentally friendly way to dispose of waste products as long as the filtration capacity of the soil is not overwhelmed.

Table 4.7 Common anthropogenic sources of and health problems associated with selected heavy metals.

HEAVY METAL	ANTHROPOGENIC SOURCES	HEALTH PROBLEMS
Hg	Electrical switches, fluorescent light bulbs, mercury lamps, batteries, thermometers, dental fillings, burning of coal and fuel oil, medical wastes, pesticides, mining	Central nervous system damage, coordination difficulties, eyesight problems, problems with the sense of touch, liver, heart, and kidney damage
Pb	Batteries, solder, ammunition, pigments, ceramic glaze, hair coloring, fishing equipment, leaded gasoline, mining, plumbing, burning of coal	Neurological impacts, lowers IQ and attention spans, impared hand-eye coordination, encephalopathy, deterioration of bones, hypertension
Cd	Zinc smelting, burning coal or Cd-containing garbage, rechargeable batteries, pigments, TVs, solar cells, steel, phosphorus fertilizer, metal plating, water pipes	Liver and kidney damage, carcinogenic, low bone density
As	Pesticides, mining and smelting of gold, lead, copper, and nickel, iron and steel production, burning of coal, wood preservatives	Gastrointestinal damage, skin damage, carcinogenic, heart, neurologic, and liver damage
Cr	Electroplating, corrosion protection, leather tanning, wood preservative, cooling-tower water additive	Carcinogenic, gastrointestinal disorders, hemorrhagic diathesis, convulsions

Source: Brevik, E.C. 2012. Soils and Human Health—An Overview. In: E.C. Brevik and L.C. Burgess (Eds). Soils and Human Health. Taylor Francis Press, Boca Raton, FL. 2013.

present in mine spoils and in the immediate surroundings of metal processing plants. **E-wastes**, or wastes associated with electronic appliances such as computers and mobile phones, are also becoming an increasing source of heavy metals such as lead, antimony, mercury, cadmium, and nickel in the soil. Urban soils are particularly susceptible to significant accumulations of heavy metals and are frequently associated with heavy metal problems, but fertilizers, manures, and pesticides have also been sources of heavy metal additions to soils in agricultural settings. In the case of fertilizers the heavy metals typically occur as impurities in the fertilizer, while heavy metals have been used in pesticides to target and kill undesired organisms. Arsenic was frequently used in pesticides in the past, and arsenic build-up in the soils of orchards in the United States has been a particular concern. Arsenic contamination may persist in orchard soils for decades or more after the application of arsenic-containing pesticides ceases.

Organic Chemicals

Organic chemicals (molecules that possess carbon-based atoms) that end up in soil are also a major health concern. The main concern with organic chemicals comes from materials known as **persistent organic pollutants** (POPs) (Table 4.8). These are organic chemicals that resist decomposition in the environment or that **bio-accumulate** through the food chain (a process producing an increase in the concentration of chemicals [usually toxicants] in the tissues of organisms with each increase in the trophic level in the food chain), and therefore pose a risk of causing adverse effects to human health and the environment. Soils and human health issues arise with organic chemicals due to the widespread use of these chemicals as pesticides in agricultural situations (Figures 4.13 and 14), for lawns and households (Figure 4.15), and through the accumulation of these organic chemicals in landfills or other disposal sites due to inadequate disposal practices. Petroleum products are another major source of organic chemicals that can end up in the soil. E-wastes are a new source of POPs such as polychlorinated biphenyls (PCBs), and burning of e-wastes can generate other POPs, such as dioxins and furans, two highly toxic organic compounds. Common routes of exposure to organic chemicals include dermal contact with soil and soil ingestion. It is important to note that the complex interactions of heavy metals and the interactions and reactions that organic chemicals undergo in the soil environment and what they mean for the toxicology of these substances are not currently well understood.

Radioactive Materials

Soils can be a reservoir of radioactive elements introduced through both natural and **anthropogenic** (produced by humans) sources. About 90% of human radiation exposure worldwide is from natural sources, but anthropogenic exposure sources can be significant in select locations. **Radon** (chemical element with symbol Rn and atomic number 86; it is a radioactive, colorless, odorless, tasteless noble gas, occurring naturally as a product of the decay of uranium) is a major source of natural radiation exposure, representing about half the natural radiation dose to humans (Figure 4.16). The ultimate source of radon is through the radioactive decay of uranium found in rocks, with **granites** (a coarse-grained igneous rock composed of quartz, feldspars, and micas), felsic **metamorphic rocks** (rocks created when heat and/or pressure changes previously existing rocks), organic-rich **shales** (a sedimentary rock composed of silt and clay-sized particles that are aligned in a parallel arrangement), and **phosphatic rocks** (rocks with a high phosphate content) particularly associated with high uranium content. However, most of the radon formed from the decay of uranium locked up in rocks remains trapped within the mineral grains and thus does not impact human health. Soils formed from parent materials high in uranium will also contain uranium, and significant amounts of the radon formed in these soils ends up in soil pore spaces where it can migrate via diffusion through soil gases or with water moving through the soil. When radon moves through the soil or degasses from radon-containing water sources, it can accumulate in enclosed spaces such as basements, cave dwellings, mines, and other enclosed structures in concentrations that negatively

Table 4.8 Some organic chemical groups that are or have been commonly used and examples of some of the specific chemicals found within those groups.

CHEMICAL GROUP	EXAMPLES	NOTES
Organochlorines[a]	para-dichlorodiphenyltrichloro-ethane (DDT)	Used in mosquito control
	Aldrin	Used in termite control
	Dieldrin	Protect crops from insect pests
	Endrin	Used in rodent control
	Chlordane	Used in termite control
	Heptachlor	Controls soil insects
	Hexachlorobenzene	Used in fungus control
	Mirex	Used in ant, termite control
	Toxaphene	Used in tick, mite control
	Polychlorinated biphenyls (PCBs)	Used in industrial applications
	Dioxines	Group of related compounds, by-product of manufacturing
	Furans	Created by heating of PCBs in the presence of oxygen
Organophosphates	Dichlorvos	Used in fly and flea control
	Parathion	Highly toxic to humans, banned in many western countries
	Diazinon	Insect control in homes, lawns
	Chlorpyrifos	Insect control in crops, lawns, and homes
	Malathion	Toxic to insects, fairly low toxicity to mammals
Carbamates	Carbaryl	Insect control on lawns, highly toxic to honey bees
	Aldicarb	Highly toxic to humans
Chloroacetamides	Alachlor	Weed control, carcinogen in animals
	Metolachlor	Weed control, suspected carcinogen in animals
	Acetochlor	Weed control
Glyphosate		Used in weed control, commercial name is Roundup
Phenoxy herbicides	2,4-D	Broadleaf weed control
	2,4,5-T	Used to clear brush along roads and powerlines

a—all of the organochlorines in this list are banned by the US Environmental Protection Agency due to adverse environmental impacts but may still be used in countries other than the United States.
Source: Brevik, E.C. 2012. Soils and Human Health—An Overview. In: E.C. Brevik and L.C. Burgess (Eds). Soils and Human Health. Taylor Francis Press, Boca Raton, FL. 2013.

Figure 4.13 Application of pesticides to a lettuce crop in Arizona. In this case, pesticide is being applied directly to both the crop and to exposed soil in-between the crop rows. Photo by Jeff Vanuga, U.S. Department of Agriculture, Natural Resources Conservation Service.

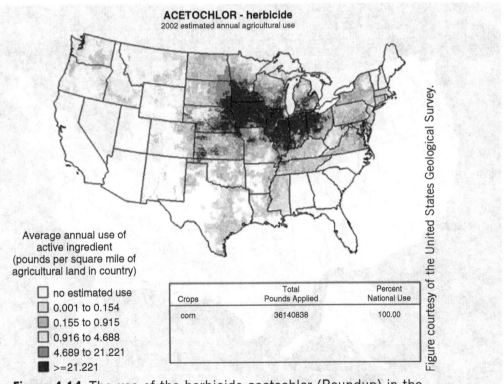

Figure 4.14 The use of the herbicide acetochlor (Roundup) in the United States in 2002. Acetochlor is a nonselective herbicide that is commonly used to control weeds in maize (corn) that has been genetically modified to tolerate it.

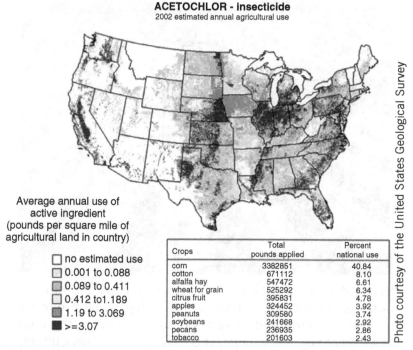

ACETOCHLOR - insecticide
2002 estimated annual agricultural use

Average annual use of
active ingredient
(pounds per square mile of
agricultural land in country)

☐ no estimated use
☐ 0.001 to 0.088
☐ 0.089 to 0.411
☐ 0.412 to 1.189
☐ 1.19 to 3.069
■ >=3.07

Crops	Total pounds applied	Percent national use
corn	3382851	40.84
cotton	671112	8.10
alfalfa hay	547472	6.61
wheat for grain	525292	6.34
citrus fruit	395831	4.78
apples	324452	3.92
peanuts	309580	3.74
soybeans	241668	2.92
pecans	236935	2.86
tobacco	201603	2.43

Photo courtesy of the United States Geological Survey

Figure 4.15 The use of chlorpyrifos in the United States in 2002. Chlorpyrifos is an organophosphate used to control insects in crops, lawns, and homes.

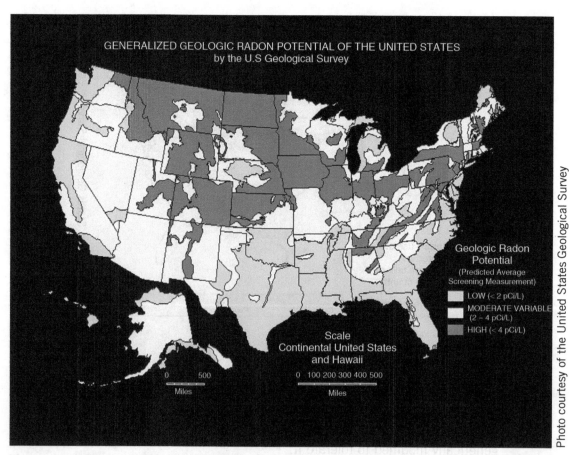

GENERALIZED GEOLOGIC RADON POTENTIAL OF THE UNITED STATES
by the U.S Geological Survey

Geologic Radon
Potential
(Predicted Average
Screening Measurement)

☐ LOW (< 2 pCi/L)
☐ MODERATE VARIABLE (2 – 4 pCi/L)
☐ HIGH (< 4 pCi/L)

Scale
Continental United States
and Hawaii

0   500
Miles

0 100 200 300 400 500
Miles

Photo courtesy of the United States Geological Survey

Figure 4.16 Map showing the potential for radon gas generation and transport through geologic materials and soils in the United States.

impact human health (Figure 4.17). Other than radon, radionuclides of significant environmental concern include isotopes of cesium, cobalt, curium, neptunium, strontium, plutonium, uranium, technetium, tritium, thorium, americium, radium, and iodine. Background radiation levels are fairly constant though most of the world, but isolated areas of higher background radiation occur in regions where high concentrations of minerals that contain radioactive elements are found and in areas containing large volumes of concentrated plant biomass such as coal. Areas of particularly high background radiation include Ramsar in Iran, Guarapari in Brazil, Karala in India, and Yangjiang in China. Important anthropogenic sources of radioactive materials in the environment include nuclear weapons manufacture and testing, accidental release from nuclear facilities such as Chernobyl and Fukushima, the burning of coal, smelting of nonferrous metals, mining activities, and medical wastes. The most common health risks from environmental exposure to radioactive materials are various forms of cancer and genetic mutations.

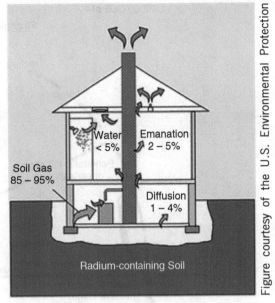

Figure 4.17 Diagram showing common points where radon enters houses.

Soil Pathogens

Most of the organisms found in soil are not harmful to humans, but soil serves as the home for a number of organisms that can cause human diseases. Soil pathogens can be classified based on what portion(s) of their life-cycles they spend in the soil (Figure 4.18, Table 4.9). Bacteria are the most abundant organisms in soil, with up to 1 billion bacteria in a single gram of soil, and perform a wide range of ecological functions. Bacteria are most numerous in warm, moist soils, but can be found in any soil on earth. Actinomycetes are similar to bacteria but have a filamentous growth pattern and are often abundant in soil. Examples of some of the disease-causing bacteria and actinomycetes found in soils are given in Figure 4.19 and Table 4.10. Approximately 300 species of fungi are known to cause disease in humans out of more than 100,000 total fungi species. Most fungi are saprophytes that absorb nutrients by aiding in the decomposition of dead organisms. As a group, fungi thrive in the upper 15 cm of moist, acidic soils, although fungi are also found in other soils. Information on

Table 4.9 Classification of soil organisms based on soil residency.

CLASSIFICATION	RESIDENCY CONDITIONS
Permanent	The organism is a permanent inhabitant of the soil that is capable of completing its entire life cycle in the soil
Periodic	The organism requires part of its life cycle to be completed in the soil
Transient	The organism may be found in the soil naturally, but the soil is not required to complete its life cycle
Incidental	Organisms that are introduced into the soil through anthropogenic activities

Source: Bultman, M.W., F.S. Fisher, and D. Pappagianis. 2005. The ecology of soil-borne human pathogens. In: O. Selinus, B. Alloway, J.A. Centeno, R.B. Finkelman, R. Fuge, U. Lindh, and P. Smedley (Eds). Essentials of Medical Geology. Elsevier, Amsterdam, The Netherlands. pp. 481–511.

LIFE CYCLE of–

Strongyloides stercoralis

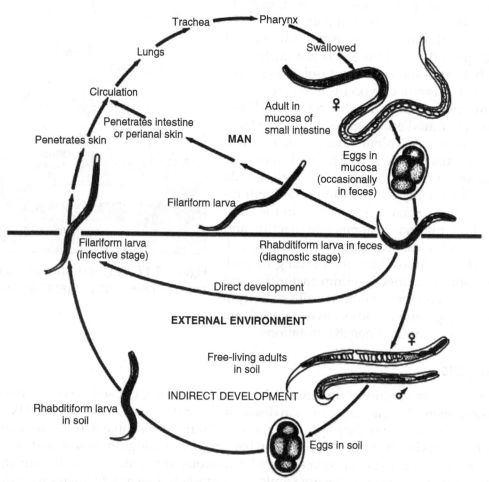

Figure 4.18 The life cycle of Strongyloides stercoralis involves the external soil environment, eggs in the soil, germination of the eggs, and development of the infective nematodes. Figure courtesy of the Centers for Disease Control and Prevention, Public Health Image Library image #5223.

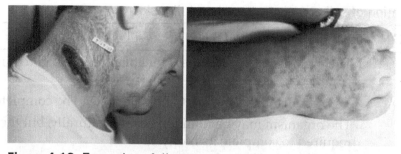

Figure 4.19 Examples of diseases caused by bacteria that spend part of their life cycle in soil. Anthrax lesion on the neck (left). Right hand and wrist displaying the characteristic spotted rash of Rocky Mountain spotted fever (right). Figures courtesy of Centers for Disease Control and Prevention, images #1934 and #1962.

Table 4.10 Some disease-causing bacteria and actinomycetes associated with the soil.

ORGANISM	DISEASE NAME	GATEWAY	ASSOCIATED PROBLEMS	SOIL RESIDENCY	INCIDENCE	GEOGRAPHIC DISTRIBUTION
Bacillus anthracis	Anthrax	Respiration, skin trauma, ingestion	Ulcer w/ black necrotic center, severe breathing problems, shock, nausea, fever, vomiting, diarrhea, abdominal pain	Periodic	Rare	South and Central America, southern and eastern Europe, Asia, Africa, the Caribbean, the Middle East
Clostridium tetani	Tetanus (Lockjaw)	Skin trauma	Painful muscle tightening	Permanent	500,000 annual deaths	Worldwide
Clostridium botulinum	Botulism	Ingestion	Vision problems, slurred speech, dry mouth, difficulty swallowing, muscle weakness	Permanent	Rare	Worldwide
Clostridium sp. (other than 2 above)	Gas gangrene	Skin trauma	Air under skin, blisters, fever, drainage, pain	Permanent	Common before antibiotics	Worldwide
Escherichia coli	Diarrhea	Ingestion	Bloody diarrhea, abdominal pain, vomiting, fever	Incidental	5 million/ year	Worldwide
Rickettsia sp.	Rocky Mountain spotted fever, other tick fevers and spotted fevers	Tick bite	Fever, nausea, vomiting, severe headache, pain, rash	Periodic	250 to 1200 cases / year in the United States	Worldwide
Salmonella sp.	Salmonellosis, typhoid fever, paratyphoid fever	Ingestion	Diarrhea, fever, abdominal pain and cramps	Incidental	2 to 4 million / year in the United States	Worldwide
Streptomyces sp.	Skin infection	Skin trauma	Redness, pain, skin becomes hot and swollen	Permanent	Extremely rare	Worldwide

Source: Brevik, E.C. 2009. Soil, Food Security, and Human Health. In: W. Verheye (Ed.). Soils, Plant Growth and Crop Production. Encyclopedia of Life Support Systems (EOLSS), Developed under the Auspices of the UNESCO, EOLSS Publishers, Oxford, UK. http://www.eolss.net.

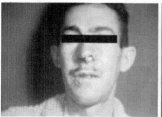
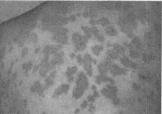
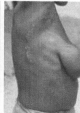

Figure 4.20 Examples of diseases caused by soil fungi. Para-coccidioidomycosis lesions on the face of a patient (left) and erythema nodosum lesions on skin of the back (center) due to coccidioidomycosis. Ringworm on the skin of the right axilla and flank due to *Trichophyton rubrum (right).* Figures courtesy of Centers for Disease Control and Prevention, images #4027, #482, and #2909).

some disease-causing soil fungi is given in Figure 4.20 and Table 4.11. Protozoa are single-celled eukaryotic organisms. Most protozoa found in soil feed on bacteria and algae, but some cause disease in humans. A typical soil contains 10,000 to 100,000 protozoa per gram. Archeozoa are similar to protozoa, but they lack mitochondria. Some common soil protozoa and archeozoa with related information are given in Figure 4.21 and Table 4.12. Helminthes are parasites that may inhabit the human intestines, the lymph system, or in some cases other tissues. Human diseases caused by helminthes are zoonotic diseases that require a nonanimal development site or reservoir for transmission, with the soil being a common development site. Some soils contain more than 10,000,000 helminthes/m^2 of soil to a depth of 10 cm. Billions of people are infected by helminthes worldwide each year, with an estimated 130,000 deaths annually. Infection generally occurs through ingestion or skin penetration, and in most cases involves infection of the intestines. Some common soil helminthes with related information are given in Figure 4.22 and Table 4.13. The soil is not a natural reservoir for viruses; however, viruses are known to survive in the soil environment. Viruses that cause human diseases are usually introduced to the soil with human wastes, such as through septic systems or sewage sludge applications. Viruses usually survive best in cool, wet soils with neutral pH and low microbial activity. The presence of clays in the soil also tends to prolong a virus's

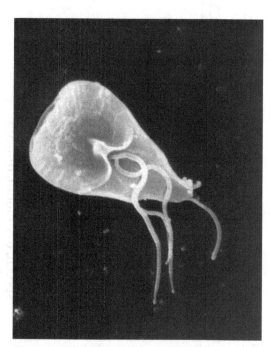

Figure 4.21 Scanning electron micrograph of the Giardia lamblia protozoan parasite. *Giardia* may be found in soil but does not require soil to complete its life cycle and is more associated with water. Figure courtesy of Centers for Disease Control and Prevention, image #8698.

ability to survive. Viruses that cause conjunctivitis, gastroenteritis, hepatitis, polio, aseptic meningitis, and smallpox have all been found in soil, in each case as an incidental organism.

Airborne Dust

Airborne dust can be another soils-related issue that impacts human health. The main direct health effect of inhaled dust is irritation of the respiratory passages and diseases such as lung cancer. However, airborne dust may carry additional materials, such as pathogens, harmful gases, organic chemicals, heavy metals, and radioactive materials, that can cause other health problems.

Table 4.11 Some disease-causing fungi associated with the soil.

ORGANISM	GATEWAY	DISEASE NAME	ASSOCIATED PROBLEMS	SOIL RESIDENCY	INCIDENCE	GEOGRAPHIC DISTRIBUTION
Coccidioides	Respiratory, sometimes trauma to skin	Coccidioidomycosis (Valley fever)	Flu-like symptoms, fever, cough, rash, headache, muscle aches	Permanent	15/100,000	Southwestern United States, northern Mexico, microfoci in Central and South America
Histoplasma capsulatum	Respiratory	Histoplasmosis	Respiratory symptoms, fever, chest pains, dry or nonproductive cough	Permanent	80% living in endemic areas have positive skin test	Eastern and Central United States, microfoci in Central and South America, Africa, India, southeast Asia
Blastomyces dermatitidis	Respiratory	Blastomycosis	Fever, chills, productive cough, myalgia, arthralgia, pleuritic chest pain	Permanent	1 to 2 /100,000	South-central, southeastern, and Midwestern United States, microfoci in Central and South America and Africa
Aspergillus sp.	Respiratory, possible through contaminated biomedical devices	Aspergillosis	Wheezing, fever, cough, allergic sinusitis, chest pain, shortness of breath	Permanent	1 to 2 /100,000	Worldwide
Sporothrix schenckii	Trauma to skin	Sporotrichosis	Bumps or nodules which open and may resemble boils, eventually lesions look like open sores	Permanent	Uncommon and sporadic	North, Central, and South America, Africa, Europe
Trichophyton sp., Microsporum sp., Epidermophyton sp.	Skin contact	Tinea corporis (Ringworm)	Itchy, red circular rash with healthy-looking skin in the middle		Common	Worldwide

Source: Brevik, E.C. 2009. Soil, Food Security, and Human Health. In: W. Verheye (Ed.). Soils, Plant Growth and Crop Production. Encyclopedia of Life Support Systems (EOLSS), Developed under the Auspices of the UNESCO, EOLSS Publishers, Oxford, UK. http://www.eolss.net.

Table 4.12 Common disease-causing protozoa and archeozoa associated with the soil.

ORGANISM	POINT OF INFECTION	DISEASE NAME	ASSOCIATED PROBLEMS	SOIL RESIDENCY	INCIDENCE	GEOGRAPHIC DISTRIBUTION
Cryptosporidium parvum	Epithelial cells of gastrointestinal tract	Cryptosporidiosis	Diarrhea	Transient-incidental	Not known	Worldwide
Cyclospora cayetanensis	Epithelial cells of gastrointestinal tract	Cyclosporiasis	Diarrhea	Incidental	15,000 / yr in USA	Worldwide, most common in tropics and subtropics
Entamoeba histolytica	Intestine	Amebiasis	Diarrhea, dysentery, liver abscesses	Incidental	40 million	Worldwide
Balantidium coli	Intestine	Balantidiasis	Acute hemorrhagic diarrhea, ulceration of the colon	Transient-incidental	Rare	Worldwide
Giardia lamblia	Large intestine	Giardiasis	Diarrhea, abdominal cramps, bloating, fatigue, weight loss	Transient-incidental	500,000	Worldwide
Isospora belli	Small intestine	Isosporiasis	Chronic diarrhea, abdominal pain, weight loss	Transient-incidental	Rare	Worldwide, most common in tropics and subtropics
Toxoplasma gondii	Eye, brain, heart, skeletal muscles	Toxoplasmosis	Flu-like symptoms, birth defects, hepatitis, pneumonia, blindness neurological disorders, myocarditis	Transient	60 million in the USA are probably carriers	Worldwide, most common in warm climate, low altitudes
Dientamoeba fragilis	Gastrointestinal tract	*D. fragilis* infection	Mild abdominal pain, gas, diarrhea	Unknown	2-4% of the population in developed countries	Worldwide

Source: Brevik, E.C. 2009. Soil, Food Security, and Human Health. In: W. Verheye (Ed.). Soils, Plant Growth and Crop Production. Encyclopedia of Life Support Systems (EOLSS), Developed under the Auspices of the UNESCO, EOLSS Publishers, Oxford, UK. http://www.eolss.net.

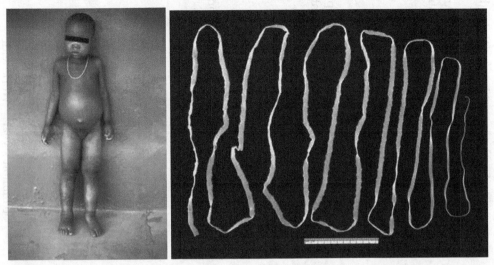

Figure 4.22. A child with hookworm showing visible signs of edema, was also diagnosed with anemia (left). An adult *Taenia saginata* tapeworm (right). Tapeworms are transient residents in soil. Figures courtesy of Centers for Disease Control and Prevention, images #5243 and #5260.

Airborne dust containing such toxins may carry these materials into the lungs, where they can enter the bloodstream. Cultivation for agricultural production and deflation (wind erosion) can introduce such dusts into the atmosphere (Figure 4.23). One of the big health concerns related to soils in North America is airborne dust from Africa. Clouds of dust from the Sahara and Sahel deserts follow the trade winds across the Atlantic Ocean (Figure 4.24). African dust has been documented in the Caribbean and all along the east coast from Florida to Maine, and the amount of Afri-

Photo by Lynn Betts, U.S. Department of Agriculture, Natural Resources Conservation Service.

Figure 4.23 Soil is deflated from a surface exposed by tillage in Iowa.

can dust making its way across the Atlantic is increasing as desertification problems in Africa become more pronounced. Influxes of African dust have been linked to elevated levels of elements such as mercury, selenium, and lead. The transatlantic transport of some viable organisms has been documented on African dust. Ultraviolet light would normally kill microbes transported through the stratosphere on dust, but modern dust levels may be so thick that they are protected from ultraviolet radiation, allowing some viable organisms to travel long distances. Asthma cases in the United States more than doubled between 1980 and 2000, and asthma rates have also increased in the Caribbean. African dust in North America has been tentatively linked to increased asthma, but much additional work is needed to investigate this possibility.

Table 4.13 Common disease-causing helminths associated with the soil.

ORGANISM	COMMON NAME	POINT OF INFECTION	DISEASE NAME	ASSOCIATED PROBLEMS	SOIL RESIDENCY	INCIDENCE	GEOGRAPHIC DISTRIBUTION
Ancylostoma duodenale	Hookworm	Intestine	Ancylostomiasis	Chronic anemia, diarrhea, cramps	Periodic	1.2 billion / year (includes *N. americanus*)	N. Africa, S. Europe, N. Asia, W. South America
Necator americanus	Hookworm	Intestine	Ancylostomiasis	Chronic anemia, diarrhea, cramps	Periodic	1.2 billion / year (includes *A. duodenale*)	Central and S. America, S. Asia, Australia, Pacific Islands
Ascaris lumbricoides	Roundworm	Small intestine	Ascariasis	Stunted growth, abdominal pain, intestinal obstruction, cough	Periodic	1.5 billion / year	Worldwide
Strongyloides stercoralis	Roundworm	Small intestine	Strongyloidiasis	Abdominal pain, diarrhea, rash	Permanent	100 million / year	Tropical, subtropical, and temperate regions
Toxocara canis, Toxocara cati	Roundworm	Organs	Toxocariasis	Fever, abdominal pain, hives, cough, wheezing, loss of vision, crossed eyes	Transient	10,000 / year	Worldwide
Enterobius vermicularis	Pinworm	Colon	Enterobiasis	Anal itching	Incidental	200 million total	Temperate regions
Trichuris trichiura	Whipworm	Large intestine	Trichuriasis	Bloody diarrhea, iron-deficiency anemia, rectal prolapse	Incidental	800 million total	Worldwide
Schistosoma sp.	Fluke	Mesenteric veins, liver	Schistosomiasis	Damage to the liver, intestines, lungs, or bladder	Periodic	200 million total	Tropical regions
Taenia saginata	Beef tapeworm	Small intestine	Taeniasis and cysticercosis	Vitamin deficiency, pain in abdomen, weakness, change in appetite, weight loss	Transient	50 million / year	Worldwide
Taenia solium	Pork tapeworm	Small intestine	Taeniasis and cysticercosis	Pain, paralysis, optical and psychic disturbances, convulsions	Transient	50 million / year	Worldwide

Source: Brevik, E.C. 2009. Soil, Food Security, and Human Health. In: W. Verheye (Ed.). Soils, Plant Growth and Crop Production. Encyclopedia of Life Support Systems (EOLSS), Developed under the Auspices of the UNESCO, EOLSS Publishers, Oxford, UK. http://www.eolss.net.

Positive Influences of Soils on Human Health

Much of the focus on soils to this point in the chapter has been on the negative impacts of soils on human health, but there are many positive aspects as well. The ability of soils to act as natural filters, purifying ground and surface waters if that filtration capacity is not overwhelmed, has already been discussed. Soils are also an important primary source of nutrients. Plants obtain nutrients from the soil which are then passed on to humans when the plants or animal products that were fed on the plants are consumed. Some important dietary sources of elemental nutrients essential to human life that originate in the soil are given in Table 4.14. Over 97% of the calories consumed by the average human have a land origin (Table 4.15), which means humans are

Figure courtesy of NASA

Figure 4.24. A dust storm that blew off of Africa, covering hundreds of thousands of square miles in the eastern Atlantic Ocean. Dust from these storms can make it all the way to the Caribbean and eastern North American coast where it is suspected to cause health problems.

Table 4.14 Some important sources of elemental nutrients essential to human life. Ultimately all these elements come from the soil, either directly from soil to plant or from soil to plant to animal.

ELEMENT	IMPORTANT PLANT SOURCES	IMPORTANT ANIMAL-PRODUCT SOURCES
Ca	Kale, collards, mustard greens, broccoli	Dairy products
Cl		Dairy products, meats, eggs
Cu	Beans, peas, lentils, whole grains, nuts, peanuts, mushrooms, chocolate	Organ meats
Fe		Meats, especially red meat
I	Vegetables, cereals, fruit	
K	Fruits, cereals, vegetables, beans, peas, lentils	Dairy products, meats
Mg	Seeds, nuts, beans, peas, lentils, whole grains, dark green vegetables	
Mn	Whole grains, beans, peas, lentils, nuts, tea	
Mo	Beans, peas, lentils, dark green leafy vegetables	Organ meats
Na		Dairy products, meats, eggs

(Continued)

Table 4.14 Some important sources of elemental nutrients essential to human life. Ultimately all these elements come from the soil, either directly from soil to plant or from soil to plant to animal. (Continued)

ELEMENT	IMPORTANT PLANT SOURCES	IMPORTANT ANIMAL-PRODUCT SOURCES
P	Nuts, beans, peas, lentils, grains	Meats, eggs, dairy products
Se	Grain products, nuts, garlic, broccoli (if grown on high-Se soils)	Meats from Se-fed livestock
Zn	Nuts, whole grains, beans, peas, lentils	Meats, organ meats

Source: Brevik, E.C. 2009. Soil, Food Security, and Human Health. In: W. Verheye (Ed.). Soils, Plant Growth and Crop Production. Encyclopedia of Life Support Systems (EOLSS), Developed under the Auspices of the UNESCO, EOLSS Publishers, Oxford, UK. http://www.eolss.net.

Table 4.15 Daily per capita food intake as a worldwide average, 2001–2003 (Table based on information from the United Nations Food and Agriculture Organization).

FOOD SOURCE	CALORIES[a]	PERCENT OF CALORIES
Rice	557	25.5
Wheat	521	23.9
Maize	147	6.7
Sorgum	33	1.5
Potatoes	60	2.7
Cassava	42	1.9
Sugar	202	9.3
Soybean Oil	87	4.0
Palm Oil	50	2.3
Milk	122	5.6
Animal Fats (raw and butter)	62	2.8
Eggs	33	1.5
Meat (pig)	117	5.4
Meat (poultry)	46	2.1
Meat (bovine)	40	1.8
Meat (sheep and goats)	11	0.5
Fish and other aquatic products[b]	52	2.4
TOTAL	2182	

a—Aquatic products data from 2003. All other data from 2001–03.

b—Includes both marine and freshwater products.

Figure 4.25. Studies have shown that humans tend to respond positively to views of attractive landscapes, such as this view from Olympic National Park in Washington (left). Preliminary results indicate contact with healthy soils (right) may have similar effects to views of attractive landscapes. Photos by Eric Brevik

consuming food loaded with nutrients from soil. Most of our current clinically relevant antibiotics come from soil organisms, and soils are rich sources of other medicines as well. About 40% of all prescription drugs have their origin in the soil, including many of our most recent cancer drugs. Antidiarrheal medicines and treatments for conditions such as diaper rash and poison ivy/oak/sumac have been derived from soil clays. Soil clays have been used in toothpaste formulas and to treat poisoning by the herbicides paraquat and diquat. And finally, there is mounting evidence to suggest that human contact with healthy soils, such as during gardening, can provide human health benefits in much the same way that exposure to green landscapes (areas displaying vegetative growth) has been shown to reduce stress, shorten recovery times from illnesses or surgery, and provide other health benefits (Figure 4.25). So while soil can cause human health problems, there are also many potential health benefits that can be derived from soil.

The Atmosphere and Air Pollution

The air that surrounds us is a complex mixture of gases. It is active and changes dramatically as you go higher up away from the surface of the earth. This air is called the atmosphere, and it is composed of 78.09% nitrogen (N_2) and 20.95% oxygen (O_2). The remaining 1% is composed mostly of argon (Ar) at 0.93%, and carbon dioxide (CO_2) at 0.039%, with lower concentrations of methane and other minor gases. Carbon dioxide and methane concentrations are increasing due to the actions of humans. The concentration of water vapor varies widely between locations and time of day, and is, on average, about 1%.

The atmosphere is held by the earth's gravity and gets less dense as the altitude increases. It becomes thinner and thinner as the distance between molecules of air increases. In all, the atmosphere is only a thin layer around the earth and is only about 1/100 of the earth's diameter. About three-quarters of the atmosphere's mass is within 11 kilometers (km) (36,000 ft) of the surface. Half of the oxygen is gone within the lower 5.5 km (18,000 ft). The atmosphere has no definite boundary with space, but at 120 km the atmosphere starts to show effects on the reentry of spacecraft and at 100 km is the **Kármán line**, which is generally regarded as the edge of space. The atmosphere is commonly divided into four layers (Figure 4.26).

Troposphere

The **troposphere** is the atmospheric layer closest to the surface and extends up to about 10 km (32,000 ft), but this can vary from 8 to 18 km (26,000–59,000 ft) depending on the position of the earth and the season of the year. This is the region of the atmosphere that is heated by the surface of the earth and can harbor life. It contains most of the water vapor in the atmosphere and is where weather occurs. The weather is due to the uneven heating of the surface of the earth and the mixing of air masses with different temperatures and water contents. This mixing is also influenced by the rotation of the earth. The temperature of the air declines with increasing altitude until it reaches roughly –52°C at the top of the troposphere and then ceases to decline with altitude. This region is called the tropopause and is the beginning of the stratosphere. At this point the mixing of the air is limited between the troposphere and the stratosphere.

Stratosphere

The **stratosphere** extends from about 11 km (36,000 ft) to 51 km (170,000 ft). In the stratosphere the temperature increases with increasing altitude. This region contains the ozone layer, which is high in O_3 or **ozone**. This region absorbs ultraviolet light radiation from the sun, thereby not only protecting life on the surface, but also warming the air in the stratosphere. Since this area has very limited mixing, the air closest to the troposphere is the coldest at about –52 to –60°C, while the top of the stratosphere may be near freezing (0°C). The top of the stratosphere is called the **stratopause** and has about 1/1000 the air pressure of sea level. It is the boundary between the stratosphere and the mesosphere.

Mesosphere

The **mesosphere** extends up to about 80–85 km (260,000–280,000 ft). In this sphere the temperature again declines with altitude and may be as cold as –100°C, with an average of –85°C. Even though the oxygen level is very low, there is still enough oxygen for meteors to burn up as they enter the atmosphere. Since the temperatures are so low, all of the water vapor is frozen, forming ice clouds called **noctilucent clouds**. They are so faint that they are usually only seen at dawn or dusk when the sun is still behind the horizon.

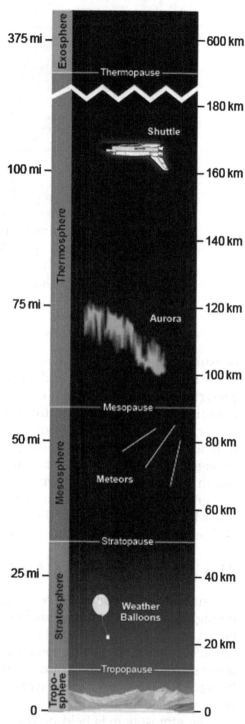

Figure 4.26. Layers of the atmosphere and approximate heights in kilometers. Figure courtesy of NOAA

Thermosphere

The **thermosphere** is the outermost layer of the atmosphere, extending from 85 to 800 km (280,000 to 2,600,000 ft) depending on solar activity and the pressure of the solar wind. The air in this area is so rarified that a molecule may have to travel a kilometer before hitting another molecule. The temperature actually increases with altitude, but since there are so few air molecules, temperature in the usual sense is not well defined. The air is poorly mixed, and usually the composition is constant. The thermosphere is where spacecraft like the International Space Station are in low orbit and the **aurora** is seen (a luminous atmospheric phenomenon appearing as streamers or bands of light sometimes visible in the night sky in northern or southern regions of the earth; it is thought to be caused by charged particles from the sun entering the earth's magnetic field and stimulating molecules in the atmosphere).

Weather and Climate

The sun sends an enormous amount of energy to the earth. Every day over 1,000 watts/m² hits the earth; 70% is absorbed and the rest is reflected into space. This solar energy heats the air that is closest to the surface, with most of the heating occurring in the troposphere. This heating is uneven due to the varied absorption and reflective properties of the surface. For example, water will absorb more heat from the sun than soil, but it returns the heat more slowly than soil, so it will lose heat over the night. This solar energy causes the air to expand and rise, evaporating water and adding water vapor to the air. As the air rises to higher altitudes, it cools and moves back toward the surface (Figure 4.27). The rotation of the planet also adds to the mixing and turbulence of the air by spinning this mixture. Air flows toward areas where the air is less dense, as from water to land during the day (this reverses at night) (Figure 4.28). These factors produce the weather and varied climates on the planet. Since the air is the most mixed component of the earth, any

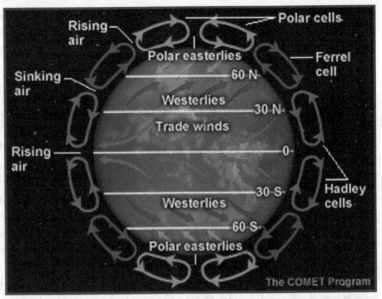

Figure 4.27. Mixing of the atmosphere due to uneven heating of the Earth due to water and land heat absorption differences and differences in the angle of the sun's rays at the equator and poles. Figure courtesy of NOAA

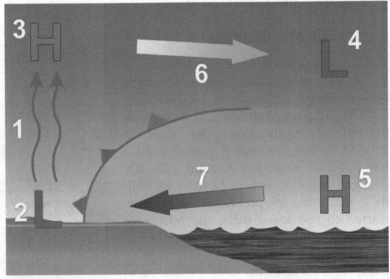

Figure 4.28. Land heats more rapidly than water during the day, creating a low-pressure center with rising air over the land. Higher-pressure air over the water moves in to replace the rising air over the land. As the low-pressure air over the land rises, it cools and moves offshore to replace the sea air that is moving onto land at lower altitudes. At night land cools more rapidly than water, and this process reverses. Figure courtesy of NOAA.

pollution added to the air will at some time be distributed throughout the entire planet. This dilutes the air pollution greatly but still causes pollution that can be detected everywhere. For example, the lead compound tetraethyl lead, which was added to gasoline to stop engines from pinging, was generally banned around the world in 2005. There are still six countries that allow the use of leaded gasoline, and it is still used in aviation gasoline for piston-driven aircraft in the United States. This lead has been found in the ice in both the Arctic and Antarctica.

Air and Life

Everyone understands that we need the oxygen in the air to survive and that plants use the carbon dioxide and produce oxygen. But the atmosphere did not have the same composition in the early days of the earth. Today's atmosphere is the third type that the earth has had. The first atmosphere was constantly being stripped away due to the solar wind until enough gases were released to stabilize the atmosphere. By using volcanic evidence, scientists have found that this first atmosphere would have contained 60% hydrogen, 20% oxygen (mostly in the form of water vapor), 10% carbon dioxide, 5% to 7% hydrogen sulfide, and traces of other gases. During this time the oceans developed due to rainfall, and this water reduced the carbon dioxide content because it was absorbed by the water. The second atmosphere had little oxygen because it was tied up due to the oxidation of iron and other compounds. Life developed during this time, but it was **anaerobic** (did not use oxygen). Anaerobic life is still present on the earth in areas that have little to no oxygen. As primitive bacteria found a way to use the sun's energy in photosynthesis, oxygen was released as a toxic byproduct. Other bacteria evolved a way of using the oxygen to help them produce energy from the breakdown of carbohydrates. These changes led to the third atmosphere, the one we have today. The oxygen concentration has gone up and down since about 1.7 billion years ago when it was produced in abundance. Oxygen content was as high as 30% at its peak 280 million years ago. Carbon dioxide, oxygen, and sulfur are in constant flux due to the action of volcanoes, plants, animals and the shifting of the continents.

Global Climatic Changes

Today's atmosphere is being changed by the actions of humans. This is called the **anthropogenic** (caused or produced by humans) **impact**. Humans have been adding pollution to the atmosphere since we learned to use fire, but it wasn't until a few hundred years ago that our influence changed the atmosphere beyond its ability to neutralize the pollutants. As humans started to use fossil fuels, the release of carbon dioxide increased dramatically. For a long time, the use of carbon dioxide by plants and its absorption by the soils and oceans mediated its build up in the atmosphere. However, over the last century the release of carbon dioxide due to the burning of fossil fuels and the release of other greenhouse gases like methane (Figure 4.29) have caused an increase in the global temperature (Figure 4.30).

Initially, humans caused a reduction in the absorbed heat of the sun due to the

Figure 4.29. Gas flaring at an oil well in southwestern North Dakota. This is a release of carbon dioxide and other gases from the burning of raw natural gas without any use of the energy. The same gas can be collected and separated into natural gas, propane, and other useable gases. Photo by Lynn Burgess

smoke, soot, and **particulates** (tiny particles of solid or liquid suspended in the atmosphere) produced from burning fossil fuels and wood. In nature this occurs from the ash and smoke from volcanoes, but by 1964 there was a switch; more **greenhouse gases** (gases in the atmosphere that absorb

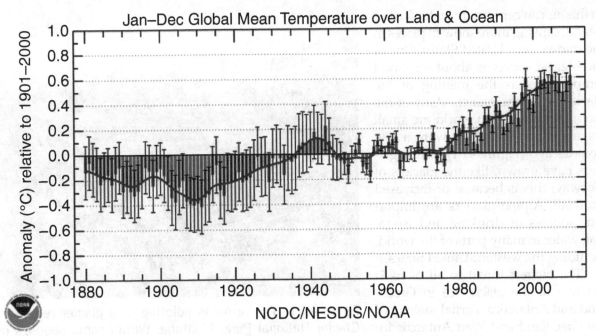

Figure 4.30. Departures of average annual temperature from the 1901–2000 average by year. Note that over the last ~25 years the average annual temperature has been above the long-term average, indicating a warming of our climate. Figure courtesy of NOAA.

and emit radiation within the thermal infrared range) were being produced, and this overrode the reflective nature of the air pollutant particulates. Also, there had been an effort to reduce particulates from burning fossil fuels.

A greenhouse gas is any gas that tends to absorb the infrared radiation from the sun. The greenhouse effect is very important; without it the earth's average temperature would be about –18°C (0°F). However, anthropogenic additions of greenhouse gases to the atmosphere may be taking the beneficial natural greenhouse effect to levels we do not desire. Water vapor is the most important and causes about 36–70% of the greenhouse effect; carbon dioxide causes 9–26%; methane causes 4–9%; and ozone causes 3–7% of the warming. Water vapor has always been in the earth's atmosphere, and ozone is important in protecting the life here from **ultraviolet radiation** (radiation in the wavelength range 4–400 nanometers).

There are also other contributors to the temperature changes that occur periodically to the earth, including volcanic activity, the sun's output of energy, and the orbital position of the earth. However, it is only the anthropogenic increases in carbon dioxide and methane that we may be able to control. Scientists think that if we put just the nonanthropogenic factors into a model of the earth's climate, it would be in a cooling and not a warming cycle.

Per capita use of fossil fuels in most developed countries has decreased in recent years, but there has been a larger matching increase in per capita energy use in developing countries such that worldwide per capita energy use has increased. Population is increasing, and, as stated previously, it is growing exponentially. Therefore, there are more cars and homes built every year that need to be fueled and heated or air-conditioned. There are adequate reserves of fossil fuels that we can use in this century (any reduction in petroleum reserves can be made up with coal reserves), so this pattern of climate change will go on unless new energy sources are utilized.

Climatic change will not just give us warmer summers and nicer winters, it will cause extreme weather. Extremes in temperature, both hot and cold, are responsible for more deaths than all other weather phenomena combined. Precipitation patterns will change, making some areas wetter and other areas drier. There are places that will have more snow because warmer air can hold more water, so this air can carry more water farther inland, causing more snow in places in the midwestern United States. One of the biggest concerns about increased temperatures is the melting of the glacial ice on the planet. Many of the mountain glaciers in world are small fragments of what they were a few decades ago (Figure 4.31). A few glaciers have grown, like the glaciers of Norway; this is because of increased snowfall. Alpine glaciers are important sources of drinking and irrigation water in many parts of the world, including the western United States.

The biggest threat to all of us is the loss of the glacial ice in Greenland and Antarctica. Partial melting of the Greenland and West Antarctic ice sheets will cause a 4–6 m (13–20 ft.) or more rise in sea level. This would flood most of the cities on both coasts of the United States and displace billions of

Figure 4.31. The arrow is pointing to a glacier remnant in Glacier National Park, Montana. Within some people's lifetime, this glacier filled the entire basin in the upper part of the photo, and in the last few centuries it filled the entire canyon. Photo by Lynn Burgess

people worldwide (Figure 4.32). Sea levels have, on average, risen 20 cm since 1980. This is due to melting ice and thermal ocean level expansion. Tuvalu, a tiny island nation in the South Pacific Ocean, is currently seeing this increase and is predicted to become uninhabitable within the century. The impact of sea level during strong storms and high tides will be significant. At present, a combination of the yearly highest tide and a category 4 or 5 hurricane could flood most of New York City or Washington, D.C.

Air Pollution

Air pollution is the addition of a gas, vapor, or particle to the atmosphere that causes harm or discomfort to a living organism. There are many sources of pollution that occur naturally, such as volcanoes and forest fires, but since these have always occurred and we have little control over them,

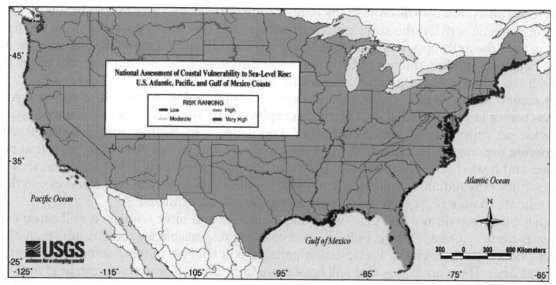

Figure 4.32. Vulnerability of U.S. coastlines to sea-level rise. Courtesy of the U.S. Geological Survey.

- "Good" AQI is 0–50. Air quality is considered satisfactory, and air pollution poses little or no risk. This region is colored green.

- "Moderate" AQI is 51–100. Air quality is acceptable; however, for some pollutants there may be a moderate health concern for a very small number of people. For example, people who are unusually sensitive to ozone may experience respiratory symptoms. This region is colored yellow.

- "Unhealthy for Sensitive Groups" AQI is 101–150. Although general public is not likely to be affected at this AQI range, people with lung disease, older adults and children are at a greater risk from exposure to ozone, whereas persons with heart and lung disease, older adults, and children are at greater risk from the presence of particles in the air. This region is colored orange.

- "Unhealthy" AQI is 151–200. Everyone may begin to experience some adverse health effects, and members of the sensitive groups may experience more serious effects. This region is colored red.

- "Very Unhealthy" AQI is 201–300. This would trigger a health alert signifying that everyone may }experience more serious health effects. This region is colored purple.

- "Hazardous" AQI greater than 300. This would trigger a health warning of emergency conditions. The entire population is more likely to be affected. This region is colored maroon.

Figure 4.33

this chapter will discuss only anthropogenic impacts. There are five major air-polluting substances released by humans. These are carbon monoxide, volatile organic compounds (hydrocarbons), particulate matter, sulfur dioxide, and oxides of nitrogen. These are called the **primary air pollutants**. In the presence of each other and sunlight, these substances can react to form **secondary air pollutants**, and these can further react with substances that occur naturally and other air pollutants to form even more compounds.

The Environmental Protection Agency (EPA) has established air quality standards for six principal air pollutants known as the **criteria air pollutants**. The criteria pollutants are carbon monoxide (CO), particulate matter (PM), sulfur dioxide (SO_2), nitrogen dioxide (NO_2), lead (Pb), and ozone (O_3). All of these are emitted directly except ozone, which is formed when nitrogen dioxide, other oxides of nitrogen, sulfur oxides (SO_x), and volatile organics react in the presence of sunlight. Increased ozone is seen more in the afternoons in areas with high automobile traffic. Particulate matter is either emitted directly or formed when nitrogen oxides, sulfur oxides, ammonia, and organic compounds react in the atmosphere. There are some compounds that are highly toxic and are emitted in small amounts in limited areas; an example is mercury (Hg) from coal-fired electric power plants. The EPA has established an **Air Quality Index (AQI)** for reporting daily air quality. The EPA calculates the AQI for five major air pollutants regulated by the Clean Air Act: ground-level ozone, particle pollution, carbon monoxide, sulfur dioxide, and nitrogen dioxide (Figure 4.33).

Carbon Monoxide

Carbon monoxide (CO) is formed when carbon compounds such as coal or gasoline are burned with inadequate oxygen. The complete burning of carbon compounds leads to the production of carbon dioxide and water, but oxygen is rarely available in high-enough concentrations to completely react with all of the carbon and carbon monoxide that is formed. In the United States, 78% of the carbon monoxide emissions come from vehicles, and most of the rest are from industrial processes and fires. Carbon monoxide causes blurred vision, headaches, and drowsiness at lower levels in the blood, but at higher levels it causes fatal asphyxia and a bright red coloring of the skin.

Carbon monoxide is both odorless and tasteless. It is very dangerous because it replaces oxygen on the hemoglobin molecule in the blood and the myoglobin molecule in the muscles. These are the molecules that carry and store oxygen for cells, and when carbon monoxide is present, less oxygen is available to the cells. Carbon monoxide will also remain bound to the hemoglobin for a long time and is lost very slowly. This is why just a very small amount of carbon monoxide is dangerous. For example, air containing 0.0001% CO can be deadly if exposure is for several hours. This means that enclosed spaces that do not get diluted with fresh air are more dangerous. In heavy traffic, tunnels can contain deadly levels of carbon monoxide if cars are stopped and people remain waiting too long. Smoking is a major source of carbon monoxide because the smokers inhale the smoke directly and the smoke contains carbon monoxide. Smokers can have 20 to 40 parts per million (ppm) of carbon monoxide in their blood depending on the time of day, the tobacco product, and the method of smoking. Nonsmokers who have exposure to second-hand smoke typically have 8 ppm of CO. The Occupational Safety and Health Administration's maximum level for carbon monoxide exposure is 50 ppm over an eight-hour period. Therefore, a heavy smoker in heavy traffic could be at dangerous levels of carbon monoxide exposure.

The reaction of sulfur dioxide to sulfuric acid

$$SO_2(g) + \tfrac{1}{2}O_2(g) ==> SO_3(g)$$
$$H_2O(l) + SO_3(g) ==> H_2SO_4(aq)$$

Sulfur dioxide is not readily oxidized to sulfur trioxide in dry air. Water droplets, however, catalyse the reaction between O_2 and SO_2 in the air producing sulfur trioixde, SO_3. This dissolves in water and produces sulfuric acid.

The reaction of nitrogen dioxide to nitric and nitrous acids

$$2NO_2(g) + H_2O(l) ==> HNO_3(aq) + HNO_2(g)$$

Nitrogen dioxide readily dissolves in water producing a mixture of nitric and nitrous acids.

Figure 4.34 The Chemistry of Acid Rain

Carbon monoxide is fortunately not a persistent pollutant, since it will combine with oxygen to form carbon dioxide. Therefore, once the carbon monoxide source is eliminated, an area can be cleared of carbon monoxide either by dilution with fresh air or by reaction with oxygen. The control of carbon monoxide emissions in the United States has been successful, with a reduction of about 70% in the last 20 years.

Sulfur dioxide

Sulfur dioxide (SO_2) is a colorless gas but has a strong odor. It is produced by the combustion of sulfur compounds found in fossil fuels, especially coal. Most of this sulfur is from cysteine and methionine, amino acids which are part of proteins. Electric power plants that burn coal account for about 70% of today's sulfur dioxide emissions. The rest is from industrial processes, such as mineral processing and gasoline and diesel combustion engines.

The biggest problem with sulfur dioxide is that it reacts with water to form sulfuric acid (H_2SO_4). This occurs readily in the atmosphere with water vapor, and then the acid falls to the surface as acid rain (Figure 4.34). Acid rain can damage structures, vehicles, and plants, with both crops and trees being affected. Lakes in some areas have become sterile due to pH changes from acid rain, and acidification of the soil can leach it of nutrients essential for crop growth. Sulfuric acid can also form in the mouth and respiratory tract of people, causing an irritation of the tissue which aggravates asthma and other respiratory conditions. Since most of the sulfur dioxide is formed from factories and power plants, it can be monitored and controlled better than some other pollutants. In the last 20 years the level of sulfur dioxide emissions has declined by 65% in the United States.

Nitrogen dioxide

Nitrogen dioxide (NO_2) is also produced from the burning of fossil fuels but not directly like sulfur dioxide and carbon monoxide. The burning of fossil fuels produces a mixture of nitrogen oxides (NO_x) which will further react with oxygen to produce mainly nitrogen dioxide. Nitrogen dioxide is a reddish-brown gas that causes the color of the haze seen over many cities. It is highly reactive and causes respiratory problems. It can produce deep lung edema at high concentrations, and it is the cause of chest pain when breathing smoggy air. Farmers can be exposed to 75 to 100 ppm of nitrogen dioxide from fresh silage, which causes shortness of breath, delayed edema, and pulmonary damage. This can be deadly and is called silo-filler's disease. Nitrogen dioxide can also come from tobacco smoke and unventilated heaters.

Nitrogen dioxide acts much like sulfur dioxide to produce nitric acid and is a component of acid rain (Figure 4.34). The most important pollution problem with nitrogen dioxide is its reactions with volatile organic compounds and ozone to produce smog (Figure 4.35).

Ozone

Stratospheric ozone (O_3) is extremely important in protecting life on earth by filtering out much of the sun's ultraviolet radiation. However, human activities cause ozone to be produced and to accumulate in the lower atmosphere, where exposure is toxic. Ozone is a respiratory tract irritant and causes epithelial cell damage. This damage is especially hard on the ciliated epithelial cells, and this makes the problem worse because the removal of particulate matter and other air pollution compounds from the respiratory tract is reduced. These particles are removed by the mucociliary escalator, which uses mucus to trap particles in the inhaled air and the ciliated epithelial cells to move them up the airway; they are swallowed to remove them from the body.

Figure 4.35 Smog over Los Angeles. The brownish color in the haze is caused by nitrogen dioxide. Photo by Eric Brevik.

Ozone is an unstable molecule that will split into oxygen gas and a free atom of oxygen. It is the single oxygen atom that damages living tissues. The single oxygen atom is also reactive with other air pollution molecules. Reactions between these pollutants in the presence of sunlight forms **photochemical smog** (photochemical smog is a type of air pollution caused by reactions between sunlight and pollutants).

Ozone is mostly a secondary air pollutant due to its formation from reactions of oxides of nitrogen and volatile organic compounds. There are other sources of ozone; the most important are electronic devices, but these do not contribute significantly to photochemical smog. Ozone from electronics can be an important cause of upper-respiratory irritation in poorly ventilated areas. Ozone is the air pollutant that most commonly exceeds the EPA standard.

Particulate matter

Particulate matter is any solid or liquid that remains suspended in the atmosphere. The EPA has set standards for particulate matter based on the size of the particle instead of the chemical composition of the pollutant. The larger particles, called **PM$_{10}$**, are 10 to 2.5 **microns** (a micron is one-millionth of a meter) and the smaller particles, called PM$_{2.5}$, are less than 2.5 microns. The PM$_{10}$ are mostly primary pollutants of the type that humans have been exposed to since our start as a species. The most common PM$_{10}$ is dust (Figure 4.36), which is about 50% of all PM$_{10}$. Much of the remainder is carbon particles called soot from fires or industrial activities that burn coal. PM$_{2.5}$ particles are mostly secondary pollutants from reactions of sulfur dioxides, nitrogen oxides, and ozone. Dust and fires can also produce fine particles but in smaller amounts than PM$_{10}$.

Particulates are also important because they are the major contributors to reduced visibility, haze, or smog. The health effects of particulates can be minor to deadly. They are irritants of the respiratory tract and eyes. The larger particles are removed by the mucociliary escalator. These ciliated cells are paralyzed by tobacco smoke; since smoking disables the escalator, smokers cannot remove the particulate matter from tobacco smoke. Without the escalator, the back-up mechanism is coughing. This is one of the reasons for the familiar condition called "smoker's cough" or "smoker's hack."

The smaller the particle size, the deeper into the lungs the particulates can go. The mucociliary escalator can remove PM_{10} efficiently, but $PM_{2.5}$ particulates are not removed very well. The ultrafine particles (< 0.1µM) are more toxic due to their smaller size. When someone increases their **ventilation** (breathing), as with exercising, this will increase the amount and depth to which the particulates enter the lungs. These particulates can be fine metal, ultrafine carbon particles, or a gas-particle interaction where gases like sulfur dioxide and nitrogen dioxide are combined with metal or carbon particles. These interactions increase the **toxicity** (the degree to which a substance can damage an organism) of the particulates.

Figure 4.36 Road dust generated by this truck is mostly larger than PM_{10} and will deposit close to the roadway, harming only the local area. The same dust also contains almost invisible dust particles that can be in the $PM_{2.5}$ range and these can carry longer distances depending on the weather conditions. Photo by Lynn Burgess

Lead

Lead (Pb) is a heavy metal of high toxicity. One may not think of it as an air pollutant, but lead is everywhere on the planet, and this distribution occurs largely as a particulate air pollutant. Due to the toxicity of lead, it was included in the criteria air pollutants by the EPA. Most of the problems with lead came from the tetraethyl lead used in gasoline until it was phased out in the 1980s by most of the world, but not all countries. The other major sources of lead are from lead paint, which has been banned in the United States and the European Union but is still a problem in older homes, and metal smelting, which releases lead and other metals as particulates. The metal releases from smelting are problematic because they usually contain sulfur dioxide and nitrogen dioxide from coal products, which create acids that make the lead easier to absorb.

Lead will accumulate in the body and is very slow to be removed. It causes malfunctions of the nervous system, blood, and the kidneys, but it can affect almost any system. The nervous system toxicity is the most important, and the effect of lead on children is critical because an extremely low concentration of lead can cause problems. Because the nervous system of young children is still developing, lead causes irreversible damage at exposure levels that will not cause any detectable problems in adults. Very low levels of lead in children will cause learning disabilities and hyperactivity. Higher levels of lead in anyone can cause blindness, loss of mental functions, kidney malfunctions, blood disorders, and death.

Volatile Organic Compounds

Volatile organic compounds (VOCs) are organic chemicals that have a high vapor pressure at ordinary, room-temperature conditions. They comprise a varied group of compounds and are a major component of air pollution and photochemical smog. These compounds are not included in the EPA's criteria air pollutants, but they represent about 13% of the air pollution in the United States. These compounds are composed mostly of hydrogen and carbon and are called hydrocarbons. Emissions from automobiles account for 44% of the VOCs, and the use of solvents accounts for 27% more. The level of VOCs indoors is about 10 times that of outdoors due to products used in homes that contain VOCs and the enclosed nature of indoor spaces. VOCs are found in paints, paint strippers and other solvents, wood preservatives, aerosol sprays, cleansers and disinfectants, moth repellents and air fresheners, stored fuels and automotive products, hobby supplies, and dry-cleaned clothing.

VOCs are a major component of photochemical smog, and they react with nitrogen oxides, sulfur dioxide, ozone, and other particulates to form smog. VOCs can be very irritating to the respiratory system and eyes. Since many are solvents, they can have neurological effects. They are a particular problem when people become sensitive to them because they trigger an allergy response. Some VOCs are carcinogenic, and they can continue to be so after forming into photochemical smog.

Indoor Air Pollution

Indoor air pollution can be composed of any of the previously discussed outdoor pollutants plus added compounds that are produced in buildings. These compounds will vary by type and age of building, the number of people in the building, and the use of the building. An office building will have different types of pollutants than a house, and a hospital will have its own unique pollutants. Indoor air is more polluted than outdoor air unless there are special filtration devices in the heating/air-conditioning system. Indoor air may appear to be cleaner and may contain less of the larger particulate matter, but this is because you can only see through a limited amount

Figure 4.37 Poorly ventilated indoor cooking fires, such as this one in India, are a common source of indoor air pollution in developing countries. Photo courtesy of Fogarty International Center, National Institutes of Health

of air, whereas outside you can see though longer distances. Indoor air has pollutants from cooking and gases given off from synthetics used in furniture, carpets, paints, solvents, tobacco smoke, and electronic equipment, to name a few. Many of these pollutants are synthetic compounds and more toxic than any of the criteria pollutants. Most of these pollutants are VOCs that evaporate from computers, printers, fax machines, and other electronics. These machines may also release metal vapors.

Smoke and vapors from cooking are a major pollutant that is more of a problem in developing countries, where people burn wood, charcoal, animal dung, or crop wastes inside their houses for cooking and heating (Figure 4.37). Along with tobacco smoke, these pollutants create an atmosphere high in particulates and carbon monoxide. In the United States, smoking, candles, wood-burning for heat, and cooking also can contribute to an unhealthy indoor environment.

Radon

Radon is a pollutant that is unique to the indoor environment because it is diluted by the outside atmosphere and is only a problem when it can collect in confined spaces like basements. Radon is a radioactive breakdown product of uranium decay and is found in the soil, water, or rocks in areas with uranium. It collects in basements and lower areas of homes and buildings after it has seeped into the building. It is colorless and tasteless, and can only be detected with the use of a special test kit. Radon is the second-eading cause of lung cancer after tobacco smoking, and it is estimated by the EPA to be above safety levels in 6% of U.S. homes. Buildings can be designed that do not let radon seep into them, and older homes can be mitigated to release the radon outside the building.

What Can Be Done to Reduce Air Pollution?

Even though modernization and technology have reduced air pollution by providing alternatives to cooking with an open fire, ways to clean some pollutants out of emissions from things like automobiles and fossil fuel powered plants, and allowing the production of electricity with green technologies like solar panels and wind turbines, most new technologies add new and very toxic pollutants. Take the example of the automobile; it is the leading contributor to air pollution in every urban area in the United States and the major generator of photochemical smog. Smog was originally caused by the burning of coal in industries and for heating homes, but it was replaced by automobile exhaust as better fuels and energy sources were developed. The use of refrigeration has saved countless lives by reducing food poisoning and provided healthier food to people, but the use of **chlorofluorocarbons** (CFCs), a class of chemicals that contain only atoms of carbon, chlorine, and fluorine, as the refrigerants caused a major problems in the ozone layer. By the 1970s over 1 million tons of CFCs were being produced annually and used

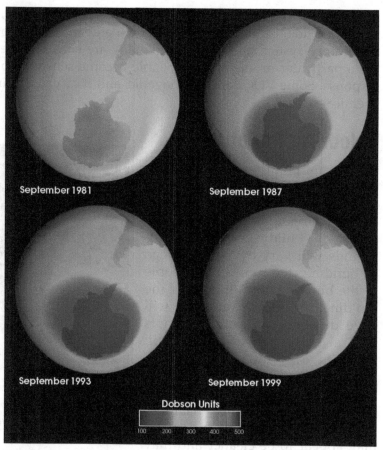

Figure 4.38 These images from the Total Ozone Mapping Spectrometer (TOMS) show the progressive depletion of ozone over Antarctica from 1979 to 1999. This "ozone hole" had extended to cover an area as large as 10.5 million square miles in September 1998. The previous record of 10.0 million square miles was set in 1996. Images by Greg Shirah, NASA Goddard Space Flight Center Scientific Visualization Studio

for refrigeration, propellants, and other uses. These CFCs were able to reach the stratosphere, where they were broken down by solar radiation creating free chlorine. The free chlorine would react with ozone and break it down. Each of the free chlorine atoms continued to react with more and more ozone molecules. A large hole in the ozone layer was detected over Antarctica in 1985 (Figure 4.38). This hole was detectable because the air in this area has the least amount of mixing of any place on the planet. The entire ozone layer was being reduced, but the hole over Antarctica was big enough to be detected. Loss of the ozone layer would allow solar ultraviolet light radiation to kill much of the planet's life. The discovery of the ozone hole led to the banning of CFCs in most developed countries, and their use has become very limited. While the hole in the ozone over Antarctica is smaller now than in the past, it still opens each spring.

The Clean Air Act

The **Clean Air Act** is actually several pieces of legislation first passed in 1970 and amended in 1977 and 1990. The act was the major legislation that allows the EPA to establish air quality standards and mandate the reduction of many air pollutants. This is why the criteria air pollutants were established and how their pollution is controlled. The act has led to the reduction of automobile emissions, acid rain, ozone depletion and most of the criteria pollutants emissions. Recently, the U.S. Supreme Court added greenhouse gases as pollutants that could be regulated by the Clean Air Act.

Water and Water Pollution

The earth is called a "water planet" and is the only known planet with liquid water on its surface. Over 70% of the earth's surface is covered with water, but 97.2% of all the water on earth is in the oceans and is salty. Humans have limited use of saltwater, since it is very energy-costly to remove the salt, so saltwater cannot be used for drinking or to grow crops. The oceans do provide a valuable source of food as seafood, but only about 2.5% of the calories consumed worldwide come from marine foods (Table 4.16). This leaves only 3% of the world's water as freshwater. Of all the earth's water, 2.15% is freshwater that is tied up in glaciers and ice caps, most of which is at the poles and not usable. About 0.62% of water is groundwater, and some of this can be pumped to the surface and used. That leaves 0.03% of the earth's water as surface freshwater, and of this 0.009% is in freshwater lakes, 0.005% in the soil, 0.001% as water vapor in the air, and 0.0001% each in organisms or rivers. This means that available freshwater to produce crops or to drink is a very scarce and unevenly distributed commodity. Consider the differences in available water between the Amazon jungle and the desert around Phoenix, Arizona, or that the Great Lakes of the United States and Canada contain 21% of the entire surface freshwater in the world. This means that water supplies are precious and water pollution is of critical importance to the environmental health field.

Water the Key to Life

Water is the key to all life. All organisms are at least 60% water, and some are over 98% water. It is the unique properties of water and its availability as a liquid that all life depends on. Water is usually polar, but it is in constant change, and for extremely brief periods of time, individual molecules are neutral. Its polarity causes water to stick together and be attracted to or to separate other molecules. It is known as the "solvent of life" and is very slow to gain or lose heat (Table 4.16). The other remarkable property of water is that it floats when it is frozen. Without this property the earth would be an ice ball, because the water would sink as it froze and everything would freeze from the bottom up, not allowing the sun to melt enough frozen water on top of the ice to support life.

Water has been used as the solvent for most of our technological or industrial processes, and water and waterways have been our way of removing and diluting wastes. We are using our oceans, rivers, and lakes as sewage ponds. Even in the most modern city, the water that is used for sewage removal and stormwater runoff is not completely treated and clean, and cannot be used as a domestic water source without passing though the ecosystem and naturally cleaned. Many of the discharge bodies of water are rivers, and then another city downstream will remove water from the river to use. It is not just human wastes that are put into water systems; industries and farms also dispose of wastewater directly or by **nonpoint source contamination** (water and air pollution from diffuse sources). Many urban areas currently use their wastewater for domestic uses such as irrigation of nonfood plants like the lawns at golf courses. Some cities use this water for their potable domestic supply, and as the population of the world increases, more cities will be doing the same thing.

Hydrologic Cycle

Water is naturally cleaned and recycled though the **hydrologic cycle** (Figure 4.39). This system is being altered by changes to the climate, and it is predicted that the distribution of freshwater will be changed dramatically. One of the more dire predictions is that the melting of the Greenland ice cap will dilute the northern Atlantic Ocean so that the circulation of warm water by the Gulf Stream from the equator to northern Europe will be disrupted and Europe will change from a mild marine

Table 4.16

Water Properties
  Facts and Figures about Water

Some of water's physical properties:

- Weight: 62.416 pounds/cubic foot at 32°F; 1,000 kilograms/cubic meter
- Weight: 61.998 pounds/cubic foot at 100°F; 993 kilograms/cubic meter
- Weight: 8.33 pounds/gallon; 1 kilogram/liter
- Density: 1 gram/cubic centimeter (cc) at 39.2°F, 0.95865 gram/cc at 212°F

Some water volume comparisons:

- 1 gallon = 4 quarts = 8 pints = 128 fluid ounces = 3.7854 liters
- 1 liter = 0.2642 gallons = 1.0568 quart
- 1 million gallons = 3.069 acre-feet = 133,685.64 cubic feet

Flow rates:

- 1 cubic foot/second (cfs) = 449 gallons/minute = 0.646 million gallons/day = 1.98 acre-feet/day

Water is unique in that it is the only natural substance that is found in all three physical states—liquid, solid, and gas—at the temperatures normally found on Earth.

Pure water (which you never really find in nature) is essentially clear in color. By "essentially" I mean that water does have a slight blue color to it, due to the way water scatters light.

Water freezes at 32° Fahrenheit (F) and boils at 212°F (at sea level, but 186.4° at 14,000 feet). Water is unusual in that the solid form, ice, is less dense than the liquid form. Thus, ice floats.

Water is called the "universal solvent" because it dissolves more substances than any other liquid. This means that wherever water goes, either through the ground or through our bodies, it takes along valuable chemicals, minerals, and nutrients.

Pure water has a neutral pH of 7, which is neither acidic (<7) nor basic (>7).

The water molecule is highly cohesive—it is very sticky. Water is the most cohesive among the non-metallic liquids.

Pure water does not conduct electricity. Water becomes a conductor once it starts dissolving substances around it.

Water has a high specific heat index—it absorbs a lot of heat before it begins to get hot. This is why water is valuable to industries and in your car's radiator as a coolant. The high specific heat index of water also helps regulate the rate at which air changes temperature, which is why the temperature change between seasons is gradual rather than sudden, especially near the oceans.

Water has a very high surface tension. In other words, water is sticky and elastic, and tends to clump together in drops rather than spread out in a thin film, like rubbing alcohol. Surface tension is responsible for capillary action, which allows water (and its dissolved substances) to move through the roots of plants and through the tiny blood vessels in our bodies.

The relative high density of water allows sound to move through it long distances (ask a whale!). In sea water at 30°C, sound has a velocity of 1,545 meters per second (about 3,500 miles per hour).

Air pressure affects the boiling point of water, which is why it takes longer to boil an egg at Denver, Colorado than at the beach. At higher altitudes the air pressure is lower, which means that the boiling point of water is lower. Thus, it takes longer to hard-boil an egg. At sea level water boils at 212°F (100°C), while at 5,000 feet, water boils at 202.9°F (94.9 °C).

Table courtesy of U.S. Geological Survey
URL: http://ga.water.usgs.gov/edu/waterproperties.html

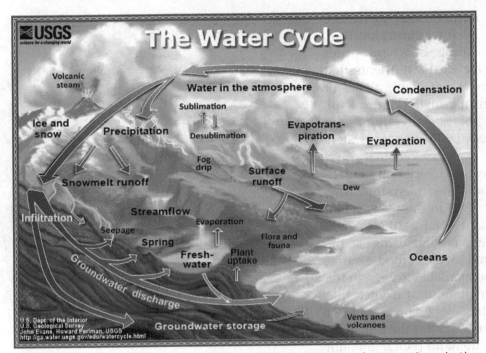

Figure 4.39 The hydrologic cycle and the movement of water though the surface of the Earth and the atmosphere. Figure is courtesy of U.S. Geological Survey

climate to a harsh cold climate like northern Canada, which is at the same latitude as northern Europe. This would, among other effects, reduce crop production in much of Europe.

Humans are changing the hydrologic cycle in ways other than climate change. One example is the use of reservoirs, where the stored water warms and evaporates during storage. This loss of water is significant and can completely empty many reservoirs during a hot summer. At the same time, the reservoir is filling with sediment causing it to become shallower, reducing holding capacity, and increasing evaporation. Impurities that are in this water are left in the sediment or remaining water when part of the water evaporates. The evaporated water is cleaned, but pollution levels increase in the water and sediments are left behind. Once the evaporated water falls as rain or snow, it starts to pick up contaminates from the air, soil, and rock that it flows over and through. Some of these are important for human health in the form of trace minerals needed by our bodies; others add the taste to the water, while still others are pollutants. Some of the pollutants are cleaned by microorganisms in the water and the material it flows though, but some pollutants persist. An example of this is water flowing through an old lead mine where it would pick up toxic levels of lead and further contaminate any other bodies of water it flowed into. Contaminated water that comes into contact with soil or sediments may transfer the lead, cleaning the water but contaminating the soil or sediment. These topics are covered in more detail in the chapter on water and wastewater.

Water Pollution

Water is polluted when harmful compounds or microorganisms are added to it though natural or human activities. The three main types of water pollution are the addition of (1) pathogenic microorganisms or parasites, (2) toxic compounds, and (3) excessive nutrients. Microorganisms and parasites are a concern for human health because of the diseases they cause. These diseases are called **waterborne** because they involve contact with or consumption of infected water. Waterborne diseases are estimated to cause 1.8 million human deaths per year and about 88% of the disease burden in the world.

A high nutrient load in surface water can lead to **eutrophication,** which is a process where water bodies receive excess nutrients that stimulate excessive plant, algae, or microorganism growth (Figure 4.40). This is a particularly important problem because eutrophic waters have lower oxygen levels that cause aquatic insect and vertebrate organisms to die. The microorganisms use the nutrients in the water along with the plants, but as the vegetation dies the microorganisms use the dead vegetation as a food source, using up the available oxygen in the process. The amount of oxygen that is used to decay a certain amount of organic matter is called the **biochemical oxygen demand** (BOD) (amount of dissolved oxygen needed by aerobic biological organisms in a body of water to break down the organic material present). The BOD in a body of water can be measured and is a method of determining if the water has been polluted by added nutrients. The added nutrients that cause the overgrowth of the vegetation are sometimes a single compound or element that is the limiting factor for vegetation growth. An example of this is phosphorus, which is added to laundry detergent to make the colors of the clothes brighter. Phosphorus does not make the clothes any cleaner, they simply appear to be brighter and look cleaner. However, phosphorus passes though waste treatment facilities and causes eutrophication if it is the element needed most by the vegetation. Phosphorus can also be added through fertilizers and manures. The other very common limiting factor is nitrates, which are most commonly added though fertilizers. Once the aerobic microorganisms have used the available oxygen, anaerobic microorganisms start to ferment the available organic matter, producing foul-smelling and bad-tasting water.

Figure 4.40 A eutrophic creek that is the result of agricultural run-off. Photo by Lynn Burgess

Pollution can enter a body of water from a single **point source** or from multiple **nonpoint sources** (Figure 4.41). A point source is a pollution source that can be traced to its origin, such as a discharge pipe from a factory sending pollutants into the water. Nonpoint sources are much harder to trace and locate, and thus reducing the pollution from them can be very difficult. Take, for example, the pollution from a roadway that runs along a river. As cars drive along this road they deposit rubber, oil, gasoline, and other wastes on the road surface. At times it rains, and the rainwater flows from the road to the river carrying the pollution with it into the river. This problem can be minimized if a barrier of plants, known as a riparian buffer, is grown between the road and the river. The buffer slows water flow, allowing the plants and soil to absorb and hopefully mitigate the pollution. The pollution may just collect in another area, but what happens depends on the pollutants present as well as the pollution load. Nonpoint source pollution can also be a result of rainfall or snowmelt moving over and through soil. As the water moves, it picks up and carries pollutants, finally depositing them into lakes, rivers, wetlands, coastal waters, and groundwaters.

All water carries some level of impurities. Trying to purify water completely is almost impossible due to the extremely strong attraction of water to other polar compounds. Even the best water purification systems will still produce water with some impurities in the range of 1–5 parts per billion (ppb). These systems are very expensive to operate, only produce limited quantities of water, and are used in laboratories and for the production of items requiring high purity like drugs. This means that water quality is a relative term. Definitions of water quality usually refer to changes in

Figure 4.41 Point source pollution is when we can identify a single location where the pollution originates, such as the pipes dumping waste into the water body in the photo on the left. Nonpoint source pollution is when we cannot identify exactly where pollutants came from. For example, in the photo on the right, if excess nutrients were identified in the river, those polluting nutrients may have originated from fertilized yards, parks, or golf courses in the city on the left side of the river, or they may have originated in the farm fields on the right side of the river. Left photo courtesy of Environmental Protection Agency, right photo courtesy of USDA Natural Resources Conservation Service.

the water content due to human activities and whether the materials added change the way the water can be used. If you look at a swamp, the water is full of organic material and living organisms varying from bacteria to alligators. The addition of heavy metals from a mining site or oil from a leaky well could seriously harm life in the swamp. Wetlands are important in cleaning and recycling water, and pollution in either of these forms would severely damage the swamp environment. Therefore, when we talk about pollution of water bodies, we must consider whether those bodies of water will still perform the same functions they did prior to being polluted. Is this lake still producing fish, do any of the fish contain high levels of a pollutant like mercury, can we still safely consume the fish? Can we drink the water from the river or is it now toxic? The water does not have to have obvious problems, such as being cloudy or smelly, to be a health hazard to humans, and the health problem does not need to affect everyone who drinks the water. Birth control drugs (made of the female hormones estrogen and progesterone) have been discovered to pass through women's bodies and out in their urine. These hormones, even after passing through a functional wastewater treatment facility, are still functional and act on the organisms living in water where these pollutants are introduced. They could possibly affect people who use the water for their drinking source. These hormones and other polluting compounds that act like hormones have been shown to cause a feminization of male reptiles, fish, and amphibians living in the water. This has reduced some of these populations by causing the males to become nonreproductive.

Water Pollution Sources

Almost anything can be a water pollutant if it can dissolve in water, stay suspended in the water column, or cover the surface of the water and prevent air from interacting with the water. The first types of pollutants are those that dissolve in water. They have some polar properties and can fit into the hydrogen bonding of the water molecules. Nonpolar compounds like oils and fats do not dissolve in water. These form droplets or a layer on top of the water. A layer of oil from an oil spill can form a barrier that stops oxygen from diffusing into the water. Pollutants can also be solids that cannot dissolve like sand, silt, or clay particles. These can cloud the water or clog fish gills and reduce the penetration of light, thereby reducing photosynthesis. Once a pollutant enters the water, it can be distributed throughout the hydrologic system. It can enter soil or rock formations and be left there. Generally, the evaporation process will clean the evaporated water molecules of a pollutant, but most of the pollutant remains in and contaminates the area where the evaporation occurred.

Urban Water Pollution

The influence of humans on the earth's waters is huge. Where people are concentrated, there is a double problem of providing drinking water and disposing of wastes and wastewater. The wastewater from an urban area can include sewage from homes and commercial building restrooms, factory or industrial wastes, and stormwater runoff.

Homes produce wastewater not only from toilets but also from kitchens and laundry. Shower and handwashing water is not very polluted and in green homes is returned to be used in the toilets. One of the major problems with domestic wastewater is the pathogenic bacteria, viruses, and parasites that are viable in this water. Some of these pathogens are easily killed or do not survive for long periods outside of the human body. Others are quite persistent and are not killed or inactivated by wastewater treatment facilities. Even after going through municipal drinking water processing some will survive. An example of this is the parasite *Cryptosporidium*, which passed though the water treatment system in Milwaukee, Wisconsin, in 1993 and sickened over 400,000 people, killing at least 100.

The stormwater runoff from city streets and buildings may have automobile wastes, acid rain, lawn fertilizer, and fecal wastes from pets and wild animals in it. Many cities flow their stormwater into their wastewater treatment systems, which can overload their systems during a large rainstorm or spring snow melt. This causes untreated wastewater, including some raw sewage, to exit the facility and enter whatever natural waterway receives the water. Other cities send their stormwater straight to the nearest lake or stream, introducing polluted water directly into the surface water system (Figure 4.42). Cities that have addressed their stormwater runoff problems have separate treatment facilities or store the water and slowly mix it into their wastewater system. Stormwater runoff can be used for certain types of irrigation because it is typically low in pollutants, so some cities store and use the water.

Industrial Water Pollution

Most industries are located in urban areas, but many industries produce large volumes of polluted water or types of pollutants that typical municipal facilities cannot handle, so they need their own treatment facilities. If the industries do dispose of their wastes into the municipal treatment system, there can be any type of waste product or pollutant in this water. Extra care must be taken to ensure that the industrial waste does not require too high a BOD, does not contain heavy metals that can kill the beneficial bacteria used to clean the wastewater, and does not contain

Figure 4.42. Signs such as this one can be placed at the inlets to storm sewers to educate people about where the wastes that flow through the storm sewer system end up. These types of signs have become common in many communities around the United States. Picture courtesy of NOAA.

Figure 4.43. Water acidified from mine wastes seeps into a creek in the Black Hills of South Dakota. The brownish-orange color characteristic of acid mine drainage is caused by iron hydroxides that coat the stream channel. Photo courtesy of U.S. Fish & Wildlife Service.

pollutants that cannot be handled by the treatment process. Pollutants that are not successfully treated will pass out into the environment where they can damage ecosystems.

Mining and metal smelting are unique industries that have numerous serious water pollution problems. Water flowing through mines or waste dump materials, both abandoned and active, can become highly acidic. Water is also commonly used in processing mining materials. Mined materials often contain pyrite and other sulfur compounds. When these compounds weather and react with oxygen and water they form sulfuric acid and create low pH water (Figure 4.43). This acidified water has the added problem of dissolving metals from mined materials, most importantly the heavy metals, which are extremely toxic, and carrying these metals with the flowing water. There are abandoned mines in many places around the world that have water flowing from them that is too acidic to touch, and if drunk, the lead, copper, zinc, or other metal would kill a person. These water sources usually mix with larger water flows and get diluted, but they can also pollute the entire water drainage system all the way to and including parts of the ocean.

Agricultural Water Pollution

A single farm or ranch can pollute local waters in the same way a city or industry can. The average-size hog farm in the United States produces the same fecal waste output as a moderate-size city. Farms have several unique pollution problems that affect the air, water, and soil. Farms apply huge amounts of pesticides (Figure 4.13) and fertilizers (Figure 4.12) to the soil and crops to maximize their food production. This production cannot be reduced or serious food shortages would occur, and therefore we need to monitor and control the use of agricultural chemicals carefully. Many of the chemicals used can wash from the soil or move into the water table below the fields. These chemicals are almost entirely water soluble, and most are applied mixed with water. When used in excess, they move easily into local water sources. This movement is increased when irrigation is used and can be extreme when nonsprinkler forms of irrigation are used. The loss of agricultural chemicals is an economic hardship on the farmer and an environmental problem for everyone. Farmers can control both the application and method of application of agricultural chemicals and can influence the flow of water from their fields. They can leave strips of natural vegetation between their fields and waterways (Figure 4.44) and leave residues from the harvested crops on their fields (Figure 4.45).

Eutrophication is a common result of farm chemical runoff into bodies of water. This problem can even extend to the oceans when rivers that have been overenriched with nutrients from agriculture reach the ocean. This is seen at the mouth of the Mississippi River, where it discharges into the Gulf of Mexico and causes a large area of "dead water" (Figure 4.46). The overloading of nutrients is not the only problem. Many farm chemicals are toxic and persistent in the environment, which means they do not break down and are not detoxified by organisms in the soil or water. Many of these can accumulate in living tissue, especially fat tissues, and increase in concentration as they move up the food chain. An example is the chlorinated hydrocarbons that have been or are still used as insecticides; these reach toxic levels in the top predators after being at almost undetectable levels in the water or soil. DDT (1,1,1-trichloro-2,2-bis(p-chlorophenyl) ethane) has liposoluble properties, it was readily absorbed and built up to toxic levels in fish, mammals, birds, and humans as it passed up the food chain. DDT's toxic action was first seen as a disruption of hormone systems. DDT was banned in the United States in 1972 but is highly persistent and is still globally distributed; it is also still used in many parts of the world. It accumulates in animals tissues because it is extremely stable, and it persists in soils and in plants. DDT has reached most groundwater and surface water sources. DDT has a reported **half-life** of > 60 years outside of organisms. A half-life is the length of time it takes for half of the compound to break down or change, but many of the breakdown products of DDT are still toxic.

Figure 4.44. This Iowa stream has rows of trees, shrubs, and grasses, known as a riparian buffer, planted between it and the surround agricultural fields. The riparian buffer serves to remove particulate material as well as dissolved nutrients and other chemicals from water coming off the fields, meaning that the water entering the stream is cleaner than if the buffer was not in place. Photo courtesy of USDA-NRCS.

Figure 4.45. Corn growing through soybean residues in Iowa. The residues slow down water flow across the field and protect the soil structure, allowing more infiltration and reducing erosion. Photo courtesy of USDA-NRCS.

Thermal Pollution

Water is not only adversely affected by the addition of chemicals, it is also affected by temperature changes. There are few if any examples of bodies of water being cooled by human activities, but humans do cause increases in water temperature in many locations around the world. With the exception of global warming, which is warming the oceans, this thermal pollution is mostly in freshwater. There are two main ways of causing thermal pollution. The first has already been mentioned in this chapter, and that is the storage of water in reservoirs, which allows more heating from the sun and evaporation of the water. Domestic and industrial uses of water also heat the water, and when the heated water returns to any natural body of water it raises its temperature.

Many industries use water to cool their operations. This ranges from cooling metal during a smelter operation to using steam during the generation of electricity. The steam is usually cooled by a local body of water and then the water is returned to its source. The addition of heat to the water causes the amount of available oxygen to decline. The increase may be only a few degrees, but it can

Figure 4.46 Gulf of Mexico Dead Zone. Less oxygen dissolved in the water is often referred to as a "dead zone" (in red above) because most marine life either dies or, if they are mobile, such as fish, leave the area. Habitats that would normally be teeming with life become, essentially, biological deserts. The Gulf of Mexico dead zone typically ranges from a low of approximately 1,197 square miles to as much as 6,213 square miles. Figure courtesy of NOAA

alter the aquatic environment. Many cold-water fish species, such as trout, cannot survive in the warmer waters and reduced oxygen levels. In other fish, a few degrees can change their reproductive cycle and either trigger or stop spawning. These changes in temperature are usually not constant but vary over time with the needs of the industry, making the thermal pollution even more disruptive. This heating can prevent lakes from freezing over and increase the growth of algae and aquatic plants, similar to the addition of excessive nutrients.

Thermal pollution can be remediated and controlled just like the other types of water pollution. Cooling waters do not have to be returned to local water sources. The industry can maintain its own separate water supply and use shallow ponds to cool the water before it is reused. Another method, the cooling tower, is used in many industrial applications. In the cooling tower the water is cooled by evaporation as it is sprayed from the top of the tower, transferring heat from the water to the atmosphere. Both of these methods lose a lot of water to evaporation. To prevent evaporation loss, water can also be cooled using a heat exchanger where the water flows though pipes with air moving over them. The heat is transferred to the atmosphere much as a radiator works in a car. Water can also be pumped though pipes underground where the heat is lost to the soil. All of these methods can cause thermal pollution in other areas (e.g., the atmosphere, soil) or overload the local atmosphere with humidity which can cause local fog or freezing rain in colder periods.

Public Health Vectors and Pest Control

5

Joe E. Beck, RS, DEASS

"House, n. A hollow edifice erected for the habitation of man, rat, mouse, beetle, cockroach, fly, mosquito, flea, bacillus, and microbe."

**—Ambrose Bierce,
The Devil's Dictionary**

Key Performance Outcome Indicators:

1. Be able to identify common rodent vectors, signs of rodent presence, and the accompanying methods of environmental, biological, chemical, and physical control of rodents
2. Be able to identify the general stages of the rodent life-cycle and discuss the major public health diseases associated with rodents
3. Understand the two basic life-cycles of arthropods; be able to identify signs of arthropod presence and the accompanying methods of environmental, biological, chemical, and physical control of arthropods
4. Understand the epidemiology of the major public health diseases associated with noted arthropods
5. Be able to identify the disease transmission cycle type of each of the significant vector-borne diseases

Introduction

Vector-borne diseases have been a major cause of human morbidity (illness) and mortality (death) for centuries. During recorded history, bubonic plague, malaria, louse-borne typhus, yellow fever, and encephalitis, to name only a few, have caused uncounted epidemics and millions of deaths. Only since the late nineteenth and early twentieth century has man discovered the sources and routes of transmission of these and many other vector-borne diseases.

The threat from vector-borne diseases is not, however, confined to the past. These diseases continue to emerge, change, and often spread to new locales. For instance, in the United States, Lyme disease, its infectious agent the spirochete bacterium, *Borrelia burgdorferi,* and its vectors (primarily members of the tick genus *Ixodes*), have all been discovered since 1975.

The epidemic threats of previous decades and centuries have by no means entirely disappeared. Vector-borne diseases, while more common in the poverty stricken areas of the world, continue to cause concern among public health officials worldwide. As world populations continue to grow, and transportation becomes more rapid and available, the pesticides that have largely kept major epidemics in check for the past 40 years become less effective and replacements are more expensive. Thus, pandemics could again threaten mankind.

The following discussion will attempt to review the ecology, surveillance, and control of some of the vectors and other pests that continue to compete with man.

General Epidemiology

Vector-borne diseases are one type of *indirect* transmission. The other major types are vehicle-borne (contaminated inanimate objects, e.g., water, food, surfaces) and food-borne. Most communicable diseases in the United States involve only two living factors: a host and a parasite. In contrast, vector-borne diseases must involve at least three factors operating within a favorable environment:

1. Susceptible host (unprotected human or animal)
2. Capable vector (mosquito, tick, flea, fly)
3. Infectious disease agent (virus, bacteria, fungus, protozoa, helminth)

In the diseases that have three participants, the host, the vector, or both may serve as the reservoir of the agent (see Figure 5.1).

Often, vector-borne diseases involve four or more participating factors operating in a favorable disease transmission environment. These include:

1. Susceptible host
2. Capable vector
3. Infectious disease agent
4. A reservoir(s). The reservoir may be a rodent, a bird, another vertebrate, an infectious disease agent from a contaminated inanimate environmental source(s), or a combination of these.

General Biology

The vast majority of vector-borne diseases are transmitted by arthropods, which belong to the Phylum *Arthropoda*, which in Greek means "jointed foot"; in reality, they have jointed legs. This group has four major subdivisions.

The largest group or class is *Insecta*, also know as insects. This includes flies, fleas, cockroaches, lice, bees, and many others. They are commonly recognized as having three distinct body parts (head, thorax, abdomen), six legs, and can possess wings (mosquito) or be wingless (lice). The mouthparts vary from a piercing proboscis (mosquito) to a sponging (housefly).

The second most prominent class is *Arachnida*, or the arachnids. They

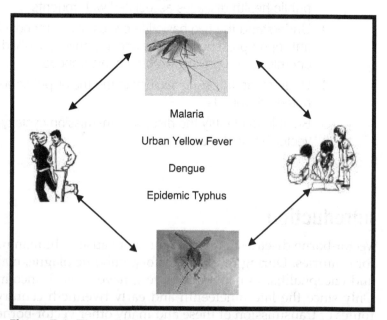

Figure 5.1 Three Living Factors in the Transmission of Insect-borne Diseases.

Silhouettes © Hanna J; mosquitoes © Henrik Larsson, 2010. Used under license from Shutterstock, Inc.

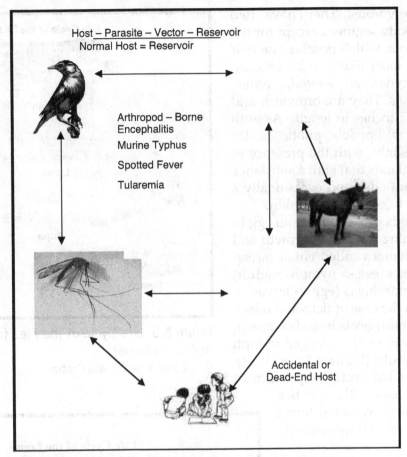

Figure 5.2 Four Living Factors in the Transmission of Vector-borne Diseases.

Silhouettes © Hanna J; mosquitoes © Henrik Larsson; animals © pinare, 2010. Used under license from Shutterstock, Inc.

are recognized with fused body parts, eight legs in the adult form, no wings, and mouthparts which include a chelicera and in some a hypostome. The former is for cutting into the victim, and the latter for anchoring and blood feeding. This class includes mites, ticks, spiders, and scorpions.

Chilopoda (centipedes) and *Diplopoda* (millipedes) are the remaining two prominent groups. The centipedes have one pair of legs per body segment, varying from 15 to 177 segments, always in odd numbers. Centipedes tend to be nocturnal and are mostly carnivorous.

Since they do not possess a waxy, waterproofing layer on their cuticle (outer layer), they are predisposed to living in moist or damp situations. Some species of centipedes have the ability to autotomize selected legs (let them fall off deliberately). This is done to divert potential predators. The American house centipede (*Scutigera coleoptera*) is approximately an inch or more in length and is found throughout the United States, but is originally from Mexico. It can be found both outside and inside the home. If inside, it is typically found in basements and other damp areas, where it feeds on spiders and insects. In contrast, the *Scololpendra gigantea* can grow to in excess of 12 inches in length. The public health implications of centipedes are minimal but are related to their ability to inflict a painful "bite" or "sting" similar to that of a bee. This bite or sting stems from the development of the legs of the first body segment into venom- bearing fangs.

The millipedes, or *Diplopoda*, are typically slower and rounder than centipedes. Like centipedes, they are nocturnal and tend to dwell in damp areas. However, they are considered herbivorous rather than carnivorous. They have two pair of legs per body segment except for the first three segments, which possess one pair each. Millipedes most likely to be encountered by householders are *Parajulus venustus* and *P. impressus*. They are brownish and approximately 1.5 inches in length. As with centipedes, the millipede's public health implications are slight, with the presence of "repugnatorial" glands that emit a substance with an unpleasant odor and occasionally a numbing effect if injected into the skin.

Most arthropods develop from an egg to adult by undergoing a series of growth and developmental changes called either *incomplete* metamorphosis (egg -> nymph -> adult) or *complete* metamorphosis (egg -> larvae -> pupa -> adult). In the case of ticks and mites, a four-stage metamorphosis includes the egg -> six-legged larvae -> eight-legged nymph -> eight-legged adult) (Figures 5.3 and 5.4). The adult stage is the vector stage of most vector-borne diseases, although tick and mite larvae and nymphal forms are involved in disease transmission.

Disease Transmission

Vector-borne disease transmission may be divided into two groups, mechanical transmission and biological transmission

Mechanical Transmission

Mechanical transmission includes simple carriage of pathogens by crawling or flying insects through soiling of the feet, mouthparts, or body parts. The process is passive in that there is no growth or stage transition of the organism during transmission. The classical vector examples of this type of transmission are cockroaches and domestic flies. While no specific disease cases have ever been directly attributed to this process, pathogens for the following diseases, among others, have been recovered from these vectors: typhoid fever, trachoma,

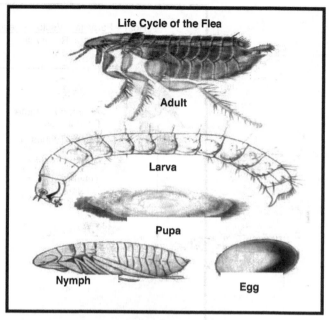

Figure 5.3 Life-Cycle of the Flea (complete metamorphosis).
U.S. Centers for Disease Control

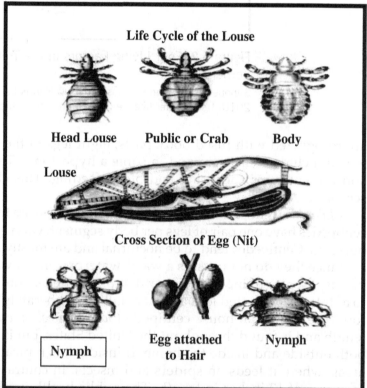

Figure 5.4 Life-Cycle of the Head Louse (incomplete metamorphosis).
U.S. Centers for Disease Control

Figure 5.5 Mechanical Transmission of Disease-causing Organisms by Flies.

cholera, and shigellosis (bacillary dysentery). It is assumed with this recovery that transmission is probable. This process is demonstrated in Figure 5.5.

Biological Transmission

Biological transmission may take one of three forms. The first is *propagative transmission*, in which the agent is within the vector but does not have a physiological or morphological change. It does, however, increase in number within the vector. This form is demonstrated by the yellow fever virus carried by the *Aedes sp.* mosquito in Figure 5.6. In this form the agent multiplies in the vector and is transmitted from the salivary gland into the bite wound. This form is also seen by the transmission of louse-borne typhus fever (*Rickettsia rowakezi*) by the body louse (*Pediculus humanus humanus*). However, in this transmission the agent is passed by contamination of the bite site by louse fecal material scratched into the wound.

The second form is *cyclo-propagative transmission*. In this form the agent not only multiplies but has a morphological or physiological change. This is confirmed by the development of the *Plasmodium sp.* (protozoa) in the *Anopheles sp.* mosquito, as demonstrated in Figure 5.7. In this the pathogen typically goes through cyclic development and multiplication of numbers before the arthropod can transmit the infective form of the agent to man. An incubation period is required following inoculation of the arthropod, usually by ingestion, before the arthropod becomes infective. Transmission to humans or other vertebrates is usually by injection of salivary gland fluids during a blood meal.

The third form is *cyclo-developmental transmission*. In this form the agent in the vector goes through a crucial part of its life-cycle without an increase in numbers. An example of this is lymphatic filariasis. In this example the parasitic, threadlike worms (*Wuchereria bancrofti* and *Brugia malayi*) develop in the mosquito and migrate to the salivary glands.

House fly eating.
Image © Subbotina Anna, 2010. Used under license from Shutterstock, Inc.

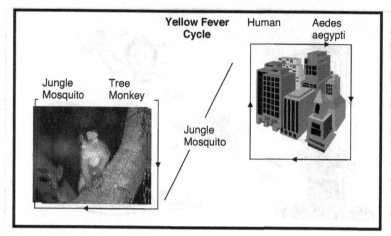

Figure 5.6 Yellow Fever Cycle.
Monkey © Henk Bentlage; city © michaeljung, 2010. Used under license from Shutterstock, inc.

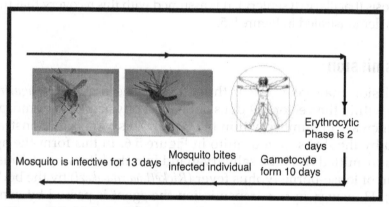

Figure 5.7 Malaria Cycle.
Mosquito © Henrik Larsson; biting mosquito © stocksnapp, 2010. Used under license from Shutterstock, Inc.

Techniques for Controlling Public Health Vectors and Pests

In recent years, pest- and vector-control personnel have adopted a strategy known as integrated pest management (IPM), which combines various compatible control methods to accomplish the best control with the least possible environmental impact.

Sanitation: Removal and proper storage or disposal of the vector's food source.

Habitat modification: Changing the habitat where the vector breeds or rests to be unfavorable for its survival (e.g., draining areas where mosquitoes breed or fluctuating water levels on a lake).

Mechanical exclusion: Screens, building design, engineering, and repair to physically exclude the vectors or pests.

Personal protection: Heavy clothing and health education to better avoid vectors and pests.

Biological control: Use of living agents that are destructive to the vector or pest organism's survival or development (e.g., the sterile male technique).

Ecological control: Utilization of natural predators by installing habitats conducive to their development.

Chemical suppression: Use of sex attractants, insect-growth regulators (juvenile hormones), and targeted pesticide applications to reduce vector populations. All restricted pesticides must be purchased and applied under the direct supervision of a licensed pest control operator, and all pesticides must be licensed by the U.S. Environmental Protection Agency (EPA) for each specific use. Because the registration of specific pesticides can vary from state to state and change periodically, check with the state pesticide authorities in your state about specific recommendations. As with the use of any chemical, it is extremely important that you read and follow pesticide label directions.

Specific Arthopods and Surveillance and Control Methods

Mosquitoes are two-winged insects varying from 1/8 inch to 1/2 inch long, depending on species. All have scales on their wing veins and fringes, and relatively long legs. Males can be separated from females by their bushy antennae and by the palpi shape and length. These insects undergo a complete metamorphosis, as described above.

Specific to the mosquito, eggs are laid on water, in areas which will flood, or in small containers which will catch and contain water, such as tree holes, garbage, and improperly disposed tires, depending on the species. The eggs are typically laid in groups of 50 to 200. As noted in Figure 5.8, *Culex sp.* glue their eggs together into rafts which are buoyant, while *Anopheles sp.* eggs are laid singularly with horizontal structures or floats which keep them from sinking. *Aedes sp.* eggs are typically laid singularly in small containers such as discarded cans. The hatching of the eggs in the spring is in response to a number of factors, which include water carbon dioxide and dissolved oxygen content, daylight length, and temperature.

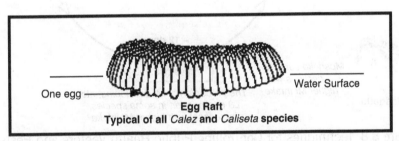

Egg raft characteristics of Culex mosquitoes.
U.S. Centers for Disease Control

The mosquito larva or wiggler has four stages (*instars*), all occurring in water. The larval stage lasts from 4 to 10 days depending upon temperature, with each stage getting progressively larger. They possess tracheal gills, but most species utilize a protracted tube (siphon) to secure air through the surface of the water. However, this is not possessed by *Anopheles* mosquitoes. This is a key element in one strategy for utilizing larvacides. Larvae are very active and continual feeders; they feed on minuscule plants and animals; thus most need to exist in somewhat contaminated waters.

The pupa or tumbler is also aquatic, much less mobile, and nonfeeding. Similarly, but less temperature dependent, this stage lasts for approximately two days.

The male and female adult stages emerge in approximately equal numbers. The former feeds on plant juices, since their mouthparts

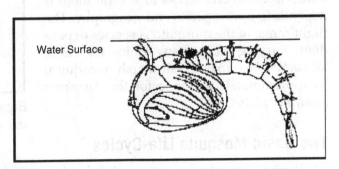

Pupa stages.
U.S. Centers for Disease Control

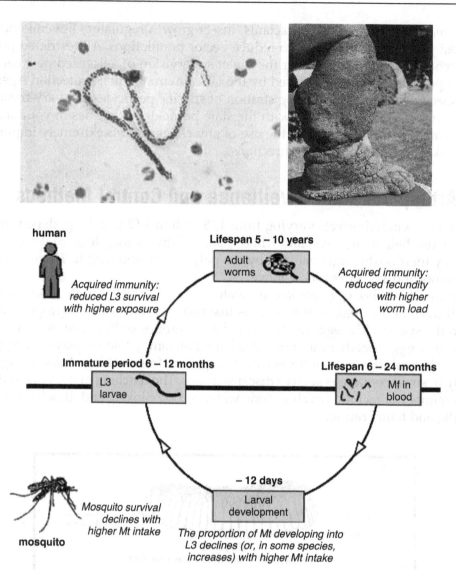

human

*Acquired immunity:
reduced L3 survival
with higher exposure*

Lifespan 5 – 10 years

Adult
worms

*Acquired immunity:
reduced fecundity
with higher
worm load*

Immature period 6 – 12 months

L3
larvae

Lifespan 6 – 24 months

Mf in
blood

– 12 days

Larval
development

*Mosquito survival
declines with
higher Mt intake*

mosquito

*The proportion of Mt developing into
L3 declines (or, in some species,
increases) with higher Mt intake*

Figure 5.8 Techniques for Controlling Public Health Vectors and Pests
U.S. Centers for Disease Control

are not adapted to piercing and sucking. The latter seek a blood meal that is normally required to produce viable eggs. Longevity varies from several weeks to several months depending upon species and geography. The flight range of the mosquito is species dependent, varying from many miles for *Aedes taeniarhynchus* (black salt-marsh mosquito) to approximately one mile for the *Anopheles quadrimaculatus*.

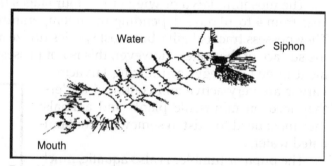

Water

Siphon

Mouth

Breathing tube.
U.S. Centers for Disease Control

Two Basic Mosquito Life-Cycles

1. *Permanentwater* mosquitoes develop in water that stands for relatively long periods of time. Females lay eggs, either singly or in masses (rafts). Most of these mosquitoes overwinter as adults.

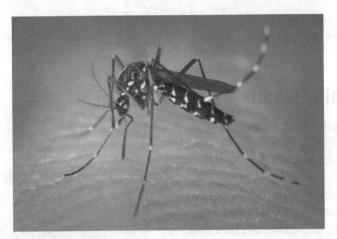

Tiger mosquito.
Image © Roger De Marfa, 2010. Used under license from Shutterstock, Inc.

2. *Floodwater* mosquitoes develop in short-term, intermittent water. Females lay eggs on damp soil, plants, debris, but not water. The eggs are resistant to drying and can survive for months or even years until they are covered by floodwater. When flooded, eggs hatch and development continues. Most of these mosquitoes overwinter as eggs.

Surveillance Activities

1. Collecting and identifying larva and adults to confirm their existence, source, importance, and best control method(s) (see Table 9.1).
2. Recording and analyzing information on kinds, numbers, locations, weather, temperature, and rainfall to help make decisions about control requirements.

Suggested Equipment for Mosquito Surveys

1. CDC miniature light trap
2. American light trap
3. Pipette for picking up larvae
4. Vial for larvae and pupae
5. Dipper for collecting larvae
6. Rubber boots
7. Flashlight for collecting adults
8. Jar for live larvae
9. Funnel
10. Aspirator for collecting adults
11. Killing tube for adults
12. Blotter disc
13. Cotton
14. Rubber bands
15. Chloroform
16. Pillbox for adults

Nonchemical Control Methods

1. Exclusion by screens or mosquito netting.
2. Habitat modification by ditching, draining, or filling low areas; disposal of water-holding containers; water management, dikes, and gate to keep salt marshes flooded.
3. Biological control by mosquito-eating fish (*Gambusia affinis*; see Figure 5.9), parasitic protozoa, nematodes, pathogenic fungus (*Lagenidium giganteum*), pathogenic bacteria (*Bacillus sphaericus*), blue-green algae transplanted with *Bacillus thuringiensis* genes, or cannibal mosquito larva.
4. Behavioral controls such as sleeping under mosquito nets, avoiding peak mosquito periods of dawn and dusk, and utilizing windy areas for camping because wind disrupts mosquito flight capability.

5. Ecological controls include the usage of habitat development for bats and purple martins.

Chemical Control Methods

1. Repellents for personal protection. The most common is N, N-diethyl-m-toluamide (DEET), recommended at 30% or less.
2. Larvacides to kill the developing mosquito before it emerges from the water. The larvacides may include petroleum fuel oils, organophosphates, pyrethrums, synthetic pyrethroids, and insect-growth regulators (IGR). The compounds may be solutions, emulsions, or granules.
3. Adulticides to kill adult mosquitoes include pyrethrums, organophosphates, carbamates, organothiocyanates, and synthetic pyrethroids. Most adulticides are aerosols, which are pesticides applied as fogs, sometimes as vapors, or rarely as dusts that contact and kill the mosquitoes. Some adulticides kill mosquitoes that land on treated surfaces. Ultra-low-volume (ULV) fogs consist of very small droplets suspended in the air that contact adults flying in the area. Small droplet size allows these particles to penetrate grass and vegetation but also is subject to drift (moving outside the target area).

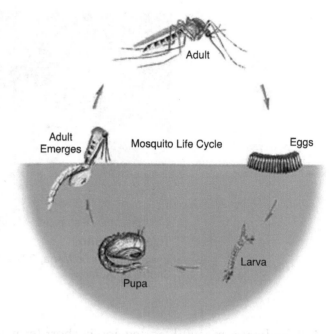

Figure 5.9 Mosquito Life-Cycle
U.S. Centers for Disease Control

Ticks

Ticks and mites are both in the order *Acarina* in the class *Arachnida*. They possess eight legs in the adult stage and six legs in the nymph and seed tick, or larvae, stage. Both sexes take blood meals, with the female's body being especially adapted to distend during feeding. This distension allows the tick to accommodate a volume of blood that can be up to 600 times its body weight when unfed, depending upon species. Tick attachment to the host in the hard tick is aided by a secretion from the salivary glands which is gluelike and essentially cements the tick to the host when feeding. Upon completion of feeding, the substance dissolves. Ticks belong to two families within the order, the *Ixodidae* (hard ticks) and the *Argasidae* (soft ticks). The families can be easily distinguished, as hard ticks possess a scutum, which is the shield behind the mouthparts on the anterior (front) dorsal (top)

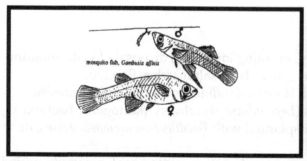

Figure 5.10 Mosquito Fish (Gambusia affinis).
Image © gualtiero boffi, 2010. Used under license from Shutterstock, Inc.

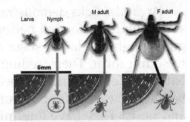

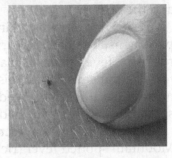

view. Also, hard tick mouthparts can be seen from the dorsal view, while soft tick mouthparts are only seen from ventral (bottom) view.

The life-cycle completion of the hard tick may be shorter than a year in equatorial regions to in excess of three years in cool climates. *Ixodidae* have several life chronologies, which can be defined by the number of hosts the tick has during its cycle. One-host ticks feed on a singular host during the larval and nymphal life stages. Upon adulthood the female falls from the host and lays her eggs. Subsequently, two-host ticks feed on one host in the larval and nymphal stages and then drop from that host to find another in the adult stage, laying eggs after falling from the second host. Finally, a three-host tick feasts on a different host at each life stage before finally dropping from the host to lay eggs. Regardless of the number of hosts, the hard tick seeks its host by demonstrating a performance referred to as *questing*. A tick in this behavior can be found moving to the tops of grass or the edges of leaves and posing with its front legs extended, especially prompted when a host passes by. The stimulus for this behavior can be movement, heat, and carbon monoxide. Mating occurs on the ground, after which the male dies. The female life ends after laying a single batch of eggs.

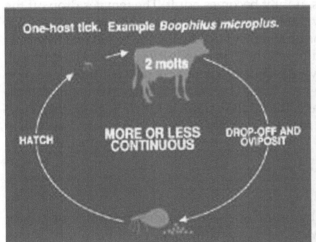

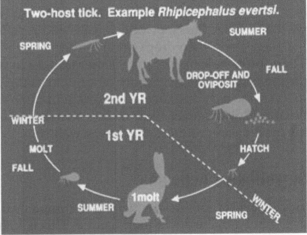

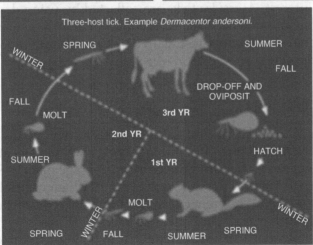

Figure 5.11 Life-Cycles of the Tick.
U.S. Centers for Disease Control

Argasidae ticks demonstrate a different life history. Their life-cycle may last several years, often surviving for extended periods without a blood meal. First, they mate on the host, and then they go through one larval stage and then five to seven nymph stages, gradually increasing in size to the adult form. Their feeding experience encompasses myriad hosts during each form, with small batches of eggs being laid between each blood meal while an adult. The questing mannerisms can be seen in some soft ticks, but the majority of the *Argasidae* live in concealed areas, such as burrows and nests. They have intermittent feeding similar to fleas, going back and forth between the nest and the host.

Regarding blood-sucking arthropods, ticks are considered to transmit the widest variety of pathogens. The hard tick transmits the majority of tick-borne diseases. An exception is tick-borne relapsing fever, which is maintained in its endemic cycle by species of the soft tick genus *Ornithodoros*. The transmission of this disease can be either through the salivary secretion to the bite wound or from coxal fluid excreted by the tick into an open wound. The epidemic cycle of this disease is spread primarily by the body louse, *Pediculus humanus*.

Hard ticks are the vectors involved in Lyme disease (spirochete *Borrelia burgdorferi*), Rocky Mountain spotted fever (rickettsia), *Rickettsia rickettsi* (tick-borne typhus), tularemia (bacteria *Francisella tularensis*), and Colorado tick fever (*Reoviridae* virus), which are currently the top four vector-borne diseases in the United States.

Hard ticks have multiple pathways to optimizing the potential of contact with a variety of potential disease-carrying host to ensure survival. The tick has tree distinct life-cycles. Some ticks use on only one host throughout all three life stages and are called one-host ticks. This type of tick remains on one host during the larval and nymphal stages, until it becomes adult. The females drop off the host after feeding to lay eggs. Other ticks use two hosts during their lives and are referred to as two- host ticks. This type of tick feeds and remains on the first host during the larval and nymphal life stages, and then drops off and attaches to a different host as an adult for its final blood meal. The adult female then drops off after feeding to lay eggs. Finally, some ticks feed on three hosts, one during each life stage, and are referred to as three-host ticks. Three-host ticks drop off and reattach to a new host during each life stage. In the last stage, the adult females lay their eggs. In each case, the fed adult stage for the female is terminal. The female dies after laying one batch of eggs. When the male has reproduced, he dies as well.

Surveillance Activities

Tick dragging for *Ixodidae* ticks is accomplished by utilizing a 1 m² rough-textured fabric (fleece or flannel) attached to a mop handle. This is known as a flag or drag. This device is pulled across vegetation in the area of interest. *Argasidae* ticks are collected by using dry ice traps. Dry ice emits carbon dioxide, which stimulates the tick to seek a host. After collection ticks are separated for identification, counted, and sent for laboratory testing to determine the presence or absence of a specific infectious agent or its antibodies.

Nonchemical Control Methods

1. Clearing brush, debris, and leaf litter, and cutting weeds to remove the habitat of ticks and their rodent hosts. Clearing leaf litter and placing wood chip barriers at the lawn perimeter has been shown to reduce nymphal tick abundance by an average of 42%–88%.
2. Avoidance of prime tick habitats if possible is important. When in tick habitats, inspection for ticks on the body, and on small children, every two hours is recommended. This should be performed during exposure periods and after.
3. Protective dress to include long sleeves, tucking in and taping of pant legs, and light-colored clothing for ease of visualization of the tick.
4. Avoidance of tick habitats, such as wooded areas, during the fall and spring tick seasons.

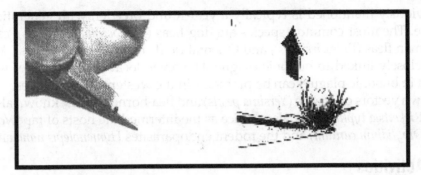

Figure 5.12 Tick Removal.
U.S. Centers for Disease Control

Chemical Control Methods

1. Tick repellents for skin and clothing (DEET 20%–30% or permethrin 0.5%).
2. Acaricidal control of ticks on rodents and area sprays for places such as yards that people frequent. Outdoor area control has been accomplished using carbaryl, chlorpyrifos, and cyfluthrin. Permethrin, diazinon, and malathion accomplish indoor control.

Proper Tick Removal

1. The first choice is to use tweezers or a commercially designed tool. If not available, the index finger and thumb can be used if protected with rubber/plastic gloves or a paper towel.
2. Grasp the tick around the area where the mouthparts enter the skin.
3. The tick should be pulled away with a slow, steady motion along the line of the skin. Care should be taken not to jerk, crush, squeeze, or puncture the tick.
4. When the tick is removed, place it in a container and disinfect the bite area.
5. The tick container should be labeled for name and date and stored at refrigerator temperature with a lightly moistened paper inside the container. The tick should be kept alive for 30 days in case tick-borne disease symptoms develop.

Fleas

Fleas are wingless, laterally compressed insects that have a complete metamorphosis (Figure 5.9) and usually vary according to species and sex from 1 to 6 mm. The life-cycle of the flea can be as short as two or three weeks, depending upon conditions of temperature, humidity, food availability, and species. Both the male and female are capillary feeders. Flea mating often occurs on the host, with eggs being deposited around feathers and hairs. The eggs will drop into bedding or the ground, since they are not sticky. Eggs normally will not hatch at temperatures of 95–100° F. The eggs are laid in successive groups after each blood meal, but only one mating is required. The larva are wormlike and live in floor cracks, rugs, and so on, and feed upon organic debris or flea feces, which contain blood. This stage may last from a week to several months depending upon environmental conditions. The pupa form is essentially a cocoon and emerges as an adult in response to vibrations, carbon dioxide, and/or humidity. The adult form is prepared to feed within 24 hours.

Figure 5.13 Flea.
Image © Carolina K. Smith, M.D., 2010.
Used under license from Shutterstock, Inc.

The flea previously mentioned is typically a year-round breeder, with generation time varying with temperature. The most common species are dog fleas (*Ctenocephalides canis*), cat fleas (*Ctenocephalides felis*), human fleas (*Pulex irritans*), and Oriental rat fleas (*Xenopsylla cheopis*). *Xenopsylla cheopis* is the flea most closely linked to bubonic plague. However, local populations of wild rodent fleas (often implicated in bubonic plague) can be problems in the western United States.

Fleas are known vectors of plague (*Yersinia pestis*) and flea-borne typhus, known also as endemic or murine typhus (*Rickettsia typhi*). They also suffice as the intermediate hosts of tapeworms such as the dog tapeworm (*Dipylidium canium*) and the rodent endoparasites *Hymenolepis nana* and *H. diminuta*.

Surveillance Activities

1. Surveillance activities involve pet areas for pest fleas, but in warm, moist climates, yards and entire buildings may be infested.
2. Surveillance of wild rodent flea populations for bubonic plague includes wild rodent observation, burrow swabs, and trapping.

Nonchemical Control Methods

1. Sanitation of pet areas.
2. Sanitation to remove food and harborage attractants for domestic rodents (rats and mice) and wild (sylvatic) rodents; exclusion or trapping of all types of rodents from house and building crawl spaces, attics, or the surrounding yard area where human contact with fleas is likely.
3. Health education to avoid wild rodents and wild rodent burrows.

Chemical Control Methods

1. Applying pesticides to pet areas, cracks, and crevices, and on pets by shampoo, spray, or flea collars. Pesticides to be applied include rotenone and pyrethrum dusts at 1% or 0.2% pyrethrum plus synergists. Malathion and carbaryl may also be used at 2%–5% dust or a 0.5% spray
2. Use of rodenticides and insecticides control rodents and their fleas living in or near the human activity area, especially the rock squirrel (*Spermophilus variegatus*) and the California ground squirrel (*S. beecheyi*), which are responsible for over 50% of human plague cases (Figures 5.10 and 5.11).
3. The use of insecticides to control fleas on wild rodents by application in their burrows if these animals are in a plague epizootic area near human residences.
4. Animal treatment may include a pill (dogs) or a liquid (cats) containing lufenuron, which prevents flea eggs from hatching; egg-stopper collars containing (methoprene or pyriproxfen), an insect-growth regulator (IGR) which keeps eggs from hatching; and "spot on" treatments applied between the shoulder blades of the animal.

Rodents of Public Health Concern

Rodent populations are unacceptable because they compete for and destroy human food, destroy property, and ultimately spread disease. Rodents serve as the vector/reservoir for babesiosis (*Babesia microtia*), Lassa fever (*Arenvirus*), Leishmaniasis (*Leishmania tropica, L. major, L. braziliensis, L. donovani*), Lyme disease (*Borrelia burgdorferi*), plague (*Yersinia pestis*), relapsing fever (*Borrellia recurrentis*), and the hantaviruses, to name a few. The three primary rodents of public health significance are the house mouse (*Mus musculus*), the Norway rat (*Rattus norvegicus*), and the roof rat (*Rattus rattus*) (Figure 5.12). Additional rodents of specific importance will be discussed with their disease of interest. Regarding the three rodents, the house mouse is the smallest (0.5–0.75 oz), is found throughout the United States, and prefers to live indoors between walls, in cabinets and furniture, and in stored goods. The Norway rat is the largest (7–18 oz); It is found throughout the temperate United States, and prefers to live in burrows. The roof rat is found across the southern parts of the United States, primarily around coastal areas, and prefers to live above ground indoors in attics, between floors, in enclosed spaces, and outdoors in trees.

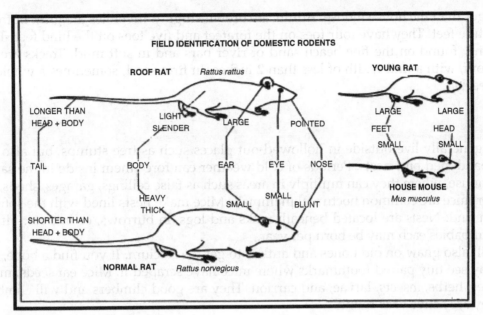

Figure 5.14 Rats and Mice
U.S. Centers for Disease Control

Nonchemical Control

1. Proper storage of refuse/garbage in tight containers with 18-in clearance from the ground, biweekly collection of garbage/refuse, and proper landfill disposal of garbage/refuse.
2. Rodent-proofing, such as sealing of exterior openings in buildings greater than 0.25 in with screens and heavy-gauge metal, and eliminating burrows.
3. Rodent trapping with spring-loaded traps.
4. Keeping pet feeding areas clean of food debris.
5. Remove all debris within the home and within a 100-ft radius of the home.

How to Dispose of Dead Rodents, Droppings, or Contaminated Material

1. Put on rubber gloves.
2. Thoroughly spray animal, droppings or nest with a mixture of 3 oz of bleach in 1 gal of water.
3. Use a paper plate, paper towels, or shovel to place disinfected material and disposable cleaning items into a plastic bag.
4. Seal or tie the bag and place in another bag.
5. Place the bag in a covered trash container for regular trash disposal. If regular trash disposal is not available, burn or bury the bag at least 2 ft deep.
6. Wash hands thoroughly with soap and water after cleanup.

Chemical Control

1. Pretreat harborage areas with insecticide to kill fleas.
2. Treat areas with rodenticides based upon type of infestation. Apply single-dose anticoagulants such as brodif *Rats and Mice.*

Deer Mouse

The deer mouse is similar in appearance to the house mouse. It can be distinguished by a two-colored body and tail. The upper side of the body is normally a darker shade of brown, while the underside is white. The tail is also covered with more fur then the house mouse, and the eyes and ears are larger than the house mouse. Adults are brownish-gray. Juveniles are gray. Both have dark eyes and white feet. They have four toes on the forefeet and five toes on the hind feet. Their tracks are commonly found on the fine beach sand of river bars and in soft mud. Tracks are usually in groups of four, with a trail width of less than 2 inches. In firm sand, sometimes a whole print will show up clearly.

Habitat

They most generally live outside in hollowed-out places such as tree stumps, but also have been found in abandoned bird nests. Periods of cold weather can force them inside in the same way as the house mouse, where they can multiply in areas such as false ceilings, garages, sheds, and crawl spaces. Deer mice are common nocturnal mammals. Mice make nests lined with the softest materials they can find. Nests are located beneath rocks and logs, in burrows, or in trees. Three or four litters of four babies each may be born per year.

Mice will also gnaw on old bones and antlers to get the calcium. If you find a bone, examine it and you may see tiny paired toothmarks where mice have scraped it. Mice eat seeds, mushrooms, fungi, berries, herbs, insects, larvae, and carrion. They are good climbers and will climb to escape danger. They are active year-round.

Deer Mice and Hantavirus

The deer mouse, also known as the white-footed mouse (*Peromyscus leucopus*), is a species that has become prominent because of the deadly disease associated with it known as hantavirus—hantavirus pulmonary syndrome (HPS). Hantavirus is rarely transmitted to people, but when it is, it can cause severe respiratory illness. Hantavirus pulmonary syndrome is a disease characterized by flu-like symptoms followed by respiratory failure. The hantavirus is believed to be a distant cousin of the Ebola virus. It has been recognized as a cause of disease in countries such as China for many years. Some hantaviruses cause kidney disease. In the United States, disease caused by hantavirus has probably always existed but in such low numbers that it was

Figure 5.15 Deer Mouse (Peromyscus maniculatus)
Image © Close Encounters Photography, 2010. Used under license from Shutterstock, Inc.

not recognized. A 1993 outbreak of fatal respiratory illness on an Indian reservation in the Four Corners area (the border of Utah, Colorado, New Mexico, and Arizona) led U.S. Public Health Service (USPHS) environmental health and epidemiologist personnel to the discovery of the hantavirus as the causative agent. Since that discovery, hantavirus disease has been reported in every western state except Washington, and in many eastern states.

Hantavirus Spread

The hantavirus is carried by rodents, particularly deer mice, and is present in their urine and feces. People contract the disease when they breathe viral particles associated with the urine, saliva, or droppings of infected rodents.

The hantavirus does not cause disease in the carrier animal, but it does in man. Humans are thought to become infected when they are exposed to contaminated dust from the nests or droppings of mice. The disease is not, however, passed between humans. Contaminated dust is often encountered when cleaning long-vacated dwellings, sheds, or other enclosed areas.

The Centers for Disease Control (CDC) reports that hantavirus-carrying rodents have been found in at least 20 national parks and that the virus may be in all of the parks. Epidemiologists at the CDC suspect that campers and hikers may have a higher chance of contracting the disease than most people. This is due to the practice of pitching tents on the forest floor and laying sleeping bags down in musty cabins.

Symptoms of Hantavirus

Those infected show flulike symptoms that turn into a pneumonia-like condition after two or three days. The initial symptoms of hantavirus disease closely resemble influenza. The disease begins abruptly with fever, chills, muscle aches (myalgia), headache, nausea and vomiting, and malaise. A dry cough may be present. The fever may be higher in younger people than in older people. For a very short period, the infected person feels somewhat better but this is followed within a day or two by an increased respiratory rate caused by seepage of fluid into the lungs. The initial shortness of breath is subtle and the patient may be unaware of it, but progression is rapid. The patient bleeds internally, and ultimately develops respiratory failure.

An effective treatment for hantavirus is not available at the time of this writing. Even with intensive therapy, over 50% of diagnosed cases have been fatal.

Hantavirus Prevention

Avoid exposure to mouse or rodent urine and feces. When hiking and camping, pitch tents in areas without rodent droppings, avoid rodent dens, drink disinfected water, and sleep on a ground cover and pad. If you must work in an area where contact is possible, follow these following recommendations from the CDC.

Cleaning Up Rodent-infested Areas

1. Use later rubber gloves.
2. Do not sweep or vacuum droppings, urine, or nesting materials.
3. Totally saturate the contaminated area with detergent. A hypochlorite solution of 1.5 cups of household bleach in 1 gallon of water may be used.

Special Precautions for Cleaning Areas with Confirmed Hantavirus Infection

1. Draw a baseline serum sample for all individuals working in the cleanup.
2. Workers are to wear disposable coveralls, rubber boots/disposable shoe covers, rubber/plastic gloves, protective goggles/facemask, and an appropriate respiratory-protection device (half-mask air purifying or negative pressure or a powered air-purifying respirator).
3. Personal protective gear is to be decontaminated upon removal, discarded or laundered as appropriate. If a laundry is unavailable, then immerse in liquid disinfectant.
4. Consult local regulations regarding infectious wastes. Burn or bury potentially infective waste material as appropriate after double bagging. Remaining waste should be disposed of in accordance with local regulations.

Domestic Flies

Flies are two-winged insects belonging to the order *Diptera*, which for public health purposes is divided into two groups. The first is *biting* flies, which includes mosquitoes, horse flies, deer flies, stable flies, black flies, punkies, sand flies, and biting midges. The second group is *nonbiting* flies, also known as synanthropic or domestic flies. Included in the latter group are house flies, little or lesser flies, blue bottle flies, green and bronze bottle flies, cluster flies, black blow flies, screwworm flies and filter or moth flies. The most common flies are the house fly (*Musca domestica*) and blow flies, with the former considered the most likely public health threat. The house fly ranges over most of the United States and is the most abundant species in homes and food areas (Figure 5.13). Flies range from 4 to 7.5 mm in length, depending on the species, with the female typically being larger than the male. They have three discrete body regions: head, thorax, and abdomen. As vectors, flies mechanically transmit diseases of the digestive system. In addition, some fly larvae live on or in an animal or human body, a condition known as *myiasis*.

Houseflies undergo a complete metamorphosis, with the life-cycle usually requiring three weeks, but varying from one to six weeks, depending on species and environmental conditions. These flies breed within three weeks of maturity, laying their eggs in batches of 75 to 150, with

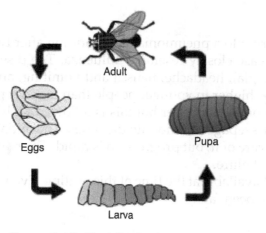

Figure 5.16 Fly Life-Cycle.
U.S. Centers for Disease Control

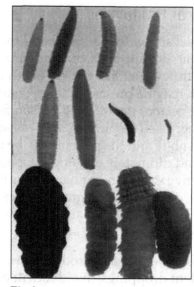

Fly Larvae.

five or six batches being laid in a lifetime. Breeding material is typically warm, moist organic material such as manure. The egg develops into the larval stage *(maggot)* within 24 hours and in warm weather will pass through three larval stages in four to seven days. The pupa stage is spent (in a capsule case) from four to five days, after which it emerges as an adult (Figure 5.14).

Figure 5.17 Common Types of Flies
Crane fly © Mark Rosteck; deer fly © Bruce MacQueen; American horse fly © zpyder, 2010.
Used under license from Shutterstock, Inc.; house fly from US Centers for Disease Control

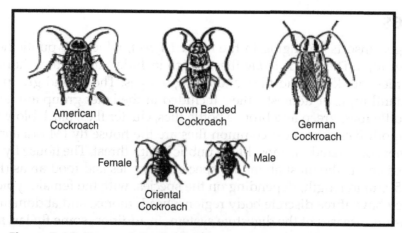

Figure 5.18 Types of Cockroaches
U.S. Centers for Disease Control

Adults feed on any food and are attracted to feces, organic material, and human foods. Because they have *sponging* mouthparts, food must be in the liquid form. This requires them to use salivary or crop secretions when testing for food. This leaves light spots, or vomit spots. As they forage for food they also leave dark spots, which are fecal material.

Flies characteristically are inactive at night and show a strong inclination for edges when resting. In flight, they wander aimlessly but can cover as much as 20 miles over a lifetime. In ideal conditions, they will live up to four weeks. Flies are very temperature dependent, being essentially inactive at 45°F and dying at 32°F. At 90°F they demonstrate maximum activity, but will suffer paralysis and death at 112°F.

Houseflies are phototropic and very sensitive to strong air currents, they are rarely seen on excessively breezy days.

Nonchemical Control Methods

1. Sanitation, including proper garbage storage, pickup and disposal.
2. Proper management and sanitary control of livestock manure, frequent disposal of pet droppings.
3. Proper sanitation and disposal of vegetable, fruit, or other food waste from commercial operations.
4. Sanitary treatment and disposal of liquid waste and sludge.
5. Screening of doors and windows, with self-closing devices on doors.
6. Air barriers, including fans over doorways, to prevent fly entry.
7. Introduction of natural enemies.

Chemical Control

This approach may be hampered by insecticide resistance but can be a useful supplement to sanitation.

Cockroaches

Cockroaches are oval and flat-bodied dorso-ventrally. A shield-like covering extends over the head. Adults, depending on the species, are from 1/2 to 2 in long. As adults, some species have functional wings, while others do not. Cockroaches develop from an egg carried in an egg capsule (*ootheca*) to a nymphal stage without wings or developed sex organs. They grow through the nymphal stage with a series of molts, eventually developing wings, with males maturing more rapidly than females. The developmental time varies from two or three months to a full year depending upon species. They are unable to reproduce or develop when the temperature is below 45°F or above 115°F. Cockroaches are typically nocturnal (active in the dark), preferring to hide when it is light, usually in warm, moist places. They are scavengers, have chewing mouthparts, and will eat almost any food. They can transmit disease by tracking filth into unprotected food and by constant defecation upon food.

The four major types of cockroaches in the United States are the German (*Blattella germanica*), American (*Periplaneta americana*), Oriental (*Blatta orientalis*), and brown-banded (*Supella longipalpa*) (Figure 5.15). *Blattella germanica* is found worldwide and is the most common cockroach found in buildings and food service operations, as well as in home pantries and kitchens. *Blatta orientalis* is mostly commonly found in sewers and damp basements and is characterized by a strong repulsive odor. Geographically it is found in the northern three-fourths of the United States and rarely along the Gulf Coast. *Supella longipalpa* is found throughout the United States, frequently in homes. However, it prefers dry, dark areas such as in televisions, radios, and within furniture. *Periplanta americana*, often called the water bug, is the largest of these four cockroaches. It has worldwide distribution and prefers warm, humid environments. It will eat nonfood items such as glue, starch, books, and pictures.

Nonchemical Control

1. Surveillance and control involves regular monitoring of the hidden areas these pests prefer, good sanitation procedures, tight-fitting screens and doors, and safe, approved pesticides.
2. Parasitic wasps (genera: *Evania, Hyptia,* and *Tetrastichus*) which lay their eggs in the cockroach eggs. The wasps eat the embryonic cockroaches.
3. A natural toxin produced by a soil-inhabiting fungus (*Streptomyces avermitilis*).

Chemical Control

1. Use of IGRs such as hydropene and fenoxycarb.
2. Use of desiccants such as diatomaceous earth and silica aerogel.
3. Use of 1% diazinon and 0.2% pyrthrins.

Sucking Lice

Figure 5.19 Nit Attached to Hair.
U.S. Centers for Disease Control

Sucking lice are found in the order *Anoplura*. The three common sucking lice of public health significance are the head louse (*Pediculus capitis*), the body louse (*Pediculus humanus corporis*), and the crab/pubic louse (*Pthirus pubis*) (Figure 5.16). Head and body lice are nearly identical, varying slightly in size and color. They are wingless and flattened. They possess short, stout legs with large claws for clasping and holding onto hairs. As adults their mouthparts are designed for piercing and sucking. These include six pairs of hooks around the mouth for attachment to the skin during feeding and piercing stylets to create an incision. Salivary secretions are injected to eliminate clotting and a pharyngeal pump sucks the blood into the stylets.

The life stages are the egg (*nit*), three nymphal stages, and the adult. The nits of the head louse and pubic louse are typically glued to the hair shaft, while the body louse nit is attached to clothing fibers. All are incubated by body heat, as the optimal temperature is 75–100°F. The head and body nymphal stage take 8–9 days, while the pubic louse takes 13–17 days when in contact with the body. However, when not in continual contact with the body, longer times are required. The life-cycle of both head and body lice is approximately 18 days. These pests are transferred from an infested person to another individual by sharing the same bed, clothing, headgear, and, in the case of body and crab lice, during sex. Lice bites cause severe itching when they bite people, and the resulting scratching can lead to secondary infections and a portal of entry for pathogenic organisms from the body louse fecal material into the human body. An infestation of lice on the body is known as *pediculosis*. The body louse is the vector of louse-borne typhus (*Rickettsia prowazeki*), trench fever (*Rickettsia quintana*), and louse-borne relapsing fever (*Borrelia recurrentis*).

Nonchemical Control

1. Education of at-risk individuals includes sanitation of all people living in the household, discouraging the sharing of personal articles of clothing, headgear, combs, brushes, and so on.
2. Dry-cleaning or laundering of headgear, clothing, and bedding.

Chemical Control

Pesticides that kill lice are available as shampoos, lotions, emulsions, or dusts. They include emulsions containing 0.2% pyrethrins, 1.0% lindane, or 12% benzyl benzoate, and insecticide dusts with 1% lindane or 1% malathion.

Mites

Mites are members of the class *Arachnida*. Due to the great morphological variances in mites, it is not possible to describe the archetypal mite. Those characteristics that can be described include a sack-like body, body segmentation that is ill defined, and the possession of *chelicerae*, which are variable in appearance and are used in identification. Most mites have four pairs of legs and breathe through their skin, although some possess *spiracles* for breathing.

Mites lay eggs that hatch into larvae having only six legs. These larvae advance through at least two nymphal stages and eventually into an adult. The mites of public health interest are discussed below.

Chigger Mite

The chigger mite is a source of discomfort. The resulting scratching of bite wounds often leads to infection. In the larval stage the *Trombicula sp.* "redbug" feed on man and other vertebrates. On people these mites attach to clothing where it fits tightly to the body, such as the waistline, ankles, and armpits. The larvae do not feed on blood but upon lymph and partially digested skin tissues. Once they become adults they do not feed on people, but upon the eggs or young of arthropods such as mosquitoes. The life-cycle is normally completed in approximately 50 days.

A second chigger mite (*Leptrotrombidium akamushi*) is responsible for the transmission of scrub typhus (*Rickettsia tsutsugamushi*). The prevalence of these mites is related to the prevalence of various species of rats and field mice. The pathogen is transmitted *transovarially* from the female to the egg and subsequently to the larval stage, which feeds on man and rodents.

Itch Mite

Sarcoptes scabiei is the mite responsible for scabies, a condition characterized by itching and irritation, and occasionally leading to secondary infections from the scratching. The female scabies mite averages 0.2 to 0.4 mm, with the male being slightly smaller. The mites mate on the skin surface, and the female burrows into the *strateum corneum* layer of the skin, feeding upon lymph. Burrows or tunnels are made in the skin by lysing of the tissue. In addition, the eggs (20–50) are laid in the burrows and fecal material (*scybala*) is deposited, which creates the intense itching. The eggs hatch in three to five days, with the young six-legged larva burrowing into the skin. The larvae develop into nymphs (1–2 instars), and by 16 days after the egg stage the adult emerges.

House Dust Mite

The house dust mite (sometimes referred to by allergists as HDM) is a cosmopolitan guest in human habitations. Dust mites feed on organic detritus such as flakes of shed human skin, and flourish in the stable environment of dwellings. House dust mites are a common cause of asthma and allergic symptoms worldwide. Some of the gut enzymes (notably proteases) produced by the house mite persist in their fecal matter, and can be strongly allergenic.

Typical mattresses can contain tens of thousands of dust mites. Nearly 100,000 mites can live in 1 square yard of carpet. A single dust mite produces about 20 waste droppings each day, each containing a protein to which many people are allergic. The proteins in the combination of feces and shed skin are what cause allergic reactions in humans. Depending on the person and exposure, reactions can range

Figure 5.20 Dust Mite.
Image © Sebastian Kaulitzki, 2010. Used under license from Shutterstock, Inc.

from itchy eyes to asthma attacks. Unlike other types of mites, house dust mites are not parasites, since they only eat dead tissue.

Beds are a prime habitat (where one-third of life occurs). A typical used mattress may have anywhere from 100,000 to 10 million mites inside (10% of the weight of a two-year-old pillow can be composed of dead mites and their droppings). Mites prefer warm, moist surroundings such as the inside of a mattress when someone is on it. A favorite food is dander (both human and animal skin flakes). Humans shed about 1/5 ounce of dander (dead skin) each week. About 80% of the material seen floating in a sunbeam is actually skin flakes. Bedroom carpeting and household upholstery also support high mite populations.

In 2005 the University of Manchester performed a medical study of pillows that found up to 16 species of fungi in a single pillow. They tested feather and synthetic pillows in a range of ages, finding thousands of spores of fungus per gram of pillow, more than is found on an average used toothbrush.

For most people, house dust mites are not actually harmful. However, the medical significance of house dust mites arises because their microscopic cast skins and feces are a major constituent of house dust that induces allergic reactions in some individuals. In addition to producing allergic reactions, dust mites can also cause nasal polyps, growths within the nose.

Dust mites are too small to be visible to the naked eye; they are only 250–300 microns in length and have translucent bodies. It takes at least a 10X magnification to be able to correctly identify them. The adult mite's cuticle (covering) has simple striations that can be seen from both the dorsal (top) view and the ventral (bottom) view. The ventral view of the house dust mite reveals long setae (hairs) extending from the outer margins of the body and shorter setae on the rest of the body. Through the microscope, one will see many oval-shaped mites scuttling around and over one another. There are eight hairy legs, no eyes, no antennae, a mouthpart group in front of the body (resembles a head), and a tough, translucent shell, giving a "fearsome appearance."

Nonchemical control

1. Elimination/reduction of reservoirs and habitats. This requires the reduction of rat, mice, and bird populations to control rat/house mice and bird mites.
2. Removing vegetation near houses and bare stripping around buildings to reduce habitat for clover mites.
3. Keeping lawns mowed, eliminating tall weeds and shrubs to control chigger mites.
4. Rotating food materials, ventilating to reduce moisture accumulation and vacuuming of storage areas to control grain and flour mites.

Dust Mite Management

To eliminate dust mite allergens, first take actions to reduce dust mite populations, and second, reduce exposure to dust. No single method has been found for reducing mites and relieving allergy suffering.

Lower humidity: Reduce humidity levels to less than 50% inside your home, especially in the bedroom. This isn't hard to do in the winter, but can be a challenge during summer months, especially in homes without air-conditioning. Studies have shown that air-conditioned homes have 10 times fewer dust mite allergens than non–air-conditioned homes. In addition to cooling the house, air-conditioning reduces the humidity dust mites need to thrive. A study has shown that using an electric blanket for eight hours each day reduced dust mites by 50% in one month.

Avoid furry or feathered pets: Pets with fur or feathers contribute to the dander in the dust and increase food source for mites. If you are a pet lover, locate the pet's sleeping quarters as far from yours as possible and furnish their sleeping area so it can be cleaned easily. Hardwood or vinyl floors with washable area rugs are ideal.

Reducing air infiltration: Airing out the house with open windows allows entry of pollen, which is another allergen as well as food for dust mites. In some climates, incoming air may be humid, which promotes dust mites.

Cleaning/heat treatments: Wash all bedding weekly. Research has shown that laundering with any detergent in warm water (77°F) removes nearly all dust mites and cat allergen from bedding. If you cannot launder blankets, dry clean them once a year. Shampoo, steam clean, or beat nonwashable carpets once a year.

Select appropriate furnishings: Avoid overstuffed furniture because it collects dust. Also avoid wool fabrics/rugs because wool sheds particles and is eaten by other insects. Use washable curtains and rugs instead of wall-to-wall carpeting. If you cannot replace carpeting, have it steam cleaned at least once a year; springtime is best. This will prevent a buildup of dust mites feeding on skin cells in the carpet during the summertime. Enclose mattresses and pillows in plastic to decrease mite populations in the bed. Replace feather pillows with synthetic ones.

Dust Management

Eliminating dust from the environment is important in reducing allergens in sensitive people.

Vacuuming: The most important tool for managing house dust and dust mites is the vacuum cleaner. Regular, thorough vacuuming of carpets, furniture, textiles, and other home furnishings such as draperies will help keep dust mite populations low. Vacuums with a water filter are preferable to those with a disposable paper bag because a water vacuum removes a greater range of particle sizes than paper-bag types. There are vacuums with highly efficient filters (HEPA) designed for use by people with allergies to dust. It is better to vacuum thoroughly once a week rather than lightly on a daily basis. Vacuum mattresses and padded furniture thoroughly; 20 minutes for each mattress is not too long.

Dusting: Dust furniture before you vacuum so the dust has time to settle on the floor, where it can be picked up by the vacuum. Do not scatter dust. Instead, dust with a damp cloth rather than dry dusting. Spraying furniture polish/dusting liquid directly on surface reduces airborne particles by 93% compared with dry dusting.

Air purifiers: A researcher at the University of Texas–Austin found that a HEPA air filter was much more effective at removing dust than ion-generating air purifiers which make particles electrically charged to remove them from circulating air. For more information on this research, visit HERE

The problem with ion-generating air filters is they emit significant amounts of ozone. Ozone irritates the lungs and can cause chest pain, coughing, shortness of breath, and throat irritation. According to the EPA, ozone may worsen chronic respiratory diseases such as asthma and compromise the ability of the body to fight respiratory infections. The EPA also states that manufacturers and vendors of ozone devices often use misleading terms to describe ozone. Terms such as "energized oxygen" or "pure air" suggest that ozone is a healthy kind of oxygen. Ozone is a toxic gas with vastly different chemical and toxicological properties from oxygen. For more information about health problems associated with ozone, check out http://www.epa.gov/iaq/pubs/ozonegen.html

Chemicals Control

No acaricides are registered for dust mite control, but benzyl benzoate or tannic acid may reduce levels of dust mites. Be careful if you decide to use these chemicals. According to the Mayo Clinic, these chemicals worsen allergies in some people. It is wise to use nonchemical dust mite control measures around people with serious allergies.

The cleaning and nontoxic approaches listed should give adequate control, except in humid, tropical regions of the world.

Chemical Control

1. Personal treatment for the scabies mite is performed using the same approach as for lice.
2. Area treatment indoors is performed using a spray of 0.5% diazinon, 0.1% lindane, 3% malathion. Outdoor treatment uses 1% toxaphene at a rate of 1 gallon per 1,000 ft^2.

Lyme Disease Review

Lyme disease is the most common vector-borne disease in the United States. It was first recognized in 1975 when researchers were investigating an atypical group of juvenile arthritis cases in coastal Connecticut. The causative agent was determined to be the spirochete *Borrelia burgdorferi*. The agent gains access to the human host by the bite of the *Ixodes* tick. In the eastern United States it is the black-legged or deer tick (*Ixodes scapularis*), and in the western coastal states it is the western black-legged tick (*Ixodes pacificus*), both of which have a two-year life-cycle. It should be noted that even if the tick is infected, not all bites transmit the infection. However, the likelihood of infection is increased by the length of the tick feeding activity, with 24–48 hours needed to transmit the pathogen adequately.

Clinically, the disease is segregated into three stages. The first stage is characterized by the *erythema migrans* rash at the site of the bite; this occurs in 60%–80% of the patients; however, less than 50% of Lyme disease patients recall being bitten. The wound averages about 15 cm, with the outer border remaining flat and bright red and the center appearing clear. Stage 2 transpires within weeks after the bite and consists of flulike symptoms along with cardiac and neurologic abnormalities. Stage 3 occurs months to years after the bite and is characterized by arthritic symptoms.

The deer tick larva is rarely infected transovarially, but will become so by feeding on an infected host, typically the white-footed mouse (*Peromyscus leucopus*). The pathogen will be passed transstadially to the nymph. This stage is exceptionally small (the size of a poppy seed), is easily missed during body examination, and is thus responsible for most human Lyme disease cases. The adult stage is active through the fall and spring when the temperature is in excess of 40°F. The infection rate of the tick larva is impacted by geography defining the larval host. The larval and nymphal host in the southern and Pacific coastal states is often a cold-blooded lizard, the western fence lizard. Cold-blooded animals are not susceptible to the pathogen. Thus, geographic variation of the larval host will impact the risk of becoming infected in a particular area. Areas of the northeast with the white-footed mouse may have tick infection rates in excess of 50%, while areas in the south and west may have only 1%–2% rates in larva and nymphs.

Nonchemical and Chemical Control

Refer to the section on ticks.

Rocky Mountain Spotted Fever Review

Rocky Mountain spotted fever (RMSF) is the most commonly reported rickettsial disease in the United States. Before the 1930s it was predominantly seen in the Rocky Mountain states, but has since become more prevalent in the south-central and southeastern states. The causative agent is *Rickettsia rickettsii*. The pathogen is transmitted by the bite of an infected tick or by contamination of the skin with tick blood or feces. This may occur through unprotected manual deticking with autoinfection via mucous membranes or eyes. In the eastern United States the primary vector is the American dog tick (*Dermacentor variabilis*). The Rocky Mountain wood tick (*Dermacentor andersonii*) is the main vector in the west, while the lone star tick (*Amblyomma americanum*) is the principal vector in the south and south- central states. It should be noted that in the tick population only 1%–5% are infected and only the adult ticks pass the pathogen to humans. Ticks may spend up to 24 hours on a human before feeding, but will liberate the pathogen from the salivary glands in 6–10 hours once feeding begins.

Clinical signs of the disease initiate within 3–12 days after the bite. In the east, children are primarily infected, while in the west it is adults. The disease is characterized by two classical triads. The most prominent is the fever + headache + rash, which occurs in 55% of cases. The rash typically starts on the wrist and ankles and proceeds centripetally to legs, arms, face, and abdomen.

Nonchemical and Chemical Control

Refer to the section on ticks.

Plague Review

Plague, otherwise known as bubonic plague, is one of the most renowned flea-borne diseases. It has a rich history, having been documented with numerous epidemics and four pandemics during the last 15 centuries. In the United States it is a "disease of the west," not known to range east of the 100th meridian. *Yersinia pestis* is the causative agent, formerly known as *Pasteurella pestis*. The pathogen is normally transmitted by the bite of an infected flea. It may also be contracted by direct contract with or by the bite of an infected animal. Numerous flea species are capable of transmitting the disease; the most notable are the oriental rat flea (*Xenopsylla cheopis*) and the human flea (*Pulex irritans*). Such fleas become blocked by the numeric growth of the organism in the *proventriculus* of the alimentary tract. This causes the blood to back into the wound, which then is contaminated by the pathogen.

The fleas live upon susceptible mammal hosts depending upon which cycle it is in. There are two epidemiologic types of plague. The first is demic plague, which alludes to the pneumonic transmission of airborne infection occurring person to person. The second type is zootic plague, which points to transmission due to the bite of infected fleas or contact through infected animals. Zootic plague is further divided into urban and rural plague. The former is the classic form in which people have close contact with domestic rats (*Rattus norvegicus and Rattus rattus*). Rural plague (sylvatic or campestral) occurs in country areas due to contact with infected mammals. There are three groups of wild animals primarily associated with this type:

1. native rats and mice
2. prairie dogs, ground squirrels, tree squirrels
3. cottontail rabbits and jackrabbits

Nonchemical and Chemical Control

Refer to the sections on fleas and on rodents.

Rabies Review

Reservoir

The rabies virus belongs to the *Rhabdoviridae* family and is a member of the genus *Lyssavirus*. It is one of the oldest documented diseases in mankind. In the United States the reservoir of the disease is geographic dependent, with numerous endemic and epidemic areas occurring throughout the country. However, other species in addition to the focus species may be contaminated and serve as reservoirs (see Figures 5.17 and 5.18). Hawaii is the only state without an indigenously acquired case of rabies in either humans or animals. The CDC reports that over 90% of all documented animal rabies cases occur in wildlife. In addition, 13 of the last 16 human cases of rabies in the United States have been identified as bat-associated genotypes of the virus related to the silver-haired bat. This bat is a solitary, tree-living insectivore. Other species of bat may be able to carry this variant of the pathogen.

Transmission and Symptoms

The transmission of the virus is typically through contaminated saliva from a host animal due to a bite wound. However, additional methods have been chronicled, including aerosol transmission, contamination of mucous membranes, and corneal transplants. The rabies virus is not hardy, and its

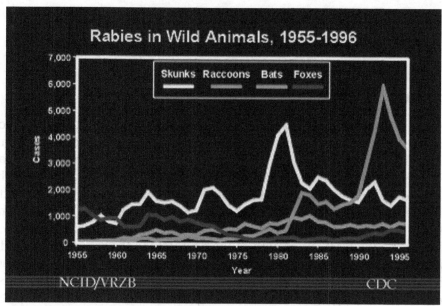

Figure 5.21 Known Carriers of Rabies and Distribution
U.S. Centers for Disease Control

resistance to environmental exposures such as drying, sunlight, heat, or chemicals is weak. The incubation period for the disease can vary from just a few days to several years. The characteristic time is one to three months. The infectious trail of the rabies virus is as follows:

1. A raccoon is bitten by a rabid animal.
2. The rabies virus enters the bitten raccoon via infected saliva.
3. The virus spreads through the nerves to the spinal cord and brain.
4. The virus incubates in the body for 3–12 weeks, during which time there are no signs of illness.
5. Upon reaching the brain, multiplication of the virus is rapid, passing to the salivary gland, and the raccoon begins to demonstrate disease symptoms.
6. The raccoon dies within seven days of symptoms.

In humans the disease is initially typified by nonspecific flulike symptoms that advance within days to neurological and behavioral symptoms, including delirium, hallucinations, and insomnia. The disease is nearly 100% fatal once clinical signs appear. Nonlethal cases have been documented, but all have included a history of either pre- or post-exposure prophylaxis.

Diagnosis and Treatment

The confirmatory diagnosis of rabies in animals is most frequently performed using the direct fluorescent antibody test (dFA). This test is performed upon the brain tissue of the animal. In order to perform the test, the removal of the animal's head and proper preservation of the specimen until arrival at the laboratory are necessary. Sacrificing the animal for such a purpose is dependent upon numerous factors, such as bite location on the body, whether the bite was provoked or not, the species of the animal, and its vaccination status. The following procedure is recommended for handling a bite case.

1. Locate the owner of the animal (dog, cat, ferret) and determine the vaccination status of the animal. Other species of animals often do not have a known viral shedding period and should be euthanized and examined immediately. Notify local law enforcement officials
2. If the animal is a stray, it may be euthanized immediately and submitted for laboratory examination. If the animal has been vaccinated, based upon the bite situation, the animal will either be confined or sacrificed. This is a decision made in concert with local law enforcement

and medical staff. If confinement is recommended, the animal should be placed under the observation of a licensed veterinarian. The confinement period is 10 days. Animals may demonstrate two types of rabies—*furious*, which demonstrates excitement and aggression, or *dumb*, in which the animal appears depressed, and shows loss of fear of humans and signs of paralysis.

3. If sacrificing the animal is necessary, it is best to have the procedure performed by a licensed veterinarian. If not possible, the following procedure should be followed.

   a. If possible, euthanize the animal humanely as possible. Care must be taken in whatever method is used to not damage the head when euthanizing or in removal. If a small animal (i.e., bat, rodent.) is suspected, submit the entire animal.

   b. To remove the head, wear protective gloves and full-face protection. Removal of the head after euthanizing the animal should be done carefully and slowly, as activity that damages the brain will render brain analysis useless.

   c. After removal, the head is to be refrigerated (not frozen. and taken to a qualified laboratory as quickly as possible, preferably within 24 hours.

Treatment for the disease can be in the form of preexposure prophylaxis and postexposure prophylaxis (PEP). The former is primarily for occupational exposure groups such as veterinarians and is a vaccine given in three doses over 28 days. PEP is indicated for persons possibly exposed to a rabid animal. This involves a single-dose regimen of immune globulin and five doses of rabies vaccine over 28 days. This is a medical decision, but it is often based upon information provided by the environmental health specialist during investigation of an incident. Such information will include vaccination status, type of animal, provoked or unprovoked, and whether the animal has been secured or is loose.

Bats

Exposure to bats and exotic animals requires a somewhat different approach. The CDC recommends that PEP be provided in any situation involving possible contact with a bat in which exposure, including mucosal or wound exposure to bat saliva, cannot be ruled out. These situations include awakening to find a bat in a room or a bat physically present in a room occupied by children with no witness to rule out contact.

Bat exclusion, also known as bat proofing, is the process of sealing all gaps and openings on the exterior of a structure to prevent any bats from entering. Bat-proofing a home or building is most often a difficult task involving high ladder work, and roofing and construction skills. One of the biggest problems involved with a bat infestation is the accumulation of bat droppings (guano). Guano accumulates in piles beneath the roosting bats and can contaminate insulation and other materials. Exposure to large quantities of bat droppings can be a serious health risk, possibly causing lung infections or a disease called histoplasmosis. An attic inspection should be done to determine the extent of damage.

Bats are known carriers of rabies, and care should be taken not to come into physical contact with them. If you or someone in your household may have come into contact with a bat, seek

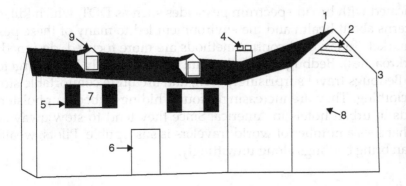

medical attention. If a bat is found in a living area of a home, the persons exposed should contact their local health department.

Bats are very beneficial to our environment and an important part of our ecosystem. A single bat can eat more than 1,000 insects every night, and a colony of bats can control an overpopulation of insects. All bats are protected species and great care should be taken to ensure a healthy bat population for the future

Figure 5.22 Other Known Carriers of Rabies and Distribution

Animal Control and Vaccination

1. Well-enforced leash laws, the removal of stray dogs, cats, and ferrets, and an active vaccination program best accomplish animal control. Strays should be confined to three days to allow owners time to pick them up. Registration/licensure can also be used to control rabies.

2. Bats should be excluded from houses and adjacent structures to prevent direct association with humans. Such structures should then be made bat-proof by sealing entrances used by bats. This means any openings larger than 1/4 in × 1/2 in. Young bats are unable to fly and will be roosted during the summer; avoid exclusion measures from May through August.

3. Animal vaccination should be restricted to use by, or under the direct supervision of, a veterinarian. Only vaccines with three-year durations of immunity should be used. A peak rabies antibody titer is reached in 30 days after primary vaccination. Dogs, cats, and ferrets should be vaccinated at three months of age, with a second vaccination occurring one year later. No parenteral vaccine is licensed for use in wild animals.

A Reemerging Pest Problem: BedBugs

Once thought to be eradicated from North America, the legendary little pests known as bedbugs have been making an unwelcome comeback in hotels and homes. Lest you think bedbugs are relegated to fleabag motels, they have been spotted in upscale facilities. Star ratings mean nothing to these little fellows.

Bedbugs are the common name for *Cimex lectularius*, a reddish-brown, oval-shaped insect that can grow to 1/4 in long. Bedbugs are wingless and survive by sucking blood from a host animal, preferably a human. Bedbugs commonly hide in mattresses, carpets, behind peeling paint or wallpaper, and in crevices in wooden furniture (e.g., cracks in the wooden headboard of a bed). Bedbugs are nocturnal and typically bite people while they sleep in an infested bed. They are usually active just before dawn.

Why Are Bedbugs Reappearing?

Bedbugs were once all but eradicated with broad-spectrum pesticides such as DDT, which killed a wide variety of bug types. Concerns about health and the environment led to many of these pesticides being removed from the market. Today, pest control methods are more focused, designed to kill a particular species (like cockroaches). Bedbugs, since they are not specifically being targeted, are slipping through the cracks. Bedbugs travel surprisingly well, and are quite comfortable stowing away in luggage and even clothing. They are increasingly found hiding in beds, upholstered furniture, and behind baseboards in urban hotels in America. Since they tend to stow away and travel with humans, any place that sees a number of world travelers is susceptible. Pilots, wealthy people, and business travelers can bring bedbugs along unwittingly.

Control of Bedbugs?

Bedbugs are large enough to see. Look particularly under the mattress and in the seams, in and around the bed frame, and along any cracks or peeling paint in the wall or picture frames. Check for bedbugs in the cracks of any wooden furniture, particularly antiques. You can also spot droppings from bedbugs, which may be tinged with blood.

Imex lectularius range in color from tan to orangish-brown. They have no wings; they can only crawl from surface to surface. If you find bedbugs hiding, say, behind a picture frame, they'll scurry quickly to another hiding place—they're quick, agile, and adaptable.

Bedbug in Mattress Seam.
US Centers for Disease Control

Photo courtesy of CDC

There are a few known possible causes of bedbug infestation, including picking up the bugs while traveling and carrying them home in or on a suitcase or clothing, or bringing in a piece of used furniture that has bedbugs already living inside it. Also, if the apartment next to you has bedbugs, any wiring holes or cracks in the walls can let them into your home too. Adult bedbugs can live up to a year without a meal, so there's no guarantee that the new apartment you move into that's been vacant for six months will be free of the little guys. Having bedbugs aren't about filth—bedbugs feed on blood, not trash. The most immaculate home can end up with bedbugs. However, a messy home does offer more places for bedbugs to hide, so cleaning up clutter is one of the first steps to getting rid of a bedbug problem.

The first step is to confirm that what you have in your home are actually bedbugs. Their bites look a lot like mosquito bites, so you (or an insect-finding professional) actually need to find one of the offending bugs and compare it to a clear picture of a bedbug before you start planning for eradication. Another positive finding is rust-colored bedbug droppings and molted shells in the creases of your sheets, the seams of your mattress, or wherever the bugs are calling home.

Once you know that you have bedbugs, the eradication process begins. Getting rid of bedbugs isn't simple, and you'll almost definitely want to call in a professional pest killer, preferably one with experience in dealing with bedbugs. These insects are tiny and wily, and the most effective pesticides against them are no longer deemed safe, so exterminators must use a combination of less effective options in order to successfully rid your home of the little parasites. A few of the treatments for bedbugs include:

- Extended exposure to temperatures above 120°F (49°C) or below 32°F (0°C)

- Heavy-duty vacuuming of all carpets, upholstered furniture, and cracks in wood and molding

- Steam cleaners, if used thoroughly, may be effective if used in combination with other actions

- Laundering affected textiles (clothing, bedding)

- Sealing an infected mattress in plastic (to suffocate the bedbugs)

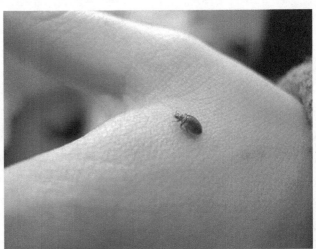
Bedbug on Arm.
US Centers for Disease Control

Photo courtesy of CDC

- Using dust insecticides, which often contain ground glass or silica powder that acts as an abrasive and drying agent to slowly kill the bugs
- Using contact insecticides that kill instantly, often containing pyrethroids or chlorfenapyr
- Using insecticides that damage bedbugs' ability to reproduce but don't necessarily kill them (insect-growth regulators)
- Fumigating the entire structure with poisonous gas

Traditional baits and traps won't work on this type of bug, so clearing your house of the infestation will require effort. You don't necessarily have to get rid of your bed or couch if that's what they've decided to call home, since heat or suffocation might get rid of the problem. But discarding those items might be the way to go if you actually want your home free of bedbugs, not just free of live bedbugs. If you do get rid of infested furniture, don't just put it on the curb where anyone with a pickup could grab your pretty couch and end up with his or her own bedbug problem. It's best to put it in a dumpster or at least deface it in a way that will stop people from wanting to take it home.

Water, Water Systems and Treatment

6

Joe E. Beck, RS, DEASS

When the well is dry, we know the worth of water.

Benjamin Franklin, (1706–1790),
Poor Richard's Almanac, 1746

In an age when man has forgotten his origins and is blind even to his most essential needs for survival, water along with other resources has become the victim of his indifference.

Rachel Carlson 1964

Key Performance Outcome Indicators:

1. *Understand how water is created, and the hydrologic cycle;*
2. Be able to discuss the magnetic nature of water and why it attracts other molecules;
3. Know what the primary elements of a sanitary survey of a water source;
4. Understand potential sources for ground water pollution:
5. Understand the difficulty of killing Guardia and Cryptosporidium in water systems;
6. Know the correct way to collect a water sample;
7. What role does prescription drugs play in our water supplies?
8. What is the best way of getting rid of unused prescription drugs?

Introduction

The quest for potable water goes back to pre-historic times. Treatment, in the form of boiling, filtration through cloth, porous vessels, sand and gravel, has been practiced for more than 2000 years. The importance of "pure water" to maintain personal hygiene and prevent disease was understood by the mid 1800s. As in early times, the quest for potable water continues today and water treatment remains a societal pre-requisite. The term *potable* describes water as being safe for human consumption and being aesthetically pleasing. Therefore, drinking water must be free of pathogens and have no odor, color or unpleasing taste. Drinking water or potable water is water of sufficiently high quality that it can be consumed or used without risk of immediate or long term harm. In most developed countries, the water supplied to households, commerce and industry, is all of drinking water standard, even though only a very small proportion is actually consumed or used in food preparation.

Essential to the survival of all organisms, water has always been an important and life-sustaining drink to humans. Excluding fat, water composes approximately 70% of the human body by mass. It is a crucial component of metabolic processes and serves as a solvent for many bodily chemicals. Health authorities have historically suggested at least eight glasses, eight fluid ounces each (168 ml), of water per day (64 fluid ounces, or 1.89 liters), and the British Dietetic Association recommends 1.8 liters. The United States Environmental Protection Agency has determined that the average adult actually ingests 2.0 liters per day.

Over large parts of the world, humans have inadequate access to potable water and use sources contaminated with disease vectors, pathogens or unacceptable levels of dissolved chemicals or suspended solids. Such water is not potable and drinking or using such water in food preparation leads to widespread acute and chronic illnesses and is a major cause of death in many countries. Reduction of waterborne diseases is a major public health goal in developing countries.

Typically, water supply networks deliver potable water, whether it is to be used for drinking, washing or landscape irrigation. One counterexample is urban China, where drinking water can optionally be delivered by a separate tap.

Currently, community access to safe drinking water is indicated by the number of people using proper sanitary sources. These improved drinking water sources include household connection, public standpipe, borehole condition, protected dug well, protected spring, and rain water collection. Sources that don't encourage improved drinking water to the same extent as previously mentioned include: unprotected well, unprotected spring, rivers or ponds, vender-provided water, bottled water (consequential of limitations in quantity, not quality of water), and tanker truck water. Access to sanitary water comes hand in hand with access to improved sanitation facilities for excreta. These facilities include connection to public sewer, connection to septic system, pour-flush latrine, and ventilated improved pit latrine. Unimproved sanitation facilities are: public or shared latrine, open pit latrine, or bucket latrine.

The most efficient way to transport and deliver potable water is through pipes. However, this can require significant capital investment in providing the infrastructure. Systems with high operating costs may fall into disrepair in both developed and undeveloped countries. The cost to replace the deteriorating water and sanitation infrastructure of industrialized countries may be as high as $200 billion a year. Leakage of untreated and treated water from pipes reduces access to water. Leakage rates of 50% are not uncommon in urban systems.

Because of the high initial investments, many less wealthy nations cannot afford to develop or sustain appropriate infrastructure and as a consequence people in these areas may pay a much higher percentage of their income on water. [2003 statistics from El Salvador, for example, indicate that the poorest 20% of households spend more than 10% of their total income on water]. In the United Kingdom authorities define spending of more than 3% of one's income on water as a hardship. It should be noted at this point that a good safe supply of potable water is equally dependent on the integrity of the distribution system. Backflow and back siphonage must always be a concern.

The EHO should be very proud of their accomplishments in the US and UK. The grim statistics below are the result of poverty and individual nations failures to focus on the problems of water and sanitation. It is truly sanitation that makes the difference between the nations of the first order and third world order. This may be where the money should be spent in the future. However, our days of unrestricted water use are also quite limited.

Meeting Global Targets for Water and Sanitation

- There are 1.1 billion people, or 18 per cent of the world's population, who lack access to safe drinking water. About 2.6 billion people, or 42 per cent of the total, lack access to basic sanitation (WHO/UNICEF, 2005: 40)

- The UN'S Millennium Development Goals (MDGs) call for halving "by 2015, the proportion of people without sustainable access to safe drinking water and basic sanitation." The MDG for safe drinking water on a global scale appears likely to be reached, in most regions, with the exception of sub-Saharan Africa (WHO/UNICEF, 2005: 26).

- Within the United Nations system, UN-Water is the inter-agency mechanism that coordinates the activities of 24 agencies of the United Nations system in the area of water resources, including sanitation.

- 1.1 billion people gained access to safe drinking water between 1990–2002. The greatest access gains were achieved in South Asia, where water access increased from 71 per cent in 1990 to 84 percent in 2002. In sub-Saharan Africa, access grew minimally, from 49 percent in 1990 to 58 percent in 2002. (WHO/UNICEF, 2004: 10).

- IIt is estimated that an additional investment of US$ 11.3 billion per year would be needed to achieve the MDGs for drinking water and sanitation at the most basic levels WHO/UNICEF, 2005: 2)

Water and sanitation

Key Water and Sanitation Statistics

- The world's population, 6.2 billion people in 2002, is expected to increase to approximately 7.2 billion people by 2015. Almost 95 per cent of the increase is expected to be in developing regions (WHO/UNICEF, 2005: 40).

Raw Sewage Near a Beach USEPA

- Only one per cent of the total water resources on earth is available for human use. While 70 per cent of the world's surface is covered by water, 97.5 per cent of that is salt water. Of the remaining 2.5 per cent that is freshwater, almost 68.7 per cent is frozen in ice caps and glaciers UN-WWAP, 2006: Fig. 4.1).

- Water withdrawals for irrigation have increased by over 60 per cent since 1960. About 70 per cent of all available freshwater is used for irrigation in agriculture. Yet because of inefficient irrigation systems, particularly in developing countries, 60 per cent of this water is lost to evaporation or is returned to rivers and groundwater aquifers UN-WWAP, 2006: 173).

- Water use increased six-fold during the 20th Century, more than twice the rate of population growth. While water consumption in industrialized countries runs as high as 380 litres/capita/day in the United States (USGS, 2004) and 129 litres/capita/day in Germany (Statistisches Bundesamt, 2000), in developing countries 20–30 litres/capita/day are considered enough to meet basic human needs.

- In parts of the United States, China and India , groundwater is being consumed faster than it is being replenished, and groundwater tables are steadily falling. Some rivers, such as the Colorado River in the western United States and the Yellow River in China, often run dry before they reach the sea.

- Freshwater ecosystems have been severely degraded: it is estimated that about half the world's wetlands have been lost, and more than 20 per cent of the world's 10,000 known freshwater species have become extinct, threatened or endangered (UN-DESA: 10).

The global water supply situation

Water scarcity: it was estimated that in 1995 about 1.76 billion people (out of approx. 5.7 billion world population (UN, 2005) were living under severe water stress (UN-WWAP, 2006: 442).

- By 2025, it is estimated that about two thirds of the world's population - about 5.5 billion people—will live in areas facing moderate to severe water stress (UN, 1997: 19).

- The areas most affected by water shortages are in North Africa and Western and South Asia. For 25 per cent of Africa's population, chronic water stress is high: 13 per cent of the population experience drought-related water stress once each generation, and 17 per cent are without a renewable supply of water (UN-WWAP, 2006, 442).

- 83 per cent of the world's population used improved drinking water sources in 2002, up from an estimated 79 per cent in 1990 WHO/UNICEF/WSSCC, 2000: 9; WHO/UNICEF, 2004: 9). Approximately 42 per cent of the people with access to water have a household connection or yard tap. However, approximately 1.1 billion people still do not have access to improved drinking water (WHO/UNICEF, 2005: 11).

- People in slum areas have very limited access to safe water for household uses. A slum dweller may only have 5 to 10 litres per day at his or her disposal, while a middle- or high-income person in the same city may use some 50 to 150 litres per day, if not more (UN-WWAP, 2006: 46).

- Up to 30 per cent of fresh water supplies are lost due to leakage in developed countries, and in some major cities, losses can run as high as 40 to 70 per cent (UN-WWAP, 2006: 150).

Global water supply situation

The global sanitation situation

- If increases in sanitation coverage stay as low as between 1990 and 2002, the world will fall short of its MDG target by over half a billion people by 2015 (WHO/UNICEF, 2005: 24).

- In 2002, 2.6 billion people—roughly 42 per cent of the world's population - had no access to improved sanitation facilities. An additional 1.8 billion people need to be provided with improved sanitation from 2002 to 2015 to achieve the MDG to halve the proportion unserved in 1990. Even if that target is achieved, still 1.8 billion people will lack adequate sanitation in 2015 due to population increase (WHO/UNICEF, 2005: 5).

- In developing countries rural communities have less than half the sanitation coverage (37 per cent) of urban areas (81 per cent) (WHO/UNICEF, 2004: 31).

- Sanitation coverage levels are lowest in the Sub-Saharan Africa (36 per cent) and South Asia (37 per cent) regions (WHO/UNICEF, 2005: 5)

About 90 per cent of sewage and 70 per cent of industrial wastes in developing countries are discharged into water courses without treatment, often polluting the usable water supply.

More than 2.2. million people, mostly in developing countries, die each year from diseases associated with poor water and sanitary conditions (WHO/UNICEF/WSSCC, 2000: V).

- At any one time, half of the world's hospital beds are occupied by patients suffering from water-borne diseases.

- Every week an estimated 42,000 people die from diseases related to low quality drinking water and lack of sanitation. Over 90 per cent of them occur to children under the age of 5 (WHO/UNICEF, 2005: 15).

- Two of the water-related diseases, diarrhoea and malaria, ranked 3rd and 4th place in the cause of death among children under 5 years old, accounting for 17 per cent and 8 per cent respectively of all deaths (WHO, 2005: 106).

- In sub-Saharan Africa, a baby's chance of dying from diarrhoea is almost 520 times the chance of that in Europe or the United States (WHO/UNICEF, 2005: 16).

- Improvements in drinking-water quality through household water treatment, such as chlorination at point of use and adequate domestic storage, can lead to a reduction of diarrhoea episodes by between 35 and 39 per cent, while hygiene interventions, such as hygiene education and promotion of hand washing, can lead to a reduction of diarrhoeal cases by up to 45 per cent (WHO/UNICEF, 2005: 13).

For a family of six, collecting enough water for drinking, cooking and basic hygiene may mean hauling heavy water containers from a distant source for an average of three hours a day. Women and girls are mainly responsible for fetching the water that their families need for drinking, bathing, cooking and other household uses (WHO/UNICEF, 2005: 11).

- Poor health resulting from inadequate water and sanitation robs the children of schooling and the adults of earning power, a situation aggravated for the women and girls by the daily chore of collecting water (WHO/UNICEF, 2005: 11).

- For pregnant women, access to enough good quality water is vitally important to protect them from serious diseases such as hepatitis (WHO/UNICEF, 2005: 20).

- Women face the challenge of maintaining basic household hygiene and keeping their own and their infants' hands and bodies clean with limited water supplies, and at the same time avoiding contamination of water stored for drinking and cooking (WHO/UNICEF, 2005: 20).

- Currently, in sub-Saharan Africa, a larger proportion of women are infected with HIV than men. When women are living with HIV/AIDS, their suffering has a double impact on their families' water problems (WHO/UNICEF, 2005: 21).

- Adoption of sustainable hygiene behaviors is strongly linked to the educational level of women. Better-educated women are more likely to adopt long-term hygiene behaviors (WHO/UNICEF, 2005: 31).

- 1.3 billion women and girls in developing countries are doing without access to private, safe and sanitary toilets. In some cultural settings where basic sanitation is lacking, women and girls have to rise before dawn, making their way in the darkness to fields, railroad tracks and roadsides to defecate in the open, knowing they may risk rape or other violence in the process (WHO/UNICEF, 2004: 21).

- The lack of adequate, separate sanitary facilities in schools is one of the main factors preventing girls from attending school, particularly when menstruating. Gender-sensitive school sanitation programmes can increase girls' enrolment significantly. In Bangladesh girls' enrolment was increased by as much as 11 per cent over a four-year period (UN-WWAP, 2006: 230), while in the Morocco Rural Water Supply and Sanitation Project of the World Bank school attendance in 6 provinces increased by even 20% in four years. Time spent on collecting water by women and young girls was reduced by 50 to 90% (World Bank, 2003).

The Economics of Investments in Water & Sanitation

- A WHO Cost-Benefit Analysis showed that every US$1 invested in improved drinking water and sanitation services can yield economic benefits of US$4 to US$34 depending on the region (WHO) (WHO/UNICEF, 2005: 4). The economic benefits of household water treatment—such as the application of chlorination, solar disinfection, filters or combined flocculation and chlorination powders—can yield benefits of US$ 5 to 140 per US$ 1 invested (WHO/UNICEF, 2005: 24 [data available in hardcopy version only]).

- The economic payback from investing US$11.3 billion per year to reach the Millennium targets for drinking water and sanitation by 2015 is estimated to be US$ 84 billion (WHO, 2004: 34).

- WHO has estimated that productivity gains from a reduction in diarrhoeal disease if the MDG drinking water and sanitation target is reached will exceed US$ 700 million a yea (WHO/UNICEF, 2005: 16).

Website development: UN Web Services Section, Department of Public Information, United Nations © 2006

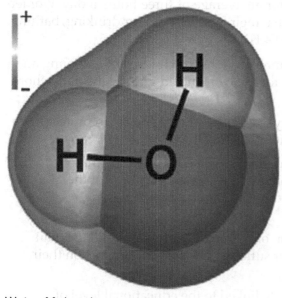

Water Molecule

Photo credits: UNICEF (Giacomo Pirozzi. Rwanda, Zambia/Jonathan Shadid, Burkina Faso), UNEP (Hlaing Thntint/Ritter/Jinda Uthaipanumas/Mazansky/Pablo Alfredo de Luca), UN Photo

The assurance of a safe water supply for human consumption has historically been a primary environmental health concern. The term "pure water" is erroneously used to describe water that has no pollutants that can cause humans to become ill. Water evaporated into the atmosphere is essentially chemically pure. However, as water travels through the atmosphere as clouds or descends as rain, gases such as oxygen, nitrogen, and carbon dioxide are dissolved into the water. Dust, smoke fumes, and microbes may also be dissolved and/or retained in suspension. Water forms in the atmosphere by condensing around particles of dust or pollutant and gains enough mass to fall from the sky; the water molecule is magnetic due to the clustering oi positively charged hydrogen on one side of the molecule and the negatively charged oxygen molecule that they form a bond. Only 3% of the planets water is available as fresh water.

Upon reaching, the earth, rainwater either sinks into the ground and becomes groundwater, flows over the ground (called runoff) into streams or pools (ponds, lakes), or evaporates back into the atmosphere. Figure 4.1 illustrates the present day hydrologic cycle. The numbers in parentheses refer to volumes of water in millions of cubic kilometers and the fluxes adjacent to arrows are in millions of kilometers of water per year. Note that fresh water is most abundant in groundwater. In comparison, surface and stream water appear to contribute very little. Water, known as the universal solvent, reacts and combines with all substances

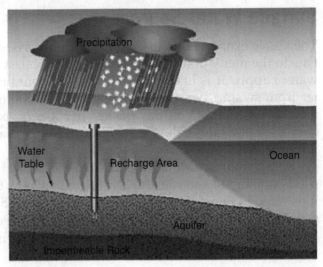

Hydrologic Cycle
USNOAA

with which it comes in contact such as; salts, organic matter, radon, or one of many inorganic compounds (minerals) in the soil. Impurities that may be present in water can be classified as *suspended* or *dissolved solids*. *Suspended solids* are those that can be removed by standard filtration techniques (coagulation, sedimentation, and filtration), whereas *dissolved solids* may require more elaborate treatment for removal such as distillation or reverse osmosis. Gases in water are not considered to be dissolved solids because they can usually be removed by aeration, heating, or similar methods.

Water Sources

Depending on local conditions, water supplies may be obtained from any number of sources . . . either singly or in combination. Commonly used water sources include underground sources such as springs or wells, and surface water sources, such as rivers, streams, or lakes. Whenever population density and the supply source are adequate, municipal facilities are utilized which provides uniform treatment and water pressure. In many cases, individual families must seek an adequate source and provide their own treatment and maintenance.

To identify a water source as usable, a sanitary survey should be conducted to determine the reliability of a water source to continuously supply safe and adequate water. The survey will furnish the data upon which one would base their decision to accept or reject the proposed water as a potential source of adequate and safe water supply. The survey must be aided by chemical and bacteriological analyses and knowledge of the significant factors involved. The sanitary survey should thus incorporate the expertise of the sanitary engineer, epidemiologist, and sanitarian and include some of the following considerations:

Sanitary Survey Should Include Identification and Assessment of:

- The total land area that contributes runoff to a stream or river, commonly known as the drainage basin or watershed
- Location of liquid or solid waste disposal sites
- Extent of agricultural activity and sources of erosion, sediment and pesticides
- Location and condition or residences
- Prevalence and location of on-site sewage disposal systems
- Location of feedlots

Surface Water Sources

The above example of what a survey should assess relates most directly to surface water sources. Due to the many potential sources of pollution, surface water may be a poor choice for a drinking water supply. It is likely to be turbid and contaminated by natural erosion, silting, organic matter from swamps, and by other natural pollutants. Surface waters may also be contaminated by animal wastes, agricultural wastes, (fertilizers, pesticides), industrial wastes, and human waste such as septic tank failures. Therefore, surface waters typically are high in suspended solids and microbes.

Because surface waters are not in close contact with rock and soils, they are lower in dissolved solids (minerals) and calcium carbonate hardness than groundwater. Unless treated by a POTW as illustrated in Figure 5.1 and described in Chapter 5, surface water in the form of creeks and streams should be avoided as a drinking water supply. Ponds and reservoirs, properly constructed, protected, and maintained may be used to supply drinking water.

Groundwater

Groundwater is water that collects underground in geologic formations called aquifers. The water generally fills the cracks and voids between rock and sand, although in limestone topography the water may be more free flowing. In these geologic formations, one would find saturated permeable material that yields water to wells and springs.

Groundwater, when available, is usually an excellent source for a drinking water supply. It is expected to be clear, cool, colorless and contains less organic material than surface water. The quality, microbiologically, is superior, but it generally contains higher concentrations of inorganic compounds (minerals) than other sources. Contamination groundwater is frequently chemical rather than microbial in nature. Common sources of chemical contamination include high concentrations of dissolved mineral solids, pesticides used in agriculture, leaking underground tanks, seepage from septic tank drainfields, garbage dumps as noted in (Figure 4.2), sanitary landfills or improper disposal of oil as illustrated.

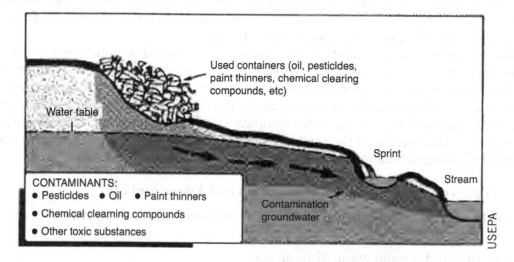

Groundwater Contaminants

Protection of groundwater must be an individual and community effort. Locating and protecting groundwater recharge areas are long term solutions to offer assurances that potable water will be there for future generations.

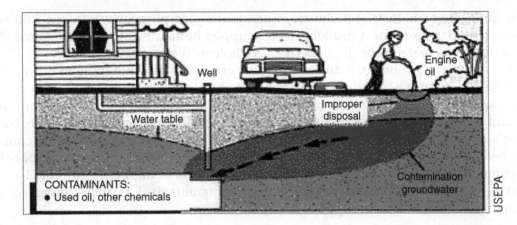

Water Contamination and Disease

The consumption of water is necessary to sustain life and for recovery from illness. In the 1950's, the newly created Indian Health Service immediately recognized that inadequate water quantity and quality for Native American homes and communities was contributing to high rates of enteric and skin diseases. Also noted were alarming levels of infant mortality from diarrhea caused by contaminated water supplies. Other traditional preventive health measures, such as immunizations, were not capable of reducing these problems.

The most effective efforts were providing Indian homes and communities with water systems for safe drinking water and sewers for adequate wastewater disposal. The availability of these essential sanitation facilities was a major factor in breaking the chain of waterborne communicable disease episodes. By no means, however, has their value been limited to disease intervention. Safe drinking water is an essential pre-condition for health promotion and disease prevention efforts. Properly fluoridated drinking water can greatly reduce tooth decay among children. Efforts by other public health specialists, such as nutritionists, alcoholism counselors, and home health care nurses, are enhanced if safe water is readily available in the home.

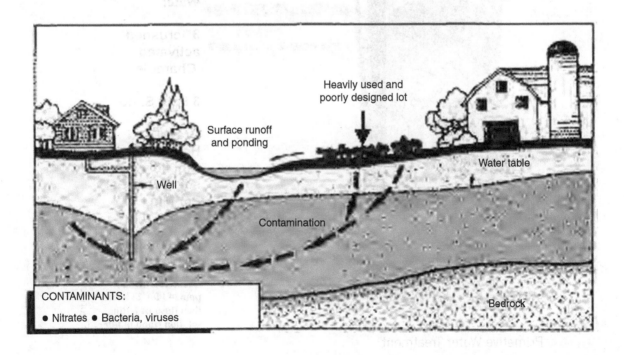

When domestic or industrial pollution is accidentally or purposely released into surface or groundwater sources used for a drinking water supply, human health is endangered. Microbial pathogens that cause waterborne illnesses such as Cholera, Typhoid fever, USEPA

Dysentery become a concern. Acute and chronic effects are possible from an array of chemical exposures. Concerns such as nitrates and microbial pathogens in water may be due to groundwater contamination from feedlots and surface impoundments as noted in Figure 4.4. When water tables are high and soil is permeable, contamination may enter individual water wells. More than half of the nation's land area possesses geological features that permit groundwater to be contaminated (Moeller, 1997) as noted in Figure 4.2, 4.3, and 4.4. As of 1992, it was estimated that more than 10% of the community well water supplies and almost 5% of rural domestic wells in the United States contained detectable concentrations of one or more contaminants. Elevated nitrates, for example, have been detected in many such supplies (Moeller, 1997).

Temporary water filtration and treatment

The primitive water treatment system below was designed by Joe Beck and can be made from relatively inexpensive materials typically found in most rural areas. The system provides relatively high quality water in volumes up to 2 gallons per minute per square foot of filter surface area. However typically the system is set at 1 gallon per minute per square foot to ensure good filtering response. A mapped of activated charcoal can be placed on the surface of the sand to remove odor and some heavy metals.

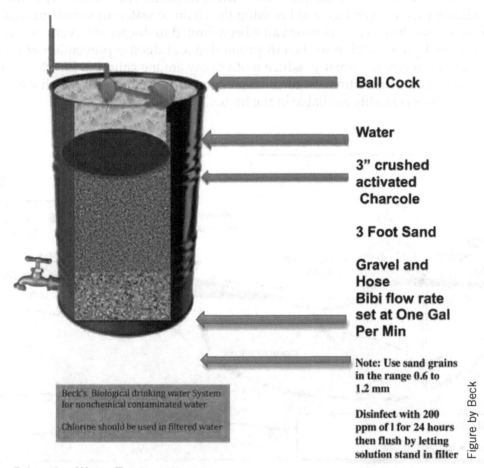

Ball Cock

Water

3" crushed
activated
 Charcole

3 Foot Sand

Gravel and
Hose
Bibi flow rate
set at One Gal
Per Min

Note: Use sand grains
in the range 0.6 to
1.2 mm

Disinfect with 200
ppm of I for 24 hours
then flush by letting
solution stand in filter

Beck's Biological drinking water System
for nonchemical contaminated water

Chlorine should be used in filtered water

Figure by Beck

Primitive Water Treatment

It is important that the barrel be cleaned thoroughly before use and heating it up to a high temperature to provide assurance that any chemical residuals be removed from the 55 gallon barrel is an added safeguard. The sand can either be soked in 200 ppm bleach or heat-treated to ensure harmful microbes are removed from the same media. It is strongly suggested that liquid bleach be used to provide at least one part per million residual at the hose bib the system will typically provide. Well filtered and pleasant drinking water from most sources, but should not be trusted to treat water that is possibly chemically contaminated.

Worst Waterborne Disease Outbreaks

More than 600 waterborne disease outbreaks have been reported to the Centers for Disease Control since 1971. CDC acknowledges that this is only a fraction of the actual numbers.

Prior to modern water treatment and subsequent use of chlorine to disinfect, waterborne diseases such as cholera and typhoid fever were responsible for widespread illness and death. These early waterborne diseases were caused by enteric bacteria derived from the improper disposal of domestic wastewater. Current concerns focus on the parasite/protozoan group, in particular Giardiasis and Cryptosporidisosis. The 1996 revisions to the Safe Drinking Water Act focus on these two microorganisms.

Table 6.1 Worst Waterborne Disec

STATE	DATE OF OUTBREAK	CAUSE OF ILLNESS	NO. OF ILLNESSES
Wisconsin	March 1993	Cryptosporidium parvum	400,000 (104 dead)
Georgia	January 1987	Cryptosporidium parvum	13,000
Michigan	June 1991	Acute gastrointeritis	1320
Tennessee	May 1990	Acute gastrointeritis	1000
Texas	May 1988	Shigella sonnei	900
Alabama	Sept. 1989	Acute gastrointeritis	700
Pennsylvania	August 1991	Cryptosporidium parvum	551
Pennsylvania	April 1987	Giardia lamblia	513
Missouri	November 1993	Salmonella	486 (4 dead)
Nevada	Jan.–April 1994	Cryptosporidium parvum	100 (19 dead)
Missouri	December 1989	E-coli 0157:H7	243

Giardiasis and Cryptosporidiosis

As noted in Table 4.1, these two waterborne illnesses have been responsible for some of the worst outbreaks in recent years. Giardiasis has been responsible for more waterborne outbreaks since 1971 than any other microorganism. Two factors make these two parasite/protozoans the primary concern of public health agencies presently.

1. They are resistant to disinfection chemicals, i.e. chlorine
2. The infective dose is low. The ingestion of only a few oocysts cause illness.

Table 6.2 Common Waterborne Diseases

Common Waterborne Diseases
Bacterial

DISEASE	SPECIFIC AGENT	RESERVOIR	SYMPTOMS	INCUBATION TIME	PREVENTION & CONTROL
Typhoid fever	Salmonella typhosa	Feces & Urine	Fever, rosy spots on body, diarrhea	7 to 21 days, average of 14 days	Protect and purify water, and isolate carriers
Paratyphoid fever	S. paratyphi A	Feces & Urine	Same as above	1 to 10 days	Same as above
Shigellosis	Shigella boydii, & dysenteriae	Feces	Acute onset of diarrhea, fever, tenemus, blood and mucus stools	1 to 7 days, average of 4 days	Same as above
Cholera	Vibrio cholera	Feces & Vomitus	Diarrhea, rice water stools, vomiting, thirst, pain and coma	Few hours to 5 days, average of 3 days	Similar to above, quarantine patients.
Campylo-bacter	Campylo-bacter jejuni	Feces & Vomitus	Watery diarrhea, abdominal pain, fever, chills, nausea, vomiting, blood in stools	2 to 5 days, possibly 10 days	Proper water filtration, prevent cross contamination
Diarrhea, entero-pathogenic (Travelers Diarrhea)	Enteropathogenic e-coli. (EEC)	Feces	Fever, mucus & bloody diarrhea, cramps, dehydration, acidosis	12 to 72 hours	Drink purified water only, scrupulous hygiene

Viruses

DISEASE	SPECIFIC AGENT	RESERVOIR	SYMPTOMS	INCUBATION TIME	PREVENTION & CONTROL
Infectious Hepatitis	Hepatitis A	Feces	Nausea, loss of appetite, fatigue, headache, and jaundice	30 to 35 days on average	Sanitary sewage disposal, assure drinking water is properly purified.
Acute Viral Gastrointestinal Illness (AGI)	Norwalk Virus	Feces	Nausea, vomiting, fever diarrhea, abdominal pain	24 to 48 hours	Same as above

Common Waterborne Diseases cont*

Parasites/Protozoans

Amebiasis	Entamoeba hystolytica	Feces of human & rodent carriers	Insidious onset, loss of appetite, abdominal pain, diarrhea or constipation, mucus & bloody stools	2 to 4 weeks	Drink only purified water, boil suspect water supplies
Giardiasis	Giardia lamblia	Feces of carriers	Prolonged diarrhea, foul gas, cramps, severe weight loss, fatigue	6 to 22 days	Drink only properly purified and filtrated water, boil suspect water supplies
Cryptosporidiosis	Cryptosporidium parvum	Feces of pets, farm animals, & humans	Mild flu-like symptoms, diarrhea	2 to 10 days	Make sure filtration units are optimally maintained. Chlorine has no effect, boil suspect water supplies
Cyclospora	C. cayetanensis	Feces	Watery diarrhea, low grade fever, abdominal pain, loss of appetite	1 to 14 days	Same as for it's coccidian cousin, cryptosporidium

Common Parasites and Protozoans

Giardiasis is caused by the protozoan, Giardia lamblia. This protozoan exists in the environment in a dormant cyst stage of life. When ingested, the stomach acids dissolve the cyst allowing the free swimming trophozoite (as it is now called) to survive in the intestines where it takes in nutrients and multiplies. Infection by Giardia does not automatically cause illness. Many people show no symptoms during an invasion, but merely become carriers.

Cryptospordiosis is caused by the protozoan, Cryptosporidium parvum. Long known as a disease among animals, it was first identified as a human pathogen in 1984. It is shed in the feces in the form of an oocyst (5 to 7 microns is size). It is, by far, the smallest protozoan observed in water. Its size has made it difficult for laboratories to detect and has allowed it to survive the coagulation and filtration treatment processes CDCCD in improperly maintained municipal water treatment facilities. A new Environmental Protection Agency (EPA) collaborative study, the *Information Collection Rule (ICR)*, requires municipal water systems serving over 100,000 people to test their source waters for cryptosporidium. If the number of these protozoa exceed a specified limit, water systems will be required to test their treated water as well. The data obtained from this study will lead EPA to develop water quality standards relating to cryptosporidium.

Chemical Contamination

The number and types of chemical hazards that can affect human health through drinking water are as numerous as the number of chemicals created. Over 60,000 toxic chemicals are now being used by various segments of U.S. industry and agriculture. These substances range from industrial

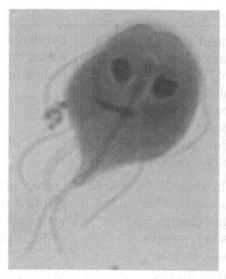

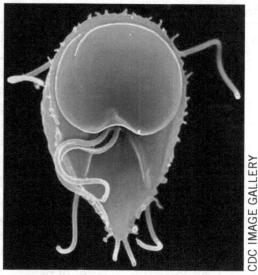

CDC IMAGE GALLERY

Two Different forms of Giardia

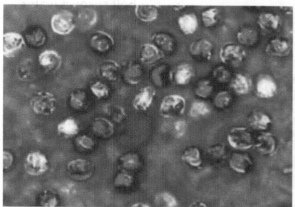

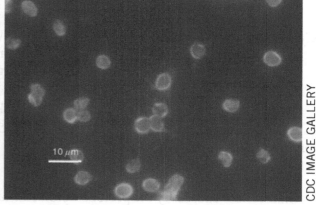

CDC IMAGE GALLERY

Cryptosporidium Seen Using Different Techniques

solvents and pesticides to cleaning preparations and septic tank degreasers. When used or discarded improperly, these chemicals can pollute ground and surface waters used as sources of drinking water. The types of illness caused by different chemicals vary widely, but can include acute and chronic toxic poisoning, cancer, or a combination of diseases. The safe levels of many chemicals are constantly being evaluated and re-evaluated. Through the National Primary Drinking Water Regulations, the Environmental Protection Agency (EPA) has established standards for many chemicals, pesticides, and radioactivity.

Desirable Characteristics of Water

Not only should water be of such quality as to present the consumer with no health threat from its direct ingestion, or indirectly when it is used for domestic or commercial processes essential to daily living activities. In addition to being potable (safe to consume), water should be pleasant to the taste (palatable), otherwise aesthetically pleasing, and present no nuisance in the form of residual stains or deposits on contact surfaces (clothes, sinks). Ironically, water may meet all the quality criteria related to palatability and aesthetics and not be potable or safe for domestic use. For this reason, it is essential that standards defining water quality be established and water quality surveillance and monitoring procedures be developed and implemented.

The Safe Drinking Water Act (SDWA)

The Safe Drinking Water Act (SDWA), Public Law 93–523, was passed in 1974 to assure that the U.S. public is provided with safe drinking water. It has been amended several times since, but the most significant and far reaching amendments occurred in 1986 – the Safe Drinking Water Act Amendments of 1986, Public Law 99–339. The SDWA authorizes the EPA to establish Federal regulations for all public water systems and to establish joint Federal-State or Federal-Tribe enforcement programs. The EPA accomplished this by setting national drinking water standards which all drinking water supplied to the public had to be in compliance.

The U.S. enforces some of the strongest drinking water standards in the world. The EPA usually is responsible for enforcing regulations on Indian lands, but under the 1986 amendments, Indian Tribes can be delegated this responsibility. Some tribes have since accepted enforcement authority responsibility, also known as "primacy." The people who supply drinking water are legally responsible for making sure the water meets the standards. The EPA, or the tribe if they have primacy, is responsible for recording sample results, conducting detailed inspections called sanitary surveys, and taking enforcement actions such as imposing fines and penalties when necessary.

Under Public Law 86–121, the Indian Sanitation Facilities Act, the Indian Health Service, Division of Environmental Health (IHS/DEH) is authorized to provide sanitation facilities for American Indians and Alaska Natives. The IHS/DEH is also authorized to provide training in operation and maintenance, but is not responsible for maintaining sanitation systems. The Indian tribes (or other non-Federal entity) and/or Indian individuals must accept the responsibility for the operation and maintenance of these systems once the project is completed and the system is providing service.

The SDWA makes the owners of public water systems responsible for complying with EPA drinking water regulations. Consequently, the Indian tribes and communities are responsible for assuring that public water systems meet these regulations. This is accomplished by a comprehensive system of water quality monitoring via scheduled sampling.

The IHS/DEH assists American Indians and Alaska Natives in the planning and construction of water supply, water treatment, and water distribution facilities on Indian lands and instructs tribal employees on the maintenance and surveillance of these facilities. IHS activities are summarized as follows:

1. Assisting tribal governments in planning and constructing new water systems.
2. Surveying existing water systems to determine existing conditions and needed repairs and encouraging proper operation and maintenance.
   a. Community Water Facilities: Follow-up surveys should be conducted twice during the first year after completion of the community water facility. Continuous consultation and assistance is provided during ongoing surveillance.
   b. Individual Water Facilities: Follow-up surveys should be made at each home once during the first year after completion of the water system and at least biennially (every 2 years) thereafter.
3. Periodic sampling and testing for the chemical and bacterial quality of water supplies used for domestic purposes and to provide recommendations for corrective action where indicated as a result of water sample analyses.

Types of Water Systems

The EPA drinking water regulations apply to community water systems (CWS), non-transient non-community water systems (NNWS), and transient non-community water systems (TNWS). They do not apply to individual water systems. The regulations governing each of these systems are slightly different. Certain contaminants cause health problems only when consumed on a regular basis over a long period of time. Therefore, these contaminants are of greater concern in systems that regularly serve the same people than in those that serve only transient users.

Community Water System. A public water system that has at least 15 service connections used by year-round residents, or regularly serves at least 25 year-round residents. Community systems include mobile home courts and homeowner associations.

Nontransient Noncommunity System. A system that regularly serves at least 25 of the same people over 6 months of the year. Examples are schools and factories.

Transient Noncommunity Systems. Systems such as restaurants, gas stations, and campgrounds that serve intermittent users. Only the maximum contaminant levels (MCLs) for turbidity, nitrate, and bacteria (coliforms) apply to transient non-community systems. These contaminants have the potential to cause illness even from short-term consumption.

Contaminant Levels

EPA sets drinking water standards that apply to community, nontransient noncommunity, and transient noncommunity water systems across the country. The enforceable standards are noted as Maximum Contaminant Levels (MCL)

MCLs are set for potentially toxic or harmful substances reflect levels That can be safely consumed in water, taking into account exposure to substances from other sources and are based on consumption of 2 liters (2 quarts) of water based fluids per day for a lifetime.

States and tribes that have "primacy" have the option to set standards which are more strict than those set by EPA.

The Safe Drinking Water Act Amendments of 1996 (PL 104–182) establish a new charter for the nation's public water systems, States, and the EPA in protecting the safety of drinking. President Clinton signed the Amendments on August 6, 1996. Copies are available from the Government Printing Office (tel. 202/512–1808; fax 202/512–2250) and by internet at:

http://www.epa.gov/OGWDW/SDWAsumm.html Revised February 12, 1999
http://www.epa.gov/ow/laws.html Revised February 22, 1999
http://www.access.gpo.gov/nara/cfr/waisidx_98/40cfr142_98.html
http://www.epa.gov/safewater/regs/cfr141.pdf (The entire SDWA)
Changes Brought About by the SDWA of 1996; The legislation:

- Requires a common-sense cost-benefit analysis be completed prior to the issuance of a drinking water standard.

- Strengthens the partnership between states, tribes, and the federal government.

- Helps small systems, whereas the original SDWA made compliance unaffordable for all but the largest of communities. Present language provides regulatory relief for systems serving under 10,000 people. Smaller systems may use less expensive alternate technologies provided they still protect public health.

- Encourages voluntary programs to control contamination of source water.

- Reduces unnecessary unfunded mandates that increase costs without improving drinking water quality. For example, the prior mandate that EPA set standards for 25 new contaminants even if there were no known health risks—has been eliminated.

- Provides financial assistance to water systems to gain compliance. A State Revolving Fund (SRF) will be established in each state according to a pre-determined formula. http://www.epa.gov/OGWDW/SDWAsumm.html#4A

- Community Right to Know: The law requires that water systems inform consumers on an annual basis on the levels of contaminants detected in tap water, what the enforceable MCLs and goals are for each contaminant and what those numbers mean. In addition, consumers will be notified of the health effects of enforceable health standards which are below MCLs, but carry a significant health concern.

Mandates a "Waterborne Disease Surveillance and Occurance Database" be maintained by EPA and the Centers for Disease Control and Prevention (CDC). The two agencies shall conduct waterborne disease investigations to determine the causes and appropriate interventions, to estimate the national occurrence of waterborne disease and to offer training and education to health care providers. The development of a national database on regulated and unregulated tap water contaminants is authorized.

National Primary and Secondary Drinking Water Regulations

National Primary Drinking Water Regulations (NPDWRs or primary standards) are legally enforceable standards that apply to public water systems. Primary standards protect drinking water quality by limiting the levels of specific contaminants that can adversely affect public health and are known or anticipated to occur in public water systems. The following Table 4.4 provides information on inorganic compounds, followed by organic chemical compounds, radionuclides and microorganisms, all of which are enforced under the NPDWR.

National Primary Drinking Water Standards
Radionuclides

CONTAMINANTS	MCLGs (MG/L) (1) (4)	MCLs (MG/L) OR TT (2) (3)	POTENTIAL HEALTH EFFECTS FROM INGESTION OF WATER	SOURCES OF CONTAMINANT IN DRINKING WATER
Beta particles and photon ememitters	None	4 millirems per year	Increased risk of cancer	Decay of natural and man-made deposits
Gross alpha Particle activity	None	15 pCi/L picocuries per liter	Increased risk of cancer	Erosion of natural deposits
Radium 226 and 228 combined	None	5 pCi/L	Increased risk of cancer	Erosion of natural deposits

Micro-organisms

CONTAMINANTS	MCLGs (MG/L) (1) (4)	MCLs (MG/L) OR TT (2) (3)	POTENTIAL HEALTH EFFECTS FROM INGESTION OF WATER	SOURCES OF CONTAMINANT IN DRINKING WATER
Giardia lamblia	Zero	TT (8)	Giardiasis, a gastro-enteric illness caused by a protozoa	Human and animal waste

(cont.)

Heterotrophic plate count (HPC)	N/A	TT (8)	HPC reflects no health threat, but indicates how effective treatment controls microbes	N/A
Legionella	Zero	TT (8)	Legionaire's Disease, commonly known as pneumonia	Found naturally in water; multiplies in heating systems
Total Coliforms (includes fecal and e-coli coliforms)	Zero	5.0% (9)	Used as an indicator that other enteric organisms may be present	Human and animal fecal waste
Turbidity	N/A	TT (8)	Reflects no health threat, but presence interferes with disinfection and provides a medium for microbial growth	Soil runoff which contains microscopic organisms and fragments of organic matter
Viruses (enteric)	Zero	TT (8)	Gastroenteric illness	Human and animal fecal waste

National Primary Drinking Water Standards

INORGANIC CONTAMINANT	MCLGs (MG/L) (1) (4)	MCL OR TT (MG/L) (2) (3)	POTENTIAL HEALTH EFFECTS FROM INGESTION	SOURCES OF CONTAMINANT IN DRINKING WATER
Antimony	0.006	0.006	Increase in blood cholesterol; decrease in blood glucose	Discharge from petroleum refineries, fire retardants; ceramics, solders
Arsenic	None (5)	0.05	Skin damage; circulatory system problems, increased risk of cancer	Discharge from semiconductor manufacturing, petroleum refining, wood preservatives, animal feed additives, herbicides, natural deposits
Asbestos (fiber < 10 μ)	7 million fibers per liter (MFL)	7 MFL	Increased risk of developing benign intestinal polyps	Decay of asbestos cement in water mains; erosion of natural deposits
Barium	2	2	Increased blood pressure	Discharge of drilling wastes, metal refineries, erosion of natural deposits
Beryllium	0.004	0.004	Intestinal lesions	Discharge from metal refineries and coal burning power plants, discharges from electrical and defense industries

National Primary Drinking Water Standards (cont.)

Cadmium	0.005	0.005	Kidney damage	Corrosion of galvanized pipes, discharge from metal refineries, runoff from waste batteries and paints
Chromium	0.1	0.1	Allergic dermatitis if exposed to excess levels for a number of years	Discharge from steel and pulp mills; erosion of natural deposits
Copper	1.3	Action level = 1.3 TT (6)	Short term exposure: gastrointestinal distress, long term exposure; liver or kidney damage.	Corrosion of household plumbing systems; erosion of natural deposits
Cyanide (as free cyanide)	0.2	0.2	Nerve damage or thyroid problems	Discharge from steel/ metal, plastic, and fertilizer factories
Fluoride	4.0	4.0	Pain and tenderness of the bones, mottled teeth in children	Water additive, erosion of natural deposits, discharge from fertilizer and aluminum factories
Lead	Zero	Action level = 0.015; TT (6)	Infants and children: Delays in mental development Adults: kidney problems, high blood pressure	Corrosion of household plumbing; erosion of natural deposits
Inorganic Mercury	0.002	0.002	Kidney damage	Erosion of natural deposits, discharges from refineries and factories; runoff from landfills and farms
Nitrate (measured as Nitrogen)	10.0	10.0	Methemoglobinemia "Blue baby syndrome" in infants under six months-life threatening without immediate medical attention, primary symptom: infant looks blue, has shortness of breath	Runoff from fertilizer use, sewage from leaking septic tanks or holding pins, erosion of natural deposits
Selenium	0.05	0.05	Hair or fingernail loss; numbness in fingers or toes, circulatory problems	Discharge from petroleum refineries; erosion of natural deposits
Thallium	0.0005	0.002	Hair loss; changes in blood; kidney, intestine, or liver problems	Leaching from ore-processing sites; discharge from electronics, glass, and pharmaceutical companies

National Primary Drinking Water Standards (cont.)

ORGANIC CONTAMINANTS	MCLGS (MG/L) (1) (4)	MCLS (MG/L) OR (2) TT (3)	POTENTIAL HEALTH EFFECTS FROM INGESTION	SOURCES OF CONTAMINANT IN DRINKING WATER
Alachlor	Zero	0.0002	Eye, liver, kidney, or spleen problems, anemia; increased risk of cancer	Runoff from herbicide used on row crops
Atrazine	0.003	0.003	Cardiovascular system problems; reproductive difficulties	Runoff from herbicide used on row crops
Benzene	Zero	0.005	Anemia; decrease in blood platelets; increased risk of cancer	Discharge from factories; leaching from underground storage tanks and landfills
Benzo(a)pyrene	Zero	0.0002	Reproductive difficulties; increased risk of cancer	Leaching from linings of storage tanks and distribution lines
Carbon Tetrachloride	Zero	0.005	Liver problems; increased risk of cancer	Discharge from chemical factories and other industrial activities
Chlordane	Zero	0.002	Liver or nervous system problems; increased risk of cancer	Residue of banned pesticides used for termites
Chlorobenzene	0.1	0.1	Liver or kidney problems	Discharges from chemical and agricultural chemical factories
2, 4-D	0.07	0.07	Kidney, liver, or adrenal gland problems	Runoff from herbicide used on row crops
1, 2-Dichloroethane	Zero	0.005	Increased risk of cancer	Discharge from industrial chemical factories
Dichloromethane	Zero	0.0005	Liver problems; increased risk of cancer	Discharge from pharmaceutical and chemical factories
Dioxin	Zero	0.00000003	Reproductive difficulties; increased risk of cancer	Emissions from waste incinerators or other combustion; discharge from chemical factories
Diquat	0.02	0.02	Cataracts	Runoff from herbicide use
Endrin	0.002	0.002	Nervous system effects	Residue of banned insecticide
Ethylbenzene	0.7	0.7	Liver or kidney problems	Discharge from petroleum factories

National Primary Drinking Water Standards (cont.)

Ethelyne Dibromide	Zero	0.00005	Stomach problems; Reproductive difficulties; increased risk of cancer	Discharge from petroleum factories
Heptachlor	Zero	0.0004	Liver damage; increased risk of cancer	Residue of banned termiticde
Lindane	0.0002	0.0002	Liver or kidney problems	Runoff/leaching from insecticide used on cattle, garden.
Methoxychlor	0.04	0.04	Reproductive difficulties	Runoff/leaching from insecticides used on fruits, vegetables, alfalfa, livestock
Polychlorinated biphenols (PCBs)	Zero	0.0005	Skin, thymus gland problems; immune deficiencies, reproductive or nervous system difficulties; risk of cancer	Runoff from landfills, discharge of waste chemicals, leaking discarded transformers
Pentachlorophenol	Zero	0.001	Liver or kidney problems; increased risk of cancer	Discharge from wood preserving factories
Styrene	0.1	0.1	Liver, kidney or circulation problems	Discharge from rubber and plastic factories; leaching from landfills
Tetrachloroethylene	Zero	0.005	Liver problems; increased risk of cancer	Discharge from factories and dry cleaners
Toluene	1	1	Nervous system, kidney, or liver problems	Discharge from petroleum factories
Total Trihalomethanes	None **(5)**	0.10	Liver, kidney, or central nervous system problems; increased risk of cancer	By-products of drinking water disinfection
Toxaphene	Zero	0.003	Kidney, liver, or thyroid problems; increased risk of cancer	Runoff/leaching from insecticide used on cotton and cattle
2, 4, 5-TP (Silvex)	0.05	0.05	Liver problems	Residue of banned herbicide
1, 2, 4-Trichlorobenzene	0.07	0.07	Changes in adrenal gland functioning	Discharge from textile finishing factories
1, 1, 1-Trichloroethane	0.2	0.2	Liver, nervous system, or circulatory problems	Discharge from industrial chemical factories
1, 1, 2-Trichloroethane	0.003	0.005	Liver, kidney, or immune system problems	Discharge from industrial chemical factories

National Primary Drinking Water Standards (cont.)

Trichloroethylene	Zero	0.005	Liver problems, increased risk of cancer	Discharge from petroleum refineries
Vinyl chloride	Zero	0.002	Increased risk of cancer	Leaching from PVC pipes; discharge from plastic factories
Xylenes	10	10	Nervous system damage	Discharge from petroleum and chemical factories

National Primary Drinking Water Standards (cont.)

Other organic chemicals and their MCLs enforced under the NPDWR include; Dalapon 0.2, 1, 2-Dibromo-3-chloropropane (DBCP) 0.0002, o-Dichlorobenzene 0.6, p-Dichlorobenzene 0.075, 1, 1-Dichloroethylene 0.007, cis-1, 2- Dichloroethylene 0.07, trans-1, 2-Dichloroethylene 0.1, 1, 2-Dichloropropane 0.005, Di(2-ethyhexl)adipate 0.4, Di(2-ethyhexl)phthalate 0.006, Dinoseb 0.007, Endothall 0.1, Epichlorohydrin TT, Glyphosate 0.7, Heptachlor epoxide 0.0002, Hexachlorobenzene 0.001, Hexachlorocyclopentadiene 0.05, Oxamyl (Vydate) 0.2, Picloram 0.5, Simazine 0.1

National Secondary Drinking Water Standards

CONTAMINANT	SMCL
Aluminum	0.05 to 0.2 mg/l
Chloride	250 mg/l
Color	15 color units
Copper	1.0 mg/l
Corrosivity (11)	Non-corrosive
Fluoride (12)	2.0 mg/l
Foaming agents	0.5 mg/l
Hexachlorocyclopentadine	0.008 mg/l
Iron	0.3 mg/l
Manganese	0.05 mg/l
Odor	3 threshold odor number
PH	6.5 – 8.5
Silver	0.1 mg/l
Sulfate	250 mg/l
Total Dissolved Solids	500 mg/l
Zinc	5 mg/l

National Secondary Drinking Water Standards

Notes accompanying Table

1. Maximum Contaminant Level Goal (MCLG) - The maximum level of a contaminant in drinking water at which no known or anticipated adverse effect on the health effect of persons would occur, and which allows for an adequate margin of safety. MCLGs are non-enforceable public health goals.

2. Maximum Contaminant Level (MCL)—The maximum permissible level of a contaminant in water which is delivered to any user of a public water system. MCLs are enforceable standards.
   The margins of safety in MCLGs ensure that exceeding the MCL slightly does not pose significant risk to public health.

3. Treatment Technique - An enforceable procedure or level of technical performance which public water systems must follow to ensure control of a contaminant.

4. Units are in milligrams per Liter (mg/L) unless otherwise noted.

5. MCLGs are yet to be established, but are mandated by the 1996 Safe Drinking Water Act Amendments. The Stage 1 D/DBP Rule will strengthen control of chemical disinfectants and their potentially cancer-causing byproducts, in drinking water. The Safe Drinking Water Act, as amended in 1996, requires EPA to develop this rule as part of a group of standards which address the risk trade-offs between microbiological contaminants and disinfection byproducts. These rules, collectively called the microbial and disinfection byproducts (M/DBP) rules, are the first to address the waterborne pathogen, Cryptosporidium, in drinking water. The Stage 1 DBP Rule and the Interim Enhanced Surface Water Treatment Rule (IESWTR), proposed in July 1994, are expected to be finalized in the near future. Therefore, there is no MCLG for this contaminant.

6. Lead and copper are regulated in a Treatment Technique which requires systems to take tap water samples at sites with lead pipes or copper pipes that have lead solder and/or are served by lead service lines. The action level, which triggers water systems into taking treatment steps if exceeded in more than 10% of tap water samples, for copper is 1.3 mg/L, and for lead is 0.015mg/L. Review Subpart I of the SDWA for monitoring frequency and exemptions for medium size water systems at http://www.epa.gov/safewater/regs/cfr141.pdf

7. Each water system must certify, in writing, to the state (using third-party or manufacturer's certification) that when acrylamide and epichlorohydrin are used in drinking water systems, the combination (or product) of dose and monomer level does not exceed the levels specified, as follows:
   Acrylamide = 0.05% dosed at 1 mg/L (or equivalent)
   Epichlorohydrin = 0.01% dosed at 20 mg/L (or equivalent)

8. The Surface Water Treatment Rule requires systems using surface or ground water under the direct influence of surface water to (1) disinfect their water, and (2) filter their water to meet criteria for avoiding filtration so that the following contaminants are controlled at the following levels:
   Giardia lamblia: 99.9% killed/inactivated

   - Viruses: 99.99% killed/inactivated
   - Legionella: No limit. EPA believes that if Giardia and viruses are inactivated, Legionella will also be controlled.
   - Turbidity: At no time can turbidity (cloudiness of water) go above 5 nephelolometric turbidity units (NTU); systems that filter must ensure that the level go no higher than 1NTU (0.5 NTU for conventional or direct filtration) in at least 95% of the daily samples in any month.
   - Heterotrophic Plate Count (HPC): No more than 500 colonies per milliliter.

9. No more than 5.0% samples total coliform-positive in a month. (For water systems that collect fewer than 40 routine samples per month, no more than one sample can be total coliform-positive). Every sample that has total coliforms must be analyzed for fecal coliforms. The presence of fecal coliforms is never to be allowed.

10. Fecal coliform and E. coli are bacteria whose presence indicates that the water may be contaminated with human animal wastes. Microbes in these wastes can cause diarrhea, cramps, nausea, headaches, or other symptoms.

11. Corrosivity is not an inorganic but is a measure of the saturation level of calcium carbonate. Under certain conditions, as calculated by the Langelier Index, calcium carbonate may be deposited onto the inside of water system pipes, protecting them from corrosion, or deposits may be stripped from water system pipes, subjecting them to greater potential for corrosion. Excessive calcium carbonate depositing will clog the pipe. Corrosivity is calculated from measurements of the pH, calcium hardness, alkalinity, temperature, and total dissolved solids (TDS). Water system owners must report the corrosivity to the EPA/state. Optimal corrosion control (maintaining a thin coat of calcium carbonate on the pipe walls) is good practice and may be required by the EPA/state regulatory agency (e.g., for lead and copper corrosion control).

12. Fluoride is a natural mineral contained in most drinking water. In the proper amounts, fluoride in drinking water prevents cavities if the water is consumed during the formative years. This is why many communities add fluoride in controlled amounts to their water supply. The maximum amount of fluoride allowed in drinking water by national standard is 4.0 mg/L (milligrams per liter). Exposure to drinking water levels above 4.0 mg/L for many years may result in some cases of crippling skeletal fluorosis or serious bone disorder. Fluoride in children's drinking water at levels of approximately 1 mg/L reduces the number of dental cavities. However, some children exposed to levels of fluoride greater than 2.0 mg/L may develop dental fluorosis, a brown staining or pitting of the teeth. EPA has set a secondary MCL of 2.0 mg/L for fluoride.

The SMCL levels noted in Table 4.6 represent reasonable goals for drinking water quality. The States may establish higher or lower levels which may be appropriate dependent upon local conditions such as unavailability of alternate source waters or other compelling factors, provided that public health and welfare are not adversely affected. [44 FR 42198, July 19, 1979, as amended at 51 FR 11412, Apr. 2, 1986; 56 FR 3597, Jan. 30, 1991], Revised July 1, 1998. These SMCLs are not federally enforced.

Synthetic Organic Chemicals (SOCs) & Volatile Organic Chemicals (VOCs)

SOCs are man-made, non-volatile, carbon-containing, chemical compounds used for a variety of industrial and agricultural purposes, usually herbicides and pesticides. Millions of pounds of pesticides are used on crop lands, forests, lawns, and gardens in the United States each year. They drain off into surface water or seep into underground water supplies. *VOCs* are man-made compounds, such as solvents, used for a variety of industrial and manufacturing purposes. They readily volatilize, or travel from water into the air. Table 4.5 lists SOCs and VOCs as Organic compounds. In January 1991, EPA established what the "Standardized Monitoring Framework (SMF)." The SMF, was based on a 9-year (calendar year) compliance cycle, with the first cycle beginning on January 1, 1993. The 9-year compliance cycle contains three, 3-year compliance periods. The first 3-year compliance period extends from 1993 to 1995. The second 9-year compliance cycle begins in 2002 and extends through 2010. Table 4.7 reflects those Organic and Inorganic compounds the IHS currently monitors with the Phase II and V compliance timetables noted. The monitoring timetables will change in the near future to reflect the 1996 amendments. The Safe Drinking Water Act (SDWA), as amended in 1996, requires the Environmental Protection Agency (EPA) to establish a list of contaminants to aid in priority-setting for the Agency's drinking water program. In establishing the list, EPA has divided the contaminants among those which are priorities for additional research, those which need additional occurrence data, and those which are priorities for consideration for rulemaking. EPA published a draft of the first Drinking Water Contaminant Candidate List (CCL) in the October 6, 1997 Federal Register (62 FR 52193). The final CCL, which was published in the March 2, 1998 Federal Register (63 FR 10273). It includes a list of 43 organic and inorganic compounds and 113 microbiological agents. A complete CCL list can be reviewed at http://www.epa.gov/OGWDW/ccl/cclfs.html

Phase II VOCs
(Volatile Organic Compounds)

CONTAMINANT	MCL-(MG/L)
Benzene	0.005
Carbon tetrachloride	0.005
1, 2 Dichloroethane	0.005
1, 1 Dichloroethylene	0.007
Para-Dichlorobenzene	0.075
1, 1, 1-Trichloroethane	0.20
Trichloroethylene	0.005
Vinyl chloride	0.002
o-Dichlorobenzene	0.6
Cis-1-2-Dichloroethylene	0.07
Trans-1-2-Dichloroethylene	0.1
1-2-Dichloropropane	0.005
Ethylbenzene	0.7
Monochlorobenzene	0.1
Styrene	0.1
Tetrachloroethylene	0.005
Toluene	1
Xylenes (Total)	10

Phase V VOCs
(Volatile organic chemicals)

CONTAMINANT	MCL-(MG/L)
Dichloromethane	0.005
1, 2, 4 Trichlorobenzene	0.07
1, 1, 2-Trichloroethane	0.005

Phase II IOCs
(Inorganic compounds)

CONTAMINANT	MCL-(MG/L)
Cadmium	0.005
Chromium	0.1
Mercury	0.002
Selenium	0.05
Barium	2

Unregulated organics: Aldacarb, Aldrin, Buta-
chlor, Carbaryl, Dieldrin, 3-Hydroxycarbofuran.
Unregulated inorganics: sulfur

Water Contaminant Candidate (cont.)

Phase V IOCs
(Inorganic compounds)

CONTAMINANT	MCL-(MG/L)
Antimony	0.006
Beryllium	0.004
Cyanide	0.2
Nickel	0.1
Thallium	0.002

Phase II SOCs
(Synthetic organic chemicals)

CONTAMINANT	MCL-(MG/L)
Alachlor	0.002
Atrazine	0.003
Carbofuran	0.04
Chlordane	0.002
Dibromochloropropane	0.0002
2,4-D	0.07
Ethylene Dibromide	0.00005
Heptachlor	0.0004
Heptachlor epoxide	0.0002
Lindane	0.0002
Methoxchlor	0.04
Pentachlorophenol	0.001
PCBs	0.0005
Toxaphene	0.003
2, 4, 5-TP	0.05

Phase V SOCs
(Synthetic organic chemicals)

CONTAMINANT	MCL-(MG/L)
Dalapon	0.2
Dinoseb	0.007
Diquat	0.02
Endothall	0.01
Endrin	0.002
Glyphosate	0.7
Oxamyl (Vydate)	0.2
Picloram	0.5
Simazine	0.004
Benzo(a)pyrene	0.0002
Di(2-ethylhexyl)adipate	0.4
Di(2-ethylhexyl)phthalate	0.00
Hexachlorobenzene	0.001
Hexachlorocyclopenta-diene	0.05
2, 3, 7, 8-TCDD (Dioxin)	3×10^{-8}

Water Contaminant Candidate

Coliform Monitoring

The maximum contaminant level (MCL) for total coliform bacteria, applicable to community and non-community water systems are as follows:

1. Compliance is based on presence/absence coliform tests, rather than a quantitative count of colonies.
2. For systems analyzing at least 40 samples per month, no more than 5 % of the monthly samples may be total coliform positive.
3. The system must analyze all total coliform cultures to determine if fecal coliforms are present. If fecal coliforms or E-coli are present, the system must notify the State by the end of the day when notified of the test results.
4. For systems analyzing less than 40 samples per month, no more than one may be total

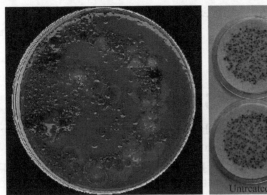

CDC Image Gallery

Coliform Test

Total Coliform Sampling Requirements According to Population Served

POPULATION SERVED	MINIMUM NO. OF SAMPLES PER MONTH	POPULATION SERVED	MINIMUM NO. OF SAMPLES PER MONTH
25 to 1,000	1	59,001 to 70,000	70
1,001 to 2500	2	70,001 to 83,000	80
2,501 to 3,300	3	83,001 to 96,000	90
3,301 to 4,100	4	96,001 to 130,000	100
4,101 to 4,900	5	130,001 to 220,000	120
4,901 to 5,800	6	220,001 to 320,000	150
5,801 to 6,700	7	320,001 to 450,000	180
6,701 to 7,600	8	450,001 to 600,000	210
7,601 to 8,500	9	600,001 to 780,000	240
8,501 to 12,900	10	780,001 to 970,000	270
12,901 to 17,200	15		
17,201 to 21,500	20		
21,501 to 25,000	25		
25,001 to 33,000	30		
33,001 to 41,000	40		
41,001 to 50,000	50		
50,001 to 59,000	60		

The monitoring requirements for total coliforms include a written sample siting plan and monthly monitoring based on population (See Table)

Laboratory Analysis and Sampling Requirements

For compliance monitoring purposes, analyses must be performed in an EPA or state-approved laboratory. To ensure proper sampling and analysis, the following guidelines should be followed:

1. Samples must be collected in proper containers and preserved as necessary. (Discuss sample and collection procedures in advance with the laboratory.)

2. Sample chain of custody must be maintained to ensure accountability.
3. The analysis must be performed within specified holding times (the period of time between sample collection and analysis).

How to Take Bacteriological Water Samples

Routine and special bacteriological samples must be taken and transferred in accordance with established procedures to prevent accidental contamination and must be analyzed by an EPA or state certified laboratory. The laboratory will usually provide specially prepared sample containers, properly sterilized and containing sodium thiosulfate to destroy any remaining chlorine. The following steps should be followed in coliform sampling:

Use only containers for bacteriological analysis that are provided by the laboratory and that have been prepared for coliform sampling. Follow all instructions for sample container handling and storage. Note: the containers are sterile; do not open them before use and do not rinse them. containing sodium thiosulfate to destroy any remaining chlorine. The following steps should be followed in coliform sampling:

1. Take a second sample and measure the concentration of the disinfectant and record relevant information (date, time, concentration, place, sampler, etc.).
2. Package the bacteriological sample for delivery to the laboratory. Record all pertinent field information on a form and on the sample container label.

Samples must be cool during shipment to the laboratory. Use insulated boxes for shipping containers, if needed, or refrigerate during transit. Note: do not allow more than 30 hours between sampling and test times. Be sure the laboratory can process the samples immediately upon receipt.

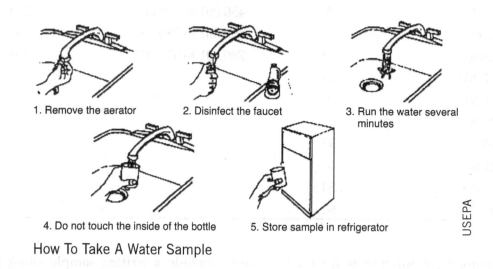

1. Remove the aerator   2. Disinfect the faucet   3. Run the water several minutes

4. Do not touch the inside of the bottle   5. Store sample in refrigerator

USEPA

How To Take A Water Sample

Public Notification if Drinking Water Regulations Are Violated

Public drinking water systems are required to notify their customers when drinking water standards are violated. The purpose of public notification is to inform consumers of any potential adverse health effects and to describe what steps consumers can take to minimize the impact. Public notification regulations are now in effect for all contaminants that a system is required to monitor. There are six violations or events that require public notification.

1. Failure to comply with an applicable maximum contaminant level (MCL).
2. Failure to comply with a prescribed treatment technique.
3. Failure to perform water quality monitoring (testing) as required.
4. Failure to comply with testing procedures as prescribed by a National Primary Drinking Water Regulation.
5. Issuance of a variance or an exemption.
6. Failure to comply with the requirements of any schedule that has been set under a variance or exemption.

Public notification by the owner or operator of the public water system is mandated in the event any of the above scenarios exists.

For communities with a daily or weekly newspaper of general circulation:

Violations notices through the newspaper must be made within 14 days of the violation and a direct notice provided by mail or hand delivered within 45 days; repeat every three months as long as the violation continues. Any violations specified by the State as posing an acute risk to human health, the owner or operator of the system shall provide notice over the television and radio within 72 hours.

Information that must be included in the public notice:

1. Provide a clear and readily understandable explanation of the violation. It must not contain unduly technical language or be in small print.
2. Information about potential adverse health effects.
3. Information about the population at risk.
4. Information about the necessity of seeking alternative water supplies, if any.
5. Preventive measures that should be taken until the violation is corrected.
6. Phone number of the owner or operator to contact at the public water system as a source of additional information.
7. Where appropriate, notices must be multi-lingual.
8. Steps being taken to correct the violation.

Record Keeping

Federal regulations require an owner or operator of a public water system to retain the following records on its premises or at a nearby location:

1. Records of bacteriological analyses made shall be kept for no less than 5 years.
   Records of chemical analyses shall be kept for not less than 10 years. Actual laboratory reports may be kept or data may be transferred to tabular summaries provided the following information is included:
   a. Date, place, time of sampling, and the name of the person collecting the sample.
   b. Identification of the sample as to whether it was a routine check sample, distribution system sample, raw or process water sample, or other special purpose sample.
   c. Date of analysis.
   d. Laboratory and person responsible for performing analysis.
   e. The analytical technique/method used.
   f. The results of the analysis.
2. Records of action taken by the system to correct violations shall be kept for not less than 3 years after the last action taken with respect to the particular violation involved.
3. Copies of any written reports, summaries, or communications relating to sanitary surveys or vulnerability assessments conducted by the system itself, a private consultant, or any local, state, or Federal agency shall be kept for a period not less than 10 years after completion. Therefore, IHS sanitary surveys should be provided to the tribes.

Records concerning a variance or exemption granted to the system shall be kept for a period not less than 5 years following the expiration of such variance or exemption.

What is Hard Or Soft Water?

In addition to EPA mandatory and recommended standards, water hardness is an important property of water, especially groundwater. Many problems, including reduced water pressure, water heater scale, soap curd, ring around the bathtub, difficulties with laundering, and clogged water pipes can be caused by hard water. Hardness is a term used to describe waters that are highly mineralized. Calcium and magnesium ions cause the largest percentage of hardness properties. The term "soft water" inversely is a term used to describe water that contains low amounts of dissolved calcium and magnesium. This is a function of the geological formations through which water flows and hence is variable depending on the location. Approximately 85 percent of the United States can be classified as hard water areas. Hardness is generally expressed in terms of milligrams per liter (mg/l) as calcium carbonate ($CaCO_3$) or grains per gallon.

0–75	mg/l as CaCO	Soft
75–150	mg/l as CaCO	Moderately hard
150–300	mg/l as CaCO	Hard
300+	mg/l as CaCO	Very hard

Photo by Beck

Sampling Drinking Water At the Well Head

Pharmaceuticals In Our Water Supplies

Are "Drugged Waters" a Water Quality Threat?

Developed to promote human health and well being, certain pharmaceuticals are now attracting attention as a potentially new class of water pollutants. Such drugs as antibiotics, anti-depressants, birth control pills, seizure medication, cancer treatments, pain killers, tranquilizers and cholesterol-lowering compounds have been detected in varied water sources.

Where do they come from? Pharmaceutical industries, hospitals and other medical facilities are obvious sources, but households also contribute a significant share. Most people dispose of unused medicines by flushing them down toilets, and human excreta can contain varied incompletely metabolized medicines. These drugs can pass intact through conventional sewage treatment facilities, into waterways, lakes and even aquifers. Further, discarded pharmaceuticals often end up at dumps and land fills, posing a threat to underlying groundwater.

Farm animals also are a source of pharmaceuticals entering the environment, through their ingestion of hormones, antibiotics and veterinary medicines. (About 40 percent of U.S.-produced antibiotics are fed to livestock as growth enhancers.) Manure containing traces of such pharmaceuticals is spread on land and can then wash off into surface water and even percolate into groundwater.

Along with pharmaceuticals, personal care products also are showing up in water. Often these chemicals are the active ingredients or preservatives in cosmetics, toiletries or fragrances.

For example, nitro musks, used as a fragrance in many cosmetics, detergents, toiletries and other personal care products, have of concern because of their persistence and possible adverse environmental impacts. Some countries have taken action to ban nitro musks. Sun screen agents have been detected in many lakes and in the fish.

Researchers Christian G. Daughton and Thomas A. Ternes reported in the December 2009 issue of "Environmental Health Perspectives" that the amount of pharmaceuticals and personal care products entering the environment annually is about equal to the amount of pesticides used each year.

Concern about the water quality impacts of these chemicals first gained prominence in Europe, where for over a decade scientists have been checking lakes, streams, and groundwater for pharmaceutical contamination. American officials and scientists are taking note.

The issue emerged in Europe about ten years ago, when German environmental scientists found clofibric acid, a cholesterol-lowering drug, in groundwater beneath a German water treatment plant. They later found clofibric acid throughout local waters, and a further search found phenazone and fenofibrate, drugs used to regulate concentrations of lipids in the blood, and analgesics such as ibuprofen and diclofenac in groundwater under a sewage plant. Other European researchers discovered chemotherapy drugs, antibiotics and hormones in drinking water sources.

In the United States, the issue might have attracted earlier notice if officials had followed up on observations made 20 years ago. At that time, EPA scientists found that sludge from a U.S. sewage-treatment plant contained excreted aspirin, caffeine and nicotine. However, no significance was attached to the findings at that time.

In Phoenix AZ about this time another event occurred that should have alerted officials that pharmaceuticals could pose a water quality threat. Herman Bouwer of the U.S. Agricultural Research Service in Phoenix recalls that clofibric acid was found in groundwater below infiltration basins that were artificially recharging groundwater with sewage effluent. Bouwer says more attention should have been paid to the finding; if clofibric acid could pass through a sewage treatment plant and percolate into the groundwater so also could many other drugs.

Europeans, have taken the lead in researching the issue. In the mid-1990s, Thomas A. Ternes, a chemist in Wiesbaden, Germany, investigated what happens to prescribed medicines after they are excreted. Ternes knew that many such drugs are prescribed, and that little was known of the environmental effects of these compounds after they are excreted. He researched the presence of drugs in sewage, treated water and rivers, and his findings surprised him.

Expecting to identify a few medicinal compounds he instead found **30 of the 60 common pharmaceuticals** that he surveyed. Drugs he identified included lipid-lowering drugs, antibiotics, analgesics, antiseptics, beta-blocker heart drugs, residues of drugs for controlling epilepsy as well as drugs serving as contrast agents for diagnostic X rays.

Results of recent research in North America also indicate reason for concern. At the June National Groundwater Association conference, Glen R. Boyd, a Tulane University civil engineer, reported detecting drugs in the Mississippi River, Lake Ponchetrain and in Tulane's tap water. Boyd and his team found in tested waters low levels of clofibric acid, the pain killer naproxen and the hormone **estrone**. Samples of Tulane's tap water showed estrone averaging 45 parts per trillion with a high of 80 parts per trillion.

At the recent American Chemical Society conference, Chris Metcalfe of Trent University in Ontario reported finding a vast array of drugs leaving Canadian sewage treatment plants, at times at higher levels than what is reported in Germany. Such drugs included anticancer agents, psychiatric drugs and anti-inflammatory compounds. North American treatment plants may show higher levels of pharmaceuticals because they often lack the technological sophistication of German facilities for water sampling.

The U.S.G.S. is currently conducting the first nationwide assessment of "emerging contaminants" found in selected streams, including the occurrence of human and veterinary pharmaceuticals, sex and steroidal hormones and other drugs such as antidepressants and antacids. One hundred stream sites were identified, representing a wide variety of geographical and hydrogeological settings. Mapping of human genome means more drugs, possibly more pollution.

Pharmaceuticals are greatly increasing in numbers and kinds, with greater likelihood of releases into the environment. Before the recent announcement of the almost complete categorization of the human genome, Christian G. Daughton and Thomas A. Ternes wrote in an article that appeared in Environmental Health Perspectives, "The enormous array of pharmaceuticals will continue to diversify and grow as the human genome is mapped. Today there are about 500 distinct biochemical receptors at which drugs are targeted. . . . The number of targets is expected to increase 20-fold (yielding 3,000 to 10,000 drug targets) in the near future." The authors warn, "This explosion in new drugs will severely exacerbate our limited knowledge of drugs in the environment and possibly increase the exposure/effects risks to nontarget organisms."

Detected contaminants include caffeine, which was the highest-volume pollutant, codeine, cholesterol-lowering agents, anti-depressants, and Premarin, an estrogen replacement drug taken by about 9 million women. Also chemotherapy agents were found downstream from hospitals treating cancer patients. Final results from the study are expected to be released in the fall. For additional information about the U.S.G.S. study check the website: toxics.usgs.gov/regional/emc.html

What risk does chronic exposure to trace concentrations of pharmaceuticals pose to humans or wildlife? Some scientists believe pharmaceuticals do not pose problems to humans since they occur at low concentrations in water. Other scientists say long-term and synergistic effects of pharmaceuticals and similar chemicals on humans are not known and advise caution. They are concerned that many of these drugs have the potential of interfering with hormone production. Chemicals with this effect are called endocrine disrupters and are attracting the attention of water quality experts.

To some scientists the release of antibiotics into waterways is particularly worrisome. They fear the release may result in disease-causing bacteria to become immune to treatment and that drug-resistant diseases will develop.

Scientists generally agree that aquatic life is most at risk, its life cycle, from birth to death, occurring within potentially drug-contaminated waters. For example, anti-depressants have been blamed for altering sperm levels and spawning patterns in marine life. Most studies of pharmaceutical and pharmaceutically active chemicals in water have mostly focused on aquatic animals.

For example, recent British research suggest that estrogen, the female sex hormone, is primarily responsible for deforming reproductive systems of fish, noting that blood plasma from male trout living below sewage treatment plants had the female egg protein vitellogenin. This finding would seem to be consistent with what U.S. researchers suspect has occurred downstream from treatment plants in Las Vegas and Minneapolis. Carp in these areas show the same effects as the British fish.

Some scientists believe arid regions of the West are especially vulnerable to the effects of drug-contaminated effluent. These areas are more likely to have streams that rely almost entirely on effluent for flow, especially during dry months. Further, effluent is extensively used in irrigation and even for recharging drinking water aquifers. Also, areas of the West have attracted large number of retired people who are likely to use more pharmaceuticals than other population segments; thus more pharmaceuticals in wastewater. The FDA advises that certain painkillers (e.g, OxyContin, Morphine, Percocet) be flushed down the toilet instead of thrown in the trash.

At his time I know of no environmentally responsible way pf disposing of left over or unwanted drugs. All of the proposed disposal methods are inadequate but listed below are the methods and their pros and cons.

Many people have and will continue to throw expired medication in the garbage. We now know, however, that medicine can actually get into our soil, creating an environmental hazard. Others tend to flush any outdated drugs. This was considered the best method because there was no danger of children and pets accidentally ingesting pills. Flushing medicine also presents an environmental hazard.

So, if we can't throw away expired medicine and we can't flush them, what can we do to ensure they're properly disposed of? Listed below are the various ways people have suggested disposal, they are well intended but each very flawed:

• Option 1 is to contact your pharmacy. A few pharmacies now have drug recycling programs in place. Some take it back at any time, others hold periodic drives to collect expired medicine. Either way, they'll take back your expired medication and see to it that they're disposed of in the proper manner. If your pharmacist doesn't take back your old drugs, he or she may have an alternate recommendation. They should be ask what they do with the returned medicines.

- Option 2 is to take any old pills and pulverize them. Return them to their child-safe container and place the container inside several thick zip lock plastic bags or a thick plastic container. This can now be tossed into the household trash. There are several problems with this method, however. Many people don't like to waste their bags and containers. Plastic doesn't always degrade so easily if at all. In addition, the medicine will eventually leak out and present a hazard. Besides, one thing we don't need is more landfill.

- Option 3, there are organizations that donate expired medicine to third world countries. Even though your medicine may have expired, it may still be good long past the printed date. (Only professionals can determine this.) Rather than have it waste away in your medicine cabinet, why not donate it where it will be put to good use? An internet search will provide you with such organizations. This is a well intentioned but very bad idea, the medicine may have turned toxic with age, may no longer be effective, and violates basic moral standards.

Since expired medicine is considered hazardous waste, it stands to reason it should be disposed as such. Contact your local hazardous waste facility to see its recommendations. If your city or town has a website, there are probably instructions on how to dispose of hazardous waste. See if medicine is listed. If it is, you can either bring it to the hazardous waste site or set it out for pick up on the designated date. Even if nothing is listed on the website, you can call the facility to either see if this is something it handles, or if it has a recommendation.

The ultimate solution is likely to be a state or federal law that who ever sells the materials will be required to dispose of it and treat like hazardous waste.

Water Systems and Treatment Karst Topography

Introduction

The primary sources of drinking water are groundwater and surface water. In addition, precipitation (rain and snow) can be collected and contained. The initial quality of the water depends on the source. Surface water, such as lakes, streams, and rivers which is the drinking water source for

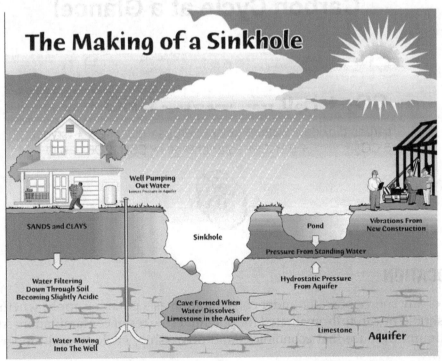

approximately 50% of our population, is generally of poor quality due to pollution and requires extensive treatment. Groundwater, which serves the other approximate 50% of our population is of better quality, but still may be contaminated by agricultural runoff, or surface and subsurface disposal of liquid waste. This includes leachate from solid waste landfills. Well water coming from sources in Kart Topography (see below) should be treated as surface water unless sanitary surveys demonstrate safety. Other sources, such as spring water and rain water, are of varying levels of quality, but each can be developed and treated to render it potable.

Most water systems consist of a water source such as a well, spring, or surface supply, some type of tank for water storage, and a system of pipes to distribute the water. Means to treat the water to remove harmful bacteria or chemicals may also be required. The system can be as simple as a well, pump, and a pressure tank to serve a single home or it may be a complex system with elaborate treatment processes, multiple storage tanks, and a large distribution system serving thousands of homes. Regardless of system size, the basic principles to assure the safety and potability of water are common to all systems. Remember the lesson from the previous chapter that water is a dipolar, magnetic molecule that does not want to stay pure. It will naturally pick up heavy metals and impurities materials until it meets its maximum in saturation (the state when a magnetic material is fully ulilized Carbonic acid is the inorganic compound with the formula H_2CO_3 (equivalently $OC(OH)_2$). It is also a name sgiven to solutions of carbon dioxide in water, which contain small amounts of H_2CO_3. The salts of carbonic acids are called bicarbonates (or hydrogen carbonates) and carbonates. It is a weak acid. Carbonic acid is sometimes confused with carbolic acid, an antiquated name for phenol. When dissolved in water, carbon dioxide exists in equilibrium with carbonic acid:

- As water infiltrates through pore spaces in the soil, it first passes through the zone of aeration, where the soil is unsaturated. At increasing depths water fills in more spaces, until the zone of saturation is reached. The relatively horizontal plane atop this zone constitutes the water table. A sustainable amount of water within a unit of sediment or rock, below the water table, in the phreatic zone is called an aquifer. The ability of the aquifer to store groundwater is dependent on the primary and secondary porosity and permeability of the rock or soil.

$CO_2 + H_2O !Ã$ The creation of water is a product of the Carbon Cycle shown below:

Carbon Cycle at a Glance!

$$CHO + O_2 \text{-----Heat---} CO_2 + H_2O$$

$$CO_2 + H_2O \text{--------------} CHO + O$$

carbon dioxide + water + solar energy -> glucose + oxygen
6 CO_2 + 6 H_2O + solar energy -> C6H12O6 + 6 O

SOURCE LOCATION

The location of any source of water under consideration as a potable supply, whether individual or community, should be carefully evaluated for potential sources of contamination. As a general practice, the maximum distance that economics, land ownership, geology, and topography will allow should separate a water source from potential contamination sources. Table 5.1 details some of the more common sources of contamination and gives minimum distances recommended to separate pollution sources from the water source

Water withdrawn directly from rivers, lakes, or reservoirs can not be assumed as being clean enough for human consumption unless receiving treatment. Water pumped from underground aquifers will require some level of treatment. To entertain the thought that surface water or soil-filtered water has purified itself is dangerous and unjustified. Clear water is not necessarily safe water. To determine what level of treatment a water source requires, one should:

1. Determine the quality needed for the intended purpose (drinking water quality needs to be evaluated under the SDWA).
2. For wells and springs, test the water for bacteriological quality. This should be done with several samples taken over a period of time to establish a history on the source. With few exceptions, surface water and groundwater sources are always presumed to be bacteriologically unsafe and, as a minimum, must be disinfected.
3. Analyze for chemical quality including both legal (primary drinking water) standards and aesthetic (secondary) standards.
4. Determine the economical and technical restraints (cost of equipment, Operation and maintenance costs, cost of alternative sources, availability of power, etc.).
5. Treat if necessary and feasible.

MINIMUM DISTANCE BETWEEN WATER SYSTEM COMPONENTS & POLLUTION SOURCES
Horizontal Distance In Feet

POLLUTION SOURCE	WELL	PRESSURE LINE	WATER SUPPLY STREAM
Sewer	50	50	50
Sewer with water tight joints	10	10	10
Septic tank	50	10	50
Subsurface pits, seepage pits, and cesspools	50	50	50
Subsurface disposal drainfield	150	50	50
Barnyard	150	50	150

MUNICIPAL WATER SUPPLIES

As described in Chapter 4, municipal water supplies can be as small as serving 15 residences or may serve a metropolitan area of millions. The level of treatment provided depends on initial quality of the water. Water treatment can involve an extremely wide variety of procedures including storage and sedimentation, aeration, filtration, mineral removal, pH control, taste and odor control, disinfection, softening, algae control, fluoridation, and a host of others. Each of these processes shall be briefly described after the following general discussion of the basics of water treatment.

Prior to the treatment processes illustrated in Figure 5.1, the following steps may have to be incorporated to physically pre-treat the water to produce a cleaner raw water product and thus make preceding treatment more efficient.

Storage & Sedimentation. When surface water is impounded, the water undergoes treatment by natural settling (pre-sedimentation), sunlight, and oxidation. It is advantageous to draw surface water from a lake or impoundment rather than a stream to allow for natural settling. Suspended solids, color, and turbidity (cloudiness) are usually reduced by this process. Algae growth may be a seasonal problem that must be dealt with in some instances.

Aeration. Aeration is a process of bringing water in close contact with air either by forcing air through water or spraying water into the air. The process is used to reduce taste and odor, reduce gases such as carbon dioxide, methane, and hydrogen sulfide as well as other treatment.

Screening. Raw water from lakes, ponds, ground or river enters through a bar screen to large debris and possibly fish from entering the POTW.

Flash mix. Water is diverted through a small basin where chemicals are added, such as coagulants, chemicals to adjust pH, and control odors are vigorously mixed with the water. *Coagulation* begins to occur as soon as chemical coagulants are added to the flash mix tank. Coaguants such as Aluminum sulfate (alum), are used to enhance the settling out of suspended solids. Suspended solids cannot be completely removed from water by natural settling. Small particles, known as colloids, will not settle out without the help of coagulants.

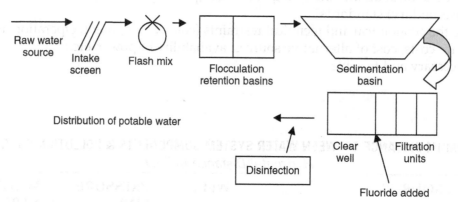

TYPICAL MUNICIPAL WATER TREATMENT FACILITY (POTW)

Flocculation. Colloidal particles stay suspended in water because they are electrostatically charged particles that repel each other when they collide. Coagulants neutralize the charged particles which causes them to adhere or "floc" together. This flocculant mass, now of greater weight, will easily settle to the bottom in the following *sedimentation basins.*

Filtration. This process is one of the most widely used processes for surface water and is used in the treatment of some ground water conditions, such as highly dissolved iron and manganese. Filtration involves the removal of various suspended particles and bacteria by allowing the water to pass through a layer or bed of porous granular material, such as sand. As the water passes through, particles become trapped or adsorbed within the pore spaces of the filter material. Regulations require nearly all surface water sources and some other sources to be filtered.

Disinfection/Chlorination. This process of adding chemicals, generally chlorine, to water to kill bacteria or oxidize organic compounds is probably the most important and widely practiced water treatment activity. All surface water sources and all community ground water sources (depending on their history) need to be continuously chlorinated. Chlorine can be added to water as free chlorine gas or in the form of chlorine compounds.

Fluoridation. It has been proven that correct levels of fluoride in drinking water reduces the number of dental caries or cavities in children by as much as 20%–40%. Extensive research over the years has demonstrated that a fluoride concentration of about 1 mg/L is effective in preventing tooth decay, especially in children without any harmful side effects. (Nathanson, 1997) Too much fluoride in drinking water can lead to dental fluorosis, a mottling or discolroration of the teeth. The maximum allowable concentration of fluoride is 1.4 mg. L in warm regions of the country and 2.4 mg/L in colder climates. Climate affects water consumption.

Other treatment processes utilized in the treatment of groundwater or possibly surface water include:

Water Softening. "Hardness" in water is caused primarily by the presence of calcium and magnesium ions, but the presence of iron, copper, manganese, zinc, lead, and barium may also cause slight increases in hardness. The two primary methods of softening water are the lime-soda process where calcium carbonate and magnesium hydroxide are formed and settled or filtered out and the zeolite or ion exchange process where calcium and magnesium ions are exchanged for sodium ions.

Corrosion Control. Some waters adversely affect the pumping and plumbing system unless properly controlled. Of particular concern are metals which are dissolved in trace amounts by corrosive waters. Lead solder used in many older systems may result in a local high lead concentration in water during periods of low use. To control corrosion it may be necessary to use nonmetallic pipes, use metal resistant to corrosion, use protective coatings on plumbing, control pH of the water, and use electrical cathodic protection which uses a metal anode to protect the rest of the metal in the tank or system.

WATER SUPPLIES FOR SMALL COMMUNITIES AND INDIVIDUAL HOMES

Many smaller communities obtain drinking water solely from underground aquifers. In addition. 25% of the people in the rural areas of the United States are on individual water supply systems. It is estimated that no less than 18 Million Americans have contaminated well water. In some sections of the country there may be a choice of individual water supply sources which will supply water throughout the year. Some areas of the country may be limited to one only one source. For their water supply. Dug wells were primarily used In the United States before the 1950s, but are still in existence in many rural areas in the U.S. and are common in underdeveloped areas of the World.

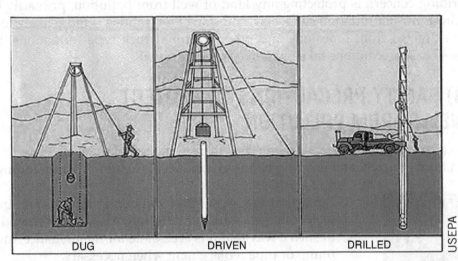

Types of Private Drinking Water Wells

- Typically, these types of wells are often built with a shovel and another pulling the dirt from the hole with a rope, pulley, and a bucket.
- The well is built below the water table until incoming water exceeds the digger's filling rate.
- Dug wells can then be lined with any of the following: stones, bricks, tile, concrete, mortar, porous concrete to prevent the well from collapsing.
- Traditionally, dug wells are quite shallow, ~25 feet deep with a large circumference hole used as a manhole for original construction.

The various sources of water include:

- Drilled wells
- Driven wells
- Jetted wells
- Dug wells
- Bored wells
- Springs
- Cisterns

Regardless of the choice for a water supply source, special safety precautions must be taken to assure the potability of the water. Since the large majority of families and communities utilize groundwater via water well development, the following section addresses the issues of placement of the well(s) sanitary design, and construction.

WELL SITE SELECTION

When determining where a water well or wells are to be located, several factors should be considered. Well site selection is based on:

- The groundwater aquifer to be developed
- Depth of the water bearing formations
- The type of rock formations one will encounter
- Freedom from flooding
- Relationship to existing or potential sources of contamination

The overriding concern is protecting any kind of well from pollution, primarily bacterial contamination. Groundwater found in sand, clay, and gravel formations is more likely to be safer than groundwater extracted from limestone and other fractured rock type formations. Whatever the strata, there are basic precautions taken when developing a well.

THREE (3) SAFETY PRECAUTIONS TO PROTECT WATER WELLS FROM POLLUTION

1. Protection against surface water entering directly into the top of the well.
2. Protection from groundwater entering below ground level without filtering through at least 10 feet of earth

3. Protection against surface water entering the space between the well casing and surrounding soil. Also, a well should be located in such a way that it is accessible for maintenance, inspection, and pump or pipe replacement when necessary.

SANITARY DESIGN AND CONSTRUCTION

Whenever a water-bearing formation is penetrated (as in well construction), a direct route of possible water contamination exists unless satisfactory precautions are taken. Wells should be provided with casing or pipe to an adequate depth to prevent caving and to permit sealing of the earth formation to the casing with water tight cement grout or bentonite clay, from a point just below the surface to as deep as necessary to prevent entry of contaminated water.

Drilled well with
submersible pump

TYPES OF WELLS FOR ACCESSING GROUNDWATER, WELL DEPTHS, AND DIAMETERS

TYPE OF WELL	DEPTH	DIAMETER	SUITABLE GEOLOGICAL FORMATIONS
Dug	0 to 50 feet	3 to 20 feet	Suitable in clay, silt, sand, gravel, and soft fractured limestone
Bored	0 to 100 feet	2 to 30 inches	Clay, silt, sand, gravel, boulders less than well diameter, soft sandstone and fractured limestone
Driven	0 to 50 feet	1.25 to 2 inches	Clay, sand, silt, fine gravel, and thin layers of sandstone
Drilled: Percussion Type	0 to 1,000 feet	4 to 18 inches	Works well in any geological Formation, including dense igneous Rock
Drilled: Rotary Type	0 to 1,000 feet	4 to 24 inches	Same as above with percussion type drilling
Jetted	0 to 100 feet	4 to 12 inches	Clay, silt, sand, small pea gravel

Types of Wells for Accessing Groundwater, Well Depths, and Diameters

Once construction of the well is completed, the top of the well casing should be covered with a sanitary seal, an approved well cap or a pump mounting which completely covers the well opening.

If pumping at the design rate causes drawdown in the well, a vent through a tapped opening should be provided. The upper end of the vent pipe should be turned downward and suitably screened to prevent the entry of insects and foreign matter.

PUMP SELECTION

A wide variety of pump types and sizes exist to meet virtually any need encountered with an individual or community water system. Depth of the well, design pressure of the system, demand rate in gallons per minute, availability of power, and economics are some of the factors considered in selecting a pump for a specific application.

SPRINGS

Another source of water for individual water supplies are natural springs. A spring is groundwater that reaches the surface due to the natural contours of the land.

Springs are common in rolling hillside and mountain areas. Some provide an ample supply of water, but most only provide water seasonally. If proper precautions are not taken, there is very good possibility that the water will be microbiologically contaminated and not considered potable.

To obtain satisfactory (potable) water from a spring, it is necessary to:

• Find the source
• Properly develop the spring

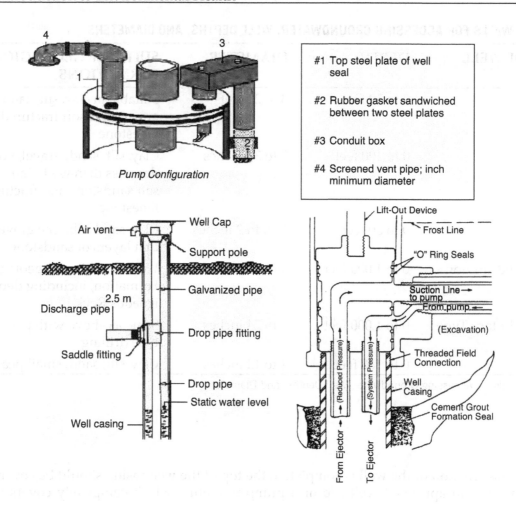

#1	Top steel plate of well seal
#2	Rubber gasket sandwiched between two steel plates
#3	Conduit box
#4	Screened vent pipe; inch minimum diameter

Pump Configuration

- Eliminate surface water outcroppings above the spring to its source
- Prevent animals from accessing the spring area

The diagram illustrates a properly developed spring. Note the water line supplying the water is well under ground, the spring box is watertight and surface water runoff is diverted away from the area.

CISTERNS

A cistern consists of a watertight underground reservoir, which is filled with rain water draining from the roof of a building(s). Cisterns will not provide an ample supply of water for any extended period of time, unless severe restrictions are made in the amount of water a family might use. Since the water is coming off the roof, one would expect the water to be polluted. However, a diversion pipe is generally installed to allow one to waste the first few minutes of rain water from the roof until the water flows clear. In any event, disinfection is of utmost importance. Since this is rain water, the water will have a low pH. This can effect plumbing pipes and fixtures if not treated.

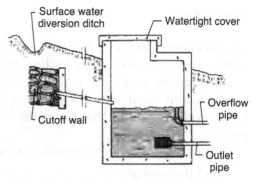

Spring Configuration

DISINFECTION OF WATER SUPPLIES

Disinfection of water supplies can be accomplished by a variety of methods including chlorination, ozonation, ultraviolet radiation, heat, and iodination. The advantages and disadvantages of each is noted below.

Disinfection Methods

DISINFECTION METHOD	ADVANTAGES	DISADVANTAGES
Boiling of Water	Readily accessible Well suited for emergencies Removes VOCs from water Effective even on giardia & crypto	Requires great deal of heat Takes time to bring to boil & cool Water tastes stale Typically limited capacity
Chlorination	Provides residual disinfectant Residual easy to test & measure Readily available; reasonable cost Low electrical requirement Useful for multiple water problems Can treat large volumes of water	Requires contact time of 30 minutes Turbidity reduces effectiveness Gives water a chlorine taste May form disinfection by products Does not kill giardia or crypto Requires careful handling & storage
Ultraviolet light	Does not change taste of water Leaves no discernable odor Kills bacteria almost immediately Compact and easy to use	High electric demand No disinfection residual Requires pre-treatment if turbid Requires new lamp annually
Iodine	Does not require electricity Requires little maintenance Provides residual treatment Residual easy to measure	Health side effects undetermined Affected by water temperature Gives water an iodine taste

Chlorine. Chlorine is the most commonly used water disinfectant. It is available in liquid, powder, gas, and tablet form. Chlorine gas is often used for municipal water disinfection, but rarely for Indian community systems as it can be hazardous if mishandled and requires more equipment. Recommended liquid, powder, and tablet forms of chlorine include:

Liquid: Chlorine laundry bleach such as Clorox, Hi-Lex, Purex, etc. (about 5% chlorine). Swimming pool disinfectant or concentrated chlorine bleach (12%–17% chlorine).

Powder: Chlorinated lime (25% chlorine). Dairy sanitizer (30% chlorine). High-test calcium hypochlorite such as HTH, PITTCHLOR, PERCHLORON, etc. (65%–75% chlorine).

Tablets: High-test calcium hypochlorite such as HTH, PIT-TABS, CHLORETS, etc. (65%–75% chlorine).

Gas: Gas chlorine is an economical and convenient way to use large amounts of chlorine. It is stored in steel cylinders ranging in size from 100–2,000 pounds. The packager fills these cylinders with liquid chlorine to approximately 85% of total volume; the remaining 15% is occupied with chlorine gas. These ratios are required to prevent rupture of the tank during high temperatures. It is important that sunlight never reach cylinders directly. It is also important that the operator or user of chlorine know the maximum withdrawal rate of gas per day per cylinder. For example, the maximum withdrawal rate from a 150 pound cylinder is approximately 40 pounds/day at room temperature discharging to atmospheric pressure.

The understanding of certain terms is necessary in talking about chlorination. Some of these are:

Chlorine Concentration. The concentration (amount) of chlorine in a volume of water is measured in parts per million (ppm). In one million gallons of water, a chlorine concentration of 1 ppm would require 8.34 pounds of 100% chlorine.

Contact Time. The time, after chlorine addition and before use, given for disinfection to occur. For groundwater systems contact time is minimal. However, in surface water systems a contact time of 20–30 minutes is common.

Dosage. The total amount of chlorine added to water. Given in ppm or milligrams per liter.

Demand. As a chlorine solution is added to water a portion is "used up." It reacts with particles of organic matter if any are present in the water, such as slimes or other chemicals and minerals that may be present. Chlorine "used up" in this manner is called chlorine demand. It is the difference between the amount of chlorine applied to water and total available chlorine remaining at the end of a specified contact period.

Parts Per Million. A weight to weight comparison. Therefore, 1 ppm equals 1 pound per million pounds. Because water weighs 8.34 pounds/gallon it takes 8.34 pounds of any substance per million gallons to equal 1 ppm. In water chemistry, 1 ppm equals 1 mg/l.

Residual. The amount of chlorine left after the demand is met is called the chlorine residual or available (free) chlorine. It is this portion that provides a ready reserve for bacteriocidal action. Both combined and free chlorine make up chlorine residual and are involved in disinfection. Total available chlorine = free chlorine + combined chlorine.

Breakpoint chlorination. A process sometimes used to ensure the presence of free chlorine in public water supplies by adding enough chlorine to the water to satisfy the chlorine demand and to react with all dissolved ammonia that might be present. The concentration of chlorine needed to treat a variety of water conditions is listed in Table 5.3

CHLORINE CARRIER SOLUTIONS

On small systems or individual wells, a high chlorine carrier solution is mixed in a tank in the pump-house and pumped by the chlorinator into the system. Table 5.4 shows how to make a 200 ppm carrier solution; by using 200 ppm only small quantities of this carrier have to be added. Depending upon the system, other stock solutions may be needed to better utilize existing chemical feed equipment.

"Rule of Thumb" Chlorination Guide for Specific Water Conditions

CHLORINATION TREATMENT FOR	TYPICAL DOSAGE RATES IN PPM
Algae	3–5
Bacteria	3–5
BOD Reduction	10
Color (Removal)	Dosage depends upon type and extent of color removal desired. May vary from 1 to 500 PPM dosage rate.
Cyanide	
Reduction to Cyanate	2 times Cyanide content
Complete destruction	8.5 times Cyanide content
Hydrogen Sulfide:	
Taste and Odor Control	2 times H_2S content
Destruction	8.4 times H_2S content
Iron Bacteria	1–10, varying with amount of bacteria to control.
Iron Precipitation	64 times Fe content
Manganese Precipitation	1–3 times Mn content
Odor	1–3
Taste	1–3

AMOUNT OF CHLORINE NEEDED TO PRODUCE 200 PPM (MG/L) CARRIER SOLUTION

CARRIER SOLUTION	AMOUNT OF CL/100 GALLONS OF WATER
5% chlorine bleach	3 pints or 1.5 liters
12% – 17% chlorine solution	1 pint or 0.5 liters
25% – 30% chlorine powder	2/3 lb.
65% – 75% chlorine powder	¼ lb.

ROUTINE WATER CHLORINATION (SIMPLE)

Most public water supplies that are chlorinated use this method. Enough chlorine is added to the water to meet the chlorine demand plus enough additional to supply about 0.2–0.5 PPM free Cl^2 when checked after 20 minutes.

Simple chlorination may not be enough to kill certain viruses. Chlorine as a disinfectant increases in effectiveness as the chlorine residual is increased and as the contact time is increased. Chlorination Management (Solution Feeders)

Mix the chlorine solution and adjust the chlorinator according to the manufacturers instructions. Chlorine solutions deteriorate gradually when standing. Fresh solutions must be prepared as necessary to maintain the required chlorine residual. Test for chlorine residual at least once a week to assure effective equipment operation and solution strengths.

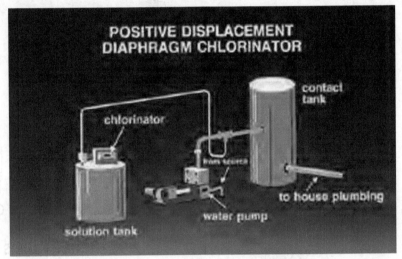

Positive Displacement Diaphragm Chlorinator

Keep a dated record of solution preparation, type, proportion of chlorine used, and residual-test results. Sensing devices are available which will automatically shut off the pump and activate a warning bell or light when the chlorinator needs servicing.

PLUMBING SYSTEMS

There are basically three piping systems in a home: (1) a water supply system, (2) a drain waste vent system (sewage system), and (3) fixtures connected to the first two.

In order to understand the environmental health problems that can occur with water and sewage systems, it is necessary to have a basic understanding of what makes up a plumbing system. The pipes in the distribution system should meet or exceed the minimum requirements of the National Plumbing Code and local codes. Always consult with these entities when constructing a facility or before renovating.

TYPES OF VALVES

It is essential that valves be used in a water system to allow functions of the system to be controlled in a safe and efficient manner. The number, type, and size of valves found in a system will depend on the size and complexity of the system. Most valves can usually be purchased in sizes and types to match the pipe sizes used in water system installations. Listed below are some of the more commonly encountered valves with a description of their basic functions.

Shutoff Valves

Shutoff valves should be installed between the pump and the pressure tank and between the pressure tank and service entry to a building. Globe, gate, and ball valves are common shutoff valves. Gate and ball valves cause less friction loss than globe valves. Shutoff valves allow servicing parts of the system without draining the entire system.

Flow-control Valves

Flow-control valves provide uniform flow at varying pressures. They are sometimes needed to regulate or limit the use of water because of limited waterflow from low-yielding wells or an inadequate pumping system. They may also be needed with some treatment equipment. These valves are often used to limit flow to a fixture. Orifices, mechanical valves, or diaphragm valves are used to restrict the flow to any one service line or complete system and to assure a minimum flow rate to all outlets.

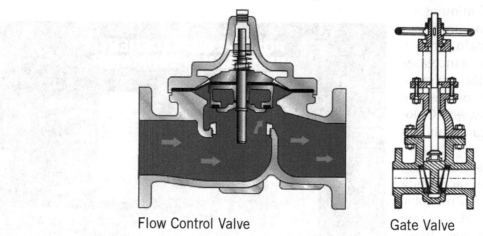

Flow Control Valve   Gate Valve

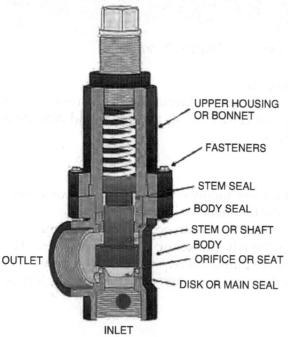

UPPER HOUSING OR BONNET

FASTENERS

STEM SEAL

BODY SEAL

STEM OR SHAFT

BODY

OUTLET   ORIFICE OR SEAT

DISK OR MAIN SEAL

INLET

Relief Valves

Relief valves permit water or air to escape from the system to relieve excess pressure. They are spring controlled and are usually adjustable to relieve at varying pressures, generally above 60 psi. Install a relief valve in systems that may develop pressures exceeding the rated limits of the pressure tank or distribution system. Positive displacement and submersible pumps and water heaters can develop these excessive pressures. Whenever there is a question of safety, a relief valve should be installed. The relief valve must be capable of discharging the flow rate of the pump. Install the relief valve between the pump and the first shutoff valve. A combined pressure and temperature relief valve is needed on all water heaters. Combination pressure and vacuum relief valves are also installed to prevent vacuum damage to the system.

Pressure Reducing Valves

A pressure reducing valve is used to reduce line pressure. On main lines, this allows the use of thinner walled pipe and protects house plumbing. Sometimes these valves are installed on individual services to protect plumbing.

Altitude Valves

Often an altitude valve is installed at the base of the tank to prevent it from overflowing. Altitude valves sense the tank level through a pressure line to the tank. An adjustable spring allows setting the level so that the valve closes and prevents more inflow when the tank becomes full.

Foot Valves

A foot valve is a special type of check valve installed at the end of a suction pipe or below the jet in a well to prevent backflow and loss of prime. The valve should be of good quality and cause little friction loss.

Check Valves

Check valves have a function similar to foot valves. They permit waterflow in only one direction through a pipe. A submersible pump may use several check valves. One is located at the top of the pump to prevent backflow from causing back spin of the impellers. Some systems utilize another check valve and a snifter valve. They will be in the drop pipe or pitless unit in the well casing. It will allow a weep hole located between the two valves to drain part of the pipe. When the pump is started, it will then force the air from the drained part of the pipe into the pressure tank, thus recharging the pressure tank.

Frost-proof Faucets

Frost-proof faucets are installed outside a house with the shutoff valve extending into the heated house to prevent freezing. After each use, the water between the valve and outlet drains, provided the hose is disconnected, so water is not left to freeze.

Frost-proof Hydrants

Frost-proof hydrants make outdoor water service possible during cold weather without the danger of freezing. The shutoff valve is buried below the frost line. To avoid submerging it, which might result in contamination and backsiphoning, the stop-and-waste valve must drain freely into a rock bed. *These hydrants are sometimes prohibited by local or State health authorities.*

Water Check Valve

Float Valves

Float valve responds to a high water level to close an inlet pipe, as in a tank-type toilet.

Miscellaneous Switches

Float switches respond to a high and/or low water level as with an intermediate storage tank.

Pressure switches with a low-pressure cutoff stops the pump motor if the line pressure drops to the cutoff point.

Low-flow cutoff switches are used with submersible pumps to stop the pump if the water discharge falls below a predetermined minimum operating pressure

High-pressure cut-off switches are used to stop pumps if the system pressure rises above a predetermined maximum.

Paddle type flow switches detect flow by means of a paddle placed in the pipe that operates a mechanical switch when flow in the pipe pushes the paddle.

Float Valve

Leaky Water Lines can Siphon

Plumbing Problems

The contamination of a public water supply from buildings, residences, and institutions by inadvertent action of users and installers of plumbing fixtures is a potential and real public health problem in all communities. Continued inspection and surveillance by environmental health personnel is necessary to ascertain whether such public health hazards exist or have developed by additions or alterations to an approved system. All environmental health specialists should learn to recognize the three general types of defects which are found in potable water supply systems; *backflow, backsiphonage, and overhead leakage* into open potable water containers. If identified, these conditions should be corrected immediately to prevent the spread of disease or poisoning from high concentrations of organic or inorganic chemicals.

BACKFLOW AND BACKSIPHONAGE

Backsiphonage is a siphon action in an undesirable or reverse direction. When there is a direct or indirect connection between a potable water supply and water of questionable quality due to poor plumbing design or installation, there is always a possibility that the public water supply may become contaminated. Some examples of common plumbing defects are:

Washbasins, sterilizers, and sinks with submerged inlets or threaded hose bibs and hose.

Oversized booster pumps which overtax the supply capability of the main and thus develop negative pressure.

Submerged inlets and fire pumps. If the fire pumps are directly connected into the water main, a negative pressure will develop.

A threaded hose bib in a health care facility is technically a cross-connection.

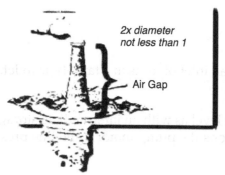

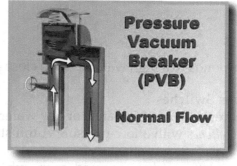

2x diameter
not less than 1

Air Gap

Airgap

Pressure Vacuum Breaker

Figure 5.5 illustrates an airgap which is a physical separation between the incoming water line and maximum level in a container of at least twice the diameter of the incoming water line. If an airgap cannot be installed, then a vacuum breaker (Figure 5.6) should be installed.

The term backflow means any unwanted flow of non-potable water into a potable water system. The direction of flow under backflow conditions is in the reverse direction from that intended by the system. Backflow may be caused by numerous factors and conditions. For example, the reverse pressure gradient may be due to either a loss of pressure in the supply main called *backsiphonage,* or by the flow from a customer's pressurized system through an unprotected cross-connection, which is called *backpressure*. A reverse flow in a distribution main or in the customer's system can be created by a change of system pressure wherein the pressure at the supply point becomes lower than the pressure at the point of use. When this happens, the water at the point of use will be siphoned back into the system thus potentially polluting or contaminating the customer's system. It is also possible that the contaminated or polluted water could continue to backflow into the public distribution system. The point at which it is possible for a non-potable substance to come in contact with the potable drinking water system is called a cross-connection.

Examples of backflow:

1. Supplemental supplies such as a standby fire protection tank.
2. Fire pumps.
3. Chemical feed pumps that overpower the potable water system pressure.
4. Sprinkler systems will backflow if connected to the potable water and the pressure falls below the pressure in the sprinkler system.

Prevention.   There are many techniques and devices for preventing backflow and backsiphonage. Some examples are:

1. Vacuum breakers, nonpressure and pressure types.
2. Backflow preventers:
   a. Reduced pressure principle
   b. Double gate—double check valves
   c. Swing-connection
   d. Airgap—double diameter separation
3. Surge tanks:
   a. Booster pumps for tanks
   b. Fire system make-up tank
   c. Potable tanks must be covered
4. Color coding in all buildings where there is any possibility of connecting two separate systems or taking water from the wrong source.
   a. Blue—potable
   b. Yellow—nonpotable
   c. Other—chemical and gases

OTHER WATER QUALITY PROBLEMS

There are various water conditions that affect water quality. As noted in Chapter 4, drinking water not only has to be safe to drink, but should be aesthetically pleasing. Table 5.6 below describes symptoms, causes, recommended action levels and, most importantly how to correct these problems.

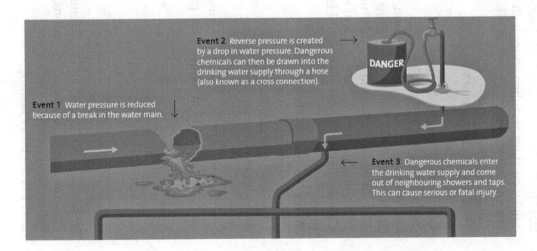

ANALYZING AND CORRECTING WATER SUPPLY QUALITY PROBLEMS

SYMPTOMS	PROBABLE CAUSE	MEASUREMENT	CORRECTIVE ACTION
Hardness- -Sticky curd forms when soap is added to water, -Causes bathtub ring. -Hard water causes one to use more soap. -Glassware appears streaked, Scale forms in pipes.	Calcium and magnesium in the water compounded with biocarbonates, sulfates, or chlorides.	Hardness test kits may measure in grains per gallon (gpg) or parts per million (ppm). 1 gpg = 17.1 ppm. 50 ppm is soft water 50–100 ppm is moderately hard 100-200 ppm is hard water 200-300 ppm is very hard over 300 ppm is extremely hard	If hardness creates problems, a sodium zeolite ion exchange water softener can be used or a reverse osmosis unit.
Red Water (Dissolved iron) -Red stains on cloths and plumbing fixtures. -Causes corrosion of steel pipes. -Water has metallic taste -Clear water just drawn begins to form red particles that settle to the bottom.	Iron, from geological formations that groundwater passes through. Water, being an excellent solvent ionizes iron and holds it in solution.	Iron measured by atomic absorption (AA) unit or one of numerous colormetric test kits measures Iron in ppm. Any measurement above 0.3 ppm will cause problems.	Iron is common in soft water and when water hardness is above 175 ppm. -To treat soft water that contains no iron but picks it up in distribution lines, add calcium to the water with calcite (limestone) units.
Iron Bacteria -Red slime appears in toilet	Caused by bacteria that act in the presence of iron.	Check under toilet tank cover for slippery jelly-like coating.	-To treat hard water containing iron ions, install a sodium zeolite ion exchange unit -To treat soft water containing iron, CO_2 must be neutralized, followed by a manganese zeolite unit. Kill bacteria by superchlorinating Pump and piping system
Brownish-Black Water -Fixtures stained black -Fabric stains black -Coff EE, tea bitter tasting	Manganese is present usually along with iron.	Colormetric tests for manganese with resulting concentrations above 0.05 mg/1 cause problems	Same method as with iron problems.

190

Problem	Condition	Test / Detail	Treatment
Acidity -Corrosion of copper and steel of pumps, fixtures, piping and tanks.	Water contains CO_2 which forms with water to form carbonic acid. Water may contain H_2SO_4, HCL, or Nitric acid, but unlikely.	Colormetric field titrametric tests for Acidity, pH and CO_2 are very affordable. Acidity test, the pH is determined at the titration end point. A PH below 6.5 causes corrosion. CO_2 should be less that 10 mg/1 or less than 5 mg/1 if alkalinity is less than 100 ppm.	-Soda ash solution-solution is fed into the well or suction line of a pump. May be fed along with chlorine solution. -Neutralizing tank-Limestone chips (calcite) are in the tank which increases alkalinity and hardness of water.
Off odors and taste -Bitter taste -Rotten egg odor -Salty taste -Flat, soda taste -Salty taste -Chlorine odor/taste	-Very high mineral content -Sulfate reducing bacteria, H_2S -High chloride levels -Bicarbonates -High Total Dissolved Solids (TDS) -High levels of di or trichloramines in water	-Excess iron, manganese, sulfate -Sulfate levels above 250 mg/1 or any trace of H_2S causes problem -Problems at levels >250 mg/1 -Carbonate hardness test -TDS levels above 500 mg/1 may cause problems -Check pH	-Methods mentioned above -Chlorinator and filter -Reverse Osmosis unit -Aeration unit -Sand filter -Activated charcoal filter
Turbidity -Water is cloudy	-Silt, -Sediment -Large number of microorganisms -Organic material	Measured in Nephelometric turbidity units (NTU) using laboratory spectrophotometers. Less than 5 NTUs is best, >10 not acceptable.	Fine filtering with sand filter or diatomaceous earth filter. For ponds, coagulation and sedimentation is needed.
Blue Stain on porcelain fixtures	Corrosion of copper pipes, fixtures due to low pH, hardness and alkalinity	Use of Langlier index to determine proper balance of pH, hardness, and alkalinity	Use methods noted above to adjust pH, hardness, and alkalinity

191

HOW TO CONDUCT AN ENVIRONMENTAL SURVEY OF A WATER SUPPLY

The definition of a Sanitary Survey, according to the 1996 Safe Drinking Water Act, is *an onsite review of the water source, facilities, equipment, operation and maintenance of a public water system for the purpose of evaluating the adequacy of the source, facilities, equipment, operation and maintenance for producing safe drinking water.*

The bacterial and chemical quality of a water source, as well as how it is protected from potential contamination, is extremely important in determining the safety of a water supply system. Sanitary precautions, proper operation and maintenance, quality construction, and bacterial and chemical surveillance are all important in any water system. This is especially true if the system receives no bactericidal treatment such as chlorination. The Water System Sanitary Survey checklist provided here is a tool one can use to complete a thorough review the aforementioned keys to a safe water system.

WATER SYSTEM SANITARY SURVEY

SOURCE COMPOUND

Condition	Yes	No	Field Notes
Compound fenced and locked			
Weed and plant growth controlled			
Absence of trash, debris, large trees			
Source out of floodplain			
Rodent burrowing, erosion observed			
Valve boxes and valves accessible			
Valves maintained			
Access road			

WELLS

Condition	Yes	No	Field Notes
Areas adjacent to well free from sources of pollution; properly drained			
Pollution sources in Recharge area			
Concrete well slab in good repair			
Sanitary seal maintained; good repair			
Well casing in good repair			
Anular grouting seal in good repair			
Air vents properly placed & screened			
Potential for backflow			
Pumping records adequate			

SPRINGS

Condition	Yes	No	Field Notes
Adjacent areas free from sources of pollution; i.e. cesspools, privies			
Area within 100 ft. protected from livestock and unauthorized persons			
Drainage diversion ditches located above spring as needed			
Catchment basin watertight;			
Catchment basin free of cracks to the outside			
Catchment basin covered & secured			
Overflow turned down & screen in place			
Interior of basin free of contaminants			
Supply outlet properly screened; not obstructed by sand and debris			
If utilized; is chlorinator maintained			

INFILTRATION GALLERIES

Condition	Yes	No	Field Notes
Area near collection system contain no sources of surface contamination			
Disinfection adequate			
Physical characteristics acceptable (color, odor, turbidity, taste)			
Covers secure			
Vents screened			
Possibility of back siponage			
Piping clogged			

SURFACE WATER SUPPLY/SOURCE

Condition	Yes	No	Field Notes
Watershed area is well protected			
Raw water quality adequate; no algae, odor, turbidity, color, ect.			
Intake screens adequate & maintained			
Deep water intake properly placed			
Potential for backflow			
Raw water disinfection			
Watershed Mgmt. Plan provided			
Water intake records provided			

STORAGE TANKS

Condition	Yes	No	Field Notes
No signs of leaks			
Vents and overflow pipes screened			
Temporary connections sealed			
Access covers locked			
Non-toxic paint on the tank interior			
Interior & exterior paint in good condition			
Depth gauge operational			
Pressure tank operational			
Freeze protection adequate			
Overall structure & condition adequate			

STORAGE FACILITY/COMPOUND

Condition	Yes	No	Field Notes
Storage tank foundation sound			
All valves maintained			
No debris; plant growth controlled			
Tools, and supplies properly stored			

PUMPS AND MOTORS

Condition	Yes	No	Field Notes
Lubrication adequate			
Pumps operational			
Overheating, excess noise observed			
Leaks in pumps/equipment observed			
Grounding is correct			
Amp. & voltage readings within specs.			

> **Control Panels Contain High and Low Electrical Voltage. It is recommended that the Surveyor not attempt to make adjustments, manipulate switches, remove or install wires or parts. The System Operator should be asked to operate the equipment allowing the surveyor to record the Electrical Measurements.**

PUMPHOUSE/BOOSTER STATION STRUCTURE

Condition	Yes	No	Field Notes
Pumphouse enclosed by locked fence			
Floor, walls, ceiling, roof in good repair			
Potential for backflow observed			
Leaking pipes observed/condensation			
Heat/freeze protection adequate			
Spare fuses/electric panel operational			
Floor drains functional			
Rodents/others pests excluded			
Building/structure maintained			
Housekeeping adequate			

CHLORINATION TREATMENT—GENERAL (GAS & HYPOCHLORITE)

Condition	Yes	No	Field Notes
Free residual Cl ^{7} 0.2 mg/l			
Records of Cl used and residual readings current			
Disinfection Chem. supply adequate			
Disinfection Chem. Storage adequate			
Chem. Storage area well ventilated			
DPD Test kit available and used			

CHLORINATION TREATMENT—(HYPOCHLORITE)

Condition	Yes	No	Field Notes
Equip. operational/secure			
Proper Solution Mixing			

CHLORINATION TREATMENT—(CHLORINE GAS)

Condition	Yes	No	Field Notes
Gas cylinders stored upright & secure			
Gas equipment operational			
SCBA available, operating properly			
Operator Trained in Use of SCBA			
Chlorine room properly ventilated			
Gas chlorine leaks monitoring system			
Chlorine gas room separation			
Warning signs posted in Chlorine Rm.			

FLUORIDATION TREATMENT

Condition	Yes	No	Field Notes
Fluoride pump controls operational			
Potential for backflow			
Equipment operational & secure			
Proper solution mixing			
Adequate supply of proper chemicals			
Safety equipment provided			
Test kit available and used			
Fluoride residual readings recorded			

OTHER WATER TREATMENT PROCESSES/UNITS

Condition	Yes	No	Field Notes
Processes and units function properly			
Cross connections controlled			
Backwash procedures are correct			
Proper disposal of chemical and back-wash wastewater			
Treatment effective; MCL			
Treatment effective; RMCL (Fe & Mn)			
Chemicals stored properly			
Process lab analysis adequate			

DISTRIBUTION SYSTEM

Condition	Yes	No	Field Notes
Potential for backflow			
Leaks noted in distribution piping			
Valve maintenance			
Appurtenances operational			
Erosion not evident/fill adequate			

UTILITY MANAGEMENT

Condition	Yes	No	Field Notes
Operator(s) trained			
Building blueprints as built accurate			
Valve/hydrant maintenance scheduled			
Record keeping adequate			

EMERGENCY MANAGEMENT

Condition	Yes	No	Field Notes
Emergency plan adequate			
Back-up source adequate			
System capacity/system needs known			
Operator has plan for water rationing & public awareness in an emergency			

References and Resources Used for Chapter 6:

1) Beck j. Barnett D.B., Fundamentals of Environmental Health Field Practice, 2010, Kendall Hunt Publishing; 1 edition, # SBN-10:0757578675 # ISBN-13: 978-0757578670.
2) American Assoc. of Vocational Instructional Material, "Planning for an Individual Water System", 4th Edition, 1973
3) Moeller, Dade W. Moeller, Environmental Health, Harvard University Press, Revised Edition, 1997
4) Foundation for Cross Contamination and Hydraulic Research, University of Southern California, 1998 http://www.usc.edu/dept/fccchr/intro.html
5) Environmental Protection Agency, Well Water Location and Condition Tutorial, 1997 http://pasture.ecn.purdue.edu/-epados/farmstead/well/src/title.html
6) Environmental Protection Agency, Publication 430/9-73-002, Cross-connection Control Manual, revised 1989.
7) Pictures used in this chapter were from USEPA and various State government water quality and protection web sites.

Talkin' Trash: An Introduction to Solid and Hazardous Waste Management

7

Jason W. Marion, PhD

"America's waste managers are the world's greatest magicians. . . . Every day they perform an amazing act by making 250 million tons of trash disappear from the eyes of most Americans."

Jason W. Marion

Key Performance Outcome Indicators:

1. Understand the differences and similarities of municipal solid waste and hazardous waste
2. Understand the history of solid waste management, particularly in the United States
3. Understand the basics of major U.S. waste management laws
4. Understand the patterns of waste generation and recycling in the United States
5. Understand the requirements of solid waste disposal defined by U.S. law
6. Understand and recognize the steps used in modern waste management practice
7. Understand the challenges associated with landfill development
8. Understand the occupational risks associated with waste management work

Introduction

The terms **trash** and **municipal solid waste** are often used interchangeably. The two terms are also applied interchangeably to mixtures of waste materials containing **hazardous waste**. There are many easily recognizable examples of municipal solid waste materials, such as leftover food, empty bottles, used newspapers, empty pizza boxes, grass clippings, used clothing, damaged furniture, packaging materials, paint cans, and dead batteries. Hazardous waste is different than municipal solid waste. Hazardous waste presents significant challenges for storage and collection, as hazardous waste products are suspected or known to be dangerous to humans and/or the environment. Examples of hazardous waste products include toxic wastes, barrels containing flammable chemicals, large volumes of paint cans, unused lead-based paint containers, and batteries.

Classifying Municipal and Hazardous Waste

It is important to recognize that some discarded materials, like paint and batteries, are considered municipal solid waste and hazardous waste. When the quantity or volume of the paint materials or batteries exceeds what is normally produced by a single- or multi-family home, then these types of waste are deemed inappropriate for treatment as municipal solid waste. These products, due to their volume, must be treated with greater caution and are treated as hazardous waste. Other products, like some very toxic solvents used for degreasing equipment in industrial operations, are only approved for industry use and should never be discarded in any quantity as municipal solid waste. Since no amount of these really toxic chemicals should be in a home environment, no amount is permissible as municipal solid waste, making these chemicals exclusively hazardous waste. For questions about what chemicals or products are acceptable for being discarded as municipal solid waste items, one should always contact the local waste management company or state/local environmental protection agency.

Any waste product deemed hazardous by law has one or more of the following properties:

1. Ignitable (easily flammable)
2. Reactive (unstable, could explode when interacting with chemicals)
3. Corrosive (destroys handles, containers, or even tissues/skin)
4. Toxic (can harm living organisms, including human life)

Waste Management History

Throughout human history, waste management has been part of the human experience. As civilizations became more established in single locations for longer periods of time, there was a greater desire and need to have waste removed from the city streets. Many ancient civilizations, particularly the Greeks, had designated locations for waste dumping outside the residential and business areas of the city. These cities and their residents knew that the buildup of waste in city streets would attract numerous nuisance animal species while also producing odors unpleasant for the residents and city guests.

Although many cities still struggled to keep their streets clean, the issue of waste accumulation peaked in Europe in the fourteenth century with the arrival of the Black Death (bubonic plague). The accumulation of rubbish in the homes and streets attracted a variety of rodents, including rats. Some of these rats were carrying rat fleas that harbored the bacterium *Yersinia pestis*. When the rat hosts died, the fleas would periodically bite humans, thus infecting some humans with the plague bacteria. In medieval England, 1.5 million people were killed in 12 years by this bacterium, which is believed to have jumped to humans while circulating in rat and flea populations. This population loss in England represented 25% of the

Example Waste Classification Scheme

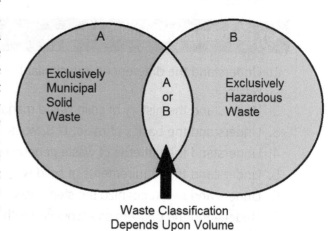

Waste Classification
Depends Upon Volume

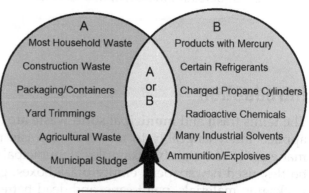

Depending Upon Volume
Paint, Motor Oil, Anti-Freeze,
Certain types of Batteries,
Pesticides, Electronics

Figure 7.1 Classifying Waste Products

total population, which is estimated to have been 4 million. Inadequate sanitation, although possibly not well recognized then, is now widely recognized as a major contributor to this horrible event in human history.

By the 1700s, waste management was still largely underappreciated by many civilizations. However, with the advent of the Industrial Revolution, numerous new products were being produced and consumed in Western Europe and the fledgling United States. Accordingly, there was a tremendous increase in the amount of rubbish being created. Furthermore, the new and growing American democracy was fueled by an Industrial Revolution, and many discoveries contributed to a more enlightened and educated society. During this era, Benjamin Franklin and others advocated for the banning of public dumps in the city of Philadelphia so that it would be free from the frequent disease epidemics, and their "liberty of breathing freely in their own houses" would be restored.[1] Over the next 100, many cities wrestled with ideas and policies on how to best manage their growing trash problem.

One remedy for dealing with the looming trash problem was incineration. In 1885, New York City constructed an incinerator on Governors Island for the purpose of destroying trash by burning. Around the United States, hundreds of incinerators were put into operation over the next 80 years in urban areas. In rural areas, trash was burned on-site, and unburned products like glass were discarded at the back of properties or in uninhabited areas. By the late 1950s and early 1960s, U.S. and European scientists were concerned about the impact of air quality on human health. Citing a number of deaths and illnesses related to air quality, scientists believed that pollution controls were needed.[2] By the 1970s and 1980s, many laws, particularly the Clean Air Act, led to the regulation of these facilities for the protection of human health. The cost of compliance with the Clean Air Act was too expensive for many incinerators and public entities. In the interest of public health, and due to the inability of most cities to implement appropriate pollution controls, most incineration facilities were shut down.

Other alternatives were present, such as sanitary and open fills. All of these practices, including hog feeding, were gaining tremendous attention by the 1930s and 1940s. Hog feeding was even common in many large U.S. cities.[3] The theory was that by feeding the hogs refuse, cities would be able to get rid of the garbage, while also being able to produce a valuable and edible product. Unfortunately, by the late 1950s, there was growing evidence that humans consuming pork from garbage-fed hogs were more likely to get ill with trichinosis,[3] which led to the eventual banning of this process from public waste-collection entities.

With incineration and hog feeding deemed unacceptable to public health, the only remaining option for municipal waste was to store or bury it. Consequently, this approach is still used, and the majority of the solid waste generated by the United States is placed in sanitary landfills and is managed at great cost. Due to the expensive nature of collecting and managing the solid waste destined for landfills, there has been an emphasis placed on the three R's, which specifically encourages citizens, businesses, and organizations to *reduce, reuse, and recycle.*

Hazardous Waste History

Lead (Pb) and mercury (Hg) have been with American populations for many years; however, since the 1920s, the United States has observed major increases in its production of synthetic chemicals, many of which can be deemed hazardous waste. For example, the chemical trichloroethylene (TCE) began replacing dry-cleaning solvents in the 1930s. The U.S. military used TCE frequently for degreasing equipment during World War II and the Korean War. Industrial applications also increased substantially as the nation became more industrialized. Like TCE, many other chemicals were developed as America and the world became more industrialized. The health effects associated with human exposure to many of these chemicals were largely unknown or only associated with anecdotal evidence, as opposed to scientific study. Consequently, many of these hazardous waste chemicals were incinerated or placed in landfills just like the waste generated by households.

The Love Canal Disaster

The most historically important hazardous waste event in U.S. history may be the Love Canal disaster. During the 1890s, a plan was proposed by William T. Love to construct a canal to connect the Niagara River to Lake Ontario. The canal was to be constructed originally for hydropower generation, and then for shipping goods by water around the very large Niagara Falls. Plans eventually fell through, but approximately one mile of the canal was dug, 50 feet wide and approximately 25 feet in depth, on average. With little use for this trench, the city of Niagara Falls, New York, decided to dedicate it as a dump site. From the 1920s until the 1940s, only the city dumped waste into the trench; but during World War II, some military wastes associated with the war effort were also dumped in the trench. By the 1950s, the Hooker Chemical Company was granted permission to dump its waste at this location, with much of the waste being in 55-gallon drums, while the city and military stopped using the site. In 1953, the dumping ceased and the canal was buried. Within several years, the school board purchased the property for $1 and constructed two schools in the area. By the 1970s, other development had occurred in the area, including the construction of homes. By the mid-1970s media outlets in the area started reporting numerous birth defects, and advocates got the attention of the newly formed U.S. Environmental Protection Administration. EPA investigations acknowledged a high frequency of chromosomal abnormalities in the people and discovered elevated concentrations of hazardous waste chemicals in the environment and even in the basements of homes. By 1978, many Americans viewed Love Canal as the worst public health disaster in American history. President Jimmy Carter declared the area a disaster area. The community in the vicinity of Love Canal was instructed to leave and was compensated by the U.S. government. The immediate site is now abandoned and has been a site of tremendous clean-up activities. The chemical company was recently ordered to pay $129 million in restitution above and beyond the homeowner lawsuits.[4]

The occurrence of events like the Love Canal disaster resulted in numerous health-related problems for the exposed people. This led to tremendous political pressure on elected officials in the Congress and on Presidents Ford and Carter to enact hazardous waste management legislation. Consequently, the Love Canal disaster brought about several major U.S. hazardous waste laws.

Waste Management Regulations

Following the growing acceptance of landfill disposal methods of solid waste, the United States passed the Solid Waste Disposal Act of 1965. This act essentially banned open-air burning of trash and required pollution controls to be utilized when incineration was being performed. It was rightfully presumed that municipalities would consider adopting alternative strategies for waste management when compliance with clean air laws related to incineration made it apparent that incineration would be very costly. In anticipation by EPA of alternative strategies being considered, the Solid Waste Disposal Act required all commercial, industrial, municipal, and household waste to be managed in an environmentally responsible manner for the protection of human health and the environment. Acknowledging some of the limitations of the Solid Waste Act, as brought to light by the Love Canal disaster, there was pressure from the citizenry to reduce waste and ensure that buried waste would be properly managed and safe for public health. Consequently, the new EPA (formed in 1970), working in concert with Congress, the president, and the states, created new legislation passed by Congress in 1976. The name of the new law, the Resource Conservation and Recovery Act, embodied the spirit of reducing waste and protecting the environment.

This new law, commonly called **RCRA** (pronounced rec•ruh), remains the most important law for governing the disposal and management of solid and hazardous waste in the United States. This law empowered and mandated the states to develop and follow plans for managing nonhazardous solid waste and municipal solid waste for the purposes of protecting the environment and human health. RCRA also created a national system for controlling and monitoring hazardous waste products from the time all new hazardous products were created until they were destroyed or ultimately disposed. This provision, pertaining to monitoring hazardous products from their creation until their destruction or ultimate disposal, is commonly called the "cradle to grave" provision (RCRA Subtitle C). RCRA also required underground storage tanks, or USTs, to be regulated. For example, gas stations with underground storage tanks are required by law to have their tanks inspected to ensure they are not leaking and are in good condition.

In summary, three programs were created by RCRA:

1. Solid waste program
2. Hazardous waste program
3. Underground storage tank program

One of the limitations of RCRA is that it was solely a preventive tool for preventing any future disasters that could be like Love Canal. RCRA dealt primarily with new waste generation; whereas there was a substantial need and desire to also deal with old hazardous waste sites created by companies, communities, and even our state, local, and federal governments, including the Department of Defense. In 1980 the U.S. Congress, with support from President Carter, passed the Comprehensive Environmental Response, Compensation, and Liability Act, also known as CERCLA (pronounced sir•cluh). Under this law, the EPA has access to and the ability to obtain financial resources for pursuing litigation against negligent parties responsible for degrading the environment and the quality of human life. Using dollars obtained through litigation, known as "Superfund" dollars, EPA can clean-up **orphan sites**. EPA adds dollars to this appropriately named fund (Superfund) through enforcement actions, consent decrees (agreements with the parties brokered while taking action through the courts), and court orders. The Superfund approach authorized through CERCLA makes it possible for to carry out expensive clean-up efforts of dangerous orphan hazardous waste without directly increasing the tax burden on ordinary citizens.

Municipal Solid Waste Management

Following the regulations laid out by RCRA and developed by individual states, municipal solid waste must be collected, transported, and discarded in a manner not harmful to the environment or public health. As of 2011, the U.S. waste management industry employed approximately 371,000 people.[5] Approximately 29,000 of this workforce were involved in hazardous materials removal, but the majority of the jobs are in nonhazardous solid waste, largely including municipal solid waste management. In the United States, there are over 45,000 truck drivers dedicated to hauling waste. Roughly 15 jobs per 1,000 people are in the waste management industry, and about 2 jobs per 1,000 are waste haulers.

It is quite understandable that this is such a big business, as Americans generate approximately 250 million tons of waste materials per year (Figure 7.2).[6] Until recently, the volume of waste production increased every year. Individually, an average American generates 4.5 pounds of trash daily, or more than 1,600 pounds per year (Figure 7.3).[6] One ton equals 2,000 pounds, and the average American generates almost one ton of trash per year! In fact, the United States generates more waste per capita (per person) than any other country in the industrialized world. Canada is the second-largest waste generator, producing about 3.75 pounds per day; whereas the Germans and Swedes produce the least among the industrialized nations by generating less than 2 pounds per person per day.[7] Consequently, waste production in the United States ends up costing citizens a lot of money that could be directed elsewhere.

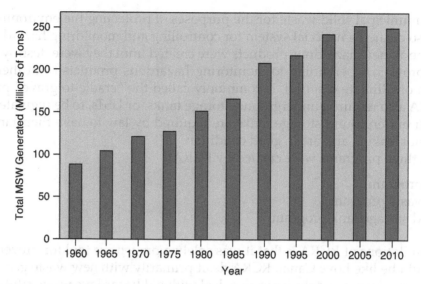

Figure 7.2 Annual Municipal Solid Waste Generation in the United States[6]

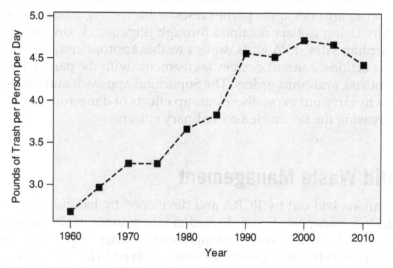

Figure 7.3 Annual per capita municipal solid waste generation in the United States[6]

Waste Management Logistics

Waste generated in a home, school, business, factory, or office must be properly managed. Proper waste management involves highly regulated processes. There are three major steps for dealing with newly created waste products.

The three major steps in waste management are as follows:

1. Collection
2. Transport
3. Disposal

Occasionally, waste is not able to be transported directly to a disposal site and may include a storage step. When a storage step is used, an additional transport step is required, making this a

Figure 7.4 Example of Rear-Tilt Trash Collection and Compaction

five-step waste management process. For situations requiring storage, the five steps would be as follows: collection, transport, storage, additional transport, disposal.

Collection

Municipal solid waste collection should be provided at a minimum of once per week. In urban environments, subdivisions, and even in small communities, curbside (house-to-house) collection methods are often available. However, in rural areas or areas with significant population densities (mobile home parks or apartment complexes), residents are expected to transport the trash to a large (usually metal) container, generally referred to as a dumpster. Some containers can be as small as 2 cubic yards (cu. yd.) or as large as 20 to 40 cu. yd.

The methods in which solid waste is collected depend upon a variety of factors such as population distribution, geography, road conditions, weather, bridge restrictions, and level of service desired. Communities, urban governments, rural governments, and for-hire waste management companies may use a variety of methods for accomplishing the task of collecting the waste and transporting the material to a suitable location for disposal. Generally, garbage trucks (often called packer trucks) are used for collecting waste. These vehicles are equipped with a packer body that contains a hydraulic system designed for compacting collected waste. By compacting the collected waste at pick-up sites, the packer body can hold more trash, thereby reducing the number of trips to the landfill (often called the dump). The dumping and compaction process associated with waste collection often enables the release of a watery substance called **leachate** (Figure 7.5), especially following rainy weather. Waste managers are encouraged to prevent the release of leachate in the environment; however, there is considerable debate on how to best manage leachate associated with collection.

Transportation

Compaction trucks (often called garbage trucks or packer trucks) transport the largest volume by far of municipal solid waste as compared to other transport methods. The packer body houses the hydraulic system for compacting the trash and also acts as

Figure 7.5 Leachate Release into the Environment Associated with Collection

the collecting bin for the trash on the truck. The size of the packer body varies, and some trucks can haul as much as 32 cu. yd. The typical truck holds 20–32 cu. yd. of trash; however, in cities where streets are narrower or weight restrictions limit truck size, the packer bodies may only hold 6–16 cu. yd. By using the hydraulic system for compaction, these compaction trucks can hold at least three times as much waste as a truck of equal size without compaction. There are a variety of packer trucks on the road, including front-, side-, and rear-loaders. When designing an approach for collecting waste, it is important to analyze the size and type of truck needed to best do the job in the safest and most cost-effective manner.

Systems using transfer stations, which often include large stationary containers, do not often have their material collected by compaction trucks. Instead, flatbed trucks with winches (a type of hoist) will lift the large 20–40 cu. yd. containers onto their flatbed for hauling to the disposal site. Some stationary containers may have a compaction system on-site to reduce the need for as many pick-ups.

Collection/transportation vehicles must be designed to maximize the safety of the operators, the safety of others, and to protect the environment. Accordingly, collection vehicles should always have the following characteristics:

1. A packer body that is covered and leak-proof.
2. A vehicle and packer body design that is cleanable.
3. A vehicle that is safe, containing proper markings, mirrors, lights, signals, back-up alarm, and other safety mechanisms for protecting operators while loading and/or unloading waste.

Disposal

Land disposal is the most common method for ultimate solid waste disposal. RCRA mandates that the only acceptable form of land disposal is through the use of a sanitary landfill. In some communities, particularly rural environments, open dumping periodically occurs. Open dumping is an unacceptable and illegal method of land disposal in direct violation of local, state, and federal laws. Open dumping is illegal and aesthetically displeasing. This activity creates many environmental and public health problems, while also presenting numerous biological, chemical, and physical hazards to human health.

Sanitary landfills are operations in which the wastes are compacted and covered with a layer of earthen material (soil) at the end of each

Figure 7.6 The Beginning Stages of an Illegal Open Dump

day's operation. Sanitary landfills are operated in a manner to prevent windblown waste scattering, while also designed to prevent the leaching or leaking of environmental pollutants into nearby environments. The goal of the sanitary landfill is to control the environmental pollution by containing potential threats. The design and daily operations of sanitary landfills are regulated by RCRA laws. The EPA has delegated authority to the state governments for regulating landfill operations and enforcing the state laws that evolved from RCRA.

Sanitary landfills have very specific requirements with regard to their construction. For all practicality, sanitary landfills rely on a high-density geomembrane liner, a layer of clay, and compacted soil to prevent the seepage or leaching of liquids and chemicals into the surrounding environment (Figures 7.7 and 7.8). Without these barriers, the risk of chemicals leaching into

Figure 7.7 Sanitary Landfill Construction Includes Laying a High-Density Geomembrane Liner
U.S. Environmental Protection Agency

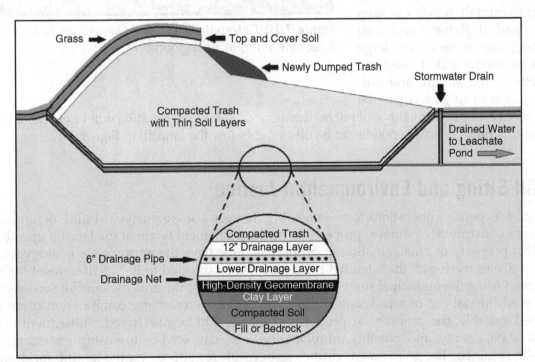

Figure 7.8 Simplified Cross-Section and Features of a Typical Sanitary Landfill

groundwater supplies would be possible; thereby potentially making the chemicals available to harm the environment or people further away from the landfill for many years during and after the landfill stops receiving waste. The local geology of where the landfill is placed is also very important for designing, constructing, and managing a landfill that does not pose significant risk to the environment or human health.

Figure 7.9 Ejection of Municipal Solid Waste from a Rear-Load Compaction Truck

At the landfill, the compaction trucks will eject their waste in areas designated for dumping by the landfill operator (Figure 7.9). This waste will often include more leachate. The landfill operator will often have machinery available to spread and compact the trash onto the existing landfill surface. Overtime, the landfill will grow substantially in size (even into what some people call mountains). In many areas of the country, landfills may be the highest elevation points in an entire county or among several counties. Consequently, landfills have a large surface area readily exposed to rainfall, which can seep into the landfill. Rainfall and even snow melt can create a very large volume of leachate that needs to seep through the landfill and ultimately escape to an area where the

Figure 7.10 Caterpillar® Landfill Compactor in Action with Leachate Pond in Background

environment and public health will not be threatened. Therefore, landfills will have leachate ponds to collect this fluid. Leachate ponds can be observed below the landfill in Figure 7.10.

Landfill Siting and Environmental Justice

Landfills are expensive operations to maintain, but they are also expensive to build. Before a landfill can even be constructed, a suitable property to be the permanent home of the landfill must be identified. This property or amalgamation of properties must have the appropriate geology and be of sufficient size to receive all the intended trash that will be directed to it. The lifetime of the landfill will depend upon the municipal solid waste generation rate of the area the landfill serves, coupled with any additional out-of-area waste received. If the property or the combination of properties is deemed suitable, the property or properties will need to be purchased. Subsequent approval from the state, county, and possibly municipal (village, city, etc.) or township governments will need to be obtained. The government entities responsible for approving the landfill for design and eventual operation will expect to see that thorough planning has occurred on the part of the waste management entity. The purchase and planning of the landfill will require a lot of financial resources for land acquisition and engineering/geotechnical studies.

During the local approval process for the landfill, community participation is required. In many cases the landfill is viewed as a "necessary evil"—needed to take the waste generated by the community, but undesirable to those who have to live near the landfill. Community meetings around landfill-related issues can be very intense, and vocal opposition is common. Nearly all people and communities acknowledge the necessity of having a landfill; however, most people do not want a landfill constructed in their backyard. This attitude is sometimes called the "Not In My Back Yard" syndrome, or **NIMBYism**. Due to the debate surrounding landfill sighting and passionate individuals potentially under the influence of NIMBYism, legal challenges can ensue, further delaying landfill development while increasing landfill development costs.

Sometimes landfill siting on the part of the owner/operator is not ideal for the community and more suitable locations could be sought. More suitable locations may have better geology for landfill development, lower population density, access to safer highway networks, or other desirable characteristics. Suitable landfill locations should be identified and purchased far in advance of landfill construction and planned operation so that there is time to gain consensus among the community members and community leadership.

Environmental Justice

Generally, whenever a landfill is constructed, some attention is given to considering the potential for **environmental justice** issues. Since waste management systems are often placed in areas that have low land values, there is always a concern that the landfill may impact the poor more than other members of society. These impacts may be real or perceived, and may involve fears or actual increased health risks, decreased property values, and/or negative impacts associated with waste transport, odors, or litter. To prevent possible environmental justice issues, the planning process should be aggressive, reaching out for input from impacted stakeholders, while also showing initiative to address area resident concerns and/or negating or mitigating for potential impacts. Such initiatives should demonstrate planned uses for the land surrounding the landfill while also illustrating plans to create economic benefits, such as increased property values. Plans to ensure the protection and safeguarding of the health of the people and the environment must also be clear. Strong consideration should be given by the landfill developer to ensure that a portion of the gains accrued from the landfill improve the infrastructure of the impacted area, including roadway improvements.

Environmental justice issues may be suspected, when certain races, ethnicities, and/or social classes are overrepresented in the homes or apartments surrounding a particular landfill or hazardous waste site. When environmental justice issues are suspected, a more thorough investigation may be warranted. The investigation may ask the following questions:

a. Which came first, the landfill or the people?
b. Did the homeowners or renters arrive before or after the landfill was planned?
c. Has the landfill or waste site caused harm, such as lower property values?

Reducing Waste Management Costs

For communities, individuals, companies, and institutions serious about reducing waste management costs associated with landfill development, waste collection, landfill monitoring, legal challenges pertaining to environmental justice issues, and many other ancillary costs associated with waste management, the three R's are an option. As stated earlier, the three R's of waste management are as follows: Reduce, Reuse, Recycle. Although recycling programs get a lot of attention, reducing the amount of waste generated is the single most important "R" of the three R's for reducing waste management costs. For health and hygiene issues, reuse may not always be possible, but should always be considered. Recycling, the last "R," is the last option for preventing a potential waste item from going into a landfill, where it may take decades or centuries to decompose.

In many communities, recycling is an essential element of the solid waste management program. In some cases, the process of separating materials for reuse from solid waste reduces the amount of waste for disposal. In some well-managed communities that are able to capture a more valuable waste stream, there may be a direct immediate economic return that may help pay for the total cost of the solid waste program.

Materials having recycle value include paper (primarily newspaper and cardboard), aluminum, glass, ferrous metals (iron and steel), plastics, batteries, used oil, and tires. Many believe that the most economical point for the separation of recyclable materials is at the household, office, or business; however, recycling programs must be adapted to the community and be flexible to the needs of the people to be most productive and valuable. Programs may include residential collection, single-material drop-off centers, or larger cen-

Figure 7.11 Universal Recycling Symbol
U.S. Environmental Protection Agency

tralized processing facilities. The most effective recycling programs provide sufficient education and have strong participation and engagement by the community.

The United States has tremendous recycling potential, as over 50% of our generated municipal solid waste is recyclable. For example, paper products, plastics, metals, and glass compose 53% of the U.S. municipal solid waste stream (Figure 7.12). Paper products alone comprise nearly 30% of all municipal solid waste. Not surprising, the United States recycles a very significant amount of waste that would once have been destined for a landfill. Currently, the United States recycles over 90 million tons of municipal solid waste annually (Figure 7.13). This is a substantial improvement over the 5–10 million tons recycled annually during the 1960s and 1970s.

Since the 1970s, much progress has been made with regard to U.S. recycling efforts. In just the last 40 years, the United States has made remarkable progress in increasing the percentage of waste being recycled, going from nearly 7% to over 30%. Just since 1990, the United States recycled about 15% of all municipal solid waster; it now recycles over 30%, representing a two-fold increase in recycling in just 20 years.

Further reductions for preventing waste from entering the landfill are possible by **composting**. Food wastes, yard trimmings, and certain types of wood make up over 25% of all U.S. municipal solid waste, and are all compostable types of waste. Paper products can also be sometimes mixed in with compost. Composted products biodegrade much faster outside landfills rather than in

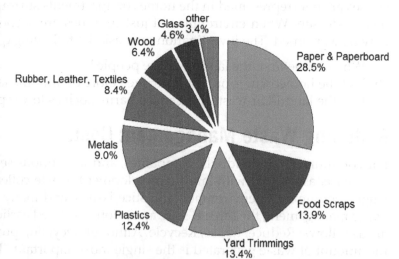

Figure 7.12 Pie Chart Characterizing U.S. Municipal Solid Waste by Material Volume[6]

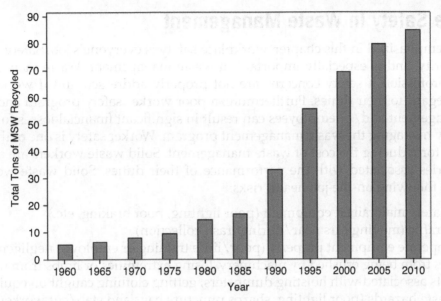

Figure 7.13 Total Tons of U.S. Municipal Solid Waste Recycled Annually[6]

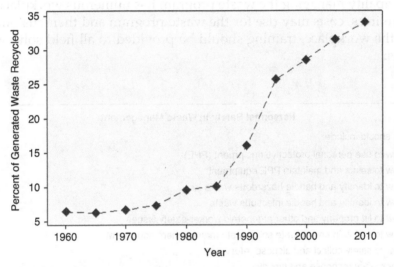

Figure 7.14 Percentage of U.S. Municipal Solid Waste Recycled Annually[6]

landfills where compaction occurs and oxygen is limited. Composting relies on microbial degradation of the waste, which is enhanced by oxygen and self-generated heat related to the actual decomposition. Some communities provide community-wide composting and may actively grind material using a massive piece of machinery called a tub grinder to further speed up decomposition. The finished decomposition product, often called compost, is rich in nutrients, has a variety of uses, and may even have market value.

Workplace Safety In Waste Management

Although not emphasized in this chapter, workplace safety is everyone's job. Safety should always be a high priority, and is especially important in waste management. Waste management can be a dangerous profession if safety concerns are not properly addressed and if workers are poorly trained with regard to their duties. Furthermore, a poor worker safety program and disinterest in safety by management and/or employees can result in significant financial losses for the company or municipality managing the waste management program. Worker safety is one of the most important strategies for reducing the cost of waste management. Solid waste workers are at considerable risk from injuries associated with the performance of their duties. Solid waste workers may be exposed to the following on-the-job health risks:

1. Inappropriately maintained equipment (poor lighting, poor braking, etc.)
2. Vehicular traffic (moving cars near/during trash collection)
3. Failure to operate equipment properly (poor/little training or employee negligence resulting in accidents from being crushed by machinery, losing extremities or limbs from numerous pinch points associated with hoisting dumpsters, getting clothing caught on equipment, etc.)
4. Hidden waste hazards (poor lighting, sharps puncture bags and stab/cut worker, unknown gases volatilized and inhaled during collection and compaction, etc.)
5. Co-workers (co-workers may not be trained properly and can accidentally hurt other co-worker(s) if not careful during team collection efforts)

If a solid waste company is deemed negligent in an accident, the costs of providing a remedy for the accident could be shifted indirectly to customers or taxpayers. Furthermore, if a solid waste company or municipality managing the waste program has numerous workplace injuries or health problems among retirees, costs may rise for the waste program and their customers. To reduce the risk of injuries in the workplace, training should be provided to all field solid waste personnel in the following areas:

Personnel Safety in Waste Management

Training should include:

- How to use personal protective equipment (PPE)
- How to select and maintain PPE equipment
- How to identify and handle hazardous waste
- How to identify and handle infectious waste
- How to lift properly and other ergonomic worker-safety issues
- How to maintain and operate solid waste management equipment
- How to safely collect and dispose refuse
- Emergency response and first aid

Management should be responsible for:

- Ensuring the workplace is alcohol- and drug-free
- Providing appropriate PPE
- Ensuring that trucks and other heavy equipment have back-up alarms
- Ensuring that factory-installed safety switches and guards are functioning properly on equipment
- Providing procedures and a place for emergency response and decontamination
- Providing and encouraging teamwork in potentially hazardous work situations
- Establishing safe refuse and disposal collection protocols.

Figure 7.15 Practices enhancing solid waste worker safety

Summary

The world and the United States have made considerable progress in managing solid and hazardous waste. Through increased reduction, reuse, recycling, and composting of potential waste materials, further progress can be made. Progress in reducing the amount of waste ending up in landfills will continue to have financial benefits by reducing the need for collecting, disposing of, and managing huge volumes of waste. These reductions will also decrease the need to consume more land for dedicated landfill purposes. Cost-savings associated with waste reduction can be directed to other beneficial programs. Waste management; however, is here to stay. Many waste materials are already in the ground and will need to be continually managed. New waste materials are going to continue to be generated daily. The need for waste collectors, waste haulers, waste managers, and environmental health professionals associated with the waste management profession will continue for many years to come. Waste management will always be important for environmental health professionals who play a major role in ensuring workplace safety while protecting the environment and human health.

References

[1]McMahon, M. 1994. Publick Service versus Mans Properties: Dock Creek and the Origins of Urban Technology in Eighteenth-Century Philadelphia." In *Early American Technology: Making and Doing Things from the Colonial Era to 1850*. ed. Judith A. McGaw (Chapel Hill: University of North Carolina Press), pp. 114–147.

[2]Flood, L. 1959. Air pollution resulting from incineration – its reduction and control. *Journal of the Air Pollution Control Association*, 9(1):63–68.

[3]Fair, G. 1959. The collection, treatment and utilization of solid wastes: practice and research in the USA. *Bulletin of the World Health Organization*, 20(4):717–724.

[4]U.S. Department of Justice. 1995. Occidental to pay $129 million in Love Canal settlement. http://www.justice.gov/opa/pr/Pre_96/December95/638.txt.html

[5]U.S. Department of Labor. 2012. Industries at a glance – waste management and remediation services: NAICS 562. http://www.bls.gov/iag/tgs/iag562.htm

[6]U.S. Environmental Protection Agency. 2012. Municipal solid waste. http://www.epa.gov/epawaste/nonhaz/municipal/index.htm

[7]U.S. Environmental Protection Agency. 2012. Focus on recycling. http://epa.gov/region4/recycle/

Changing Agricultural Practices and Their Impact on Disease Control

8

David McSwane, HSD, REHS, CP-FS, DAAS

Agriculture in the United States contributes to the health and welfare of its citizens by producing approximately 80% of the food it eats, providing many different types of jobs, and contributing significantly to the nation's economy. The U.S. agriculture system plays a major role in the safety of the foods consumed in this country as well as the food exported to hundreds of countries worldwide. The safety and wholesomeness of foods intended for human consumption is influenced by production and handling at the farm, ranch, orchard and many other points of contact. Therefore, food safety interventions must be implemented at a variety of points from farm to table. In addition, one must not lose sight of the fact that the safety and quality of finished products is typically no better than the foods and ingredients that are used to produce them.

Key Performance Outcome Indicators:

- Describe some ways that agriculture impacts the health and economy of our nation
- Identify some disease-causing microorganisms that have been linked to foodborne illness in produce
- Provide some examples of Good Agricultural Practices (GAPs) and describe how they are used to reduce the risk of microbial contamination in produce
- Describe concentrated animal feeding operations (CAFOs) and explain how they have contributed to human exposure to antimicrobial resistant pathogens
- Identify some sanitation measures that must be taken on dairy farms to reduce the risk of contamination of raw milk

Agriculture is a major source of the food we eat and a leading contributor to the nation's economy. According to the U.S. Department of Agriculture (USDA), the U.S. agricultural system provides American consumers with 80% of the food they consume and at a price that is lower than in most countries throughout the world. In addition, one in twelve jobs in this country is directly or indirectly affiliated with U.S. agriculture.[1]

The U.S. food and agriculture system is both vast and complex. It encompasses approximately 2.2 million farms covering more than 1 billion acres of land.[2] In addition, there are approximately 900,000 companies and more than a million facilities that work with food from farm to table.[3] The food and agriculture system is commonly divided into preharvest and postharvest components. The preharvest component includes crop, plant, and livestock production. Crops and plants include commodities such as fruits and vegetables intended for human consumption, and grains and forage that is fed to livestock. Livestock production provides food animals and animal products, such as milk, and includes species such as beef cattle, dairy cattle, swine, goats, and sheep. Other farm-raised food animals include chickens, turkeys, and other types of poultry as well as some species of fish and shellfish that are raised using aquaculture.

The postharvest segment includes the portions of the food supply chain that involve processing, packaging, warehousing, and distribution to restaurants, retail stores, institutional food establishments, and other types of retail food establishments. Distribution is an essential and complex component of the farm-to-table continuum. It encompasses transportation, storage, and logistics, both domestically and internationally. Approximately 21 million trucks transport products, including a majority of food and agricultural commodities, across the United States every day. Rail transportation is also an important part of the domestic food distribution system.[4]

The goal of food safety is to protect food throughout the various stages of production from the farm to the table. What occurs at the farm will have a direct bearing on the safety of the foods that are supplied to retail food establishments and ultimately to consumers. The focus of this chapter is on food safety interventions being implemented by food producers (farmers, ranchers, etc.) to reduce the risk of foodborne illness associated with their products. While it would be impossible to study all types of food producers, this chapter will cover interventions used at produce and animal farms to ensure the safety and wholesomeness of their food products. Protecting the safety and integrity of the U.S. agricultural and food supply system is essential to safeguard public health and preserve the security of the nation's economy.

The Agriculture System as a Source of Plant Foods

People of all ages are eating more fruits and vegetables as part of a healthy, well-balanced diet. However, as consumption of produce has increased, so has the number of foodborne disease outbreaks, cases of foodborne illness, and food recalls that are associated with these types of food products. Two disease-causing agents most commonly associated with produce are *Salmonella* and *E. coli* O157:H7 bacteria. However, foodborne illness has also been caused by other pathogens linked to fruits and vegetables. Some examples of these pathogens and the produce items they were linked to during foodborne disease outbreaks are noted in Table 8.1.

Table 8.1

DISEASE-CAUSING MICROORGANISMS	FRUITS AND VEGETABLES LINKED TO FOODBORNE DISEASE OUTBREAKS
Cyclospora parasite	raspberries and strawberries
E. coli O157:H7	apple cider/juice, cabbage, celery, coleslaw, cucumbers, green onions, lettuce, mushrooms, potatoes, radishes, salad items, spinach
Hepatitis A virus	green onions
L. monocytogenes	coleslaw, green onions, lettuce, strawberries, cantaloupe
Norovirus	lettuce and fresh fruits.
Salmonella spp.	alfalfa sprouts, cantaloupe, lettuce, orange juice, green peppers, leafy greens, tomatoes
Shigella spp.	cantaloupe, scallions, sprouts, tomatoes, watermelon

The increased incidence of foodborne disease associated with fruits and vegetables is likely due to a combination of factors. First, as previously noted, people are eating more produce because of its nutritional benefits. Second, most produce is eaten raw or is considered ready-to-eat, which means it will be eaten by consumers without being cooked, washed, or prepared in some way to make it safe. Finally, a large portion of the produce consumed in the United States is imported from countries all over the world. Some of these are developing countries where sanitation standards are low and government oversight of food production facilities is minimal or nonexistent.

Reducing the incidence of foodborne illness in produce requires interventions at many levels of the produce food chain. The first interventions will occur at the farm where produce is grown and harvested. There are many potential sources of contamination that can be introduced during planting, growing, and harvesting. The primary sources of contamination are manure, animals, people, pesticides, as well as polluted water, soil, and air.

Biological hazards are the most common cause of foodborne illness and food spoilage. Biological hazards include bacteria, viruses, and parasites. These organisms are so small they are not visible without a microscope. They are frequently referred to as the "invisible challenge" because of their extremely small size and the fact that they are everywhere in our natural and man-made environment. Bacteria and viruses are the most common causes of foodborne illness related to most food products, including produce. It is important to remember that the microbial pathogens that cause foodborne illness usually do not alter the appearance, odor, texture, or taste of food. Therefore, people consume contaminated food because they are unaware that it is contaminated and unsafe to eat.

Good Agricultural Practices

In 1998, the U.S. Food and Drug Administration (FDA) published a *Guide to Minimize Microbial Food Safety Hazards for Fruits and Vegetables* which provides nonbinding recommendations for growers, packers, and shippers to use Good Agricultural Practices (GAPs) and Good Manufacturing Practices (GMPs) in those areas over which they have control to prevent or minimize microbial food safety hazards in fresh produce.[5] The FDA also published a related document in 2008 entitled *Guide to Minimize Microbial Food Safety Hazards of Fresh-cut Fruits and Vegetables*, which specifically addresses "fresh-cut" fruits and vegetables. These are produce products that have been minimally processed (e.g., no lethal kill step), and altered in form by peeling, slicing, chopping, shredding, coring, or trimming, with or without washing or other treatment, prior to being packaged for use by the consumer or a retail establishment.[6] These documents have proven to be valuable tools for many segments of the produce industry.

A training program to support the Good Agricultural Practices (GAPs) program was developed for farm workers and the produce distribution chain by Cornell University and collaborating universities (http://www.gaps.cornell.edu/). This initiative was funded by the USDA and FDA. The GAPs program provides the basis for reducing the risk of microbial contamination in produce grown in the United States.

Once fruits and vegetables are contaminated, it is difficult to remove or eliminate the pathogens from the products. Therefore, prevention is the key to assuring the safety of produce. Growers must have GAPs in place that are tailored to their commodities and management practices in order to effectively reduce microbial risks and prevent contamination on the farm every day.

Contamination with microbial pathogens can occur when fruits and vegetables are in the fields or orchards as well as during harvesting and transport. Therefore, GAPs must be implemented when preparing fields, planting and managing crops, harvesting produce, and during postharvest operations. The GAPs that have been created to reduce biological contamination during production and harvest focus on (1) water used for irrigation and cleaning, (2) source, use, and handling of manure, (3) employee training and hygiene, and (4) proper sanitation of farm equipment.

Irrigation and Wash Water

Water is used on the farm and orchard for many purposes, including irrigation, mixing with pesticides, and produce washing and cooling. It is possible for raw water from surface and groundwater sources to contain pathogens such as *E. coli*, *Salmonella*, *Giardia*, and *Cyclospora*. Some large, multistate outbreaks of foodborne illness have been linked to produce that was contaminated with polluted water.

Farm and orchard operations are commonly divided into agricultural and postharvest operations. Agricultural operations include activities such as irrigation and pesticide applications. Water of lesser quality can be used for these purposes if the water does not have direct contact with produce or contact

Figure 8.1 Field of Cabbage.
Courtesy of David McSwane

occurs before fruits and vegetables are positioned on the plant. However, irrigation procedures that expose produce to polluted water can increase the risk of microbial contamination. In these situations, it is important to minimize direct contact between irrigation water and produce by using drip or furrow irrigation instead of spray irrigation.

The use of reclaimed or recaptured wastewater for crop irrigation is not uncommon in areas where there are chronic water shortages and water conservation programs have been implemented. The reclaimed water has been treated using standard wastewater treatment processes and technologies and is considered safe for irrigation purposes.

Some postharvest operations use water for washing, rinsing, and carrying produce from one stage of the process to another. Potable water should be used in these types of operations because the water is likely to come into direct contact with the fruits and vegetables. In addition to using potable water, antimicrobial agents are frequently added to the water used during postharvest operations to ensure that it is of the highest quality possible.

Some additional GAP recommendations to farm and orchard operators to enhance the quality of water used in agricultural and postharvest operations include:

• Know the source of the water and its intended use
• Evaluate the irrigation method
• Be certain wells are properly located and constructed
• Test water quarterly for fecal coliform bacteria and keep records of all water test results
• Be active in local watershed management efforts to reduce the potential for pollution of ground water and surface water sources.

Manure Source, Use, and Handling

Animal manure is a valuable source of nutrients for crops, but it also can be a source of pathogens such as *E. coli* O157:H7, *Salmonella*, and *Campylobacter* bacteria. These organisms can remain viable in manure for several weeks. When improperly aged or treated manure is used as fertilizer, it can increase the risk of microbial contamination of produce. If manure comes into contact with fruits and vegetables or water containing pathogens from manure splashes onto produce, it can contaminate the food and increase the risk of foodborne illness.

Growers can reduce the risk of contamination from manure by making certain it is stored, handled, and applied properly. Manure should be stockpiled away from areas where fresh produce is grown, and, when possible, barriers should be installed to prevent runoff of manure. Growers can also compost the manure to kill most of the pathogenic bacteria. The high temperature and aerobic environment associated with the composting process produce a high-quality, stable compost.

Growers can reduce the risk of contamination from manure by carefully timing its application. Manure should be applied in the fall or at the end of the growing season to reduce exposure to crops. If it is necessary to apply manure at the start of a growing season, the GAPs recommend that the manure be applied at least two weeks before planting and 120 days before the produce will be harvested. Once manure is applied to a field, it should be incorporated into soil immediately to reduce the number of harmful pathogens that survive in soil.

Growers must also take measures to prevent contamination from manure from animals confined in adjoining fields as well as wild and domestic animals that may enter the growers' fields or orchards to graze. This can be best accomplished by diverting runoff from nearby fields away from the fields where produce is grown and placing fences around the perimeter of the fields to keep out animals.

Employee Training and Hygiene

Good personal hygiene by farm workers is critical, especially during harvest and postharvest operations. Pathogens can be easily spread to produce by workers who are ill or have contaminated hands. Workers with nausea, vomiting, or diarrhea symptoms should not handle food or any surface that comes in contact with food. Open wounds are also likely sources of contamination. If a wound cannot be adequately covered with a waterproof bandage, the worker should be assigned duties that do not involve direct contact with fruits and vegetables as well as with the surfaces of equipment that come into contact with produce.

Convenient access to restroom facilities with handwash stations helps promote good personal hygiene by workers. Workers must understand how poor personal hygiene increases the risk of spreading pathogens that can cause foodborne illness. They need to be trained about food safety hazards and the consequences of improper hygiene and sanitation. They should also receive training on the grower's sanitation standards and hygiene policies and practices. Training should be conducted in a way that all workers can understand the information. Whenever possible, trainers should demonstrate good hygiene practices, such as proper handwashing techniques. It may be necessary to provide bilingual instructions and visual aids to enhance training. It is important to train all new workers on sanitation and hygiene practices, and it is equally important to conduct refresher training programs for experienced workers.

Farm workers must know how and when to wash their hands. They should wash their hands before starting work; after breaks; after eating, drinking or smoking; after using the restroom; after blowing their nose or touching their face or hair; after handling dirty or raw materials; after performing maintenance on equipment; and after picking up objects off the ground. Workers should wash their hands with soap and warm running water. Hands are washed by briskly rubbing them

Figure 8.2 Handwashing Station in a Produce Field.
Courtesy of David McSwane

Figure 8.3 Toilet Facilities in a Produce Field.
Courtesy of David McSwane

together for 15–20 seconds. Proper handwashing includes scrubbing the front and back sides of the hands as well as between fingers and under fingernails. Washed hands should be rinsed with clean, running water and dried with single-use paper towels.

Growers must provide adequate and convenient toilet and handwashing facilities for employees who are harvesting produce in fields and orchards. Workers who relieve themselves in the field can undermine food safety, but having convenient toilet facilities will help discourage this practice. Convenient locations may include setting up toilet facilities at the end of the field. However, if harvesting is occurring in large fields that cover many acres or in constantly changing areas of a field, the grower may want to provide portable toilet facilities that can be moved as needed to remain close to the areas of the field where harvesting is taking place. Toilet facilities must be maintained in a sanitary condition. Maintenance of these facilities typically involves picking up trash; cleaning and disinfecting toilets, urinals, floors, and walls; and collecting and disposing of sewage in a manner that will not permit leakage or spillage in the field.

Handwashing facilities must be supplied with potable water, soap, and single-use hand towels. A soap dispenser is preferred over a bar of soap to prevent the spreads of germs. Containers used to store and transport water for handwashing sinks should be emptied, cleaned, sanitized, and refilled with potable water on a regular basis. If possible, a container should be provided to collect dirty water from handwashing sinks rather than letting it fall to the ground. If hand sanitizers are provided at a handwashing facility, workers should be taught that the hand sanitizers are to be used in addition to handwashing and not as a replacement for it.

Farm and Equipment Sanitation

Properly designed and constructed equipment and containers (bins) help keep crops free from contamination that can promote disease and product spoilage. Equipment and containers should be made of nontoxic materials and constructed to be smooth, seamless, durable, and easily cleanable. Nonwashable materials such as wood, burlap, and reused cardboard are not permitted because they are porous and can harbor microbes that cause disease and spoilage.

Growers should develop and follow a cleaning schedule for equipment such as tables, bins, buckets, brushes, and hand tools. Dirt and organic matter on surfaces of equipment and containers prevents sanitizers from destroying bacteria and viruses. Therefore, it is important that surfaces of equipment and containers be cleaned before they are sanitized. Equipment and containers should be cleaned with a detergent, rinsed, and sanitized with a commercial product that contains chlorine or quaternary ammonium compounds. Bins should be stored in the full sun when possible to promote drying. In addition, UV light from the sun will help destroy pathogens. Growers should also inspect for signs of insect, rodent, and bird infestation. These pests pose a potential source of contamination and should be dealt with as quickly as possible.

GAPs have also been created to minimize the risk of biological contamination during the postharvest stage of production. These GAPs target the following areas:

- Worker hygiene
- Design and sanitation of the packinghouse
- Washing operations
- Produce cooling and cold storage
- Packing lines
- Transportation of produce from farm to market
- Implementing a traceback system.

Figure 8.4 Bin of Freshly Picked Green Peppers.

Courtesy of David McSwane

Worker Hygiene

Workers in postharvest operations pose the same risks as workers in the field, and many of the personal hygiene practices that are required in the field must also be followed in the packinghouse. Workers who are ill and show symptoms of nausea, vomiting, and diarrhea must not be allowed to work directly with produce. The cleanliness of a worker's hands during processing and packing is vitally important to the safety of the food. Packinghouse workers must know when and how to wash their hands. In addition, properly equipped toilet facilities must be provided, and handwashing stations must be conveniently located throughout the production area. Whenever a packing line worker has an open wound on his or her hand, it should be covered with a waterproof bandage and a disposable glove. Workers should be taught to change gloves whenever they become contaminated and to wear hair restraints and aprons as needed to protect produce from contamination.

Design and Sanitation of the Packinghouse

Figure 8.5 Tomato Sorting and Culling Operation.
Courtesy of David McSwane

In some instances, a packinghouse will be located in or near a grower's field and will be used to process fruits and vegetables from a single farm. In other cases, the packinghouse is located off-site and processes produce from a number of different growers in the area. In either scenario, a properly designed packinghouse can help eliminate conditions that lead to contamination and cross-contamination of the food being processed.

The floors, walls, and ceilings of a packinghouse should be constructed of materials that are durable, smooth, and easily cleanable. Floors should be sloped to allow drainage, and floor drains should be installed in a manner that will facilitate cleaning and sanitizing and be covered with a metal screen or cover to prevent the entry of rodents into the facility.

The packinghouse should be constructed to prevent the entry of pests such as insects, rodents, and birds. Windows and doors should be tight-fitting and properly screened. Large openings like the loading dock should be equipped with air curtains and electrocution devices to prevent the entry of flying insects. When closed, the loading dock doors should provide a tight seal to prevent the entry of crawling insects, rodents, and birds.

Shatterproof light bulbs and/or properly shielded light fixtures should be installed to prevent contamination of food by glass fragments which are a physical hazard.

The food-processing equipment inside a packinghouse should be laid out and installed so that finished and unfinished products are kept separate and never come into contact with the same surfaces or each other. An ideal design for a packinghouse permits produce from the farm to enter the building at one end and the finished products to emerge at the opposite end of the building.

Processing equipment should be designed and constructed to permit effective cleaning and sanitizing. Equipment should be easily disassembled for cleaning and inspection. Bins, containers, packing line belts, and conveyors used to transport food products from one area to another in the packinghouse must be properly maintained and repaired to prevent them from becoming potential sources of contamination.

Washing Operations and Packing Lines

Produce washing is the first step that occurs at the packinghouse. The washing process removes soil and other types of foreign material from the surface of the fruits and vegetables. The washwater must be sanitary, and a sanitizer such as chlorine is frequently added to the washwater to reduce pathogens on the surface of the produce. Dirty washwater reduces the effectiveness of sanitizer. Therefore, the process water should be replaced when it gets dirty or after several hours of operation. Workers should use a sanitizer test kit to monitor the chlorine level in the washwater, and the correct amount of the sanitizer should be added to achieve the desired concentration in the washwater. Packers should ensure

Figure 8.6 Potato Washing Operation.
Courtesy of David McSwane

that the temperature of the washwater is not more than 10°F cooler than the produce to prevent infiltration which can allow bacteria on the produce or in the water to be drawn inside the produce. This concern is greatest for tomatoes, peppers, apples, and potatoes.

Biofilm is a type of foreign material that poses significant challenges for produce growers and packers. Biofilm forms when bacteria and other types of microbes stick to the surface of the produce and food-processing equipment. These microbes produce waste products that gradually form a very thin layer of a slimy, gluelike substance. Biofilms can stick to all kinds of materials including metals, plastics, and biological tissues. Biofilms pose a challenge for the food industry because they are hard to remove from the surface of food and equipment, and they can shield pathogenic microorganisms from the effects of the chemical sanitizers that are used during the produce-washing process. Biofilm is believed to have contributed to two large multistate foodborne disease outbreaks linked to cantaloupe in 2011 and 2012. Food scientists are currently searching for better ways to remove the biofilms that are created by microbes found on the surface of certain foods and the food contact surfaces of equipment.

Produce Cooling and Cold Storage

Fruits and vegetables need to be cooled quickly to minimize the growth of pathogens and maintain optimal quality. If ice is used to cool produce, it must be made from potable water. Cooling rooms equipped with mechanical refrigeration should be maintained at 45°F or below. Packinghouse workers must make certain the cooling capacity of cooling rooms and cold storage areas is not exceeded. Coolers should be emptied periodically in order to clean and sanitize the floors, walls, ceiling, and cooling unit. An effective sanitation program for cooling rooms and walk-in coolers will help control *Listeria monocytogenes* and other microbial pathogens of concern in a refrigerated environment.

Packing Lines

Packing materials must be stored in a dry area away from processing equipment and used in a sanitary manner. Packing line belts, conveyors, and other food contact surfaces must be washed at the end of

Figure 8.7 Strawberries in a Walk-in Cooler Awaiting Shipping.
Courtesy of David McSwane

each day to prevent contamination. Packing materials must be removed from the packing area before equipment is cleaned and sanitized and floors, walls, and ceilings are cleaned.

Regular cleaning and maintenance of the exterior portion of the building and grounds is necessary to maintain the sanitary conditions at the facility. In addition, trash and garbage should be stored in containers with tight-fitting lids. These measures are important to avoid attracting insects and rodents and to reduce the risk of contamination being brought in from outside the facility.

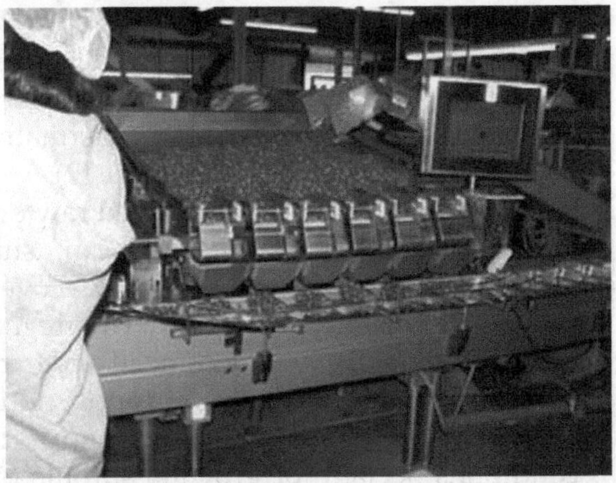

Figure 8.8 Packing Line for Cherry Tomatoes. Courtesy of David McSwane

Transportation of Produce from Farm to Market

Produce must only be shipped in trucks which have a clean cargo area. Dirty vehicles can contaminate produce with harmful microorganisms. Growers and packers should avoid shipping fruits and vegetables in trucks that have been used to transport livestock or hazardous materials. If this cannot be avoided, the cargo area of the trucks must be thoroughly cleaned and sanitized before transporting the produce.

Implementing a traceback system

Traceback is the ability to trace a fruit or vegetable back to its field of origin. Being able to trace a product back to its source in a short period of time has become the standard for many food companies. The produce industry recently began implementing traceback and traceforward tracking systems to follow the movement of fruits and vegetables through specified stages of production, processing, and distribution. These systems permit food companies and food regulatory agencies to identify where a food came from (one step back) and where it goes to (one step forward) at any stage in the food flow. This is a valuable source of information that can be used during product recalls and foodborne disease outbreak investigations. Growers and packers should make certain that each package that leaves a farm or packinghouse can be traced to the field or farm of origin and the date it was packed. In addition, they should maintain records of lot numbers for all loads and packaged produce leaving a farm or packinghouse.

Sprouts Pose Unique But Manageable Food Safety Challenge

The amount of raw sprouts consumed in the United States has increased significantly in recent years. Sprouts are an excellent source of fiber, protein, vitamin C, and B complex vitamins. However, with increased sprouts consumption have come more cases of foodborne illness associated with this product. The Centers for Disease Control and Prevention (CDC) reports more than 30 outbreaks of foodborne illness associated with sprouts since 1996. (1)

Contaminated sprouts have been linked to both multistate and multinational foodborne disease outbreaks and numerous product recalls. Alfalfa, clover, and mung bean are the most common types of sprouts, and they have been most frequently implicated in sprout-associated foodborne disease outbreaks. *Salmonella* and *E. coli* bacteria are the disease-causing agents in most of the outbreaks. In 2011, a multinational foodborne disease outbreak was caused by a

(Continued)

rare form of *E. coli* (O104:H4) linked to bean sprouts. According to the World Health Organization, the outbreak caused 4,075 cases illness and 50 deaths in 14 countries in Europe as well as Canada and the United States. Germany was at the center of the outbreak and experienced 3,935 cases of illness and 48 deaths. (2)

Sprouts are typically consumed raw or lightly cooked. This raises their risk as a vehicle of foodborne illness. Healthy adults can usually eat sprouts with minimal risk of infection, and those who may become ill usually recover without treatment. However, people in high-risk groups (young children, the elderly, pregnant women, and those with weakened immune systems) are more likely to become ill and experience the most severe symptoms. For this reason, individuals in these high-risk groups should avoid eating raw sprouts of any kind.

Sprouts production poses a unique challenge for food safety because the warm, humid conditions needed for growing sprouts from seeds are ideal for bacteria to flourish. *Salmonella*, *E. coli*, and other pathogenic bacteria can reach levels capable of causing illness without affecting the appearance of the sprouts. Another unique feature about sprouts is that the seeds used to produce them are the most likely source of microbial contamination. According to FDA, damage to seeds or treatments that scratch the surface of the seeds are most likely to increase pathogens within the seed and make disinfection more difficult. (3) A few bacteria on the seeds can grow to high numbers of pathogens on the sprouts in a relatively short period of time.

FDA created a guidance document for the sprouts industry that provides recommendations for reducing the risk of contamination of sprouts by harmful bacteria. (4) These nonbinding recommendations identify preventive controls that FDA believes should be taken by seed producers, conditioners, distributors, and sprout growers to reduce the risk of raw sprouts as a source of foodborne illness. A brief summary of FDA's recommendations is as follows:

Seed Production: By implementing GAPs, seed suppliers can reduce the pathogen levels in seeds that will be used for sprout production. Seed suppliers should also sample every batch of seeds and test them for *Salmonella* and *E. coli* bacteria.

Seed Conditioning, Storage, and Transportation: Seeds used for sprouting should be conditioned, stored, and transported in a way that minimizes the likelihood that the seeds will become contaminated. Seed should be stored in bags or covered containers off the floor and away from walls. Seed storage areas should be kept clean, dry, and free of pests.

Sprout Production: Sprout growers should implement good manufacturing practices (GMPs) during production, packaging, and finished product storage to ensure that sprouts are produced under sanitary conditions. Sprouts growers must utilize good sanitation practices throughout all stages of production. The production facility must be supplied with potable water and have proper sewage disposal. Workers must follow safe and hygienic food-handling practices, and equipment and facilities must be maintained in a sanitary condition that will reduce the likelihood of the sprouts being contaminated with pathogens.

Seed Treatment: FDA guidelines state that at least one approved antimicrobial treatment should be applied to the seeds immediately before sprouting. Calcium hypochlorite at 20,000 ppm for 15 minutes with agitation is the preferred method. To achieve the desired kill step, sprouts growers must use the correct concentration of disinfectant, ensure proper contact time, and regularly verify the concentration of the antimicrobial solution used to treat their sprout seeds. Sprout producers should carefully follow all label directions when mixing and using antimicrobial chemicals.

Testing for Pathogens: The antimicrobials currently approved for use with sprouts seeds have not proven effective at eliminating all pathogens. Therefore, FDA recommends that sprout producers conduct microbiological testing of spent irrigation water from each batch of sprouts to ensure that contaminated product is not distributed. The recommended testing procedures are described in the FDA guidance document entitled *Sampling and Microbial Testing of Spent Irrigation Water During Sprout Production*. (5) On the second day after planting the seeds, a sample of seed irrigation water is collected and tested for *Salmonella* and *E. coli*. Because laboratory testing for pathogens can be done with irrigation water as early as 48 hours into the growing process, producers should be able to obtain test results before shipping product without losing product shelf-life. **Absolutely no sprouts should be shipped until negative results are obtained**. Testing, whether done by the producer or contracted out, should be done by trained personnel, in a qualified laboratory, using validated methods. In addition, correct interpretation of the test results is vital to ensuring the safety of the product before it enters the marketplace.

Traceback: Traceback cannot prevent foodborne illness. However, being able to quickly trace a food back to its source can limit the public health and economic impacts of an outbreak, if it occurs. Information gained in traceback investigations may also help prevent future outbreaks. Sprout producers, seed producers, conditioners, and distributors should develop and implement systems to facilitate traceback and recalls in the event of a problem. All parties should test their systems in advance of a real problem.

Food safety regulatory agencies are working with the sprouts industry to enhance the safety of sprouts and protect consumers by keeping contaminated sprouts out of the marketplace. Sprout producers are routinely inspected by federal and/or state food safety regulatory agency personnel to assure compliance with food safety standards and protocols. Sprout producers frequently implement a Hazard Analysis and Critical Control Point (HACCP) food safety system and use third-party audit services to supplement regulatory inspections.

Food retailers can also implement measures to promote the quality and safety of raw sprouts. Some examples of things retailers should do are:

- Purchase sprouts only from reputable suppliers (growers, packers, coolers, transporters, etc.) that use GAPs, GMPs, and other appropriate food safety practices from farm to store.

- Assure sprouts are at the proper temperature when received and maintain proper product temperature throughout storage and display. When kept at 32°F (0°C), most sprouts may be expected to maintain acceptable quality for five to nine days. Shelf-life at 36°F (2.5°C) is less than five days and at 41°F (5°C) is less than two days. (6)

- Protect sprouts and all ready-to-eat foods from cross-contamination.

- Provide a consumer advisory that informs people in high-risk groups to avoid eating raw or lightly cooked sprouts of any kind.

- Inform consumers that they can cook sprouts to reduce the risk of foodborne illness.

Like any fresh produce that is consumed raw or lightly cooked, sprouts carry a risk of foodborne illness. However, sprouts are unique in that the seeds used to produce them are the most likely source of contamination. Nonetheless, by strictly following FDA guidelines and proper food safety practices, firms can produce and retailers can sell sprouts that will be safe for "most" consumers to eat.

References

1. Centers for Disease Control and Prevention. (2011, February 10) *Investigation Update: Multistate Outbreak of Human Salmonella I 4,[5],12:i:- Infections Linked to Alfalfa Sprouts*. Retrieved from http://www.cdc.gov/salmonella/i4512i-/021011/index.html

(Continued)

2. World Health Organization. (2011, July 22) *Outbreaks of E. coli O104:H4 infection: update 30.* Retrieved from: http://www.euro.who.int/en/what-we-do/health-topics/emergencies/international-health-regulations/news/news/2011/07/outbreaks-of-e.-coli-o104h4-infection-update-30

3. United States Food and Drug Administration. *Sprouts: What You Should Know.* http://www.foodsafety.gov/keep/types/fruits/sprouts.html

4. United States Food and Drug Administration. 1999. *Guidance for Industry: Reducing Microbial Food Safety Hazards for Sprouted Seeds.* http://www.fda.gov/Food/GuidanceComplianceRegulatoryInformation/GuidanceDocuments/ProduceandPlanProducts/ucm120244.htm

5. Food and Drug Administration. 1999. *Guidance for Industry: Sampling and Microbial Testing of Spent Irrigation Water During Sprout Production.* http://www.fda.gov/Food/GuidanceComplianceRegulatoryInformation/GuidanceDocuments/ProduceandPlanProducts/ucm120246.htm

6. Trevor Suslow and Marita Cantwell. 2009. *Seed Sprouts—Recommendations for Maintaining Postharvest Quality.* University of California, Davis, CA. http://postharvest.ucdavis.edu/Produce/ProduceFacts/Veg/seedsprouts.shtml Edited version of article by same name reprinted with permission of the National Registry of Food Safety Professionals, E-Zine, May, 2011. Accessed August 23, 2012. http://www.nrfsp.com/E-Zine/Archived%20Issues/2011/May%202011%20Issue.aspx

Agriculture System as a Source of Food Animals and Animal Products

In addition to producing food crops, the U.S. agriculture system provides large quantities of food animals and animal products for human consumption. Food animals include a variety of meat and poultry species such as beef, pigs, goats, sheep, chickens, turkeys, ducks, geese, and ostriches. Recent advances in aquaculture have resulted in increased production of farm-raised fish and shellfish. Some common examples of animal products are eggs, milk, and milk products.

Agriculture has changed dramatically since the middle of the twentieth century. Genetic engineering, mechanization, and increased use of antibiotics and hormones have enabled livestock farmers to increase production to previously unheard of levels. These changes have resulted in the vast majority of animals and animal products being produced by a smaller number of very large farming operations in the United States The era of the family farm is largely a thing of the past.

Meat and milk will be used in this chapter to illustrate how animal and animal products are produced by the U.S. agriculture system.

Meat Production

Meat and poultry production practices in the United States have changed dramatically in recent years. Rather than using a free-range approach for raising the animals, producers today are raising animals in confined spaces to promote rapid weight gain by the animals and to minimize the amount of land area required for the production facility.

According to the U.S. Environmental Protection Agency (EPA), an animal feeding operation (AFO) is an enterprise where animals are kept and raised in confined conditions for at least 45 days in a 12-month period and there is no grass or other vegetation in the confinement area during the normal

Figure 8.9 Cattle in a Confined Animal Feeding Operation.
Courtesy of U.S. Geological Survey
Source: http://toxics.usgs.gov/photo_gallery/emercont_all.html

growing season.[7] Feed is brought to the animals raised in an AFO rather than allowing them to graze in pastures, fields, or on rangeland. AFOs are designed to permit animals, feed, manure and urine, dead animals, and production operations to be confined on a small parcel of land.

The EPA has established criteria for concentrated animal feeding operations (CAFOs) through the Clean Water Act. CAFOs are animal-production facilities that meet the definition of an AFO plus certain size criteria as denoted in Table 8.2. A large CAFO confines at least the number of animals described in Table 8.2. Small CAFOs confine fewer than the number of animals listed in the table but have been designated as CAFOs because they are considered to be a significant contributor of pollution that can threaten surface water supplies in the area. A medium CAFO falls within the size range in Table 8.2 and has either a man-made ditch or pipe that carries manure or wastewater to surface water or the animals come into contact with surface water that passes through the area where they are confined.[8]

Air quality can be harmed by emissions of ammonia, hydrogen sulfide, and particulate matter from CAFOs. These and other air pollutants contribute to respiratory problems, such as asthma and difficulty breathing, for workers at the CAFO as well as people living in the vicinity of these operations. Ammonia and hydrogen sulfide also produce strong odors that can result in serious health impacts for workers and nuisances for nearby residents. Proper ventilation of CAFOs is vital to protect the health of the animals and workers. However, it can cause problems for the local environment.

Table 8.2 EPA Criteria for Large, Medium, and CAFOs

ANIMAL SECTOR	SIZE THRESHOLDS (NUMBER OF ANIMALS)		
	LARGE CAFO	MEDIUM CAFO[a]	SMALL CAFO[b]
Cattle or cow/calf pairs	1,000 or more	300–999	less than 300
Mature dairy cattle	700 or more	200–699	less than 200
Veal calves	1,000 or more	300–999	less than 300
Swine (weighing over 55 pounds)	2,500 or more	750–2,499	less than 750
Swine (weighing less than 55 pounds)	10,000 or more	3,000–9,999	less than 3,000
Horses	500 or more	150–499	less than 150
Sheep or lambs	10,000 or more	3,000–9,999	less than 3,000
Turkeys	55,000 or more	16,500–54,999	less than 16,500
Laying hens or broilers (liquid manure handling systems)	30,000 or more	9,000–29,999	less than 9,000
Chickens other than laying hens (other than liquid manure handling systems)	125,000 or more	37,500–124,999	less than 37,500
Laying hens (other than liquid manure handling systems)	82,000 or more	25,000–81,999	less than 25,000
Ducks (other than liquid manure handling systems)	30,000 or more	10,000–29,999	less than 10,000
Ducks (liquid manure handling systems)	5,000 or more	1,500–4,999	less than 1,500

[a] Must also meet one of two "method of discharge" criteria to be defined as a CAFO or may be designated.
[b] Never a CAFO by regulatory definition, but may be designated as a CAFO on a case-by-case basis.
Source: U.S. Environmental Protection Agency, Region 7 Concentrated Animal Feeding Operations (CAFOs), http://www.epa.gov/npdes/pubs/sector_table.pdf

Impairments to water quality from manure pollution are another public health concern associated with CAFOs. The animals confined in these operations produce large amounts of urine and manure. CAFO operators typically use lagoons, pits, and similar structures to store manure. If not properly handled and stored, this waste can pollute surface and groundwater sources near the CAFO. Bacteria and chemicals improperly released from CAFOs can contaminate ground and surface waters. This can negatively affect aquatic life in surface waters and the drinking water supplies of people living near or downstream from CAFOs when manure spills occur. The manure storage facilities must be properly managed to prevent spills and accidental discharges that can harm public health and environmental quality.

The role of CAFOs in increasing antibiotic resistance among bacteria and the emergence of new strains of viruses is the subject of growing scientific inquiry. Animals living in CAFOs can become stressed as a result of living in confined spaces such as stalls, pens, and cages. Living in close proximity also facilitates the spread of disease-causing organisms from one animal to another. This has prompted the operators of CAFOs to deliver low doses of antimicrobial drugs to healthy animals for nontherapeutic purposes. The drugs are administered through the animals' feed or water in an effort to keep healthy animals healthy amid the stressful and sometimes unhygienic conditions found in AFOs and CAFOs. Antimicrobial refers to drugs that are effective against microorganisms such as bacteria, viruses, and parasites. Antibiotics are a narrower category of drugs that are effective against bacteria in particular.[9] According to Nicholas Kristof, the FDA reports that 80% of the antibiotics administered in the United States is given to livestock and 90% of these antibiotics are administered to prevent healthy animals from getting sick when they are confined in CAFOs.[10] Antimicrobials also combat the increased risk for illness that results from the altered diet that is fed to animals raised in CAFOs. Finally, antibiotics are given to farm animals to stimulate growth and promote uniformity. In most instances, low levels of antimicrobials are administered to the animals over the entire course of their lifespan.

Antimicrobial resistance is the ability of bacteria or other microbes to resist the effects of a drug. Antimicrobial resistance occurs when bacteria change in some way that reduces or eliminates the effectiveness of drugs, chemicals, or other agents designed to cure or prevent infections.[11] Antimicrobial resistance (AR) is not a new phenomenon; however, the current magnitude of the problem and the speed with which new resistance phenotypes have emerged elevates the public health significance of this issue in the United States and worldwide. Since the 1940s, physicians have used antibiotics to turn life-threatening bacterial infections into treatable conditions, resulting in a dramatic reduction in illness and death. However, many of the antibiotics administered to animals in CAFOs are also commonly used when treating human illness. Growth of antibiotic resistant bacteria occurs when bacteria are exposed to low doses of an antibiotic that kill only a portion of the bacteria present. Some of the bacteria that survive will transfer one or more resistant genes to their offspring, and they become more resistant to the effect of the drug. The development of antibiotic-resistant microbes is occurring more rapidly than the development of new antimicrobial drugs. The scarcity of new antimicrobial drugs limits treatment options, particularly for patients with infections caused by multidrug-resistant organisms. When this occurs, another drug that the bacteria do not exhibit a resistance to will have to be administered.

In early 2012, staff at the Centers for Disease Control and Prevention (CDC) reported a multistate outbreak of *Salmonella typhimurium* linked to the consumption of contaminated ground beef. A particularly disturbing aspect of this outbreak was the fact that the outbreak strain of *Salmonella typhimurium* was resistant to several commonly prescribed antibiotics, such as amoxicillin, ampicillin, ceftriaxone, cefoxitin, kanamycin, streptomycin, and sulfisoxazole. Many of these antibiotics are commonly used by physicians to treat infections in their patients. Some of the salmonella bacteria were also resistant to tetracycline. The antibiotic resistance exhibited by these organisms increased the risk of hospitalization and possible treatment failure in infected persons.[12]

Though the problems associated with commercial farm production are unintentional, failure to address these issues may result in worsening public health, increased environmental damage, declining animal health, and dwindling consumer confidence. If the spread of antibiotic-resistant bacteria is not controlled, the pharmaceutical field may find itself involved in a race to produce new antibiotics faster than bacteria can acquire resistance to them.

Improvements in animal production practices have had both positive and negative effects on food safety. The amount of meat and poultry produced in the United States is at an all-time high, and the rate of growth of these animals is faster than ever. In addition, some diseases such as trichinosis have largely become a thing of the past as the diet of the animals and the safety of their feed is strictly controlled. However, controversy among the scientific and medical communities surrounds the use of nontherapeutic antibiotics to promote growth and prevent disease. Further research is needed to determine if this is in fact a risky, and perhaps unnecessary, practice.

Milk Production

The terms "milk" and "milk products" are used by the dairy industry to cover a wide range of foods, such as fluid milk, cultured fluid milk, cream, yogurt, sour cream, butter, ice cream, cheese, and other manufactured foods. Depending on the region of the world, liquid milk and milk used to make milk products may come from cows, goats, sheep, water buffalo, reindeer, and other species of animal.

Dairy Farms

The production of milk and milk products begins at the dairy farm. Dairy farm sanitation consists of several elements, including keeping the dairy herd healthy and the buildings and grounds clean. In addition, it is important to keep milking equipment clean and sanitary while using proper milking procedures, including promptly cooling raw milk in a clean milkhouse. Preventing contamination with proper ventilation and effective pest control are also very important.

The health of a dairy herd is a prerequisite to the safety of milk and milk products. Herd health is very important because there are a number of pathogens that can be transmitted by raw milk and improperly pasteurized milk and milk products. Raw milk, improperly pasteurized milk, and cheese made from raw milk have been implicated in recent foodborne disease outbreaks of *Salmonella*, *Campylobacter*, *Listeria monocytogenes*, and *E. coli* O157:H7. Disease-causing bacteria such as *Brucella*, *Campylobacter*, *Salmonella*, and *Mycobacterium tuberculosis* can be found in the raw milk of apparently healthy animals.

Bovine mastitis is a highly communicable disease of the udder in dairy cattle caused by microorganisms, usually bacteria, which invade the udder, multiply, and produce toxins that are harmful to the mammary gland. These pathogens are spread by contaminated milking equipment or human hands during milking or by flies that may be present in the milkhouse. The symptoms include inflammation of the udder and clotted, bloody milk. Control of the disease requires sanitary facilities, proper milking procedures, and the segregation of affected animals. The disease is typically now treated by penicillin in combination with a sulfa drug and other antibiotics.

Dairy animals which produce abnormal milk based on bacteriological, chemical, or physical examination should be milked last or with separate equipment, and the milk must be discarded. In addition, animals which have consumed or been treated with medicinal, chemical, or radioactive agents which are capable of being excreted in milk and may be deleterious to human health must be milked last or with separate equipment and the milk must be discarded.

Figure 8.10 Healthy Dairy Cattle.
Courtesy of David McSwane

The standard components of a dairy farm are the cowyard, the milking barn, and the milkhouse. The cowyard is the area adjacent to the barn in which the animals congregate prior to milking. The milking barn is the building in which the herd is housed during the milking process. The milkhouse is an area where the raw milk is cooled and stored and milking equipment, utensils and containers are cleaned and stored until the next use.

Figure 8.11 Dairy Cattle in a Cowyard Awaiting Milking.
Courtesy of David McSwane

Cowyard

The cowyard must be graded and properly drained to prevent standing water and wet conditions that are conducive to fly breeding and make it difficult to remove manure and keep the animals clean prior to milking. Dairy animals have a tendency to lie down which can cause their udders and flanks to be soiled with manure and other pollutants. This filth can contaminate the milk they produce and spread disease among the herd. Therefore, manure from the animals and feces-containing wastes from the milking barn must not be allowed to accumulate in the cowyard.

Milking Barn

The milking barn, also called a stable or parlor, is provided to house the herd during milking operations. The milking barn should provide separate stalls for the animals and should not be overcrowded. Swine and fowl must not be allowed in the milking barn to prevent the spread of disease. The milking barn must be constructed to facilitate cleaning and sanitation. Floors in the building are constructed of concrete or another impervious material, and the walls and ceilings are smooth, durable, and maintained in good repair. The milking barn must be provided with adequate natural and/or artificial lighting to support the milking operations. From a sanitation perspective, adequate lighting is required to show when surfaces are soiled and when they have been properly cleaned. Adequate air space and air circulation must be provided in the milking barn to prevent condensation and excessive odors. Feed for the animals must be stored in a manner that will not increase the dust content of the air or interfere with the cleaning of the floor. A clean interior in the milking barn reduces the chances of contamination of the milk and milking equipment. The outside of milking equipment located in the milking barn must be kept clean, and all equipment used during the milking process must be stored above the floor.

Any person who is milking animals must have clean hands and clothing. The animals' flanks, udders, and tails need to be clean at the time of milking. Udders must be cleaned, sanitized, and dried immediately prior to milking to reduce the opportunity for the milk produced by the animal to be contaminated.

Milkhouse

A milkhouse must be conveniently located to the milking barn. This facility is used to handle, strain, and cool the raw milk, and to clean, sanitize, and

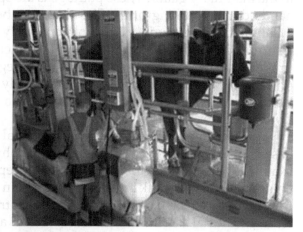

Figure 8.12 Dairy Cow Being Milked in a Milking Barn.
Courtesy of David McSwane

store equipment and utensils used during the milking process. The milkhouse can only be used for these purposes, and there cannot be a direct opening into a milking barn unless it is covered with a solid, tight-fitting, self-closing door. The milkhouse may not open directly into a room used for domestic purposes such as sleeping and cooking.

As was the case with the milking barn, the milkhouse must be designed and constructed to facilitate cleaning and sanitation but with even more stringent requirements. Floors in the milkhouse must be smooth, impervious, and maintained in good repair. They must also be graded to a floor drain to facilitate the disposal of liquid wastes in a sanitary manner. The walls and ceilings must be constructed of a smooth, easily cleanable material that is light-colored or painted a light color. All work areas in the milk-

Figure 8.13 Sink Used to Clean and Sanitize Equipment in a Milkhouse.
Courtesy of David McSwane

house must be adequately lighted by natural and/or artificial sources, and ventilation must be provided to minimize odors and condensation. The construction of the milkhouse must be sufficiently tight to prevent the entrance of pests such as houseflies and rodents. Flies can be kept out of the milkhouse by installing screens over windows and installing self-closing on outer openings. Only approved pesticides may be used and stored in the milkhouse. Medicinals, antibiotics, and approved pesticides may only be kept in the milkhouse when separate tight cabinets or containers are provided.

A supply of potable water must be piped under pressure to the milkhouse, and the facility must be equipped with adequate water-heating equipment. The milkhouse must also be equipped with a two-compartment sink that is used for cleaning and sanitizing equipment and utensils.

Raw milk produced by disease-free animals and in clean surroundings usually contains a relatively low number of bacteria immediately after milking. However, these bacteria can multiply to very large numbers within a few hours unless the raw milk is cooled properly. The Grade A Pasteurized Milk Ordinance calls for raw milk for pasteurization to be cooled to 50°F (10°C) or less within four hours or less after the milking process begins and to 45°F (7°C) or less within two hours after the milking process is finished. The temperature of blended batches of raw milk from different milking sessions should never exceed 50°F (10°C).[13] A bulk milk tank is frequently used to cool and/or store milk at a dairy farm. The tank should be located in a room that is adjacent to but not a part of the milkhouse. The construction, lighting, drainage, pest control, and general maintenance of the room where the raw milk is stored should meet the same standards as those required for the milkhouse.

The sanitary measures taken at a dairy farm to protect raw milk are just the beginning. Once the raw milk leaves the farm, it must be shielded from contamination and kept cold while being transported to a milk-processing plant. At the milk plant, the raw milk is pasteurized to reduce the number of pathogens that cause milk-borne disease to safe levels and destroy enzymes that cause milk to spoil, thereby increasing its shelf life. The pasteurized raw milk can be sold as liquid milk or is converted into its basic components of skim milk and cream. The milk can also be used to make a variety of dairy products such as cheese, cottage cheese, butter, and ice cream.

Figure 8.14 Milk Storage Tank in a Milkhouse.
Courtesy of David McSwane

Food Safety Regulation in Agriculture

Government agencies are responsible for setting food safety standards, conducting inspections to ensure that standards are met, and undertaking enforcement when regulated entities fail to comply with standards. Federal oversight of food safety from farm to table is divided among 15 agencies that administer more than 35 major laws related to food safety. Three federal agencies with significant responsibilities for food safety on the farm are the U.S. Department of Agriculture (USDA), the Food and Drug Administration (FDA), and the Environmental Protection Agency (EPA). The USDA is responsible for the safety of meat, poultry, and eggs; while the FDA is responsible for the safety of all other domestic and imported products including produce, dairy, and seafood.

The USDA has implemented a variety of food safety initiatives to reduce foodborne hazards from farm to table. The Animal and Plant Health Inspection Service (APHIS) is the unit within the USDA that is responsible for preventing the introduction of foreign pests and diseases and promoting the health of U.S. agriculture. The APHIS employs a cadre of scientists, veterinarians, biologists, and other professionals to protect and improve plant and animal health. The Veterinary Services branch of APHIS protects and improves the health, quality, and marketability of domestic animals, animal products, and veterinary biologics by preventing, controlling, and/or eliminating animal diseases, and monitoring and promoting animal health and productivity. The Plant Protection and Quarantine (PPQ) program within APHIS safeguards agriculture and natural resources from the entry, establishment, and spread of animal and plant pests and noxious weeds into the United States. Another important unit within the USDA is the Food Safety Inspection Service (FSIS), which ensures that meat, poultry, and egg products from the United States are safe, wholesome, and properly labeled and packaged. Though the FSIS does not typically work with farmers and growers, it does have a significant impact on the U.S. agriculture and food system. It enforces the Federal Meat Inspection Act (FMIA), the Poultry Products Inspection Act, and the Egg Products Inspection Act, which require federal inspection and regulation of meat, poultry, and processed egg products prepared for human consumption. The FSIS also verifies and enforces industry compliance with the Humane Methods of Slaughter Act, which requires that all livestock inspected under the FMIA are handled humanely.

The EPA is responsible for regulating pesticides and setting safety standards for pesticide residues in food. EPA conducts risk assessments for pesticides and establishes acceptable risk for carcinogenic pesticides. The agency has given particular attention to the health and safety of children by establishing a tenfold safety factor for children when setting tolerances (maximum legally permissible levels) for pesticide residues in food. For example, if EPA determines that the threshold level for a particular pesticide is to be 100 parts per million (ppm), then the allowable limit would be set at 10 ppm to protect children. In all cases, pesticide residue is prohibited in the edible portion of food.

The role of the FDA in food safety was drastically changed as a result of the Food Safety Modernization Act (FSMA) which was signed into law by President Obama on January 4, 2011. The FSMA represents the most sweeping reform of our nation's food safety laws in more than 70 years. It aims to ensure the safety of our nation's food supply by shifting FDA's focus from detecting contamination to preventing it. Prevention is not a new concept, but through FSMA Congress has given the FDA authority to use the tool more broadly to regulate the production and processing for domestic and imported foods. Through FSMA, Congress directed the FDA to develop science-based minimum standards for the safe production and harvesting of fruits and vegetables. It is anticipated that these standards will be developed based on prioritization of known risks. As such, it is likely that low-risk fruit/vegetables will be exempted from the rule. Farm markets and roadside stands that sell produce locally and directly to consumers and small farmers that have annual sales under $500,000 are likely to be exempted from the rule. This exemption can be withdrawn if a foodborne illness outbreak is directly linked to an exempted farm. The provisions of FSMA do not pre-empt state and local food safety laws. In addition, food must be labeled with the name and business address of the farm to facilitate the traceback of products.

Summary

The U.S. food and agriculture system is large, complex, economically significant, geographically dispersed, and globally important. Consumers expect their food to be safe, wholesome, nutritious, and taste good. Ensuring the safety of food requires interventions at multiple points in the flow from farm to table. Federal, state, local, and tribal food safety regulatory agencies are working with many different entities in the U.S. food and agriculture system to reduce the risk of food contamination. By doing so, the United States will continue to have one of the safest food supplies in the world, thereby meeting consumers' expectations and preserving consumer confidence.

Resources Used

1. U.S. Department of Agriculture. (n.d.). *USDA Accomplishments 2009–2011*. Accessed August 4, 2012. http://www.usda.gov/documents/Results-Ag-Production.pdf.

2. U.S. Department of Agriculture. (February 2012) *Farms, Land in Farms, and Livestock Operations–2011 Summary*. Accessed August 4, 2012. http://usda01.library.cornell.edu/usda/nass/FarmLandIn//2010s/2012/FarmLandIn-02-17-2012.pdf.

3. U.S. Food and Drug Administration. (May 2007). *Food: Critical Infrastructure and Key Resources Sector-Specific Plan as Input to the National Infrastructure Protection Plan*. Accessed August 4, 2012. http://www.usda.gov/documents/nipp-ssp-ag-food.pdf

4. U.S. Food and Drug Administration. Last modified on September 1, 2011. *Guidance for Industry: Guide to Minimize Microbial Food Safety Hazards for Fresh Fruits and Vegetables*. Accessed August 12, 2012. http://www.fda.gov/Food/GuidanceComplianceRegulatoryInformation/GuidanceDocuments/Produceand PlanProducts/ucm064574.htm

5. U.S. Food and Drug Administration. Last modified on August 24, 2011. *Guidance for Industry: Guide to Minimize Microbial Food Safety Hazards of Fresh-cut Fruits and Vegetables*. Accessed August 12, 2012. http://www.fda.gov/Food/GuidanceComplianceRegulatoryInformation/GuidanceDocuments/Produceand PlanProducts/ucm064458.htm

6. U.S. Environmental Protection Agency, Region 7. Last modified on September 10, 2012. *What is a Concentrated Animal Feeding Operation?* Accessed September 15, 2012. http://www.epa.gov/Region7/water/cafo/index.htm

7. U.S. Environmental Protection Agency, Region 7. (n.d.). *Regulatory Definitions of Large CAFOs, Medium CAFO, and Small CAFOs*. Accessed September 15, 2012. http://www.epa.gov/npdes/pubs/sector_table.pdf

8. Centers for Disease Control and Prevention Interagency Task Force on Antimicrobial Resistance. (2012). *A Public Health Action Plan to Combat Antimicrobial Resistance—2012 Update*. Accessed September 15, 2012. http://www.cdc.gov/drugresistance/pdf/public-health-action-plan-combat-antimicrobial-resistance.pdf

9. Nicholas D. Kristof, "When Food Kills," *New York Times*, June 11, 2011, accessed September 15, 2012, http://www.nytimes.com/2011/06/12/opinion/12kristof.html?_r=1

10. Joshua M. Sharfstein, M.D. (July 14, 2010). *Antibiotic Resistance and the Use of Antibiotics in Animal Agriculture*. Accessed September 16, 2012. http://www.fda.gov/NewsEvents/Testimony/ucm219015.htm

11. Centers for Disease Control and Prevention. (February 1, 2012.) *Investigation Update: Multistate Outbreak of Human Salmonella Typhimurium Infections Linked to Ground Beef*. Accessed September 16, 2012. http://www.cdc.gov/salmonella/typhimurium-groundbeef/020112/index.html

12. U.S. Department of Health and Human Services, Public Health Service, Food and Drug Administration. *Grade "A" Pasteurized Milk Ordinance–2011 Version*. Accessed September 22, 2012. http://www.fda.gov/downloads/Food/FoodSafety/Product-SpecificInformation/MilkSafety/NationalConferenceon InterstateMilkShipmentsNCIMSModelDocuments/UCM291757.pdf

Food Safety and Security

9

Thomas H. Hatfield

"Tell me what you eat, and I will tell you what you are."

—Anthelme Brillat-Savarin
(The Physiology of Taste, 1825)

Key Performance Outcome Indicators:

1. Define food safety terms, especially as they relate to the diagnosis of food-related illness
2. Identify environmental factors in the growth of pathogens
3. List some of the major food-related illnesses, especially in terms of their diagnosis, risk, and controls
4. Prescribe different control measures for preventing food-related illnesses
5. Analyze the risks and benefits of chemical food additives, and the legal challenges they present

Brillat-Savarin's statement may have more meaning today than it did nearly 200 years ago: chemicals bio-accumulate up food chains, microbes interact with immune systems, and dietary choices have diverse effects on our weight and health. Physically, chemically, and biologically, we continue to discover new ways in which we are indeed what we eat. Moreover, the infrastructure for managing food risks in this country—now more than ever—says something about the diverse sources of food we draw from, the broad range of risks we face, and the various ways in which we manage those risks. Indeed, the more recent literature has adopted the term *food security* in reference to the deliberate contamination of food sources for the purpose of terrorism.

Food safety may be one of the least recognized but greatest opportunities for reducing morbidity and mortality. Whether the risks are deliberate or accidental, food-related illnesses in the United States account for 48 million illnesses per year, with about 180,000 hospitalizations and 3,000 deaths per year (*New York Times*, December 2010). Food-related illnesses are transmitted in our restaurants, grocery stores, various other food facilities, and our own homes. The risks, of course, are not limited to pathogens. When a chemical is released into the air, water, or soil, our most likely exposure is through food. Thus, we must study food risks from the chemical as well as microbial perspective.

On the one hand, the modernization of our food supply system has delivered a more reliable quantity and quality of foods. On the other hand, modern techniques raise entirely new questions regarding potential contamination. Consider just a few initial examples:

1. Ground beef is typically produced from large, centralized facilities. A study in 1998 (R.P. Clayton and K.E. Belk) found that a single 4-ounce ground beef patty, on average, may come from 55 to 1,082 different cows. How does this change the way we evaluate potential contamination, when a single hamburger may originate from over a thousand cows?

2. In 1994, genetically modified tomatoes were introduced that lack polygalacturonase, an enzyme involved in fruit softening. The idea was that the tomatoes could be left to ripen on the vine and still have a long shelf life. These tomatoes, however, disappeared from the market after peaking in 1998. How do we evaluate new genetic versions of food and, in the process, sort out marketing issues from genuine public health issues?

3. "Pink slime" caused a media stir not too long ago, some say mostly because of its disconcerting name. Referred to in the industry as "lean finely textured beef" and "boneless lean beef trimmings," it is used mostly as a food additive for ground beef (typically as a cheap filler, or to reduce the overall fat content of the product). In the midst of a media frenzy, how do we sort out media labels from the genuine risks?

While these are important questions in the developed world, the impacts are magnified for the rest of the world. Food supplies have become increasingly international, and the food on your plate today may have originated from halfway around the world. The need to sort out risks from hype has never been greater. While this chapter will not completely resolve these and many other emerging issues, it will nevertheless provide a framework for bringing more sense to a rapidly developing and increasingly challenging area of study.

Our first task, then, is to define some basic terms. **Food poisoning** shows up in headlines, and you can probably anticipate the objection to this term. It suggests that poisons are the only cause for illness from food, and we know that's not true—illnesses can certainly be from chemical poisons, but can also be from biological or chemical agents. The limitations to the term "food poisoning" are not because it doesn't exist—it certainly does—but because the term is incomplete. It doesn't address the wider range of reasons for why we get sick from food. Over the years, however, the term has been accepted as taking on a broader meaning. Besides, we're unlikely to see TV and newspapers change anytime soon from using this term.

The better term is **foodborne illness**, and I have to admit that I've used this term for most of my career. Notice that the term is broader in its meaning; it says your illness is borne out of the food, and it leaves open the possibility that it's not just a poison, but could be any kind of other cause.

The preferred term, however, as defined by the Centers for Disease Control and Prevention, is **food-related illness**. To put it as broadly as possible, any event that has some kind of relationship with food can then be worthy of study. Notice that the terms are even more generalized. Why the fuss over these definitions? My real objective is not simply to define these terms—far more importantly, these are concepts that can guide us in the investigation and diagnosis of the broad range of food-related illnesses.

Agents of Food-Related Illnesses

With these definitions in mind, we start with the different kinds of agents, and the first of these is **chemical agents**. There are any number of chemical poisons that find their way into food, and it does not always happen because of some kind of criminal activity. It's not someone slipping arsenic into your food in a devious manner. The fact is that if you walk into any kitchen—including your own at home—you will find a number of cleaning agents. Usually you find them underneath the sink: it might be scouring powder, window cleaner, or drain cleaner. It might be any number of cleaners that you use to clean the kitchen, and that's fine except for one thing: all of those chemical agents, if they find their way into the food in any significant concentrations, clearly can make you sick. So the first step in thinking about any agent—especially chemical agents—is to walk around any kitchen. When you do, look up and look down; look around with a fresh set of eyes to see all the chemical agents that might potentially find their way into food.

The second agent is **physical agents**, and a lot of people forget about this. We become so enamored with the idea of microbes fighting with their food that we forget that there are some really simple physical agents that can get into food and make people sick. For example, you might be surprised how often glass will find its way into food. If you're in a commercial restaurant and a light bulb breaks, it can easily end up falling into the food. Restaurants are very busy places—so they may witness the breakage but not get around to removing it fast enough—and so not only glass but broken equipment can get into the food. When meat is on the bone being processed, sometimes bones can be split and bone fragments can find their way into food. Other examples include fingernails or hair. That's not a very fun topic to talk about, but we have to recognize the reality that restaurants and grocery stores are very busy places, and sadly these things can find their way into the food.

The third agent, of course, is **biological agents**. Before we get into the wide variety of biological agents that can find their way into food, I should immediately recommend a wonderful online source from the Food and Drug Administration (FDA). It's called *The Bad Bug Book*, and it'll tell you all about the different pathogens that can find their way into food. One of the reasons I'm excited about this reference is that instead of reading about this in a textbook, which can go out of date almost immediately, this is a website maintained by the FDA. It's constantly updated to include all the pathogens that find their way into food, and what we can do to control the risks.

Biological agents can be divided into several categories. The first of these categories is **infection**. Infection refers to microbial action *inside* the host *after* eating the food. That might seem obvious to you, but bear in mind that the real reason people get sick as a result of foodborne infection is that the agent multiplies *inside* the host after the host consumes the food.

Compare this with **intoxication**. Whenever I talk about foodborne intoxication in the field with laypeople, what I sometimes hear is, "I didn't have any beer that night—I didn't have any alcohol." I have to smile and say that's fine, but intoxication is a much broader term than you know. We talk about being intoxicated from alcohol, but the fact is you can be intoxicated from a wide range of toxins, and microbes can produce toxins. What usually happens is those microbes can sit inside the food—typically at room temperature—and they're just digesting the food. As a result of digesting the food, they produce toxins. Now here's the catch: you can end up killing every last microbe. For example, let's say we sterilize the food. All the microbes are gone but the toxins remain. Those toxins, in far too many cases, can make you sick—sometimes very sick. So notice the distinction I'm making here. An infection says that you might have just a relatively small number of microbes sitting inside the food, and if you eat the food, they can multiply inside the host to make you sick. Whereas, intoxication is a very different story. Most of the action that really causes someone to get sick from the foodborne intoxication has happened well before they ever consume the food—we'll talk a little bit later about incubation. It'll start to make sense that on average the **incubation period** for foodborne infections tends to be longer than the incubation periods for foodborne intoxication gamble began to that a little bit later it's not a hard-and-fast rule but as far as the diagnosis of food-related illnesses if you have a much longer incubation. It's probably more likely going to be a foodborne infection.

There is a wide range of toxins. The first of these is the **exotoxin**. An exotoxin is released into the food by the microbes when the cell is alive. In other words, when the pathogen is alive, it's producing a toxin and it is naturally released into the food. A classic example of this is *Staphylococcus aureus*. We'll be getting to that little bit later on. It's a gram-positive bacteria again. If you don't know gram-positive bacteria, don't worry about it. It's something the chastity about microbiology but many of the gram-positive bacteria tend to produce exotoxins. An exotoxin is the key toxin involved in food-related intoxication's account makes sense if you think about it because these microbes are releasing that toxin into the food while they're alive, so they really have the capacity to build up a lot of intoxication in any given kind of food.

The second kind of toxin is the **endotoxin**, and endotoxins are released into the food at the death of a cell and that because these toxins are in our art these toxins are contained inside the cell wall of gram-negative bacteria. again on I cannot hold you to it in terms the gram-negative and gram-positive because there are exceptions to the rule but a classic example of an endotoxin is salmonella. Salmonella is a gram-negative bacteria, and its toxins are released into the food only when the pathogen dies, so that leads me to the question, What is it about foodborne infections that makes you sick? Is it due to the endotoxins being produced or is it something else? And of course the answer is in a foodborne in talk of story hidden in innate foodborne infection you get sick because the pathogens attack the body that's what you get sick and not because of the endotoxins Now in time, as some of those cells die off and release endotoxins, that may happen to the health effect from an infection. But generally speaking, foodborne infections make you sick because of the action of the bacteria in the pathogen, the different pathogens whereas foodborne intoxication make you sick because of the exotoxin's will.

The next one is a lot easier to discuss: **enterotoxin**. You probably can figure out by now that in our toxins are toxins that act on the intestines. A classic example of this *is vibrio cholera*, which is an agent we will talk about a little bit later on that causes cholera. The key thing is, you cannot tell if something is an enterotoxin simply by the symptoms. In other words, if there's diarrhea, which implies a toxic action on the intestines, it's probably a good chance that there's an enterotoxin involved. But it's not a guarantee—sometimes there are exceptions to the rule. Similarly, we know that neurotoxins act on the nervous system. One of the classic examples here is *Clostridium botulinum*, which is an agent that causes botulism. So, clearly that is a very potent group of neurotoxins that act on the human body. But again you can have neurological effects caused by enterotoxins, and you can have intestinal effects caused by neurotoxins, so again you cannot tell just by the symptoms. Still, there seems to be a general correlation between the two. I also want to add the **pyrogens** because it is typical that a fever is a sign of an infection. This is a true statement, but you can't necessarily conclude that if there is a fever, it cannot be an intoxication because pyrogens are a toxin that can cause the fever. You notice a trend going on here—we have general rules but we have exceptions to those rules. The pyrogen is the exception to the rule, because an intoxication can indeed cause a fever, at least in some cases.

Finally, as long as we are talking about we need to point out that there is a very wide world of **poisonous plants and animals**. One example I'll give is mushrooms. Later on. I'll talk about certain kinds of mushroom poisonings that can be very deadly in some cases. This chapter does not have the space to get into all the different kinds of poisonous plants and animals that are out there—I only want to emphasize at this point that they would fall under the category of intoxications as well. As I said at the very beginning, food-related illnesses are widespread. We see food-related illnesses all the time, and hopefully these terms will get you started to think like a detective in investigating food-related illnesses.

Foodborne Infections

The purpose of this section is not to provide a comprehensive list of foodborne infections. A more complete list of foodborne infections would be beyond the scope of this chapter; moreover, the list is constantly evolving. Instead, the spirit of this list is:

1. To address the broad diversity of foodborne diseases;
2. To encourage an awareness of these diseases in order to improve the detective skills of environmental health professionals; and
3. To think systematically about the controls that can prevent these illnesses.

Salmonellosis (*Salmonella typhimurium*, *Salmonella enteritidis*)

Salmonella is one of the best-known and most common of foodborne infections. Roughly one-third of all chickens in the United States are contaminated with salmonella, and a common vehicle for the spread of this infection is cutting boards. More specifically, preparation of raw chicken on cutting boards followed by cross-contamination with cooked chicken is a simple and often-repeated means contamination.

With an incubation period of about 12 to 36 hours, salmonella produces gastroenteritis (vomiting and diarrhea) that is common to so many of these foodborne illnesses. *Salmonella enteritidis* is associated with raw eggs even when they are uncracked and undamaged.

Campylobacter *Campylobacter jejuni*

Campylobacter may be one of the most common foodborne infections that you never heard of! One of the most common of infections, it has an incubation period of about five days. The agent grows more slowly than most other pathogens, making it harder to isolate. It was often misidentified as a Shigella in the 1960s, and can be found in raw milk, chicken, pork, and various meats.

Listeriosis *Listeria monocytogenes*

Listeria is found in roughly 5% of all raw red meat. Coincidentally, 5% of all Americans are carriers of Listeria. The flulike symptoms range from fever and headache to vomiting, and pregnant women are especially susceptible to this illness area.

Hepatitis type A

Hepatitis refers to inflammation of the liver, and of course this can come from many sources. Type A is the so-called infectious hepatitis, caused by the Type A infectious hepatitis virus. This illness is most closely associated with eating raw oysters. Because oysters are filter feeders, they are able to concentrate the virus from infected waters.

Brucellosis (Undulant Fever)

Brucellosis is an important illness because it is associated with improper pasteurization. Brucella has a reservoir in cattle, swine, goats, sheep, and even dogs. It can be transmitted by direct contact with infected meets and can even spread through airborne infection, but it is most commonly associated with raw milk. Symptoms range from fever and headache to chills. It actually has a low case fatality rate, but the disease can be disabling and last for over a year.

Anisakiasis

This illness is associated with raw fish, particularly sushi and sashimi, but also with raw herring and seviche in other parts of the world. It gets its name from the *Anasakidae* family, a family of parasitic worms that normally reside in fish. They would be easily killed by cooking, but it's the raw serving of fish that causes this problem. More specifically, the worms live in the guts of the host fish, and upon the death of the fish, the worms migrate from the intestines to the muscle tissue. When humans consume the cooked muscle tissue, the worm can be easily transmitted. This is an interesting illness because the means of prevention raise important questions: Thoroughly cooking the fish can easily kill the worms, but this would defeat the entire purpose behind sushi. Gutting the fish soon after they are caught would prevent the worms from migrating into the muscle tissue, but unfortunately this is not a universal practice.

Foodborne Intoxications

As you might expect from the preceding discussion, foodborne intoxications are caused primarily by exotoxins.

Staphyloccoccus *Staphyloccoccus aureus*

This is one of the most common of foodborne intoxications. A large percentage of healthy humans carry Staphylococcus. If introduced into food and allowed to sit at room temperature, it produces toxins that can cause a nasty gastroenteritis.

With a distinctive incubation period of about two to four hours, the illness is intense but normally doesn't last long.

Botulism *Clostridium botulinum*

The good news is that this illness is fairly rare in this country these days. The bad news, as almost everyone knows, is that botulism can kill you if you don't receive the antitoxin in time. The early symptoms include dizziness and double vision, but as a potent neurotoxin about one-third of all cases result in death. The root of the problem is that *Clostridium* is an anaerobic spore former. Being an anaerob, it can survive the limited oxygen in canned foods. Moreover, the spores are highly resistant to boiling. The transmission of botulism is mostly through improper home canning, although significant cases of infant botulism can be traced to the low-acid stomachs of infants. The acid normally found in older children and adults is enough to kill off the spores, but the low-acid stomachs of infants leave them susceptible to this spore. Indeed, sudden infant death syndrome has been associated with relatively small amounts of *Clostridium* spores making their way into the infant stomach.

Perfringens *Clostridium perfringens*

This is another agent in the *Clostridium* family. The good news is that it is not nearly as deadly as botulism. The bad news is that it is far more prevalent. Symptoms are generally mild, including diarrhea and nausea, and the case fatality rate is very low. This raises an interesting question about how we control food-related illnesses: Do we fight the rare but deadly diseases, or do we fight less fatal but far more prevalent diseases? Fortunately, the answer has always been that we fight both. The toxin of this agent is heat sensitive, as is the toxin with botulism, and thorough heating of the food would therefore lower the incidence of this disease. On the other hand, in the case of botulism, it is best to follow the advice "When in doubt, throw it out."

Poisonous plants/animals

Favism *Vicia faba*

Favism gets its name from the fava bean, which is commonly used in falafels. If the bean is eaten when it is too raw, the symptoms include anemia, jaundice, and blood in the urine. This illness can be easily prevented if there is adequate knowledge about preparation of the fava bean.

Snake root *Eupatorium*

Snake root refers to a weed. If cows eat these particular weeds, you can get sick from drinking the cow's milk. Symptoms include vomiting, constipation, extreme thirst, and various allergic reactions.

Paralytic shellfish poisoning

This illness is part of the group referred to as pelagic paralysis, which also includes the puffer fish and ciguatera (discussed below). Pelagic simply refers to the ocean. Paralytic shellfish poisoning stems from the filtering abilities of clams and mussels that are harvested in a red tide. A red tide is rich in dinoflagellates, which can produce a neurotoxin associated with this illness. The incubation is very short, ranging from 5 to 30 minutes, and the symptoms include respiratory paralysis. Early symptoms might include facial spasms, and loss of control of the neck and extremities. Thus, immediate reaction is required in these cases. Inducing vomiting can sometimes help, and may even save a life.

Ciguatera

Ciguatera is related to paralytic shellfish poisoning, but is a much milder form. The same toxins found in a red tide accumulate in fish. More commonly, it is found in fish that feed on poisonous reef algae (again, rich in dinoflagellates). Because the concentrations are much lower than paralytic shellfish poisoning, there is a much lower case fatality rate. Symptoms tend to be less severe, and include numbness, facial stiffness, spasms, and gastroenteritis

Scombroid

Scombroid is a poisoning from histamines in certain fish. Especially common to California and Hawaii, it gets its name from the *Scombridae* family, which includes tuna, mackerel, and mahi-mahi. Because these fish have high concentrations of the amino acid histidine, surface bacteria can convert large amounts of histidine to histamines.

The incubation period can be as short as five minutes, and the symptoms include gastroenteritis, dizziness, facial swelling, fever, and various allergic responses. The treatment, as you might guess, is the use of antihistamines. However, this condition can be prevented by refrigerating the fish after they are caught.

Vibrio parahemolyticus

The reservoir for *Vibrio parahemolyticus* is the oceans. Transmission is typically from poorly cooked seafood. Symptoms include diarrhea and abdominal cramps. Unlike its better-known cousin, *vibrio cholera*, this agent is rarely fatal. However, it is significant for this discussion because it represents an agent that is resistant to salty environments.

Copper poisoning

Copper poisoning is caused by transmission copper in prolonged contact with acid foods or carbonated beverages. For example, improperly constructed vending machines that have carbonated water in contact with copper lines were at one time a notorious source. Symptoms include vomiting and weakness within one hour of consumption, and often within minutes.

Potentially Hazardous Foods

The discussion of food-related intoxications leads me to this much larger issue. The question is not simply what microbes can do in terms of harm. Now the question is where do they grow best—what is the environment that is most supportive of these food-related illnesses? That, of course, leads me to the term **potentially hazardous food,** which is defined as foods capable of supporting rapid and progressive growth of pathogens. One of the most commonly asked questions in an interview with county health department people is, What is a potentially hazardous food? Some foods may support meager growth, but we are looking for the highest-risk foods, the ones that support rapid and progressive growth of pathogens.

Just as soon as I give you the definition, I have to say there's an exception to that rule, and the exception is *Clostridium botulinum*. The reason for this is that *Clostridium botulinum* produces botulism, and it does it by way of intoxication. The *Clostridium botulinum* toxin is so potent that you don't need rapid and progressive growth of the *Clostridium botulinum* agent—even the most modest kind of growth of the agent can produce enough toxin to be deadly. So we have to remember that exception, but otherwise we are talking about the foods that support the quickest and fastest growth of pathogens, and it make sense that the foods we want to pay attention to are the ones that can cause an outbreak.

Even if the food is not potentially hazardous, it can cause outbreaks. For example, orange juice and cookies are not normally considered potentially hazardous foods, but I have the newspaper headlines to prove they have caused illnesses. Still, when we want to serve the public, we want to spend our time on the foods that are most likely to cause food-related illnesses, which means we focus more of our time and more of our attention on the potentially hazardous foods. By the way, as long as I'm talking about orange juice and cookies, you already know that broken glass, cleaning agents, and even some pathogens can survive in orange juice and cookies, but we would have to acknowledge those are lower risks that can happen. The foods that are very supportive of growth are the potentially hazardous foods that we want to pay attention to.

So, there is a danger zone for potentially hazardous foods and we have to talk about what that danger zone is: it is **41°F** to **135°F**. You'd better be ready to know that number in any interview that you go into, especially with county health departments. When potentially hazardous foods are held at a temperature between 41°F and 135°F, those are nice modest temperatures that tend to encourage the growth of pathogens; therefore we don't want to store potentially hazardous foods in this danger zone. Potentially hazardous foods should either be refrigerated or you should heat them up to a pretty high temperature. So to be a little more specific about this, 41°F to 135°F is within six hours. The law says you cannot store potentially hazardous foods for a total of six hours actively on and off, but if it cumulatively adds up to six hours in this danger zone, we know those foods are going to be dangerous. We also are a little more specific in the law saying that 135°F to 70°F should be cooled off within two hours. I hope that can make sense to you because you know the human temperature of 98.6 is an environment that human pathogens love to grow in, and so it stands to reason that a really moderate temperature range of around 98.6 is the range that is the most dangerous for the storage of potentially hazardous foods. We want them to get out of that temperature range in two hours and then make it the rest of the way in the additional four hours, and remember that is the total cumulative time.

Before I go any further in this discussion, I just want to pose a few questions: Do McDonald's restaurants have the finest cuisine on the planet? Most people would say no. Let me ask the next question: Do you think that McDonald's has relatively safe food, and why? And while you're pondering that, I would say that there is a difference between fancy food and safe food. McDonald's is, in fact, a relatively safe food. This does not mean that McDonald's can't have an outbreak, but in terms of the risks, McDonald's is less likely to have an outbreak. The reason is McDonald's is what we refer to as fast food, and fast food is the kind of food we serve quickly. We get food out to the customer as quickly as possible, and now you can see that fast food works in our favor in terms of the storage of potentially hazardous foods, McDonald's doesn't want that food to wait around six hours or even two hours; they want to get it out as quickly as possible, and so that works to the advantage of food safety. To me, the most dangerous restaurants in town are often the fanciest ones. For example, if you have a fancy French restaurant where the chef has slaved over the sauces for so many hours to get them perfect, and has worked with them all afternoon long—think about what that means! All afternoon long means that sauces have the potential to sit out in that danger zone between 41°F and 135°F. I might add that the fanciest restaurants in town tend to be dimly lit—you won't have that nice romantic feel going to a restaurant without the dim lights, which is why environmental health professionals bring flashlights. You can see an awful lot when you get your flashlight out to look into those fancy restaurants, whereas McDonald's is well lit everywhere. If it seems as if I'm having a little bit of fun here, there is nevertheless a bit of truth to what I say— the fanciest places that slave over their foods and recipes for hours at a time are often the ones that are highest-risk. Again, I'm not saying that fast food is the most nutritious, and I'm not saying that it is the best cuisine, but in terms of the growth of pathogens and the danger zone of potentially hazardous foods, McDonald's and all those fast foods generally have a much better time.

So the question then becomes, What are the exempted foods? In other words, we will consider all foods to be potentially hazardous unless we know otherwise, whereas many consider them potentially hazardous foods that must be kept out of the danger range of 41°F to 135°F.

So what are the foods that are exempted? The first has to do with water activity and is represented by the variable **Aw**. **Water activity** can also be defined as the percentage of water, so think of it as the mole fraction of the water. Or if you want to be simpler about the percentage of water that's in the food, and if Aw is less than 0.85, then it's a smaller fraction of water and therefore it would be exempted in the human body is mostly water and so therefore most of the pathogens begin to the human body really preferable in an environment of mostly water so then the question becomes, if you want to lower the water activity if that exempts the food what can you do to lower the water activity course I have listed there as dehydration or adding a lot of sugar or adding a lot of salt adding sugar and salt affects the osmotic concentration and ultimately lowers the water activity so again bacteria are about 80% water and so we would want to provide an environment that doesn't support the growth of all those different bacteria the smoking of foods the drying of foods and again, if you if you go into any of a number of restaurants in Southern California, we have such an international cuisine that you have to sometimes ask a lot of questions. You know it might be a district you've never seen before, and even if it's a familiar dish, it might be prepared in ways very different than what you've seen before, and so you go step-by-step. Basically what you do next what he did next and when you see that they're adding a time of sugar or a ton assault under the food you know that that's lowering the water activity and lowering the risk.

The second category of exempted foods is **pH,** and if the pH is less than 4.6 or equal to 4.6, then you have a pretty acidic food, right? So very acidic foods, such as pickles or orange juice, they're less of a risk; they are not considered exempt, they are not considered potentially hazardous foods, and so when we add acidic materials we end up lowering the risk and a lot of people of vastly will with the pH is very high it is very difficult to find foods that have a very high pH I believe you can find him but it's far more common to see foods with the lower pH and that's before those of the foods that would be exempted.

Our next category of the foods that are exempted from being called potentially hazardous are those that have a limited **oxygen content,** and I again want to underline that because how do we limit the oxygen in him food while canning is pretty much the traditional way that we do it but anytime we seal off foods ceiling their canning is a way of limiting the oxygen content in the course if I asked the question what kind of bacteria are affected by limiting the oxygen content, you already know that the aerobic bacteria so we lower the risk by limiting the oxygen content by lowering the risk of anaerobic pathogens having an a chance to grow inside the food now stars the canning is concerned canning works because of more than just a limited oxygen content certainly the cancer which you call hermetically sealed and for those of you who don't know hermetically sealed, it is not a very fancy term, it just means watertight. Hermetic means watertight, but along with being watertight it is sealed off from the oxygen content, and as we will talk about a little bit later on, canning typically involves heating up the food to 240°F for 30 minutes. Believe me, you don't have to worry about writing that down right now, we will get to it, but heating up the food kills off a lot of the agents and having it sealed off and limited oxygen content all turns it into an exempted food. Remember what this means if you see foods and a restaurant or grocery store that are exempted. You don't have to refrigerate them the commercially sterilized as I have your 240°F for 30 minutes and hermetically sealed.

Number four is a more recent addition: **cooked eggs.** These include eggs that are cooked in their shells, are intact, and haven't been broken—in other words, hard-boiled or pasteurized eggs. These eggs are exempted. The reason that this category was developed in more recent times is because of a specific kind of salmonella—*Salmonella enteritidis*—which is known to be found in whole fresh eggs.

The next category of exempted foods is **radiation,** and we have discovered over the years that very small amounts of radiation, whether in the form of ultraviolet or gamma radiation or X-rays, it turns out that they're very good at killing bacteria. If you irradiate the foods, you can exempt the food because you've really lowered the risk by killing off any potential agents that might be there.

Finally, something called a **microbial challenge study** is a way that you can exempt any kind of food. So if someone says, for example, "My food does not meet the previous five categories of exempted foods but I think my food should not be considered a potentially hazardous food, and I'm willing to conduct a microbial challenge study," what that would mean is this. It is possible to grow pathogens in a certain kind of food prepared a certain way and if the microbial challenge study shows that they don't really grow within the food, then you can end up having the food exempted. Probably the most famous example of an exempted food by microbial challenge studies is the Chinese dish Peking duck. I remember from long ago that Peking duck was once considered a potentially hazardous food, and we would end up and bar going the food that was not started appropriate temperatures and what I heard way back then from all the cooks I talked with is that Peking duck has been prepared much the same way for centuries and we haven't seen massive outbreaks of food-related illness from Peking duck over the centuries, and you know, what I said at the time was that you might want to use a microbial challenge study to prove that all turns out. They eventually did, and now Peking duck is an exempted food, and has to do with the way they did is prepare the chicken of course is still a, started. It is still a potentially hazardous food, but it's the preparation of the Peking duck that is exempted. their canning here I'm trying to show in this picture is that there is a concave lid. In other words, we're trying to limit the oxygen content inside any type of canned food.

Temperature Controls

There are several important exceptions to the basic rule that potentially hazardous foods can cause illness in the danger zone. First, freezing usually does *not* kill *existing* bacteria. While it will often prevent further growth, the microbes they still be viable and pathogenic thawed. This is why most food codes prohibit the refreezing of frozen goods.

The second exception is that heating cannot kill many spores or resistant toxins. We see countless examples where the bacteria themselves have been completely killed off, but any remaining spores may be viable, and their toxins may not have been denatured. Again, while keeping foods out of the danger zone will prevent further growth, it does not guarantee that the existing growth has been removed.

Third, there is a whole range of processes that are referred to as pasteurization. *Pasteurization* can be defined as controlling pathogens without affecting taste. Pasteurization temperatures are generally in a milder temperature range, because the taste of the food becomes an additional consideration in the process. We will discuss this a little later in the chapter.

Finally, a knowledge of the danger zone is not enough to fully understand the importance of heating and cooling procedures in a food facility. Now that we have established that temperature in the danger zone is a critical factor to food-related illness, it's important to analyze why high-volume operations such as restaurants and grocery stores are so vulnerable to this issue.

The key measure is something called the *surface-to-volume ratio*, expressed as S/V. Intuitively, we can understand that larger volumes of food at a given temperature can contain greater amounts of heat. We can also understand that heat loss from foods depend on the surface area. Consider, for example, a cup of coffee that cools off at a given rate. If we spilled that same cup of coffee onto the floor, the coffee now covers a much larger surface area and the temperature loss would be much faster. But finally, it is the surface-to-volume ratio itself that influences the rate of heat loss. We start with the simplest derivation: Consider a perfect cube with the variable x for the length of each side (as shown below).

The surface-to-volume ratio can be derived as follows:

- The volume of this cube is simply x^3
- The area of one face on the cube is simply x^2
- Since there are six faces on any cube, the total surface area is $6x^2$
- Therefore, the S/V ratio of a perfect cube is $6x^2/x^3$, or $6/x$

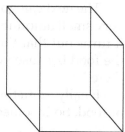

Now that we know that the S/V ratio of a cube is $6/x$, we can turn our attention to the *size* of the cube (i.e., the value of x). As x gets larger, the surface-to-volume ratio gets smaller. In other words, as objects get larger, not only do they contain more heat, but they lose that heat less rapidly.

Although the perfect cube may be the easiest derivation, the surface-to-volume ratio of *any* object will have some form of x^2 in the numerator (surface), and some form of x^3 in the denominator (volume). Therefore, x will be in the denominator for the surface-to-volume ratio of any object. As a result, for any object that gets larger, the surface-to-volume ratio will get smaller.

Why is this concept so important to large-volume operations? It is because the heating and cooling of foods in large-volume operations will take considerably longer than household operations, especially due to the surface-to-volume ratio. Consider a pot of soup, and then compare it to a barrel of soup. The additional time to cool is not simply because of the added volume, but because of the reduced surface-to-volume ratio.

So how do we appropriately guard against this natural condition? We have a variety of strategies. First, we can avoid using large containers! Second, we can adjust the shape of these containers to add more surface area. For example, shallow containers will generally have a greater surface-to-volume ratio. But perhaps most important of all, it is critical for everyone involved with food operations to understand the basic concept of surface-to-volume ratio.

All of this discussion begs the question: How do we verify these temperatures? This is accomplished by the use of a stem thermometer (also called a probe thermometer), as shown below. Thermometers are required in all refrigerators that store potentially hazardous foods. The law stipulates that the thermometer should be readily visible, at the warmest part of the unit (usually in the front and top, near the opening of the door). Finally, the thermometer should be accurate within 1°C. This is typically calibrated in ice water (obviously at 32°F) and boiling water (of course, 212°F). There is usually a nut behind the temperature display that can be turned right or left to change the dial.

Dishwashing, Canning

Appropriate dishwashing facilities are required whenever multiuse utensils are used (single-use utensils are plastic and other utensils intended to be discarded after one use). There are two generally approved methods of dishwashing. The first is the *manual method*, which requires a three-compartment sink. The first sink contains detergent and warm water. Detergent is not a particularly good bactericidal, but it is good at removing bacteria. From the standpoint of preventing food-related illness, it is the most important step in dishwashing.

The second compartment of a three-compartment sink is intended for the rinse. It is in this step that the detergent is removed from the dishes before applying the sanitizer.

The third compartment of a three-compartment sink is intended for the sanitizer. Contrary to popular belief, the sanitizing step should be considered a "polishing" step, in order to kill off the last remaining microbes that might be present. There are two basic ways in which this is achieved. The first way is simply by the use of hot water, which requires a minimum of 180°F for 30 seconds. However, as the cost of energy continues to increase, many restaurants have long opted for the use of various chemicals along with warm water (at a minimum of 75°F). Probably the most common example of a sanitizer used in dishwashing is chlorine, with a minimum requirement of 100 ppm for 30 seconds. An alternative is quaternary ammonia, with a requirement of 200 ppm for 1 minute. Yet another option is iodine, with a minimum requirement of 25 ppm for 1 minute.

The second form of approved dishwashing is the *machine method*, referring to the wide array of dishwashing machines. However, for use in a commercial food facility, dishwashing machines must meet the standards of the National Sanitation Foundation. While there are many requirements for the construction of an NSF-certified dishwasher, the wash temperature must be in the range of 140°–160°F, and the rinse temperature must be 180°F for at least 10 seconds at a minimum water pressure of 15–25 psi. Alternatively, a chlorine rinse of at least 50 ppm is required.

Hazard Analysis and Critical Control Point (HACCP)

Originally developed by the Pillsbury Company for NASA astronauts in 1960s, HACCP has since been adopted by FDA, USDA, and of the Department of Commerce. The key concept behind HACCP is to predict hazards and control them before they happen. The name itself includes some of the key steps.

The first step is to identify hazards (i.e., biological, chemical, and physical hazards). The focus is on identifying potentially hazardous foods, which we have already discussed, with the added step of assessing the risk (e.g., high, medium, low, or negligible).

The second step is to identify critical control points, defined as any point in an operation where the hazard can be eliminated, prevented, or minimized. This is accomplished by observing the handling of food throughout its lifetime. This includes identifying: sources of contamination, and the potential for microbes to survive or grow.

The third step is to establish controls. At a minimum, this includes identifying control criteria (e.g., temperatures) and corrective action.

The fourth step is to monitor the entire process. More specifically, to monitor the critical control points and record the data.

The fifth step is to establish corrective action, which also includes actions when criteria are not met.

The last step is to verify that HACCP is functioning.

Food Safety Controls

I'm starting off with a rather provocative question: How do you regulate a $1 trillion industry? If you combine all the different industries and services that are involved with producing food and providing food to the consumer, it really does come up to about a $1 trillion industry. So how well do we regulate it? Evidently, not very well. If you even ask who does what (for food safety) in the federal government, there is still a great deal of confusion. Now, with the recently passed Food Safety Modernization Act, the FDA has some new tools that it didn't have before. But before we get into that discussion, we have to look at the backdrop for regulating the food industry. Experts every-where say that federal law is hopelessly fragmented. For example, the last time I checked, there were at least 35 federal laws related to food safety, at least 12 major agencies involved in food safety, and at least 51 interagency agreements. Now I will say up front that these numbers are a few years old, but the point is not the exact numbers but that this is very fragmented approach to regulating the overall food industry, and by the way this is not counting all the different federal-state interagency agreements, and of course it doesn't count all the different state and local laws.

But at the very least, to guide you through this maze, we will talk about the six biggest agencies—the six major agencies involved with regulating food. We start at the federal level with the Food and Drug Administration (**FDA**). I would have to say that the FDA is the little agency that could. I know it is a major agency, but you'll see in a moment that relative to other agencies it is taking on a lot of titans. Remember, we're talking about $1 trillion industry, and the FDA has done some wonderful work. We will get to that in terms of the laws in just a moment. Most state codes are modeled after the FDA model food code.

The second group involved in regulating food and it makes sense is the Environmental Protection Agency (**EPA**). The EPA gets involved, for example, with pesticides, and pesticides can be involved with food, and so the EPA works with the FDA and a coordinate in terms of coming up with regulations that make sense so far that seems like it's possible that we could have some good regulation. The third group is the National Marine Fisheries Service, and by the time we get into regulating the fish industry, a cats a little more difficult I won't say that it's an adequate certainly the national Marine Fisheries Service work :-) in terms of coming up with the standards and enforcing the standards to protect food safety.

The U.S. Department of Agriculture (**USDA**) is by far the biggest regulator of food. At first glance you'd say it probably should be—after all, we are talking about agriculture in the United States. There are actually three major agencies within the U.S. Department of Agriculture. The first of these is the **Food Safety and Inspection Service**. This group is involved with the international aspects of food. It worries about regulating foods coming into the United States. In case you didn't know, food in the United States is already a very international market. And so the Food Safety Inspection Service plays a role in looking at that safety. The second group is the **Agricultural Marketing Service**. The name tells the whole story; it tries to market agriculture, and so it gets involved in talking about standards for food safety, and that's where the issues get pretty interesting. Finally there's the **Federal Grain Inspection Service**.

The USDA receives about three-quarters of all the federal funding involved with food and food safety, so it's the one that gets the most money. The FDA is second with about an eighth of the total federal funds.

There are number of different major laws that you should know about. The first is the Food, Drug and Cosmetic Act. The next law is the Egg Products Inspection Act. The Public Health Service Act created a group called the Public Health Service, and the Public Health Service is one of the uniformed services of the United States of America. Now you may think of the uniformed services as the military, and you'd be correct in that way—the uniformed services include the Army, Navy, Marine Corps, Air Force, and Coast Guard. Don't forget them, but there are two other uniformed services that are not military. They are part of the uniformed services. One is the National Oceanic and Atmospheric Administration. But it's the seventh uniformed service that deserves our greatest attention: the Public Health Service. This may be the finest group in this country that is devoted to all aspects of environmental health. In fact, there is even one specialized group within the Public Health Service that is strictly devoted to environmental health.

Under most state codes, significant authority is given to the environmental health specialist. With that in mind, let's talk a bit about enforcement strategies. So you are charged with going out and doing good and improving food safety around the community. Do you simply take everyone to court or put everyone in jail? You know the answer to that already. If we did that, everyone would be in jail, but more than that, we can't afford to spend all of our time in court when we have the ability to get these things done in other ways. So that's why I say it's more than just enforcing the law—there is an element of psychology here.

So let me start off with what I mean by the psychology. Item number one is called a **re-check out**. What is a re-check? Simply put, you go out to inspect the facility, you list its violations under the code, and you say I'm coming back in one week to see if you have corrected these violations. Obviously, if there was an imminent threat to the public's health, you can take other actions. But there are many violations that are not going to be corrected in three minutes anyway. It can take a lot of work on the part of the restaurant owner and manager, and so doing a re-check is a beautiful first step at getting things done.

Number two is called a **notice of violation,** and this is very broadly used. A notice of violation is essentially a letter—a letter to the owner of a food facility that says this is to inform you that you have violated these sections of the code. You are to take care of these violations or face further action. Notice that it is just a letter, but there's a psychology here, and I don't think the psychology is missed by most of the people in the business. What we're really doing is due process. Due process is where we show the court that we were thorough; we were complete; we were eminently fair; we sent a letter to the owner showing clearly what the violations are. Certainly we said if you have any questions, give us a call. Owners will know the notice of violation is the next step of a process. Once again, if it's an imminent threat to the public's health, then a notice of violation is not going to be good enough.

So let's move down to the next category, and this list of strategies is in increasing order of severity. The third category includes fines, grades, and scores. **Fines** are not very popular these days in environmental health when it comes to food facilities, and the reason is that fines can lead to bribes.

If the inspector says you will be fined $500, the operators may be tempted to say, Hey, I'll give you $200 and let's pretend it never happened. Very sadly, this has happened over and over again. That's generally the criticism for fines.

Grades and scores correspond with each other—for example, scores of 90 or above usually correspond to a grade of A, 80 to 89 to a grade of B, and so on. I've co-authored a series of articles on grading systems that highlight a number of issues.

The next technique is called **VC&D**. The VC&D stands for voluntary condemnation and destruction. The way it works is this: Suppose I'm walking through a restaurant and I see a potentially hazardous food and it's sitting on the floor. Cockroaches are crawling out of it, it's been at room temperature all afternoon, and I say to the manager or the owner, Look at that—you have potentially hazardous food at room temperature with cockroaches crawling all over it. Would you like to voluntarily condemn and destroy that food? Most operators are shrewd enough that they get the hint and say Absolutely—we believe in quality in this restaurant, and of course I will voluntarily condemn and destroy. But every once in a while, you get the guy who asks, What if I say no? What if I don't voluntarily condemn and destroy? In that case, we do have the power of embargo. You say, if you do not voluntarily condemn and destroy, then I will embargo this product, which says you cannot serve this food. Generally the way that works is you have to box it up, tape it up, initial your name or sign your name all over the box, and you announce that if there's any other evidence of tampering with this box, you are going to have to explain to a judge why you violated the embargo. The thinking that goes along with embargo generally is you take a sample of that food, the sample generally is taken back to a lab at the jurisdiction that you work, and they will proceed with testing to see if it is contaminated. Whenever the results are returned, you can then inform the restaurant owner if you have a clearance on this product. The vast majority of restaurant operators, once they understand that, will say, If you can embargo it anyway, then yes I will go ahead and voluntarily condemn and destroy.

Story: By the way, the VC&D has its own stories too. I went to one place and it had canned goods. It's a long story, but basically they were bad and they had to be opened up and thrown away. There are called swells. So there's gas production in inappropriate canning. I asked about the voluntarily condemn and destroy, and the owner said yes. I said let's take the cans out by the dumpster, so what they had to do is open up each can, dump it into the dumpster. I really don't know why I did this at the time, but I just had my instincts tell me to do this. They will have all these cans and they started destroying them and throwing into the dumpster and so I said I have the paperwork here, I see that you are proceeding with the VC&D, so I got into my car, I drove around the block and drove right back to the restaurant. I was gone maybe one minute, and you can guess what happened. They were not throwing the cans into the dumpster anymore—they were taking the cans out of the dumpster and bringing them back with the idea of still using them! So I said, look at this—you have violated a VC&D. I'm going to embargo this product and you're going to meet with our authorities at the county health department to explain why you violated the VC&D. They learned a lesson, that we really mean business with the VC&D. Normally if you have the VC&D you stay the entire time to verify the condemnation and destruction, but once again they sign a document in which they promise in writing to voluntarily condemn and destroy. I had a lot of fun with that particular issue.

A lot of people think of **quarantine** as a rare power (Typhoid Mary comes to mind, for example) and wonder it there isn't a lot of trauma when you issue quarantines. In my experience, quarantines are actually not dramatic at all, and maybe it has something to do with the modern era. The way it works is that a doctor finds that a patient has a communicable disease. If the patient works in a restaurant, by law they are to be quarantined from working in that food facility. It's really not as bad as you might think, because in most cases it just means the patient has to receive adequate medical treatment. Our job as environmental health professionals is to verify that the disease is gone and the quarantine can be lifted. It doesn't have to be a big deal, so why is it not such a dramatic deal? At least in my experience, the reason is that by the time I issue a quarantine, the employee of that food facility is long gone. If they're contagious, they know that they should not be working the food facility and so they voluntarily leave. Another good reason is that no matter how shrewd a manager or owner might be, if someone with a communicable disease is working in the kitchen, that's just not good business. In fact, that's the best way to destroy a business. So the vast majority of owners and managers, upon reading a quarantine statement, will honor it. We end up showing up well after the fact. But life being what it is, there are times when people will violate quarantines, and yes indeed, we do have the authority to enforce law.

The next item is **suspension of permit,** and suspension of permit says that you are no longer permitted to operate this food facility. When you suspend a permit, it's often followed up by court action, so we're talking about serious actions at this point. Obviously if there is an imminent threat to the public's health, it may lead immediately to a suspension of a permit, so we bypass the previous six steps, and we just say flat out, you are not allowed to operate. Have I issued suspensions of permits? Yes, many of them. I've been in places where there were serious problems—the owner knew it, the manager knew it, and I said, Under the law, you know I have to suspend your permit. I almost say this almost apologetically and the owner says, Yes I understand. So the permit is suspended. Often, the suspension of permit will last a day or two, because obviously there hustling to correct the problem before they can reopen their facility. But clearly this is an action that has some real teeth to it. I like to say that the *knowledge* that a permit can be suspended is enough to motivate many if not most food facility operators. Finally **court action**: yes, we can and do go to court. When people have failed to heed all of the instructions and advice given by the environmental health officer, we have that tool: we go to court all the time. But I think that many more times, we *don't* go to court because people have the knowledge that we can indeed do this.

To finish up, let's talk a little bit about **pasteurization**. As mentioned before, pasteurization is heating up a product to kill off microbes without destroying the taste, and I wanted to give you some different kinds of pasteurization as it relates to milk products. So the first of these is **ultra-pasteurization**, and I want you to write down that it's greater than 280°F for a period of over two seconds, so we are heating up the milk product to this very high temperature not stuff for very long but to earn 80° is extremely high temperature can kill a lot of things A second kind of pasteurization is ultra-high-temperature pasteurization, and if you look on a lot of products you'll see UHT I've seen a lot of this in Europe but think if you have a sharp ideals look at your products and see **UHT** I know that the little cups of cream that you see at a restaurant in a little miniature cups of creamer if you look at those labels, sometimes you will see ultra-pasteurized or UHT. Anyway, it's for 191°F to 212°F for a period of 1.0 to 0.01 seconds, so what that means is if the milk is at boiling temperature to earn 12°F for 0.01 seconds, that's enough to adequately pasteurize the product, and as we talked about before, it's not going to kill every product in the milk but it certainly makes the milk a whole lot safer. Again, ultra-high-temperature pasteurization is abbreviated UHT The next kind of pasteurization is the high-temperature short-time pasteurization often abbreviated **HTST,** and it's 161°F for 15 seconds.

Finally, the old-fashioned pasteurization we do still see it out there. It's called a **holder pasteurizer.** A holder pasteurized or is 145°F for 30 min. All of this leads to the question of how do you know that you're going to have the milk at a temperature for 0.01 seconds or, for that matter, for even 15 seconds, and the answer is that a lot of the processing of milk it goes through some very high speed processing by very large processors, so what you have is the milk shooting through pipes and a very rapid speed, and you have this one really narrow range of high that has the temperature, let's say, up to two or 12°, and you have a thermometer there to verify that the temperature is there for that location, but since the water is shooting through at a very high speed ,we can make calculations and determine that it reached that temperature for 0.01 seconds.

But there's an even better way to verify pasteurization. This is important, because what if people say, I have this product, and I'm afraid that it might be unsafe? How then do you know if it has had adequate pasteurization? The answer is the phosphatase test. This is a really excellent test—I won't go into all the details, but I will say it's a colorimetric test. You add the ingredients, and I believe it turns blue if it's bad, and it's basically that kind of test. Why is it so important? Because phosphatase is an enzyme found in all milk, and phosphatase is destroyed by pasteurization. If phosphatase is present in the milk, then we know pasteurization was not adequate. If the phosphatase is gone, if we can't find it in the milk but we know there was adequate pasteurization, we can't tell whether there has been subsequent contamination—for example, the milk may have been perfectly well pasteurized, but then becomes contaminated later on in the process. But at least we can tell whether pasteurization was done adequately at one time.

Food Additives

There are many food additives, so the topic here is definitely selected food additives, but I've selected some of the more dramatic ones and the ones that I think teach us a lesson about what we've done in terms of regulating food additives.

The first one is **DES**, which stands for **diethylstilbestrol.** DES was used for a long time as a synthetic estrogen. It was used to fatten cattle and chickens. As it turns out, we learned later that it really didn't add any extra meat—it really did literally add fat, and so it was something that might have added to the profits of the business. It certainly didn't provide anything useful to the consumer. Its effects, we later discovered, were that it was a carcinogen and a mutagen, and the FDA banned DES in 1977. What I like about this particular example is that it's so straightforward—by the time we got information about cancer, we had the information that it was carcinogenic as well as mutagenic, DES was banned, and that was it.

But compare that to our next food additive, **monosodium glutamate**, or **MSG**. Monosodium glutamate also goes by a lot of other different names. It may surprise you to learn the different names you will see for monosodium glutamate, including "flavor enhancer"! Monosodium glutamate is indeed used to enhance flavors, but it's also been called "natural flavoring." You could look at that and ask how it could possibly be harmful. Monosodium glutamate is a natural product and does not need to be synthesized. It is naturally present in nature, and the problem here is that just because an ingredient is natural doesn't mean that it's not harmful. The other name it goes under is **hydrolyzed vegetable protein**, so if you walk down the canned goods and you look carefully at the ingredients, you're going to find a lot of different products that contain monosodium glutamate. Some people are sensitive, some not so sensitive—but those who are sensitive, they can have headaches, nausea, diarrhea, burning sensation, chest pains, and a very long list of other effects. My favorite is that MSG causes brain lesions in monkeys and mice. So you have to ask why MSG was not banned. The answer is, it doesn't cause cancer. It might cause brain lesions in monkeys and mice, but we wouldn't worry about a brain lesion or two! This really highlights the fact that food additives are regulated in sometimes inconsistent ways. The risk from MSG could be a serious one to those who are sensitive, and yet it is still a legal product, so what we do? We give you an accurate label—a label on a product should be able to identify MSG, and if you're sensitive to it you can stay away from it. So here's my challenge: look at the labels in a typical grocery story, and see where you find MSG.

Story number two: Many years ago, when I first started studying the role of food additives, I remember having many sinus headaches during my studies, particularly in the afternoon. Like many people with allergies, I simply attributed it to unknown allergens in the air. But on one particularly painful day, I decided to look at the labels on the food I ate. It was an eye-opener! Like a lot of young men with less than stellar diets, I discovered MSG in many of the junk foods I consumed. More than that, I slowly became horrified by the wide range of additives that I had not only studied but indeed had consumed. Finally, I began to notice all the times that I consumed food from restaurants and other establishments that simply had no labels at all! Many years later, I cannot claim to have an ideal diet—not by any means! But all those years ago, my new awareness of MSG dramatically lowered my incidence of sinus headaches, and I challenge you to do the same for about a week. You truly can learn a lot about yourself by closely monitoring the foods you eat.

Our next food additive is **sodium nitrite**, and I start off with the idea that it is sometimes used to mask food. Of course, it's illegal to mask the effects on food, so how is it used when it's used in illegal ways? It interferes with the browning of meat. If hamburger meat is left to sit out a long enough time, the oxygen will react with the meat and it turns brown. But what is sodium nitrite? Does sodium nitrite interfere with that process, and how does it do it? It combines with myoglobin to form met-myoglobin, which cannot combine with oxygen. Therefore the oxygen will not brown the meat. In other words, since browning is an indicator of the age of the meat, sodium nitrite is sometimes used illegally to mask the aging of meat. I should add that sodium nitrite is used routinely in luncheon meats. If you like bologna or salami, it is very likely that it will contain sodium nitrite. So what's the story going on here? Sodium nitrite deters the spoilage from different organisms but also deters botulism, especially with cured meats such as the luncheon meats. So as it turns out, while there might be a small risk from sodium nitrite, there is a much greater risk of botulism in these cured meats, and so it ends up being used legally.

The effects of sodium nitrite for those who are sensitive to it is they tend to get headaches and sometimes hives, and dermatitis for those who are allergic to sodium nitrate. There is one potential concern about nitrites, and that is the potential of being converted into nitrosamines, which are known to be carcinogenic. So if it's carcinogenic and the law is so sensitive about cancer, why wouldn't we ban nitrates? The answer is, we find nitrates throughout nature. We find nitrites in a lot of different natural foods. We can find it in spinach, for example, and so if we end up banning sodium nitrite as an additive to food, not recognizing that many natural foods may contain nitrites, then we don't really have a very consistent regulation of the product, because we end up introducing nitrites into the system anyway. So the last point that I would want to make is that the reason the cancer card is used here is that there is no evidence of increased cancer from sodium nitrites. We can make the connection biochemically that it might cause cancer, but no such epidemiological evidence has been shown.

The next additive is **aspartame,** which is composed of aspartic acid and phenylalanine. Aspartame is, of course, an artificial sweetener. Aspartame is sensitive only for specific people called phenylketonurics. They are people who cannot metabolize phenylalanine and as a result they develop phenylketonuria. Phenylalanine is one of the ingredients in aspartame. Aspartame was developed in 1965 and fully approved by the FDA in 1983. So we really are talking about a sweetener that has gained approval in the more modern era. So what we found out is that this very small group of people called phenylketonurics should stay away from aspartame. By the way, phenylketonuria starts in infancy, and it includes mental retardation if it's not caught (and is usually one of the first signs). In other words, if someone is a phenylketonuric, they probably know it already, or their family knows. So what are the effects of aspartame? Sensitive persons have a lot of swelling—swelling of the eyelids, of the lips, the hands, or the feet. There have, however, been a variety of complaints from aspartame, including headaches, dizziness, high blood pressure, chronic fatigue syndrome, various kinds of digestive disorders, insomnia, asthma, and the list goes on. Most of these have ultimately been dismissed by the FDA as inconsistent and anecdotal, but what this tells us about the regulation of food additives is that even with the most highly studied food additives, there are likely to be issues for any food additive.

Our next additive is **sulfites.** Sulfites have a variety of effects for those who are sensitive to it—they may have abdominal cramps, diarrhea, and variety of other effects, including low blood pressure, elevated pulse, lightheadedness, chest tightness, asthma, hives, and allergies. In 1986 the FDA banned the use of sulfites on raw fruits and vegetables or fish. In 1987 the FDA required labels any time a product contains more than 10 ppm of sulfites. So what this tells us is that increasingly we are seeing an advisory approach for food additives. Some people are sensitive to it, some are not. Probably the biggest example of a single label where the product contains sulfites is wine, especially red wine. So if you see the label, you know you're sensitive to it, but you are advised and you can make the appropriate decisions.

Food Security

According to the 1996 world food Summit, "Food security exists when all people, at all times, have physical and economic access to sufficient safe and nutritious food that meets their dietary needs and food preferences for an active and healthy life."

From this definition, we can identify four main dimensions of food security:

1. Physical availability of food: this dimension addresses the "supply side" of food security and is determined by the level of food production, stock levels, and net trade.
2. Economic and physical access to food: an adequate supply of food at the national or international level does not in itself guarantee household-level food security.
3. Food utilization refers to how the body makes the most of various nutrients in the food. This depends on such factors as food preparation, diversity of the diet, and the distribution of food within the home. Combined with biological utilization of the food consumed, this determines the *nutritional status* of individuals.
4. Stability of the other three dimensions over time. Adverse weather, political instability, or economic factors may affect food-security status. For food security to be achieved, all four dimensions must be fulfilled simultaneously.

Food insecurity can be either chronic or transitory. This makes planning more difficult and requires different capacities and types of intervention, including early warning capacity and various safety nets.

From the standpoint of food safety, virtually all of the concepts discussed previously in this chapter apply to the questions of food security. However, it does signal the start of a new era where not all food-related illnesses are due to accidents or negligence. The notion that food-related illnesses would be deliberately cultivated adds to the difficulty of our investigations and our safety measures.

Summary

Food-related illness is sometimes called foodborne illness and even food poisoning, and is generally divided into intoxications (including a range of toxins), infections, and chemical poisonings. A wide range of pathogens are involved with food-related illnesses, including salmonella, *Campylobacter*, Listeria, hepatitis virus, *Brucella*, *Staphylococcus*, anisakiases, *Clostridium* (botulinum and perfringens), scombroid, vibrio, paralytic shellfish poisoning, ciguatera, and bacillus.

Food controls include pasteurization, dishwashing, canning, thermometers, and temperature controls. We distinguish between sterilize, disinfect, and sanitize.

Food additives include a broad range of chemical agents representing diverse risks to health. We discussed MSG, sulfites, nitrites, DES, and aspartame.

Further Reading

Devereux, S. 2006 *Distinguishing Between Chronic and Transitory Food Insecurity in Emergency Needs Assessments.* Rome: SENAC. WFP.

Dilley, M., and T.E. Boudreau. 2001. Coming to terms with vulnerability: A critique of the food security definition. *Food Policy*, 26, 3, pp. 229–247(19).

FAO. 2003. Focus on food insecurity and vulnerability—A review of the UN System Common Country Assessments and World Bank Poverty Reduction Strategy Papers. FIVIMS Secretariat and Wageningen University and Research Centre: www.fao.org/DOCREP/006/Y5095E/Y5095E00.htm

Sen, A.K. 1981. *Poverty and Famines: An Essay on Entitlements and Deprivation.* Oxford. Clarendon Press.

Stamoulis, K., and A. Zezza. 2003. A conceptual framework for national agricultural, rural development, and food security strategies and policies. ESA Working Paper No. 03–17, November 2003. Agricultural and Development Economics Division, FAO, Rome. www.fao.org/documents/show_cdr.asp?url_file=/docrep/007/ae050e/ae050e00.htm

WFP. 2005. *Emergency Food Security Assessment Handbook.* http://www.wfp.org/operations/emergency_needs/EFSA_section1.pdf

This document is available online at: www.foodsec.org/docs/concepts_guide.pdf

For more resources see: http://www.foodsec.org/pubs.htm

QUIZ—T/F:

1. Food intoxications are generally by exotoxins.
2. The danger zone for PHF is 45–140°F.
3. As objects get larger, their S/V ratio gets larger.
4. Pasteurization is sterilization.
5. As the S/V ratio gets larger, foods thaw faster.
6. Holder pasteurizers = 145°F for 15 minutes.
7. Boiling kills all food microbes.
8. Intoxications generally have shorter incubation periods than infections.
9. Intoxications never cause fever.

1. Foods are not considered potentially hazardous with a pH less than
   - ❑ 6
   - ❑ zero
   - ❑ 2
2. Foods are not considered potentially hazardous with a water activity less than
   - ❑ 0.50
   - ❑ 0.15
   - ❑ 0.85
3. Foods are not considered potentially hazardous when they are
   - ❑ high in protein
   - ❑ stored at room temperature
   - ❑ canned (in hermetically sealed and commercially sterilized containers)
4. Foods considered to be potentially hazardous may be exempted
   - ❑ True: exemptions can occur by appropriate microbial challenge studies
   - ❑ False: no potentially hazardous foods may be exempted
   - ❑ False: no foods may be exempted
5. An exception to the "rapid and progressive growth" requirement for potentially hazardous foods is
   - ❑ Salmonella typhimurium
   - ❑ Clostridium botulinum
   - ❑ Staphylococcus aureus
6. Bacterial food intoxications are caused primarily by
   - ❑ endotoxins
   - ❑ antitoxins
   - ❑ exotoxins
7. Staphylococcus has an incubation period of about
   - ❑ 15 minutes
   - ❑ 3 hours
   - ❑ 5 days
8. A poisoning from histamines in certain fish is
   - ❑ Scombroid
   - ❑ Snake root
   - ❑ Ciguatera

9. Snake root is associated with
   - ❏ vomiting
   - ❏ numbness and tingling
   - ❏ respiratory paralysis

10. Copper poisoning is usually caused by prolonged contact with
    - ❏ acid foods
    - ❏ basic foods
    - ❏ neutral foods

11. Sterilization is normally achieved at
    - ❏ 165°F for 5 minutes
    - ❏ 140°F for 20 minutes
    - ❏ 240°F for 30 minutes

12. A sterilization step in canning is
    - ❏ Retort processing
    - ❏ Exhausting
    - ❏ Blanching

13. Flat sour refers to a group of
    - ❏ thermophilic pathogens
    - ❏ psychrophilic pathogens
    - ❏ thermophilic spoilage agents

14. Dishwashing sanitization can be achieved by water at
    - ❏ 140°F for 30 seconds
    - ❏ 160°F for 10 seconds
    - ❏ 180°F deg. 10 seconds

15. HTST pasteurization can be achieved at
    - ❏ 145 deg. F for 15 seconds
    - ❏ 161°F for 15 minutes
    - ❏ 161°F for 15 seconds

16. The earliest step of HACCP is to
    - ❏ identify potentially hazardous foods
    - ❏ identify critical control points
    - ❏ institute controls

17. A point in an operation where risks can be minimized is called a(n)
    - ❏ critical control point
    - ❏ endpoint
    - ❏ hazard

18. In establishing controls under HACCP, it is necessary to identify both the criteria and the
    - ❏ corrective action
    - ❏ data point
    - ❏ endpoint

19. HACCP requires the actual recording of data
    - ❏ false: data must only be considered
    - ❏ false: data must only be recognized
    - ❏ true

20. Under HACCP, the role of the environmental health professional is to
    - ❏ take corrective action
    - ❏ verify that HACCP is functioning
    - ❏ record the data

21. Federal regulation of food safety is integrated into a well-coordinated legal and administrative system.
    - ❑ The legal system is sound but the administrative system is fragmented
    - ❑ False
    - ❑ The administrative system is sound but the legal system is fragmented

22. In terms of federal funding, the largest agency involved in food safety is the
    - ❑ EPA
    - ❑ FDA
    - ❑ USDA

23. In terms of federal funding, the second-largest agency involved in food safety is the
    - ❑ EPA
    - ❑ USDA
    - ❑ FDA

24. The Pesticides Monitoring Improvements Act is enforced by the
    - ❑ USDA
    - ❑ EPA
    - ❑ FDA

25. The Food, Drug and Cosmetic Act is enforced by the
    - ❑ USDA
    - ❑ FDA
    - ❑ EPA

26. A synthetic estrogen once used to fatten cattle and chickens is
    - ❑ sodium nitrate
    - ❑ diethylstilbestrol
    - ❑ MSG

27. The natural browning of meat with oxidation is slowed by
    - ❑ diethylstilbestrol
    - ❑ MSG
    - ❑ sodium nitrate

28. Hydrolyzed vegetable protein contains
    - ❑ diethylstilbestrol
    - ❑ MSG
    - ❑ sodium nitrate

29. Brain lesions in monkeys and mice are caused by
    - ❑ diethylstilbestrol
    - ❑ MSG
    - ❑ sodium nitrate

30. Aspartame is specifically harmful to
    - ❑ phenylketonurics
    - ❑ diabetics
    - ❑ epileptics

Discussion Questions

Imagine you are inspecting Joe's Diner, a hypothetical restaurant that I have discussed in many years of my classes. Imagine further that Joe's Diner recently had a suspected food-related illness.

1. What questions would you ask Joe?
2. What issues would you want to examine in the restaurant?
3. What questions would you ask of the individuals who complained of getting sick?

WEBSITES

1. Food Protection ("Bad Bug Book")
2. Food Additives, Pesticides & Chemical Contaminants
3. Government Food Safety Information
4. Cleaning the henhouse

REFERENCES

author? *Infectious Diseases: A Treatise of Infectious Processes.*

Philadelphia: Lippincott, 1994.

author? *Antimicrobials in Foods*. New York: M. Dekker, 1993.

Conner, 1st initial?, et al. Growth, inhibition and survival of Listeria monocytogenes as affected by acidic conditions, *Journal of Food Protection* 53(8): 652 (August 1990).

Ewald, Paul W. *Evolution of Infectious Disease*, New York, Oxford University Press, 1994.

Frank, J.F., et al. Surface adherent growth of *Listeria* monocytogenes, *Journal of Food Protection* 53(7): 550 (July 1990).

Giesecke, Johan *Modern Infectious Disease Epidemiology*. London: Edward Arnold, 1994.

Gumbo, T., S.M. Gordon, and K.A. Adal Cyclospora: Update on an emerging pathogen. *Cleveland Clinic Journal of Medicine* 64(6): 299 (1997).

Hatfield T.H. Environmental health databases on the World Wide Web. *Journal of Environmental Health*, 57(10): 30–33 (1995).

Hatfield, T.H. Environmental health bulletin board systems and databases. *Journal of Environmental Health* 57(5): 30–31 (1994).

Hatfield T.H. A risk communication taxonomy for environmental health. *Journal of Environmental Health* 56(8): 23–28 (1994).

Hatfield T.H. The failure of sanitarians. *Journal of Environmental Health* 53(5): 23–25 (1991).

Hatfield T.H. Risk factors and non-differential misclassification, *American Journal of Public Health* 80(8): 1000–1001 (August 1990).

Hatfield T.H. Restaurant inspections may *not* predict outbreaks of foodborne illness, *American Journal of Public Health* 79(12): 1678 (December 1989).

Jones, Julie Miller *Food Safety*. St. Paul: Eagan Press, 1992.

Lopez A. *A Complete Course in Canning*. Canning Trade, 1981.

Millstone, E. *Food Additives*. Penguin, 1986.

Robinson C.L., and T.H. Hatfield. Labeling of microbial risks, *Journal of College Science Teaching* 24(6): 407–409 (1995).

Rosenkranz, H.S., and G. Klopman. Natural pesticides present in edible plants are predicted to be carcinogenic, *Carcinogenesis* 11(2): 349–53 (Feb. 1990).

Chemistry: The Benefits and Hazards

10

Carolyn Harvey, RS, DAAS, CIH, PhD

The scientist is not a person who gives the right answers, he's one who asks the right questions.
—Claude Lévi-Strauss

Key Performance Outcome Indicators:

1. *Understand the carbon cycle and the essential benefits and hazards to humanity*
2. *Understand how chemicals get into the body*
3. *Understand the nature of chemical threats found in the home environment*
4. *Understand when your body is trying to warn you of environmental hazards*
5. *Understand how hazardous chemicals end up in your drinking water and food*
6. *Understand the sources of volatile organic compounds (VOCS) in the home or work environment and their effect on the body*
7. *Be knowledgeable about federal agencies and federal laws governing chemicals and their use in today's society*

Our Dependence on Chemistry

Modern society could not exist without chemicals: From hard plastics to flexible plastics, from pesticides to inks and other organic compounds, chemicals are everywhere. Want to run an engine, that oil you put in it is a mixture of organic molecules designed to extend engine life. Get a bacterial or fungus infection, that antibiotic is a synthetic organic molecule. Chemicals that form plastics, paints, dyes/pigments, the coatings on your household wiring are at the very fabric of our society. The world and modern society would literally grind to a halt without organic molecules.

Basic Chemistry at Work in Nature

The carbon cycle is the biogeochemical cycle by which carbon is exchanged among the biosphere, exosphere, geosphere, hydrosphere, and atmosphere, and it is one of the many important cycles of the earth (see Figure 10.1). It allows for carbon to be recycled and reused throughout the biosphere .

Carbon Cycle

The cycle in its fundamental simplicity looks like this:

First part of cycle: CHO, a basic **carbohydrate, O_2,** oxygen from air, heated, produces **CO_2, carbon dioxide molecule, the O_2** and **H_2O molecule,** a basic water molecule.

Second part of cycle: Water molecule H_2O mixes with CO_2 in plants process of photosynthesis and yields **CHO** carbohydrate and O_2 oxygen.

While this cycle is quite simple and fundamental, its simplicity hides astounding other realities. For example, if there is not enough oxygen to complete the cycle, then carbon monoxide, which is a very toxic gas, forms.

Exposure to carbon monoxide gas can result in death from the carbon monoxide locking up the hemoglobin in the blood so that the hemoglobin will no longer carry oxygen to the cells.

The cycle is often referred to as the hydrologic cycle and used to process <u>word missing?</u>, the extra carbon will attach to the water and form formaldehyde, a simple but toxic sugar and a carcinogen.

It appears that one of the few actual solutions to global warming lies in the carbon cycle by using photosynthesis to explain the creation and movement of water within the eco-system. The actual basics of the hydrologic diagram can be seen in the following diagram of the carbon cycle.

At the same time, if there is leftover carbon and excessive carbon dioxide in the combustion remove the CO_2 from the air by locking it up as CHO, carbohydrates. The carbon cycle was initially discovered by Joseph Priestley and Antoine Lavoisier, and popularized by Humphry Davy in 1772.

Research or Accidental Chemical Discoveries?

The often true but not often told story about chemical discoveries is that many of them occur by accident and not design in the process of researching something else. This has been true with many food additives, plastics, and numerous other civilization-changing materials.

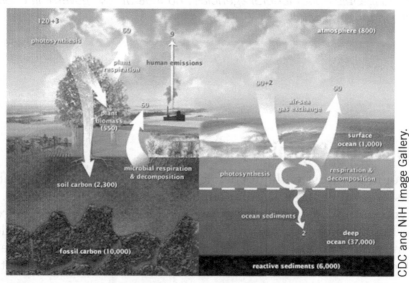

Figure 10.1 Carbon Cycle.

Many of the chemicals used today that were discovered by accident also have hidden human risks associated with them and may have been precipitously used as additives in food or in materials in contact with the human body. Plastics, Teflon, polycarbonates, and artificial sweeteners are prime examples of some of these new products. The GRAS list discussed below tells you how many of these substances have been used in food.

Generally Recognized as Safe (GRAS)

GRAS is an acronym for the phrase "**G**enerally **R**ecognized **A**s **S**afe." Under sections 201(s) and 409 of the federal Food, Drug, and Cosmetic Act, any substance that is intentionally added to food is a food additive that is subject to premarket review and approval by FDA, unless the substance is generally recognized, among qualified experts, as having been adequately shown to be safe under the conditions of its intended use, or unless the use of the substance is otherwise excluded from the definition of a food additive.

Under sections 201(s) and 409 of the act, and FDA's implementing regulations in 21 CFR 170.3 and 21 CFR 170.30, the use of a food substance may be GRAS either through scientific procedures or, for a substance used in food before 1958, through experience based on common use in food.

Serendipity means a "happy accident" or "pleasant surprise"; specifically, the accident of finding something good or useful Serendipity has played a big part in many of chemistry's major discoveries, from electrically conducting polymers to mauve dye, to the discovery of penicillin, and Teflon . The prototype chemical that made the photocell possible involved the catalyzed linking up of acetylene molecules. It was a routine synthesis, but the new lab worker misunderstood the instructions and added one thousand times too much catalyst. The result was something that didn't look like polyacetylene at all. Normally, it was a black powder, but here instead was a rubbery film with silvery metallic sheen. The Lab manager had never seen anything like it. But instead of throwing it into the bin and starting again, he decided to investigate.

The prototype chemical that made the photocell possible involved the catalyzed linking up of acetylene molecules. It was a routine synthesis, but the visitor misunderstood the instructions and added one thousand times too much catalyst. The result was something that didn't look like polyacetylene at all. Normally, it was a black powder, but here instead was a rubbery film with a silvery metallic sheen. Shirakawa had never seen anything like it. But instead of throwing it into the bin and starting again, he decided to investigate. Might the metallic appearance betray metallic properties? In fact, this material didn't turn out to be a particularly good electrical conductor, but in 1976 Shirakawa, collaborating with Alan Heeger and Alan MacDiarmid in the United States, added iodine to the films, turning them golden and boosting their conductivity about a billion-fold. This was the first electrically conducting polymer-the precursor to a generation of plastic electronic and, later, light-emitting devices that are now promising to make electronics cheap and literally flexible. More can be read about this amazing story at: http://science.howstuffworks.com/dictionary/famous-scientists/chemists/hideki-shirakawa-info.htm

Interesting polymers have a history of turning up in unexpected ways. In 1938, chemist Roy Plunkett at DuPont's Jackson Laboratory in New Jersey, was studying fluorohydrocarbon gases related to Freon refrigerants. When he opened a steel cylinder containing one of these, tetrafluoroethylene, under pressure, no gas came out. Perplexed, Plunkett sawed the cylinder in half and found inside a white, waxy residue. This was polytetrafluoroethylene, marketed by DuPont as Teflon and later to become the key to making a good fried egg. In 1938, Roy Plunkett capitalized on an accident and invented one of the best-known and most widely used polymers of all time—Teflon, a product now under serious investigation for health risk.

"Now for the rest of the story" New tests conducted by a university food safety professor, a generic non-stick frying pan preheated on a conventional, electric stovetop burner, reached 736°F in three minutes and 20 seconds, with temperatures still rising when the tests were terminated. A Teflon pan reached 721°F in just five minutes under the same test conditions as measured by a commercially available infrared thermometer.

A Teflon pan reached DuPont studies show that the Teflon off gases toxic particulates at 446°F. At 680°F the Teflon pans release at least six toxic gases, including two carcinogens, two global pollutants, and MFA, a chemical lethal to humans at low doses. At temperatures that DuPont scientists claim are reached on stovetop drip pans (1000°F), non-stick coatings break down to a chemical warfare agent known as PFIB, and a chemical analog of the World War II nerve gas phosgene gases, an issue worth thinking of the next time you pull out a frying pan for those eggs and bacon!

Polystyrene was also discovered by accident in 1839. A German apothecary called Eduard Simon discovered polystyrene. Eduard Simon isolated the substance from natural resin, but he did not know what he had discovered.

It took another German organic chemist, Hermann Staudinger, to realize that Simon's discovery, comprised of long chains of styrene molecules, was a plastic polymer that had many uses.

In 1922, Hermann Staudinger published his theories on polymers, stating that natural rubbers were made up of long repetitive chains of monomers that gave rubber its elasticity. He went on to write that the materials manufactured by the thermal processing of styrene were similar to rubber. They were the high polymers including polystyrene. In 1953, Hermann Staudinger won the Nobel Prize for Chemistry for his research.

However, polystyrene can be recycled, and has the number "6" as its recycling symbol. Increasing oil prices have increased the value of polystyrene for recycling. No known microorganism has yet been shown to biodegrade polystyrene, and it is often abundant as a form of pollution in the outdoor environment, particularly along shores and waterways, especially in its low-density cellular form. As a result it is both a major eyesore and a major pollutant of oceans and waterways.

It seems no product goes without risk. There is evidence that styrene causes cancer in animals also. Women exposed to low concentrations of styrene vapors in the workplace are known to have a variety of neurotoxic and menstrual problems. Read about the hazards of polystyrene https://www.osha.gov/SLTC/styrene/

Penicillin, most of us have heard how this was an accidental discovery, originally noticed by a French medical student, Ernest Duchesne, in 1896. Penicillin was rediscovered by accident by bacteriologist Alexander Fleming working at St. Mary's Hospital in London in 1928. He observed that a plate culture of Staphylococcus had been contaminated and that colonies of bacteria adjacent to the mold were being dissolved. Curious, Alexander Fleming grew the mold in a pure culture and found that it produced a substance that killed a number of disease-causing bacteria. Naming the substance penicillin, Dr. Fleming in 1929 published the results of his investigations, noting that his discovery might have therapeutic value if it could be produced in quantity.

Many Hidden Risks

Many of the chemicals used today that were discovered by accident have hidden human risk associated with them and may have been precipitously used as additives in food or in materials in contact with the human body. Artificial sweeteners are prime examples of some of these problems.

Saccharine is an artificial sweetener that has been found to be a carcinogen that is so popular with the American public that the federal agency given regulatory power has decided not to prohibit its use in spite of the Delany Clause in the Food and Drug Act that prohibits cancer-causing materials in our foods. The substance benzoate sulfilimine does not allow itself to be metabolized and provides effectively no food energy but is much sweeter than sucrose, but it has a bitter metal aftertaste and high concentrations. It is frequently used to sweeten products such as drinks, cookies, medicines, and toothpaste.

Saccharin was first produced in 1978 by Constantin Fahlberg, a chemist working on cold tar derivatives at Johns Hopkins University. The sweet taste of saccharin was discovered when he noticed a sweet taste on his hands one evening, and then he connected the sweet taste with the material that he had been working on that day.

Saccharine is unstable when heated, but it does not react chemically with other food ingredients. However, it stores well. Blends of saccharine with other sweeteners are often used to compensate for each sweetener's weaknesses. Saccharine is now considered by many to be a health risk!

Starting in 1907, the USDA began investigating saccharin as a direct result of the Pure Food and Drug Act. Harvey Wiley, then the director of the Bureau of Chemistry for the USDA, viewed it as an illegal substitution of a valuable ingredient (sugar) by a less valuable ingredient. In a clash that had career consequences, Wiley told President Theodore Roosevelt that "Everyone who ate that sweetened product was deceived. He thought he was eating sugar, when in point of fact he was eating a coal tar product totally devoid of food value and extremely injurious to health." Controversy was stirred in 1969 with the discovery of files from the FDA's investigations of 1948 and 1949. These investigations, which had originally argued against saccharin use, were shown to prove little about saccharin's being harmful to human health. In 1972, the USDA made an attempt to completely ban the substance. However, this attempt was also unsuccessful because of public nonacceptance of the science, and so the sweetener continued to be widely used in the United States. It is now used the most after sucralose and aspartame.

Cyclamate was discovered in 1937 at the University of Illinois by a graduate student. He was working in the lab on the synthesis of anti-fever medication. He put his cigarette down on the lab bench, and, when he put it back in his mouth, he discovered the sweet taste of cyclamate. Further research resulted in a 1969 study that found the common 10:1 cyclamate/saccharin mixture increased the incidence of bladder cancer in rats. The released study was showing that 8 out of 10 rats fed a mixture of saccharin and cyclamates, at levels of humans ingesting 350 cans of diet soda per day, developed bladder tumors. Other studies implicated cyclohexylamine in testicular atrophy in mice. On October 18, 1969, the FDA banned its sale in the United States with citation of the Delaney Amendment after reports that large quantities of cyclamates could cause liver damage, bladder cancer, birth mutations and defects, reduce testosterone, or shrivel the testes.

Aspartame was discovered by accident in 1965 by James M. Schlatter working at the G. B. Searle Company. He was working on an anti-ulcer drug and accidentally spilled some aspartame on his hands. When he licked his finger, he noticed that sweet taste. Because of its intense sweetness, little of it is needed to produce a sweet taste in whatever food it is added. At low temperatures it converts to toxic wood alcohol. Please read more about this food ingredients and the recent attempt to add it to your child's milk, http://www.bing.com/news/search?q=artifisal+sweeteners&qpvt=artifisal+sweeteners&FORM=EWRE

Polyvinyl Chloride (PVC) was accidentally discovered at least twice in the nineteenth century, first in 1835 by Henri Victor Regnault and then in 1872 by Eugen Baumann. On both occasions the polymer appeared as a white solid inside flasks of vinyl chloride that had been left exposed to sunlight. In the early twentieth century the Russian chemist Ivan Ostromislensky and Fritz Klatte of the German chemical company Griesheim-Elektron both attempted to use PVC in commercial products, but difficulties in processing the rigid, sometimes brittle polymer blocked their efforts. Waldo Semon and the B. F. Goodrich Company developed a method in 1926 to plasticize PVC by blending it with various additives. The result was a more flexible and more easily processed material that soon achieved widespread commercial use. Major cancer concerns have arisen over its widespread uses.

Polyvinyl chloride is a useful material because of its inertness, and this inertness is the basis of its low toxicity: There is little evidence that PVC powder itself causes any significant medical problems. The main health and safety issues with PVC are associated with VCM, its carcinogenic precursor, the products of its incineration (dioxins under some circumstances), and the additives mixed with PVC, which include heavy metals and potential endocrine disruptors. "Fear of litigation . . . have all but eliminated fundamental research into VCM polymerization."

Phthalate Esters

In 2004 a joint Swedish-Danish research team found a statistical association between allergies in children and indoor air levels of DEHP and BBzP (butyl benzyl phthalate), which is used in vinyl flooring. In December 2006, the European Chemicals Bureau of the European Commission released a final-draft risk assessment of BBzP which found "*no* concern" for their use. Other studies have shown the material to be very hazardous. Phthalic acids are mainly used as plasticizers (substances added to plastics to increase their flexibility, transparency, durability, and longevity). They are used primarily to soften polyvinyl chloride (PVC). Phthalates are being phased out of many products in the United States, Canada, and the European Union over health concerns.

Phthalates are used in a large variety of products, from baby bottle nipples to enteric coatings of pharmaceutical pills and nutritional supplements to viscosity-control agents, gelling agents, film formers, stabilizers, dispersants, lubricants, binders, emulsifying agents, and suspending agents. End-applications include adhesives and glues, electronics, agricultural adjuvants, building materials, personal-care products, medical devices, detergents and surfactants, packaging, children's toys, modeling clay, waxes, paints, printing inks and coatings, pharmaceuticals, food products, and textiles.

Phthalates are easily released into the environment because there is no covalent bond between the phthalates and the plastics in which they are mixed. As plastics age and break down, the release of phthalates accelerates. People are commonly exposed to phthalates, and most Americans tested by the Centers for Disease Control and Prevention have metabolites of multiple phthalates in their urine. Because phthalate plasticizers are not chemically bound to PVC, they can easily leach and evaporate into food or the atmosphere. Phthalate exposure can be through direct use or by indirect means through leaching and general environmental contamination. Diet is believed to be the main source of di-2-ethyl hexyl phthalate (DEHP) and other phthalates in the general population. Fatty foods such as milk, butter, and meats are a major source. Please read the paper by Brian Amato, Sarah Karl, and Carla Ng at: http://www.eng.buffalo.edu/Courses/ce435/2001ZGu/Phthalate_Plasticizers/PhthalatePlasticizersReport.htm

Air Fresheners

Many people assume that the delightful fragrance coming from the spray cans and containers of air freshener are made from the purest of organic materials such as roses and various other flowers. The harsh reality is that these smells are simply complex chemical compounds that have been discovered to smell like these natural systems. Many of these so-called air fresheners are acute and chronic hazards to the lungs, and many of them are also irritants to the eyes nose and skin. In addition the aerosol cans also pose a risk to the ozone layer of the earth. Most air fresheners are simply odor-masking compounds which hide the biological growth in decomposition that produces foul smells.

There are two broad air freshener categories: continuous action and instant action. Continuous action products include scented candles and devices which use a candle flame or some other heat source to heat and vaporize a fragrance formulation, incense burners, wall plug-ins which either use piezoelectric technology to aerosolize fragrance or heat to vaporize it, fragrance-impregnated gels which release fragrance as the gel evaporates, sometimes with the help of an electric fan; wick and reed diffusers which release fragrance by evaporation from fragrance-soaked wicks or wooden reeds; and fragrance-impregnated materials like floor wax, paper, plastics, wood which release fragrance by off-gassing; and lastly nebulization systems which convert liquid fragrances into a vapor in a cold process without the use of heat.

Basic ingredients in air fresheners typically include volatile organic compounds (VOCs) such as formaldehyde, aerosol propellant, petroleum distillates, and p-dichlorobenzene. Air freshener preparations often also include terpenes such as limonene. Aldehydes, ketones, esters, alcohols, and other synthetic fragrances are also used. A report issued in 2005 by the Bureau Européen des Unions de Consommateurs (BEUC) found that many air freshener products emit allergens and toxic air pollutants, including benzene, formaldehyde, terpenes, styrene, phthalates, and toluene. Air fresheners may also contain phosphates, chlorine bleach, or ammonia.

Research at the University of California found that the prominent products of the reaction of terpenes found in air fresheners with ozone included formaldehyde, hydroxyl radical, and secondary organic aerosol. Many air fresheners employ carcinogens, volatile organic compounds, and known toxins such as phthalate esters in their formulas. A Natural Resources Defense Council (NRDC) study of 13 common household air fresheners found that most of the surveyed products contain chemicals that can aggravate asthma and affect reproductive development.

Candles

The burning of candles in the homes is claimed to have beneficial health impacts while being a health hazard. The burning of the wick and the wax as the temperature becomes sufficient to vaporize lead poses a lead hazard to anyone in reasonable proximity to the candle. Often the chemicals put in the candles to produce the smells are both allergy producing, and carcinogenic.

Drywall

Because of the extensive construction effort demanded by the hurricane that hit New Orleans, a major shortage of drywall has plagued our building industry. This required it to import vast quantities of drywall from around the world. Some of this drywall has been found to release a toxic gas when exposed to the high humidity of the southern United States. In these cases the drywall has ruined the potential for human habitation of the house and either the drywall must be removed or the house torn down. The drywall in question often has its origin in China and contains a naturally occurring allotrope of elemental sulfur—orthorhombic cyclooctasulfur (S_8).

Chemical Exposure

Many people experience chemical exposure every day, in the home, while out shopping, on the job, or even at their local playground. Lawsuits have now become common over people wearing perfume or strong cologne in office or classroom environments.

In today's industrialized world, chemicals are everywhere, and while they cannot be escaped, the exposure to them can be limited. However, that can only occur if one understands the ins and outs of chemical exposure, including whether one has been exposed to toxins at all!

As a quick primer, the following are some recent chemical exposure statistics that have been generated from various national databases on chemical exposure. Though they are only estimates, they might surprise you.

Even highly educated individuals are not aware that virtually all synthetic materials in the home and workplace off-gas! The term off-gassing means that as a material ages it continues to give off molecules of its composition into the atmosphere around it. For example, the shards of wood in particleboard are glued together with ureaformaldehyde. When it gets wet, , the process of decomposition speeds up off-gassing the VOC formaldehyde.

Health Effects

Eye, nose, and throat irritation, headaches, loss of coordination, nausea, damage to liver, kidney, and central nervous system. Some organics can cause cancer in animals; some are suspected or known to cause cancer in humans. Key signs or symptoms associated with exposure to VOCs include conjunctival irritation, nose and throat discomfort, headache, allergic skin reaction, dyspnea, declines in serum cholinesterase levels, nausea, emesis, epistaxis, fatigue, dizziness.

The ability of organic chemicals to cause health effects varies greatly from those that are highly toxic to those with no known health effect. As with other pollutants, the extent and nature of the health effect will depend on such factors as level of exposure and length of time exposed. Eye and respiratory tract irritation, headaches, dizziness, visual disorders, and memory impairment are among the immediate symptoms that some people have experienced soon after exposure to some organics. At present, not much is known about what health effects occur from the levels of organics usually found in homes. Many organic compounds are known to cause cancer in animals; some are suspected of causing, or are known to cause, cancer in rats.

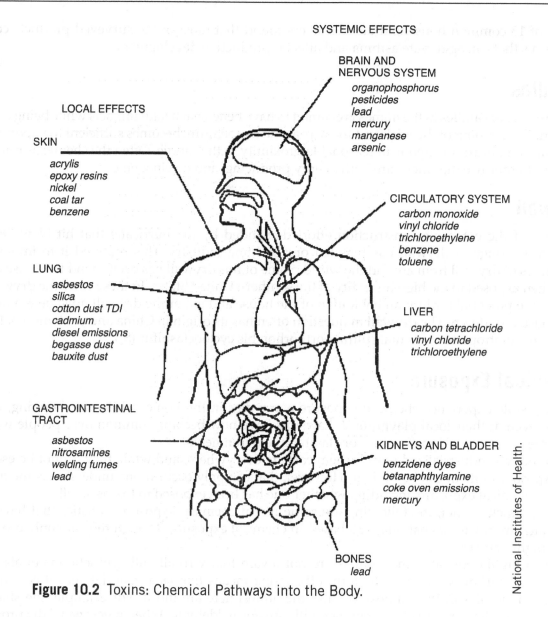

SYSTEMIC EFFECTS

BRAIN AND
NERVOUS SYSTEM
*organophosphorus
pesticides
lead
mercury
manganese
arsenic*

LOCAL EFFECTS

SKIN
*acrylis
epoxy resins
nickel
coal tar
benzene*

CIRCULATORY SYSTEM
*carbon monoxide
vinyl chloride
trichloroethylene
benzene
toluene*

LUNG
*asbestos
silica
cotton dust TDI
cadmium
diesel emissions
begasse dust
bauxite dust*

LIVER
*carbon tetrachloride
vinyl chloride
trichloroethylene*

GASTROINTESTINAL
TRACT
*asbestos
nitrosamines
welding fumes
lead*

KIDNEYS AND BLADDER
*benzidene dyes
betanaphthylamine
coke oven emissions
mercury*

BONES
lead

National Institutes of Health.

Figure 10.2 Toxins: Chemical Pathways into the Body.

Laws Governing Hazardous Chemicals

Environmental illness shares characteristics with common diseases. For example, cyanide-exposure symptoms include weakness, headache, nausea, confusion, dizziness, seizures, cardiac arrest, and unconsciousness. Influenza and heart disease have the same symptoms. Cyanide is one of the most toxic substances known to man. Failure to obtain proper disclosure is likely to lead to improper or ineffective medical diagnosis and treatment. This can contribute to prolonged illness and death.

Safe Chemicals Act proposed 2011 Legislation (pending)

The Safe Chemicals Act would overhaul the 35-year-old Toxic Substances Control Act (TSCA), which is widely perceived to have failed to protect public health and the environment. Specifically the act would:

- Require EPA to identify and restrict the "worst of the worst" chemicals, those that persist and build up in the food chain;

- Require basic health and safety information for all chemicals as a condition for entering or remaining on the market;
- Reduce the burden of toxic chemical exposure on people of color and low income and indigenous communities;
- Upgrade scientific methods for testing and evaluating chemicals to reflect best practices called for by the National Academy of Sciences; and
- Generally provide EPA with the tools and resources it needs to identify and address chemicals posing health and environmental concerns.

The Toxic Substances Control Act (TSCA)

A law passed by the United States Congress in 1976 that regulates the introduction of new or already existing chemicals. It grandfathered most existing chemicals. Contrary to what the name implies, TSCA does not separate chemicals into categories of toxic and nontoxic. Rather, it prohibits the manufacture or importation of chemicals that are not on the TSCA Inventory (or subject to one of many exemptions). Chemicals that are listed on the TSCA Inventory are referred to as "existing chemicals." Chemicals not listed are referred to as "new chemicals." Generally, manufacturers must submit premanufacturing notification to the U.S. Environmental Protection Agency (EPA) prior to manufacturing (or importing) new chemicals for commercial purposes. There are notable exceptions, including one for research and development, and for substances regulated under other statutes, such as the Federal Food, Drug, and Cosmetic Act and the Federal Insecticide, Fungicide, and Rodenticide Act.

Passed in 1976, TSCA's presumption that chemicals should be considered innocent until proven guilty was a sharp departure from the approach taken with pharmaceuticals and pesticides. Since then, an overwhelming body of science has shown that presumption to be unfounded. Published studies in peer-reviewed journals have shown that many common chemicals can cause chronic diseases and can be toxic even at low doses.

Workplace Right to Know. Each grants certain rights to those groups. The "right to know" was a movement made popular by Rachel Carson with her book Silent Spring.

Material Safety Data Sheet (MSDS)

The Occupational Safety and Health Administration requires that MSDS be available to employees for potentially harmful substances handled in the workplace under the hazard communication regulation. The MSDS is also required to be made available to local fire departments and local and state emergency-planning officials under Section 311 of the Emergency Planning and Community Right-to-Know Act.

It is intended to provide workers and emergency personnel with procedures for handling or working with that substance in a safe manner, and includes information such as physical data (melting point, boiling point, flash point, etc.), toxicity, health effects, first aid, reactivity, storage, disposal, protective equipment, and spill-handling procedures. MSDS formats can vary from source to source within the country depending on national requirements.

MSDSs are a widely used system for cataloging information on chemicals, chemical compounds, and chemical mixtures. SDS information may include instructions for the safe use and potential hazards associated with a particular material or product. These data sheets can be found anywhere where chemicals are being used.

There is also a duty to properly label substances on the basis of physico-chemical, health, and/or environmental risk. Labels can include hazard symbols such as the European Union standard black diagonal cross on an orange background, used to denote a harmful substance.

Comprehensive Environmental Response, Compensation, and Liability Act of 1980 (CERCL)

A federal law designed to clean up sites contaminated with hazardous substances.[1] Superfund created the Agency for Toxic Substances and Disease Registry (ATSDR), and it provides broad federal authority to clean up releases or threatened releases of hazardous substances that may endanger public health or the environment. The law authorized the Environmental Protection Agency to identify parties responsible for contamination of sites and compel them to clean up the sites. Where responsible parties cannot be found, the EPA is authorized to clean up sites itself, using a special trust fund

Agency for Toxic Substances and Disease Registry (ATSDR)

A public health agency within the U.S. Department of Health and Human Services that focuses on minimizing human health risks associated with exposure to hazardous substances. It works closely with other federal, state, and local agencies, tribal governments, local communities, and health care providers. Its mission is to "Serve the public through responsive public health actions to promote healthy and safe environments and prevent harmful exposures." ATSDR was created as an advisory, nonregulatory agency by the Superfund legislation and was formally organized in 1985.

Although ATSDR is an independent operating division within the Department of Health and Human Services, the Centers for Disease Control and Prevention (CDC) performs many of its administrative functions. The CDC director also serves as the ATSDR administrator, and ATSDR has a joint office of the director with the National Center for Environmental Health (NCEH). The ATSDR headquarters is located in Atlanta, Georgia, at the CDC Chamblee campus. In fiscal year 2010, ATSDR had an operating budget of $76.8 million and roughly 300 full-time employees (not including contractors).

HAZWOPER (acronym for Hazardous Waste Operations and Emergency Response)

This refers to many types of hazardous waste operations and emergency responses conducted in the United States under Occupational Safety and Health Administration (OSHA) Standard 1910.120 "Hazardous Waste Operations and Emergency Response." The standard contains the safety requirements employers and their subcontractors or public sector responders must meet in order to conduct clean-ups or emergency response operations.

Occupational Safety and Health Administration (OSHA)

An agency of the U.S. Department of Labor. Congress established the agency under the Occupational Safety and Health Act, which President Richard M. Nixon signed into law on December 29, 1970. OSHA's mission is to "assure safe and healthful working conditions for working men and women by setting and enforcing standards and by providing training, outreach, education and assistance." OSHA is also charged with enforcing a variety of whistleblower statutes and regulations.

The Occupational Safety and Health Act allows OSHA to issue workplace health and safety regulations. These regulations include limits on chemical exposure, employee access to information, requirements for the use of personal protective equipment, and requirements for safety procedures.

In its first year of operation, OSHA was permitted to adopt regulations based on guidelines set by certain standards organizations, such as the American Conference of Governmental Industrial Hygienists, without going through all of the requirements of a typical rulemaking.

In 2000, OSHA issued an ergonomics standard. In March 2001, Congress voted to repeal the standard through the Congressional Review Act. The repeal, one of the first major pieces of legislation signed by President George W. Bush, is the only instance of Congress successfully using the Congressional Review Act to block a regulation.

Between 2001 and 2011, OSHA issued just four new health and safety standards; during this period, the agency promulgated regulations at a far slower rate than during any other decade in its history.

U.S. Environmental Protection Agency (EPA or sometimes USEPA)

An agency of the federal government which was created for the purpose of protecting human health and the environment by writing and enforcing regulations based on laws passed by Congress. The EPA was proposed by President Richard Nixon and began operation on December 2, 1970, after Nixon submitted a reorganization plan to Congress and it was ratified by committee hearings in the House and Senate. The agency is led by its administrator, who is appointed by the president and approved by Congress.

The EPA has its headquarters in Washington, D.C., regional offices for each of its 10 regions, and 27 laboratories. The agency conducts environmental assessment, research, and education. It has the responsibility of maintaining and enforcing national standards under a variety of environmental laws, in consultation with state, tribal, and local governments. It delegates some permitting, monitoring, and enforcement responsibility to the states and to Native American tribes. EPA enforcement powers include fines, sanctions, and other pollution-prevention programs and energy conservation efforts.

The agency has approximately 17,000 full-time employees and engages many more people on a contractual basis. More than half of EPA's human resources are engineers, scientists, and environmental protection specialists; other are legal, public affairs, financial, and information technologists.

Dry-Cleaning Chemicals

These chemicals include methyl chloroform and brand names Chloroethene NU, Aerothene TT, and Perchloroethylene (tetrachloroethylene). They are found primarily in dry-cleaning chemicals and some metal degreasing products. easily detected by the human nose (1 ppm). These chemicals primarily enter through the skin and respiratory system. They are all listed as strong carcinogens.

Household Products and Glues

N-hexane is a derivative of crude oil that is combined with other chemicals to make solvents. While the main use of n-hexane is making vegetable oils, it is also an ingredient in glues, rubber cement, and gasoline. N-hexane is a derivative of crude oil. When combined with other chemicals to make solvents it is very volatile. It enters the body through the respiratory system."Huffing" n-hexane-containing products can result in nerve damage and paralyzed arms and legs. Benzene is a proven carcinogen causing acute myeloid leukemia. It is found mainly in tobacco smoke, paints, and fuel, Exposure of >365 days has been linked to anemia, irregular menstrual periods, and shrinking ovaries.

How Do I Lower My Risk of Exposure?

Rely on common sense and knowledge of risk. If you smell it, the concentration is usually much too high. Increase ventilation!!! The old idea of "baking" a new building is untrue; circulate fresh air for two or three days in a new home, a month in a building. Read and follow the directions for use on the label. Store products in an area with little human traffic (garage, etc.). Don't keep excess products on hand. The best way is to be an informed consumer and ventilate your house, air your laundry in your garage before you wear it even if it smells pleasant, do not breath more than you must. It is likely a carcinogen, an irritant, or an allergen.

References

What do the numbers refer to? Should there have been footnote callouts in the text?

1. *The Carbon Cycle*, updated primer by NASA Earth Observatory, 2011.
2. The story of serendipity, http://undsci.berkeley.edu/article/serendipity
3. "US FDA Website Guidance Documents". cfsan.fda.gov.
4. "FDA's response to European Aspartame Study."
5. Toby J. Sommer, "'Bahramdipity' and Scientific Research," *The Scientist*, 1999, 13(3), 13.
6. "poly(tetrafluoroethylene) (CHEBI:53251)". Retrieved July 12, 2012.
7. "Are Tang, Teflon, and Velcro NASA spinoffs?" source?
8. "History Timeline 1930: The Fluorocarbon Boom". DuPont. Retrieved 10 June 2009. Merck Index, 11th Edition, 8282.
9. Chemicals Delisted Effective April 6, 2001 as Known to the State to Cause Cancer, California Office of Environmental Health Hazard Assessment.
10. Vernal S. Packard, (1976). *Processed Foods and the Consumer: Additives,*
11. *Labeling, Standards, and Nutrition.* Minneapolis: University of Minnesota Press. pp. 332.
12. Susan Budavari, ed. (1989). "861. Aspartame." In *The Merck Index* (11th ed.). Rahway, N.J.: Merck & Co. p. 859.
13. Charles A. Harper, ed., *Handbook of Plastics, Elastomers, and Composites*, 4th ed. McGraw-Hill, 2002.
14. Directive 2004/42/CE of the European Parliament and of the Council of 21 April 2004 on the limitation of emissions of volatile organic compounds due to the use of organic solvents in certain paints and varnishes and vehicle refinishing products EUR-Lex, European Union Publications Office.
15. Agency for Toxic Substances and Disease Registry, http://www.atsdr.cdc.gov/
16. Rachel Carson, *Silent Spring.* Houghton Mifflin, 1962, pp. 13, 278.
17. *Pesticide User's Guide.* Ohio State University, http://ohioline.osu.edu/b745/b745_4.html
18. Occupational Health and Safety. US department of Labor, http://www.osha.gov/
19. HAZWOPER, http://en.wikipedia.org/wiki/HAZWOPER

Industrial Hygiene: CSI for the Workplace

11

D. Gary Brown, CIH, RS, DAAS

Safety is not an intellectual exercise to keep us in work. It is a matter of life and death. It is the sum of our contributions to safety management that determines whether the people we work with live or die.

—Sir Brian Appleton, after *Piper Alpha* Accident

Key Performance Outcome Indicators:

1. *Understand what an industrial hygienist is*
2. *Understand how an industrial hygienist protects members of the workforce and public*
3. *Understand the difference between injuries and illnesses*
4. *Understand the anticipation, recognition, and control of hazards*
5. *Understand gases and solvents*
6. *Understand particulate and fibers*
7. *Understand ionizing and nonionizing radiation*
8. *Understand ergonomics*
9. *Understand thermal stress*

Introduction

Industrial hygiene is forensic science for the workplace. Crime scene investigators are detectives who investigate a crime scene to solve mysteries. Industrial hygienists are scientists who investigate biological, chemical, or physical hazards in the workplace which can cause an employee an injury or illness. Industrial hygienists also work protect members of the community. As a good detective an industrial hygienist investigates the whole workplace—from the procurement of raw materials to production, maintenance, and waste disposal.

The American Industrial Hygiene Association (AIHA) defines industrial hygiene as the "science and art devoted to the anticipation, recognition, evaluation, prevention, and control of those environmental factors or stresses arising in or from the workplace which may cause sickness, impaired health and well-being, or significant discomfort among workers or among citizens of the community." The "science" in the definition is having an education that includes biology, chemistry, math, and physics along with formal education in industrial hygiene. The "art" is deciding who or what to monitor, when to monitor, and the various aspects of dealing with people.

If you would be interested in a job which is never the same and always evolving, then industrial hygiene is for you. Twenty-five years ago nanotechnology, the utilization of small particles to manufacture products, was not a concern for industrial hygienists. If you like science and enjoy television shows showing how products are manufactured, then industrial hygiene is a field you would enjoy. I have been in factories which make cereal, cookies, dog food, automobiles, implantable medical devices, liquor, laundry detergent, beer, furnaces, paint, chemicals, and various other products. Industrial hygienists get to see what most people do not. I have walked the steel on construction sites; been in and under the Brooklyn Bridge; worked inside coal-burning power plant boilers; and been on military bases.

Industrial hygienists communicate with people at all levels of an organization, from the production worker to corporate executives. An industrial hygienist's first and foremost job is to protect the health and safety of the worker. Industrial hygienists practice public health, the science of preventing disease. Preventing a disease is less expensive than treating the disease. The goal of industrial hygienists is to prevent occupational injury or illness by preventing workers or members of the community from experiencing an environment or hazard which can harm them. By protecting the health and safety of the worker, the industrial hygienist is also protecting the best interests of the corporation.

Industrial hygienists need formal education in industrial hygiene. Undergraduate programs which fulfill the educational requirement include bachelor of science degrees in environmental health science and industrial hygiene. Information on environmental health programs can be found on the website of the Environmental Health Accreditation Council (EHAC). Information on bachelor of industrial hygiene programs can be found on the American Board of Engineering Technology (ABET) website. For the last 20 years, the National Institute of Occupational Health and Safety (NIOSH) has provided free tuition, and in many cases a stipend, to students at NIOSH educational resource centers (ERCs) pursuing their master and doctoral degrees in industrial hygiene.

Becoming a certified industrial hygienist (CIH) increases one's marketability in the field. A CIH is very similar to a professional engineer. People who have the proper education along with the necessary professional experience may take a certification examination administered by the American Board of Industrial Hygiene.

The final piece of the puzzle in order to become a competent industrial hygienist is professional experience. No matter what one's credentials are, there is no way a person watching someone do a particular job for a day or even a week, will know that job as well as the person who has been doing it for years. I know numerous doctors who are CIHs, and they are great theoretical industrial hygienists, but are not very good in the field. Conversely, I know numerous industrial hygienists who are not certified and have a bachelor's degree, but are wonderful field industrial hygienists. As in any field, having the credentials provides the opportunity to advance your career, but having these credentials does not necessarily mean you can perform the job. Industrial hygienists are employed by universities, teaching, consulting firms, government, manufacturing, and in many other areas.

History

In ancient Greece, Hippocrates, the father of medicine, was the first person to attempt to explain disease occurrence on a rational rather than a supernatural basis. He identified environmental and lifestyle influences, including where a person worked, to explain the occurrence of disease. Hippocrates identified lead poisoning in mine workers. Hippocrates also noticed that tinners would eventually become deaf from the repeated exposure to the sound of hammering metal. Tinnitus, which is a constant ringing or buzzing in the ears, was named in honor of Hippocrates. In Roman times, Pliny the Elder developed the first know respirator, made from an animal bladder, to protect workers from the hazards of mining copper.

Paracelsus (1453–1541), a physician, published some of the earliest works on the relationship between respiratory disease and the mining and smelting industries. The father of occupational medicine, Bernardino Ramazzini (1633–1714), devoted his medical practice to the study of occupational diseases and the avocation of improving the well-being of the working class.

Percivall Pott (1714–1788) identified that scrotal cancer in chimney sweeps came from exposure to hydrocarbons on their scrotum. In England, the boys who were chimney sweeps were poor. In order to keep their clothes clean, they would take them off before going into the chimney. While cleaning the chimney they would get the soot on their scrotum, which led to scrotal cancer. This is why today mechanics put their oily rags in their back pocket.

Figure 11.1 "National Library of Medicine "Changing the Face of Medicine"

Industrial hygiene is a relatively new science, and became a formal science in the 1900s. The annual industrial hygiene conference began in 1961. Industrial hygiene's founding mother is Dr. Alice Hamilton (see Figure 11.1). Dr. Hamilton became a resident of Hull House, which was a settlement founded by the social reformer Jane Addams. Living at Hull House, Dr. Hamilton became aware of the problems faced in the workplace by the residents, leading her to research workplace dangers. Dr. Hamilton published the results of her studies, bringing the issue of dangers in the workplace to the public's eye.

In the United States, the first formal organization of industrial hygienists was the Independent National Conference of Governmental Industrial Hygienists (NCGIH), which convened on June 27, 1938, in Washington, D.C. The original goal was "to encourage the interchange of experience among industrial hygiene workers and to collect and make accessible such information and data as might be of aid to them in the proper fulfillment of their duties." In 1946, the organization changed to its present name, the American Conference of Governmental Industrial Hygienists (ACGIH®). In 1946 the ACGIH started publishing the Threshold Limit Values for Chemical Substances (TLVs), which had earlier been called the Maximum Allowable Concentrations. The ACGIH annually publishes a TLV booklet that includes revisions of TLVs. TLVs are still utilized by industrial hygienists around the world.

The Occupational Safety and Health Administration (OSHA) was formed in 1970. When OSHA was formed, it adopted the 1968 TLVs as the permissible exposure limits (PELs). The permissible exposure limits have not been updated since they were adopted in 1970. Attempts to update them in the late 1990s were unsuccessful.

Injuries vs. Illnesses

Most people assume that injuries cause more harm to workers than occupational illnesses, but unfortunately this is not true. The first global estimates of occupational mortality were published in 1999. They estimated that approximately 100 million occupational injuries (100,000 deaths) and

11 million occupational diseases (700,000 deaths) occur in the world each year. A person who experiences an occupational injury usually knows right away. The problem with a person who develops an occupational disease is that the disease often takes years to develop and at that point the worker may not attribute the disease to something that happened in the workplace.

An acute health hazard is one which causes an adverse health effect after a short duration of exposure, such as when an employee is burned with acid. The employee knows immediately that they have been burned by the acid. The employee doesn't realize two months later they were burned with acid.

A chronic health hazard is a hazard which takes exposure over many months or years before an adverse health effect occurs. If you were to smoke 10,000 cartons of cigarettes in one month, you would not develop cancer the next month. Cancers take a long time to develop, usually 20–30 years, which is called the latency period.

In addition, workers are more willing to protect themselves from an acute health hazard. If employees are exposed to a chemical in which their ears would fall off immediately if they are overexposed, they are likely to protect themselves. If the same chemical took 20–30 years before effects took place, then the workers are much less likely to protect themselves. This is the same problem facing public health officials who attempt to get people to stop smoking. No one starts smoking to get cancer; they do it for the pleasure received from it. Smokers think that cancer will not happen to them.

Anticipation of Hazards

Major functions of an industrial hygienist include anticipating hazards. The anticipation/recognition of potential or actual hazards is accomplished through knowledge of materials, operations, processes, and conditions. This can include being involved in the design of a new process or even a new facility. For a company, it is much easier to attempt to prevent a hazard before a process or factory is built than to deal with the problem after the fact.

An example of anticipation of hazards can be seen in the design and location of sports facilities. New sports arenas are built with wider walkways, stair which are not as steep, better lighting, and numerous rest rooms. These features help enhance the fans' experience during the event, but also improve their safety and health. Another area of predesign which arena designers take into account is how people will get into and out of the arena either by personal vehicle or public transportation.

Recognition of Hazards

Industrial hygienists recognize hazards through their familiarity with work operations and processes. They must understand the industrial process, including the materials used, the processes involved, including setup, manufacturing, cleanup, and maintenance, and personal protective equipment (PPE).

When people think of hazards in a workplace, they usually think of safety hazards, such as getting hurt by a machine, a crane, or a forklift. OSHA has developed the focus-four hazards for construction, since these four hazards cause approximately 75% of the deaths experienced by construction workers. The focus-four hazards are electrical, struck by, falls, and caught in between.

Industrial hygienists have an educational background in biology, chemistry, mathematics, and physics which helps them perform their job. Having knowledge of chemistry helps industrial hygienists recognize chemical hazards, which can include gases, liquids, vapors, and dusts. Knowledge of physics assists an industrial hygienist in identifying physical hazards, including noise, radiation, and thermal. Biological hazards include molds, fungi, and infectious agents.

Ergonomics is the science of fitting the task to the person, as opposed to the person having to fit the task. Ergonomics is utilized every day in your home. An example can be seen in your car. Today's car seats are designed to be more comfortable and adjust to accommodate all sizes of people. Car seats adjust not only back and forth, but also up and down. In addition, the seat incline adjusts. In the past a car seat only moved forward and backward. Ergonomic hazards are determined utilizing biomechanics and work analysis.

Evaluation of Hazards

The evaluation of hazards involves measuring workplace hazards and comparing the results to experience and/or standards. Parameters industrial hygienists are concerned with include toxicity of substance, concentration in the breathing zone, manner of use, length of exposure, controls already in place and their effectiveness, and any special susceptibilities of the employees.

Industrial hygienists can use either direct-reading instruments or equipment that takes a sample and then is sent into a laboratory for analysis. A direct-reading instrument takes in a sample of the material of concern and provides an instantaneous reading.

Most people think only about chemicals when they are thinking about measuring workplace hazards. Numerous other hazards can be measured, including physical hazards such as noise, heat, and nonionizing and ionizing radiation. Biological hazards can also be measured.

When evaluating a space for mold, an industrial hygienist does not always need to sample. If a wall is covered in mold, there is no reason to sample; the hazard exists. Industrial hygienists measure to determine if a hazard exists. When evaluating a space for mold, the industrial hygienist is investigating whether the total mold in the space or any one species in the space is elevated compared to measurements taken outside the space that day. Unfortunately, there are many charlatans who claim to be mold experts, but do not have the knowledge on how to properly evaluate a space.

Control of Hazards

The best method of controlling hazards is to engineer the hazard out; the next-best course of action is to utilize administrative controls; and personal protective equipment is the last resort. Unfortunately, too many people automatically decide that the best and cheapest option is to put workers in PPE.

Here is an example of how it can be more cost-effective in the long run to fix a problem. A company has a noisy piece of equipment and 20 people work in the area of the equipment. The cost to install engineering controls to reduce the noise to acceptable levels would be $5,000. This is the best option, because if the piece of equipment's noise is lowered, then no employees are exposed. The next-best course of action would be an administrative control, such as utilizing the equipment when fewer employees are working. The problem is, workers are still exposed and will have to be put in PPE. The final option is to utilize PPE.

Most people do not realize the true cost of PPE utilization. If you have 20 employees who will be working in the area for 30 years, you need to calculate the true cost of using PPE. For all employees to conduct annual audiograms (hearing tests), it will cost $1,000, annual training will cost $1,000, and the cost of supplying personnel with ear plugs will cost $1,000. The annual cost will be $3,000 times 30 years working for a true cost of $90,000. OSHA will cite an employer if the cost of placing personnel in PPE is greater than the cost of engineering out the hazard. Another issue with PPE is that people do not like to wear it; this is why the United States has a teen pregnancy problem. Young people are not saying, I enjoy wearing condoms so much, I am going to wear four of them before I have sex.

Engineering controls can include the isolation of a process or operation, substitution of less toxic materials, ventilation, utilization of shielding, and using wet methods to reduce dusts. Administrative controls include written procedures, good housekeeping, and training. A general rule of thumb is that companies with good housekeeping have good safety.

Occupational Exposure Limits

There are numerous sources of occupational exposure limits (OEL) available to the industrial hygienist. Since we are dealing with workers' health, an industrial hygienist will always utilize the lowest OEL. The organizations within the United States which publish OELs include OSHA, NIOSH, ACGIH, AIHA, and company standards. There are OEL standards published by other countries which industrial hygienists will also utilize. OSHA publishes permissible exposure limits (PELs) which are the only standards a company must adhere to by law. The ACGIH publishes threshold limit values (TLVs) which are recommendations. NIOSH publishes recommended exposure limits, and the AIHA publishes workplace employee exposure levels (WEELs) which are recommendations. In addition companies may publish OELs which are their recommendations for what an employee can be exposed to.

OELs are based upon best available information from industrial experience, experimental human studies, and experimental animal studies. Information gathered from industrial experience usually is a result of the substance having such harmful effects that numerous workers experience adverse health effects. The majority of our information comes from animal studies.

OELs refer to the concentration of a substance to which nearly all workers may be exposed day after day for a working lifetime without adverse effects. A time-weighted average (TWA) is the concentration for a normal 8-hour workday and 40-hour workweek, to which nearly all workers may be repeatedly exposed day after day, without adverse effect. TWAs are not to be used for other purposes, including the evaluation or control of community air pollution hazards. OELs are designed so that a worker is exposed for 8 hours and has 16 hours of nonexposure along with weekends and holidays to recover. If an employee works more than 8 hours, the OELs must be reduced, since there is greater exposure time and less recovery time. Community air pollution standards are designed for people who spend their entire time in the community, therefore they are breathing the same air 24 hours a day 365 days a year.

A short time exposure limit (STEL) is a 15-minute TWA exposure which should not be exceeded at any time, even if the 8-hour TWA is within the OEL. A STEL represents the concentration to which workers can be exposed continuously for a short period of time without suffering from irritation, chronic or irreversible tissue damage, or narcosis of sufficient degree to increase the likelihood of accidental injury, impair self-rescue, or materially reduce work efficiency. STELs should not be longer than 15 minutes and should not occur more than four times a day; and there should be 60 minutes between successive exposures in this range.

A ceiling (C) is a concentration that can never be exceeded. Ceilings are appropriate for chemicals causing acute disease. If a chemical has a skin (S) notation, it means that the substance can be absorbed by the skin. If a chemical has an SEN notation which means that it can cause sensitization. The OEL for sensitizers is designed to protect workers from becoming sensitized, not for those who are already sensitized.

IH Programs

Unfortunately, too many companies do not pay enough attention to occupational health. They do not utilize a systematic approach to occupational health, and instead choose to conduct industrial hygiene monitoring either due to employee complaints or employees experiencing health effects. The minimum elements of a comprehensive industrial hygiene program include identification of health hazards, evaluation of health hazards, and control of health hazards. Additional components include recordkeeping, employee training, and periodic program review.

The AIHA has developed a systematic exposure assessment strategy allowing the ranking of risks based on several key parameters (chemical hazard, exposure) which ultimately decides whether exposures are acceptable, unacceptable, uncertain, or that further information is needed. The advantages of utilizing a systematic assessment include establishing a systematic approach to IH monitoring, better prioritization of control efforts and expenditures, and a better understanding of worker exposure.

The basic steps in an industrial hygiene assessment begin with a facility tour to understand the process. The industrial hygienist interviews workers, managers, engineers, and others to determine which tasks are routine or nonroutine. The industrial hygienist reviews records, including material safety data sheets (MSDSs) and any existing sampling data. The last step is to determine which OEL to utilize.

The industrial hygienist groups workers into similar-exposure groups (SEGs). A SEG is a group of employees who have the potential for similar exposures. A SEG can be grouped by location, job classification, or chemical hazard. An example of a SEG can be employees working in the spray booth. The results for several operators can be conveyed to other similarly exposed operators.

IH Sampling

Industrial hygienists are not the same as environmental scientists. There are differences in education. Industrial hygienists take courses including epidemiology, ergonomics, health physics, indoor air quality, industrial hygiene, occupational health, physics, risk assessment, safety, toxicology, and ventilation.

The exposure environmental exposure period is 168 hours per week for a person's entire life (24 hours × 7 days), while the occupational exposure period is 40 hours a week for 50 weeks a year for 30 years (8 hours × 5 days). In addition, the equipment for sampling is different. Environmental sampling for air containments requires much higher flow rates and the collection of greater volumes of air. The standards in industrial hygiene are higher than environmental due to the healthy worker factor. The healthy part of the population is in the workforce.

Gases

Gasses are materials that are in the gaseous state at normal temperature and pressure. For industrial hygienists, normal temperature and pressure is 25°C and 760 mm mercury. In the workplace, industrial hygienists are usually, but not always, facing a situation where a contaminant is dispersed in air. A newly released gas will quickly disperse evenly and uniformly by diffusion and turbulence.

The vapor pressure of a substance is related to the temperature pressure exerted by a vapor. Materials with a low boiling point, such as gasoline, have high vapor pressures. Substances which have high vapor pressures (readily evaporate) are generally more hazardous than materials with a low vapor pressure. For example, if a gallon of gasoline and a gallon of motor oil spill, the gasoline will evaporate very rapidly, while the motor oil will take a long time. Therefore, the people working in the area of the gasoline would have a greater exposure due to evaporation than the people near the motor oil.

Never depend on your nose to let you know if there is a hazard present. After approximately 10 minutes in any smell, your body stops detecting the smell due to olfactory fatigue. Your body knows the smell is present, so there is no need to waste energy detecting the smell any longer. This is why some people take a bath in perfume or cologne. They put the perfume on and after some time they can no longer smell it, think they did not put enough on, and so they douse themselves with more.

Gases have a property called flammability or explosivity range which is the range of the percentage of materials to reach an explosive or flammable level. The lower flammable or explosive limit is when there is not enough concentration of vapors in the air to catch on fire or explode. For example, if there was a small cup of gas in a corner of a 50 ft × 50 ft room, and in the opposite corner there was a lit match, the gas would not catch on fire, because there are not enough vapors in the air. The upper flammable limit or explosive limit is when there is so much of the material that it displaces the oxygen in the air, preventing ignition. A fire or explosion occurs within the flammability range.

Compressed gases possess special hazards, including fire hazards. Cryogenic gases also present unique hazards, including great expansion ratios and extreme cold temperatures. Gases can be oxidizing, like peroxides. An oxidizer is a chemical which provides oxygen to a fire. In addition, gases can be pyrophoric or air reactive. Gases are usually expressed in parts per million (ppm).

Solvents

Solvents are liquids in which something, called a solute can be dissolved; solids may also be suspended in solvents. Water is a polar solvent. A rule of thumb regarding solvents is that "like likes like," meaning that polar materials like to dissolve in polar materials. So if something will dissolve in water, such as alcohol, it is polar. If a material such as oil does not mix with water, it is nonpolar. So oil, a nonpolar solvent, will mix with diesel fuel, another nonpolar solvent.

Another rule of thumb is that lipophilic substances stay in the body longer than water-soluble or hydrophilic substances. Lipophilic substances absorb into the body's fat cells. In addition, lipophilic substances are absorbed by the skin. This is why hand lotion is oily and greasy and not watery. To have young-looking skin, people do not rub water on their faces.

Solvents have several characteristics in common, including a low boiling point, meaning that they evaporate easily. Because of environmental concerns, corporations that utilize solvents try to minimize the loss by refrigerating the solvent tanks and having vapor-recovery systems installed on the exhaust stacks. In an effort to reduce waste costs, companies will install a distillation unit to distill the solvent and leave the dissolved substance behind. The company will reuse the solvent until it loses its effectiveness. The company will then recycle the used solvent, reducing the amount and cost of waste.

Solvents are not very reactive. The solvent should not react chemically with the material or the dissolved compounds it comes in contact with. In addition solvents have a characteristic odor. Solubility is the maximum amount of a compound that is soluble in a specific volume of solvent. Solvents are used at home and in industry. Nail polish remover contains acetone; laundry detergents contain citrus terpenes; and paint thinner usually contains toluene.

Particulates

The first known air pollution was from particulates produced during combustion (smoke from a fire). A general rule for particulates is, the higher the energy used to create the particulate, the smaller the particle. For example, gasoline energy operates at much higher temperature and pressure than a diesel fuel engine. You can see the particulate coming from a diesel engine much more easily than from a gasoline engine.

Dusts are produced by mechanical action on larger pieces of the material. Common dusts include quarry dust, cutting stone such as tile, and tunneling in rock. A common method to reduce dust is to wet the surface to be cut and applying water while cutting. Mists are droplets of liquid created by breaking liquid into small particles. Mists include ocean spray. Fumes are formed by evaporation and rapid condensation of metal vapors; welding fumes are an example. Smoke is the product of incomplete combustion of organic materials.

In nature there are a greater number of smaller particles, but the larger particles have more mass, as can be demonstrated if you have 1,000 BBs and one bowling ball. Since particles in nature are not perfectly round, industrial hygienists utilize aerodynamic diameter to predict where in the respiratory tract a particle will deposit. Aerodynamic diameter is also used to determine how slow or fast a particle will settle. Industrial hygienists are interested in particle size because the size of the particle is the factor which determines where a particle will deposit in the respiratory tract.

The ACGIH states that "an inhalable particulate mass is a particle which is deposited anywhere in the human respiratory tract." Inhalable particles are 100 microns or less in diameter. A thoracic particulate mass is a particle which is deposited anywhere within the lung airways and the gas-exchange region of the human respiratory tract. Thoracic particles are 10 microns or less in diameter. A respirable particulate is a particle which is deposited in the gas-exchange region of the human respiratory tract. Respirable particles are 4 microns or less in diameter. Particulates are usually expressed in milligrams per cubic meter (mg/m^3).

There are numerous diseases caused by particulates. Hypersensitivity pneumonitis is one such disease, usually caused by exposure to bacteria or mold. Examples of hypersensitivity pneumonitis include farmer's lung, from exposure to moldy hay; bagassosis, from exposure to moldy sugar cane fiber; and cheese worker's lung, from exposure to cheese mold. Bird fancier's lung is the most common type of hypersensitivity pneumonitis in children. As the name implies, bird fancier's lung is associated with birds. Exposure to birds can come from having them as pets, raising them for food, and exposure to birds in the wild.

Pneumoconosis means "dusty lung." People who are exposed to certain dusts can develop pneumoconiosis. The dust evades phagocytosis; phagocytic cells are like little Pac-Man cells in your lungs eating harmful materials. People who get a pneumoconiosis lose lung function. Picture your lung as a balloon. Every time you inhale particles, it is like cutting the balloon. The balloon keeps getting cut and sewn back together, which in turn reduces the size of the balloon. The same thing happens with your lungs; your lung function is reduced. Common pneumoconiosis include byssinosis from exposure to cotton dust, baritosis from exposure to barium dust, chalicosis, known as stonecutter's disease, and silicosis, caused by exposure to silica.

Welders can get metal fume fever from welding galvanized steel. Exposure to the zinc in the galvanizing causes this condition. Several hours after exposure to the fumes, the worker will feel like he has the flu.

Fibers

Asbestos is not a particle, but a fiber. Asbestos was used in a variety of products due to its chemical and fire-resistant properties. Asbestos can be found in insulation, floor tiles, gaskets, and numerous other products. Exposure to asbestos can cause can cause numerous diseases, including asbestosis, lung cancer, and mesothelioma (cancer of the lining of the lung). Mesothelioma is only caused by exposure to asbestos.

Noise

Society as a whole is getting noisier. Noise is all around us; iPods, videogames, car stereos, and surround sound for televisions are just a few examples. The National Institutes of Health recently concluded a study demonstrating that children today have 20% worse hearing than children years ago. Unfortunately, the 4 Ps of hearing loss apply. Hearing loss is painless; you do not realize you losing your hearing. Hearing loss is progressive, because it happens gradually over time. Hearing loss is permanent, and it can be prevented.

Some rules of thumb to know if you are overexposed to noise include whether normal speech can't be heard, ringing occurs (tinnitus), or you experience a threshold. Another rule of thumb is that if you have to raise your voice to be heard by someone who is three feet or less away, then the environment is too loud. People losing their hearing tend to miss the higher frequencies, such as the telephone or the doorbell. In addition, they have a harder time with a higher-frequency letters such as *r*, *s*, and *t*; while they have an easier time with a lower-frequency letters such as *a*, *e*, and *o*. People losing their hearing have a harder time with little children's voices and women's voices, but they can hear you when you whisper because you do not whisper in a high frequency.

Sociocusis is hearing loss from nonoccupational sources, such as traffic, music, or even television. The problem with hearing loss is that once you lose your hearing, you have lost it for life. People who lose their hearing due to occupational reasons will continue to have their hearing deteriorate as they lose their hearing due to old age, known as presbycusis.

There are three parts to your ear; outer, middle, and inner ear. The outer consists of your pinna, whose function is to direct the noise into your ear. You could still hear without your pinna. The middle ear consists of the three smallest bones in your body; the hammer, anvil, and stirrup. The three bones transmit the energy from your outer ear to your inner ear. Your inner ear is where hearing takes place and where you lose your hearing due to noise overexposure. Your inner ear consists of the cochlea, a seashell-shaped fluid-filled mechanism containing tiny hair cells. The cochlea is where hearing takes place. The movement of your middle ear bones causes the fluid in the cochlea to move, which in turn causes the hair cells to move, transmitting the movement to your auditory nerves. Different hair cells respond to different frequencies. The hair cells which wear out first due to overexposure to noise are those that correlate with 4,000 Hz. People who experience hearing loss due to overexposure to noise get a 4,000 Hz notch in their audiogram.

Industrial hygienists utilize decibels to measure noise, because the decibel scale correlates roughly to what the human ear can hear. A 10 dB increase sounds twice as loud. For example, going from 50 to 60 dB sounds twice as loud. Also, going from 60 to 70 dB sounds twice as loud. A standard threshold shift is when people have experienced a 10 dB drop in their hearing; meaning that everything for the rest of their life will sound twice as soft.

Industrial hygienists consider noise to be any sound that has the potential to damage hearing. Currently, the OSHA PEL for noise is 90 dB; the action level is 85 dB, while personnel in the military and those working in nuclear facilities can be exposed to a PEL of 85 dB with an action level of 80 dB, which is much more protective of hearing. The problem with the OSHA limits for noise is that a percentage of personnel exposed at or above the action level will have an appreciable drop in their hearing.

In the United States according to OSHA, any employee exposed to 85 dB or more must be included in the hearing conservation program. People in a hearing conservation program must receive an annual audiogram, annual training, and be provided with hearing protection if exposed to 85 dB, but must wear it when exposed to 90 dB or more or have an appreciable drop in their hearing. Training must include how to properly wear hearing protection and how to know that you have achieved the proper fit. Other aspects of the hearing conservation program include a written program, a key person in charge of the program, signs, and reduction of noise exposure through the use of engineering, administration, or personal protective controls.

Remember, you need to protect your hearing at home and at work. If you can hear somebody else's iPod, it is too loud. In the morning, when you turn on your car radio and it seems extremely loud, you have experienced a temporary threshold shift. The hair cells in your cochlea were beaten down the night before due to overexposure to noise; while you were sleeping they recovered.

Ionizing Radiation

Ionizing radiation is radiation that carries enough energy to knock out one or more electrons from an atom. This is the radiation most people think of when they think of radiation. Unfortunately, most people do not realize that the major sources of exposure to radiation are the earth and the sun for the majority of people.

There are three types of radiation; alpha, beta, and gamma. Alpha radiation is particles of small fast-moving bits of atoms. Alpha radiation can be shielded by human skin or thick piece of paper. Radon is an alpha particle. The problem with alpha particles is they are the most damaging internally. If you breathe in an alpha particle, it cannot escape the lung, causing major damage.

Beta radiation is negative electrons that are fast-moving in a medium energy. Beta radiation can penetrate material well, but can be stopped by 100–250 pieces of paper or a 0.5–1 cm of water. Acute exposure to beta radiation is uncommon, but can come from sources such as an abandoned industrial instrument. Chronic effects are more common, the main health effect being cancer. X-ray electromagnetic radiation is produced when electrons collide with a metal target.

Gamma radiation is high-frequency electromagnetic radiation similar to light, X-rays, and radio waves. Gamma radiation is usually accompanied by beta and some alpha rays. Gamma radiation is highly penetrating and can be stopped by about 1 cm of lead or 5–15 cm water. Gamma rays are considered the primary hazard to the population during most radiation emergencies. Radiation sickness is almost always caused by gamma radiation. Other radiation includes neutrons found in nuclear reactors and high-energy particles coming from cosmic radiation. The half-life is the time for half of the sample to decay.

The current federal regulation for a worker's limit is 5 roentgen equivalents in man (rems) per year. Industrial hygienists want to keep workers' exposure to radiation "as low as reasonably achievable" (ALARA), which is achieved through time, distance, and shielding. Radiation dose is directly proportional to time spent in the field; therefore the less time spent exposed to radiation, the lower the dose. The radiation dose depends on the proximity to the source or distance. Distance has a greater influence than time on dose and is much more important. The radiation dose received is inversely proportional to the square of the distance of separation $(1/d^2)$. Shielding is used to minimize the amount of radiation that reaches people. If the shield is thick enough, the radiation will use its energy before it gets through the shield.

Nonionizing Radiation

Nonionizing radiation is radiation that is not powerful enough to cause the release of an electron; instead electrons become excited. This can be demonstrated by a microwave in which the food is heated up through the water molecules becoming excited. Nonionizing radiation is becoming a greater concern to industrial hygienists because of its more frequent use. One item that no student can survive without is a cellphone, which gives off nonionizing radiation. Cellphones emit radio frequency energy (radio waves), a form of nonionizing radiation.

Lasers are a form of nonionizing radiation. Laser light is coherent, meaning the light waves are all the same frequency, the same wavelength, and in phase with each other. The wave from the laser is also monochromatic, meaning the waves are all the same length. The main hazard from a laser is to the eyes, and the secondary hazard is to the skin.

The nominal hazard zone refers to the area where the maximum permissible exposure limit would be exceeded. In the nominal hazard zone, employees must wear proper PPE. There are four different classes of lasers. Class I and II lasers are found in numerous consumer settings, including laser pointers, supermarket scanners, laser printers, and CD players. Class II lasers require caution labeling. Class II lasers will not burn skin but can cause damage after direct long-term exposure.

The lasers utilized in medicine and industry are Class III and Class IV. They require numerous controls, including signs, activation keys, and interlocks on the doors. These lasers can cause permanent eye damage from direct exposure and direct reflections. They are also capable of producing injury from intrabeam of viewing, which is looking at the laser from a side view not directly into the beam. Class IV lasers can also cause damage from spectral reflections. There are numerous types of lasers, including solid-state, gas, excimer (excited and dimers) which use reactive gases mixed with another gas, dye, and semi-conductor.

Another form of hazardous nonionizing radiation is light, including sunlight. Unfortunately, many of my students go to tanning beds believing there are safe. The greater the exposure to sunlight, the greater the chance you have of getting skin cancer. The U.S. Department of Health and Human Services has placed tanning beds in the same cancer-causing category as tobacco. In addition, being exposed to some chemicals and medicines may make you more sensitized to their effects.

You need to be especially careful in the sun if you burn easily, spend a lot of time outdoors, or have numerous moles freckles, fair skin, or blonde, red, or light brown hair. To protect yourself from the sun, cover up by wearing loose-fitting, long-sleeve shirts and long pants, use sunscreen with a sun protection factor (SPF) of at least 30, wear a hat, wear UV absorbent sunglasses, and limit exposure. Residents of Caribbean islands know the tourists, because they're the ones with the tans. People who live in hot climates naturally avoid the sun, especially during the most intense periods between 10 a.m. and 2 p.m. Additional forms of nonionizing radiation include static magnetic fields, microwaves, HF or short waves, and radio waves.

Ergonomics

Ergonomics is the science of fitting the workplace to the worker. Ergonomics is a way to work smarter not harder by designing tools, equipment, and workstations. As jobs get more specialized, workers are performing the same motions repeatedly. An example of this is a baseball pitcher. When a pitcher is young, his arm is lively, but as he gets older he loses speed off his fastball, as his pitching arm gets worn out from repeated use.

Humans were not designed to perform the same task repeatedly day after day. We evolved from cavemen who had a variety of tasks to perform each and every day. Cavemen did not say, "For the next six weeks we will just pick corn, for eight weeks we will fish, and for two weeks we will make arrows." If you watch children when they are very small, two or three years old, you will notice that they do not sit still. Little kids do not like to sit in the same position for a very long time or to sit in a chair the way adults do. This is because they still have their natural instincts.

The key to good ergonomics is to maintain a neutral position by keeping your body in its natural alignment. The four greatest risk factors for ergonomic-related diseases, also known as cumulative trauma disorders (CTDs), are repetition, awkward postures, force, and static load. The greater the number of risk factors present during a task, the greater the possibility that the worker will develop CTD. Static load is staying in one position for too long, causing an overload of muscles, reduction of blood flow, and increased pressure on sensitive tissues and joints. Additional risk factors include localized contact stresses, vibration, and temperature extremes.

Musculoskeletal disorders are characterized by discomfort, impairment, and disability or persistent pain in joints, muscles, tendons, and other soft tissues. Work-related musculoskeletal disorders (WMSDs) are the fastest-growing injury/illness category. Causes of increased incidence of WMSDs include higher production rates, shifting jobs, medical knowledge, greater reporting, expanded compensation law, and knowledge of causes.

Cumulative trauma disorders are the group of disorders characterized by wear and tear on muscles and sensitive nerve tissue. A cumulative trauma disorder is a musculoskeletal disorder that is additionally characterized by repeated long-term micro-trauma. Both CTDs and WMSDs are related to activities that require continuous use of a few different motions over an extended period of time.

Symptoms of CTDs include pain and discomfort, numbing and tingling sensations, limited range of motion, weakness or clumsiness, redness and swelling, pins-and-needles sensation, cracking noises, fingers becoming pale, and pain at night—enough to wake you. Examples of CTDs include bursitis, carpal tunnel syndrome, epicondylitis, tendonitis, and trigger finger.

Many small and inexpensive improvements can be made to help reduce the risk of CTDs. Engineering controls include workplace redesign, such as designing for variability and the addition of handles or fixtures. Administrative controls include training, job rotation, job enlargement, work methods, and rest cycles. The key is to have the support of both management and the employees. Due to the hazards in meatpacking, OSHA has developed ergonomic guidelines for that industry. The elements include worksite analysis, hazard prevention and control, medical management and surveillance, and training and education.

Thermal Stress

Heat stress is a much greater hazard to workers than cold stress. Workers can utilize clothing and other means to protect themselves from the cold. There are no OSHA standards for heat stress because it would greatly hamper work done in the southern part of the United States.

When exposed to cold, our body shivers, blood vessels vasoconstrict, and our metabolic rate increases. We lose body heat through respiration, evaporation, conduction, radiation, and convection. Normal body temperature is 98.6°F; cold stress occurs when our body temperature drops to below 95°F. Hypothermia kills in two distinct steps: exposure to cold and wind, and exhaustion.

People who are at increased risk to cold stress are those with predisposing health conditions such as heart disease and diabetes, on medications, in poor physical condition, or who have alcohol in their system. Frostbite is the most common injury resulting from exposure to cold, usually affecting our outer extremities: fingers, toes, ears, and nose. People experiencing severe hypothermia (body temperature 82–90°F) are in serious trouble and need to be the transported to the hospital.

Protection from hypothermia includes being properly clothed. Today's synthetic fabrics make this much easier than in years past. Wear a warm head covering, waterproof insulated boots, gloves/mittens, and layered clothing. Drink plenty of fluids, avoiding beverages with alcohol or caffeine. Train workers to recognize conditions that lead to and the signs and symptoms of cold-induced injuries and illnesses. Have workers take frequent breaks in warmer areas. Ensure that workers wear proper clothing and headwear.

Stress factors in heat stress include environmental conditions, clothing, workload, and individual worker characteristics. Our body automatically handles heat by varying the rate and amount of blood circulation to the skin and perspiration of our major cooling mechanism. Evaporation is the body's major cooling mechanism, emitting large quantities of heat from the body. The problem is when the air temperature is greater than the body temperature, meaning that our body surface cannot lose heat. If the air temperature is greater than 35°C, do not use fans, because that will only increase the load on the person. Your body is always generating heat, passing it on to the environment. The harder you work, the more heat your body has to lose.

Heat stress is usually a concern in warmer climates or in warmer seasons. The TLV is loosely designed to keep the core body temperature from being heated by 1°C. The longer a person does hard work in the heat, the better their body becomes at keeping itself cool. If you're not used to working in the heat, you must take a week or two to get acclimatized or used to the heat. If a person is experienced on the job, limit their time in a hot environment to 50% of the shift on the first day, 80% of the second day, working a full shift on the third day. If the person is not experienced on the job, have them work 20% of the time in the hot environment on the first day and increase their exposure by 20% each following day. Another method to get people acclimatized is reducing the physical demands of the job for a week or two. If a person is ill or away from work for a week or two, they can lose their acclimatization.

Heat rash is caused by a hot humid environment. Heat cramps are caused by heavy sweating, draining the body of salt, which cannot be replaced by just water. Heat exhaustion is caused by inadequate salt and water intake, causing a person's cooling system to fail. Heat stroke is when a person's body has used its reserve of water and salt, causing it to stop sweating, which causes the body temperature to rise. People with heatstroke need medical attention immediately; call an ambulance. Alcohol, caffeinated beverages, very cold beverages, and carbonated beverages should be avoided when working in the heat. Alcoholic beverages can cause dehydration. Caffeinated beverages increase the heart rate. Cold or carbonated beverages can cause cramps. A rule of thumb is that your urine should be the color of what you are drinking, ideally water. If your urine is a dark color, you are not getting enough fluid intake.

How to Conduct an Industrial Hygiene Survey

This is a rough guide to what an industrial hygienist will do to conduct an industrial hygiene survey. It is an attempt to provide you with an idea of what an industrial hygienist does.

The first step is to investigate the industry. You want to check out prior industrial hygiene surveys either from OSHA or a private entity. In addition, you want to investigate the hazards found in that industry from sources such as OSHA, NIOSH, or the Canadian Center for Occupational Health and Safety (CCOHS). Ask the employer if they have done any medical monitoring. If they have medical records, review the records. Investigate any employee health complaints; for example, common health effects associated with overexposure to lead include neuromuscular, wrist drop, weakness, loss of appetite, metallic taste, and clumsiness. Are multiple employees experiencing symptoms? Are the employees exposed to multiple chemicals?

The evaluation of hazards is based on toxicity of the substance, concentration in the breathing zone, matter of use, length of time of exposure, controls already in place and effectiveness, and any special susceptibilities of employees. You need to conduct a plant walk-through looking for the materials the employees may be exposed to in the greatest quantity. Ask the employees how they usually use the material. Look for the materials that may cause the greatest risk when the employees are exposed; these may not be found in large quantities. One gallon of hydrogen cyanide is more dangerous than 500 gallons of isopropyl alcohol in terms of health effects. Ask employees what materials they use that cause the worst health effects. Ask the employees what materials they do not like to work with. Look for employees with special susceptibilities such as being pregnant.

Investigate engineering controls, such as ventilation automation. Are the engineering controls being used or look like they have been used? Are the employees wearing their PPE properly? How is the housekeeping, how is material stored and handled, and waste disposed of? You also need to look at setup, maintenance, and cleanup. Review the material safety data sheets (MSDSs) of the materials utilized by the facility. Investigate which materials have the greatest potential to cause adverse health effects. From your plant walk-through and a review of materials used, determine which materials you should conduct an industrial survey on.

Observe the work practices and if necessary conduct screening samples. Before sampling, utilize the NIOSH occupational exposure sampling strategy manual to determine the number of samples to take. The number of samples taken depends on the error of measurement and differences in results. Take a sufficient number of samples to obtain a representative estimate of exposure. Contaminant concentrations vary seasonally with weather, production levels, location, and/or job class.

Utilize the NIOSH analytical methods to determine which media to use, flow rate, limit of detection, and sample volume. Call your lab for information. Order your media; if sampling seven employees, remember you need at least eight sampling media—seven employees and one blank. Order 12, just to have some extra on hand. You need one blank for every 1 to 10 samples. For 11 employees you would need at least 13 media, 11 employees and 2 blanks; order 18. Always order at least three more media than you think you need.

Prepare blanks during the sample period for each type of sample collected. They should be handled in the same manner as any sampling media used to sample air contaminants, with the exception that no air is drawn through them. One blank will suffice for up to 10 samples for any given analysis/sampling period, except asbestos, which requires a minimum of two field blanks.

The day before you sample, charge the sampling pumps and/or the noise dosimeters. Calibrate the flow rate you need and place them back on the charger. Use the media in line with the sampling pump in the calibrator. The morning of the survey, when you get to the industry, turn on all your sampling pumps for at least 10 minutes before calibrating. Calibrate the flow rate recording the information. Do at least five flow rates for each sampling pump, average the flow rate, and record the time calibrated. After calibration, place the sampling pumps on the employees to be sampled and record the starting time.

Determine which employee should be sampled, if you cannot monitor a sufficient number of employees due to financial constraints or other reasons, try to pick out worst-case scenarios. Discuss the purpose of sampling, informing the employee when and where the equipment will/can be removed. Always be honest with the employees. Place the sampling equipment on employees where it does not interfere with their work performance. Always ask employees if they are right or left-handed because that is where you should put the microphone, cassette, or tube. Place the pump on their nondominant side or on the area of their back that will not interfere with their work. When you place a collection device on an employee, try to place it as close as practical to the nose and mouth. You want to try to get in an area within 1 foot of their nose and mouth. The sample inlet should always be in a downward vertical position to avoid gross contamination.

Record the sampling pump and sample that is on each employee and label the sample. Record the employee's job title, workstation, and tasks performed. Ask the employees to keep a record of how many parts they completed and approximately how long they performed each task. For example, a welder ground for two hours, welded for four hours, and brazed for an hour. Ask the employee to complete 110 parts if they normally complete 100 parts. Turn on the pump on recording the starting time, observing the operation of the pump for a short time.

Check the pump every hour, recording any relevant observations, such as work practices. In addition, make sure the sample integrity is maintained. Tell the employees that if the pump/vibrator starts humming, they should contact you right away. More frequent checks may be necessary when heavy filter loading is possible, such as employees working in a very dusty environment. Turn off and remove the sampling pumps immediately prior to employee leaving a potentially contaminated area, such as going to lunch or a break in a clean area. If the clean areas also appear contaminated and are considered part of the workplace, assess the need for surface contamination measurements. You always want to record what the employees doing, trying to be as detailed as possible and if possible take pictures. If pictures are not possible, try to make a diagram. You want to note such things as visible airborne contaminants, work practices, potential interferences, movements, and other conditions. These will assist in determining appropriate engineering controls. In addition, if you see any safety hazards, you want to note these as well.

At the end of the sampling period record the time you shut off the pump. Record the number of parts completed, including the type, model, and so forth. Record what the employee did that day. Postcalibrate the pumps, completing the same number of flows as the precalibration. Remember that you need to use the media line with the sampling pump and the calibrator.

Calculate the average flow rate, taking the pre- and post-averages for each sampling pump. To calculate sample volume, take the number of minutes sampled multiplied by the average flow rate. For example, an 80-min sample × a 2 L average flow rate = a 960 L sample. Ensure that the samples are properly labeled and complete the chain of custody.

When writing a report, remember that anyone should be able to read it in the future and know exactly what was going on when the industrial hygiene sampling occurred. Who was monitored? For example, was a welder, machinist, or maintenance worker being sampled? What were they doing? What equipment were they using—a MIG welder, a three-quarter horsepower grinder? What parts or products were they making—welded 52 rear differentials for mighty trucks? What were they in—welding booth number seven?

References

Anna, Daniel H. *The Occupational Environment: Its Evaluation and Control and Management*. 3rd ed. <place?>: American Industrial Hygiene Association, 2011.

Choi B., L. Tennassee, and J. Eijkemans. Developing regional workplace health and hazard surveillance in the Americas., *Pan American Journal of Public Health*, 10(6), 2001, 376–381.

Goldwater, L.J.: *Historical Highlights in Occupational Medicine* (Readings and Perspectives in Medicine, Booklet 9). Durham, N.C.: Duke University Medical Center, 1985

Plog, Barbara A., and Patricia Quinlan. *Fundamentals of Industrial Hygiene*. Itasca, Ill.: National Safety Council, 2002.

2012 TLVs and BEIs: Based on the Documentation of the Threshold Limit Values for Chemical Substances and Physical Agents & Biological Exposure Indices. Cincinnati: ACGIH Signature Publications, 2012.

ACGIH: Industrial Hygiene, Environmental Occupational Safety and Health Resource, 2012. American Conference of Governmental Industrial Hygienists. http://www.acgih.org/home.htm

AIHA: American Industrial Hygiene Association, 2012. American Industrial Hygiene Association. http://www.aiha.org/Pages/default.aspx

CDC: Centers for Disease Control and Prevention; CDC 24/7 *Saving Lives. Protecting People*.

National Institute for Occupational Safety and Health (NIOSH): *Providing National and World Leadership to Prevent Workplace Illnesses and Injuries*, 2012. http://www.cdc.gov/niosh/

Occupational Health and Safety Administration. 2012. http://www.osha.gov/>OSHA

National Environmental Health Association (NEHA), 2012. http://www.neha.org/index.shtml

Association of Environmental Health Academic Programs, 2012. http://aehap.org/>

National Environmental Health Science & Protection Accreditation Council (EHAC), 2012. http://www.ehacoffice.org/

ABET, 2012. ABET. http://www.abet.org/

Living with Radiation, Its Benefits and Risks

12

Douglas Draper, CHP

If radiation causes cancer, have you ever wondered why radiation is used in the treatment of cancer?

Key Performance Outcome Indicators:

1. Identify the common types of radiation and interactions of each type
2. Consider example control processes for radiation and radioactive sources
3. Study basic biological effects of radiation exposure and dose management
4. Review some of the issues regarding waste management of radioactive materials
5. Learn about the field of health physics and its employment opportunities

---

Introduction

Radiation is ubiquitous in nature. Radiation that affects people originates in the stars, from the earth, and through man-made inventions. Scientists who need to take nuclear measurements make great efforts to minimize the radiation that surrounds us constantly, and although this ambient radiation can be reduced, it cannot be eliminated. Radiation, because of its properties, can be useful for various common applications. The very properties of radiation that make it unique and potentially useful are the same properties that, if used unwisely, can cause physical harm to people and the environment. **Health physics** is the field of study that is focused on the protection of people and the environment from the harmful effects of radiation while it is being used in an appropriate application.

Atomic Structure

Matter is composed of atoms. A simple approach to understanding the atom is based on the Bohr model, where a nucleus, containing positively charged protons and neutrons with no electrical charge, is surrounded by negatively charged electrons that occupy shells. Virtually all of the mass of an atom is found in the nucleus. The proton, which is almost equivalent to the neutron in mass, is approximately 2,000 times the mass of the electron. The number of protons in the nucleus determines the chemical element. An atom with six protons is a carbon atom; an atom with 47 protons is a silver atom. Atoms of an element may have different numbers of neutrons. For example, an atom of sulfur with 16 protons may have 16 neutrons, and be called sulfur-32. If an atom of sulfur has 18 neutrons, it would be sulfur-34. Two atoms of the same element that have different numbers of neutrons are called isotopes.

A neutral atom has a number of electrons equivalent to the number of protons, so that the positive charges of the protons are canceled by the negative charges of the electrons.

Protons and neutrons are held together in the nucleus by the strong nuclear force which only operates over short distances, perhaps two times the diameter of a proton. This force is sufficient to overcome the electrostatic repulsion of the positive charges on the protons. However, the stability of the nucleus depends on the ratio of protons to neutrons. Enough neutrons are necessary to allow the strong nuclear force to act, but too many neutrons cause instability in the nucleus, just as too few neutrons. Isotopes with too many or too few neutrons for the number of protons in the nucleus are unstable, and in order to gain stability change the structure of the nucleus by releasing nuclear radiation and energy. Atoms that change in this manner are radionuclides.

Energy

Radiation is one of the many natural processes for transferring energy. Examples include visible light and dental X-rays. Life as we know it would not exist without the ability to transfer energy through radiation. Electromagnetic radiation is described by its wavelength or frequency, which is related through the equality

$$v = \lambda * f$$

where the velocity is the speed of light, or $3 (10^8)$ m/sec in free space, the wavelength, λ is measured in meters, and the frequency, f, is measured in $\sec^{-1}$. Therefore, at a given velocity, the shorter the wavelength, the higher the frequency. Electromagnetic radiation is one of the primary means of transferring nuclear energy to matter.

The spectrum of electromagnetic energy varies from very long wavelengths, as found in radio waves, to very short wavelengths, such as gamma rays.

Energy is also found in other forms. For example, chemical energy is contained in the process of bond making and bond breaking, leading to the creation of different molecules. Gravitational effects exist due to the attraction of different masses. They are responsible for holding the moon in orbit around the earth. Gravitational attraction occurs over great distances.

Nuclear energy originates in the nucleus of unstable atoms and is emitted from the nucleus as waves or particles.

Energy is measured in a number of quantities, including the joule and the calorie. In radiological terms, the unit of energy commonly used is the electron volt, or the amount of energy required to move the charge on one electron through a resistance of one volt. This amount of energy is equivalent to $1.6 (10^{-19})$ joules. Energy associated with typical radiation of interest in the protection of people ranges from a few electron volts, or ev, to thousands of electron volts, or kev, to millions of electron volts, or Mev.

Radiation

In radiological protection, radiation is described as energy transmitted as waves or particles. The waves or particles interact with matter and can change the physical or chemical properties of the matter with which they interact. When an atom emits radiation in the form of particles or waves, it is said to "decay." It is no longer the same atom it was before it emitted the radiation; its chemical and or physical properties have changed; it has transmuted to a new nuclide which may or may not be radioactive. In this manner, it is possible to change one element to another; for example, mercury to gold. However, because of the effort required to make this occur, it is not economically feasible at this time.

When a radioactive atom decays, it emits radiation. This radiation can then interact with other atoms. The interactions cause these atoms to change chemically and/or physically. It is the changes in matter produced by radiation which make it useful, and if not properly controlled, can cause damage or harm.

Ionizing/nonionizing

Ionizing radiation has sufficient energy to dislodge orbital electrons, thereby producing ions. Examples include alpha, beta, gamma, neutron, and X-rays. Nonionizing radiation does not have sufficient energy to dislodge orbital electrons. Examples include visible light, infra-red, microwaves, radio waves, and radar.

Nuclear radiation in the form of charged particles can cause ionization in matter by the process of removing electrons from neutral atoms by electrostatic attraction or repulsion. The electrons that are removed from matter may have sufficient energy imparted to them that they can subsequently interact with electrons in adjacent atoms and cause those electrons to be removed. This is an example of secondary ionization. As an example, a typical alpha particle emitted from a radioactive nucleus may have energy of 4 Mev, or 4 million electron volts. In air, it typically requires approximately 33.7 electron volts to cause the ionization of one atom. Theoretically there is enough energy from one alpha particle to ionize more than 100,000 atoms in air.

Half-life

There are more than 3,000 known radionuclides. Each has unique properties, including the type of radiation that it emits, the energy of the radiation, and how quickly it emits the radiation. Each time an atom emits radiation, it changes its physical and or chemical properties, it is no longer the same atom it was. Each radionuclide emits radiation at a predictable rate based on a large number of decays. The rate is expressed in terms of time. The time required for half of the radioactive atoms of a radionuclide to decay is called its half-life.

Each radionuclide has a specific half-life. Some radionuclides have very long half-lives, thousands of years or longer. Some have very short half-lives, on the order of fractions of a second. The shorter the half-life, the faster a radioactive material decays and the quicker it becomes nondetectable.

Types of Decay

When a radionuclide decays, it can emit a number of different types of radiation. Generally there are four types of nuclear radiation, as will be discussed in this chapter: alpha, beta, gamma, and neutron radiation.

Alpha Particle Emission

When a radionuclide decays by emission of an alpha particle from the nucleus, it changes the number of protons and neutrons in the nucleus. An alpha particle has two protons and two neutrons. When it is emitted, it interacts primarily with electrons of adjacent atoms. The two protons, each positively charged, attract electrons from the adjacent atoms and pull them from their orbits, causing ionization of those atoms. Eventually the alpha particle, with its two positive charges, picks up two electrons and becomes an atom of helium. Sometimes a helium detector is used around the seal of an alpha source to ensure that it is still properly sealed, since helium would escape if there were any small breaks.

The radionuclide that emits the alpha particle now has two fewer protons and two fewer neutrons. An atom of radium that has 88 protons and 138 neutrons that decays by the emission of an alpha particle now has 86 protons and 134 neutrons. That nuclide would be radon-222. It is the alpha decay of radium-226 that creates radon-222, which in some parts of the country can cause a potential hazard in poorly ventilated areas.

Not all alpha interactions cause ionization. If an alpha particle is too far away to attract an electron sufficiently out of its orbit, it may still have enough attraction to pull an electron from its current shell to a higher-energy shell. The electron will eventually fall to a lower-energy shell and in the process emit a weak X-ray. When an alpha particle causes an electron on an adjacent atom to go to a higher energy level, the process is called "excitation." Alpha particles interact with matter by two processes: ionization and excitation.

Alpha particles give up their energy over relatively short distances, on the order of a few centimeters in air, a few microns in water. Because of this, alpha particles have low penetrating power. In fact, alpha particles can be stopped by a sheet of paper. Alpha particles may be able to just penetrate the dead layer of skin, so these particles cause little if any harm to an exposed individual. However, if a source of alpha particles is inhaled or ingested, the alpha particles give their energy up over short distances, and can cause significant damage to living cells, especially if the alpha particle is emitted inside the nucleus of a cell. Alpha-emitting radionuclides are referred to as internal health hazards.

Beta Particle Emission

A radionuclide can decay by emission of a beta particle from the nucleus. A beta particle is formed within the nucleus when a neutron converts to a proton and emits a negative particle the size and charge of an electron. Beta emission is always accompanied by the emission of another particle which shares its energy; a neutrino. Neutrinos interact with matter very weakly and are extremely difficult to detect. A neutrino can pass through the earth without interacting with any of the atoms along its path. The beta particle, on the other hand, interacts with other electrons of adjacent atoms. The negative charge on a beta particle repels the electron of an adjacent atom and can cause ionization by "kicking" the electron out of its orbit.

Beta particles interact with adjacent atoms through the processes of ionization and excitation. In addition, beta particles can interact with other atoms in a third type of process, *Bremsstrahlung*, which means "braking radiation." In this process, a beta particle with negative charge passes close to the nucleus. The direction of the beta particle is changed by the attractive force of the nucleus, causing deceleration of the beta. When the direction of the beta particle is changed, an X-ray is emitted from the beta particle, resulting in a lower energy of the beta particle. The more protons in the nucleus, the more potential *Bremsstrahlung* produced. The energy of the X-ray varies with the energy of the beta particle, so the more energetic beta particles produce *Bremsstrahlung* X-rays with a higher average energy. Because of this effect, beta-emitting radionuclides are normally shielded with plastic or aluminum. These two materials each have a nucleus with a small average number of protons. Lead or other dense materials may be used for an external shield over the plastic or aluminum.

Beta particles generally are less effective at ionizing air than alpha particles; therefore they have a greater range in air, and have a greater range in other forms of matter, depending on the energy of the beta particle. Beta particles are normally considered an internal hazard rather than an external hazard, although most beta-emitting radionuclides produce beta particles with sufficient energy to penetrate the skin or lens of the eye.

Gamma Ray Emission

The third type of nuclear radiation that will be discussed in this chapter is gamma radiation. Gamma radiation originates in the nucleus. It often is produced concurrently with the emission of a beta particle, and may accompany the emission of an alpha particle. Unlike alpha and beta radiation, gamma radiation is not a particle, it is an electromagnetic wave. It does not have a charge, and has no mass. However, it can transfer its energy to matter through three different processes.

One process in which gamma rays interact with matter occurs when a gamma ray is completely absorbed by an electron, and transfers all of its energy to that electron. Called a photoelectric interaction, it usually results in the removal of the electron from the atom, creating an ionized atom. The ionized electron may subsequently cause secondary ionizations. Photoelectric interactions are most common with gamma rays of lower energy.

Another gamma ray interaction process is similar to the photoelectric interaction. The Compton interaction occurs when a gamma ray impinges on an electron but only transfers some of its energy to the electron. The electron may be excited to a higher energy level or ionized. Following the Compton interaction, there is a resulting gamma ray of lower energy. The total energy before the Compton interaction and after the interaction remains the same, but a transfer of energy has occurred. Gamma rays of intermediate energy normally interact with matter through Compton interactions.

The third interaction of gamma rays with matter is pair production. This occurs when a high-energy gamma comes close to the nucleus. As the gamma ray passes, the influence of the nucleus causes the energy of the gamma ray to convert to mass. A pair of electrons is produced, one a typical electron with a negative charge, the other, a positive electron called a positron. The positron is actually an example of antimatter; it is an antiparticle of an electron. When the positron subsequently interacts with another electron, the two annihilate with the conversion of mass to energy, creating a pair of X-rays.

Because gamma rays interact weakly with matter, they can travel long distances in air. These radiations are shielded effectively by dense materials such as lead and tungsten. Actually, any type of material can shield gamma rays, but some materials are more effective than others. The thicker the shield, the more effective it is at reducing the exposure to gamma rays.

Gamma rays are electromagnetic waves that originate in the nucleus of unstable atoms. X-rays are electromagnetic waves also, but do not originate in the nucleus; rather, they originate in the electron shells. Because of this distinction, X-rays are not considered nuclear radiation, but are ionizing radiation just like gamma rays, but with a different source.

Gamma rays and X-rays are considered to be external hazards. The best protection from gamma rays and X-rays is to avoid them using appropriate radiological controls.

Neutron Emission

Neutrons are emitted from the nucleus. These are particles, but unlike alpha and beta particles, neutrons have no charge. Therefore, interactions of neutrons are based primarily on their interactions with other nuclei rather than on their interaction with electrons. Neutron interactions are influenced by their energy. For slow neutrons, there are three primary interactions. One of these interactions is fission. In this case, the neutron interacts with the nucleus of another atom, the neutron is absorbed, and the nucleus, now unstable, splits into smaller nuclei, usually with the emission of more neutrons. Another possible interaction of slow neutrons is charged particle interactions. In this case, the slow neutron is absorbed by the nucleus of another atom which then becomes unstable, and emits a charged particle, either an alpha, beta, or another type of particle. In the other possible case of slow neutron interactions, the neutron is absorbed by the nucleus of another atom, and the unstable nucleus emits an electromagnetic ray. This is called radioactive capture.

Fast neutron interactions are dominated by two processes. The first is the elastic collision. In this case, the neutron collides with a lightweight nucleus, perhaps a hydrogen nucleus which has approximately the same mass as the neutron, and the neutron transfers some of its energy to the nucleus and retains some of its energy. The kinetic energy of the two is equivalent to the kinetic energy of the two before the collision. This is similar to the reaction when a billiard ball is struck by a cue ball. In the other interaction process, an inelastic collision occurs whereby some of the energy of the impacting neutron is converted to internal energy within the nucleus. In both of these cases, the energy of the neutron is reduced until it becomes a slow neutron which can then react by the mechanisms discussed.

Neutrons can also be made by other means. An alpha particle that reacts with an atom with only a few protons can produce a neutron. Called the "alpha-n" reaction, it provides a means to generate neutrons that can be used for various purposes. High-energy accelerators are another source of neutrons. Usually, neutrons produced in this manner are a byproduct of the accelerator and are considered a nuisance. Another source of neutrons is from radionuclides that undergo spontaneous fission. Radionuclides that produce significant quantities of neutrons by this method are somewhat rare; most common among them is californium-252.

Neutrons are shielded by materials that include atoms with low numbers of protons. Examples include water, with two atoms of hydrogen in each molecule, organic materials such as plastics, and wet soil.

Biological Effects and Risk

The biological effects of radiation can be attributed directly to the types of interactions that each type of radiation can induce. In general, few biological effects are caused by the direct ionization of a molecule within the body. Most of the biological effects are caused by the formation of free radicals following the ionization of a molecule. Since most of the human body is water, the most prevalent of the free radicals is the hydroxyl radical. This radical causes chemical changes to other molecules. If that molecule happens to be a strand of DNA, the DNA is damaged.

When damage occurs within the human body, repair mechanisms can repair the damage. In some cases apoptosis can cause cell death. In some cases it is possible that incomplete or inaccurate repair can lead to mutation within the affected molecule. The mutation may or may not be able to replicate. The function that is performed by the mutated molecule may or may not be performed correctly.

Some argue that no amount of exposure to radiation is safe; that because of the ionization that occurs in atoms within the body, every event has a probability of giving rise to cancer. Indeed, because of the large number of potential agents in the environment that can cause cancer, approximately 25% of the U.S. population will die from cancer. One of these potential agents is exposure to radiation. Exposure to large amounts of radiation has been shown to cause cancer in animals and humans.

The effect of radiation is similar to exposure of a number of other stressors to the human body. Generally, at low doses, the exposure has a stochastic effect. In other words, the exposure has a corresponding probability of an event; in this case, cancer. At high doses, the exposure has corresponding deterministic effects, the larger the dose, the more severe the effect.

Consider the analogy of smoking. Tobacco has a number of toxins that are inhaled during smoking; one of these toxins is nicotine. We have all heard someone say, "My grandmother/ grandfather smoked for 50 years and didn't get cancer." On the other hand, we know that smoking tobacco causes cancer. The more a person smokes, the greater the probability that the person will contract cancer. This is an example of a stochastic effect.

Nicotine is a chemical found in tobacco. At low exposures, it may cause, or contribute to the cause of cancer. Perhaps 1 mg of nicotine is incorporated into the body per cigarette. At higher concentrations, nicotine increases blood pressure and pulse rate. When the concentration in humans approaches 1 mg/kg body weight, nicotine can be lethal. The higher the concentration in the body, the more severe the effect. This is an example of a deterministic effect.

At some low exposures, we normally do not consider nicotine to have any lasting effect. A person who smokes one cigarette at age 16 and does not like it may give up smoking altogether. If that person dies of lung cancer 50 years later, most people would not think that the person died from cigarette smoking, although perhaps it is possible.

At low doses, it is not expected that exposure to radiation causes health effects, either short-term or long-term. As the dose increases, the probability of an effect such as cancer increases. At a high dose, exposure to radiation can cause manifest effects, including death.

Dosimetry

Radiation is generally easy to detect because of its interaction with matter. This provides a means to measure radiation exposure from sources of radiation, and to quantify the amount of radioactive material that may be incorporated into the body through inhalation, ingestion, absorption, and injection through cuts and open wounds.

External Dosimetry

People who may be exposed to radiation because of their work, are monitored in accordance with regulations. Monitoring for radiation considers the type of radiation, the energy of the radiation, the quantity of radiation, and the portions of the body that are exposed.

Gamma and neutron radiations are considered external radiological hazards. Beta radiation can also cause harm to living tissues. Current dosimeters are designed to monitor for these types of radiation. Filters are sometimes used to provide information on the energy of the radiation. Personnel dosimeters are normally small, sealed packages that can be decontaminated if necessary. These assigned dosimeters provide dose records for exposed individuals, typically radiation workers. Normally, the dose report takes a number of days to prepare after the dosimeter is submitted to allow for processing and calculations. Dosimeters are routinely exchanged on a quarterly or monthly schedule. In emergency situations, dosimeter processing can be expedited.

For personnel that enter high radiation fields, additional dosimetry is required that can provide a real-time measurement. Usually, these are electronic alarming, self-reading dosimeters. Electronic dosimeters of today typically have an alarm setpoint for dose rate and total dose, so that an individual is notified either when the field dose rate is higher than permitted or if the total dose exceeds a predetermined amount. Although useful for personnel protection, these electronic dosimeters are not used for dose of record because of the potential inaccuracies, but they can be used for dose investigations if the assigned dosimeter is compromised.

Internal Dosimetry

When radiation workers are required to enter areas with elevated contamination or airborne radiation, it may be necessary to monitor the individual for intake of radioactive materials. This is normally accomplished through a bioassay program. Bioassay includes both *in vivo* and *in vitro* analyses; *in vivo* analyses include direct monitoring of sensitive organs, such as the thyroid, for radioiodine exposures, lung counting for inhalation of transuranics, and whole-body counting for exposure to radiocesium and other radionuclides that disperse throughout the body.

In vitro measurements are performed on bodily samples, including urine, feces, blood, hair, breath, and other types of samples. *In vitro* samples are collected, packaged, then analyzed by a specialized laboratory. Based on biokinetic models, the uptake is estimated, and a dose derived from calculation algorithms. *In vitro* measurements are performed if *in vivo* measurements are not sensitive enough. This occurs if the uptake limit is too low to be easily measured, if the radionuclide in question does not have sufficient energy to be easily measured, or if an exposure may have occurred at some time in the past, and it is too late for *in vivo* measurements to be effective.

Detection and Measurement, Instrumentation

Ionizing radiation has the ability to ionize neutral atoms; this characteristic is used to detect radiation and the presence of radioactive materials. At environmental levels, radiation cannot be seen, tasted, smelled, heard, or felt; therefore, radiation must be detected by the use of instrumentation.

Instruments consist of three basic components:

- a component where ionization occurs
- another component to collect the ionized particles
- a component used to count the ionized particles

Radiation detection instruments can be simple devices or quite complex, depending on how accurate the measurement needs to be, the expected radiation exposure levels, the type of radiation, and the energy of the radiation.

Radiation measurement devices are used to monitor radiation worker exposures, environmental contamination, and are used in industry for controlling application processes. Instruments are normally portable and suitable for field operation or may be larger or more sensitive and suitable for laboratory use or process control.

Calibration

Instruments respond to radiation by detecting ionization in the detector. Not all ionizing events are detected by the instrument; only a fraction of them. Therefore, to be able to use an instrument to measure a particular type of radiation, the instrument requires calibration. The instrument is placed in a known radiation environment that includes the type of radiation, energy of the radiation, scatter effects, and other parameters that might affect the response, including temperature, atmospheric pressure, humidity, and others. Then the response of the instrument is noted. In some cases, the meter is adjusted to read out in the quantity being measured, such as microsieverts (μSv) per hour. The instrument can then be used, within the tolerance factors from the calibration, to measure similar fields. Cesium-137 is often used to calibrate gamma-measuring instruments. The instrument then responds linearly to other fields of cesium-137 radiation. However, if a field of cobalt-60 radiation is encountered, the instrument may overrespond or underrespond. Also, if another cesium-137 field of much greater strength is encountered, the instrument may not respond correctly.

Functional Checks

Instruments need to be checked on a regular basis. Instruments may stop working correctly for a variety of reasons, including weak batteries and damaged detectors. Typically, an instrument is verified using a check source before use and after use. If the instrument passes the source check at the beginning of its use, but does not pass at the conclusion of its use, then an evaluation of what measurements were valid is necessary. If it cannot be reasonably determined what caused the instrument to malfunction and when, then it may be necessary to perform the measurements again with a functional instrument.

Common Sources: Natural and Anthropogenic

Radiation is ubiquitous. It has been part of the environment since the creation of the earth. Cosmic radiation from the sun and other stars causes significant radiation exposures in space. Man also produces radioactive sources.

Terrestrial radiation is caused by primordial radionuclides that were incorporated into the earth as it was forming. Many of the shorter-lived primordial radionuclides have long since decayed away. However, primordial radionuclides with long half-lives continue to exist in the earth. For example, uranium-238 has a half-life of approximately 4.5 billion years. If the earth is 4.5 billion years old, about one half of the uranium that was present when the earth was formed is still present. Uranium-238 decays to a radioactive progeny, thorium-234. The decay of uranium-238 leads to 13 radioactive progeny before decaying to a stable isotope of lead. These progeny include alpha-, beta-, and gamma-emitting radionuclides, including radium-226 and radon-222. This is called the uranium-238 decay series. Two other extended naturally occurring decay series exist. These are the thorium-232 decay series and the uranium-235 decay series. In addition to the decay series, other long-lived primordial radionuclides are present in the earth, including potassium-40. This radionuclide is incorporated into growing plants such as grass, fruits, and vegetables. Bananas are a good source of potassium and hence a source of potassium-40. Cows eat grass and incorporate the potassium into milk. Milk and milk products are sources of potassium-40. When we eat bananas and drink milk, we are incorporating the radionuclide potassium-40 into our bodies as part of the potassium.

Cosmogenic radionuclides are continually created in the upper atmosphere through interactions of cosmic radiation with stable isotopes such as nitrogen-14 and oxygen-16. Important cosmogenic radionuclides include carbon-14 and tritium, or hydrogen-3. These radionuclides precipitate out of the atmosphere and are eventually incorporated into living cells. Carbon-14, with a half-life of 5,470 years, provides a useful way to determine the age of certain relics and remains.

With the dawn of the nuclear age in the 1940s, man developed the ability to create large numbers of radionuclides in nuclear reactions. The first nuclear reactions were created in nuclear reactors. Later, nuclear reactions were created in the use of nuclear weapons. These nuclear reactions have created a number of useful radionuclides, such as technicium-99m, which is used in millions of diagnostic medical procedures each year around the globe, and also highly toxic radionuclides, including plutonium-239 with a 24,600-year half-life.

Useful Applications of Radiation

Radioactive materials have many applications in science, medicine, and industry. They are used in a wide variety of applications in everyday life. Research laboratories, medical centers, industrial facilities, food irradiation plants, and many consumer products all use or contain radioisotopes. A promising new use of radiation is in the effective treatment of water.

Energy

The most commonly known use of radioactive materials is nuclear power generation. Nuclear power plants produce 20% of the electricity used in the United States, and 16% worldwide. Nuclear reactors are also used to power submarines, aircraft carriers, and spacecraft. Heat from reactors can be used to desalinate ocean water to make it potable. Radioisotope thermoelectric generators (RTGs) use the energy emitted from radioisotopes to boil water and generate power for remotely located weather stations and navigational buoys. Early pacemakers were also powered by radioactive materials and may still be in use today.

Medicine

Radioisotopes are used to diagnose and treat many medical conditions and diseases, including cancer and thyroid disorders. Imaging procedures such as kidney and bone scans often use radioactive materials because these materials are absorbed by particular parts of the body. Thyroid conditions are diagnosed and treated using radioactive iodine, which concentrates in the thyroid. Bone scans use radioactive phosphorous, and muscle imaging uses potassium. The workings of the digestive and cardiovascular systems can also be seen by eating or injecting special radioactive materials and using a special camera to record the paths these materials take through the body.

All of these treatments are classified as nuclear medicine procedures. Overall, more than 11 million nuclear medicine procedures are performed in the United States each year. Around 100 million medical laboratory tests on body fluid and tissue samples use radioactive materials.

In addition, radioactive materials are used to sterilize blood before it is used in treatment. Radiation is also used to sterilize bandages, medical devices such as scalpels, and other operating room items.

Industry

Radioactive materials allow many industrial processes to be performed cheaper, faster, easier, and more effectively. Radioactive tracers make it possible to find blockages and leaks in pipes and to determine how quickly materials flow through them. They also allow corrosion and wear-and-tear on mechanical equipment to be monitored. In addition, radioactive materials are employed in external industrial imaging applications to determine metal content and quality in steel and to show cracks and faults in engines, bolts, and structural assemblies.

Paper and sheet metal manufacturers use radioisotopes to monitor the sheets to ensure that the proper thickness is attained. The height of liquid in beverage containers and large tanks is tested in a similar fashion.

The mining, oil, and gas industries rely on radioactive materials to find and map mineral and hydrocarbon deposits. Road surface density is also measured using radioisotopes.

Agriculture

Radiation is used to kill bacteria, molds, and other microorganisms in strawberries, onions, potatoes, meats, and spices, preventing the food from spoiling, and making it safer to eat.

Radiation is also used to sterilize insect pests. The sterilized insects are then released to unsuccessfully mate with other insects. This has proven effective in the reduction of swarms of pests.

Fertilizers often contain radioactive materials. Potassium, phosphorus, and nitrogen are important ingredients in these fertilizers. Potassium contains naturally occurring potassium-40, which is incorporated into living organisms that have potassium. Phosphorous is often derived from potash, which may contain uranium or its progeny.

Food often contains trace quantities of radioactive materials, including potassium-40 and carbon-14. Water also contains various primordial and cosmogenic radionuclides, including tritium.

Consumer Products

Many smoke detectors contain a radioactive americium source, while some photocopiers use radioactive polonium to prevent static buildup. Cosmetics, baby powder, and contact lens solution are sterilized by radiation.

Common Radioisotopes and Their Uses

The most common radioisotopes seen in everyday life are tabulated on the following pages with their main uses, half-life, and emission types.

Radiation sources provide critical capabilities in the oil and gas, electrical power (utilities), construction, manufacturing, and food industries. They are used to treat millions of patients each year in diagnostic and therapeutic procedures and also are used in a variety of military applications. In addition, academic, government, and private institutions use radioactive sources in technology research and development. These materials are as diverse in geographic location as they are in functional use.

—From transmittal letter to president of EPACT Radioactive Source
Protection and Security Task Force Report

The radionuclides most commonly used in industry are listed below:

Americium-241

Used in many smoke detectors for homes and businesses to measure levels of toxic lead in dried paint samples, ensure uniform thickness in rolling processes like steel and paper production, and help determine where oil wells should be drilled.

Cadmium-109

Used to analyze metal alloys for checking stock and scrap sorting.

Californium-252

Used to inspect airline luggage for hidden explosives, gauge moisture content of soil in the road construction and building industries, and measure the moisture of materials stored in soils.

Carbon-14

Used as an important research tool. In pharmaceutical research it is used as a tracer to ensure that potential drugs are metabolized without forming harmful byproducts. It is also used in biological research, agriculture, pollution control, and archeology.

Cesium-137

Used to treat cancerous tumors, measure correct patient dosages of radioactive pharmaceuticals, measure and control the liquid flow in oil pipelines, tell researchers whether oil wells are plugged by sand, and sure the right fill level for packages of food, drugs, and other products. (The products in these packages do not become radioactive.)

Cobalt-60

Used to sterilize surgical instruments and to improve the safety and reliability of industrial fuel oil burners. Used in cancer treatment, food irradiation, gauges, and radiography.

Curium-244

Used in mining to analyze material excavated from pits and slurries from drilling operations.

Iridium-192

Used to test the integrity of pipeline welds, boilers, and aircraft parts and in brachytherapy/tumor irradiation.

Iron-55

Used to analyze electroplating solutions and to detect the presence of sulfur in the air. Used in metabolism research.

Krypton-85

Used in indicator lights in appliances such as clothes washers and dryers, stereos, and coffee makers; used to gauge the thickness of thin plastics and sheet metal, rubber, textiles and paper, and to measure dust and pollutant levels.

Nickel-63

Used to detect explosives, and in voltage regulators and current surge protectors in electronic devices, and in electron capture detectors for gas chromatographs.

Plutonium-238

Has powered more than 20 NASA spacecraft since 1972.

Polonium-210

Reduces the static charge in production of photographic film and other materials.

Promethium-147

Used in electric blanket thermostats, and to gauge thickness of thin plastics, thin sheet metal, rubber, textiles, and paper.

Radium-226

Makes lighting rods more effective.

Sodium-24

Used to locate leaks in industrial pipelines, and in oil well studies.

Sulphur-35

Used in survey meters by schools, the military, and emergency management authorities. Also used in cigarette-manufacturing sensors and medical treatment.

Thallium-204

Measures the dust and pollutant levels on filter paper, and gauges the thickness of plastics, sheet metal, rubber, textiles, and paper.

Thoriated Tungsten

Used in electric arc-welding rods in the construction, aircraft, petrochemical, and food-processing equipment industries. Produces easier starting, greater arc stability, and less metal contamination.

Thorium-229

Helps fluorescent lights last longer.

Thorium-230

Provides coloring and fluorescence in colored glazes and glassware.

Tritium (H3)

Used in self-luminous aircraft and commercial exit signs, for luminous dials, gauges, and wrist-watches, to produce luminous paint, and for geological prospecting and hydrology.

Uranium-235

Fuel for nuclear power plants and naval nuclear propulsion systems, and used to produce fluorescent glassware, a variety of colored glazes, and wall tiles.

From *The Regulation and Use of Radioisotopes in Today's World* (NUREG/BR-0217, Rev. 1), U.S. Nuclear Regulatory Commission.

Radiological control

Radiation has proven to be useful and effective in many applications that enhance the quality of life. However, because of the unique properties of radiation, it must be controlled to minimize undesirable effects on workers, the public, and the environment.

Regulations

Standards are developed by various internationally recognized organizations for the control and monitoring of radiation in the environment. These standards are peer reviewed and published. Countries of the world develop legislation based on the standards. The legislation is then codified as regulations. Because regulations for each country are based on international standards, there is generally agreement on the limits and control measures, such as transportation of radioactive materials.

Time, Distance, and Shielding

Protection from unwanted exposure to radiation is usually accomplished through the three basic tenets of radiation safety: time, distance, and shielding. Exposure to a source of radiation is based on the quantity and type of radiation and the time of the exposure. Much as exposure to sunlight can cause sunburn, if one limits the time directly exposed to the sun, then the chances of sunburn is minimized. The longer one is exposed to the sun, the greater the sunburn. Similarly, the longer one is exposed to a source of radiation, the greater the exposure.

Another principle of radiation safety is distance. The farther from an unshielded source, the less exposure one gets from the source. As one reaches for a hot burner on the stove, as the hand approaches the hot surface, it is obvious from the heat that one feels. As the hand is withdrawn, the heat becomes imperceptible. Of course, in a large fire, one must be pretty far back to not feel the heat. So it is with radioactive sources. Near a small source, one doesn't have to get very far away to minimize exposure, but one must be relatively far back from a large source to minimize the exposure.

The third method commonly used to reduce exposure to a source is through the use of shielding. Radiation interacts with matter. When a material is placed between you and a radioactive source, some of the radiation interacts with the material. The more material, the more the radiation interacts with the material. How effective a material is at shielding depends on a number of factors, including the type of radiation, the energy of the radiation, and the amount of material that is used for shielding.

By judiciously applying time, distance, and shielding, harmful effects of radiation can be controlled.

ALARA

When radiation is used for a purpose, it is important to maximize the usefulness of the radiation while at the same time reducing its negative or harmful effects. The principle that describes this is ALARA, or "As Low As Reasonably Achievable." Use of radiation is controlled so as to use the minimum amount necessary to achieve the desired results. However, that aspect alone is not protective of the worker or public.

The ALARA principle is applied through the use of justification, optimization, and limitation. Justification is the evaluation of technology to assure that the use of radiation or radioactive materials will achieve the desired results, and that no other technology can cost-effectively perform the task as well as the use of radiation. Optimization is the process that assures that the exposures from the use of the radiation are optimized. In other words, the radiation is efficiently used to achieve its intended purpose. Don't use too much, but make sure you use enough. Limitation is the third technique of the ALARA principle. If an application for radiation is justified, and the use has been optimized, the radiation cannot be used for the intended purpose if the use will cause a person to exceed a regulatory threshold, or limit.

Measuring the effectiveness of an ALARA program requires an understanding of the operation, the technologies available, the incorporation of time, distance, and shielding into the planning and conduct of the operation, exposure monitoring, and continual improvement based on new methods and technologies.

Waste Management

The residues from activities that generate or use radioactive materials create waste that must be addressed in an environmentally acceptable manner. International treaties and agreements have brought most of the world into consensus for dealing with radioactive waste, with each country responsible for developing and managing its waste treatment and disposal programs.

Some very low levels of activity are released from stacks into the atmosphere or discharged into sewers or released to streams and other bodies of water through regulated permits. These releases include residues from medical administrations. These discharges are not considered waste.

Some radioactive materials that are used in common household devices have been reviewed and determined not to pose a hazard to the environment when disposed at a landfill. These include certain compact fluorescent lights that contain small quantities of krypton-85. Some devices are to be returned to the manufacturer for recycle or proper disposal, including exit signs powered by tritium.

Most radioactive waste that is generated in large volumes is classified as low-level waste. This type of waste is normally disposed in shallow land-burial facilities. It includes used protective clothing that may be contaminated, analytical glassware and chemical residues, and contaminated building materials such as concrete, roofing, flooring, and structural materials.

Some radioactive materials have short half-lives, on the order of minutes to perhaps days and weeks. These can be stored in secure locations until the radioactivity has decayed to a sufficiently low level that it can then be disposed as regular household trash.

Radioactive sources are reused if possible. Worldwide there are a number of programs that coordinate the transfer of an unwanted radioactive source to an authorized user that would like the source. If a source is unwanted, it is disposed as radioactive waste.

Certain types of radioactive waste have unique characteristics that must be addressed by the disposal option. This includes transuranic waste, a higher-activity-level waste that typically emits alpha radiation, with a relatively long half-life. In the United States, waste of this nature is disposed at the Waste Isolation Plant Project located near Carlsbad, New Mexico.

High-level radioactive waste is a type of high-hazard radioactive waste generated by the reprocessing of spent fuel that is removed from reactors. Reprocessing allows certain useful radionuclides to be extracted, including uranium and plutonium that can then be used in reactors to provide power. The waste stream from reprocessing contains significant quantities of radioactive materials that create high radiation levels. In the United States this type of waste is generated and disposed by the government. There are no facilities in the commercial industry for disposing of this type of waste.

The United States has another serious radioactive waste issue: how to deal with tons of spent fuel. Spent fuel is a high-hazard, high-activity material that is created by nuclear reactors. As the fuel is used in a reactor, it generates waste products which may include useful radionuclides and radionuclides with no apparent use. At this time, spent fuel is stored on site at the locations where they were generated or at other authorized sites. Yucca Mountain was the proposed site for disposal of these materials, but has since been canceled. It is estimated that the earliest a facility can be built to receive the spent fuel is 2027. The spent fuel pools at Fukushima contributed to the releases of radioactive contamination that covered the countryside.

Summary

Radiological health is a fascinating field that offers abundant opportunities to work in a number of areas for the protection of workers, the public, and the environment. Radioactive materials have existed since the dawn of time, they are ubiquitous in nature. Radiation from the stars and the earth is part of the makeup of the universe. Man uses the natural radioactive materials and creates man-made radionuclides to provide power, medical diagnostics and therapy, research studies, and in industry, exploration, and other endeavors to improve our world.

Health Physicist

The Job

Among the scientists essential to the nuclear industry is the health physicist, who is responsible for the protection of persons and their environment from the damaging effects of ionizing radiation.

While health physics is now one of the required phases in the training of industrial hygienists who concern themselves with industrial and environmental hazards of all kinds, the health physicist is concerned entirely with problems created by radiation.

The term health physics is sometimes referred to as "radiation science and protection" by those employed in the field. Most people are more familiar with the former usage. Health physicists work in three areas of activity: research, consulting, and education and training. Some may specialize in only one area, but most often they are involved in all three.

Health physicists may be employed in a reactor operation, an accelerator program, a state public health department, a hospital, or a medical center. They may be involved with basic research in radiobiology, radiogeology, ecology, or shielding and critical assembly studies. In a nuclear plant, the health physicist devises and directs research, training, and monitoring programs to protect plant personnel from radiation hazards.

Health physicists in a public health department plan and conduct studies and investigations of radiological health hazards in industrial, medical, dental, and laboratory situations where radioactive materials or ionizing radiation is used. Within the area of jurisdiction they provide consultation and assistance to personnel who use or produce ionizing radiation.

As research scientists, health physicists may study applied science and engineering programs, basic research, or anything in-between. Radiation ecologists study the effects of radiation exposure on the environment, while other health physicists study internal dosage affects or radiation. New methods of waste disposal and soil seepage of radionuclides are also under study by engineers in health physics.

All health physicists participate to some degree in the following duties: developing inspection standards, safe working methods, and decontamination procedures; assisting in designing and modifying health physics equipment and advising builders on the best facilities for radiation safety; developing standards of permissible concentration of radiation in a given area; and keeping accurate records of radiation hazards and reports of program status.

Working Conditions

Jobs for health physicists exist in research establishments (both government and private), in plants processing nuclear fuels, in firms manufacturing reactors or employing reactors to generate power, in public health services, military establishments, aerospace agencies, and in hospitals where radiation-emitting devices are used. Working conditions vary widely.

Health physicists associated with a public health agency may have a great deal of field work and public contact work and may have to travel extensively. At a uranium mill they may spend much of the time in remote areas, performing duties in a dusty atmosphere while wearing protective clothing. Research work is generally conducted indoors, where temperatures are controlled, lighting is excellent, and safety is monitored carefully.

Physical requirements are light, but the job usually requires the ability to do a good deal of walking.

Employment Outlook

The following information is from the California Projections of Employment published by the Labor Market Information Division. The figures represent the broad occupational group of medical scientists, which includes health physicists.

Estimated number of workers in 1990: 2,100
Estimated number of workers in 2005: 2,650
Projected growth 1990–2005: 26%
Estimated openings due to separations by 2005: 1,080
(These figures do not include self-employment or openings due to turnover.)

Health physicists enjoy a favorable job market, but growth is slowing. These scientists are a small but essential part of the atomic energy field. Every large firm that uses some nuclear power needs radiation safety personnel.

Jobs are becoming available for physicists with state and county public health departments as more equipment emitting radiation is installed and utilized.

As educational institutions, medical centers, and manufacturing plants acquire more equipment using radiation, health physicists will be needed to see that hazards of overexposure to radiation are under control.

Wages, Hours, and Fringe Benefits

Salaries are comparable to those for engineers and scientists, ranging from $28,000 to $45,000 a year for beginning jobs and from $35,000 to $82,000 for well-qualified physicists with experience.

In large firms, promotion to supervisory jobs is possible. Senior management or research-directing positions are examples of these jobs, and salaries are approximately $45,000 to $100,000 a year. Salaries may reach $110,000 or more for an outstanding health physicist with years of experience.

Medical and life insurance, paid vacations, and retirement programs are customary fringe benefits in firms employing health physicists.

The hours may vary from 37 to more than 50 per week depending on the needs of the employer.

Entrance Requirements and Training

Those interested in becoming health physicists should have capacity for analysis and other traits characteristic of a research scientist. They should be able to adjust well to changes and to incorporate new devices and methods into their work, because the development of safety procedures is steadily improving. They must also be able to express views well, both orally and in writing. Much of the work entails persuading management to take certain safety precautions and maintaining technical reports and directives. A health physicist is often asked to speak before groups and to contribute to publications.

Health physicists must be capable of planning and directing programs, be able to supervise activities, and must be able to make decisions regarding physical safety from radiation. Since most of this work is either government-sponsored or -supervised, a security clearance is usually necessary.

Education for health physicists usually requires at least an A.B. or a B.S. degree in physics, chemistry, engineering, biology, or related field. Most health physicists hold graduate degrees. Graduate work can sometimes be funded through government fellowships in selected institutions.

Suggested Reading

U.S. Environmental Protection Agency. *Radiation Protection at EPA: The First 30 Years*, EPA 402-B-00-001. Washington, D.C., August 2000.

Moe, Harold J., *Operational Health Physics Training*, ANL-7291

U.S. Nuclear Regulatory Commission, *Radioactivity in Consumer Products*, NUREG/CP-0001, Washington, D.C., August, 1978.

National Council on Radiation Protection and Measurements, *Radiation Exposure of the U.S. Population from Consumer Products and Miscellaneous Sources*, NCRP Report No. 95. Bethesda, Md., 1987.

U.S. Nuclear Regulatory Commission, *Systematic Radiological Assessment of Exemptions for Source and Byproduct Materials*, NUREG-1717, Washington, D.C., 2001. This report is currently available at http://www.nrc.gov/reading-rm/doc-collections/nuregs/staff/

International Atomic Energy Agency, *The Management System for the Disposal of Radioactive Waste*, Safety Guide GS-G-3.4. Vienna, Austria, 2008.

The Health Physics Society website (http://www.hps.org) contains a wealth of information about radiation and radioactivity, including an "Ask the Experts" feature where specific questions about radiation and radioactivity will be answered.

Environmental Justice

13

Sheila Davidson Pressley
Eastern Kentucky University

"All communities and persons across this Nation should live in a safe and healthful environment."

President Bill Clinton,
February 11, 1994

Key Performance Outcome Indicators:

1. *To define environmental justice problems, especially as they relate to environmental health impacts.*
2. *To identify environmental justice principles as they relate to law and policy.*
3. *To explain some of the major environmental justice events.*
4. *To explain different prevention measures as the basis for preventing injustice in communities*

The term, environmental justice, is defined by the U.S. Environmental Protection Agency (EPA) as *the fair treatment and meaningful involvement of all people regardless of race, ethnicity, income, national origin or educational level with respect to the development, implementation, and enforcement of environmental laws, regulations, and policies.* The premise of environmental justice (EJ) is that African Americans and other racial or ethnic communities bear a disproportionate amount of exposure to a variety of environmental burdens and hazards. This exposure causes adverse environmental health effects that often result in lower life expectancies and other health disparities among U.S. racial and ethnic groups. Significant health disparities exist between U.S. racial and ethnic groups in terms of key health indicators such as low birth weight, infant mortality, death rates, and cancer. Although communities like Love Canal and Times Beach, Missouri received national press coverage for their environmental insults, the many incidents of environmental insults in minority communities are not often shared in the same way.

The History of the Environmental Justice Movement

The EJ movement was ignited in 1982 when a rural, poor, and mostly African American county in North Carolina was selected as the location for a polychlorinated biphenyls (PCBs) landfill. PCBs are a mixture of individual chlorinated chemicals used as coolants and lubricants in transformers and other electrical equipment. According to ATSDR's toxic profile for PCBs, the production of PCBs was stopped in the United States in 1977 because of evidence that showed harmful human effects, but they are still found in the environment today. In fact, the EPA and the International Agency for Research on Cancer have determined that PCBs are probably carcinogenic, or cancer causing to humans. Warren County, North Carolina was chosen as a PCB landfill site because developers saw it as an easy target with the least amount of resistance. The builders of the landfill assumed that rural, poor, black residents would not be able to fight such a development. As described by Robert Bullard in his book, *Dumping In Dixie*, the residents of Afton, North Carolina formed the Warren County Citizens Concerned About PCBs, gathered over 400 protesters, and voiced their disapproval of the landfill. It was during these demonstrations that the term, environmental racism was born. Environmental racism is racial discrimination in environmental policymaking. This term was used frequently in the beginning and at the height of the EJ movement; however, EPA later coined other terms such as environmental equity and environmental justice to reflect its efforts in addressing environmental racism.

In 1972, before the incidents in Afton, The United Church of Christ Commission for Racial Justice, a faith-based organization, voiced its disapproval of the Warren County PCB landfill and other sites like it in the nation. With the Commission's voice, the Congressional Black Caucus, and many other civic and political supporters pushing for justice, the U.S. Government Accounting Office (GAO) conducted a study in 1983 of where hazardous waste landfill sites were located. The GAO study revealed a strong relationship between the citing of hazardous waste landfills and the race and socioeconomic status of surrounding communities. The states in this study included North Carolina, South Carolina and Alabama. Emelle, Alabama in Sumter County is another well-known example of environmental injustice. The population of Emelle is mostly African American and the majority of the residents live below the poverty line. Emelle is often described as the economically impoverished Black belt of western Alabama. In 1978, the citizens of Emelle were told that a safe, new industry, which would provide jobs to replace the diminishing agricultural economy of the area, was coming to their town. However, only a small portion of local residents were offered jobs at the site and ChemWaste (a subsidiary of Waste Management) proceeded to run its hazardous waste treatment, storage, and disposal facility in Sumter County. Emelle became the home for the nation's largest hazardous waste landfill.

The North Carolina Department of Environment and Natural Resources contracted with Shaw E & I, Inc. to detoxify 81,500 tons of PCB-laced soil at the landfill site. Soil containing small amounts of PCBs is still buried deep in the landfill pit.

Hazardous waste—wastes are divided into listed, characteristic or universal wastes. Characteristic hazardous waste includes ignitability, corrosivity, reactivity, and toxicity.

In 1987, the United Church of Christ Commission for Racial Justice released its groundbreaking study entitled, *Toxic Wastes and Race in the United States*. The findings of this study showed that communities with greater minority percentages were more likely to be the sites of commercial hazardous waste facilities. This study was another spark in the EJ movement, and it spurred conversations and questions among academicians, politicians, and other grassroots organizations. The study found that three out of five African Americans live in communities with abandoned toxic waste sites. In 1992, the EPA followed with its final release on a report entitled *Environmental Equity: Reducing Risks For All Communities.* This report showed that there were clear differences between racial groups in terms of disease and death rates. The report also showed that racial minority and low-income populations experience higher than average exposures to pollutants and hazardous waste facilities.

Chemwaste landfill in Emelle, Alabama

Executive Order 12898

On February 11, 1994, the leaders of the EJ movement and six government agencies convened the first federal symposium on environmental justice. At this symposium, President Clinton signed Executive Order 12898: Federal Actions to Address Environmental Justice in Minority Populations and Low-Income Populations. The Order focused federal attention on the environmental and human health conditions of minority and low-income populations with the goal of achieving environmental protection for all communities. The primary intent of Executive Order 12898 was three fold. First, it was to assist federal agencies in recognizing environmental justice as an issue, thereby leading to the formation EJ workgroups and the formation of Office of Environmental Justice at EPA Head-quarters. Second, it required EPA and the other federal agencies to have a written plan to address EJ issues germane to their organizations. Third and most importantly, the executive order gave impacted communities a chance to gain awareness and be educated about environmental health issues. Through the executive order, communities can apply for small grants and be a part of solving and preventing environmental injustice in their communities. The Order directed federal agencies to develop environmental justice strategies to identify and address disproportionately high and adverse human health or environmental effects of their programs, policies, and activities on minority and low-income populations. The Order is also intended to promote nondiscrimination in federal programs substantially affecting human health and the environment, and to provide minority and low-income communities access to public information on, and an opportunity for public participation in, matters relating to human health or the environment. The Presidential Memorandum accompanying the Order underscores certain provisions of existing law that can help ensure that all communities and persons across this nation live in a safe and healthful environment. A copy of the Federal Register announcement of Executive Order 12898 can be found at the end of this chapter.

Federal Legislation

A federal bill labeled as HR1103—the Environmental Justice Act of 2007 was proposed to the 110th Congress, 2007–2009, but it never became a law. The last action by Congress on the bill was on October 4, 2007 when the House Energy and Commerce Committee held a hearing. The legislation, introduced by Congresswoman Hilda Solis (D-Calif.) and others, would have been used to codify Executive Order 12898 on environmental justice. Moving forward with environmental justice will require more enforcement from the EPA and the Department of Justice in order for communities to see relief from disproportionate and cumulative pollution burdens. Along with Executive Order 12898, there are also federal statutes that can be used to address environmental justice concerns. Here's a list of existing federal environmental statutes that have enabled authorities and communities to address various environmental justice issues:

- The National Environmental Policy Act (NEPA)
- The Federal Water Pollution Control Act (Clean Water Act)
- The Resource Conservation and Recovery Act (RCRA)
- The Comprehensive Environmental Response, Compensation, and Liability Act (CERCLA)
- The Federal Insecticide, Fungicide, and Rodenticide Act (FIFRA)
- The Federal Food, Drug, and Cosmetic Act (FFDCA)
- The Safe Drinking Water Act (SDWA)
- The Toxic Substances Control Act (TSCA)
- The Emergency Planning and Community Right-to-Know Act (EPCRA)

Brownfields

In addition to the existing federal laws, the EPA Brownfields Program that started in 1995 has grown into a program with a proven track record on empowering states to change the way contaminated property is perceived, addressed and managed. A brownfield is the expansion, redevelopment or reuse of property that has the presence or the perceived presence of a hazardous substance, pollutant, or contaminant. According to EPA, there are more than 450,000 brownfields in the United States, with many of those sites in or near environmental justice communities. Through the passage of the Small Business Liability Relief and Brownfields Revitalization Act, effective policies that EPA developed over the years were passed into law. Brownfields grants continue to serve as the foundation of EPA's Brownfields Program and as a means to address the cleanup needs of some environmental justice communities.

Environmental Justice Communities In Appalachia

In addition to African American, Latino, Native American and Asian communities, environmental justice has also affected people residing in Appalachia. The communities in Appalachia are mostly composed of rural whites and African Americans, but the African Americans in Appalachia are often forgotten because these communities are usually portrayed in books and media as poor and white. Some history textbooks do not mention the fact that some slaves retreated to the mountains to be free and that many labored in the coalmines along with white miners. As time went on, African Americans stayed in Appalachia and made the mountains their home. According to the book, *Blacks in Appalachia*, more than 1.3 million blacks lived in the Appalachian region reaching from Mississippi to New York in 1974. African Americans in Appalachia were considered to be a "neglected minority within a neglected minority." This circumstance was only worsened by environmental injustices such as extracting coal using mountaintop removal. This practice became popular in the mid 1970's and was also known as strip mining or surface mining. The mountaintop removal method was almost exclusively conducted in Kentucky and West Virginia. Communities in Eastern Kentucky and West Virginia know about the impact of such practices all too well. Mountaintop removal involves removing the cap of a mountain to extract coal while the masses of earth and rock are shoved into nearby lakes, streams and rivers that pollute the water and kill aquatic life. The removal creates black water or sludge that is kept in dams that are not always safe and may cause flooding in the valleys. Both blacks and whites have endured substandard treatment from coal mining companies for decades, but much of the story remains untold.

After two decades, the detoxification of the PCB landfill in Warren County, North Carolina began in 2001. The cleanup activity ended in 2003 and a park was constructed on the site of the old landfill. Despite numerous regulatory violations, worker exposure, offsite water contamination, local opposition and the involvement of grassroots organizations, the landfill in Emelle remains open. Cases like those of Afton and Emelle are plentiful and their struggles continue.

Many of the communities labeled as EJ communities, are located in small southern towns or neighborhoods like Afton and Emelle with very little political power, and even fewer financial and educational resources. There is an enormous need for community based participatory research related to the health disparities and the environmental impacts of residents in these areas. There are many untold stories and facts surrounding environmental justice. The United Church of Christ Commission for Racial Justice conducted its own study and sought environmental justice for everyone, but other communities around the nation and internationally are still fighting for their rights to a cleaner, safer environment.

References

Institute of Medicine (IOM). (1999). *Toward Environmental Justice: Research Education and Health Policy Needs*. Washington, DC: National Academy Press.

Bullard, Robert D. (1994). *Dumping In Dixie: Race, Class, and Environmental Quality*. Boulder: Westview Press.

U.S. Department of Health and Human Services (HHS). (2001) *ToxFAQs for Polychlorinated Biphenyls (PCBs)*. Agency for Toxic Substances and Disease Registry (ATSDR) Website. Available at http://www.atsdr.cdc.gov/tfacts17.html. Accessed on February 28, 2012.

Environmental Justice Study Questions

1. The term environmental justice refers to:
    a. a clean environment
    b. fair treatment of all people
    c. meaningful involvement of all people
    d. all of the above
2. Where was the environmental justice movement really ignited?
    a. Times Beach, Missouri
    b. Love Canal, New York
    c. Afton, North Carolina
    d. Dallas, Texas
3. In 1987, the United Church of Christ Commission for Racial Justice released a study entitled:
    a. *Reducing Risks for all Communities of Color*
    b. *Environmental Equity: Reducing Risks*
    c. *Dumping In Dixie*
    d. *Toxic Wastes and Race in the United States*
4. Based on the Government Accounting Office study in 1983:
    a. There was a strong relationship between the citing of hazardous waste landfills, race and socioeconomic status.
    b. There was no relationship between the citing of hazardous waste landfills, race and socioeconomic status.
    c. The citing of hazardous waste landfills was fair and inclusive of all people regardless of race.
    d. None of the above

5. Which small southern town was the home of the nation's largest hazardous waste landfill in the late 1970's?
    a. Afton, North Carolina
    b. Emelle, Alabama
    c. Alsen, Louisiana
    d. Bell Buckle, Tennessee

Environmental Justice Discussion Questions

1. Explain the evolution of the term environmental racism.

2. What federal regulations should be considered when identifying environmental justice communities?

3. How did Executive Order 12898 change the process for helping environmental justice communities?

4. What is the next step environmental justice legislation?

5. How can environmental health practitioners uphold the principles of environmental justice?

tle 3—

he President

Executive Order 12898 of February 11, 1994

Federal Actions To Address Environmental Justice in Minority Populations and Low-Income Populations

By the authority vested in me as President by the Constitution and the laws of the United States of America, it is hereby ordered as follows:

Section 1–1. *Implementation.*

1–101. *Agency Responsibilities.* To the greatest extent practicable and permitted by law, and consistent with the principles set forth in the report on the National Performance Review, each Federal agency shall make achieving environmental justice part of its mission by identifying and addressing, as appropriate, disproportionately high and adverse human health or environmental effects of its programs, policies, and activities on minority populations and low-income populations in the United States and its territories and possessions, the District of Columbia, the Commonwealth of Puerto Rico, and the Commonwealth of the Mariana Islands.

1–102. *Creation of an Interagency Working Group on Environmental Justice.* (a) Within 3 months of the date of this order, the Administrator of the Environmental Protection Agency ("Administrator") or the Administrator's designee shall convene an interagency Federal Working Group on Environmental Justice ("Working Group"). The Working Group shall comprise the heads of the following executive agencies and offices, or their designees: (a) Department of Defense; (b) Department of Health and Human Services; (c) Department of Housing and Urban Development; (d) Department of Labor; (e) Department of Agriculture; (f) Department of Transportation; (g) Department of Justice; (h) Department of the Interior; (i) Department of Commerce; (j) Department of Energy; (k) Environmental Protection Agency; (l) Office of Management and Budget; (m) Office of Science and Technology Policy; (n) Office of the Deputy Assistant to the President for Environmental Policy; (o) Office of the Assistant to the President for Domestic Policy; (p) National Economic Council; (q) Council of Economic Advisers; and (r) such other Government officials as the President may designate. The Working Group shall report to the President through the Deputy Assistant to the President for Environmental Policy and the Assistant to the President for Domestic Policy.

(b) The Working Group shall: (1) provide guidance to Federal agencies on criteria for identifying disproportionately high and adverse human health or environmental effects on minority populations and low-income populations;

(2) coordinate with, provide guidance to, and serve as a clearinghouse for, each Federal agency as it develops an environmental justice strategy as required by section 1–103 of this order, in order to ensure that the administration, interpretation and enforcement of programs, activities and policies are undertaken in a consistent manner;

(3) assist in coordinating research by, and stimulating cooperation among, the Environmental Protection Agency, the Department of Health and Human Services, the Department of Housing and Urban Development, and other agencies conducting research or other activities in accordance with section 3–3 of this order;

(4) assist in coordinating data collection, required by this order;

(5) examine existing data and studies on environmental justice;

(6) hold public meetings as required in section 5–502(d) of this order; and

(7) develop interagency model projects on environmental justice that evidence cooperation among Federal agencies.

1–103. *Development of Agency Strategies.* (a) Except as provided in section 6–605 of this order, each Federal agency shall develop an agency-wide environmental justice strategy, as set forth in subsections (b)–(e) of this section that identifies and addresses disproportionately high and adverse human health or environmental effects of its programs, policies, and activities on minority populations and low-income populations. The environmental justice strategy shall list programs, policies, planning and public participation processes, enforcement, and/or rulemakings related to human health or the environment that should be revised to, at a minimum: (1) promote enforcement of all health and environmental statutes in areas with minority populations and low-income populations; (2) ensure greater public participation; (3) improve research and data collection relating to the health of and environment of minority populations and low-income populations; and (4) identify differential patterns of consumption of natural resources among minority populations and low-income populations. In addition, the environmental justice strategy shall include, where appropriate, a timetable for undertaking identified revisions and consideration of economic and social implications of the revisions.

(b) Within 4 months of the date of this order, each Federal agency shall identify an internal administrative process for developing its environmental justice strategy, and shall inform the Working Group of the process.

(c) Within 6 months of the date of this order, each Federal agency shall provide the Working Group with an outline of its proposed environmental justice strategy.

(d) Within 10 months of the date of this order, each Federal agency shall provide the Working Group with its proposed environmental justice strategy.

(e) Within 12 months of the date of this order, each Federal agency shall finalize its environmental justice strategy and provide a copy and written description of its strategy to the Working Group. During the 12 month period from the date of this order, each Federal agency, as part of its environmental justice strategy, shall identify several specific projects that can be promptly undertaken to address particular concerns identified during the development of the proposed environmental justice strategy, and a schedule for implementing those projects.

(f) Within 24 months of the date of this order, each Federal agency shall report to the Working Group on its progress in implementing its agency-wide environmental justice strategy.

(g) Federal agencies shall provide additional periodic reports to the Working Group as requested by the Working Group.

1–104. *Reports to the President.* Within 14 months of the date of this order, the Working Group shall submit to the President, through the Office of the Deputy Assistant to the President for Environmental Policy and the Office of the Assistant to the President for Domestic Policy, a report that describes the implementation of this order, and includes the final environmental justice strategies described in section 1–103(e) of this order.

Sec. 2–2. *Federal Agency Responsibilities for Federal Programs.* Each Federal agency shall conduct its programs, policies, and activities that substantially affect human health or the environment, in a manner that ensures that such programs, policies, and activities do not have the effect of excluding persons (including populations) from participation in, denying persons (including populations) the benefits of, or subjecting persons (including populations) to discrimination under, such programs, policies, and activities, because of their race, color, or national origin.

Sec. 3–3. *Research, Data Collection, and Analysis.*

3–301. *Human Health and Environmental Research and Analysis.* (a) Environmental human health research, whenever practicable and appropriate, shall include diverse segments of the population in epidemiological and clinical studies, including segments at high risk from environmental hazards, such as minority populations, low-income populations and workers who may be exposed to substantial environmental hazards.

(b) Environmental human health analyses, whenever practicable and appropriate, shall identify multiple and cumulative exposures.

(c) Federal agencies shall provide minority populations and low-income populations the opportunity to comment on the development and design of research strategies undertaken pursuant to this order.

3–302. *Human Health and Environmental Data Collection and Analysis.* To the extent permitted by existing law, including the Privacy Act, as amended (5 U.S.C. section 552a): (a) each Federal agency, whenever practicable and appropriate, shall collect, maintain, and analyze information assessing and comparing environmental and human health risks borne by populations identified by race, national origin, or income. To the extent practical and appropriate, Federal agencies shall use this information to determine whether their programs, policies, and activities have disproportionately high and adverse human health or environmental effects on minority populations and low-income populations;

(b) In connection with the development and implementation of agency strategies in section 1–103 of this order, each Federal agency, whenever practicable and appropriate, shall collect, maintain and analyze information on the race, national origin, income level, and other readily accessible and appropriate information for areas surrounding facilities or sites expected to have a substantial environmental, human health, or economic effect on the surrounding populations, when such facilities or sites become the subject of a substantial Federal environmental administrative or judicial action. Such information shall be made available to the public, unless prohibited by law; and

(c) Each Federal agency, whenever practicable and appropriate, shall collect, maintain, and analyze information on the race, national origin, income level, and other readily accessible and appropriate information for areas surrounding Federal facilities that are: (1) subject to the reporting requirements under the Emergency Planning and Community Right-to-Know Act, 42 U.S.C. section 11001–11050 as mandated in Executive Order No. 12856; and (2) expected to have a substantial environmental, human health, or economic effect on surrounding populations. Such information shall be made available to the public, unless prohibited by law.

(d) In carrying out the responsibilities in this section, each Federal agency, whenever practicable and appropriate, shall share information and eliminate unnecessary duplication of efforts through the use of existing data systems and cooperative agreements among Federal agencies and with State, local, and tribal governments.

Sec. 4–4. *Subsistence Consumption of Fish and Wildlife.*

4–401. *Consumption Patterns.* In order to assist in identifying the need for ensuring protection of populations with differential patterns of subsistence consumption of fish and wildlife, Federal agencies, whenever practicable and appropriate, shall collect, maintain, and analyze information on the consumption patterns of populations who principally rely on fish and/or wildlife for subsistence. Federal agencies shall communicate to the public the risks of those consumption patterns.

4–402. *Guidance.* Federal agencies, whenever practicable and appropriate, shall work in a coordinated manner to publish guidance reflecting the latest scientific information available concerning methods for evaluating the human health risks associated with the consumption of pollutant-bearing fish or wildlife. Agencies shall consider such guidance in developing their policies and rules.

Sec. 5-5. *Public Participation and Access to Information.* (a) The public may submit recommendations to Federal agencies relating to the incorporation of environmental justice principles into Federal agency programs or policies. Each Federal agency shall convey such recommendations to the Working Group.

(b) Each Federal agency may, whenever practicable and appropriate, translate crucial public documents, notices, and hearings relating to human health or the environment for limited English speaking populations.

(c) Each Federal agency shall work to ensure that public documents, notices, and hearings relating to human health or the environment are concise, understandable, and readily accessible to the public.

(d) The Working Group shall hold public meetings, as appropriate, for the purpose of fact-finding, receiving public comments, and conducting inquiries concerning environmental justice. The Working Group shall prepare for public review a summary of the comments and recommendations discussed at the public meetings.

Sec. 6-6. *General Provisions.*

6-601. *Responsibility for Agency Implementation.* The head of each Federal agency shall be responsible for ensuring compliance with this order. Each Federal agency shall conduct internal reviews and take such other steps as may be necessary to monitor compliance with this order.

6-602. *Executive Order No. 12250.* This Executive order is intended to supplement but not supersede Executive Order No. 12250, which requires consistent and effective implementation of various laws prohibiting discriminatory practices in programs receiving Federal financial assistance. Nothing herein shall limit the effect or mandate of Executive Order No. 12250.

6-603. *Executive Order No. 12875.* This Executive order is not intended to limit the effect or mandate of Executive Order No. 12875.

6-604. *Scope.* For purposes of this order, Federal agency means any agency on the Working Group, and such other agencies as may be designated by the President, that conducts any Federal program or activity that substantially affects human health or the environment. Independent agencies are requested to comply with the provisions of this order.

6-605. *Petitions for Exemptions.* The head of a Federal agency may petition the President for an exemption from the requirements of this order on the grounds that all or some of the petitioning agency's programs or activities should not be subject to the requirements of this order.

6-606. *Native American Programs.* Each Federal agency responsibility set forth under this order shall apply equally to Native American programs. In addition, the Department of the Interior, in coordination with the Working Group, and, after consultation with tribal leaders, shall coordinate steps to be taken pursuant to this order that address Federally-recognized Indian Tribes.

6-607. *Costs.* Unless otherwise provided by law, Federal agencies shall assume the financial costs of complying with this order.

6-608. *General.* Federal agencies shall implement this order consistent with, and to the extent permitted by, existing law.

6-609. *Judicial Review.* This order is intended only to improve the internal management of the executive branch and is not intended to, nor does it create any right, benefit, or trust responsibility, substantive or procedural, enforceable at law or equity by a party against the United States, its agencies, its officers, or any person. This order shall not be construed to create any right to judicial review involving the compliance or noncompliance of the United States, its agencies, its officers, or any other person with this order.

THE WHITE HOUSE,
February 11, 1994.

[FR Citation 59 FR 7629]

Sustainability Basics

14

Priscilla Oliver, PhD
Sheila D. Pressley, PhD, REHS, DAAS

"You must be the change you wish to see in the world."

Mahatma Gandhi

Key Performance Outcome Indicators:

1. *Define sustainability terms, especially as they relate to environmental health*
2. *Identify environmental influences on health, economics, and social aspects of living*
3. *List some of the major sustainability methods for various aspects of life, work, schools, community, and home*
4. *Prescribe different control measures as the basis for preventing the degradation of air, land, and water resources*
5. *Analyze the risks and benefits of sustainability*

The first law of nature is well known to be self-preservation. This law is learned very early in life, some say in the "terrible twos." It is very evident when the baby learns to say "It is mine." Self-preservation is the precursor to the current buzz word "sustainability." Sustainability is a broader term that takes into account the individual and the group in the environmental field.

Sustainability was left out of environmental health in the past. The term may not even be mentioned in the curriculum. Sustainability is described as the practice of preserving, conserving, restoring, reducing, expanding, protecting, and creating conditions such that there are longer-term benefits or resources for future use. Sustainability is the futuristic approach to make sure there are quality products and/or services left to keep it going and strong in existence. The process of sustaining is allowing for the continuation of the future use of resources. Sustainability has come out of the environmental pollution-prevention movement and has been replaced by some of the similar terms. A major component in sustainability that may have been left out of other terms is economics. Sustainability means that social factors and economic savings are also considered.

Environmental health scholars have provided a foundation for the sustainability movement. Linda Lair described how Rachel Carson's classic book *Silent Spring* (1962) gave a wake-up call to the degradation and environmental pollution, stating that Rachel felt it was important to sustain the human spirit. The wake-up call discussed in her book exposed the problems with harmful chemicals and the coverup and uncertainty of the impacts.

Another environmental health scholar, Dr. Martin Luther King, Jr., exposed the importance of what is now known as environmental justice by coming to the rescue of the trash collection crew in Memphis, Tennessee, in 1968. Human civil rights needed to be protected to protect the environment. The "use of public transportation by all" was a precursor for curbing pollution and promoting sustainability efforts. Trash collection is imperative, and the equal treatment of workers is all-important to sustainability.

The value of other authors: Aldo Leopold, who wrote *A Sand County Almanac*, and Stewart Udall, who wrote *The Quiet Crisis*, embodied this same spirit, all leading to the involvement of the federal government in environmental issues. The National Environmental Policy Act of 1968 was created, and several agencies and states have taken on the task of cleaning up the environment. Environmental health became a public health issue. The profession has grown, and the population and cities and towns are continually growing. The sustainability concept has added consideration of social and economic impacts.

The energy crises of 1973 and 1979 prompted the realization that important resources, such as petroleum (oil), are limited. The continual rise in gas prices has further enforced that. Alternative fuel usage is marketed to reduce harmful air pollution. Vehicles have been modified through the years to promote the use of alternative fuels to reduce the negative impacts. The regulations placed on emission standards are tied to the car tag registration in some states. Policy and technology advances have joined forces to create the need for sustainability in the transportation industry.

The formal merging of sustainability into the culture occurred with the United Nations meetings in Nairobi, Kenya, in 1987, with the introduction of the Brundtland Report. The chairman, Gro Harlem Brundtland (from Norway) of the United Nations World Commission on Environment and Development, introduced *Our Common Future*. The document contained a chapter entitled "Toward Sustainability Development." It explained environmental degradation worldwide, calling for sustainable human intervention to reduce harm to the environment and sustainable improvements for the future. Problems mentioned were deforestation, air and water pollution, poverty, growth of noxious chemicals, declining factory working conditions, and a reduction in the quality of life.

The charge is to include sustainability in the conversation and in the academic curriculum. Some schools have begun to include classes, certificate programs, and degrees. For years the topic was not in the curriculum. With the inclusion of economics, several fields have begun to discuss sustainability. Environmental health as a profession has thus begun to work with others in such fields as geography, math, social and political science, transportation, business administration, business, economics, and agriculture. The relationship with the sciences and engineering has been enhanced and strengthened. New topics include climate change, recycling, organic gardening, and composting. Sustainability is all-inclusive. The field has the interest of children, teens, and adults. It is not uncommon for elementary and middle school children to get involved in recycling and composting projects as a part of the school curriculum. These science or interdisciplinary projects are real, relevant, and can be income-producing. Children are growing up to be sustainable adults.

Sustainability may be the topic for the family and the community. Community gardens, Earth Day celebrations, neighborhood clean-ups, charity runs/walks, prescription drug take-backs, block parties, and special festivals all offer possibilities for accenting sustainability and getting all ages of children, teens, and adults involved. The range of persons interested in sustainability has no income limitations. It is very inspiring to see the homeless and the elderly involved in sustainability efforts. Most people now recycle soda cans and plastic bottles. Churches and sports arenas are also involved in sustainability.

Work Environment

The workplace has the greatest burden of addressing sustainability. The focus is on economics generally, but the good will of preserving resources for future uses is also important. Energy conservation and reduction of the carbon footprint are components. Corporations have taken on this responsibility from the top down. Wildlife preserves, demonstration and pilot programs, and fundraising projects have been utilized to get employees and citizens involved in sustainability. Emergency and disaster events such as Hurricane Katrina have spurred companies to spring forward to donate services and funding to contribute to the clean-up and sustainability efforts.

Corporations and companies are **"going green."** Going Green is defined as the process of adopting policies to reduce waste, streamline processes, recycle, and utilize less harmful chemicals, reducing the carbon footprint and reducing economic costs. The government, academic organizations, non-profit organizations, and healthcare facilities have joined in going green. The use of Energy Star (energy efficient) appliances and equipment is important to sustainability. The use of and recycling of fluorescent light bulbs are common. Business recycling is utilized for goodwill, to save money, and to increase profits. Some industries are now reusing all byproducts of production to make additional items for sale and distribution. There is zero waste with no expensive costs for removal of unwanted materials.

Leadership in Energy and Environmental Design (LEED) certification, developed by the U.S. Green Building Council (USGBC), has been obtained since 1995. Various levels of gold, silver, and platinum status are obtained to denote the compliance, efficiency, and design of the building to distinguish it from other buildings. The status symbol denotes leadership. LEED Certified means that the company and building have become leaders in construction, design, operations, maintenance, and sustainability. The upfront construction cost may be high, but the future cost savings is what drives the efforts.

Environmental management systems (EMS) are adopted and may involve a part of or the total organization. The system allows for better planning, maintenance, and management of operations and processes within the organization. Control measures are in check to prevent losses and destruction. The EMS process may involve all pf the organization's employees from the top down.

Academic Environment

School projects in science can clearly focus on sustainability and green projects. The interest of elementary and middle school youth and of college environmental groups has done much to get the message of sustainability to the younger generation. These communication messages are important to the sustainability of the environmental movement. There is a drive to call for more sustainability in the curriculum of elementary, postsecondary, and college educational programs. The interdisciplinary approach involving all fields and subjects is strongly suggested.

Grants have been awarded to organizations (academic institutions, churches, and businesses) to increase their sustainability efforts. Partnership relationships are encouraged. Innovations and creative efforts are encouraged. The grants are given by foundations, governmental agencies, and companies.

It is a strategy to involve college students and below to ensure that sustainability is ingrained into their future. Sustainability is a curricular component that is wanted by policymakers. Some schools have gotten ahead on this effort: Brown University, Emory University, and George Washington University. The concept of having students live in dorms has expanded. Some campuses are varying the type of housing offered to upperclassman students to include apartments and suites to keep students on the enclosed campuses yet give them the feeling of independence they want. Colleges have gone green in transportation, living, and recycling of cans and other products. Students may study sustainability as they live in the concept.

Community Environment

Many cities and local governments have adopted the sustainability approach to managing resources. Elements of the process may be, but are not limited to, neighborhood nature trails, parks, transportation routes, rail service, streetcar service, bike trails, organic gardening, rain barrels, and more sidewalks. Some newer cities are being designed with sustainability at the helm of planning. Revitalizations of neighborhoods have taken this approach also. The idea of putting living, shopping, recreation, and places of work in close proximity with sidewalks and parking is very much in place to increase the human ability to walk and exercise. The built environment may reduce health problems. The shopping center concept is revisited.

Sustainability has an important role in recreation. Marketing has been placed on gaming machines in arcades to influence the youth to consider sustainability. More and more nature areas are being created to preserve the natural environment in community settings. Wildlife preserves, nature trails, walking trails, bike trails, neighborhood parks, pet parks, gardens, highway adoptions, organic gardens, and fish ponds are a few creations. Corporate sponsorships and grant funding are also available as support for some of the projects. An appreciation of nature and ecology is encouraged in many communities.

Recycling is probably the most common practice. Several cities have provided recycling bins for citizens, and regular collections are scheduled. Items collected are paper, plastics, and glass containers. The cost of recycling has generated funds for cities and local governments.

Home Environment

Sustainability has no exclusivity on participation. All of us can participate in sustainability efforts in our homes or apartments. The campaign to recycle cans and paper is common. There is much that can be recycled or reused. Paper, cardboard, glass, plastics, and clothing can be recycled or reused. There are organizations (recycling center, reuse centers) in the community that accept various items.

Composting is defined by Friis as the degradation of natural resources, no meat, in a confined space such that it can be reused as fertilizer or fill in another setting. Constructive reuse of the compost is important to this process. Composting can be done on a small or large scale. Composting is the collection of appropriate waste materials that, when decomposed, offer nutrient materials to sustain growth of living organisms, plants in particular. Composting is the act of creating renewable resources. The waste material is reused and becomes a valuable resource. Composting materials are commonly used for gardening of plants for food, landscaping, and flower beds. On a large scale, industries may use composted materials for reconstruction and in large-scale agricultural production.

The recycling of food waste with the garbage disposal in the home sink is a sustainable effort. The recycling of food waste on a larger scale offers great potential in sustainability. There is a need for additional innovative techniques in this industry.

Equipment and Supplies

In recent years sustainable equipment and supplies have been developed and distributed for industrial, academic, community, and home use. Some examples are Energy Star, LEED Certified, and Environmentally Preferable Products (EPP). These items are made from reusable, biodegradable, ecofriendly, and less harmful components that will not cause harm to life. Green cleaners and biodegradable flooring and carpets are common to hospitals, schools, governmental buildings, industrial facilities, and businesses. The loss of work time from being out sick has been reduced because of the use of green cleaners and better sustainable products. Less harmful products have been labeled so that consumers can make better choices and chose sustainable products.

Technology

Materials that are not reused or recycled need to be taken to the landfill. Some of these products are computer related. There is an effort to save our landfills. Space is limited and there is the concept of "not in my backyard" (NIMBY). Computers, printers, and electronic devices are subject to some reuse, but not always. Checking with local handlers is a good idea to see what is available in the area. Some programs periodically collect used computers, printers, and electronic devices for recycling. The concern with leaving these items around living organisms is the exposure and leaking of chemical components such as lead, mercury, cadmium, beryllium, aluminum, and chromium. The negative impacts are unwanted.

Individuals and organizations are going green at a rapid rate. Here are some steps to consider in going green.

Sustainability Project: Steps to Going Green

New sustainable products are being developed daily. It is true: One man's trash is another man's treasure. There is truly treasure in trash.

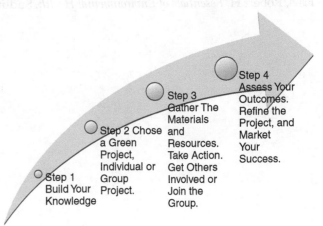

Step 1 Build Your Knowledge

Step 2 Chose a Green Project, Individual or Group Project.

Step 3 Gather The Materials and Resources. Take Action. Get Others Involved or Join the Group.

Step 4 Assess Your Outcomes. Refine the Project, and Market Your Success.

Further Reading

Bach, David. 2008. *Go Green. Live Rich*. New York: Broadway Books.

Schendler, Auden. 2009. *Getting Green Done*. New York: Public Affairs.

Sivertsen, L. and Sivertsen, 2008. *Generation Green*. New York: Simon Pulse.

Bongiotno. L. 2008. *Green Greener Greenest*. New York: Pergee Books.

Summary

Sustainability is a product of the environmental movement and the implementation of federal regulations. Thus it has resulted from the environmental degradation through pollution of the air, water, and land. Sustainability came from pollution prevention to reduce, reuse, and recycle waste, reducing what is sent to landfills and improving the quality of life.

Sustainable activities are commonly practiced individually, at school, work, and in the home. Some activities may include recycling cans, paper, cardboard, plastics, glass, organic gardening, use of alternative fuels, use of biodegradable products, and composting.

The need for sustainability is to make sure that resources are not depleted for future generations. Sustainability can be a part of daily life and can be incorporated in various parts of living.

Websites

http://www.neha.org/sustainability/index.html

http://www.epa.gov/sustainability/

http://www.sustainability-recycling.com/sustainability-recycling/Home.html

http://www.usda.gov/oce/sustainable/index.htm

http://www.lm.doe.gov/Office_of_Site_Operations/Environmental_Management_System/Sustainability_Programs.aspx

http://www.un.org/en/sustainability/

http://www.who.int/gho/mdg/environmental_sustainability/en/index.html

http://en.wikipedia.org/wiki/Brundtland_Commission

http://en.wikipedia.org/wiki/Leadership_in_Energy_and_Environmental_Design

References

Carson. Rachel. *Silent Spring*. 1962. New York: Houghton Mifflin Harcourt.

Friis, Robert H. *Essentials of Environmental Health*. Sudbury, Mass. 2012.

Recreation

15

Joe E. Beck, RS, DEASS

Roman Baths:
I find that the old Roman baths of this quarter, were found covered by an old burying ground,
belonging to the Abbey; through which, in all probability, the water drains in its passage; so that
as we drink the decoction of the living bodies at the Pump-room, we swallow the strainings of
rotten bones and carcasses at the private bath—I vow to God, the very idea turns my stomach!

—Tobias Smollett,
The Expedition of Humphry Clinker

Chlorine is my perfume.

—Author Unknown

Key Performance Outcome Indicators:

1. *Understand the engineering used for pool equipment*
2. *Know the design elements of a public pool*
3. *Understand the measurement and proper use of disinfectants*
4. *Understand the relationship of chlorine levels and pH*
5. *Know how to measure water hardness and alkalinity*
6. *Know how to use the Langelier Saturation Index*
7. *Understand how to calculate turnover and filter loading rates*
8. *Understand the limitations of UV and ozone disinfection systems*

INTRODUCTION

The environmental health officer (EHO) must be capable of understanding the total engineered
system and be capable of identifying all equipment, valves, and piping systems. The piping system
for a pool should be color coded to assist both the operator and the EHO in determining the

proper protocols of operation of the swimming pool. This chapter will provide the EHO with the critical formulas for determining the design and equipment adequacy of the facility and for a basic understanding of the individual components of the system to ensure effective problem-solving.

The specific goal for the EHO is to ensure that the bottom-line expectations of the public are met as related to the protection of the public health. These are to ensure:

Clean, clear water
Water free of disease agents
Safe recreational environment
Effective, properly operating equipment
Sound, effective maintenance and operation

PUBLIC HEALTH ISSUES

Current epidemiological evidence indicates that properly constructed and operated swimming pools that are not a major public health problem are a preferable option to bathing beaches due to the engineered controls designed into pools. Poorly designed or operated pools can be major public health hazards. The issues below are a few of those concerns:

Diseases and Other Pool Issues

A. **Diseases of Concern**
   1. Intestinal diseases: *E. coli* O157:H7, typhoid fever, paratyphoid fever, amoebic dysentery, leptospirosis, Cryptospordosis (highly chlorine resistant), and bacillary dysentery can be a problem where swimming waters are polluted by domestic or animal sewage or wastes. Swimming pools have also been implicated in outbreaks of leptospirosis.
   2. Respiratory diseases; Colds, sinusitis, and septic sore throat can spread more readily in swimming areas due to close contact, coupled with lowered resistance due to exertion.
   3. Eye, ear, nose, throat, and skin infections: The exposure of delicate mucous membranes, the movement of harmful organisms into ear and nasal passages, the excessive use of water-treatment chemicals, and the presence of harmful agents in the water can contribute to eye, ear, nose, throat, and skin infections. Close physical contact and the presence of fomites also help to spread athlete's foot, impetigo, and dermatitis.
B. **Injuries**
   1. Injuries and drowning deaths are by far the greatest problem at swimming pools. Lack of bather supervision is a prime cause, as is the improper construction, use, and maintenance of equipment. Some particular problem areas are:
      • Loose or poorly located water diving board
      • Slippery decks or pool bottom surfaces
   2. Poorly designed or located water slides.
   3. Projecting or ungrated pipes and drains. resulting in hair or body-part traps.
   4. Drain grates of inadequate size.
   5. Improperly installed or maintained electrical equipment.
   6. Improperly vented chlorinators and mishandled chlorine materials.

Calculations for Pools

Swimming pools are engineered systems, with demanding safety and sanitary requirements that result in sophisticated design standards and water-treatment systems. The size, shape, and operating system of the pool is based upon:

1. The intended use of the pool and the maximum expected bather loading;
2. The selection of skimmers, scuppers, or gutters dependent upon the purpose, size, and shape of the pool;

3. The recirculation pump, its horsepower, and impeller configuration are based on the distance, volume, and height of the water to be pumped;
4. The filters are sized on the volume of water to be treated and the maximum gallons of water per minute that can be delivered by the pump and the type of filter media selected; and
5. The chemical feeder sizes and types are based upon the chemicals used, the total quantity of water in the system, expected use rates, and external environmental factors such as quantity of sunlight and wind impacting the system.

It is not unusual for pools built prior to regulatory programs to fail to meet minimum performance standards required to protect health and safety. Occasionally equipment is replaced without consultation with the EHO and as a result is inappropriately sized. In these circumstances, smaller than required is often inadequate and too large often overloads some other part of the pool treatment system. An oversized pump may increase the turnover rate but will not fit the pipe's carrying capacity or may overload the filter, causing permanent damage or the forcing through of dirt and grime. In order to determine if the pool design meets minimum design requirements, the EHO must be able to perform basic calculations required for inspection of swimming pools:

Nonmetric Equivalents for Calculation Purposes

1. 1 cubic foot of water contains 7.48 gallons.
2. 1 cubic foot of water weighs 62.4 pounds.
3. 1 gallon of water weighs 8.33 pounds.
4. 1 part per million (ppm) represents 8.3 pounds of chemical per million gallons of water.
5. To convert Celsius (C) to Fahrenheit (F), multiply by 9, divide by 5, add 32; or $F = {}^9/_5 C = 32$.
6. To convert Fahrenheit (F) to Celsius (C) , subtract 32, multiply by 5, divide by 9; or $C = {}^5/_9 (F - 32)$.
7. 1 pound per square inch (psi) is equal to the pressure of a column of water 2.31 feet high.
8. A column of water 1 foot high creates a pressure of 0.433 psi.
9. 1,000 square feet of water 1 inch deep contains 625 gallons.

Metric Equivalents for Pool Calculations

1. 1 liter = 0.2642 gallons
2. 1 gallon = 3.786 liters
3. 1 foot = 0.3048 meter
4. 1 yard = 0.914 meter
5. 1 square yard = 0.836 square meter
6. 1 meter = 39.37 inches or 3.2808 feet or 1.093 yards
7. 1 cubic meter = 264.2 gallons
8. 1 cubic meter = 1.308 cubic yards or 35.314 cubic feet

The EHO must be able to perform the following calculations:

- calculation of acceptable bather loads
- calculation of sq. ft. of surface area
- calculation of pool volume in pools of various shapes
- calculation of pool contents turnover rate base on pool volume and pump size
- calculation of filter surface areas
- calculation of filter loading rates
- calculation of required filter loading rate maximums for specific types of filters such as high rate, rapid rate, and diatomaceous earth
- calculation of amount of chlorine/disinfectant required to raise a specified pool volume to a specific level;
- know how much chlorine is typically found in the various solids, liquids and gas and used for disinfectant.

Calculation of Pool Surface Area

Basic formulas can be used in combination to calculate the surface area of most swimming pools. These are the formulas used to determine the areas of rectangles, triangles, and circles. The following potential pool shapes indicate a few of these applications:

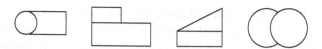

Symbols for Calculations

A = Area   r = radius, or 1/2 diameter
L = Length   π = pi, or 3.14
W = Width   π r2 = area of a circle
H = Height

1. The perimeter of any figure is equal to the entire distance around the figure.
2. The area of a triangle equals one-half the product of the base and the height.
3. The area of a square is equal to the square of one of its sides.
4. The area of a rectangle equals the base multiplied by the height.
5. The area of a trapezoid equals half the sum of the parallel sides multiplied by the height.
6. The area of any parallelogram can be converted to a rectangle without changing its area.

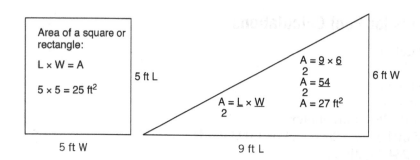

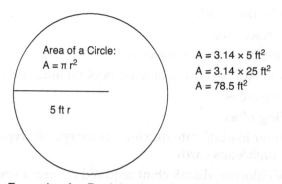

Formulas for Pool Surface Area Calculations

Bather Loading Standards

The maximum bather load of a pool is based on the addition of the area of the diving area, the swimming area, and the nonswimming area of the pool.

1. A maximum of 12 persons is the standard for within 10 ft of a diving area or platform.
2. The swimming area should be designed for a minimum of 24 ft^2 of area per person.
3. The nonswimming area should be designed for a minimum of 10 ft^2 of area per person, This area should equal from 60% to 80% of the pool if the pool is not exclusively dedicated to diving.

Bather Loading Calculations

1. Start with your **total square footage of pool area** _____;
2. Number of diving boards, calculating 10 ft on each side of board and 10 ft for the length of the board and 10 ft for the length beyond board equals **20 × 20, or 400 ft^2, for each diving board** (allow *12 persons per diving board 400 ft^2 area*);
3. For the area of the pool less than 5 ft deep the formula would be:
   square feet of nonswimming area divided by 24 ft^2 (allowed for each person) = number of persons allowed in nonswimming area;
   • How many square feet of surface area remains after subtracting the surface area claimed by the diving area and the nonswimming area of the pool? (total surface area of pool) – (sq. ft. of surface required for diving area) + (total sq. ft of nonswimming area) = (area of nondiving swimming sq. ft.). Allow 24 ft^2 for each swimmer in nondiving area (**area of nondiving swimming sq. ft. divided by 24), this gives you the number of persons allowed for this area ;**
4. **Add the number of swimmers allowed in items 2, 3, and 4** and you obtain the sum of the number of people allowed in the pool at one time, or the maximum bather load.

Allowable bather load may vary according to local codes. The information given above and the calculations below are taken from the HHS publication *Swimming Pools, Safety and Disease Control through Proper Design and Operation*, USPHS, 1983, Publication No. (CDC) 83–8319.

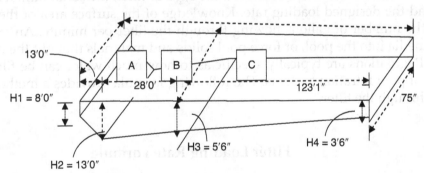

Calculation of the Volume of a Rectangular Pool

(applying the formula to the pool above)
Step 1: Divide the pool into sections as indicated above.

Step 2: Volume in cu ft = volume A × $\dfrac{H1 + H2}{2}$ + volume B × $\dfrac{H2 + H3}{2}$ + volume C × $\dfrac{H3 × H4}{2}$

$(13 \times 75) \times \underline{8 + 13} + (28 \times 75) \times \underline{13 + 5.5} + (123 \times 75) \times \underline{5.5 \times 3.5}$

$= 71,175$ cubic feet

Step 3: Pool volume, gal = cubic feet × gallons per cubic feet = 71,175 cu ft × 7.48 gal/cu ft
= 532,289 gallons

How much makeup water do you need to add to fill your pool after backwashing or to make up for leaks or other causes of pool water loss?

Measure the inches of water need for filling the pool, multiply it by the pool surface area in feet, and then multiply that outcome by 0.625, and it will equal the number of required gallons to be added to the pool. Or in other words use the formula:

Inches of water needed × area of pool in sq. ft. × 0.625 = water needed in gal.

Calculation of Pool Contents Turnover Rate

The number of times the pool contents can be filtered though a pool's filtration equipment in a 24-hour period is referred to as the turnover rate of the pool. Since the filtered water is diluted with the nonfiltered water of the pool, the turbidity continually decreases. One the pool water has reached equilibrium with the sources of contamination, a 6-hour turnover rate will result in 98% clarification if the pool is properly designed. A *typical use* pool should have a pump and filtration system capable of pumping the entire contents of the pool though the filters every 6 hours. To determine compliance with this 6-hour turnover standard, the following formula is used:

Therefore, the pool shown above would not meet the required turnover rate of 6 hours. The cause of this could be improperly sized piping or restrictions in the piping, undersized pump, or filters that are undersized or clogged. This turnover rate would likely result in cloudy water if the pool is used at the normal bather load. The decreased circulation would also result in difficulty in the disinfecting equipment meeting the required levels.

Calculation of Filter Loading Rates

The specification plate on the side of approved commercial swimming pool filters contains considerable information, such as the manufacturer, the type of filter, the serial number, the surface area of the filter, and the designed loading rate. Knowledge of the surface area of the filter allows you can calculate the number of gallons flowing through the filter per minute. An excessive flow rate can push the media into the pool, or force pool solids and materials thought the media resulting in turbid water. Regulations are typically specific as to how much water can be filtered through the various types of pool filtration systems. The following formula provides a method of determining the flow rate through the filter:

Filter Loading Rate Formula

$$\text{Filter loading rate (GPM per sq. ft)} = \frac{\text{(gpm)} \quad \text{Flow Rate}}{\text{Surface Area of Filter (sq. ft.)}}$$

Filter Loading Rates

The specification plate on the side of approved residential or commercial swimming pool filters contains such information as the manufacturer, type of filter, serial number, surface area, and designed loading rate. Knowing the surface area of the filter permits calculation of the number of gallons flowing through the filter per minute. An excessive flow rate can push the media into the pool or force pool solids and materials thought the media, resulting in turbid water.

The Filtration Rate is measured in Cubic metres of water per Square metre of Filter Surface Area per Hour—(CuMtrs/SqrMtr/Hr or m3/m2/hr) OR Gallons per Square Foot of Filter Surface Area per Hour—(Gall/SqFt/Hr or gal/ft2/hr

$Turnover\ Rate = \dfrac{Pool\ Volume}{Flow\ Rate}$	turnover rate or time
$Pool\ Volume = Turnover\ Rate \times Flow\ Rate$	pool volume or size
$Flow\ Rate = \dfrac{Pool\ Volume}{Turnover\ Rate}$	pump flow rate

Table 15.1 Disinfectant Levels Required at Different pH Values:

Disinfection Type	7.2–7.49 pH Range		7.5–7.79 pH Range		7.8–8 pH Range	
	Pool	Spa	Pool	Spa	Pool	Spa
Bromine	2.0 ppm	3.5 ppm	2.5 ppm	4.0 ppm	3.5 ppm	5.0 ppm
Stabilized Chlorine	1.5 ppm	3.0 ppm	2.0 ppm	3.5 ppm	2.8 ppm	4.3 ppm
Chlorine	1.0 ppm	2.5 ppm	1.4 ppm	2.9 ppm	1.8 ppm	3.3 ppm

Disinfectants Used in Pools

There are many disinfectants that are used in pools around the world, but the greatest experience is with halogen-based compounds. Those used most often are chlorine, bromine, and iodine, each having advantages and limi tations. Table 15.1 provides a concise summary of the advantages of many of the commonly used disinfectants.

The effective use of halogen disinfectants is based on the pH, hardness, and alkalinity of the water. Improper water balance can render high levels of disinfectant useless in the killing of disease-causing organisms. The table demonstrates the levels of disinfectants required at different pH values. Levels required to achieve similar results with differing pH values are listed in the table.

Effect of pH On Killing Power of Chlorine Disinfectants

The ideal pH from the perspective of eye irritation is 7.3. Bactericidal or algae killing effectiveness is improved with an even lower pH. National standards typically recommend that the range of 7.2 – 7.6 is ideal and will be more cost effective. Table 15.2 demonstrates the loss of effective disinfectant as the pH rises:

Why is pH important? Two reasons. First, the germ-killing power of chlorine varies with pH level. As pH goes up, the ability of chlorine to kill germs goes down. Second, a swimmer's body has a pH between 7.2 and 7.8, so if the pool water isn't kept in this range, then swimmers will start to feel irritation of their eyes and skin. Keeping the pH in this range will balance chlorine's germ-killing power while minimizing skin and eye irritation.

Chlorine was first discovered in the sixteenth century, and today is one of the most produced chemicals in the United States, finding its way into a multitude of products. Chlorine is so deeply intertwined into industry that finding alternatives would indeed change our daily lives. When chlorine is added to water, another dissociation occurs. When we add Cl2 (chlorine) + H2O (water), we get a reaction which leaves us with HOCl (hypochlorous acid) + HCl (hydrochloric acid). Hypochlorous acid is the active, killing form of chlorine. This is what does the real sanitizing work. The chlorine molecule or ion kills microorganisms by slashing through the cell walls and destroying the inner enzymes, structures, and processes. When this occurs, the cell has been deactivated, or oxidized. The hypochlorous molecule continues this slash-and-burn until it combines with a nitrogen or ammonia compound, becoming a chloramine, or it is broken down into its component atoms, becoming deactivated itself.

A **bleach** is a chemical that removes colors or whitens, often via oxidation. Common chemical bleaches include household chlorine bleach, a solution of approximately 3–6% sodium hypochlorite (NaClO), and oxygen bleach, which contains hydrogen peroxide or a peroxide-releasing compound such as sodium perborate, sodium percarbonate, sodium persulfate, tetrasodium pyrophosphate, or urea peroxide together with catalysts and activators; for example, tetraacetylethylenediamine and/or sodium nonanoyloxybenzenesulfonate. Bleaching powder is calcium hypochlorite. Many bleaches have strong bactericidal properties, and are used for disinfecting and sterilizing.

Table 15.2 Optimum pH Increases the Effectiveness of Chlorine Disinfection

HOCl ⟷	H^+	+	OCl^-

Hypochlorous Acid *More* Results in increased Effectiveness	Hydrogen Ion	Hypochlorite Ion *More* Results in Reduced Effectiveness as
% of Chlorine as HOCl	pH	% of Chlorine as OCl
90%	6.5	10%
73%	7.0	27%
66%	7.2 IDEAL	34%
45%	7.6 IDEAL	55%
21%	8.0	79%
10%	8.5	90%

Table 15.3 Pool and Beach Disease-Causing Organisms

ILLNESS	ORGANISM	TRANSMISSION
Athlete's Foot	Trichophyton rubrum Epidermophyton flocosum	Shower room floors, foot baths, pool deck.
Granulomas	Mycobacteria	Skin scraping against pool sides or deck.
Ear Infections	Pseudomonas aeruginosa	Bacteria entering ear canals.
Skin rash	Staphylococcus or Pseudomonas	Direct contact width contaminated water or towels and suits.
Eye infections	Streptococcus or Adenoviruses	Direct contact with contaminated water or infected individual.
Respiratory illnesses	Legionella, rhinovirus, adenovirus.	Swallowing water and direct contact.
Systemic infections and Gastroenteritis	Bacteria (E coli, shigella, salmonella) Protozoa (Giardia, Cryptosporidum) many other bacteria and viruses.	

According to the results of the pool water tests, we may need to add chemicals to bring the pool water back into the ideal balance for swimmer safety and visual clarity. We are required to regularly adjust the pH and chlorine levels as these tend to fluctuate according to the weather conditions and swimming pool use.

It is extremely important to adjust the pH before adding the chlorine. When the pH is 8.0, the chlorine is only 20% effective, and at a pH of 8.5 the chlorine is only 8% effective. Chlorine becomes overactive when the pH is lower than 7.0. Despite a balanced pool water system, the swimming pool can sometimes become cloudy and lose its sparkle. This is usually a result of minute suspended particles of dirt in the water that are too small to be trapped in the filter. These particles can usually be cleared using a flocculant/coagulant, which clumps them together, allowing them to be removed from the pool.

Chlorine Disinfectants

The options for selection of the form of chlorine disinfectant for use in pools is quite varied and the choices complex. Table 15.4 demonstrates the properties of each form; the relative cost is less with the gas chlorine and more expensive as you move right across the page. The cost of the disinfectant tends to be less with the higher concentration of available chlorine. The safety issues are more complex than they might appear. The hazards of gas chlorine are well known and that in some ways mitigates the hazard when using the gas form.

Note that the solid forms of chlorine, such as calcium hypochlorite, are quite reactive and when exposed to organic compounds generate a great deal of heat and are potentially explosive. Because it seems quite inert to the untrained worker, you will often find it stored beside motor oil, gasoline, or left in areas where moisture can start a chemical reaction. The simple act of a pencil with a graphite core dropping from a shirt pocket can, under the right circumstances, begin a chemical reaction leading to a fire releasing free chlorine gas.

Langelier Saturation Index

In order to understand the proper maintenance procedures for the prevention/elimination of water-quality problems in swimming pools, spas, and fountains, it is necessary to understand the process used to determine the chemical aggressiveness of water. The process is used to determine when water needs additional treatment. Water that is out of balance can result in many negative outcomes, from toxic water to damaged and ruined equipment, such as nonfunctional pumps to leaky pipes, solid concrete like media in filters, and clogged or leaky heaters. Water has a tremendous appetite to dissolve and carry materials when it is not saturated with materials resulting in equilibrium between pH, temperature, alkalinity, and hardness factors that determine the carrying capacity of water. This balance controls the water's ability to create scale or to dissolve material. If we fulfill the saturation needs of the water with harmless or beneficial substances such as calcium, then the threat of damage can be mitigated. The Langelier method, developed in the early 1930s, is used in boiler management, municipal water treatment, and swimming pools.

A. Pool Water Hardness
1. Ideal range for a plaster pool is 200–275 ppm.
2. Ideal range for a vinyl, painted, or fiberglass surface is 175–225 ppm.
3. Excess causes scaling, discoloration, filter inefficiency.
4. Less than recommended causes results in corrosion of most contact surfaces

B. Pool Water Alkalinity
1. Alkaline compounds produce basic solutions.
2. Should be 80–120 ppm
3. High levels cause scale and high Cl demand.
4. Low levels cause unstable pH.
5. Cloudy water if over 200 ppm
6. Sodium bicarbonate will raise it.

Table 15.4 Forms of Chlorine Typically Used in Swimming Pools

	GAS CHLORINE	SODIUM HYPOCHLORITE	CALCIUM HYPOCHLORITE	DICHLORO	TRICHLORO
Percent Chlorine	100%	10–15%	65–70%	56–62%	90%
Impacts on pH	Lowers pH	Raises pH	Raises pH	Neutral Impact	Lowers pH
Sunlight Impacts	Considerable	Yes	Yes	Little loss	Little loss
Physical Form	Gas	Liquid	Granular or Tablets	Granular only	Granular or Tablets

Table 15.5 Swimming Pool Operational Parameters

WATER CLARITY	MINIMUM	IDEAL	MAXIMUM	COMMENTS
Crystal-clear water at all times is the goal.	Main Drain Visible	Crystal-clear; object the size of dime easily seen from pool deck at main drain, water sparkles	No maximum parameter	Lack of clarity is often due to malfunctioning or undersized filters. Other problems may be improperly sized pump, air collecting in the filter shell, or operator not running filter 24 hours per day.
Disinfectant levels	Minimum	Ideal	Maximum	Comments
Free Chlorine (ppm)	.5	1–1.5	2	Continuous levels Superchlorinate when combined level exceeds 0.2
Combined Chlorine (ppm)	None	None	0.2	Superchlorinate indicators: Sharp chlorine level, eye irritation, or algae growth
Bromine (ppm)	2.	3–5	5	Continuous levels
Iodine (ppm)	Consult manufacturer of product			
Ozone, ultraviolet light, hydrogen peroxide, and others	Consult manufacturer of product			The use of these also requires a residual forming disinfectant for the approval of most health jurisdictions.
pH	7.2	7.3	7.6	Ideal range 7.2–7.6
Total alkalinity ppm as CaCO3 (ppm)	60	80–100	180	
Dissolved solids (ppm)	300	Not often a problem in swimming pools.	2,000	Excess solids may lead to hazy water and corrosion of fixtures (partial water replacement may be required)
Hardness (ppm) CaCO3'	150	200–400	500 +	If difficult to control, using a different disinfectant may be suggested.
Heavy metals	None	None	None	Check algaecide for heavy metal presence or byproducts of corrosion (partial water replacement may be required).
Stabilizer Cyanuric Acid (ppm)	10	30–50	100	Action required: if level exceeds 100 ppm, then partial water replacement may be required.
Algae, Bacteria	None	None	None	Shock treat and maintain required levels of disinfectant and 7.2–7.6 pH.

Table 15.6 Pool Water Quality Problem-Solving

WATER QUALITY ISSUE (SYMPTOMS)	POTENTIAL PROBLEMS (ROOT CAUSES)	CORRECTIVE APPROACHES (ACTIONS)
Air bubbles coming from inlets.	1. Air in Filter Shell (easy fix).	Bleed air off of top of filter shell.
	2. Leak in hair and lint strainer, pipe, valves, or fittings on suction side of pump (may be difficult).	First check seal around opening of hair and lint strainer; locate leaking fitting and seal.
Foam on water, around floating objects, and on sides of pool.	1. Low hardness of water (easy fix)	Maintain a minimum of 200 ppm of calcium hardness but less than 400 ppm.
	2. Effect of algaecides (do not need)	Do not use algaecides but maintain 1 ppm of free Cl at minimum and a maximum pH of 7.6. It is preferable that pH be 7.2 for algae-free water.
	3. Spillage of detergent into pool.	Backwash filters for extended time and add makeup water. If foam still a problem, add defoaming agent.
Cloudy water	1. Inadequate turnover rate. 2. Filter media corrupted/channeled or creviced.	Check pump capacity and flow rate. If sand, clean filter media and replace media if necessary. If DE filter, wash filter bags in weak acid solution.
	3. Excessive filter pressure.	Backwash filter, bleed air pressure from filter shell, check pump for proper sizing.
	4. High pH and/or alkalinity above 150 ppm.	Reduce pH to max. of 7.6 and alkalinity to less than 150 ppm.
Milky water (uniform water color with white, opaque appearance).	DE entering pool from DE filter leakage	Check filter bags for tears or holes and the mounting of the bags on the filter septa. Expect 24-hours minimum filtering to clear water.
Dull green color, varying density	Algae growth	Superchlorinate and then maintain pH at 7.6, preferably 7.2, and disinfectant level of 1 ppm or higher.
Bright green color	Dissolved iron	Adjust pH to 7.2–7.6 range, adjust disinfectant level to 1–1.5 ppm. Iron should precipitate to ferrous state (brown), backwash repeatedly to remove. Expect 24–46 hour. filtering to clear water.
Bluish green color	Copper damage from low pH	Raise pH to 7.6, increase hardness to 200 ppm, and alkalinity of at least 150 ppm. Perform a saturation index calculation and adjust water to slightly above +0.5 to achieve scale-forming water to isolate prior equipment damage.
Reddish-brown water, uniform in color and texture.	Precipitated iron (ferrous)	Adjust pH and disinfectant level and backwash filter as needed until clear.

Breakpoint Chlorination

Excessive Chlorine is not the typical cause of eye irritation. Complaints from patrons that there is an excessive amount of chorine in the pool causing eye irritation and/or because of the strong smell of chlorine around the pool is more likely due to increasing chloramine. The resolution of this issue is to add more chlorine to the pool and destabilize the chloramine. Figure 15.1 is an example of the process of slow buildup of these compounds and their destruction.

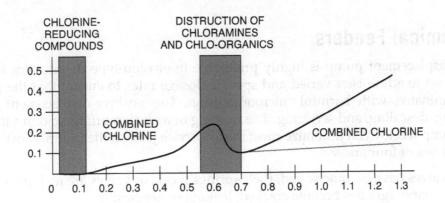

Breakpoint Chlorination
Superchlorination
In order to achieve breakpoint chlorination You must
Raise pool chlorine level to 10 x the combined
chlorine level!

When using granular chlorine
(approximate 65%) available chlorine
Use 2 ounces of chlorine per 10,000
Gallons pool water to raise the level 1 ppm
The Chemical Destabilization of Combined Chlorine
(Shock Treatment)

How Chlorine Oxidizes Organics and Produces Irritating Chloramines

$Cl_2 + H_2O = HCl + HOCl$
Chlorine + Water = Hydrochloric Acid + Hypochlorous Acid

$HOCl + NH_3 = H_2O + NH_2Cl$
Hypochlorous Acid + Ammonia = Water + Monochloramine

$HOCl + NH_2Cl_2 = H_2O + NHCl_2$
Hypochlorous Acid + Monochloramine = Water + Dichloramine

$HOCl + NHCl_2 = H_2O + NH_3$
Hypochlorous Acid + Dichloramine = Water + Nitrogen Trichloride

Gas Chlorination Injection System

This system is typically used when chlorine gas is the selected disinfectant. The advantages of gas chlorine are the relative cost of the gas chlorine and the minimal effect that gas chlorine has on pH. The pH effect is to lower the water pH slightly. The safety issues are the negative aspects of its use. The cylinders must be secured and chained to the wall at all times when in use, the safety caps must be installed over the brass valves when not in use, and the cylinders still must be secured from overturning and be protected from extreme heat and sunlight.

Liquid Chemical Feeders

The positive displacement pump is highly preferable to erosion-type disinfectent feeders. These pumps can be set to administer varied and specific dosage rates to ensure that the pool does not become contaminated with harmful microorganisms. The positive-displacement pump needs routine cleaning, descaling, and servicing. The running of a weak muriatic acid or vinegar solution thought the pump weekly can minimize most major service jobs on the pump. Most service on the pump involves one of four areas:

1. The check valves have become scaled, their springs weak, or valves are no longer flexible.
2. The flexible diaphragm has become cracked, leaking or nonflexible.
3. The cake needs replacement or adjustment.
4. The motor requires replacement.

Errosion and Flow-Through Feeders

These feeders work through the erroding of a solid cake of chlorine by the action of moving water around the cake. The feeders work quite well for smaller pools but require considerable care and maitenance. The variables that impact the effectiveness of errosion feeders are:

1. Soluabiltiy of the chlorine cake or tablet.
2. Size or surface area or the cake or tablet.
3. Amount of water flowing around the cake or tablet.
4. Concentration of chlorine in the cake or tablet.
5. Number of cakes or tablets in the feeder.

Design and Construction Guidelines

- **Water Supply**
  - Water must be from an approved source in compliance with EPA Safe Drinking Water Act requirements.
  - Backflow prevention is required either by an air gap, pipe-applied atmospheric vacuum breaker, pressure-type anti-siphon vacuum breaker, or reduced pressure principle backflow preventer.

- **Sewer System:**
  - Wastewater system must be of approved construction and sufficient capacity to treat wastewater/backwash water from the pool and associated equipment.
  - No direct connection between wastewater system and pool drains.
  - Backflow water piped to an approved public or private sanitary sewer.

- **Construction Materials**
- **Smooth and easily cleanable materials.**

- Easy-to-clean surfaces that are slip resistant.
- Sand or earth bottoms not permitted.

- **Submission of Plans**
  - Prior to construction, alteration, remodel, or renovation of any swimming pool, plans should be submitted and reviewed for compliance with the following requirements.
  - Plans should include a site plan, sectional views, piping diagrams, and structural/mechanical details.
  - Plans should be prepared and have a seal from a registered professional engineer or architect.
- **Design Details**
  - Hydrostatic relief valve strongly recommended.
  - Minimum pool depth is 3 feet. Except for special use pools (i.e. wading, handicap).
  - In pools with a depth of >5 feet a life line should be installed to separate deep and shallow ends.
  - The bottom slope in water depths <5 feet should be not more than 1 foot vertical in 12 feet horizontal. Bottom slopes in water depths >5 feet should be 1 foot vertical for every 3' in distance.

Table 5.7 Diving Area Requirements

Elevation of diving board above water (feet)	Minimum depth of water under end of board (feet)	Minimum depth of water 6 ft behind, 20 ft forward, and 8 ft to either side of end of diving board.
1–4 ft	10 ft*	10 ft*
4–10 ft	12 ft	10 ft
Above 10 ft (platforms)	15–18 ft	12 ft
* Bottom may not be horizontal but must be sloped to permit drainage.		

- Diving Boards
  - Diving board supports should be anchored firmly to the decking.
  - A minimum of 16 ft of headroom must be provided above the diving board.
  - Handrails are required if the board is more than 2 ft above the water level.

- **Pumps/Piping**
  - Turnover rate for the pool water at least four times every 24 hours.
  - Return flow should be through an overflow system/surface skimmers, and main drain.
  - Piping should be color-coded
  - Strainer basket should be accessible and cleaned daily.
  - A system is needed for cleaning of pool sides and bottom.
  - A rate-of-flow indicator installed on filtered water line capable of measuring flows of 1.5 times the designed flow rate.
  - Pumps should be sized to adequately circulate water and backwash filters. Dynamic head of 50 ft for sand filters and 80 ft for diatomaceous/cartridge type of filters.
  - Thermometers provided for heated pools near heater outlet/Inlets should be adequate in number and location to facilitate water flow and prevent stagnant water pockets. Number of inlets required is 1/600 ft^2 of water surface area or 1/15,000 gallons of pool volume. Eyeball fitting should be installed in the inlets to allow correction of any flow problems.
  - At least one drain located in the deepest portion of the pool is required.
  - The main drain grate must be a minimum of 4 x the size of the main drainpipe.

- The surface overflow/skimmer system should be designed to handle 100% of the circulation flow from the pool.
  - Skimmers are used at least 1/500 ft² of water surface area.
- **Filters**
  - Sight glass should be required on the backwash line to determine water clarity.
  - Air relief valve and pressure gauge needed on filter(s).
- **Disinfectant/Chemical Feeders**
  - Automatic disinfectant feeder required
  - Chlorine gas cannot feed directly to pool, pool piping system, water supply system, or swimming pool enclosure.
  - Chlorine gas should utilize a solution feeder capable of delivering chlorine solution at its maximum rate without releasing gas into the atmosphere.
  - Gas chlorine cylinders and equipment should be installed in a separate well-ventilated room. The door to this room should open to the outside.
  - Chlorine cylinders should be anchored to prevent them from falling and installed on a scale when in use.
  - When the cylinders are not in use, they should be stored with the protective cap on away from direct sunlight.
  - Adequate personal protective equipment should be provided for all personnel working in areas that may contain high concentrations of chlorine gas. PPE should be stored outside the chlorine room and in a secure place. Personnel should be fit tested for PPE and trained on proper use, storage, and maintenance.
  - Door to the chlorine room should be labeled DANGER: CHLORINE GAS.
  - Disinfectant feeders should be capable of providing the equivalent of 1 lb. chlorine/ 8 hours/10,000 gallons of pool water.
- **Ladders/Steps/Stairs**
  - Pools over 2 ft deep should have stairs or steps located at the shallow end of pool.
  - Pools over 30 ft wide should have recessed steps or ladders on either side of the deepest portion of the pool.
  - Stairs should be slip-resistant and a minimum of 12 in deep with a maximum of 10 in rise between steps.
  - Recessed steps should be slip-resistant and have a maximum rise of 10 in.
  - Ladders should have slip-resistant treads and provide a handhold. A clearance of <5 in and >3 in should be provided between the ladder and the pool wall.
  - Steps inserted into the walls should have a minimum tread of 5 in and a minimum width of 14 in.
  - If stepholes or ladders are provided within the pool, a handrail should be provided on each side and extend over the coping or edge of the deck.
- **Decking**
  - Decks should be constructed of an impervious material and should be slip-resistant.
  - Decks should be sloped at a grade of 1/4–1/2 in per foot to a deck drain. Deck drains should not connect to the pool circulation system.
  - Outdoor pool decking should be at least 8 ft wide at all points. Indoor pool decking should be at least 5 ft wide at all points.
  - At least 5 ft of deck should be provided behind the diving board.
- **Depth Markings**
  - The pool deck should be clearly and appropriately marked with the depth of the pool in large and easy-to-see locations: 18 in from water's edge using 4 in contrasting colored letters showing slopes of 2 ft and also marked on the vertical sides of the pool visible from the distant side.

- Markings should be provided at the deep and shallow ends, at the point of change from shallow to deep water, at each 2 ft increment of water depth, and every 25 ft around the perimeter of the pool.
- Markers should be in Arabic numbers at least 4 in high and in a color contrasting to the background.
- Where it is physically impossible to place depth markers on pool walls and decking, other means should be used, provided markings are clearly visible to persons using the pool.
- Markings can be placed along the bottom of the pool to identify when the slope of the bottom changes.

- **Lighting**
  - When used, underwater lighting should be a minimum of 0.5 watts/sq ft of swimming pool water surface area.
  - When pools are used at night, lighting should be provided so that all portions of the pool, including the bottom, can be seen.
  - When underwater lighting is provided, surface area lighting should provide at least 30 foot-candles (fc) of lighting on the pool surface and deck. If underwater lighting is not provided, surface area lighting should provide at least 50 fc in these areas.
  - Underwater lights must be individually grounded and the circuit protected by a ground fault interrupter (GFI).
  - There should be no overhead electrical wiring within 20 ft of the swimming pool enclosure.
  - Electrical circuits located within 15 ft of a pool should be provided with GFIs conforming to the latest editions of the National Electric Code and the Life Safety Code.
  - Adequate natural or mechanical ventilation, or a combination of the two, should be provided for all indoor pools, equipment rooms, bathhouses, dressing rooms, shower rooms, and toilet areas.

- **Dressing Rooms, Toilets, and Showers**
  - Facilities should be provided within 150 ft of the pool. Separate dressing rooms, toilets, and showers should be provided for men and women. Walls and partitions should be constructed in compliance with the most recent Uniform Building Code and should have a smooth and impervious finish. Floors should be finished with a smooth, slip-resistant surface, impervious to moisture, and sloped to floor drains. Floors may be covered with an artificial recreational surface.
  - Facilities should be designed so that bathers will pass through the shower area on their way to the pool from the changing area and from the toilet rooms.

- **Fences and Enclosures**

  Outdoor pools should be secured by a fence, wall, or other enclosure to ensure the following conditions are met:
  - No external handholds or footholds.
  - Six-ft minimum height around the entire pool area.
  - Horizontal space between vertical bars not to exceed 2 in.
  - Any opening under the bottom of the fence, wall, or enclosure should be less than 2 in.
  - All gates and doors should be provided with self-closing, positive-latching closure devices.
  - Latches should be at least 3 ft above the ground and equipped with permanent locking devices.
  - A minimum of one drinking fountain should be provided in the swimming pool area.

- **Safety Equipment and Facilities**
  - Pools with a surface area <2,250 ft² should be provided with a minimum of one elevated lifeguard chair or platform. Pools with a surface area of 4,000 ft² should be provided at least two lifeguard chairs or platforms and one additional chair/platform for each additional 2,500 ft² of surface area.

- One unit of life-saving equipment should be provided for every 2,000 ft² of water surface area. A unit of life-saving equipment consists of one ring buoy not more than 15 in diameter or similar flotation device attached to a 60-ft length of 3/16-in rope; one life pole or shepherd's crook type pole with blunt ends and a minimum length of 12 ft.
- First aid kit supplied and ready for use. Containing the following:
  - 1-in adhesive compress (2)
  - 2-in bandage compress (2)
  - 3-in bandage compress (2)
  - 4-in bandage compress (2)
  - 3 × 3 in plain gauze pad (2)
  - gauze roller bandage (2)
  - eye dressing packet (2)
  - plain absorbent gauze yd² (4)
  - plain absorbent gauze 24 × 72 in (3)
  - triangular bandages, 40 in (4)
  - bandage scissors, tweezers (1)
  - hydrogen peroxide 6 oz (1)
- Pools with a maximum water depth of less than 8 ft should have NO DIVING signage posted, easily readable, and placed in prominent locations in the pool area.
- Semi-public pools that do not have a lifeguard should post warning signs, WARNING: NO LIFEGUARD ON DUTY in a readily visible location. A sign stating CHILDREN UNDER THE AGE OF 16 SHOULD NOT SWIM WITHOUT SUPERVISION FROM AN ADULT should also be provided if there is no lifeguard.
- Two wading pools
- Should not be attached directly or physically connected to any swimming pool.
- Should have a separate circulation system, pump, piping, filter, disinfectant feeder, and inlet and outlet fittings from the swimming pool. should be no deeper than 2 ft and have a main drain at the deepest point.
- Separated from the swimming pool by a fence or other physical barrier or located in the vicinity of the shallow end of the main pool.
- There should be no more than one child for every 10 ft2 of water surface area.
- Fill and draw pools should not be used.

- Swimming Pool Operation and Maintenance
  - Pool area and enclosure should be maintained in good repair, clean and sanitary.
  - Dressing rooms, shower rooms, fixtures, equipment, and structures should be maintained clean and in good repair.
  - Soap and towels from dispensers should be provided in lavatories.
  - Floors, walls, and ceilings should be maintained and in sanitary condition. Floors should be disinfected at least once per day and more if bather use dictates.
- **Water-Quality Standards**
  - Chlorine levels should be maintained between 0.5 and 1.5 ppm *free available* residual chlorine.
  - Combined chlorine levels should be maintained below 0.2 ppm. Concentrations over 0.2 ppm indicate a need to superchlorinate the water to oxidize and reduce the combined residual chlorine.
  - pH (hydrogen ion concentration) should be maintained between 7.2 and 7.6.
  - If water samples are collected for microbiological analysis, they should be taken during use of the pool, residual disinfectant deactivated, and examined in accordance with *Standard Methods for the Examination of Water and Wastewater.*
  - Not more than 15% of samples taken during a 30-day period should contain more than 200 colonies/ml of water as determined by standard plate count, or test positive in any of the five 10 ml samples tested when using multiple fermentation method, or more than 1 coliform organism/50 ml when using membrane filter test, or test positive using colilert testing methods.

- Total alkalinity should be maintained between 80 and 150 mg/l.
- Water should be maintained clear enough to easily see the grate on the main drain in the deepest portion of the pool.
- Manual application of chemicals requires chemicals to be mixed prior to adding to pool water. During these applications, pool use should be discontinued, allowed to diffuse throughout the system, and the chemical content checked to ensure proper levels prior to reopening of the pool.
- Every swimming pool should have an operator assigned to test and examine the water to ensure that chemical levels are correct. A test kit should be provided capable of testing at least total and free residual chlorine, pH, total alkalinity, and cyanuric acid (if used).
- During hours of operation, pool water should be tested at least once during the first hour of operation and then at least every three hours from two different locations within the pool.

- **General Safety**
  - Results of tests conducted on pool water should be recorded by the operator and maintained in file for review.
    All public pools should have at least one attendant (lifeguard) trained in first aid, life saving, and resuscitation for every 75 bathers in the pool.
  - Personal protective equipment should be provided and used by pool operators responsible for using or mixing chemicals.
  - Smoking should not be permitted in chemical storage areas and equipment rooms.
  - Safety rules should be posted in visible locations around the pool.

- **Food Service**
  - Food service should be designed, constructed, operated, and maintained in accordance with the most recent FDA food code or the local administrative code.
  - Consumption of food and beverages should be restricted and not allowed on the swimming pool deck or in the pool.

General Inspection Points for Swimming Pools
Recommended Chemical Levels

- pH: 7.2–7.8
- Chlorine: 1.0–2.0 ppm
- Total Alkalinity: 80–120 ppm
- Calcium Hardness: 180–220 ppm, though some say 200–400.
- Cyanuric Acid: 25–50 ppm
- Total Dissolved Solids: 500–5,000 ppm

Pool Disese Prevention, Safety, and Injury Prevention
A. **Disease Control**
   1. Water must be clear, bottom main drain easily visible.
   2. Disinfectant level above 1 ppm. and less than 2 ppm.
   3. pH level optimum when between 7.2 and 7.3.
   4. Stabilizer (cyanuric acid) levels below 100 ppm.
   5. Persons with open wounds or bandages not allowed in pool.
   6. Diaper-aged children not allowed in the pool.
   7. Clean suits and towels required.
   8. All bathers must take hot, soapy showers.
   9. Showers, locker rooms, floors, and pool decks cleaned and disinfected daily.
   10. Majority of water flows though gutters or skimmers rather than main drain.
   11. Disinfectant level in pool a minimum of 1 ppm at all times.

12. Pool equipment operates 24 hours a day.
13. No food or drink allowed in pool area.
14. No glass or brittle plastics or other such materials allowed in pool area.
15. Litter, gum, and personal items controlled throughout pool area.
16. Ensure maximum effectiveness of pool disinfectants.
17. Footbaths not used or, if used, flowing water and a clean basin.

B. **Safety**
   1. Check all drain openings, grates, skimmers, and gutters for potential opportunities for hair and body-part entrapment.
   2. Make sure all showers and lavatories are equipped with scald-prevention valves.
   3. Never add any chemical directly to the pool when patrons are present.
   4. Do not wear ties or loose clothing around pool operation equipment.
   5. All skimmer openings must have the designed cover firmly in place when the pool is in operation.
   6. Appropriate fencing must enclose the pool in accordance with the inspection jurisdiction and the liability insurance requirements.
   7. A shepherd's crook, appropriate life rings, lifeguard tower, and other safety equipment.
   8. Properly certified and trained lifeguards are on duty and in appropriate numbers,
   9. All activities should be kept within the design specifications of the pool. If diving is allowed, it should be confined to the designated locations in the pool.
   10. The pool deck, shower floor, and pool floor should be monitored for slick surfaces and appropriately treated if found to be a hazard.
   11. Glass doors should have shatterproof glass and be marked with decals to ensure that they are easily visible at all times and in all light.
   12. The pool deck should be clearly and appropriately marked, with the depth of the pool in large and easy-to-see locations: 18 in from water's edge using 4 in contrasting colored letters showing slopes of 2 ft and also marked on the vertical sides of the pool visible from the distant side.
   13. A lighting level of 30 fc is recommended for pool equipment rooms.
   14. Maintain a Red Cross–approved or equivalent first aid kit for pool areas.
   15. Main drains and skimmers must be designed to prevent entrapment and have the appropriate safety guards installed.
   16. Telephone available and accessible near the pool.
   17. No power lines or other unprotected electrical devices are located near the pool.
   18. No trees or branches overhang the pool.
   19. The pool deck and pool bottom have a nonslip texture.

C. **Chemical Management**
   1. Read and maintain all material safety data sheets.
   2. Read all containers and keep the chemicals in the original container until use.
   3. Uses appropriate personal protective equipment (PPE), such as safety glasses, and, if provided, training in the use and maintenance of gas mask for chlorine.
   4. Beware of both gas and solid forms of chlorine and use as the label indicates.
   5. Always pour acid into water slowly; when diluting never add water to any chemical.
   6. Lawn supplies and equipment are not stored in the pool operation or chemical treatment areas. Pool chemicals must be stored in clean, dry, well-ventilated areas.
   7. A minimum lighting level of 30 fc is recommended for pool equipment rooms.
   8. All chemical spillage is immediately cleaned up and neutralized.
   9. All chemical container covers are replaced and nothing is set on their lids.
   10. Chlorine gas room properly vented and has an observation port.

Table 5.8 Spa and Hot-Tub Operational Parameters

DISINFECTANT LEVEL	MINIMUM	IDEAL	MAXIMUM	COMMENTS
Free chlorine (ppm)	2	3–5	5	Continuous levels Superchlorinate when combined level exceeds 0.2
Combined chlorine (ppm)	None	None	0.2	Superchlorinate indicators: Sharp chlorine level, eye irritation, or algae growth
Bromine (ppm)	2.	3–5	5	Continuous levels
Iodine (ppm)	Consult Manufacturer			
Ozone, ultraviolet light, hydrogen peroxide, and others	Consult manufacturer of product			The use of these also requires a disinfectant for the approval of most health jurisdictions.

CHEMICAL VALUE	MINIMUM	IDEAL	MAXIMUM	COMMENTS
pH	7.2	7.3	7.6	Ideal Range 7.2 – 7.6
Total alkalinity ppm as CaCO3	60 (ppm)	80 – 100 (ppm)	180 (ppm)	
Dissolved solids (ppm)	300	—	2,000	Excess solids many lead to hazy water and corrosion of fixtures (may need partial water replacement)
Hardness (ppm) CaCO3'	150	200–400	500+	If difficult to control, using a different disinfectant may be suggested.
Heavy metals	None	None	None	Check algaecide for heavy metal presence or byproducts of corrosion (partial water replacement may be required).
Stabilizer cyanuric acid (ppm)	10	30–50	100	If level exceeds 100 ppm, then partial water replacement may be required.
Algae, bacteria	None	None	None	If observed, shock treat and maintain required levels of disinfectant and appropriate pH.

Covers

All drain covers must be compliant with the ANSI/ASME A112.19.8 performance standard, or the successor standard ANSI/APSP-16 2011.

Pool and spa owners and operators can either have older covers tested against the standard to determine if they comply, or replace these covers with new compliant drain covers. If covers are field fabricated, then a Registered Design Professional or a licensed professional engineer (PE) must specify the covers meet the ASME/ANSI A112.19.8 standard.

As of Jan. 30, 2009, Underwriters Laboratory, the National Sanitation Foundation and the International Association of Plumbing and Mechanical Officials (IAPMO) are conducting third-party testing and certification of drain covers.

While there is no requirement in the Act that there be a specific marking on drain covers, the CPSC has asked manufacturers to mark them "VGB 2008." Since Nov. 12, 2008, drain covers should have the "VGB 2008" marking.

Some drain covers manufactured during the summer of 2008 used the ASME symbol and/or the "ASME/ANSI A112.19.8 " mark. And in the fall of 2008, no marking was placed on drain covers made to comply with the standard.

The drain cover manufacturer should provide a certification document with each drain cover stating that it complies with the requirements of the VGB Act. If there is no mark or you are otherwise in doubt, contact the manufacturer and ask for a copy of the certificate. The CPSC encourages you to keep a record of where and when you purchased the cover and its installation.

The ASME standard requires covers to display:

- Use—single or multiple
- Flow rate GPM
- Life or the number of years
- Wall and/or floor mount
- Manufacturer's name
- Model number
- Flow Rates and Single Drains

Drain cover ratings are based on allowable flow in gallons per minute (GPM). Covers are tested in the laboratory to determine maximum flow rate, which can result in velocities through the open area of the cover that are greater than 1.5 feet per second (fps).

Drain cover manufacturers determine approved flow rates, but some state standards require that the water velocity through grates not exceed 1.5 feet per second (fps) with one drain 100 percent blocked.

Given the pool volume and turnover rate required by the state/local authority, the minimum required GPM should be known and the cover GPM determined based on the number of covers present.

Generally, to calculate flow for multiple drains, you subtract one drain (presuming it is blocked) so the total flow through the remaining drains should meet the system requirements.* Flow rate calculations for single drain would be:

- One drain = total system flow (plus a secondary anti-entrapment system if the single main drain is not unblockable)

    Note: The flow-rate calculations are independent of 'unblockable.'
    *This is a CPSC staff position that coincides with the ANSI/APSP-7 Entrapment

Avoidance standard. The Act does not reference APSP-7 and owners/operators/service companies should comply with the ASME/ANSI standard first and foremost.

Bathing Beach Standards

Illnesses associated with swimming in waters receiving runoff and/or other pollutants include eye and ear infections and gastroenteritis. Swimming and other water-contact activities are never a zero-risk activity, even in pristine bathing beach waters. Swimming pools are a preferable recreational option due to the engineering controls that are designed into those facilities. Compliance with the guidelines listed in the following material will reduce the health risks to a reasonable level.

Beach monitoring is required for each designated beach. Monitoring is recommended for other beaches that are heavily used (40 or more people per 100 ft of shoreline). Specific requirements for each beach in the program include:

1. Doing a sanitary survey.
2. Preparing a beach-monitoring plan.
3. Sampling for enterococcus or *Escherichia coli* bacteria levels.
4. Issuing swimming advisories when bathing beach waters exceed the bacterial standards.

Sanitary Surveys of Beaches

The sanitary survey is a health-risk evaluation of the swimming beach and surrounding area to determine whether the beach is safe for water-contact activities such as wading, swimming, and snorkeling. The survey takes into consideration all factors that have an actual or potential bearing on the microbial quality of the water. It includes potential sources of pollution, physical factors that can affect the distribution and concentration of microorganisms, and the microbial quality of the water at the time of the survey. Potential sources of human-caused bacterial contamination include, but are not restricted to, sewage outfalls, storm drains, raw sewage overflows from manholes, septic tanks, and sewage treatment plants, boating activities, and people using the beach. Potential sources of animal-caused microbial contamination include, but are not limited to, streams, animal enclosures, feedlots, and forage areas for both domestic and wild animals.

Also of concern are potential sources of chemical contamination or hidden waste sites that could impact the swimming areas. The monitoring of solid waste and litter disposal around such areas is increasingly a issue of health concern. Medical waste such as bandages, syringes, and other sharps must be part of an effective sanitary survey and the routine monitoring of the water and the bathing beach.

Physical factors that have a bearing on water quality include precipitation, topography, runoff patterns, prevailing winds, tides, and currents. Water quality is also affected by characteristics of the receiving water, such as thermal and salinity stratification, water depth, and surface area.

A sanitary survey should be conducted annually before the beginning of the beach season. It will help you in selecting sampling locations for your beach-monitoring program. It will also help you identify potential source(s) and pathway(s) of contamination.

Beach-Monitoring Protocol

Each area with designated or heavily used beaches should develop a written beach-monitoring protocol. The protocol should include the names of beaches to be sampled, sampling station locations, a map or sketch of each beach showing the location of each sampling station,; bacterial standard used, and the name of the laboratory doing the bacterial analyses.

1. Data Form
   The development of a data form for consolidating your beach monitoring data should be developed. It should include information about the location, time, date, and bacterial densities of each water sample.

2. Sampling Location.

Sample locations should reflect the water quality within the entire recreational zone. The majority of samples should be taken in areas of heaviest use. They should include sites that potentially can be affected by point discharges and surface runoff. Sampling should be conducted at the areas of most probable contamination. Examples are locations adjacent to drains and natural contours that could discharge stormwater collections or septic waste. The total number of samples taken at a bathing beach will depend on the size and intensity of use. A minimum of three sampling stations per beach is recommended. The use of the new GPS identifying systems can be of great value in identifying sampling locations for future resampling and potential evidence collection.

3. Sampling Frequency.

Water samples should be collected as early as possible in the morning to accurately reflect the baseline bacterial quality. The first set of samples should be collected approximately two weeks before the beginning of the recreational season. This will provide sufficient time to resample if the initial samples indicate the bacterial standards have been exceeded. A weekly set of samples should be taken beginning with the first week and continuing through the last week of the recreational season. A minimum of one water sample should be collected for each beach-sampling station each week.

4. Sampling Procedures.

Samples should be collected in conformance with the most recent edition of the American Public Health Association's *Standard Methods for the Examination of Water and Wastewater.*

5. Sample Analysis.

Analysis should be done in conformance with the most recent edition of the *Standard Methods for the Examination of Water and Wastewater,* using the enterococcus or fecal cloakroom membrane filter techniques. A certified microbiological laboratory should be used for the analysis. Often the same laboratory that analyzes your drinking water parameters will also be certified to do these analyses. Upon receipt of the laboratory results, transcribe the bacterial densities onto the beach data form.

Bacterial Standards

For governmental units that do not have their own bathing beach standards, enterococcus is the recommended bacterial indicator. However, you may not be able to use enterococcus if laboratory analysis is not readily available. In that case, the recommended standard is *E. coli.* Two types of bacterial density standards are recommended. One standard is the geometric mean. The geometric mean should be calculated weekly for each sampling station beginning with week five. It is a running mean calculated using the most recent five weekly samples. The second bacterial density standard is the maximum standard. It is the bacterial density that should never be exceeded, even by one sample. It is the only standard available from the beginning of the sampling period until week five when the first geometric mean can be calculated. Transcribe the bacterial density data (colonies/100 ml) onto your beach data form.

Water Appearance

Water clarity should be such that a Secchi disk (20 cm in diameter divided into four quadrants painted alternating black and white) is visible to a minimum depth of 4 ft. No film should be visible on the surface of the water, and the water should have no lasting foam with no abnormal color evident.

Table 5.9 Recommended Marine and Freshwater Bacterial Standards

1. **Marine Water Bathing Beaches**
   a. Enterococci
      1) **35 enterococci/100 ml.** (geometric mean) **or**
      2) **104 enterococci/100 ml.**
         Not to be exceeded by any one sample.
2. **Freshwater Bathing Beaches**
   a. Enterococci
      1) **33 colonies/100 ml.** (geometric mean) **or**
      2) **61 colonies/100 ml.**
         Not to be exceeded by any one sample.
   b. *E. coli*
      1) **126 colonies/100 ml.** (geometric mean) **or**
      2) **400 colonies/100 ml.**
         Not to be exceeded by any one sample.

Beach Sampling Protocols

1. Collect samples using bottles provided by your laboratory.
2. Collect samples as early as possible in the morning before visitors begin using the beach. Wade out into the surf about thigh-deep and face the current, if any. Collect the sample from an incoming wave, taking care to avoid getting debris into the sample.
3. The object is to avoid capturing surface water, and to collect from at least 1 ft depth. Grasp the bottle near its base with one hand and remove the cap with the other. Be careful to avoid touching the inside of the cap or the rim of the bottle. Rotate your wrist so the mouth of the bottle is pointing downward at about a 45-degree angle. Rapidly plunge the bottle to a depth of about 1 ft. Rotate your wrist so the mouth of the bottle points up, loses its air bubble, and fills with water. Replace the bottle cap while still under water.
4. Lift the capped bottle out of the water. Remove the cap and pour out enough water to leave a 1/2-in air space. Replace the cap. Be careful not to touch the lip of the bottle or the inside of the cap.
5. Immediately place the bottle in an upright position in a covered cooler containing sufficient ice to keep the samples cool until they arrive at the laboratory.
6. Record the sample bottle number, station name, date and time of sampling, sampler's name, and other appropriate information on the field data sheet.
7. Transport the sample to the laboratory on ice, in a covered cooler, preferably within six hours but no longer than 24 hours of sampling.

Major Inspection Points for Bathing Beaches

1. Uniform slope to bottom and free of hidden submersed obstacles and hazards.
2. Bathing waters meet bacterial standards.
3. Algae and aquatic weeds not a problem.
4. Bathhouse with appropriate number of fixtures available.
5. Animals such as dogs and horses not permitted in beach area.
6. Depth markers provided and wading area clearly visible.
7. Children with diapers excluded from bathing waters.
8. Water clarity should be such that a Secchi disk (20 cm in diameter divided into four quadrants painted alternating black and white) is visible to a minimum depth of 4 ft.
9. No film should be visible on the surface of the water, and the water should have no lasting foam.

Resources and References

Beck, Joe E. *Hazard Analysis and Reduction Program for Healthy Homes*, September 29, 2004

Beck, Joe E. *Healthy Housing Reference Manual.* Joint publication of CDC, HHS, HUD, and EPA, 2004.

Beck, J.E., D.B. Barnett, and W. Johnson. *Fundamentals of Environmental Health Practice*, Kendall Hunt / Little Brown, April 2010.

Environmental Health Practice in Recreational Areas. U.S. Public Health Service, Publication No. (CDC) 77-8351, January 1977.

Federal Manual and Interactive Computer Inspection Program.

Kowalsky, L., ed. *The Pool / Spa Operators Handbook.* San Antonio: National Swimming Pool Foundation, 1990.

Pool Operator's Manual. Washington State Public Health Association and Washington State Environmental Health Association, 1997.

Standard Methods for the Examination of Water and Wastewater, 18th ed. American Public Health Association.

Suggested Health and Safety Guidelines for Public Spas and Hot Tubs. U.S. Public Health Service, Publication No. (CDC) 99–960, January 1985.

Swimming Pools, Safety and Disease Control through Proper Design and Operation. U.S. Public Health Service, HHS Publication No. (CDC) 83–8319, 1983.

Future Roles and Challenges for the Environmental Health Workforce

16

Larry J. Gordon, MS, MPH, DHL, DEAAS

Keep away from people who try to belittle your ambitions. Small people always do that, but the really great make you feel that you too can become great.

—Mark Twain

Key Performance Outcome Indicators:

1. Understand why the issues that create employment demand will continue to increase
2. Understand why a broad-spectrum education is necessary
3. Be aware of the diversity and necessity for a broad array of agencies to have environmental health oversight
4. Understand why the local level of government will remain where most field activities will occur

---

Environmental health will continue to be *the art and science of protecting against environmental factors that may adversely impact human health or the ecological balances essential to long-term human health and environmental quality. Such factors include, but are not limited to: air, food and water contaminants; radiation; toxic chemicals; disease vectors; safety hazards; and habitat alterations.*

Committee on the Future of Environmental Health[1]

The Committee on the Future of Environmental Health developed the preceding definition after widespread peer review and input from such groups as the NEHA, CDC, NCEH, HRSA, EPA, ATSDR, ASPH, CLEHA, various state and local health departments, ASTHO, and NACCHO. The definition recognizes that with rare exceptions, environmental health and environmental protection activities are the same, varying only by the titles of the agencies responsible for the programs. Health departments and the U.S. Public Health Service spawned most of the activities of state and federal environmental protection agencies, but magically, the terminology changed with the transfer of responsibilities from health departments.

Utilizing the peer-reviewed definition of environmental health developed by the Committee on the Future of Environmental Health will continue to be essential to marketing. In the absence of this widely referenced definition, practitioners will not know if they are marketing a buggy whip or a rocket ship. Environmental health must be consistently marketed in an organized fashion to ensure understanding and support of the public, including the media, civic leaders, and elected officials. Environmental health is valuable, environmental health is essential, and environmental health is marketable.

Environmental health is one of the two basic components of the field of public health, the other being *personal* public health. Environmental health services are essential components of the health services continuum, and precursors to the efficacy of other components of the range of health services. Other health services include personal public health services (population-based disease prevention and health promotion) and health *care* (diagnosis, treatment, and/or one-on-one patient rehabilitation).

Environmental health programs have traditionally been justified, designed, and administered based on a narrow public health rationale. As environmental problems, priorities, public perceptions and involvement, goals, and public policy have evolved, *ecological* considerations have become increasingly important. Whatever long-term health threats exist, the public and public policy leaders also know that pollution kills fish, limits visibility, creates foul stenches, ruins lakes and rivers, degrades recreational areas, and endangers plant and animal life.

Practitioners Will Increasingly Be Multidisciplinary

Environmental health will continue to be an effort engaged in an assortment of practitioners within an array of organizations. Such practitioners will manage the environmental factors that may adversely impact human health or the ecological balances essential to long-term human health. The practitioners should minimally include environmental health specialists, sanitarians, engineers, architects, chemists. biologists, economists, toxicologists, physicists, radiological health personnel, epidemiologists, laboratory scientists, physicians, dentists, veterinarians, social scientists, nurses, political scientists, attorneys, meteorologists, statisticians, educators, geologists, and entomologists.

The environmental health workforce will continue to require a spectrum of practitioners—from subbaccalaureate surveillance and inspection personnel through masters- and doctoral-level scientists and policymakers.

A Spectrum of Agencies Will Deliver Services

The trend to organizationally diversify environmental health programs will continue in response to the priorities of environmental health and protection, the demands of environmental advocates, and the tendency for many health departments to become significantly involved in health *care* to the detriment of environmental health and other public health priorities.

It is unrealistic to develop programmatic relationships between water pollution control, for example, and health care (treatment and rehabilitation) programs. Increased health care responsibilities of federal, state, and local health departments may translate to inadequate understanding, leadership, and primacy for environmental *health* within health departments.[1] Additionally, many health departments will continue to find it difficult to deal with the *ecological* aspects of environmental health.

Such organizational diversification signifies that environmental health is a basic component of *public* health. While each community or state has only one health department, every community and state will have many other agencies delivering environmental health services.

Organizational diversification of environmental health responsibilities will continue due to the ever increasing priority and complexity of environmental health problems and programs.

Federal

In addition to the U.S. Environmental Protection Agency, other significant federal environmental health agencies will remain, including the following:

- Occupational Safety and Health Administration of the U.S. Department of Labor;
- U.S. Public Health Service, including
  - National Institute of Environmental Health Sciences
  - Centers for Disease Control and Prevention,
  - Indian Health Service,
  - Food and Drug Administration
  - Agency for Toxic Substances and Disease Registry
  - National Institute for Environmental Health and Safety
- U.S. Coast Guard, Geological Survey, National Oceanographic and Atmospheric Administration
- Nuclear Regulatory Commission
- U.S. Army Corps of Engineers
- Departments of Transportation, Agriculture, and Housing and Urban Development

State

At least 85% of state-level agencies, other than state health departments, already have major environmental health responsibilities.[2] This percentage will probably increase. Every state indicated that multiple agencies were involved in environmental health activities. Data from the Johns Hopkins study, coupled with data published by the Public Health Foundation,[3] suggests that state expenditures for environmental health approximates that of all other public health activities combined. Another study, conducted by the University of Texas School of Public Health, leads to similar conclusions.[4] Environmental health will continue to the largest single component of the field of public health. Regardless of names, environmental health agencies are components of the broad field of public health, as their programs fall within common definitions of environmental health and are based on attaining public health goals. State agencies have various names, such as environment, environmental protection, ecology, labor, agriculture, environmental quality, natural resources, and pollution control.

In general, state environmental health agencies are most likely to have responsibility for water pollution control, air pollution control, solid waste management, public water supplies, meat inspection, occupational health and safety, pesticide regulation, and radiation protection.[5]

Local

The majority of local environmental health services will remain the responsibility of local health departments. Local activities tend to differ from those assigned to state agencies. They focus on food protection, swimming pool inspection, lead poisoning, onsite liquid waste disposal, groundwater contamination, asbestos surveillance, water supplies, animal/vector control, radon testing, illegal dumping, hazardous material spills, emergency response planning, health impact statements, and nuisance abatement. Some local jurisdictions administer comprehensive indoor and ambient air pollution control programs. Other local health departments indicate activities in water pollution control, solid waste management, radiation control, and hazardous waste management.[6,7]

Most local governments have already assigned certain environmental health functions to agencies such as public works, housing, planning, councils of government, solid waste management, special-purpose districts, and regional authorities.[8]

A number of jurisdictions have authorized local environmental health departments, and many important responsibilities will continue to be assigned to local and regional agencies other than traditional local health departments. The 1996 "Survey on the Organization of Local Environmental Departments" conducted by Public Technology, Inc., revealed that agencies other than local health departments are playing increasing roles in such environmental health areas as air pollution control, noise pollution control, water pollution control, groundwater contamination, industrial discharges, accidental spills, fish and shellfish sanitation, drinking water contamination, brownfields clean-up and redevelopment, hazardous materials control, leaking fuel storage tanks, hazardous waste sites, and pollution prevention.

Why Federal, State, or Local?

Environmental health services should be administered as close to home as possible. Local agencies can do a better job of protecting the local environment than distant bureaucracies.[9] Principles that will determine the responsibilities of government levels include:

- Problems of an *interstate* nature, such as protection of food and food products, solid and hazardous waste transportation, water pollution control, pesticide regulation, radioactive waste disposal, and air pollution resolution, will continue to be administered by appropriate federal agencies.

- The federal government will retain partial or sole authority to administer many activities that are federally mandated or funded, including certain aspects of radioactive waste management, water pollution control and facilities construction, air pollution control, meat inspection, occupational safety and health, and safe drinking water. State and local governments will continue to accept primacy for administering some of these activities, subject to adhering to federal requirements.

- State agencies or special districts will find it easier to administer certain issues on a "problem-shed" (geographic area that contains a complex of interrelated polluters) basis, rather than a local jurisdiction basis. Examples include water pollution control, air pollution control, solid waste management, and milk sanitation.

- In sparsely populated states as well as rural areas of other states, the state agency will exercise direct administrative authority in all program areas.

- Many state agencies will provide technical and consultative support to local environmental health agencies.

- State as well as federal agencies will develop criteria, standards, and model legislation for state and/or local adoption.

- State agencies will administer state and federal grant-in-aid funds for local agencies.

- Some local agencies will not have expertise in certain specialized areas, such as epidemiology, toxicology, radiological health, industrial hygiene, public health assessment, and risk assessment.

The Art of Environmental Health Practice

The practice of environmental health is both an art and a science. The *art* includes mentoring, organizational issues, politics and public policy, public relations, marketing, leadership, the benefits of environmental health, ensuring a comprehensive vision, and understanding the future of the field of practice.

Environmental health practitioners must understand that organizations, programs, problems, and public expectations are dynamic, and change will continue.

Environmental health practitioners must lead changes in programs, organizations and personnel; otherwise, the responsibility for untended environmental health problems will be claimed by others.

Environmental health will continue to demand organizational support, visibility, and effectiveness that may translate to organizational change—and environmental health advocates and elected officials frequently demand such change. Environmental health is easily marketable and demanded by the public, the media, and public policy leaders.

Practitioners should expand their horizons, stretch their imaginations, and develop comprehensive visions of their field of practice.

There is no standard model for the organization and delivery of environmental health services. There are no data to indicate that one organizational or service-delivery model is superior to others. Environmental health may be effectively served by agencies separate from health care, such as state and local EPAs.

Environmental health practitioners should consider the health impacts along with the impacts on agriculture, recreation, wildlife, ecology, environmental quality, and the economy. When health departments do not address such relevant problems, other agencies lacking tunnel vision compunctions are eager to take the entire program.

Environmental health practitioners must lead in striving for improvements in programs, priorities, organizational patterns, and laws rather than waiting for someone else to lead.

Experience, education, initiative, vision, and the courage to question the status quo—and to think and practice outside the box—will bring novel perspectives generating constructive ideas.

Components of a Vision for Environmental Health

A vision for environmental health should include environmental health measures that contribute substantially to preventing disease and disability, as well as reducing health care costs. The foresight should also incorporate *communities* in which:

- Environmental health is considered to be an important entitlement for the common good of all residents and visitors.
- Environmental health problems should be measured and defined prior to designing and implementing control measures.
- Environmental health efforts should be based on risk assessment, risk communication, and risk management.
- The primacy of prevention measures should be understood and practiced.
- Environmental health measures should be designed for optimal net impact rather than zero risk.
- Ecological considerations should be understood to be components of environmental health, because in the long run, a deteriorated environment is a threat to public health and the economy.
- Citizens understand that a quality environment is an important factor in economic vitality and productivity.
- Environmental health outcomes contribute to minimizing social problems.
- The quality of the environment contributes to educational achievement.
- Quality of life is enhanced by effective environmental health services.
- Environmental health practitioners should possess the broad array of competencies needed to address the community's environmental health problems.
- Broad environmental health communication bridges should be constantly traveled by the public, the media, and policymakers.

- Public policy leaders should seek the input of environmental health practitioners prior to developing policies that impact environmental health.
- Environmental health agencies should have missions of protecting public health and environmental quality rather than missions of protecting and promoting the interests of a narrow segment of society.

The environmental health mission, goal, objectives, program design, priorities, and public support should be based on the foregoing elements of a vision.

Workforce Education

Environmental health academic programs must inculcate students with the competencies to address current as well as future problems. Efforts to adequately educate students for leadership and policy roles will be vastly more effective than spending funds on cookie-cutter methodologies designed to make all agencies uniform rather than striving for creativity and diversity.

A small percentage of today's environmental health practitioners are being educated in accredited environmental health programs or schools of public health, but the vast majority will continue to be products of other essential curricula, disciplines, and professions.

Career-long learning should be available for the environmental health workforce, no matter the agencies involved. Such learning should take many forms—and the continuing education content will vary considerably, depending on the audience. Some will need training in the public health sciences; others in leadership, management, planning, marketing, policy and politics, public relations, and finance. Training should be a cooperative venture between major federal environmental health agencies.

The changes in environmental health problems that have been accompanied by adjustments to curricula include:

- Decreases in communicable diseases as major causes of death,
- Aging of our population with associated increase in chronic diseases,
- Changing lifestyles relating to exercise, obesity, smoking, and nutrition with their implications for public health,
- Increased recognition of the relationship between environmental pollutants and stresses in terms of cancer, heart disease, and genetic effects.

The increasing realization that the best answer to environmental health problems lies in prevention should continue to have an effect on environmental health curricula

Environmental health workforce requirements will include not only those working in and managing such programs, but also academicians who educate such person-power and research scientists who develop essential information. The spectrum of people-power will range from inspectional-level subbaccalaureate personnel doing routine inspection and sampling through the baccalaureate, masters, and doctoral levels required for the more complex aspects of policy, leadership, management, research, and education.

Developing and pursuing a meaningful vision for environmental health that is more than blurred imagination would help to invoke support of those charged with financing and educating the workforce. As an important part of a comprehensive vision, educational programs should be developed in which students learn that environmental health services substantially contribute to reduced disease and disability, as well as to:

- Enhanced community educational achievement,
- Fewer social problems,
- Enhanced quality of life in a more livable environment,
- Lower health care costs,
- Enhanced community economic vitality, and
- Enhanced productivity.

If educational programs embrace the foregoing benefits as important components of a vision for environmental health, education for environmental health practitioners will be developed to achieve the vision. Environmental health practice is based on risk assessment, risk communication, and risk management applied to one or more of the following problems.

Plethora of Problems

- Ambient air quality
- Indoor air quality
- Radon exposure
- Asbestos contamination
- Community noise pollution
- Radiation exposure
- Tanning parlors
- Water pollution
- Safe drinking water
- Liquid wastes
- Water supply cross-connections
- Eating and drinking establishments
- Food wholesalers
- Food retailers
- Itinerant food establishments
- Fish sanitation
- Shellfish production and sanitation
- Pure food control
- Slaughterhouses
- Poultry processing
- Milk sanitation
- Industrial hygiene and safety
- Disaster planning and response
- Bioterrorism
- Healthful housing
- Educational facilities
- Health care facilities
- Daycare facilities
- Correctional facilities
- Unintentional injuries
- Body art establishments
- Amusement parks
- Temporary mass gatherings
- Migrant workers health
- Swimming pools and spas
- Beaches
- Parks and recreational areas
- Solid wastes
- Hazardous wastes
- Toxic chemicals
- Lead poisoning
- Pesticides
- Fertilizers
- Weeds
- Hazardous spills
- Brownfields restoration
- Leaking storage tanks
- Insects and rodents
- Public health nuisances
- Animal bites
- Bioengineering of food
- Global climate change
- Stratospheric ozone depletion
- Global toxification

Spectrum of Program Activities

Many types of activities are necessary, including:

- Warnings
- Surveillance
- Sampling
- Monitoring
- Inspection
- Embargoes
- Environmental impact requirements
- Court preparation/testifying
- Consultation
- Pollution prevention

- Regulation
- Administrative hearings
- Permits
- Grading
- Compliance schedules
- Variances
- Injunctions
- Administrative and judicial penalties
- Networking and community involvement

- Plan and design review
- Economic and social incentives
- Public information and education
- Problem prioritization
- Program marketing
- Strategic planning
- Public policy development and implementation

Also, planning for prevention of environmental health problems through effective involvement during the planning, design, and implementation stages of:

- Energy production and utilization,
- Land use,
- Transportation systems,
- Resource development and consumption, and
- Product and facility design.

Many environmental health practitioners consider only the health aspects of environmental health problems. This has led to fragmentation of environmental health programs and has often resulted in the creation of special districts and/or single-purpose agencies designed to deal with specific issues such as air pollution control, mosquito abatement, or solid wastes in a comprehensive fashion.

Embracing the Comprehensive Field of Practice

Another important challenge for the future of environmental health is to embrace the comprehensive field of practice. Many educational programs, agencies, associations, and practitioners have tunnel vision with regard to the breadth, depth, and benefits of the field of practice. Too many feel it begins and ends in health departments and the U.S. Public Health Service, and self-serving definitions are disturbingly narrow. Environmental health is practiced in scores of local, state, and federal agencies, as well as the private sector and voluntary organizations. Academicians and practitioners must expand their horizons and visions.

The rotatable concentric wheels shown in Figure 16.1 depict the interdependent relationships between environmental stresses (e.g., pesticides), environmental factors (e.g., water), areas of contact (e.g., industries), and human safety, health, comfort, and well-being.

The Primacy of Prevention

Environmental health practitioners should be educated to become involved in prevention when initial decisions are made regarding land use, resource utilization, energy alternatives, global environmental health problems, transportation methodologies, economic development, and public education. To do this will require that personnel trained in environmental health fill leadership and policy roles throughout the public, private, and voluntary sectors.

Market Research and Analysis

Market research and analysis would significantly improve the practice of environmental health. Market research and analysis are universally utilized in the private sector, but have been ignored as essential tools to achieve the objectives of environmental health. Marketing research and analysis

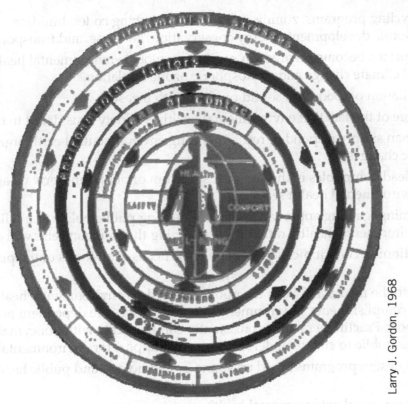

Larry J. Gordon, 1968

Figure 16.1 Interdependent Environmental Relationships

are the functions that link the public to the marketer through information designed to identify and define marketing opportunities and problems, generate, refine, and evaluate marketing actions, produce actionable insights, and improve marketing as a process.

A simple definition of *marketing* for the field of environmental health is:

The process of planning and executing the conception, the promotion, and the distribution of information and services that satisfy environmental health objectives.

Environmental health is valuable, environmental health is essential, and environmental health is marketable. However, effective marketing research and analysis should be conducted for the field of environmental health. The market should be analyzed and understood, and marketing efforts should have defined targets in sight that have failed to reach and effectively impact the market. Many practitioners view market research and analysis tools with disdain. Many confuse marketing with public information. News releases, pamphlets, leaflets, media appearances, and other similar tools are valuable—but are only tactical elements of an effective strategic marketing discipline.

Future Challenges and Opportunities

Following are samples of challenges and opportunities obvious at this time:

- Become constructively involved in basic environmental health prevention measures such as the planning stages of energy production, land use, transportation modes, facilities construction, resource utilization, and product design.
- Promote alternative energy measures, including wind, solar, nuclear, and hydrogen.
- Make a difference by being informed, getting involved, networking, and promoting environmental health actions and policies—even in the absence of statutory authority. Environmental health administrators should stimulate action in long-range community

planning, recycling programs, zoning ordinances, plumbing codes, building codes, waste systems, economic development, energy conservation, land-use, and transportation systems.

- Where appropriate, become involved in preventing global environmental health problems such as global climate change and stratospheric ozone depletion.
- Promote irradiation of foods as a sound public health measure.
- Take advantage of the fact that environmental health is widely considered to be an entitlement.
- Lead rather than simply respond in recommending environmental health organizational and programmatic changes.
- Compete for leadership roles in the complex spectrum of public and private agencies delivering environmental health services.
- Lead in designing, gaining approval, and implementing public policy that will improve the quality of environmental health, rather than assuming that someone else will do it for you.
- Maintain continuing communication with policy officials at all levels of the public and private sectors.
- Cooperate with the media and keep the public advised on environmental health problems, needs, and accomplishments. Environmental health services are dependent on public and political support. Practitioners must consistently communicate with policymakers, news media, and the public to ensure understanding and support for environmental health.
- Prioritize and design programs based on sound epidemiology and public health risk assessment.
- Engage in controversial environmental health issues as appropriate.
- Understand that the public is barraged with sensational weekly catastrophes related to environmental risk coupled with a paucity of critical scientific inquiry. There would be many times the actual morbidity and mortality if all the predicted catastrophes were factual. Practitioners should be scientifically critical, routinely questioning policies, standards, regulations, and proposals to ensure that all measures reflect scientifically valid priorities and needs.

The efficacy of environmental health services will depend on developing and utilizing constantly traveled communication bridges and networks connecting a variety of groups and agencies involved in the struggle for a quality environment and enhanced public health. A few such interests include land use, energy production, transportation, resource development, the medical community, public works, agriculture, conservation, engineering, architecture, colleges and universities, economic development, chambers of commerce, environmental groups, trade and industry groups, and elected officials. These relationships should be dictated by organizational policy rather than chance or personalities.

Environmental health will continue to increase in complexity—and the public will increasingly deserve and demand problem prevention and amelioration. Demographic changes, resource development and consumption, product and materials manufacturing and utilization, wastes, global environmental deterioration, technological development, bioterrorism, evolving disease patterns, changing patterns of land use, transportation methodologies, resource development and utilization, and continuing organizational diversification of environmental health services will create unanticipated challenges. Environmental health will continue to be basic to the health of the public and the quality of our environment. Environmental health problems, programs, service-delivery organizations, and educational needs will evolve in unforeseen ways. Ensuring an adequate supply of environmental health practitioners qualified to handle the policy, leadership, managerial, technical, research, and scientific issues of the future must be of the highest priority.

The career heights to which environmental health practitioners may aspire will be as great as an individual's capabilities and desires. While it was once assumed that there was a career ceiling over environmental health practitioners, time and experience have proven that individual capabilities equal those of other professions. Environmental health practitioners have a solid record of achievement in the public sector, academia, and the private sector—as well as professional and voluntary organizations.

Practitioners aspiring to lead will do well to *take the road less traveled*, and not be concerned about being out of step with their peers. Only dead fish move with the current.

And as Peter Drucker wrote, *"The best way to predict the future is to create it."*

Study Guide for Students

❑ Understand the definition and scope of environmental health, and name at least *ten* problems addressed by environmental health.

❑ Discuss why ecological considerations are important to environmental health and protection.

❑ List at least *ten* disciplines/professions involved in environmental health.

❑ Name at least *five* federal agencies having environmental health responsibilities.

❑ List at least *five* major state environmental health agencies.

❑ List at least *ten* programs commonly delivered at the local level.

❑ Discuss the principles of determining why programs are assigned to various levels of government.

❑ Understand and discuss the art of the environmental health practice.

❑ Understand and discuss various aspects of a vision for environmental health.

❑ Discuss the types of institutions involved in developing the environmental health workforce.

❑ Understand and discuss the benefits and values of environmental health, other than health benefits.

❑ Be able to list at least *twenty* environmental health problems addressed by environmental health practitioners.

❑ Be able to list at least *thirty* different environmental health activities.

❑ Discuss involvement in the comprehensive field of practice.

❑ Discuss the primacy of prevention.

❑ Discuss market research and analysis, and how it differs from public information.

❑ Discuss the myriad future challenges and opportunities in the field of environmental health.

Useful links:

http://hsc.unm.edu/library/resources/spc/biography.html

http://www.sanitarians.org/gordon/

http://www.deltaomega.org/memberSpotlight/Gordon.cfm

1. Committee on the Future of Environmental Health, "The Future of Environmental Health, Part One," *Journal of Environmental Health* 55(4): 28–32 (1993).

2. Thomas A. Burke, M. Nadia Shalauta, and Nga L. Tran, *The Environmental Web: Services, Structure, Funding.* Rockville, Md.: U.S Department of Health and Human Services, Health Resources and Services Administration, Bureau of Health Professions, Public Health Branch. January 1995.

3. *Public Health Agencies 1991: An Inventory of Programs and Block Grant Expenditures.* Washington, D.C.: Public Health Foundation, December 1991.

4. Center for Health Policy Studies, *The Professional Public Health Workforce in Texas.* Houston: University of Texas School of Public Health, 1996.

5. Larry J. Gordon, "The Future of Environmental Health, and the Need For Public Health Leadership," *Journal of Environmental Health* 56(5): 38–30 (1993).

6. *National Profile of Local Health Departments.* Washington, D.C.: National Association of County Health Officials, 1990.

7. *Current Roles and Future Challenges of Local Health Departments in Environmental Health.* Washington, D.C.: National Association of County Health Officials, 1992.

8. *National Profile of Local Health Departments.* Washington, D.C.: National Association of County Health Officials, 1990.

9. Carol Browner, "Public Health—An EPA Imperative," EPA Insight Policy Paper EPA-175-N-93-025, November 1993.

The Energy Conundrum: Roles for Environmental Health Practitioners

17

Larry J. Gordon, MS, MPH, DHL, DEAAS

A star is drawing on some vast reservoir of energy by means unknown to us. This reservoir can scarcely be other than the subatomic energy which, it is known exists abundantly in all matter; we sometimes dream that man will one day learn how to release it and use it for his service. The store is well nigh inexhaustible, if only it could be tapped. There is sufficient in the Sun to maintain its output of heat for 15 billion years.

—Sir Arthur Stanley Eddington

Comparatively few environmental health practitioners have a working concept of their roles in the technical and policy aspects of energy production and utilization.

Most environmental health professionals are narrowly oriented to their particular programs—and with few exceptions, the issue of energy has not been programmed into their roles. Likewise, undergraduate and graduate educational institutions usually have not incorporated energy problems into environment health curricula.

Larger operating agencies like the U.S. Public Health Service and the U.S. Environmental Protection Agency have developed cadres of personnel to ensure that the environmental health aspects of energy issues are properly considered. However, at the state and local levels, few agencies have allocated positions for personnel competent in the environmental health technical and policy aspects energy production and utilization.

Despite this relative inactivity on energy problems by academia and operating agencies, most environmental health practitioners agree that energy is a critical component of environmental health.

The energy conundrum has evaded solution for decades. While not the first, THE following is an example of early environmental health policy recommendations developed in 1972 as a policy proposal for the American Public Health Association:

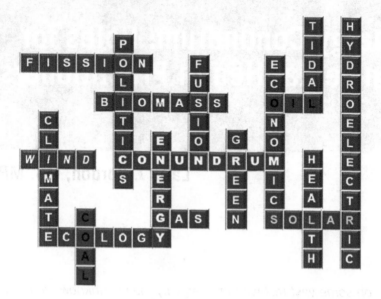

American
Public Health
Association

Proposed Energy Policy
1972

The problems relating to an adequate supply of energy are matters of grave concern for this and future generations of Americans. While a safe, dependable energy supply is of the utmost importance to the national economy and individual well-being, the byproducts of energy production are well known as detrimental factors to human health and well-being, and to the quality of the environment. Because of the many and varied relationships between energy, health and environmental quality, the American Public Health Association finds that:

- Most experts agree we must look to energy sources other than fossil fuels as early as possible.

- Although energy produced from fission may produce less pollution than that of fossil fuels, it is still by no means clean energy. As yet, adequate solutions have not been found for the disposal of radioactive waste and the problems of thermal pollution in an aquatic environment.

- There is a need for early massive research and demonstrations in the area of geothermal energy, fusion, solar energy, and fuel cells.

- The proliferation of freeways increases the tempo of fossil fuel utilization and significantly adds to pollution, disrupted patterns of living, community eyesores, environmental injuries, and undesirable patterns of land use. Rapid mass transportation is a "must" not only for urban areas but as alternatives for many interstate freeways.

- Proper land use and subdivision designs are also necessary to solve the problem of misuse of energy and the resulting impact on environmental quality.

- Population stabilization is a basic component in stabilizing energy production and decreasing the resulting pollution problems.

- Citizens are increasingly and properly concerned about power plants, not only with the adverse health effects of certain pollutants, but also with the impact upon the aesthetic environment (i.e., natural beauty and visibility).

- The National Power Plant Siting Act only serves to transfer pollution from overpopulated urban areas to relatively clean areas of the Nation. This ultimately results a uniform blanket of smog to the detriment of all citizens of the United States.

- Controls for pollution from energy production must be based on need, rather than the "state-of-the-art" or the latest limits of technology.

Respectfully submitted,

Larry J. Gordon

Larry J. Gordon
Member, APHA Executive Board

And in 1981, the following was published as the APHA President's Column:

The American public and their political leaders have finally become acutely and painfully aware that the burgeoning appetite for energy is taking an unreasonable toll of the economic pie and is creating unacceptable health and environmental problems. The problem is world-wide and the underlying predisposing issues include a rapidly expanding population and gluttony of energy from non-renewable sources. The U.S. Government has failed to place priorities and make the necessary commitment to develop renewable energy sources which ultimately must be developed if our technology, civilization, and standard of living are to survive. The majority of our political leaders still seem to be insufficiently informed and motivated to act against interests which continue us on the ultimately self-defeating course of relying on non-renewable energy sources. The official agency charged with the responsibility of providing expertise and leadership in energy matters (the Department of Energy), has changed its course little, if any, from the course of its predecessor agency, the Atomic Energy Commission.

Federal proposals for energy development have continued to recommend larger and larger governmental support for energy development from such short-term and non-renewable sources as synfuels and nuclear fission, with only a pittance for the energy needed from renewable sources on a long-term basis. Political leaders continue to recognize renewable energy resources as the best and ultimate, but the political reaction has been rhetoric rather than funding and action.

Solutions to the energy crisis must take due notice of the underlying issues of over-population, non-renewable energy resources, and the lack of a realistic conservation ethic.

The United States has no comprehensive energy policy or rational leadership in energy matters. There exists a patchwork of bumbling plans and confusion, largely designed to appease powerful interests. Recommendations and decisions are being made largely by those technocrats representing such powerful interests. The technocrats have understandable but inappropriate biases and conflicts of interests, and are not pursuing a mission of serving the public welfare.

Conservation of energy offers an immediate and effective methodology for significantly reducing energy consumption. There is no tight or predetermined correlation between energy use and economic vitality, and a healthy economy can be maintained with a greatly reduced reliance on energy. Conservation through technical improvement, "meticulous engineering," and personal sacrifice, could result in zero energy demand growth beyond 1985. For example, automobiles can travel twice or three times as far on a gallon of gas, and such improvements are already being made. Other technological changes are involving computers, advances in steel and aluminum processing equipment, fuel cells, heat pumps, etc. Changes in consumer behavior including such things as insulation, mass transit, decreased travel, decreased electric lighting, and car-pooling are being increasingly utilized. Price incentives, tax incentives, regulatory controls, alteration of advertising, educational campaigns, and changes in research and development emphasis offer conservation improvements which have barely been considered or addressed.

Solar resource systems could provide energy as solid fuels (wood); liquid fuels (from grain); gaseous fuels (methane from manure or plant residues); hydroelectric power; photovoltaic electricity; wind-generated electricity; and direct heat for home, businesses, industries, and institutions. The mix of solar resource systems could be varied and integrated for different climatic areas. Solar energy does not involve an economy of scale, local solar systems reduce or eliminate transmission costs and losses, and solar systems are less likely to create unacceptable health and environmental problems.

It will take 25 to 50 years of transition to bridge the gap from the current non-renewable energy sources to renewable solar resource energy. Bridging energy during this period must be derived from a changing transitional mix of fossil fuels and fission until the required level of solar energy systems are functioning. The United States has recognized the need for solar systems for more than a decade, but has only responded for funding non-renewable systems at a disparate rate while essentially ignoring the long-term needs for renewable solar energy. Only recently (January, 1980) did the U.S. Government make a crash commitment to alcohol production, and this was the right decision for the wrong reasons (subsidizing the Agricultural interests rather than rationally developing alcohol production).

The self-interest of the majority of our citizens and future generations would be best served by the solar resource alternative.

Larry J. Gordon

Both of the foregoing would have to be altered if rewritten in light of current information (2012). They are included simply to indicate that national and international public and private sector policymakers have failed to make the necessary difficult decisions for many decades.

Energy-based Environmental Health Problems

Energy is vital to our modern society, but it has public health, environmental, economic, political, and security considerations. Every proposal for a unified energy policy has been met with opposition from environmental advocates, public health interests, other citizen groups, economic interests, NIMBY concerns, or elected officials. Such groups do not share a common interest and frequently work at cross-purposes.

Every source of energy has environmental health ramifications, and none is entirely clean or green. Such ramifications include land use, solid wastes, hazardous wastes, noise, atmospheric visibility, toxic chemicals, geothermal problems, global climate change, atmospheric pollution, safety, bioterrorism, and transportation issues.

There is a positive correlation between air pollution created by the burning of fossil fuels and human health impacts, including cardiovascular disease, respiratory disease, asthma, reduced lung function, lung cancer, and premature death. Air pollution resulting from the burning of fossil fuels—including greenhouse gases such as CO_2—accumulate in the atmosphere and contribute significantly to increasing global mean temperatures and global climate change.

The secondary impacts of global climate change, including food insecurity and population displacement due to increased incidence of extreme weather events and other climatic changes, may result in social and economic disruption, increasing susceptibility to political unrest and violent conflicts. Our energy infrastructure and the extraction of oil and other fossil fuels create heavy environmental and public health impacts—and have been a target for attack and sabotage throughout the world, resulting in oil spills, habitat destruction, and human casualties. The U.S. energy infrastructure is vulnerable to such attacks.

The production of energy by nuclear power plants also creates numerous environmental health and security vulnerabilities that remain unresolved, including appropriate siting, secure construction of facilities, disposal of radioactive waste, proliferation concerns, the threat of nuclear accidents, acts of God, terrorist attacks, and other acts of sabotage. A nuclear power plant accident or attack could result in the release of radiation leading to radiation sickness, genetic mutation and cancer, and the contamination of large tracts of land.

Involvement of Environmental Health Practitioners

Environmental health practitioners have a solid record of achievement in a wide variety of environmental health issues. However, most have not been involved in energy production and utilization. Most environmental health practitioners are competent to engage in such technical issues related to energy production as solid wastes, hazardous wastes, toxic chemicals, air pollution, noise pollution, and water pollution. And some are competent to deal with the land use and transportation aspects of energy production.

Needs and opportunities for involvement of qualified environmental health practitioners abound in every area of energy production and utilization. Such opportunities are in technical issues as well as in policy and leadership roles. Unless prohibited by policy, practitioners should become involved even in the absence of specific authorization.

Education and Training Essential

Continuing education/short courses and relevant curricula are not available except in a few isolated cases. Such training should be developed by universities, official agencies, professional associations, and the private sector to enable environmental health practitioners to offer quality services and become effectively involved in technical issues as well as to influence public policy. Some training related to the various technical issues and well as public policy is available through the public, private, and academic sectors, as well as such associations as the American Public Health Association, the National Association of Boards of Health, the National Association of County and City Officials, the Association of State and Territorial Health Officials, and the National Environmental Health Association.

Venturing into Energy Policy

Energy policy is developed at all levels of the public and private sectors, but the most critical energy policy issues are the responsibility of elected officials.

- **Politics determines who gets what, when and why. The results are policy**. Practically every environmental health practitioner engages in politics in some manner, but the politics of elected officials are vital.
- Every energy policy issue is deemed "critical" by one important cohort or another.
- Elected officials focus primarily on the needs and desires of their constituents. A case must be made to indicate the impact of the policy recommendation on such constituents.
- Elected officials are much more likely to be influenced by thoughtful, individually worded letters than by "canned" letters and postcards that are usually ignored as obviously emanating from a single source.
- Practitioners who have developed an ongoing relationship with elected officials and the media are more likely to have their requests considered.
- Elected officials receive masses of requests daily, so only the well-justified requests will be seen by the elected official rather than by an aide.

Some Policy Actions to Be Supported

Scores of energy policies related to environmental health are worthy of support by environmental health practitioners, and the following rank high for individual and organizational political action:

- America's current and future energy needs must be met through a balanced approach that protects our economy and supports fundamental environmental health values. Energy policy must reduce our country's dependence on imported oil and shift our focus to renewable forms of energy. Transportation issues must be a critical component of a comprehensive policy. The nation's transportation sector, which is 95% reliant on oil, is a major contributor to greenhouse gas emissions and is a large contributor to our need for foreign sources of oil.

- Environmental health practitioners should support investments in alternative energy technologies and abundant domestic energy sources, like natural gas, as part of a comprehensive domestic energy portfolio. Our nation needs to employ an approach to our energy challenges that incorporates a spectrum of domestic energy solutions, including incentives for growth in renewable energy and energy conservation programs, support of domestic natural gas, and implementation of conservation incentives.

- Environmental health practitioners should play a role in ensuring that our country relies increasingly on a diverse energy supply, especially energy we can produce ourselves. It will be better for environmental health to develop relatively clean energy sources, such as wind, solar, nuclear, tidal, agricultural biomass, hydroelectric, and geothermal.

- Environmental health practitioners should advocate a deliberate transition to an energy strategy that includes the promotion of energy conservation, including the adoption of responsible fuel-economy standards, improvements in energy efficiency, the development of renewable fuel sources for energy production, strengthened controls for greenhouse gas emissions and air-hazardous pollutants, and the expedited institution of safe and renewable energy sources.

- Environmental health practitioners should support immediate legislative and regulatory efforts to reduce adverse health impacts and to mitigate global climate change, particularly through multipollutant control strategies that encompass health-protective limits on emissions of hazardous air pollutants, including carbon dioxide and other industrial greenhouse gases, in manufacturing, transportation, energy production, and, where feasible, other sources.

- Environmental health practitioners should support adequate funding for research, development, and utilization of renewable energy technologies.

- Environmental health practitioners should ensure development of educational opportunities to learn more about the environmental health and global effects of energy policy through educational institution curricula developing personnel for the environmental health workforce.

- With a burgeoning population and rapidly increasing energy demand, "all of the above" will continue to be necessary.

In 2012, wile not speaking specifically about the energy conundrum, U.S. Senator Olympia J. Snowe (Maine) noted her frustration with the Congress. *"It's become all about the politics, and not the policy. It's not about governing; it's about the next election."* Senator Snowe's statement characterizes the energy conundrum.

Thought-provoking References

American Public Health Association: Affirming The Necessity of a Secure, Sustainable, and Health Protective Energy Policy, 11/9/2004 http://www.apha.org/advocacy/policy/policysearch/default.htm?id=1289

Bill Gates on energy innovating to zero http://www.ted.com/talks/bill_gates.html

Debate: Does the world need nuclear energy? http://www.ted.com/talks/debate_does_the_world_need_nuclear_energy.html

Energy Sources, Part A, Recovery, Utilization, and Environmental Effects http://www.tandf.co.uk/journals/titles/15567036.asp

Hidden Health and Environmental Health Costs of Energy Production and Consumption in U.S. http://www8.nationalacademies.org/onpinews/newsitem.aspx?RecordID=12794

International Journal of Green Energy http://www.tandf.co.uk/journals/ljge

IOM.edu: The Health Impact Assessment of New Energy Sources: Shale Gas Extraction http://www.iom.edu/Activities/Environment/EnvironmentalHealthRT/2012-APR-30.aspx

Rob Hopkins: Transition to a world without oil http://www.ted.com/talks/rob_hopkins_transition_to_a_world_without_oil.html

Steven Cowley: Fusion is energy's future http://www.ted.com/talks/steven_cowley_fusion_is_energy_s_future.html

World Economic Forum http://www.weforum.org/issues/energy